District Gazetteers of India Series 24

BENGAL DISTRICT GAZETTEERS

THE COOCH BEHAR GAZETTEERS

District Gazetteers of India Series 24

BENGAL DISTRICT GAZETTEERS

THE COOCH BEHAR GAZETTEERS STATISTICS

52 VOLUMES

(VOL. 13th)

GYAN

Published by

Gyan Publishing House
5, Ansari Road
Daryaganj, New Delhi-110002
Phone: 011-47034999, 9811692060
E-mail: books@gyanbooks.com

Distribution Network
gyanbooks.com
India, USA, Canada, UK, Australia, France

ISBN: 978-93-6208-915-1 (Set) 52 Volumes
978-81-212-5941-5 (PB)

First Published, 1947

2nd Impression 2024

Printed at: Gyan Press, Delhi.

BENGAL DISTRICT GAZETTEERS (VOL. 13th)

LIST OF VOLUMES

S. NO.	ISBN NO.	VOLUME	TITLE	AUTHOR	PRICE	PAGES
			ASSAM DISTRICT GAZETTEERS			
1	9788121285926	1st	Cachar	B. C. Allen	600	300
2	9788121285919	2nd	Sylhet	B. C. Allen	750	378
3	9788121285902	3rd	Goalpara	B. C. Allen	400	203
4	9788121285896	4th	Kamrup	B. C. Allen	675	344
5	9788121285889	5th	Darrang	B. C. Allen	725	364
6	9788121285872	6th	Nowgong	B. C. Allen	560	280
7	9788121285865	7th	Sibsagar	B. C. Allen	675	343
8	9788121285858	8th	Lakhimpur	B. C. Allen	690	347
9	9788121285841	9th	Naga Hills and Manipur	B. C. Allen	580	294
10	9788121285834	10th	The Khasi And Jaintia Hills, The Garo Hills And The Lushai Hills	B. C. Allen	675	363
11	9788121285827	11th	The Sadiya and Balipara Frontier Tract	B. C. Allen	375	190
			BENGAL DISTRICT GAZETTEERS			
12	9788121218672	1st	Angul	L. S. S. O'Malley	340	168
13	9788121259637	2nd	Bakarganj	J. C. JACK	970	194
14	9788121218696	3rd	Balasore	L. S. S. O'Malley	450	228
15	9788121259590	4th	Bankura	L. S. S. O'Malley	1000	199
16	9788121218375	5th	Bhagalpur	J. Byrne	390	194
17	9788121218290	6th	Birbhum	L. S. S. O'Malley	300	150
18	9788121259651	7th	Eastern Bengal and Assam - Bogra	J. N. Gupta	940	188
19	9788121218351	8th	Burdwan	J. C. K. Peterson	450	227
20	9788121259538	9th	Calcutta District Gazetteer - Statistics, 1901 - 02		340	68
21	9788121218313	10th	Champaran	L. S. S. O'Malley	410	205
22	9788121259613	11th	Eastern Bengal District Gazetters - Chittagong	L. S. S. O'Malley	1080	216
23	9788121259552	12th	Chota Nagpur Tributary		130	26
24	9788121259415	13th	The Cooch Behar Gazette: Statistics		1460	292
25	9788121218412	14th	Cuttack	L. S. S. O'Malley	490	248
26	9788121261357	15th	Eastern Bengal District Gazetteers Dacca	B. C. Allen	400	207
27	9788121218436	16th	Darbhanga	L. S. S. O'Malley	360	180
28	9789362089335	17th	Darjeeling	L. S. S. O'Malley	500	248
29	9788121259453	18th	Eastern Bengal District Gazetteers - Dinajpur	F. W. Strong	890	178
30	9788121259392	19th	Faridpur	L. S. S. O'Malley	700	140
31	9788121218474	20th	Gaya	L. S. S. O'Malley	540	270
32	9788121214032	21st	Bihar and Orissa District Gazetteer: Hazaribagh	E. Lister	715	234
33	9788121218337	22nd	Hooghly	L. S. S. O'Malley	680	340
34	9788121218191	23rd	Bengal District Gazetteer Howrah	L. S. S. O'Malley	390	199
35	9788121259293	24th	Eastern Bengal and Assam - Jalpaiguri	John F. Gruning	890	178
36	9788121259279	25th	Jessore	L. S. S. O'Malley	960	192
37	9788121259231	26th	Khulna	L. S. S. O'Malley	1100	220
38	9788121259217	27th	Malda	G. E. Lambourn	670	134
39	9788121267854	28th	Manbhum	H. Coupland	600	313
40	9788121218498	29th	Midnapore	L. S. S. O'Malley	500	252
41	9788121218597	30th	Monghyr	L. S. S. O'Malley	560	280
42	9788121259156	31st	Murshidabad	L. S. S. O'Malley	1250	250
43	9788121259576	32nd	Bengal District Gazetteers - Muzaffarpur	L. S. S. O'Malley	940	188
44	9788121259132	33rd	Mymensingh	F. A. Sachse	960	192
45	9788121259118	34th	Nadia	J. H. E. Garrett	1070	214
46	9788121259095	35th	Eastern Bengal and Assam - Noakhali	J. E. Webster	580	115
47	9788121218450	36th	Feudatory States of Orissa	L. E. B. Cobdenramsay	790	395
48	9788121259071	37th	Pabna	L. S. S. O'Malley	710	142
49	9788121218511	38th	Palamau	L. S. S. O'Malley	380	190
50	9788121218634	39th	Patna	L. S. S. O'Malley	500	250
51	9788121218535	40th	Puri	L. S. S. O'Malley	650	328
52	9788121218757	41st	Purnea	L. S. S. O'Malley	440	220
53	9788121258937	42nd	Rajshahi	L. S. S. O'Malley	1080	216
54	9788121256681	43rd	Bihar and Orissa District Gazetteers: Ranchi	M. G. Hallett	1350	278
55	9788121258913	44th	Eastern Bengal and assam - Rangpur	J. A. Vas	890	178
56	9788121218559	45th	Sambalpur	L. S. S. O'Malley	480	242
57	9788121214056	46th	Santal Parganas	L. S. S. O'Malley	940	308
58	9788121218610	47th	Saran	L. S. S. O'Malley	380	190
59	9788121218658	48th	Shahabad	L. S. S. O'Malley	380	190
60	9788121256704	49th	The Gazetteer of Sikhim	H. H. Risley	960	481
61	9788121218573	50th	Singhbhum, Saraikela And Kharsawan	L. S. S. O'Malley	560	280
62	9788121259439	51st	Eastern Bengal District Gazetteers - Tippera	J. E. Webster	730	146
63	9788121259033	52nd	24 Parganas	L. S. S. O'Malley	1420	284

S. NO.	ISBN NO.	VOLUME	TITLE	AUTHOR	PRICE	PAGES
			CENTRAL PROVINCES DISTRICT GAZETTEERS			
64	9789362081728	1st, Vol. A	Akola (Descriptive)	A. E. Nelson, C. Brown	870	436
65	9789362085481	2nd, Vol. A	Amraoti (Descriptive)	S. V. Fitzgerald, A. E. Nelson	1050	524
66	9789362089267	3rd,Vol. A	Balaghat (Descriptive)	R. V. RUSSELL	430	216
67	9789362083494	4th, Vol. A	Betul (Descriptive)	R. V. RUSSELL	610	306
68	9789362085146	5th, Vol. A	Bhandara (Descriptive)	R. V. RUSSELL	580	292
69	9789362088390	6th, Vol. A	Bilaspur (Descriptive)	R. V. RUSSELL	870	434
70	9789362086044	7th, Vol. A	Buldana (Descriptive)	A. E. Nelson	1090	543
71	9789362089014	8th, Vol. B	Chanda (Descriptive)	R. V. RUSSELL	470	234
72	9789362086938	9th	Chhattisgarch Feudatory State	E. A. De Brett	880	440
73	9789362082961	10th	Chhindwara (Descriptive)	R. V. RUSSELL	550	274
74	9789362089342	11th, Vol. A & B	Damoh (Descriptive and Statistical Tables 1891-1901)	R. V. RUSSELL	830	414
75	9789362081230	12th, Vol. A	Durg (Descriptive)	A. E. Nelson	460	232
76	9789362086037	13th, Vol. A	Hoshangabad (Descriptive)	R. V. RUSSELL	860	430
77	9789362086792	14th, Vol. A	Jubbulpore (Descriptive)	A. E. Nelson	950	474
78	9789362089663	15th, Vol. A & B	Mandla (Descriptive and Statistical Tables 1891-1901)	R. V. RUSSELL	370	186
79	9789362086419	16th, Vol. A	Nagpur (Descriptive)	R. V. RUSSELL	790	394
80	9789362080646	17th, Vol. A	Narsinghpur (Descriptive)	R. V. RUSSELL	510	257
81	9789362084835	18th, Vol. A	Nimar (Descriptive)	R. V. RUSSELL	600	299
82	9789362087737	19th, Vol. A	Raipur (Descriptive)	A. E. Nelson	790	396
83	9789362080264	20th, Vol. A	Saugor (Descriptive)	R. V. RUSSELL	570	285
84	9789362081117	21st, Vol. A	Seoni (Descriptive)	R. V. RUSSELL	460	232
85	9789362084965	22nd, Vol. A	Wardha (Descriptive)	R. V. RUSSELL	600	302
86	9789362083401	23rd, Vol. A	Yeotmal (Descriptive)	R. V. RUSSELL	550	277
87	9789362080325	24th, Vol. I, Pt. I	Gwalior (Text and Tables)	R. V. RUSSELL	980	489
88	9789362087133	24th, Vol. I, Pt. II	Gwalior (Maps)	R. V. RUSSELL	400	198
89	9789362086341	24th, Vol. I, Pt. III	Gwalior (Village List)	R. V. RUSSELL	810	406
90	9789362085467	24th, Vol. I, Pt. IV	Gwalior (Photos)	R. V. RUSSELL	1400	698
91	9789362087393	25th, Vol. II	Indore (Text and Tables)	C. E. Luard	1050	524
92	9789362084422	26th, Vol. III	Bhopal (Text and Tables)	C. E. Luard	540	272
93	9789362086815	27th, Vol. IV	Rewah (Text and Tables)	C. E. Luard	500	250
94	9789362087584	28th, Vol. V, Pt. A	Western States - Malwa (Text)	C. E. Luard	1520	762
95	9789362087300	29th, Vol. VI, Pt. A	Eastern States - Bundelkhand (Text)	C. E. Luard	930	463
96	9789362082169	30th, Vol. VI, Pt. B	Eastern States - Bundelkhand (Tables)	C. E. Luard	830	417
			GAZETTEER OF THE BOMBAY PRESIDENCY:			
97	9788121283441	1st, Part I	History of Gujarat	Ed.: James M. Campbell	3220	644
98	9788121285582	1st, Part II	History of the Konkan Dakhan and Southern Maratha Country	Ed.: James M. Campbell	4200	840
99	9788121285568	2nd	Gujarat, Surat and Broach	Ed.: James M. Campbell	2990	598
100	9788121285544	3rd	Kaira and Panch Mahals	Ed.: James M. Campbell	1690	339
101	9788121285520	4th	Ahmedabad	Ed.: James M. Campbell	1860	372
102	9788121285506	5th	Cutch, Palanpur, and Mahi Kantha	Ed.: James M. Campbell	2390	478
103	9788121285483	6th	Rewa Kantha, Narukot, Cambay, and Surat States	Ed.: James M. Campbell	1450	290
104	9788121285469	7th	Baroda	Ed.: James M. Campbell	3260	652
105	9788121285445	8th	Kathiawar	Ed.: James M. Campbell	3790	758
106	9788121285421	9th, Part I	Gujarat Population - Hindus	Ed.: James M. Campbell	3170	636
107	9788121285407	9th, Part II	Gujarat Population - Musalmans and Parsis	Ed.: James M. Campbell	1520	304
108	9788121285384	10th	Ratnagiri and Savantvadi	Ed.: James M. Campbell	2500	501
109	9788121285360	11th	Kolaba and Janjira	Ed.: James M. Campbell	2550	513
110	9788121285346	12th	Khandesh	Ed.: James M. Campbell	3190	638
111	9788121285322	13th Part I	Thana	Ed.: James M. Campbell	2050	413
112	9788121285308	13th Part II	Thana	Ed.: James M. Campbell	1770	357
113	9788121285285	14th	Thana - Places of Interest	Ed.: James M. Campbell	3290	659
114	9788121285261	15th Part I	Kanara	Ed.: James M. Campbell	2340	348
115	9788121285247	15th Part II	Kanara	Ed.: James M. Campbell	1740	348
116	9788121285223	16th	Nasik	Ed.: James M. Campbell	3490	698
117	9788121285209	17th	Ahmadnagar	Ed.: James M. Campbell	3860	772
118	9788121285186	18th Part I	Poona	Ed.: James M. Campbell	2930	586
119	9788121285162	18th Part II	Poona	Ed.: James M. Campbell	2680	537
120	9788121285148	18th Part III	Poona	Ed.: James M. Campbell	2500	503
121	9788121285124	19th	Satara	Ed.: James M. Campbell	3450	692
122	9788121285100	20th	Sholapur	Ed.: James M. Campbell	2730	547
123	9788121285087	21st	Gazetteer of the Bomaby Presidency: Belgaum	Ed.: James M. Campbell	2570	514
124	9788121285063	22nd	Dharwar	Ed.: James M. Campbell	4200	841
125	9788121285049	23rd	Gazetteer of the Bombay Presidency:Bijapur	Ed.: James M. Campbell	3550	712
126	9788121285025	24th	Kolhapur	Ed.: James M. Campbell	2250	450

S. NO.	ISBN NO.	VOLUME	TITLE	AUTHOR	PRICE	PAGES
127	9788121285001	25th	Botany	Ed.: James M. Campbell	2040	408
128	9788121284981	26th, Part I	Materials Towards a Statistical Account of the Town and Island of Bombay - History	Ed.: James M. Campbell	2500	504
129	9788121284967	26th, Part II	Materials Towards a Statistical Account of the Town and Island of Bombay - Trade and Fortifications	Ed.: James M. Campbell	2690	538
130	9788121284943	26th, Part III	Materials Towards a Statistical Account of the Town And Island of Bombay - Administration	Ed.: James M. Campbell	2450	702
131	9788121284929	27th	General Index	Ed.:R. E. Enthoven	2190	428
			MADRAS DISTRICT GAZETTEERS			
132	9788121258814	1st	Anantapur	W. Francis	1140	227
133	9788121258555	2nd	Malabar	C. A Innes & F. B Evans	3010	602
134	9788121258791	3rd	Bellary	W. Francis	1890	377
135	9788121258777	4th	Statistical Appendix For Chingleput		280	56
136	9788121258753	5th	Coimbatore	K. N. Krishnaswami Ayyar	3420	628
137	9788121232814	6th	Madras District Gazetteers District Gazetteer Cuddapah	C. F. Brackenbury	1120	285
138	9788121258715	7th	Statistical Appendix For Ganjam		370	73
139	9788121256766	8th, Vol. 1st	Godavari District Gazetteer	F. R. Hemingway	650	320
140	9788121256803	8th, Vol. 2nd	Godavari District Gazetteer	F. R. Hemingway	160	83
141	9788121258678	9th	Statistical Appendix For Kistna		640	127
142	9788121258654	10th	Statistical Appendix For Kurnool		270	54
143	9788121258616	11th	Madura	W. Francis	1900	379
144	9788121258579	12th	Statistical Appendix For Madura		740	148
145	9788121258630	13th	The Nilgiris	W. Francis	2190	437
146	9788121234276	14th	Madras District Gazetteers Gazetteer Of The Nellore District Brought Upto 1938		1150	386
147	9788121258517	15th	North Arcot		590	118
148	9788121258494	16th, Vol. 1, Part I	Salem	F. J. Richards	1710	343
149	9788121258593	16th, Vol. 1, Part II	Salem	F. J. Richards	1800	360
150	9788121258456	17th	South Arcot	W. Francis	2400	480
151	9788121258470	18th	Statistical Appendix For South Canara		400	80
152	9788121258432	19th, Vol. 1st & 2nd	Tanjore: Main Volume and Statistical Appendix		2070	401
153	9788121258395	20th	Tinnevelly	H. R. Pate	2740	547
154	9788121258418	21st	Statistical Appendix For Tinnevelly		320	64
155	9788121258371	22nd, 1st & 2nd	Trichinopoly: Main Volume and Statistical Appendix	F. R. Hemingway	2440	487
156	9788121241953	23rd	Vizagapatam District Gazetteer	W. Francis	760	385
			PUNJAB DISTRICT GAZETTEERS			
157	9788121255943	1st	Ambala District 1883-84		620	124
158	9788121255967	2nd	Amritsar		1180	236
159	9788121255981	3rd	Delhi		1300	260
160	9788121256001	4th	Ferozepore		950	188
161	9788121256025	5th	Faridkot		350	70
162	9788121256049	6th	Gujranwala 1893-94		1270	254
163	9788121256063	7th	Gujrat	C. E. Luard	1140	228
164	9788121256087	8th	Gurdaspur 1891-92		1260	252
165	9788121256100	9th	Gurgaon 1883-4		1020	203
166	9788121256124	10th	Hazara	H. D. Watson	2290	458
167	9788121256148	11th	Hissar district and Lohar State		1840	367
168	9788121256162	12th	Hoshiarpur		1420	283
169	9788121256186	13th	Jhang		1070	213
170	9788121256209	14th	Jhelam		1010	202
171	9788121256223	15th	Jalandhar District 1883-84		540	108
172	9788121256247	16th, Vol. XIV-A	Jullundur District, with maps and Kapurthala		1990	398
173	9788121256261	17th, Pt. I	Kangra (Proper)		1450	290
174	9788121256285	17th, Pt. II	Kangra (Kulu, Lahual, Spiti)		1800	357
175	9788121256308	18th	Karnal		1930	386
176	9788121256322	19th	Kohat		1540	307
177	9788121256346	20th	The Lahore District 1883-84		1220	244
178	9788121256384	21st	Ludhiana and Maler Kotla		1680	335
179	9788121256407	22nd	Lyallpur		735	147
180	9788121256421	23rd	Mianwali		1170	234
181	9788121256445	24th	Montgomery	P. J. Fagan	1590	318
182	9788121258364	25th	Multan (1901-02)	E. D. Maclagan	2400	480
183	9788121258708	26th	The Rohtak District 1883-84		980	196
184	9788121258746	27th, Vol. III A	Dujana State 1904		500	16
185	9788121256483	28th	Shahpur District		1780	356
186	9788121256506	29th	Simla District		800	159

S. NO.	ISBN NO.	VOLUME	TITLE	AUTHOR	PRICE	PAGES
187	9788121256520	30th	The Chamba State		2040	408
188	9788121256544	31st	The Chenab Colony 1904		1550	310
189	9788121256568	32nd	Kalsia State		270	53
190	9788121256582	33rd	Suket and Mandi		770	154
191	9788121256605	34th	Phulkian States, Patiala Jind And Nabha 1904		2070	414
192	9788121256643	35th	Simla Hill States		2220	443
193	9788121256667	36th	Sirmur		920	183
			RAJPUTANA DISTRICT GAZETTEERS			
194	9789362088994	1st, Vol. I-A & B	Ajmer-merwara (Text and Statistics Tables)	C. C. Watson	1230	246
195	9789362080882	2nd. Vol. II-A & B	Mewar Residency (Text and Statistics Tables)	K.D. Erskine	1700	339
196	9789362088444	3rd, Vol. III-A & B	The Western Rajputana States Residency And The Bikaner Agency	K.D. Erskine	3590	718
			UNITED PROVINCES OF AGRA AND OUDH DISTRICT GAZETTEERS			
197	9789362087560	Vol. I	Agra	H. R. Nevill	2260	452
198	9789362082466	Vol. II	Aligarh	H. R. Nevill	1300	260
199	9789362089779	Vol. III	Allahabad	H. R. Nevill	2050	409
200	9789362081346	Vol. IV	Almora	H. G. Walton	1670	333
201	9789362085658	Vol. V	Azamgarh	D. L. Drake Brockman	1750	349
202	9789362080547	Vol. VI	Bahraich	H. R. Nevill	1410	281
203	9789362085214	Vol. VII	Ballia	H. R. Nevill	1750	350
204	9789362084668	Vol. VIII	Banda	D. L. Drake Brockman	1750	349
205	9789362086518	Vol. IX	Bara Banki	H. R. Nevill	1720	344
206	9789362084101	Vol. X	Bareilly	H. R. Nevill	1640	327
207	9789362086631	Vol. XI	Basti	H. R. Nevill	1610	321
208	9789362083814	Vol. XII	Benares	H. R. Nevill	2290	458
209	9789362086105	Vol. XIII	Bijnor	H. R. Nevill	1820	363
210	9789362081674	Vol. XIV	Budaun	H. R. Nevill	1890	378
211	9789362086891	Vol. XV	Bulandshahr	H. R. Nevill	2100	419
212	9789362081520	Vol. XVI	Cawnpore	H. R. Nevill	2210	442
213	9789362088031	Vol. XVII	Dehra Dun	H. G. Walton	1710	342
214	9789362088710	Vol. XVIII	Etah	E. R. Neave	1600	320
215	9789362082992	Vol. XIX	Etawah	D. L. Drake Brockman	1390	277
216	9789362082220	Vol. XX	Farrukhabad	E. R. Neave	1620	324
217	9789362083869	Vol. XXI	Fatehpur	H. R. Nevill	1890	377
218	9789362085962	Vol. XXII	Fyzabad	H. R. Nevill	1700	339
219	9789362087997	Vol. XXIII	Garhwal	H. G. Walton	1270	254
220	9789362089892	Vol. XXIV	Ghazipur	H. R. Nevill	1600	320
221	9789362085436	Vol. XXV	Gonda	H. R. Nevill	1650	330
222	9789362080271	Vol. XXVI	Gorakhpur	H. R. Nevill	1890	378
223	9789362086129	Vol. XXVII	Hamirpur	D. L. Drake Brockman	1390	277
224	9789362087638	Vol. XXVIII	Hardoi	H. R. Nevill	1680	336
225	9789362081636	Vol. XXIX	Jalaun	D. L. Drake Brockman	1180	236
226	9789362084309	Vol. XXX	Jaunpur	H. R. Nevill	1750	350
227	9789362084187	Vol. XXXI	Jhansi	D. L. Drake Brockman	1960	391
228	9789362089168	Vol. XXXII	Kheri	H. R. Nevill	1650	330
229	9789362086778	Vol. XXXIII	Lucknow	H. R. Nevill	1760	352
230	9789362088635	Vol. XXXIV	Mainpuri	H. R. Nevill	1740	348
231	9789362080424	Vol. XXXV	Meerut	H. R. Nevill	2170	434
232	9789362081087	Vol. XXXVI	Mirzapur	D. L. Drake Brockman	2430	486
233	9789362085443	Vol. XXXVII	Moradabad	H. R. Nevill	1900	380
234	9789362082763	Vol. XXXVIII	Muttra	D. L. Drake Brockman	2140	428
235	9789362089915	Vol. XXXIX	Muzaffarnagar	H. R. Nevill	2260	451
236	9789362086143	Vol. XL	Naini Tal	H. R. Nevill	1890	377
237	9789362086761	Vol. XLI	Partabgarh	H. R. Nevill	1560	312
238	9789362081124	Vol. XLII	Pilibhit	H. R. Nevill	1570	314
239	9789362084453	Vol. XLIII	Rai Bareli	H. R. Nevill	1610	322
240	9789362088284	Vol. XLIV	Rampur	H. R. Nevill	1170	234
241	9789362083654	Vol. XLV	Saharanpur	H. R. Nevill	2190	438
242	9789362083142	Vol. XLVI	Shahjahanpur	H. R. Nevill	1510	302
243	9789362083623	Vol. XLVII	Sitapur	H. R. Nevill	1590	317
244	9789362089939	Vol. XLVIII	Sultanpur	H. R. Nevill	1330	266
245	9789362080851	Vol. XLIX	Unnao	H. R. Nevill	1530	305

BENGAL DISTRICT GAZETTEERS.

The Cooch Behar Gazette.

STATISTICS

1947.

No. 17 of 1947

Registered No. C 1085

The Cooch Behar Gazette.

Published by Authority.

১৫ই ভাদ্র সোমবার] MONDAY, SEPTEMBER 1, 1947. [১৩৫৪ সাল ৪৩৮ রাজশক]

PART I.

CONTENTS.

Notifications and Orders by His Highness the Maharaja Bhup Bahadur, His Highness the Maharaja Bhup Bahadur in Council, the Chief Minister and other Ministers and the High Court.

HUZUR SECRETARIAT

The Maharaja's Office, Cooch Behar.

NOTIFICATION.

The 20th August, 1947.

It is notified for general information that the Shooting Camp godown will henceforth be designated 'The Farashkhana.'

By order,
R. Singh,
Major,
Household Minister, Cooch Behar.

HEAD QUARTERS, COOCH BEHAR STATE FORCES, COOCH BEHAR.

Dated, Cooch Behar, the 26th August, 1947.

Reference.—*Cooch Behar Gazette* Notification of 19th August, 1947 :—

The following amendments may please be made :—

Under Head "APPOINTMEMT & TRANSFER-(B) NG" please delete the word "To be Comdt".

By Order,
Raj Singh,
Major,
Offg. Dy. Chief Comdt,

ORDERS BY HIS HIGHNESS THE MAHARAJA BHUP BAHADUR, COOCH BEHAR.

CHARGE.—*The 20th August, 1947.*—Mr. S. Stern, Chief Engineer and Secretary, P. W. D., and the Electricity Department will make over his charges including Darjeeling Estate to Rajkumar G. Narayan, Deputy Chief Engineer, P. W. D., on the afternoon of the 1(t)h September, 1947.

By Command,
J. C. GOON,
Assistant Secretary, General Secretariat, Cooch Behar.

ORDERS BY HIS HIGHNESS THE MAHARAJA BHUP BAHADUR IN COUNCIL, COOCH BEHAR.

EXTENSION.—*The 10th August 1947.*—Srijut Nirmal Chandra Mustafi, B. L., Treasury Officer, Cooch Behar, (now officiating Fouzdari Ahilkar) is granted an extension of service for one year with effect from the 16th December, 1947.

J. C. GOON,
Assistant Secretary,
General Secretariat, Cooch Behar.

THE STATE COUNCIL, COOCH BEHAR.

GENERAL AND EXECUTIVE DEPARTMENT.

NOTIFICATION.

(Forest).

No. G/28.—*Dated the 8th August, 1947.*

It is notified for general information that the State Council have been pleased to sanction the following revised schedule of rates for forest produce in supersession of the previous orders in this connection. The rates will come in force with effect from its publication in the *Gazette* :—

Schedule of Rates for Forest Produce.

1. TIMBER.

Pieces of wood 8 feet and over in length in (a) Logs and (b) Poles.

Timber is classified as follows :—

CLASS A.—Teak.
CLASS B.—Sal, Sisoo and Khair.
CLASS C.—Simul, Pitali, Kadam, Lampati, Panisaj, Chikrassi, Toon, Gamari.
CLASS D.—Kainjal, Lali, Saj, Chhatian.
CLASS E.—All other trees.

(A) LOGS.

Girth at 4½ feet from the thick end.

Class.	3 feet & less than 4 feet. Per Cft.			4 feet & less than 5 feet. Per Cft.			5 feet and over. Per Cft.			
	Rs.	As.	P.	Rs.	As.	P.	Rs.	As.	P.	
Class A ...	1	8	0	2	0	0	3	0	0	The cubic contents of logs will be calculated by multiplying the square of the quarter girth taken in the middle of the log (after removal of the bark) by the length of the log.
Class B ...	1	2	0	1	8	0	2	4	0	
Class C ...	0	6	0	0	8	0	0	10	0	
Class D ...	0	4	0	0	6	0	0	8	0	
Class E ...	0	3	0	0	4	0	0	5	0	

(B). Poles for each piece (maximum length of piece must be less than 18 feet.)

Girth at 4½ feet from the thick end.

Class:	Under 1 foot.			1 foot & less than 1 foot 6 inches.			1 feet 6 inches & less than 2 feet.			2 feet & less than 2 feet 6 inches.			2 feet 6 inches & less than 3 feet.		
	Rs.	As.	P.	Rs.	As.	P.	Rs.	As.	P.	Rs.	As.	P.	Rs.	As.	P.
Class A ...	0	8	0	1	0	0	2	0	0	6	0	0	8	0	0
Do. B ...	0	4	0	0	8	0	1	8	0	2	8	0	5	0	0
Do. C ...	0	2	0	0	3	0	0	4	0	0	6	0	0	10	0
Do. D ...	0	1	6	0	2	0	0	4	0	0	4	0	0	6	0
Do. E ...	0	1	0	0	1	0	0	2	0	0	2	0	0	4	0

Note.—The casual sale of dead, dry, fallen or small plots of trees may be sanctioned by the Conservator of Forests up to a limit of Rs. 200 in each case as laid down in Paragraph 13 of Mr. Ahmad's report.

II. FIREWOOD

(a) Green Firewood (from coupes and plantation only).

Pieces of wood below 8 feet in length.

Species	Locality.		Rate per 100 cubic feet stacked.			Rate per Cart Load.		
			Rs.	As.	P.	Rs.	As.	P.
Kukat firewood	all forests	...	2	0	0	1	0	0
Teak, Sal, Sissu and khair branch wood.	All forests	...	4	0	0	2	0	0

(b). Dry Firewood.

	Rs.	As.	P.	
Per monthly cooly ticket (to remove one cooly load daily.	1	12	0	The use of *dao* only is allowed.
Per cart load	1	0	0	
Per cooly load	0	1	0	
*Per one ton lorry load ...	4	0	0	

* For 2 ton motor lorries the rate will be double and so on.

(c). Drift—firewood.

	Rs	As.	P.	
Per monthly cooly ticket (to remove one cooly load daily.	1	12	0	Cutting instruments will be allowed.
Per 100 cubic stacked ...	2	0	0	
Per cart load	1	0	0	
Per cooly load	0	1	0	
Per one ton lorry load ...	4	0	0	

(d). Charcoal.

Per cart load	... Rs. 4	When manufactured by the purchasers.

III. BAMBOOS

Kind.		Rate per hundred.		
		Rs.	As.	P.
Borobans or Bombas	...	20	0	0
Makla or Mahlbans ..	...	18	0	0
All other Bamboos ...	...	12	0	0

IV. GRAZING AND FODDER.

Description.	Rate. Rs.	As.	P.	
Grass and other kinds of fodder per cooly load.	0	1	0	Lopping of trees is prohibited.
Monthly permit for one cooly load of grass and other kinds of fodder only.	0	12	0	
Grazing buffaloes, each per month ...	1	8	0	No grazing will be allowed without permission from the Minister in charge of the forest Department.
Grazing cattle and ponies, each per month	0	8	0	
Elephant, each per diem, includes one load fodder	0	2	0	
Passing fees for buffaloes, bullocks, pony and cow each.	0	2	0	
Passing fees for goats, sheep and pigs each	0	1	0	

V. MINOR FOREST PRODUCE.

Description of Produce.	Rs.	As.	P.	
Ekra, Khagra or other reeds, per cooly load	0	2	0	
Ekra, Khagra or reeds, per cart load ...	1	0	0	
Thatch grass per cart load	1	0	0	
Thatch grass, per cooly load	0	2	0	
Leaves per cooly load	0	2	0	
Long pepper, per monthly ticket ...	5	0	0	If not sold by tender.
Stones (quarried), per 1,000 Cft. ...	5	0	0	
Sand or stones from river beds, per 1,000 Cft.	2	8	0	
Leaf mould (manure) or cowdung, per cart load.	0	8	0	
Leaf mould (manure) or cowdung, per lorry load.	2	0	0	
Leaf mould (manure) or cowdung, per cooly load or maund.	0	1	0	
Lime stone, per 100 Cft.	8	0	0	
Sand or stone from river beds, per cart load	0	2	0	
Sand or stone from river beds, per lorry load	0	8	0	
Potter's clay, per cart load	0	8	0	
Fruit per maund	0	2	0	
Simul cotton, per maund	1	0	0	

Note:—Seed and seedlings may be sold at rates fixed by the Conservator of Forests, from time to time.

General Note:—For produce or quantities mentioned in the Schedule, the Conservator of Forests, may charge up to 50 per cent more according to circumstances in special cases. The reasons for so doing to be reported to the Minister in charge of the Forest Department.

J. C. GOON,
Assistant Secretary, General Secretariat, Cooch Behar.

ORDERS BY THE STATE COUNCIL, COOCH BEHAR.

POWERS.—*The 14th August, 1947.*—The Commissioner of Excise is empowered to grant leave of any kind to non-gazetted subordinates under him without any limit in respect of pay drawn by these officers, in partial modification of powers given to him in the Books of Powers.

LEAVE.—*The 21st August, 1947.*—Mrs. Renula Lahiri, Lady Supervisor, Sudder Hospital, Cooch Behar, is granted privilege leave for one month with effect from the 1st September, 1947.

By order,
J. C. Goon,
Assistant Secretary, General Secretariat, Cooch Behar.

THE STATE COUNCIL, COOCH BEHAR.
GENERAL AND EXECUTIVE DEPARTMENT.
NOTIFICATION.

No. R/24—*Dated the 13th August, 1947.*

It is notified for the information of those whom it may concern that Mr. A. K. Roy Moulik of Messrs Roy Moulik & Co "Naren Villa" Jalpaiguri was enrolled on the eighth day of August 1942 on the Register of Accountants maintained under the authority of the State Council under Rule 8 of the Auditors Certificate Rules, 1942. This enrolment will remain valid until the thirty first day of March, 1948.

By order,
J. C. Goon,
Assistant Secretary, General Secretariat, Cooch Behar.

THE STATE COUNCIL, COOCH BEHAR.
GENERAL AND EXECUTIVE DEPARTMENT.
Circular Order No. G. B/7
(General Sanad)

The 20th August, 1947.—In modification of the orders contained in Circular Order No. 7 dated the 12th March, 1945 published in the *Cooch Behar Gazette* of the 2nd April, 1945, the State Council have been pleased to authorise the Assistant Secretary, General Secretariat, Cooch Behar, to register all Lakheraj and Mokarari Sanads received in the State Council, until further orders.

By order,
J. C. GOON,
Assistant Secretary,
General Secretariat, Cooch Behar.

ORDERS BY THE CHIEF MINISTER, COOCH BEHAR.

LEAVE.—*The 22nd August, 1947.*—Sjt. Jyotish Chandra Biswas, Assistant Audit and Finance Officer, Cooch Behar, is granted an extension of privilege leave for one month and 15 days with effect from 22nd August, 1947 in continuation of the privilege leave already granted to him.

By order,
J. C. GOON,
Asstt. Secretary, General Secretariat, Cooch Behar.

GENERAL SECRETARIAT, COOCH BEHAR.
GENERAL & EXECUTIVE DEPARTMENT.
NOTIFICATION No. T. 6
The 14th August, 1947.

The Durbar have been pleased to fix the number of free studentships in all the State M. E. Schools (excluding the Sudder M. E. School and including Junior Madrasahs) at the rate of 20% on the Roll strength of each school.

This modifies the orders contained in paragraph 1(d) of the Regency Council Notification dated the 21st September, 1934 published in this behalf in the *Cooch Behar Gazette* of the 1st October, 1934.

The award of free studentships will however continue to be governed by the rules already in force under cover of the aforesaid Regency Council Notification.

S. C. ROY SINGHA SARKAR,
Public Health & Education Minister,
Cooch Behar.

THE STATE COUNCIL, COOCH BEHAR.
GENERAL & EXECUTIVE DEPARTMENT.
(Notification).
No. G/30—*dated the 7th August, 1947.*

The Durbar is pleased to order that in cases where the Journey is made by the employees of the State including those of the Chaklajat Estates, Darjeeling Estates etc., by a service open to the public on hire, the mileage allowance shall not exceed twice the actual fare charged. This rule will apply to all officers excepting the 4th class officers who will get only the actual fare plus daily allowance as they get in case of Railway Journey.

J. C. GOON,
Assistant Secretary,
for Chief Minister, Cooch Behar.

THE STATE COUNCIL, COOCH BEHAR.

GENERAL AND EXECUTIVE DEPARTMENT.

NOTIFICATION

(Rationing)

No. R/26.—*Dated the 25th August, 1947.*

It is notified for general information that in view of the fact that the supply of cheap rice or paddy now given to the State servants and their families does not afford any relief to the Cooch Behar town people generally, the State Council have been pleased to order that as a temporary measure six chattaks of rice or nine chattaks of paddy in lieu of rice per head per diem at the rate of Rs. 19 and Rs. 10-10 per maund respectively plus the usual administration duly as was sanctioned for the State servants and their families will be supplied to all the existing Ration Card holders in the Cooch Behar Town. No rice or paddy will be supplied to children of two years of age or below but half the quantity will be supplied to children between ages two and twelve years.

The State Council have further been pleased to order that the supply of rice or paddy as above will be made only to the existing Ration Card holders in the Cooch Behar town and that no new Ration Cards for supply of rice or paddy to the new comers will be issued except to the State servants newly appointed or transferred or to such other persons as the Civil Supplies Commissioner thinks fit and desirable. The supply of rice or paddy is being introduced purely as a measure of temporary relief and not by way of rationing so that with its introduction the Durbar do not take the responsibility of feeding the town people of Cooch Behar and that this privilege can be withdrawn at any time.

As regards the supply of cheap rice or paddy to the mofussil towns, *i. e.* in the towns other than Cooch Behar, the State Council have been pleased to order that the State servants and their families in the mofussil towns only will continue to get the privilege of cheap rice or paddy as now but in their cases also no rice or paddy will be supplied to children of two years of age or below but those between two to twelve years will be given half the prescribed rate of rice or paddy. The privilege of supply of cheap rice or paddy will not however be extended to the Posts and Telegraphs and Railway employees but the municipal employees will be given it.

By order,
J. C. GOON,
Asstt. Secretary, General Secretariat, Cooch Behar.

No. 18 of 1947

Registered
No. C 1085

The Cooch Behar Gazette.

Published by Authority.

৩১শে ভাদ্র মঙ্গলবার] TUESDAY, SEPTEMBER 16, 1947. [১৩৫৪ সাল ৪৩৮ রাজশক]

PART I.

CONTENTS.

Notifications and Orders by His Highness the Maharaja Bhup Bahadur, His Highness the Maharaja Bhup Bahadur in Council, the Chief Minister and other Ministers and the High Court.

COOCH BEHAR STATE FORCES ORDERS
BY
HIS HIGHNESS THE CHIEF COMMANDANT.

Cooch Behar, the 1st September, 1947.

LEAVE :

The following leave is granted :—

Rank, Name & Unit :	*Nature :*	*Duration :*
Reference CBSF Order 71/47 dated 1st July, 1947.		
Lt. B. K. Bhattacharjee N. G.	PRIVILEGE	15 days extension w. e. f. 23rd August, 1947.
Lt. Bhagwan Singh 1 CBI	FURLOUGH	2½ months w. e. f. 25th August 1947 or date of availing.

By order,
RAJ SINGH,
MAJOR,
Offg : Dy. Chief Commandant.

THE STATE COUNCIL, COOCH BEHAR.

General and Executive Department.

NOTIFICATION.

No. R/27—*Dated the 30th August, 1947.*

It is notified for the information of those whom it may concern that Mr. Asit Baran Rudra of No. 3, West Gumtee, Jalpaiguri was enrolled on the 30th day of August 1947 on the register of Accountants maintained under the authority of the State Council under Rule 8 of the Auditor's Certificate Rules, 1942. This enrolment will remain valid until the 31st day of March 1948.

By order,
J. C. Goon,
Assistant Secretary,
General Secretariat, Cooch Behar.

THE STATE COUNCIL, COOCH BEHAR.

General & Executive Department.

(Notification).

No. G/31—*Dated the 9th September, 1947.*

In continuation of State Council Notification No. G-23 dated the 9th July 1947, published in *Cooch Behar Gazette* (Extraordinary) dated the 17th July 1947, the Durbar is pleased to direct, in exercise of relevant powers, that all other process fees realisable under any other rule or notification made or issued by the State Council are hereby enhanced by 50% with immediate effect.

By order,
J. C. Goon,
Assistant Secretary, General Secretariat, Cooch Behar.

ORDERS BY THE STATE COUNCIL, COOCH BEHAR.

Appointment.—*The 9th September, 1947.*—Sjt. Arun Kumar Banerjee, M. A., is appointed as Lecturer in History and Economics, Victoria College, Cooch Behar, with effect from the 4th September, 1947, *i. e.* the date on which he joined the appointment.

S. C. Roy Singh Sarkar,
Public Health & Education Minister,
Cooch Behar.

No. 19 of 1947

Registered
No. C 1085

The Cooch Behar Gazette.

Published by Authority.

১৫ই আশ্বিন বুধবার] WEDNESDAY, OCTOBER 1, 1947. [১৩৫৪ সাল ৪৩৮ রাজশক]

PART I.

CONTENTS.

Notifications and Orders by His Highness the Maharaja Bhup Bahadur, His Highness the Maharaja Bhup Bahadur in Council, the Chief Minister and other Ministers and the High Court.

ORDERS BY THE STATE COUNCIL, COOCH BEHAR.

Powers.—*The 18th September 1947.*—The Assistant Civil Judge will exercise all powers granted to officers in Group II of class (e) subordinate officers in the book of powers.

Extension.—*The 16th September, 1947.*—Probationary period of service of Sjt. Tarapada Talukdar, B. L., Superintendent of Excise, Cooch Behar, is further extended upto 31st December, 1947 on the expiry of the period of extension as sanctioned under State Council orders dated the 21st May 1947.

Extension.—*The 16th September 1947.*—Probationary period of service of Sjt. Santi Bhusan Bhattacharjee, B.A., Jailor, Cooch Behar Central Jail, is further extended upto 31st December, 1947.

Extension.—*The 17th September 1947.*—Sjt, Nagendra Nath Roy, B. L., Maleutchery and Debutter Naib Ahilkar, Cooch Behar, is granted a further extension of service upto the 19th December 1947 inclusive.

By Order,
J. C. Goon,
Assistant Secretary,
Geneal Secretariat, Cooch Behar.

THE STATE COUNCIL, COOCH BEHAR.
GENERAL AND EXECUTIVE DEPARTMENT.
NOTIFICATION.
(Stamp)
No. L/14.—*Dated the 17th September, 1947.*

In exercise of the powers conferred by the Cooch Behar Stamp Act II of 1943, the Durbar is pleased to amend the Rules under the Cooch Behar Stamp Act II of 1943 published at pages 85 to 95, Part I of *Cooch Behar Gazette* 1946 as follows :—

In the second proviso in Rule 3(a), after the words—"under Schedule B to the said Act" insert the words—"or under these Rules".

By order,
J. C. GOON,
Asstt. Secretary, General Secretariat, Cooch Behar.

THE STATE COUNCIL, COOCH BEHAR.
GENERAL AND EXECUTIVE DEPARTMENT.
NOTIFICATION.
No. L/15.—*Dated the 18th September, 1947.*

The Durbar is pleased to order that the Registrar of Companies, Cooch Behar, be authorised under section 8(1) of the Cooch Behar Foreign Companies (Controlling) Act, 1946 to accord sanction for prosecution under the Act.

He will be charged with the duty generally, of enforcing the provisions of the aforesaid Act.

By order,
J. C. GOON,
Assistant Secretary,
General Secretariat, Cooch Behar.

THE STATE COUNCIL, COOCH BEHAR.
GENERAL AND EXECUTIVE DEPARTMENT.
NOTIFICATION.
(Treasury)
No. G/33—*Dated the 11th September, 1947.*

It is notified for information of those whom it may concern that all Sub-treasuries with Sadar Treasury will be kept open on every Monday from 10 A. M. to 2 P. M. for receiving deposits of the Special Excise Duty and Export Duty and Excise Duty collections during the ensuing Mahalaya and the Durga Puja holidays commencing from the 18th October 1947 and ending with the 2nd November 1947.

By order,
J. C. GOON,
Assistant Secretary, General Secretariat,
Cooch Behar.

ORDERS BY THE STATE COUNCIL, COOCH BEHAR.

APPOINTMENT.—*The 12th September, 1947.*—Sjt. Sasanka Mohan Ganguli, B. L., Sub-Registrar and Tehsildar, Haldibari, is appointed as a member of the Haldibari Town Committee for a period of 3 years with effect from the 1st August, 1947.

S. C. ROY SINGH SARKAR,
Public Health & Education Minister,
Cooch Behar.

THE LEGISLATIVE COUNCIL, COOCH BEHAR.

Dated, Cooch Behar, the 11th September, 1947.

The following report of the Select Committee on Bill Nos. I and II of 1947 (The Cooch Behar Industrial Employment (Standing Orders) Bill, 1947 and the Cooch Behar Ware House Bill, 1947) is published for general information :—

No. 87 C. J.

To

His Highness the President, Cooch Behar Legislative Council, Cooch Behar.

Dated, Cooch Behar, the 9th September, 1947.

YOUR HIGHNESS,

We the undersigned members of the Select Committee to which the marginally noted two Bills were referred at the last sitting of the Legislative Council, beg to report as follows :—

1. Bill No. I of 1947.—Cooch Behar Industrial Employment (Standing Orders) Bill, 1947.
2. Bill No. II of 1947—Cooch Behar Warehouse Bill, 1947.

1. The Bills were published in the *Cooch Behar Gazette* on the 17th March, 1947 and the 16th April, 1947 respectively :—

2. In the unavoidable absence of the Chairman, the Chief Minister, but at his desire, we met on the date, *viz.*, 8th September, 1947 and at the place appointed by him and adopted the following modifications of the two Bills.

3. We do not however consider it necessary to republish the Bills as amended beyond publication of this report with the proposed amendments and supplying each member of the Council with a copy thereof.

Modifications proposed.

I. Bill No. I of 1947.

Cooch Behar Industrial Employment (Standing Orders) Bill, 1947.

1. In clause 2 (a) of the Bill the following words be inserted after the word "means" :—

"an Industrial Court, if any exists, or in its absence".

2. In Clause 6 (1) of the Bill, in place of the words "on which copies are" the following words be substituted :—

"of delivery or tender to him or his agent or prescribed representative of copies".

3. In clause 13 (1) a printing mistake be corrected by substituting the word "submit" in place of the printed word "submitted".

II. Bill No. II of 1947.

Cooch Behar Warehouse Bill, 1947.

1. In clause 8 (1) of the Bill after the words "show cause" the words "within a reasonable time to be fixed in the notice" be inserted.

2. In clause 8(2) after the word "offered" the following words be inserted—"within the time fixed in the notice".

3. In clause 9, the present clause be renumbered as sub-section (1) of the clause and the full stop at the end be substituted by a comma, and the following words be added thereafter :—

"and if any deposited goods be still lying in his warehouse at the time, the prescribed authority shall forthwith, on notice to the depositor or depositors, arrange either for return of the deposited goods to the depositor or depositors, if possible, or for sale of the same at public auction with reasonable notice at his discretion, unless the depositor or depositors concerned immediately transfers or transfer the same to other licensed warehouses at his or their own costs, but till the warehouse concerned is cleared of the deposited goods as above, the duties and liabilities of the warehouse man in respect of the same under the law shall continue subject to payment of legitimate charges due to him under the law".

4. After clause 9 thus renumbered as clause 9(1), the following clause (2) be added :—

"(2) No suit or other proceeding shall lie against the prescribed authority or any officer acting under his orders, for any act of commission or omission, in good faith done in respect of goods referred to in sub-section (1) above."

5. In clause 13(1) the words "and damp free" be omitted.

6. Before the word "grader" and the word "graders" wherever either of them occurs, the words "classifier or" or classifiers or", as the case may be, be added.

We have the honour to be,
Your Highness'
Most obedient servants,

P. C. Mustafi,
G. M. Dutt,
Amanatulla Ahmed,
Lalit Mohan Baksi,
Surendra Kanta Basu Majumder,
S. C. Dutt.

By authority,
J. C. Goon,
Assistant Secretary,
General Secretariat, Cooch Behar.

ORDERS BY THE CHIEF MINISTER, COOCH BEHAR.

General Secretariat.

Leave.—*The 11th September, 1947.*—Sjt. D. P. Chakravarti, B. A., Assistant Secretary, General Secretariat, Cooch Behar is granted an extenision of medical leave for the period of one month and 27 days with effect from the 15th August 1947 with permission to avail himself of Sunday the 12th October 1947 and also of the ensuing Mahalaya and Durga Puja holidays. During his absence on leave, the existing arrangement will continue,

By order,
J. C. Goon,
Assistant Secretary, General Secretariat, Cooch Behar

No. 19 of 1947

Registered
No. C 1085

The Cooch Behar Gazette.

SUPPLEMENTARY.

Published by Authority.

১০ই আশ্বিন বুধবার] WEDNESDAY, OCTOBER 1, 1947. [১৩৫৪ সাল ৪৩৮ রাজশক]

PART I.

CONTENTS.

Notifications and Orders by His Highness the Maharaja Bhup Bahadur, His Highness the Maharaja Bhup Bahadur in Council, the Chief Minister and other Ministers and the High Court.

ORDERS BY THE STATE COUNCIL, COOCH BEHAR.

No. R-28.—CANCELLATION OF RATION DEALERS' LICENSES.—*The 24th September, 1947.*

It is notified for general information that Bahadur Mandal and Debendra Barman, Ration Shop-keepers of Sahibgunj taluk in the Dinhata Subdivision have, on investigation, been strongly suspected of malpractices, *viz.*, black-marketing and smuggling. Hence their licenses have been cancelled.

By order,
J. C. GOON,
Asstt. Secretary, General Secretariat, Cooch Behar.

THE STATE COUNCIL, COOCH BEHAR.

GENERAL & EXECUTIVE DEPARTMENT.

(Notification).

No. 7—*Dated the 17th September, 1947.*

In supersession of all previous orders, the working hours of the State Library, Cooch Behar, will be as follows with effect from the 1st October, 1947 :—

7 A. M. to 9 A. M.
&
4 P. M. to 8-30 P. M.

By order,
J. C. GOON,
Assistant Secretary, General Secretariat, Cooch Behar.

ORDERS BY THE CHIEF MINISTER, COOCH BEHAR.

LEAVE.—*The 24th September, 1947.*—Sjt. Suresh Chandra Ghosh, Examiner of Local Accounts, Audit Department, Cooch Behar, is granted privilege leave for 19 days with effect from the 3rd November 1947 with permission to prefix Mahalaya and Durga Puja holidays and to affix the Jagaddhatri, Mahurrum etc. holidays upto the 30th November 1947.

By order,
J. C. GOON,
Assistant Secretary,
General Secretariat, Cooch Behar.

NOTIFICATION.

(Arms).

No. G/34—*The 11th September, 1947*

It is hereby notified that it is not imperative for license-holders of arms to appear personally at the ammunition dealer's shop and sign a receipt for the ammunition purchased. The dealer will henceforth sell or supply ammunition to the license-holders even through the latter's servant or agent on production of the license in which the quantity of ammunition sold or supplied will be recorded by him.

H. SINGH,
Chief Minister, Cooch Behar.

No. 20 of 1947

Registered
No. C 1085

The Cooch Behar Gazette.

Published by Authority.

২৯শে আশ্বিন বৃহস্পতিবার] THURSDAY, OCTOBER 16, 1947. [১৩৫৪ সাল ৪৩৮ রাজশক]

PART I.

CONTENTS.

Notifications and Orders by His Highness the Maharaja Bhup Bahadur, His Highness the Maharaja Bhup Bahadur in Council, the Chief Minister and other Ministers and the High Court.

ORDERS BY THE STATE COUNCIL, COOCH BEHAR.

STATUS—*The 28th September 1947.*—Major Rajkumar Gautam Narayan, Acting Chief Engineer of the State will also function as the Secretary, P. W. Department and the Electricity Department for such period as he works as Acting Chief Engineer.

LEAVE—*The 3rd October, 1947.*—Rai S. C. Dutta Bahadur, B.L. Chief Justice, High Court, Cooch Behar is granted privilege leave for 3 days from the 19th to 21st November 1947 with permission to prefix the Puja holidays ending on the 18th November 1947 and to suffix the other holidays from the 22nd November 1947.

During his absence on leave the Puisne Judge, High Court, Cooch Behar will remain in charge in addition to his own duties.

By order,
J. C. GOOH,
Assistant Secretary, General Secretariat, Cooch Behar.

THE STATE COUNCIL, COOCH BEHAR.

GENERAL AND EXECUTIVE DEPARTMENT.

NOTIFICATION.

(Advisory Sub-Committee).

No. G/37—*Dated the 24th September, 1947.*

It is notified for general information that the Durbar are pleased to sanction the formation of Sub-divisional Advisory Sub-Committees for improvement of village communications and rural water supply under the Presidentship of Sub-divisional Officers. The Durbar are also pleased to nominate the members to serve on the Sub-Committees as under :—

Sudder Sub-division.

1. Sjt. Prem Kanta Sarkar, Moamari (south-east).
2. Munshi Mahammad Ali Pramanic, Haldimohan (south).
3. Sjt. Swarneswar Chakrabarty, Maghpala (west).
4. ,, Benoyendra N. Adhicari, Kalarayerkuti (north-west).
5. Munshi Sabaruddin Ahmed, Kaljani (north-east).
6. Sjt. Sashi Kanta Karjee, Hatiduba (north).

Dinhata Sub-division.

1. Sjt. Dinesh Pramanik of Barabangla.
2. ,, Jogendra Nath Das of Bara Adabari.
3. ,, Maheswar Hisabia of Jarabari.
4. Mlv. Bakter Uddin Mia of Patharsori.
5. ,, Badar Uddin Mia of Seuti Part I.
6. Sjt. Kailash Chandra Roy Singh Sarkar of Dighaltari.

Mathabhanga Sub-division.

1. Sjt. Tarakeswar Roy Basunia of Kheti.
2. ,, Gajendra Narayan Roy Basunia, M.L.C.
3. Md. Abul Hossain Mia of Baro Simulguri.
4. Sjt. Ram Mohan Adhikari, Siktibari.
5. Moulvi Karimuddin Basunia, Nalgram.
6. Sjt. Birendra Nath Pramanik, Paglimari.

Mekliganj Sub-division.

1. Sjt. Akhya Kumar Roy of Dhulia.
2. Md. Pashar Uddin Sarkar of Kuchlibari.
3. Md. Badir Uddin Sadagar of Nagar Changrabandha.
4. Sjt. Ananda Patwari of Hemkumari
5. Md. Khaybar Uddin Sarkar of Bara Haldibari.
6. Sjt. Bhabendra Nath Roy of Permekliganj.

Tufanganj Sub-division.

1. Sjt. Harish Chandra Sarkar, Singimari.
2. Kumar Tikendra Narayan, M L C., Balarampur.
3. Md. Mabaruddin Bepari, Champuta.
4. Sjt. Satish Chandra Knor, Salbari.
5. ,, Ramani Mohan Sarkar, Jaigirchilakhana.
6. Sjt. Har Sing Sarkar, Bhanukumari.

By order,
J. C. GOON,
Asstt. Secretary, General Secretariat, Cooch Behar.

THE STATE COUNCIL, COOCH BEHAR.

GENERAL AND EXECUTIVE DEPARTMENT.

NOTIFICATION.

(Food Control).

No. R/29.—*Dated the 3rd October, 1947.*

In continuation of State Council Notification No. R/25 dated the 28th March 1946, published at page 25 of *Cooch Behar Gazette*, Part I, dated the 1st April 1946, the Durbar is pleased to order that the fee for the renewal of a license shall be Rs. 4 if the application for renewal is not made immediately after the previous license expires.

By order,
J. C. GOON,
Assistant Secretary,
General Secretariat, Cooch Behar.

No. 21 of 1947

Registered
No. C 1085

The Cooch Behar Gazette.

Published by Authority.

১ই কার্ত্তিক শনিবার] SATURDAY, NOVEMBER 1, 1947. [১৩৫৪ সাল ৪৩৮ রাজশক]

PART I.

CONTENTS.

Notifications and Orders by His Highness the Maharaja Bhup Bahadur, His Highness the Maharaja Bhup Bahadur in Council, the Chief Minister and other Ministers and the High Court.

ORDERS BY THE STATE COUNCIL, COOCH BEHAR.

LEAVE.—*The 14th October 1947.*—Moulvi B. Rahaman, B. L., Civil & Sessions Judge, Cooch Behar is granted privilege leave for 22 days from 31st October to 21st November 1947 with permission to prefix the Puja holidays from 19th October 1947 to 30th October 1947 and affix the holidays from the 22nd November 1947 to 25th November 1947.

During his absence on leave, Sjt H. Biswas, M. A., B. L., Civil Supplies Commissioner, Cooch Behar will officiate as Civil & Sessions Judge, Cooch Behar in addition to his own duties.

EXTENSION.—*The 15th October 1947.*—Sjt. Debendra Mohan Dutta Gupta, Inspector of Excise, Cooch Behar has been granted an extension of service for a further period of one year with effect from the date his present term of service expires *i. e.* 22nd October 1947 on the existing terms.

By order,

APPOINTMENT.—*The 31st October 1947.*—With effect from the 31st October 1947, the Council is pleased to appoint Mr. N. C. Mustafi, B. L., as Additional Fouzdari Ahilkar, Cooch Behar with jurisdiction throughout the whole State until further orders, in addition to his own duties as Treasury Officer.

Mr. N. Sen Gupta, M. A., B. L., has taken over charge of the post of Fouzdari Ahilkar with effect from the forenoon of 31st October 1947.

By order,
J. C. GOON,
Assistant Secretary, General Secretariat, Cooch Behar.

ORDER.

The State Council have been pleased to order the removal of Sjt. Durgakinkar Bhattacharjee, Professor of the Victoria College, Cooch Behar (under suspension) from State service with effect from the afternoon of the 17th October, 1947 for taking active part in political activities in contravention of Rule 16 (1) of the State Servants' Conduct Rules.

STATE COUNCIL COOCH BEHAR,
17th October, 1947.

H. SINGH,
Chief Minister, Cooch Behar State.

ORDER.

Mr. Himadriballav Biswas may be allowed to go during the holidays and Mr. L. M. Baksi may take charge of the routine duties of the Civil and Sessions Judge during that period. On Mr. H. B. Biswas' return from holidays on 31st October, 1947 he will officiate as Civil and Sessions Judge in addition to his duties as the Civil Supplies Commissioner.

H. Singh,
Chief Minister, Cooch Behar State,
Cooch Behar.

THE STATE COUNCIL, COOCH BEHAR.

GENERAL AND EXECUTIVE DEPARTMENT.

Circular Order No. 3.

(Education).

Dated the 9th October, 1947.

The Durbar have been pleased to order that the restrictions, on the admission of students in the State Educational Institutions, as sanctioned in Circular Order No. 1 dated the 24th April, 1947 shall apply to Mofassil H. E. Schools of the State as well.

S. C. ROY SINGH SARKAR,
Public Health & Education Minister,
Cooch Behar.

STATEMENTS IN CONNECTION WITH STRIKES AND PICKETING OF SEPTEMBER—OCTOBER, 1947.

The following resolution passed unanimously at a meeting of the Peace Committee held on 19th October, 1947 is published for general information :—

"We are of opinion that discipline should be maintained in all our educational institutions, that the duty of a student is to devote his whole time to his studies and to the development of his body, and that it is not in his interest to fritter away his precious time in any political movement. Academic associations and societies, literary and religious, are not to be treated as political movements".

Sd. H. Singh, (*Chief Minister*).
,, S. K. Chakraverty, M. L. C.
,, D. Bhattacharyya, *Advocate*.
,, Mvi. Ismailuddin Chowdhury, *Advocate*.
,, N. N. Roy, *Advocate*.
,, Asruman Das Gupta, (*Controller, Household Department*).
,, Prafullya Ch. Barma.

H. SINGH,
Chief Minister.
31st October, 1947.

The following declaration made by Mr. Chunilal Mookerjee, President, Cooch Behar Chamber of Commerce and Messrs. Govinda Mohan Dutta, M. L. C., R. G. Banik, Malchand Bhadani, Madan Chand Manik Chand Bothra, Ramlal Tularam, Ismailuddin Ahme , Keshablal Banik, Tularam Dalam Chand, Manmatha Nath Pal and 73 other members of the Cooch Behar Chamber of Commerce is published for general information in the *Cooch Behar Gazette* :—

"We, the members of the Cooch Behar Chamber of Commerce declare our disapproval of and dissociation from the acts of lawlessness during the last ten days. In our opinion strikes in schools and the college are harmful to the students themselves, but apart from this the coercion exercised against boys and girls who do not wish to join strikes is, in our view, wholly improper and may lead to breach of peace.

"Any kind of picketing is a dangerous act likely to disturb the public tranquillity which we oppose whole-heartedly; we are also opposed to any kind of coercion for compelling the State to act in a particular way.

"We offer our full co-operation to the State in maintaining law and order and we hope that the State authorities will exercise effective control over persons who break laws and disturb the peace.

"At the same time we have to emphasise the necessity of taking prompt steps to counteract the various false and distorted reports about the actions of the State circulated amongst the public here as well as outside, by efficient publicity work. In these days of widespread unrest it is not enough to act quite justly with firmness, but it is also absolutely necessary to convince the public about the justification of the steps taken by the Administration. In fact we cannot over-emphasise the necessity of prompt and efficient publicity work, among the public as well as outside".

H. SINGH,
Chief Minister.
31st October, 1947.

The following letter submitted to His Highness the Maharaja Bhup Bahadur by Messrs. L. M. Bakshi, Srish Chandra Ray, Basudeb Bhattacharjee, Nalini Mohan Bakshi, Himadri Ballabh Biswas, Satish Chandra Roy, Birendra Chandra Ghosh, Sushil Kumar Chakravarty, Asraman Das Gupta, Dwijendra Chandra Sen, Promode Ranjan Ghosh, Nagendra Nath Roy, N. C. Mustafi, Byomkesh Banerjee, Principal—Profulla Ranjan Dhar, and Professors—A. R. Gupta, Radha Kishore Ghosh, Tara Prosad Chatterjee, Debi Prosad Sen, Jitendra Nath Das Gupta, Madhu Sudhan Paramanik and 24 other gentlemen residing in Cooch Behar is published in the *Cooch Behar Gazette* for general information :—

"We, the undermentioned peace loving loyal subjects of Your Highness, have been greatly pained to see the recent disturbances committed by a section of the student community which have upset the tranquillity of the Cooch Behar State. We condemn these recent strikes and picketing of the Schools, College, Bazars and Offices unequivocally and sincerely believe that these activities are harmful to the interest of the students themselves. We also want to make it abundantly clear that we entirely disapprove and have no sympathy with this student movement which we believe is against the best interests of the country and we offer our co-operation with the authorities in the maintenance of law and order. We have made Cooch Behar our hearth and home and we sincerely desire that the proverbial peace and tranquillity of Cooch Behar may be restored."

H. SINGH
Chief Minister.
31. 10. 47.

The Cooch Behar Gazette.

Published by Authority.

১লা অগ্রহায়ণ সোমবার] MONDAY NOVEMBER 17. 1947.[১৩৫৪ সাল ৪৩৮ রাজশক।

PART I.

CONTENTS.

Notifications and Orders by His Highness the Maharaja Bhup Bahadur, His Highness the Maharaja Bhup Bahadur in Council, the Chief Minister and other Ministers and the High Court.

COOCH BEHAR STATE FORCES ORDERS BY HIS HIGHNESS THE CHIEF COMMANDANT.

Dated, Cooch Behar, the 18th October, 1947.

STAFF DUTY :

During absence on leave of Capt. A. P. Deexit, Staff Captain, HQ, Cooch Behar SF, Lt., B. K. Bhattacharjee, Narayan Guards, will officiate as Staff Captain with effect from 15th October, 1947.

LEAVE :

The following are granted leave :—

Rank, Name & Unit :	Nature :	Duration :
Capt. A. P. Deexit. Staff Captain, HQ. Cooch Behar SF.	PRIVILEGE.	1 month with effect from the 15th October, 1947.

COMMAND :—During absence on P. L. of Capt. A. P. Deexit, OC W/T Section, Lt. B. K. Bhattacharjee, NG, will officiate as OC W/T Section with effect from 15th October, 1947.

By order,
B. P. WALAWALKAR,
Lt. Colonel,
Deputy Chief Commandant.

COOCH BEHAR STATE FORCES ORDERS
BY
HIS HIGHNESS THE CHIEF COMMANDANT.

Dated, Cooch Behar, the 1st November, 1947.

COMMAND:

During absence on leave (FURLOUGH) of Major Raj Singh, Commandant, 1st Cooch Behar Infantry, Capt. M. S. Majumder, 1st Cooch Behar Infantry will Officiate as Commandant and will sign bills pertaining to 1st Cooch Behar Infantry with effect from 31st October, 1947.

LEAVE:

The following are granted leave :—

Rank, Name & Unit :	Nature :	Duration :
Major Raj Singh, Commandant, 1st Cooch Behar Infantry.	FURLOUGH.	2 months with effect from 31st October, 1947.

By order,
B. P. WALAWALKAR,
LT. COLONEL,
Dy. Chief Commandant.

THE STATE COUNCIL, COOCH BEHAR.
GENERAL AND EXECUTIVE DEPARTMENT.
NOTIFICATION.
(Khas Mehal).

No. G/42—*Dated the 18th October 1947.*

It is hereby notified for general information that, in modification of clause (I) of the State Council Notification (Khas Mehal) dated 22nd September 1941 published in the *Cooch Behar Gazette* dated 16th October 1947 prescribing the procedure for the transfer of a pattani holding or of a part thereof by private sale, gift, will or mortgage, the State Council have been pleased to order that, in future, transfers etc. and auction purchase in certificate sales of pattani holdings or parts thereof shall be restricted to Cooch Beharis as defined in State Council notification No. 114 dated the 15th August 1941.

By order,
J. C. GOON,
Assistant Secretary,
General Secretariat, Cooch Behar.

THE STATE COUNCIL, COOCH BEHAR.
GENERAL AND EXECUTIVE DEPARTMENT.
Circular Order.

No. G. B/12.—*Dated the 27th October, 1947.*

It is notified for information of those whom it may concern that the State Council have been pleased to order that it should henceforth be the responsibility of the occupiers of the State houses to supply the P. W. D. with all necessary information *viz.* (1) the pay they draw (2) the date of their occupying the houses (3) increment in their pay and (4) the date when the houses are vacated, to enable the P. W. D. to assess their rents correctly.

By order,
J. C. GOON,
t. Secretary, General Secretariat, Cooch Behar.

THE STATE COUNCIL, COOCH BEHAR.

GENERAL AND EXECUTIVE DEPARTMENT.

NOTIFICATION.

No. L/17.—*Dated the 17th October, 1947.*

Under section 15 of the Cooch Behar Motor Vehicles Tax Act, 1947 (No. III of 1947) the Durbar is pleased to exempt the following motor vehicles from payment of the tax.

S. No.	Name of owners and address.	Registration mark.	Horse power.	Kind of vehicles.	Maker's name.
1	His Highness the Maharaja Bhup Bahadur of Cooch Behar.	C. B. 2	45	Light car	Rolls Royce
2	Do	C. B. 3	20	Do	Austine
3	Do	C. B. 4	16	Do	Do
4	Do	C. B. 5	10	Do	Do
5	Do	C. B. 6	25	Do	Vàxhaul
6	Do	C. B. 17	12	Do	Austine
7	Do	C. B. 18	12	Do	Do
8	Do	C. B. 20	45	Light Bus	Isatta
9	Do	C. B. 21	7	Light Car	Austine
10	Do	C. B. 23	30	Do	Ford
11	Do	C. B. 24	30	Do	Do
12	Do	C. B. 27	30	Motor Bus	Dodge
13	Do	C. B. 29	25	Light Car	Bently
14	Do	C. B. 30	30	Do	Packard
15	DO	C. B. 31	30	Do	Dodge
16	Do	C. B. 32	25	Do	Do
17	Do	C. B. 34	30	Do	Crysler
18	Do	C. B. 39	36	Do	Buick
19	Do	C. B. 40	36	Do	Do
20	Do	C. B. 8	25	Do	Rolls Royce
21	Do	C. B. 36	16	Do	Willeys
22	Do	C. B. 150	30	Do	Chevrolet
23	Major Rajkumar G. Narayan, Cooch Behar.	C. B. 25	28	Do	Railton
24	Do	C. B. 138	13	Jeep Car	Ford
25	Chief Minister of the State, Cooch Behar.	C. B. 28	95	Light Car	Chevrolet
26	Do	C. B. 169	26·3	Do	Studebekar Commander.
27	Commissioner of Police, Cooch Behar.	C. B. 38	24	Lorry	Ford (Fire Brigade.)
28	Do	C. B. 131	29	Do	Dodge (Do)
29	Household Minister, I/C, Military Department, Cooch Behar.	C. B. 42	29·5	Do	....
30	State Engineer, P. W. D., Cooch Behar.	C. B. 95	15	Do	Chevrolet (State Car).
31	Vice Chairman, Town Committee, Cooch Behar.	C. B. 50	56	Lorry	Bed Ford (Disel).
32	Do	C. B. 51	17	Do	Chevrolet
33	Do	C. B. 52	21	Do	Do
34	Do	C. B. 53	21	Do	Do
35	Do	C. B. 54	90	Do	Do
36	Deputy Chief Commandant, C. B. State Forces, Cooch Behar.	C. B. 106	29·4	Do	Do
37	Do	C. B. 116	29	Do	Do
38	Do	C. B. 117	1	Motor Cycle	B. S. A Solo
39	Do	C. B. 118	29	Lorry	Chevrolet
40	Honorary Controller, Guest Department Cooch Behar.	C. B. 152	10	Light Car	Hillman Minx

By order,
J. C. GOON,
Assistant Secretary, General Secretariat, Cooch Behar.

ORDERS BY THE STATE COUNCIL, COOCH BEHAR.

APPOINTMENT.—*The 5th November, 1947*—Sjt. Somen Bose who has been serving temporarily in the P. W. D. as "Architectural Draftsman" is appointed as Assistant to Town planner in the rank of Gazetted Officers in the scale of pay of Rs. 150-10/2-200 with effect from the 13th November 1947 *i. e.* the date on which his services as "Architectural Draftsman" in the P. W. D. will terminate.

APPOINTMENT—*The 6th November 1947*—Mr. R. C. Kar, M. A., is appointed State Archaeologist in connection with collection of the historical materials in the State temporarily for six months with effect from 16th October 1947.

LEAVE—*The 6th November 1947*—Mr. A. C. Datta, Commissioner of Excise, Cooch Beharis granted an extension of privilege leave for 7 days from 12th October to 18th October 1947 in continuation of privilege leave for 2 months with effect from 12th August 1947 with permission to suffix the Puja holidays already granted to him.

LEAVE—*The 10th November 1947*— Lt. Col. Maharajkumar I. Narayan Deputy Development Commissioner, Cooch Behar is granted extension of medical leave for 18 days from 1st October to 18th October 1947 with permission to affix the Puja holidays from 19th to 30th October 1947, in continuation of the leave granted to him from 7th June 1947 to 30th September 1947.

POWERS.—*Dated the 15th October, 1947.*—Sjt. H. Biswas, M.A., B.L., Civil Supplies Commissioner is vested, as a special case, with the same powers as are enjoyed by the Secretaries to the Government as defined in the Book of Powers.

POWERS.—*The 19th October, 1947.*—Mlv. Matiar Rahaman, B. L., Additional Naib Ahilkar on probation, is posted to Sadar with powers of a Naib Ahilkar in the Revenue and Registration Departments. He is vested with the powers of a 3rd class Magistrate and also with the powers to try civil and rent suits. He is further permitted to do such work as will be given to him from time to time by the Revenue Minister of the State.

By order,
J. C. GOON,
Asstt. Secretary, General Secretariat, Cooch Behar.

THE STATE COUNCIL, COOCH BEHAR.

GENERAL AND EXECUTIVE DEPARTMENT.

NOTIFICATION.

No G/48—*Dated the 1 th November, 1947.*

It is notified for general information that the State Council is pleased to order that a State Motor Transport service will be run from the 1st December 1947 by the Development Department from Cooch Behar to Tufanganj and Tufanganj to Cooch Behar. The fares to be charged are fixed as follows :—

	Fare.	Luggage and Parcels per Md.
Cooch Behar to Kaljani.	1 0 0	0 10 0
Kaljani to Tufanganj.	0 8 0	0 5 0
Cooch Behar to Tufanganj.	1 4 0	0 12 0

Free allowance of 20 seers of luggage will be given per passenger.

By order,
J. C. GOON,
Assistant Secretary, General Secretariat,
Cooch Behar.

ORDERS BY THE CHIEF MINISTER, COOCH BEHAR.

LEAVE—*The 19th October. 1947.*—Sjt. Suresh Chandra Ghosh, Examiner of Local Accounts, Audit Department, Cooch Behar is granted privilege leave for 22 days with effect from 31st October 1947 with permission to prefix Durga Puja holidays and to affix the casual holidays from 22nd November to 25th November 1947 instead of 19 days with effect from 3rd November with permission to prefix and affix the holidays previously granted to him, according to the recent orders of the State Council published in the *Cooch Behar Gazette* dated 7th October 1947.

By Order,
J. C. GOON,
Assistant Secretary,
General Secretariat, Cooch Behar.

ORDERS BY THE CHIEF MINISTER, COOCH BEHAR.

GENERAL SECRETARIAT,

The 6th November, 1947.

LEAVE—Sjt. D. P. Chakravarti, B.A., Assistant Secrtary, General Secretariat, Cooch Behar, is granted further extension of medical leave for the period from the 12th October 1947 to 31st January 1948.

During his absence on leave, the existing arrangement will continue.

By order,
J. C. GOON,
Asstt. Secretary, General Secretariat, Cooch Behar

PUBLICITY DEPARTMENT.
COOCH BEHAR.

The 17th October, 1947.

The following extracts from an article by Sir Jadu Nath Sarkar, D. Litt. published in the Modern Review of September, 1947 will be of interest to teachers and parents and guardians of students and are republished in the earnest hope that students will be called back to their legitimate duties :—

"On the first day of India's independence, what causes the greatest anxiety to a thoughtful patriot is the politicians' corruption of our immature lads. The most alarming threat to the new world which we wish to create in India is the lawlessness which has become ingrained in a certain section of our students. It is true that less than a quarter of our student community make political work a pretext for neglecting their legitimate duties and spurning at discipline. But they are backed by a certain type of political leaders (in whose election campaigns they assist as "camp followers" without pay), and the educational authorities are publicly humiliated and the 75 per cent of dutiful students are overborne by this boisterous minority.

For twenty years now, ever since the visit of the Simon Commission, students, even school children in their teens, have been deliberately employed as "soldiers in the war of national liberation" and glorified as heroes and martyrs, while educationists have been publicly censured as tyrants. In consequence academic discipline and even order and peace in educational institutions, have vanished from India, most of all from Bengal. Very frequently, on flimsy grounds, sometimes on no ground that one can see (euphemistically called sympathetic strikes), the hustling minority in our schools and colleges—working in federations through the province—declare strikes; they block the gates of the schools and colleges and forcibly prevent the teachers and dutiful students from entering and doing their work; teachers are assaulted in the streets, even in the examination halls invigilators and examiners have been man-handled and desks overturned to interrupt the University examination work. Their elders raise no voice of protest or moral condemnation against such antics, and hence there is nothing to disabuse these young minds of the false idea that they are thus doing national service or showing true patriotism. These students are our political leaders by forming their own Federations, holding periodical conventions, issuing free communiques, conducting party journals, and even indulging in faction fights between rival groups at public meetings. (Bose party *versus* Sen party, miniature edition).

* * * * * * *

* * * * * * *

On sober reflection it will appear that in instigating and continuing the employment of immature lads in political agitation (miscalled national work) and destroying the peace and efficiency of our schools and colleges, we are acting exactly like the foolish farmer who eats up the seed-corn for his next year's harvest so that his fields lie untilled and barren in future.

Where is the remedy? Where is the honest and strong Education Minister (or Vice-Chancellor) who will face initial unpopularity with a noisy section by calling students back to their legitimate duties, remove the enemies of academic peace and efficiency from the temples of Saraswati and thus enable the country to rise higher and higher in the work of learning and science? Remember that the young Buddist Bhikhus (monks and novices) of old by their violation of discipline (*vinaya*) and defiance of the "Council of elders" broke up the monstaries of India and at last Buddhism itself perished in the land of its birth."

J. C. GOOW,
Publicity Officer, Cooch Behar.

১৯৪৭ সনের সেপ্টেম্বর মাসের মডার্ণ রিভিউ পত্রিকায় প্রকাশিত সার যদুনাথ সরকার, ডি-লিট মহাশয়ের লিখিত প্রবন্ধের নিম্নলিখিত উদ্ধৃত অংশ শিক্ষক, পিতামাতা ও ছাত্রের অভিভাবকগণের হিতার্থে লিখিত এবং উহা ছাত্র-সমাজকে ন্যায় ও কর্ত্তব্যের পথে চালিত করিবে এই একান্ত আশায় পুনঃ প্রকাশিত হইল :—

"ভারতের স্বাধীনতার প্রথম দিবসেই চিন্তাশীল ও দেশ সেবকের মনে গভীর উদ্বেগ জাগিয়া উঠে কি ভাবে রাজনীতিজ্ঞদের হস্তে অপ্রাপ্তবয়স্ক বালকদের নৈতিক অবনতি ঘটিয়াছে। ছাত্রসমাজে আইন ভঙ্গ করিবার প্রবৃত্তি যেরূপ দৃঢ় ভিত্তি লাভ করিয়াছে তাহাতে নিশ্চিত মনে আসে আমরা যে সকল পরিকল্পনা সিদ্ধ করিতে চাই—তাহা অতীব সুদূর পরাহত।

এ কথা সত্য যে ছাত্রসমাজের এক চতুর্থাংশের কিছু কম বিধিসঙ্গত কর্ত্তব্যের প্রতি অবহেলা ও শৃঙ্খলা রক্ষার প্রতি পদাঘাত প্রদর্শনের জন্যই রাজনৈতিক কর্ম্মের সুবিধা গ্রহণ করে ও তাহাতে লিপ্ত থাকে। তাহারা একশ্রেণীর রাজনৈতিক নেতা দ্বারা সমর্থিত হয় (এই নেতাগণের নির্ব্বাচন অভিযানে এই ছাত্রগণ বিনাবেতনে শিবির অনুগামীর কাজ করে) ও শিক্ষা প্রতিষ্ঠানগুলিকে লোকচক্ষে হেয় প্রতিপন্ন করে। এই হাঙ্গামাপ্রবণ সংখ্যালঘুদের দ্বারা অবশিষ্ট শতকরা ৭৫ জন কর্ত্তব্যপরায়ণ ছাত্রগণ অপচালিত হইতে বাধ্য হয়।

বিগত বিশ বৎসরকাল এই দেশে সাইমন কমিশনের আগমনের পর হইতে ছাত্ররা এমন কি স্কুলের একান্ত অপ্রাপ্তবয়স্ক ছাত্ররা স্থিরসিদ্ধান্তভাবেই "দেশমুক্তির সংগ্রাম সৈন্য" হিসাবে নিয়োজিত হইতেছে এবং বীর ও শহীদএর ন্যায় পূজ্য বলিয়া গন্য হইতেছে। অপরপক্ষে শিক্ষাবিদ্‌গণকে অত্যাচারী আখ্যা দিয়া সর্ব্বসমক্ষে হীন বলিয়া প্রতিপন্ন করা হইতেছে যাহার ফলে শিক্ষা প্রতিষ্ঠানের নিয়ম পালন এবং শান্তি ও শৃঙ্খলা ভারতবর্ষ হইতে এবং বিশেষ করিয়া বঙ্গদেশ হইতে একেবারে দূর হইয়াছে। প্রায়শঃই অতিসামান্য কারণে এবং একেবারে অকারণে (যাহাকে নামভাষায় সহানুভূতিসূচক ধর্ম্মঘট বলা হয়) সংখ্যালঘু স্কুল ও কলেজের ছাত্রগণ আন্তঃপ্রাদেশিক যোগসাজসে ধর্ম্মঘট ঘোষণা করে। তাহারা স্কুল কলেজের দ্বারদেশ বন্ধ করিয়া দেয় এবং বলপূর্ব্বক শিক্ষক ও কর্ত্তব্যপরায়ণ ছাত্রগণকে নিজ নিজ কাজে যোগদানে বাধা দেয়। শিক্ষকগণ রাস্তায় প্রহৃত হন এমনকি পরীক্ষাগৃহের পরিদর্শকগণ ও পরীক্ষকগণ প্রহৃত হন। কখনও বা বিশ্ববিদ্যালয়ের পরীক্ষা কার্য্যে ব্যাঘাত ঘটাইয়া ডেস্ক প্রভৃতি উল্টাইয়া দেওয়া হয়। তাহাদের বয়োজ্যেষ্ঠগণ এই প্রকার অন্যায় কার্য্যের বিরুদ্ধে কোন আন্তরিক নিন্দা বা প্রতিবাদ প্রকাশ করেন না। কাজেই এই সকল অপরিণতদের মনে মিথ্যা ধারণা হইয়াছে যে তাহারা দেশের সেবা করিয়া প্রকৃত দেশসেবকের কার্য্য করিতেছে এই ভ্রম সংশোধনের কোন চেষ্টাই করা হইতেছে না। এই সকল ছাত্র তাহাদের নিজেদের সঙ্ঘগঠন করিয়া নিয়মিতভাবে মাঝে মাঝে সভা আহ্বান, দ্বিধাহীনভাবে প্রচারপত্র প্রকাশ ও দলীয় পত্রিকা পরিচালনা করে এবং এমন কি জনসভায় প্রাতিদ্বন্দ্বীপক্ষের সহিত দলায়দ্বন্দ্বে লিপ্ত হয়। ইহারাই এখন আমাদের রাজনৈতিক নেতা।

গভীরভাবে চিন্তা করিলে ইহা প্রতিভাত হয় যে রাজনৈতিক আন্দোলনে (বিকৃত রাজনীতিতে) অপ্রাপ্তবয়স্ক বালকদিগকে প্ররোচিত ও নিয়োজিত করিয়া ও স্কুল কলেজের শান্তি ও শৃঙ্খলা নষ্ট করিয়া, যে সকল নির্ব্বোধ কৃষক তাহাদের আগামী বৎসরের শস্য বীজ খাইয়া ফেলার দরুণ ভবিষ্যতে তাহাদের জমি অকর্ষিত ও শূন্য অবস্থায় ফেলিয়া রাখে, আমরা তাহাদের ন্যায় কার্য্য করিতেছি।

ইহার প্রতিকার কোথায়? কোথায় সেই সৎ ও শক্তিশালী শিক্ষামন্ত্রী (অথবা ভাইস চ্যান্সেলার) যিনি ছাত্রদের—তাহাদের এই প্রকার দুষ্কর্ম্ম হইতে ফিরিতে বলিয়া, বাক্‌দেবীর মন্দির হইতে শিক্ষার শত্রু ও বিশৃঙ্খলাকে বিদূরিত করিয়া দেশকে শিক্ষা ও বিজ্ঞানের কার্য্যে উন্নত হইতে উন্নত স্তরে লইয়া যাইতে সাহায্য করিয়া আন্দোলনকারী সম্প্রদায়ের অপ্রীতিভাজন হইতে সাহস করেন?

স্মরণ রাখিতে হইবে যে প্রাচীনকালের তরুণ বৌদ্ধভিক্ষু (সন্ন্যাসী ও অদীক্ষিত শিষ্যগণ) শিষ্টাচার (বিনয়াদি) অমান্য করিয়া এবং "প্রাচীনদের মতবাদ" অগ্রাহ্য করিয়া ভারতের মঠীয় বংশ [illegible]"

The Cooch Behar Gazette.

Published by Authority.

১৫ই অগ্রহায়ণ সোমবার] MONDAY, DECEMBER 1, 1947. ১৩৫৪ সাল ৪৩৮ রাজশক

PART I.

CONTENTS.

Notifications and Orders by His Highness the Maharaja Bhup Bahadur, His Highness the Maharaja Bhup Bahadur in Council, the Chief Minister and other Ministers and the High Court.

COOCH BEHAR STATE FORCES ORDERS BY HIS HIGHNESS THE CHIEF COMMANDANT.

Cooch Behar, the 15th November, 1947.

COMMAND:

(i) Capt. R. K. Chatterjea, OC, MH, on return from leave took over command of Military Hospital from Lieut. B. Chakraborty with effect from 1st November, 1947 (A. N.).

(ii) Capt. A. P. Deexit, Staff Captain, Cooch Behar SF, on return from leave took over command of W/T Section from Lieut. B. K. Bhattacharjee, with effect from 15th November, 1947 (F. N.).

STAFF DUTIES:

Capt. A. P. Deexit, Staff Captain, Cooch Behar SF, on return from leave took over charge of Staff Captain from Lieut. B. K. Bhattacharjee with effect from 15th November, 1947 (F.N.).

Lieut. B. Chakraborty, M H.	PRIVILEGE.	21 days w. e. f. 10th November. 1947.

(ii) **The following leaves are cancelled :**

(a)	Ref. CBSFO 132/47 Capt R. K. Chatterjee, O.C., M.H.	Unavailed period from 2.11.47 (FN) to 18.11.47 (AN).
(b)	Ref. CBSFO 120/47 Lieut. Bhagwan Singh, 1 CBI.	Unavailed period from 5.10.47 (F.N.) to 8.11.47 (AN).

By order,
B. P. WALAWALKER,
LT. COLONEL,
Dy. Chief Commandant.

ORDERS BY THE STATE COUNCIL, COOCH BEHAR.

LEAVE.—*The 10th November 1947.* —Lt. Col. B. P. Walawalker, Deputy Chief Commandant, Cooch Behar State Forces, Cooch Behar, is granted an extension of furlough by 2 days in addition to the furlough already granted to him.

LEAVE.—*The 18th November, 1947.*—Dr. S. C. Chatterjee, Chief Medical Officer, and Secretary, Medical and Public Health Departments, Cooch Behar, is granted privilege leave for one month with effect from the 10th December, 1947.

During his absence on privilege leave, the work of the Sudder Hospital will be carried on by Dr. A. S. Sen, Surgeon Superintendent, in addition to his own duties with the usual allowance admissible under rules with the help and assistance of other Medical Staff. He will also sign and countersign all bills relating to the Medical Department.

The charge of the Public Health Department will lie with the Public Health and Education Minister.

CORRIGENDUM—*The 19th November 1947.*—Please read "15th November 1947" in place of "16th November 1947" in the State Council Order dated 5th November 1947 under "Appointment" as published in Part I of the *Cooch Behar Gazette* dated 17th November 1947 at page 128.

By Order,
J. C. GOON,
Assistant Secretary,
General Secretariat, Cooch Behar.

THE STATE COUNCIL, COOCH BEHAR.
GENERAL & EXECUTIVE DEPARTMENT.
NOTIFICATION.
(Town Committee).

No. T. 8 —*Dated the 16th November, 1947.*

It is notified for information of those whom it may concern that the Durbar have been pleased to levy a tax of Rs. 4 per mensem on every tea stall and sweetmeat shop situated in the Mathabhanga Town Committee with effect from the date of publication of this notification in the Gazette.

S. C. ROY SINGH SARMAR,
Public Health & Education Minister,
Cooch Behar.

The Cooch Behar Gazette.

SUPPLEMENTARY.

১৬ই আষাঢ়, মঙ্গলবার ; TUESDAY, JULY 1, 1947 [১৩৫৪ সাল ৪৩৮ রাজশক]

PART II.

NOTICES.

রাজকীয় প্রাপ্য আদায় বিষয়ক ১৯৪৩ ইং সনের ১০ আইনের ২ সিডিউলের ৪৬ নিয়মের ঘোষণাপত্র।

রাজ্য কোচবিহারের সদর খাস মহাল আদালত।

এতদ্দ্বারা সর্ব্বসাধারণকে জানান যাইতেছে যে দায়ীকগণের নিম্নলিখিত সম্পত্তি আগামী ১৯৪৭ ইং সনের ১৬ই জুলাই মোঃ ১৩৫৪ সনের ৩১শে আষাঢ় তারিখে দিবা ১ ঘটিকার সময় তুফানগঞ্জ খাস মহাল আফিসে খাস মহাল তহশীলদার কর্ত্তৃক প্রকাশ্য নিলাম আরম্ভ হইবে।

৬ নং সার্ট ১৯৪৬।৪৭ ইং। বাঃ ডিঃ ২৸৶০ মোঃ।

সরকার বাহাদুর বঃ কদম আলী মণ্ডল।

তপশিল সম্পত্তি।

পং তুফানগঞ্জ নং ১৪৩ থাক তাং বলরামপুর মধ্যে ২২৪ নং তৌঃ লিখিত ১৫৮২ কাঠা জমির কাত বাঃ ১৩৶ আনা জমার পঃ স্বত্ব।

৭ নং সার্ট ১৯৪৬।৪৭ ইং। বাঃ ডিঃ ৩০৸৶৯ মোঃ।

সরকার বাহাদুর বঃ আতর আলী ব্যাপারী।

তপশিল সম্পত্তি।

পং তুফানগঞ্জ নং ১৪৩ থাক তাং বলরামপুর মধ্যে ২২৮ নং পঃ তৌঃ লিখিত ১৮৮২।০ খুর জমির কাত বাঃ ১৩৶ আনা জমার পঃ স্বত্ব।

৪৮ নং সার্ট ১৯৪৬।৪৭ ইং। বাঃ ডিঃ ৬৮/০ মোঃ।

সরকার বাহাদুর বঃ নেহ দাস গং।

তপশিল সম্পত্তি।

পং তুফানগঞ্জ নং ১৮২ থাক তাং দেওচড়াই মধ্যে ১২০৩ নং পঃ তৌঃ লিখিত ২৩।৩/০ খুর জমির কাত বাঃ ২২।০ আনা জমার পঃ স্বত্ব।

৭১ নং সার্ট ১৯৪৬।৪৭ ইং। বাঃ ডিঃ ৮৲ মোঃ।

সরকার বাহাদুর বঃ আলীমুদ্দিন সেখ।

তপশিল সম্পত্তি

পং তুফানগঞ্জ নং ১১০৫ থাক তাং বালাভূত মধ্যে ৪৮৫ নং পঃ তৌঃ লিখিত ৫/৬/০ খুর জমির কাত বাঃ ৬৶০ আনা জমার পঃ স্বত্ব।

৭২ নং সাট্ট ১৯৪৬।৪৭ ইং। বাঃ ডিঃ ১০৲ মোঃ।

সরকারবাহাদুর বঃ রহিমুদ্দিন সেখ গং।

তপশিল সম্পত্তি।

পং তুফানগঞ্জ ১১০৫ নং থাক তাং বালাভুত মধ্যে ৪৮৬ নং পঃ তৌঃ লিখিত ৩/২৮৵০ ধুর জমির কাত বাঃ ৫৮০ আনা জমার পঃ স্বত্ব।

৮০ নং সাট্ট ১৯৪৬।৪৭ ইং। বাঃ ডিঃ ৩২৴৩ মোঃ।

সরকারবাহাদুর বঃ বিলাতু সেখ গং।

তপশিল সম্পত্তি।

পং তুফানগঞ্জ ১১০৬ নং থাক তাং ঝাউকুটি মধ্যে ৪৯১ নং পঃ তৌঃ লিখিত ২০৮৩৷৵০ ধুর জমির কাত বাঃ ১৫৮৴ আনা জমার পঃ স্বত্ব।

১০১ নং সাট্ট ১৯৪৬।৪৭ ইং। বাঃ ডিঃ ৩৯৲ মোঃ।

সরকারবাহাদুর বঃ রেজাল সেখ।

তপশীল সম্পত্তি।

পং তুফানগঞ্জ নং ১১১১ থাক তাং মানসাই মধ্যে ১৪৩২ নং পঃ তৌঃ লিখিত ১০৮২৮০ধুর জমির কাত বাঃ ১৩৷০ আনা জমার পঃ স্বত্ব।

১৫৭ নং ১৯৪৬।৪৭ ইং। বাঃ ডি. ৩৫৷৵০ মোঃ।

সরকারবাহাদুর বঃ মনসর দাস গং।

তপশিল সম্পত্তি।

পং তুফানগঞ্জ ১১৮৮ নং থাক তাং ছাট অনকা মধ্যে নং ১৯১ পঃ তৌঃ লিখিত ৩৯৷০৵০ধুর জমির কাত বাঃ ১৫৲ টাকা জমার পঃ স্বত্ব।

১৭৩ নং সাট্ট ১৯৪৬।৪৭ ইং। বাঃ ডিঃ ৫।৴০ মোঃ।

সরকারবাহাদুর বঃ আবদুল গফুর সেখ গং।

তপশিল।

পং তুফানগঞ্জ নং ১১৯৩ থাক তাং ফলিমারী মধ্যে ২৯০৩ নং পঃ তৌঃ লিখিত ১০৷৪৵০ ধুর জমির কাত বাঃ ২৵ আনা জমার পঃ স্বত্ব।

১৭২ নং সাট্ট ১৯৪৬।৪৭ ইং। বাঃ ডিঃ ৮৷৴০ মোঃ

সরকারবাহাদুর বঃ আবদুল গফুর সেখ।

তপশিল সম্পত্তি।

পং তুফানগঞ্জ নং ১১২৩ থাক তাং ফলিমারি মধ্যে ২৮৩৮ নং পঃ তৌঃ লিখিত ১৭৴৫৷৵০ ধুর জমির কাত বাঃ ২৮৴ আনা জমার পঃ স্বত্ব।

১৭৯ নং সাট্ট ১৯৪৬।৪৭ ইং। বাঃ ডিঃ ১০৮৴৩ মোঃ।

সরকারবাহাদুর বঃ পিয়ারউদ্দিন আহাম্মদ গং।

তপশিল সম্পত্তি।

পং তুফানগঞ্জ ১১৪৮ নং থাক তাং নেপাল মধ্যে ৭৯৪ নং পঃ তৌঃ লিখিত ৩৯।৪৷৵০ ধুর জমির কাত বাঃ ২৬০ আনা জমার পঃ স্বত্ব।

৪০ নং সাট্ট ১৯৪৬।৪৭ ইং। বাঃ ডিঃ ২১৮৴৩ মোঃ।

সরকারবাহাদুর বঃ তরণীকান্ত দাস গং

তপশিল সম্পত্তি।

পং তুফানগঞ্জ নং ৯৪১ থাক তাং বলরামপুর মধ্যে ৮৬৫ নং পঃ তৌঃ লিখিত ১৭।৫৷৵০ ধুর জমির কাত বাঃ ৷৵ আনা জমার পঃ স্বত্ব।

DWIJENDRA CHANDRA SEN, *Certificate Officer.*

MALCUCHERY NOTICE.

ইস্তাহারনামা কাছারী মাল মোতালকে নিজ বেহার, সন ১৩৫৭ তারিখ ২৯শে জুন
মোতাবেক বাঙ্গালা ১৩৫৪ সন তারিখ ৯ই আষাঢ়।

পরগণে মাথাভাঙ্গা এলাকাধীন ৩৯০ নং থাক তাং শৌলমারী অন্তর্গত কোচবিহার চা বাগানের জন্য অত্র আদালতের ১৯৭৭৪৮ ইং সনের ৮ নং ভূমিগ্রহণের মোকদ্দমায় ২০।৬।৪৭ ইং তারিখের আদেশ সূত্রে নিম্নলিখিত বিবরণযুক্ত ভূমি ১৩৫৩ সনের শেষ ৬ মাস হইতে সরকারে গৃহীত হইয়া উক্ত কোচবিহার চা বাগানের শামিল হওয়ায় সর্ব্বসাধারণের অবগতি জন্য এই ইস্তাহার প্রচারিত হইল। ইতি

১। পঃ মাথাভাঙ্গা ৩৯০ নং থাক তাং শৌলমারী ১০ নং বঃ ২৪৩৬ নং তৌঃ ৯৭ নং স্বত্ব জোত মালচাঁদ পিং দৌলতরাম ভাদানী হরেকচাঁদ পিং গোলাপচাঁদ ভাদানী মোঃ মাথাভাঙ্গা বর্ত্তমান জমি ২৯৩/৮ কাঠা জমা ২০৮/০ আনা গৃহীত জমি ২৯৪,৮০ কাঠা জমা ২০৮ ০ আনা।

বিবং

৯৮ নং স্বত্ব চুকানী ঠাকুরদীন পিং সূর্য্যপ্রসাদ তেওয়ারী সাং কালাকাটা জিঃ জলপাইগুড়ী বর্ত্তমান জমি ২০১/৫।/০ ধুর জমা ১৩৯৮/০ আনা সিট নং ২ গৃহীত জমি ২০১/৫।/০ ধুর জমা ১৩৯৮/০ আনা।

বিবং

৯৯ নং স্বত্ব দরচুঃ সবরণ নেছা বিবি নাঃ পক্ষে উঃ পিতা খয়রউদ্দিন তাহাম্য সাং মেটি কেলী ভাণ্ডানী তৌঃ কালাকাটা জিঃ জলপাইগুড়ী বর্ত্তমান জমি ১৪২৮।৶০ ধুর জমা ১৩০।৶০ আনা সিট নং ২ গৃহীত জমি ১৪২৮১৶০ ধুর জমা ১৩০॥৶০ আনা।

বিবং

নিজ দখল দাগ নং ১৪—৩৩, ৪৩—৪৮, ৫৪, ৫৫, ২২৯—৩১, ৯৩৭, ৯৪৭, ৯৫৩, ৯৫৫, ৯৪৬, ৯৯৯—১৫২, ১০১৬, ১০১৭, ১০১৯, ১০২০ গৃহীত জমি ৮৫/১৶০ ধুর।

১০০ নং স্বত্ব কৃষিপ্রজা নতি মামুদ পিং নছিমামুদ নস্য বর্ত্তমান জমি ২৯।৪ ৶০ ধুর জমা ৩৫৮/০ আনা সিট নং ২ দাগ নং ৩৫, ৩৯—৪১, ৫৩, ৫৬, ৮৪৪, ৯৩৬, ৯২৮—৯৪১, ৯৪৪ গৃহীত জমি ২৯।৪।৶০ ধুর জমা ৩৫৮/০

১০১ নং স্বত্ব কৃষিপ্রজা ফুলমামুদ পিং বিতাব সেখ বর্ত্তমান জমি ৩১।০॥৶০ ধুর জমা ৪০।/০ আনা সিট নং ২ দাগ নং ৩৬—৩৮, ৪২—৪৫, ৪৯—৫২, ৯২০, ৯৩২—৯৩৫, ৯৪৭, ৯৪৮, ৯৫৩, ৯৫৭ গৃহীত জমি ৩১।০॥৶০ ধুর জমা ৪০।/০ আনা।

১০২ নং স্বত্ব দরচুঃ ব্রজনাথ পিং ছিরাম বর্ম্মণ সাং নিজ বর্ত্তমান জমি ৫৮।২৶০ ধুর জমা ৩২৮৶০ আনা সিট নং ২ দাগ নং ৩৪, ৮২—৮৪, ২১৮, ১০১৫, ১০১৮ গৃহীত জমি ৫৮।২৶০ ধুর জমা ৩২৮৶০ আনা।

১০৩ নং স্বত্ব চুকানী ব্রজনাথ পিং ছিরাম বর্ম্মণ সাং নিজ বর্ত্তমান জমি ১৯২।২।৶০ ধুর জমা ১৪১৲ টাকা সিট নং ২ দাগ নং ৫৭—৮১, ১০৯, ২১৯, ১০০৯—১০১৪ গৃহীত জমি ১৯২৮২।৶০ ধুর জমা ১৪১৲ টাকা।

চৌঃ—উঃ সীঃ জিলা জলপাইগুড়ী থানা কালাকাটা তাং রায়চেঙ্গা পুঃ সীঃ মাথাভাঙ্গা কালাকাটা রাস্তা দঃ সীঃ ১০৮, ১০৭, ১০৩, ১০০৬, ৯৯ ও ১০১৪ নং দাগের জমি পঃ সীঃ ৩ নং সিট ৯৫৫, ১৩ নং দাগের জমি।

২। পঃ মাথাভাঙ্গা ৩৯০ নং থাক তাং শৌলমারী ১২ নং বঃ ২৪১৮ নং তৌঃ ১০৬ নং স্বত্ব জোত মালচাঁদ পিং দৌলতরাম ভাদানী হরকচাঁদ ভাদানী পিং গোলাপচাঁদ ভাদানী মোঃ মাথাভাঙ্গা সিট নং ২ বর্ত্তমান জমি ১১০৮।৩।/০ ধুর জমা ৫৭৶০ আনা গৃহীত জমি ৫৮।৮৶০ ধুর জমা ৬॥৫ পাই।

নিজং

১০৭ নং স্বত্ব চুকানী চন্দ্রকা পিং গুল দাস সিট নং ২ দাগ নং ১৫৪, ১৫৫ বর্ত্তমান জমি ৪৬৮১ কাঠা জমা ৫১।০ আনা গৃহীত জমি ১৭।১।৶০ ধুর জমা ১,৬ পাই।

১০৮ নং স্বত্ব চুকানী গুরুচাঁদ নাঃ পক্ষে উঃ মাতা রুক্মাবতী দাস্যা জঃ শীতল বর্ম্মণ নারায়ণ ও চন্দ্র পিং রূপ বর্ম্মণ সিট নং ২ দাগ নং ৪৫৭, ৮৪১, ৮৪২ বর্ত্তমান জমি ৬৬/২॥০ ধুর জমা ৫৯।০ আনা গৃহীত জমি ৬।১॥০ ধুর জমা ৮,৩ পাই।

চৌঃ—উঃ সীঃ ১৬২, ৪১৫ নং দাগ পূঃ সীঃ ৬—৬২, ৪৫৮, ৪৫৬, ৪৫৫, ৯০৫, ৪৫২, ৪৬৯, ১৫৬ নং দাগের জমি দঃ সীঃ ৪৬৩ নং দাগের জমি পঃ সাং মাথাভাঙ্গা কালাকাটা রাস্তা।

৩। পঃ থাক তাং ৩০।১৩ নং বঃ ২৪৩৯ নং তৌঃ ১ ৯ নং স্বত্ব জোত হেমেন্দ্রকুমার, জ্ঞানেন্দ্রকুমার পিং হীরেন্দ্র কুমার রায় চৌধুরী শিশিরকুমার পিং শচীন্দ্রকুমার রায় চৌধুরী বীরেন্দ্রকুমার, জিতেন্দ্রকুমার পিং রাজেন্দ্রকুমার রায় চৌধুরী মোঃ মাথাভাঙ্গা তৌঃ সূত্রে ৫ প্রাপ্ত নাগ জঃ জিতেন্দ্রচন্দ্র নাগ ইন্দুবালা সাহা জঃ শচীন্দ্রকুমার সাহা সিট নং ২ বর্ত্তমান জমি ৪৮৮।২ ৶০ ধুর জমা ২৯৭৶০ আনা গৃহীত জমি ১১৩।১ ৶০ ধুর জমা ৭৫৮/৭ পাই।

৩। পরগণে মাথাভাঙ্গা ৩৯০ নং থাক তাং শৌলমারী বঃ ১৩ নং ১৪১৯ নং তৌঃ বদীনাথ পিং রামপ্রসাদ দাস বর্ত্তমান জমি ৪১০॥২।৶০ ধুর জমা ৩৫২।৶০ আনা স্বত্ব ১১০ নং সিট ২ নং দাগ নং ১৫৭—১৬১ ৪১৭, ৪৪৫, ৫৬৩, ৪৬৪, ৪৬২, ৬৬৭, ৬৬৮, ৬৬৯, ৭১২—৭১৫, ৭১৭, ৭১৮, ৯০৮, ৪১৮, ৬৬১ গৃহীত জমি ১০৪৮১।/০ ধুর জমা ৯১।৶৬ পাই।

কৃষিপ্রজা খোনা, বেচেশ্বর ও ভবেশ্বর পিং টুলু দাস বর্ত্তমান জমি ২।৪/ ধুর জমা ৫৮৶০ আনা ১১১ নং স্বত্ব সিট ২ নং ৪৪৯—৪৫১ গৃহীত জমি ২.৪/০ ধুর জমা ৫৮৶০ আনা।

দরচুকানী টেপ্পা পিং সজীব বর্ম্মণ ও নাঃ পক্ষে উঃ পিতামহী শাকালী দাস্যা বর্ত্তমান জমি ২।৭৮/০ ধুর জমা ২৬৮৶০ আনা ১১২ নং স্বত্ব ২ নং সিট ৪১২, ৯৯১, ৯৯২, নং দাগ গৃহীত জমি ২৮০/০ ধুর জমা ৬॥৶৫ পাই।

দরচুকানী জয়নাথ বর্ম্মণ পিং কাছিন দাস বর্ত্তমান জমি ১৯/৪/৶ ধুর জমা ২৪৮৶০ আনা ১১৩ নং স্বত্ব ২ নং সিট ৪৫৯, ৯০৪, নং দাগ গৃহীত জমি ১।১।৶ ধুর জমা ২৮৫ পাই।

দরচুকানী সোনাতন, হরিশঙ্কর পিং ভুখিয়া বর্ম্মন বর্ত্তমান জমি ১৭৮৪৸৵০ খুর জমা ২১৷/০ আনা ১১৫ নং খত ২ নং সিট ১৫৬, ৪৪৬, ৪৪৭, ৪৪৮, নং দাগ বর্ত্তমান জমি ৩ ১৵০ খুর জমা ৬৷০ পাই

দরচুকানী শিবা পিং হাণ্ডিয়া বর্ম্মন বর্ত্তমান জমি ৪৭৷১৪৶০ খুর জমা ৩৮৵০ আনা ১১৬ নং খত ২ নং সিট ৬১৯, ৬৬০, ৬৯১, ৬৯২—৭০৬, ৭১৬, ৭১৯, ৯০৭, ৯১৮, ৯০৮, ৯১৯, নং দাগ গৃহীত জমি ৪৭৪৷৶০ খুর জমা ৩৮৵০ আনা।

দরচুকানী দীন দস্তা অঃ অধোয়া বর্ম্মন বর্ত্তমান জমি ১৮৬৷০ খুর জমা ২৭৵০ আনা ১১৭ নং খত ২ নং সিট ৪৫৩, ৪৫৫, ৪৫৬, ৪৫৮, ৯০৫, নং দাগ বর্ত্তমান জমি ৫৪০/৸০ খুর জমা ১৫/১১ পাই।

দরচুকানী নিপুচাপিং টেপু দাস বঃ জমি ৩০৷১৮৶০ খুর জমা ২৪ টাকা ১১৮ নং খত ২ নং সিট ৩৫৪, নং দাগ গৃহীত জমি /৩ কাঠা জমা ।৫৩ পাই।

চুকানী দর্পনাথ পিং রামপ্রসাদ দাস বঃ জমি ৫৩২/।৶০ খুর জমা ৩০।৶০ ১২০ নং খত ২ নং সিট ৬৬২, ৬৬৫, ৬৬৬, ৯০৯, ৯১০, গৃহীত জমি ৩/।৶০ খুর জমা২।/২ পাই।

চুকানী হরেকচাঁদ পিং গোলাপচাঁদ ভাদানী, মালচাঁদ পিং দৌলতরাম ভাদানী, মোঃ মাথাভাঙ্গা বর্ত্তমান জমি ২৫৮৪৷৶০ খুর জমা ১৮/০ আনা ১২১ নং খত ২ নং সিট গৃহীত জমি ৪।৩৸৶ খুর জমা ৸০ আনা

বিক্তং

দরচুকানী হরিপ্রসাদ পিং নেন্দা বর্ম্মণ সাং রামঠেঙ্গা বর্ত্তমান জমি ২৫৮৪৷৶০ খুর জমা ২৩৶০ আনা ১২২ নং খত ২ নং সিট ৭১০, ৭১১, নং দাগ গৃহীত জমি ৫।৩৸৶০ খুর জমা ৮৶২ পাই।

চৌঃ—উঃ সীঃ ৬৮১, ৬৮২, ৯১৬, ৬১৩, ৯১১, ৬৭০, ৬৬৪, ৬৬০, ৯০৬, ১৮২, ১৮০, ৪১১—৪১৬ নং দাগ পুঃ সীঃ ৪০৮, ৪০৯, ৪২১, ৪৪৭, ৪৪৪, ৪৬৭, ৯৯৩ নং দাগের জমি দঃ সীঃ ৪৮০, ৮৪২, ৭২১ নং দাগের জমি ও ৭২০ নং দাগের মুজনাই নদী পঃ সীঃ ৭০৭ নং দাগ মুজনাই নদী ৪ নং সিট।

৪। পঃ মাথাভাঙ্গা ৩১০ নং থাক তাং শৌলমারী ১৪ নং বঃ ২৪৪০ নং তৌঃ ১২৩ নং খত ২ নং সিট জোত লালবিহারী মিছির পিং বিকারী মিছির মোঃ মাথাভাঙ্গা বঃ জমী ১৫৯/৪৸৶০ খুর জমা ১২৪৶০ গৃহীত জমী ৪৪৪৸৶০ খুর জমা ৮৫২ পাই।

চৌঃ সূত্রে—গুরুপ্রসাদ ও প্রয়াগ দত্ত হুকুম।

বিক্তং

চুকানী মালচাঁদ পিং দৌলতরাম ভাদানী, হরেকচাঁদ পিং গোলাপচাঁদ ভাদানী, মোঃ মাথাভাঙ্গা বঃ জমি ১৪৩/৩।/০ খুর জমা ১৬৬৷৵০ আনা ১২৪ নং খত ২ নং সিট গৃহীত জমী ৪৪৮/৸৷০ খুর জমা ৮৵২ পাই।

বিক্তং

দর চুঃ অধোয়া পিং পাটিয়া বর্ম্মণ বঃ জমী ২৩৷২৷৶০ খুর জমা ৪১৷০ আনা ১২৫ নং খত ২ নং সিট গৃহীত জমী ৪৪৪৸৶০ খুর জমা ২৷৵৩ দাগ নং ৪৬০, ৪৬১, ৪৬২, ৪৭০, ৪৭১।

চৌহদ্দী—উঃ সীঃ ৪৪৫ নং দাগ রাস্তা, পুঃ সীঃ ৪৭২, ৪৭৩, ৪৭৪ ও ৪৭৫ নং দাগের জমী, দঃ সীঃ ৪৬৯ নং দাগের জমী, পঃ সীঃ ৪৬৩, ৪৬২, ৪৬২ ও ৮৪১ নং দাগের জমী।

৫। পঃ মাথাভাঙ্গা ৫৯০ নং থাক তাং শৌলমারী ১৬ নং বঃ ২৪৫২ নং তৌঃ জোত মালচাঁদ পিং দৌলতরাম ভাদানী হরেকচাঁদ পিং গোলাপচাঁদ ভাদানী মোঃ মাথাভাঙ্গা বর্ত্তমান জমী ১৬৭।১৸৶০ খুর জমা ৪৬৸৶০ আনা খত নং ১৫৯ সিট নং ২ গৃহীত জমী ১৬/৩ ০ খুর জমা ২।৬ পাই।

বিক্তং

চুঃ রুদী পিং রামপ্রসাদ দাস, গেন্দা পিং সাদামামুদ নস্ত মহেন্দ্রনাথ বর্ম্মণ পিং নোকয় দাস বর্ত্তমান জমী ১৬৭।১৸৶০ খুর জমা ৬৩।০ আনা ১৪০ নং খত ২ নং ২২৭/১ দাগ গৃহীত জমী ১৬/৩৵০ খুর জমা ৩ ৩ পাই।

বিক্তং

কৃষিপ্রজা চলকা পিং গুল দাস তারিনী পিং পুটকনা দাস সাং মিল বর্ত্তমান জমী ৫৮/।৶০ খুর জমা ২৬০ আনা ১৪১ নং খত ২ নং সিট দাগ নং ২২০/২, ২২১/৩, ২২৬/২ গৃহীত জমী ২৷২।৶০ খুর জমা ২।/২ পাই।

চৌহদ্দী—উঃ সীঃ ২২৭ নং দাগ পুঃ সীঃ ২২০, ২২১, ২২২ ও ২২৭ নং দাগ দঃ সীঃ ২১৮ নং দাগ পঃ সীঃ মাথাভাঙ্গা কলাকাটা রাস্তা।

K C GANGULI,
Revenue Minister of the
Cooch Behar State.

The Cooch Behar Gazette.

১৬ই আষাঢ়, মঙ্গলবার ; TUESDAY, JULY 1, 1947 [১৩৫৪ সাল ৪৩৮ রাজশক]

PART II.

NOTICES.

রাজকীয় প্রাপ্য আদায় বিষয়ক ১৯৪৩ ইং সনের ১০ আইনের ২ সিডিউলের ৪৬ নিয়মের ঘোষণাপত্র ।

রাজ্য কোচবিহারের সদর খাষ মহাল আদালত ।

এতদ্দ্বারা সর্ব্বসাধারণকে জানান যাইতেছে যে দায়ীকগণের নিম্নলিখিত সম্পত্তি আগামী ১৯৪৭ ইং সনের ৫ই জুলাই মোঃ ১৩৫৪ সনের ২০শে আষাঢ় তারিখে দিবা ১ ঘটিকার সময় মেখলীগঞ্জ খাষ মহাল আফিসে খাষ মহাল আফসার কর্ত্তৃক প্রকাশ্য নিলাম আরম্ভ হইবে।

১১৫ নং সার্ট ১৯৪৬।৪৭ ইং। বাঃ ডিঃ ২১৭৸/১০ মোঃ।

সরকার বাহাদুর বঃ আমানউদ্দিন খাঃ।

তপশিল সম্পত্তি

পঃ মেখলীগঞ্জ ৪৫ নং থাক ৩২৮২ নং তৌঃ তাং তিস্তানদীর পয়স্তী মধ্যে ১২১৸৩৷৷৴০ খুর জমির কাত বাঃ ১১৭৸৴০ আনা জমার পঃ খব।

১১৯ নং সার্ট ১৯৪৬।৪৭ ইং। বাঃ ডিঃ ৫৫৶০ মোঃ।

সরকার বাহাদুর বঃ সফিরুদ্দিন মহম্মদ।

তপশিল সম্পত্তি।

পঃ মেখলীগঞ্জ ১২৪ নং থাক ৯১৭ নং তৌঃ তাং ফুলকাডাবরী কাশিয়াবাড়ী মধ্যে ১৭/২১৷৴০ খুর জমির কাত বাঃ ১৬৸৴০ আনা জমার পঃ খব।

১২৫ নং সার্ট ১৯৪৬।৪৭ ইং। বাঃ ডিঃ ৮৶৩ মোঃ।

সরকার বাহাদুর বঃ বোবাই মহম্মদ।

তপশিল সম্পত্তি।

পঃ মেখলীগঞ্জ ১২৫ নং থাক ১৭৫৩ নং তৌঃ তাং ধরলাবাড়ী মধ্যে ২।৪ কাঠা জমির কাত বাঃ ৩৶০ আনা জমার পঃ খব।

১২৭ নং সার্ট ১৯৪৬।৪৭ ইং। বাঃ ডিঃ ২৸০ মোঃ।

সরকার বাহাদুর বঃ মহাজনী বর্ম্মণী খাঃ।

তপশিল সম্পত্তি

পঃ মেখলীগঞ্জ ১১১৩ নং তৌঃ তাং বালাপুখরী ১৩।১০ খুর জমির কাত বাঃ ১৩।০ আনা জমার পঃ খব।

১২৯ নং সার্ট ১৯৪৬।৪৭ ইং। বাঃ ডিঃ ৩০৸৴০ মোঃ।

সরকার বাহাদুর বঃ মহাজনী বর্ম্মণী খাঃ।

তপশিল সম্পত্তি।

পঃ মেখলীগঞ্জ ১১২৯ নং তৌঃ তাং বালাপুখরী মধ্যে ১১৪৩।০ খুর জমির কাত বাঃ ১৫।৴০ আনা জমার পঃ খব

১৪২ নং ১৯৪৬।৪৭ ইং। বাঃ ডিঃ ২৬।৵৬ মোঃ।

সরকার বাহাদুর বঃ ৻খবলু মহম্মদ।

তপশিল সম্পত্তি।

পঃ মেখলীগঞ্জ ১৪৭ নং থাক ২০৭৫ নং তৌঃ তাং ভোটবাড়ী মধ্যে ২৫৴২৮০ ধুর জমির কাত বাঃ ৩৬॥৶০ আনা জমার পঃ স্বত্ব।

১৪৪ নং ১৯৪৬।৪৭ ইং। বাঃ ডিঃ ৬৩৫৸৶০ মোঃ।

সরকার বাহাদুর বঃ যোগেন্দ্র দ. স গঃ।

তপশিল সম্পত্তি।

পঃ মেখলীগঞ্জ ১৫২ নং থাক ১৭৮৬ নং তৌঃ তাং পানীশালা মধ্যে ২১॥৩॥৴০ ধুর জমির কাত বাঃ ১৫৲ টাকা জমার পঃ স্বত্ব।

১৪১ নং ১৯৪৬।৪৭ ইং। বাঃ ডিঃ ৫৮॥০ মোঃ।

সরকার বাহাদুর বঃ অক্ষয়চরণ বর্ম্মণ।

তপশিল সম্পত্তি।

পঃ মেখলীগঞ্জ ২০৯ নং থাক ৭৬ নং তৌঃ তাং বুরাবুরী পাটছড়া মধ্যে ২৮৮০।৶০ ধুর জমির কাত বাঃ ৩০৶০ আনা জমার পঃ স্বত্ব।

১৬৪ নং ১৯৪৬।৪৭ ইং। বাঃ ডিঃ ৪৮॥৩ মোঃ।

সরকার বাহাদুর বঃ অবলা খাতুন গঃ।

তপশিল সম্পত্তি

পঃ মেখলীগঞ্জ ৯৬ নং থাক ১৩৫৭ নং তৌঃ তাং কুলকাড়াবরী মধ্যে ১৩।১॥৶০ ধুর জমির কাত বাঃ ২০।৶০ আনা জমার পঃ স্বত্ব।

১৬৫ নং ১৯৪৬।৪৭ ইং। বাঃ ডিঃ ৫৫।৶০ মোঃ।

সরকার বাহাদুর বঃ অবলা খাতুন গঃ।

তপশিল সম্পত্তি।

পঃ মেখলীগঞ্জ ১০১ নং থাক ১৩৫৫ নং তৌঃ তাং কুলকাডাবরী মধ্যে ২০॥০৸৶০ ধুর জমির কাত বাঃ ২০॥৶০ আনা জমার পঃ স্বত্ব।

১৬৬ নং ১৯৪৬।৪৭ ইং। বাঃ ডিঃ ৩৮।৶০ মোঃ।

সরকার বাহাদুর বঃ আছিরউদ্দিন।

তপশিল সম্পত্তি।

পঃ মেখলীগঞ্জ ৯৬ নং থাক ২৩৫৮ নং তৌঃ তাং কুলকাডাবরী মধ্যে ১২॥২৸৶০ ধুর জমির কাত বাঃ ১৬৶০ আনা জমার পঃ স্বত্ব।

২৭২ নং ১৯৪৩।৪৪ ইং। বাঃ ডিঃ ১৮॥৶০ মোঃ।

সরকার বাহাদুর বঃ হজরত মহম্মদ।

তপশিল সম্পত্তি।

পঃ মেখলীগঞ্জ ১০৪ নং থাক ৯৮৭ নং তৌঃ তাং কুলকাডাবরী মধ্যে ১০৴৪৸৶০ ধুর জমির কাত বাঃ ৬৶০ আনা জমার জমার পঃ স্বত্ব।

১৫৭ নং ১৯৪৬।৪৭ ইং। বাঃ ডিঃ ৩১৶০ মোঃ।

সরকার বাহাদুর বঃ হীরামামুদ গ।

তপশীল সম্পত্তি।

পঃ মেখলীগঞ্জ ১০৯ নং থাক ৩১০৭ নং তৌঃ তাং বাঃ কুচলিবাড়ী মধ্যে ১২৴৩॥৶০ ধুর জমির কাত বাঃ ১৪৸৴০ আনা জমার আং পঃ স্বত্ব।

৯৭০ নং ১৯৪২।৪৩ ইং। বাঃ ডিঃ ৪॥৩ মোঃ।

সরকার বাহাদুর বঃ সিবিন বর্ম্মণ গঃ।

তপশিল সম্পত্তি।

পঃ মেখলীগঞ্জ ১১১ নং থাক ৪ নং তৌঃ তাং বাজেজমা কুচলিবাড়ী মধ্যে ৮৩৶০ ধুর জমির কাত বাঃ ।৶০ আনা জমার পঃ স্বত্ব।

DWIJENDRA CHANDRA SEN, *Certificate Officer*,

দেওয়ানী কার্য্যবিধি আইনের ২১ হুকুম, ৬৬ নিয়মের ঘোষণাপত্র।

জারীর মহকুমা মেখলীগঞ্জের দেঃ আদালত।

এতদ্বারা সর্ব্বসাধারণকে জানান যাইতেছে যে, দায়ীকগণের নিম্নলিখিত সম্পত্তি আগামী ১৯৪৭ সনের ৭ই জুলাই মোঃ ১৩৫৪ সনের ২২শে আষাঢ় তারিখে দিবা ১২ ঘটিকার সময় প্রকাশ্য নিলাম আরম্ভ হইবে।

৩ নং ১৯৪৭।৪৮ ইং। বাঃ ডিঃ মোঃ।

ডিঃ—ভ বস্তুনাথ রায় সরকার সাং কাজলদিঘী ষ্টেঃ হলদিবাড়ী।

দেঃ—প্রসন্নকুমার রায় প্রামাণিক গং সাং কাজলদিঘী ষ্টেঃ হলদিবাড়ী।

তপশিল সম্পত্তি।

পঃ মেখলীগঞ্জ ৩৭ নং ছিট তাং কাজলদিঘী মধ্যে ১২৮২ নং তৌঃ লিঃ ৪৬।১।৫/০ দুর জমির কাত বাঃ ৫৫৮৵০ আনা জমার আংশিক চুঃ।

২০ নং ১৯৪৬।৪৭ ইং। বাঃ ডিঃ ১৩২।৩ মোঃ

ডিঃ—জগনাথ সিংহ সাং তিস্তা নদীর পয়স্তী ষ্টেঃ মেখলীগঞ্জ।

দেঃ—আছরউদ্দিন মহম্মদ সাং তিস্তানদীর পয়স্তী ষ্টেঃ মেখলীগঞ্জ।

তপশিল সম্পত্তি।

পঃ মেখলীগঞ্জ ২৫ নং থাক তাং তিস্তা নদীর পয়স্তী মধ্যে ৫১২ নং তৌঃ লিঃ ২/০ বিঘা জমির কাত বাঃ ।. ৬ পাই জমার চুঃ।

১ নং ১৯৪৬।৪৭ ইং। বাঃ ডিঃ ১১০৩৮/৬ মোঃ

ডিঃ—আশুতোষ পাল সাং মেখলীগঞ্জ।

দেঃ—যামিনীমোহন সিংহ সাং মেখলীগঞ্জ।

তপশিল সম্পত্তি।

পঃ মেখলীগঞ্জ ১২৩ নং থাক তাং অন্দরান খড়খড়িয়া মধ্যে ৯ নং মেঃ তৌঃ লিঃ ২৪৯.৩।৫/০ জমির কাত বাঃ ২১৯।৫/০ আনা জমার জোত।

KUMAR P. NARAYAN, *Naib Ahilkar.*

ইং ১৯১০ সালের ৫ আইনের ৫৩ ধারার ২ প্রকরণ মতে নিলামী ইস্তাহার।

রাজ্য কোচবিহারের এঃ সিঃ জজ আদালত।

এতদ্বারা সর্ব্বসাধারণকে জানান যাইতেছে যে, প্রতিবাদীর দাবীর বাকী খাজনা আদায় না করায় তাহার নিম্নলিখিত ক্রোকী সম্পত্তি আগামী ১৩৫৪ সনের ২২শে আষাঢ় মোতাবেক ১৯৪৭ সনের ৭ই জুলাই, তারিখে বেলা ১ ঘটিকার সময় প্রকাশ্য নীলাম আরম্ভ হইবে।

৩০৪ নং ১৯৪৬।৪৭ ইং। বাঃ খাঃ ১২৩।৵০ মোঃ।

ডিঃ—দি কোচবিহার ব্যাঙ্কিং করপোরেশন লিঃ মোঃ বেহার ষ্টেঃ কোতয়ালী।

দেঃ—প্রফুল্লকুমার রায় রাঃ গং সাং মদনমোহন ষ্টেঃ কোতয়ালী।

তপশিল সম্পত্তি।

পঃ বেহার ৮২৮ নং থাক তাং ব্রঃ কশালডাঙ্গা মধ্যে ৭৩৸০ কাঠা জমির কাত বাঃ ৭৩৸০ আনা জমার আংশিক জোত।

৩০৩ নং ১৯৪৬।৪৭ ইং। বাঃ খাঃ ৩৫০।০ মোঃ।

ডিঃ—কোচবিহার ব্যাঙ্কিং করপোরেশন লিঃ মোঃ বেহার ষ্টেঃ কোতয়ালী।

দেঃ—ভোলানাথ বর্ম্মণ গং সাং ব্রঃ কশালডাঙ্গা ষ্টেঃ কোতয়ালী।

তপশিল সম্পত্তি।

পঃ বেহার ৮২৮ নং থাক তাং ব্রঃ কশালডাঙ্গা মধ্যে ৫২।১।/০ দুর জমির কাত বাঃ ১০৮/০ আনা জমার চুঃ।

F. AHMED, *Offg. Ass.. Civil Judge.*

দেওয়ানী কার্য্যবিধি আইনের ২১ হুকুম, ৬৬ নিয়মের ঘোষণাপত্র।

জারীর মহকুমা মাথাভাঙ্গার নাঃ আ দেওয়ানী আদালত।

এতদ্বারা সর্ব্বসাধারণকে জানান যাইতেছে যে, দায়ীকগণের নিম্নলিখিত সম্পত্তি আগামী ১৯৪৭ সনের ৭ই জুলাই মোঃ ১৩৫৩ সনের ২২শে আষাঢ় তারিখে দিবা ১ ঘটিকার সময় প্রকাশ্য নিলাম আরম্ভ হইবে।

৫১ নং ১৯৪৬।৪৭ ইং। বাঃ ডিঃ ৫২৩৵ মোঃ

ডিঃ—হরিলাল সাহা মোঃ ও ষ্টেঃ মাথাভাঙ্গা।

দেঃ—পিতাম্বর অধিকারী গং সাং পাঃ ছড়া গোপালপুর।

তপশিল সম্পত্তি।

পঃ মাথাভাঙ্গা ২২৮ নং থাক তাং পাটছড়া গোপালপুর মধ্যে ২৯ নং তৌঃ লিঃ ২০৬২।/০ দুর জমির কাত বাঃ ৩৮৵০ আনা জমার আংশিক জমি।

৫০ নং ১৯৪৬।৪৭ ইং। বাঃ ডিঃ ৬৫০৶০ মোঃ।

ডিঃ—কেশরীচাঁদ তাবানী মোঃ ও ষ্টেঃ মাথাভাঙ্গা।

দেঃ—বিপিনকান্ত মুরজীয়া পঃ সাং ভাউয়াগুড়ী ষ্টেঃ মাথাভাঙ্গা।

তপশিল সম্পত্তি।

১। পঃ মাথাভাঙ্গা ৪০০ নং থাক তাং ভাউয়াগুড়ী মধ্যে ১৫৬২ নং তৌঃ পিঃ ৪৪।৪৮৶০ ধুর জমির কাত বাঃ ৫০।০ আনা জমার চুঃ।

২। পঃ, থাক, তাং, তৌঃ তথা মধ্যে ৪০৸৶০ ধুর জমির কাত বাঃ ২৸৶০ আনা জমার দরচুঃ।

MANABENDRA NATH BHATTACHARJYA, *Naib Ahilkar.*

দেওয়ানী কার্য্যবিধি আইনের ২১ হুকুম, ৬৬ নিয়মের ঘোষণাপত্র।

রাজ্য কোচবিহারের এঃ সিঃ জজ আদালত।

এতদ্বারা সর্ব্বসাধারণকে জানান যাইতেছে যে, দাবীকগণের নিম্নলিখিত সম্পত্তি আগামী ১৯৪৭ সনের ৭ই জুলাই মোঃ ১৩৫৪ সনের ২২শে আষাঢ় তারিখে দিবা ১ ঘটিকার সময় প্রকাশ্য নিলাম আরম্ভ হইবে।

৯১ নং ১৯৪৫।৪৬ ইং। বাঃ ডিঃ ৫৪৩৸৶৩ মোঃ।

ডিঃ—সুরেন্দ্রমোহন চক্রবর্ত্তী মোঃ বেহার ষ্টেঃ কোতয়ালী।

দেঃ—রাজেন্দ্রনাথ সাহা মোঃ বেহার ষ্টেঃ কোতয়ালী।

তপশিল সম্পত্তি।

পঃ বেহার ৯১০ নং থাক তাং গুড়িয়াহাটী মধ্যে ৫৫৪১।৶০ ধুর জমির আংশিক জমি।

৯২ নং ১৯৪৬।৪৭ ইং। বাঃ ডিঃ ৪৫০৶৯ মোঃ।

ডিঃ—শচীলাল বণিক পঃ মোঃ বেহার ষ্টেঃ কোতয়ালী।

দেঃ—অহরমামুদ মিঞা সাং দেওয়ানহাট মওয়ামারী ষ্টেঃ কোতয়ালী।

তপশিল সম্পত্তি।

১। পঃ বেহার ৯০৪ নং থাক তাং মওয়ামারী মধ্যে ১৬৫৬ নং তৌঃ পিঃ ৫।২।৶০ ধুর জমির কাত বাঃ ১০।৶০ আনা আনা জমার কৃষিপ্রজা।

২। পঃ, থাক, তাং তৌঃ তথা মধ্যে ২৶।০ ধুর জমির কাত বাঃ ৫।৶০ আনা জমার কৃষিপ্রজা।

F. AHMED, *Asst. Civil Judge.*

ইং ১৯১০ সালের ৫ আইনের ৫৩ ধারার ২ প্রকরণ মতে নিলামী ইস্তাহার।

জারীর মহকুমা মেখলীগঞ্জের মাল আদালত।

এতদ্বারা সর্ব্বসাধারণকে জানান যাইতেছে যে, প্রতিবাদীর দাবার বাকী খাজানা আদায় না করায় তাহার নিম্নলিখিত ক্রোকী সম্পত্তি আগামী ১৩৫৪ সনের ২২শে আষাঢ় মোতাবেক ১৯৪৭ সনের ৭ই জুলাই তারিখে বেলা ১ ঘটিকার সময় প্রকাশ্য নিলাম আরম্ভ হইবে।

১৪ নং ১৯৪৭।৪৮ ইং। বাঃ খাঃ ৭৭।৶৯ মোঃ

ডিঃ—রহিমদ্দীন সরকার পঃ সাং ২য় খণ্ড নিজতরফ [illegible]।

দেঃ—নেগেন্দ্র দাস নাঃ।

তপশিল সম্পত্তি

পঃ মেখলীগঞ্জ ১৪ নং থাক তাং ২য় খণ্ড নিজতরফ মধ্যে ৬০ নং তৌ পিঃ ১।৸৶০ ধুর জমির কাত বাঃ ১৬৸৶০ আনা জমার কৃষি প্রজা স্বত্ব।

১৩ নং ১৯৪৭।৪৮ ইং। বাঃ খাঃ ১০৮৷৶৩ মোঃ।

ডিঃ—মৌঃ মোসারফ হোসেন প্রধান পঃ সাং কিসমত কুচলিবাড়ী।

দেঃ—জয়চন্দ্র রায় বসুনীয়া সাং পানবাড়ী।

তপশিল সম্পত্তি।

পঃ মেখলীগঞ্জ ৮ নং থাক তাং ভোটবাড়ী মধ্যে ৫৫৬ নং তৌঃ পিঃ ১৩।৸৶০ ধুর জমির কাত বাঃ ৫।১০ আনা জমার কৃষি প্রজা স্বত্ব।

১৮ নং ১৯৪৭।৪৮ ইং। বাঃ খাঃ ২২৬৶৯ মোঃ।

ডিঃ—গিরিধারীমল বয়েদ মোঃ বেহার।

দেঃ—কিরিণচন্দ্র রায় বসুনিয়া পঃ সাং ফুলবাড়ী।

তপশিল।

পঃ মেখলীগঞ্জ ১০২ নং থাক তাং উদ্দারপুরবাড়ী মধ্যে ৫৩০ নং স্বত্ব পিঃ ২০৯৸৪৶০ ধুর জমির কাত বাঃ ২৩৬৶০ আনা জমার আং চোক স্বত্ব।

১৯ নং ১৯৪৭।৪৮ ইং। বাঃ খাঃ ৩০৩।৶৩ মোঃ।

ডিঃ—গিরিধারীমল মহেশ মোঃ বেহার।

দেঃ—আমানতুল্যা প্রধান গঃ সাং গোলাবারী।

তপশিল সম্পত্তি।

পঃ মেখলীগঞ্জ ১৪১ নং থাক তাং কামতাচাংরাবান্ধা মধ্যে ১৩০ নং স্বত্ব লিঃ ২০০৮০।৶০ দুর জমির কাত বাঃ ১৬৯৮০ আনা জমায় জোত স্বত্ব।

২১ নং ১৯৪৭।৪৮ ইং বাঃ খাঃ ৩১৮০ মোঃ।

ডিঃ—আনন্দমোহন সিংহ মোঃ মেখলীগঞ্জ।

দেঃ—বিন্ধ্যাচলপ্রসাদ চৌবে গঃ সাং হেমকুমারী।

তপশিল সম্পত্তি।

পঃ মেখলীগঞ্জ ৩৯ নং থাক তাং নিজতরফ মধ্যে ৭৭১ নং চৌঃ লিঃ ৮।১৶০ দুর জমির কাত বাঃ ১০।৶০ আনা জমার চুকানী স্বত্ব।

২২ নং ১৯৪৭।৪৮ ইং। বাঃ খাঃ ৩২।৶৩ মোঃ।

ডিঃ—আনন্দমোহন সিংহ মোঃ মেখলীগঞ্জ।

দেঃ—বিন্ধ্যাচলপ্রসাদ চৌবে গঃ সাং হেমকুমারী।

তপশিল সম্পত্তি।

পঃ মেখলীগঞ্জ ৫৪ নং থাক তাং হেমকুমারী মধ্যে ৯২৯ নং চৌঃ লিঃ ৬/২৶০ দুর জমির কাত বাঃ ৮৮৶০ আনা জমার চুকানী স্বত্ব।

২৩ নং ১৯৪৭।৪৮ ইং। বাঃ খাঃ ৩৯৸৶৪ মোঃ।

ডিঃ—আনন্দমোহন সিংহ মোঃ মেখলীগঞ্জ।

দেঃ—বিন্ধ্যাচলপ্রসাদ চৌবে সাং হেমকুমারী।

তপশিল সম্পত্তি।

পঃ মেখলীগঞ্জ ৫৫ নং থাক তাং হেমকুমারী মধ্যে ৯২৯ নং চৌঃ লিঃ ৭৮২।০ দুর জমির কাত বাঃ ১২।০ আনা জমার চুকানী স্বত্ব।

২৪ নং ১৯৪৭।৪৮ ইং। বাঃ খাঃ ৪৯৸৶৫ মোঃ।

ডিঃ—আনন্দমোহন সিংহ মোঃ মেখলীগঞ্জ।

দেঃ—বিন্ধ্যাচলপ্রসাদ চৌবে গঃ সাং হেমকুমারী।

তপশিল সম্পত্তি।

পঃ মেখলীগঞ্জ ৫৫ নং থাক তাং হেমকুমারী মধ্যে ৯২৯ নং চৌঃ লিঃ ১১।২৷৷০ দুর জমির কাত বাঃ ১৬৭৶০ আনা জমার চুকানী স্বত্ব।

২৫ নং ১৯৪৭।৪৮ ইং। বাঃ খাঃ ৫৩।০ মোঃ।

ডিঃ—আনন্দমোহন সিংহ মোঃ মেখলীগঞ্জ।

দেঃ—বিন্ধ্যাচলপ্রসাদ চৌবে গঃ সাং হেমকুমারী।

তপশিল সম্পত্তি।

পঃ মেখলীগঞ্জ ৫৫ নং থাক তাং হেমকুমারী মঃ ৯২৯ নং চৌঃ লিঃ ১২৶৸৶০ দুর জমির কাত বাঃ ১৮৭৶০ আনা জমার চুকানী স্বত্ব।

২৬ নং ১৯৪৭।৪৮ ইং। বাঃ খাঃ ৫৮৸৶৯ মোঃ।

ডিঃ—আনন্দমোহন সিংহ মোঃ মেখলীগঞ্জ।

দেঃ—বিন্ধ্যাচলপ্রসাদ চৌবে গঃ সাং হেমকুমারী।

তপশিল সম্পত্তি।

পঃ মেখলীগঞ্জ ৩৯ নং থাক তাং নিজ তরফ মধ্যে ৭৭১ নং চৌঃ লিঃ ১৯৷৷২/০ দুর জমির কাত বাঃ ২৯৶০ আনা জমার চুকানী স্বত্ব।

২৭ নং ১৯৪৭।৪৮ ইং। বাঃ খাঃ ২৪৶৯ মোঃ।

ডিঃ—আনন্দমোহন সিংহ মোকাম মেখলীগঞ্জ।

দেঃ—বিন্ধ্যাচলপ্রসাদ চৌবে গঃ সাং হেমকুমারী।

তপশীল সম্পত্তি।

পঃ মেখলীগঞ্জ ৫৫ নং থাক তাং হেমকুমারী মধ্যে ৯২৯ নং চৌঃ লিঃ ৬/৩৶০ দুর জমির কাত বাঃ ৯৬৶০ আনা জমার চুকানী স্বত্ব।

২৮ নং ১৯৪৭।৪৮ ইং। বাঃ খাঃ ৮৩৪৶০ মোঃ।

ডিঃ—আনন্দমোহন সিংহ মোঃ মেখলীগঞ্জ।

দেঃ—বিন্ধ্যাচলপ্রসাদ চৌবে গঃ সাং হেমকুমারী।

তপশীল সম্পত্তি।

পঃ মেখলীগঞ্জ ৩৯ নং থাক তাং নিজ তরফ মধ্যে ৭৭১ নং চৌঃ লিঃ ২৮৷৷৪৶০ দুর জমির কাত বাঃ ৪২৶০ আনা জমার চুকানী স্বত্ব।

২৯ নং ১৯৪৭।৪৮ ইং। বাঃ খাঃ ৮০।৩ মোঃ।

ডিঃ—আনন্দমোহন সিংহ মোঃ মেখলীগঞ্জ।

দেঃ—বিন্ধ্যাচলপ্রসাদ চৌবে গঃ সাং হেমকুমারী।

তপশিল সম্পত্তি

পঃ মেখলীগঞ্জ ৩৯ নং থাক তাং নিজ তরফ মধ্যে ১৭১ নং চৌঃ লিঃ ৩৩৮৩।৵০ ধুর জমির কাত বাঃ ৪২৶০ আনা জমার চুকানী স্বত্ব।

৩০ নং ১৯৪৭।৪৮ ইং। বাঃ খাঃ ৪৭৮৭ মোঃ।

ডিঃ—আনন্দমোহন সিংহ মোঃ মেখলীগঞ্জ।

দেঃ—বিন্ধ্যাচলপ্রসাদ চৌবে গঃ সাং হেমকুমারী।

তপশিল সম্পত্তি।

পঃ মেখলীগঞ্জ ৩৯ নং থাক তাং নিজ তরফ মধ্যে ১৭১ নং চৌঃ লিঃ ৫২।২।৶০ ধুর জমির কাত বাঃ ১৯৶৪ পাই জমার চুকানী স্বত্ব।

৩২ নং ১৯৪৭।৪৮ ইং। বাঃ খাঃ ৩৫।৶৪ মোঃ।

ডিঃ—মোসাররফ হোসেন প্রধান সাং কিঃ ফতেমামুদ।

দেঃ—হাকিম উদ্দীন মহাম্মদ সাং ছোঃ হলদিবাড়ী।

তপশিল সম্পত্তি

পঃ মেখলীগঞ্জ ২৭ নং থাক তাং ছোট হলদিবাড়ী মধ্যে ৬৫১ নং চৌঃ লিঃ ৫৮২ কাঠা জমির কাত বাঃ ৯৶৩ পাই জমার দরচুকানী স্বত্ব।

৩৪ নং ১৯৪৭।৪৮ ই বাঃ খাঃ ১৬৮৬ মোঃ।

ডিঃ—বেগম ফাতেমা খাতুন সাং কিসমত ফতেমাহন।

দেঃ—মহাম্মদ নুরল হক গঃ সাং বড় হলদিবাড়ী।

তপশীল সম্পত্তি।

পঃ মেখলীগঞ্জ ১ নং থাক তাং বড় হলদিবাড়ী মধ্যে ৬৫ নং চৌঃ লিঃ ২০।০৫০ ধুর জমির কাত বাঃ ৫২৴৩ পাই জমার দরচুকানী স্বত্ব।

KUMAR P. NARAYAN, *Naib Ahilkar.*

MALCUCHERY NOTICE.

ইস্তাহার নামা কাছারী মাল মোতাবেক নিজবেহার সন ১৯৪৭ তারিখ ২৪শে মে
মোতাবেক বাঙ্গালা ১৩৫৪ সন তারিখ ৯ই জ্যৈষ্ঠ।

পরগণে কোচবিহার এলাকাধীন ৯৫৪ নং থাক তালুক খড়িমালাখাগড়াবাড়ী অন্তর্গত এগ্রিকালচারাল কার্য্যের নালার জন্য অত্র আদালতের ১৯৪৭।৪৮ ইং সনের ২ নং ভূমিগ্রহণের মোকদ্দমায় ৭।৫।৪৭ইং তারিখের আদেশ সূত্রে নিম্নলিখিত বিবরণযুক্ত ভূমি ১৩৫৩ সনের শেষ ৬ মাস হইতে সরকারে গৃহীত হওয়ায় সর্ব্বসাধারণের অবগতি জন্য এই ইস্তাহার প্রচারিত হইল। ইতি

১। পঃ কোচবিহার ৯৫৪ নং থাক তাং খড়িমালাখাগড়াবাড়ী ২০৯২ নং জোত রায় চৌঃ সতীশচন্দ্র ॥০ আনা সুরেশচন্দ্র ॥০ আনা পিং বৈকুণ্ঠচন্দ্র মুস্তফী মোঃ বেহার। বর্ত্তমান জমি ১৯।১॥০ ধুর জমা ৩২৶০ আনা ২ নং সিট গৃহীত জমি ৴।৶০ ধুর জমা ৻৭ পাই।

৭২ নং স্বত্ব চুঃ খালসা ॥০ আনা পিং বোদং দাস সাং নিজ মনসা ওঃ মহেশ্বরী দাস্যা ।০ আনা অং প্রিয়নাথ দাস সাং ভোটেশ্বরপাড়। বর্ত্তমান জমি ১০৮২।৶০ ধুর জমা ১৫॥৶০ আনা ২ নং সিট গৃহীত জমি ৴॥০ ধুর জমা ৻৭ পাই।

৭৬ নং স্বত্ব দরচুঃ সফরুল্যা মহম্মদ পিং দিদারমামুদ মিঞা নাঃ পং উক্ত ভ্রাতা ফজলিন মহম্মদ। বর্ত্তমান জমি ২।৫৶০ ধুর জমা ৪৶০ আনা ২ নং সিট গৃহীত জমি ৴।৶০ ধুর জমা ৻৭ পাই।

৭৮ নং স্বত্ব কৃষিপ্রজা গঙ্গাধর পিং শুকদেব কৈবর্ত্ত নাঃ পঃ উক্ত মাতা খাবলিয়া কৈবর্ত্তনী। বর্ত্তমান জমি ১॥১॥৶০ ধুর জমা ২।৶০ আনা ২ নং সিট ১৫৪৴৮ নং দাগ গৃহীত জমি ৴॥৶০ ধুর জমা ৻৮ পাই।

২। পঃ থাক তাং তথা ২৭৯৭ নং চৌঃ ১০২ নং স্বত্ব জোত ললিতমোহন ॥০ আনা পিং গোপীরাম মজুমদার, রজনীমোহন ॥০ আনা পিং কেশরীমোহন মজুমদার। চৌঃ সূত্রে সহকারীর দাখিল বর্ত্তমান জমি ৮৩৴২ কাঠা জমা ৮৮।০ আনা ২ নং সিট গৃহীত জমি ৴৪৶০ ধুর জমা ৶১১ পাই।

বিভাগ

১০৩ নং স্বত্ব চুঃ সুরেন্দ্রনাথ পিং রামচরণ নন্দী মোঃ বেহার। বর্ত্তমান জমি ৩৪॥১ কাঠা জমা ৫০॥৶০ আনা ২ নং সিট গৃহীত জমি ৴৪৶০ ধুর জমা ৶১১ পাই।

বিতং

১০৫ নং স্বত্ব দরচুঃ সাতার উদ্দিন ॥০ আনা বাতার উদ্দিন ॥০ আনা পিং পাত মিঞা। বর্ত্তমান জমি ১৯৮।৮/০ ধুর জমা ৩৮।৶০ আনা ২ নং সিট ৪০৪/.৯ নং দাগ গৃহীত জমি /৩ কাঠা জমা ।৬ পাই।

১০৭ নং স্বত্ব দরচুঃ আলিমামুদ পিং ভেলা মিঞা মোঃ বেহার। বর্ত্তমান জমি ৮৪॥৶০ ধুর জমা ১৫॥/০ আনা ২ নং সিট ৪৭০/১৭ নং দাগ গৃহীত জমি /১৶০ ধুর জমা ৴২ পাই।

৩। পঃ থাক তাং তথা ২৮১১ নং তৌঃ ১৭৮ নং স্বত্ব জোত গোপালচন্দ্র ॥০ আনা নাঃ পঃ উঁছি পিতা সম্ভুনাথ দাস রবি।০ আনা পিং সনাতন দাস, অছারী দাদা।০ আনা জঃ নবীন দাস। বর্ত্তমান জমি ৬।২॥৶০ ধুর জমা ৯।/০ আনা ২ নং সিট গৃহীত জমি /৫॥৶০ ধুর জমা ।৫ পাই।

বিতং

১৭৯ নং স্বত্ব চুঃ নিজাম উদ্দিন ওঃ ফাকুসা মিঞা পিং গরিবুল্যা মিঞা। বর্ত্তমান জমি ৩৮৩॥৶০ ধুর জমা ৬৬৷০ আনা ২ নং সিট ২০৪/১ নং দাগ গৃহীত জমি /১৮/০ ধুর জমা ৶৪ পাই।

১৮৯ নং স্বত্ব চুঃ গঙ্গাধর ।০ আনা গদাধর ॥০ আনা পিং গোপিনাথ দাস। বর্ত্তমান জমি ৩০৩॥৶০ ধুর জমা ৭॥৶০ আনা ২ নং সিট গৃহীত জমি /১৮/০ ধুর জমা ৶৭ পাই।

বিতং

১৯১ নং স্বত্ব দরচুঃ আয়মন বেওয়া ওঃ ইমাইমামুদ। বর্ত্তমান জমি ৮১৮৶০ ধুর জমা ২৫৶০ আনা ২ নং সিট ৭৩০/২, ৭৩১/৩ নং দাগ গৃহীত জমি /১৮/০ ধুর জমা ।৩ পাই।

৪। পঃ থাক তাং তথা ২৮০৩ নং তৌঃ ১৩৮ নং স্বত্ব জোত নিস্তারিনী ।/৩। = ক্রান্তি জঃ চন্দ্রকুমার ঘোষ রুহিনীকুমার ।/৩॥= ক্রান্তি পিং কৃষ্ণকুমার ঘোষ, ক্ষিরোদকুমার ওরফে হরিদাস ৶১৩।— ক্রান্তি নাং পঃ উঁছ মাতা মৃনালিনী ঘোষ জঃ নবকুমার ঘোষ, হরকুমার ৶১৩— ক্রান্তি পিং রাজকুমার ঘোষ। বর্ত্তমান জমি ২২।২।৶০ ধুর জমা ২৫।৶০ আনা ২ নং সিট গৃহীত জমি ।৷৶০ ধুর জমা ।/১ পাই।

বিতং

১৪২ নং স্বত্ব চুঃ স্বর্গেশ্বরী দাস্যা ।০ জঃ জীবধন দাস সাং গোঁহারঝাড় গগনচন্দ্র ॥০ পিং গৌরচন্দ্র অধিকারী বর্ত্তমান জমি ১৬৮।১।৶০ ধুর জমা ২৩।০ সিট নং ২ গৃহীত জমি /৩ কাঠা জমা ৶১০ পাই।

বিতং

১৫৩ নংস্বত্ব দরচুঃ খলিসা ॥০ পিং বেহেৎ দাস মনসা ওঃ মনেশ্বরী দাস্যা ॥০ জঃ প্রিয়নাথ দাস সাং ডোডেয়ারপাড় বর্ত্তমান জমি ১২/৶০ ধুর জমা ২২৮/০ সিট নং ২ দাগ নং ৭১৯/১১ গৃহীত জমি /৩ কাঠা জমা ।৬ পাই।

১৪৬ নংস্বত্ব চুঃ নিস্তারিনী ঘোষ ।/৩॥= ক্রান্তি জঃ চন্দ্রকুমার ঘোষ রোহিনীকুমার। ৬= ক্রান্তি পিং ক্ষিরোদকুমার ওঃ হরিদাস ৶১৩।— ক্রান্তি নাঃ পক্ষে উঁছি মাতা মৃনালিনী ঘোষ জঃ নবকুমার ঘোষ হরকুমার ৶১৩।— ক্রান্তি পিং রাজকুমার ঘোষ বর্ত্তমান জমি ৫॥১৶০ ধুর জমা ৭৸০ আনা সিট নং ২ গৃহীত জমি /।৶০ ধুর জমা ৶০ আনা।

৪। পঃ কোচবিহার ৯৫৭ নং থাক তাং খড়িমালা খাগড়াবাড়ী ২৮০৩ নং তৌঃ ১৪৭ নং স্বত্ব দরচুঃ খলিসা ॥০ পিং বেহেৎ দাস সাং নিজ মনসা ওঃ মনেশ্বরী দাস্যা ॥০ জঃ প্রিয়নাথ দাস সাং ডোডেয়ারপাড় বর্ত্তমান জমি ৫॥১।/০ ধুর জমা ৯৶০ সিট নং ২ দাগ নং ৪৮০/১৩ গৃহীত জমি /২।৶০ ধুর জমা ৶৭ পাই।

৫। পঃ থাক তাং তথা ২৮১৩ নং তৌঃ ২০১ নং স্বত্ব জোত গঙ্গাধর পিং গোপীনাথ দাস বর্ত্তমান জমি ১৩৮২॥৶০ ধুর জমা ১৬॥০ আনা সিট নং ২ গৃহীত জমি /৩ কাঠা জমা ৶১০ পাই।

বিতং

২০২ নং স্বত্ব চুঃ গঙ্গাধর ।০ গদাধর ॥০ পিং গোপীনাথ দাস বর্ত্তমান জমি ১৩৮২॥৶০ ধুর জমা ২২।০ সিট নং ২ দাগ নং ৪৬৬/১৮ গৃহীত জমি /৩ কাঠা ৶১০ পাই।

৬। পঃ কোচবিহার ৯৫৪ নং থাক তাং খড়িমালা খাগড়াবাড়ী ১১২ নং তৌঃ ২৩৪ নং স্বত্ব জোত সুরেন্দ্রনাথ ।/৩॥= ক্রান্তি ত্রৈলক্যনাথ ।/৩॥= ক্রান্তি প্রফুল্লচন্দ্র ।/৩॥= ক্রান্তি পিং হরিশ্চন্দ্র সাহা মোঃ বেহার বর্ত্তমান ৪৮/৫০ ধুর জমা ৪৩।৶০ আনা সিট নং ২ গৃহীত জমি /৪।০ ধুর জমা ।০ আনা।

বিতং

২৫৮ নং স্বত্ব চুঃ লোপ দরচুঃ প্রিয়নাথ পিং স্বর্গনাথ দাস বর্ত্তমান জমি ৮/৫৮৶০ ধুর জমা ১২৮/০ আনা সিট নং ২ দাগ নং ৪৪০/২০ গৃহীত জমি /৪।০ ধুর জমা ।/১১ পাই।

৭। পঃ থাক তাং তথা ৩৭১৫ নং তৌঃ ৯৯ নং স্বত্ব জোত কণ্ঠনাথ।০ বৈকুণ্ঠনাথ।০ কীর্ত্তিনাথ।০ কুলনাথ।০ পিং কাশীনাথ কামার সাং চণ্ডিশাল বর্ত্তমান জমি ৮৮৪॥৶০ ধুর জমা ৮৮/০ আনা সিট নং ২ গৃহীত জমি /৩ কাঠা জমা ৶১ পাই।

১০০ নং স্বত্ব চুঃ গঙ্গাধর ।০ গদাধর ॥০ পিং গোপীনাথ দাস বর্ত্তমান জমি ৮৮৪॥৶০ ধুর জমা ১১৮৶০ আনা সিট নং ২ দাগ নং ৩৭৪/১৪ গৃহীত জমি /৩ কাঠা জমা ৶১০ পাই।

৮। পঃ থাক তাং তথা ৩৭১৮ নং তৌঃ ১২৭ নং স্বত্ব জোত শরৎকুমার দেব ॥০ পিং রতিদেব বকসী অমূল্য ৶১৩।— ক্রান্তি অপূর্ব্ব ৶১৩।— ক্রান্তি অনিল ৶১৩।— ক্রান্তি পিং প্রসন্নকুমার দেব বকসী মোঃ বেহার। পত্তন হস্তে মনোমোহন চৌধুরী ম্যানেজার পক্ষে দি কোচবিহার ব্যাঙ্কিং করপোরেশন লিঃ মোঃ বেহার বর্ত্তমান জমি ১৫।১৮০ ধুর জমা ১৫॥/০ আনা সিট নং ২ গৃহীত জমি /৫॥৶০ ধুর জমা ৶৬ পাই।

১২৮ নং স্বত্ব চুঃ দিদার মামুদ পিং মজর মামুদ মিঞা বর্ত্তমান জমি ১৫৷১৶৹ ধুর জমা ২১/৹ আনা সিট নং ২ গৃহীত জমি /৩॥৶৹ ধুর জমা ।৯ পাই।

৮। সদর কোচবিহার ৯৫৪ নং থাক খড়িমালা খাগড়াবাড়ী ২৮০১ নং তৌঃ ১২৯ নং স্বত্ব দরচুকানী খোদন পিং হরদেব দাস বর্ত্তমান জমি ৭/৸৶৹ ধুর জমা ১৩৶৹ আনা ২ নং সিট ৪৭১/১৬, ৪৭২/১৫ নং দাগ গৃঃ জমি /৩॥৶৹ ধুর জমা ।/৭ পাই।

৯। পঃ থাক তাং তথা ২৮০৮ নং তৌঃ ১৮০ নং স্বত্ব জোত মফির উদ্দীন ॥৹ হবতুল্যা ॥৹ পিং নবু মিঞা বর্ত্তমান জমি ৩৮৪।৹ ধুর জমা ৩৸৹ ২ নং সিট গৃঃ জমি /১৶৹ ধুর জমা /২ পাই।

বিতং

১৬১ নং স্বত্ব চুকানী মহমুদ পিং বাহার সেখ বঃ জমি ৮২॥/৹ ধুর জমা ১৸৶৹ ২ নং সিট ৩৭১/১০ নং দাগ গৃঃ জমি /১৶৹ ধুর জমা /৭ পাই।

১০। পঃ তথা মধ্যে ৯৫৪ নং থাক খড়িমালা খাগড়াবাড়ী ৪৪৬৮ নং তৌঃ ৩৭৯ নং স্বত্ব জোত গোপাল চন্দ্র দাস নাঃ পক্ষে উহি পিতা শম্ভুনাথ দাস রবি পিতা সনাতন দাস আহ্লাদী দাস্যা জঃ নবীন দাস সাং নিজ বর্ত্তমান জমি ৪।৩৶৹ ধুর জমা ৪৶৹ ২ নং সিট গৃহীত জমি /২।৶৹ ধুর গৃহীত জমা ৶২ পাই।

৩৫০ নং স্বত্ব চুকানী নিজাম উদ্দিন পিং গাবুল্যা মিঞা বর্ত্তমান জমি ৩/২৸৶৹ ধুর জমা ৫॥/৹ ২ নং সিট ৮৭৮/৪, ৮৫৩/৫, ৮৭২/৭, নং দাগ গৃহীত জমি /১৸৹ ধুর জমা ৵২ পাই।

৩৫৩ নং স্বত্ব চুকানী আয়মন বেওয়া জঃ ইয়ার মামুদ বর্ত্তমান জমি ৮২৸৹ ধুর জমা ১।৶৹ ২ নং সিট ৮৫৭/৬ দাগ নং গৃহীত জমি /॥৶৹ ধুর জমা ৴৯ পাই।

১১। পঃ কোচবিহার ১০৬ নং তৌঃ ২৫০ নং স্বত্ব জমাভুক্ত রাজেন্দ্রনাথ ।/৬৷= ভুমিন্দ্রনাথ ।/৬৷= পিং চন্দ্রনাথ চক্রবর্ত্তী নরেন্দ্রনাথ ।/৬৷= পিং ধীরেন্দ্রনাথ চক্রবর্ত্তী বর্ত্তমান জমি ২॥২/৹ ধুর ২ নং সিট গৃহীত জমি /২।৶৹ ধুর।

বিতং

২৫১ নং স্বত্ব জোত সরলাবালা দাস্যা জঃ ধীরেন্দ্রনাথ দাস ইষ্টেট পক্ষে কোর্ট অফ ওয়ার্ডস বর্ত্তমান জমি ২॥২/৹ ধুর জমা ৩৲ ২ নং সিট গৃহীত জমি /২।৶৹ ধুর জমা ৶১ পাই।

১১। পঃ কোচবিহার ২৫৪ নং থাক তাং খড়িমালা খাগড়াবাড়ী ১০৬ নং তৌঃ ২৫২ নং স্বত্ব চুকানী আবদুল্যা পিং দিদার মামুদ বর্ত্তমান জমি ২॥২/৹ ধুর জমা ৪/৹ আনা ২ নং সিট ৪৭৫/১২ গৃহীত জমি /২৶৹ ধুর জমা ৶৹ আনা।

১২। পঃ কোচবিহার থাক তাং তথা মধ্যে ৬৯, ৭০, ৭১ নং তৌঃ ২৫৫ নং স্বত্ব জায়গীর জগদীশ ॥৹ অমূল্য ॥৹ পিং কামেশ্বর দাস উক্ত নাবালক পক্ষে উহি নন্দন দাস বর্ত্তমান জমি ১০৩।১৶৹ ধুর ২ নং সিট ৪৭৭/৯ নং দাগ গৃহীত জমি /৩ কাঠা।

চৌঃ—১ নং ডেনের ২০৪/১, ৭৩০/২, ৭৩১/৩ নং দাগের উত্তর সীমানা এগ্রিকালচার কাম দক্ষিণ সীমানা সরকারী খাস রাস্তা পূর্ব্ব সীমানা ২০৪ ও ৭৩০ নং দাগের ভুমি পশ্চিম সীমানা ২০৪ ও ৭৩০ নং দাগের ভুমি।

২ নং ড্রেনের ৮৭৮/৪, ৮৫৩/৫; ৮৫৪/৬, ৮৭২/৭ নং দাগের উত্তর সীমানা এগ্রিকালচারাল কারম দক্ষিন সীমানা সরকারী খাস রাস্তা পূর্ব্ব সীমানা ৮৭২ ও ৫৬ নং দাগের ভুমি পশ্চিম সীমানা ৮৭১, ৮৫৩, ও ১৫৪ নং দাগের ভুমি।

৩ নং ড্রেনের ১৫৪/৮, ৪৭৭/৯, ৩৭৫/১০ দাগের উত্তর সীমানা এগ্রিকালচারাল কারম দক্ষিন সীমানা সরকারী খাস রাস্তা পূর্ব্ব ও পশ্চিম সীমানা ১৫৪, ৪৭৭, ৩৭৫ নং দাগের ভুমি।

ইস্তাহারনামা কাছারী নাল মোতাল্লেক নিজ বেহার, সন ১৯৪৭ তারিখ ২৬শে মে মোতাবেক বাঙ্গালা ১৩৫৪ সন তারিখ ১১ ই জ্যৈষ্ঠ।

পরগণে কোচবিহার এলাকাধীন ৯৩৬ নং থাক তালুক বড়বরিয়া ২য় খণ্ড অন্তর্গত একটী গ্রাম্য রাস্তা প্রস্তুতের জন্য অত্র আদালতের ১৯৪৭।৪৮ ইং সনের ৪ নং ভুমি গ্রহণের মোকদ্দমায় ২১।৫।৪৭ ইং তারিখে আদেশ সূত্রে নিম্ন লিখিত বিবরণযুক্ত ভুমি ১৩৫৩ সনের সুরু হইতে সরকারে গৃহীত হওয়ার সর্ব্বসাধারণের অবগতির জন্য এই ইস্তাহার প্রচারিত হইল।

১। পঃ কোচবিহার ৯৩৬ নং থাক তাং বড়বরিয়া ২য় খণ্ড ৮ নং বন্দোবস্ত ২৫৮৯ নং তৌঃ ৭৩ নং স্বত্ব জোত কাঙ্গালীচরণ সাহা পিং দীনবন্ধু সাহা মোঃ বেহার তৌঃ সূত্রে শচিলাল বণিক এবং শম্ভুনাথ বণিক নাঃ পিং মৃত কাঙ্গালীচরণ সাহা উক্ত নাঃ পক্ষে উহি মাতা কিরণশশি বণিক জঃ মৃত কাঙ্গালীচরণ সাহা ও গোলকবাসিনী বণিক জঃ মৃত অমিয়কুমার বণিক বর্ত্তমান জমি ৩১৯৸০৸৹ ধুর জমা ৩৭৪॥৹ গৃহীত জমি ॥৹ ধুর জমা ।৹ আনা

বিতং

৭৪ নং স্বত্ব চুকানী কাঙ্গালীচরণ সাহা পিং দীনবন্ধু সাহা বর্ত্তমান জমি ৩১৫৸০।৹ ধুর জমা ৫০৫৶৹ আনা গৃহীত জমি ।৸৹ ধুর জমা ।/৫ পাই।

বিবরণ

১১০ নং খং বন্দুঃ সর্বনাথ দাস পিং পুষ্ট দাস সাং নিজ বর্তমান জমি ৮৩৷৪৴০ খুর জমা ১২৫৲ টাকা সিট নং ৩ দাগ নং ১০০৮/১ গৃহীত জমি ।২।০ খুর জমা ৷৵৫ পাই।

চৌহদ্দী—উত্তর দক্ষিণ সীমানা ১০০৮ নং দাগ বাবদ ভূমি পূর্ব ও পশ্চিম সীমানা রাস্তা বাবদ ভূমি।

ইস্তাহারনামা কাছারী মাল মোতালকে নিজ বেহার সন ১৯৪৭ তারিখ ২৩শে মে মোতাবেক বাঙ্গালা ১৩৫৪ সন তারিখ ১৯ই জ্যৈষ্ঠ।

সরগণে কোচবিহার এলাকাধীন ৯১৪ নং থাক তালুক সহর কোচবিহার মধ্যে সরকারী কাজের জন্য অত্র আদালতের ১৯৪৭।৪৮ ইং সনের ৩ নং ভূমিগ্রহণের মোকদ্দমায় ২৪।৩।৪৭ ইং তারিখের আদেশ সূত্রে নারায়ণ গার্ডস্ ব্যারাকের পূর্ব্বপার্শ্বস্থ নিম্নলিখিত বিবরণযুক্ত ভূমি ১৩৫৪ সনের সুরু হইতে সরকারে গৃহীত হওয়ায় সর্ব্বসাধারণের অবগতির জন্য এই ইস্তাহার প্রচারিত হইল। ইতি

১। পঃ কোচবিহার তাং সহর কোচবিহার ১২৯৫ নং তৌঃ ৩০২ নং খং দখলি স্বত্ব মহাবীর রায় পিং বেণীমাধব রায় মোঃ বেহার বর্তমান জমি ৮৪৷৷৴০ খুর জমা ১০৲ সিট নং ৪ দাগ নং ১০৪ গৃহীত জমি ৮৪৷৷৴০ খুর জমা ১০ টাকা।

২। পঃ তাং তথা ৩১ নং তৌঃ ৩০৩ নং খং দখলি স্বত্ব আব্দুল গফুর পিং এছাহক উদ্দিন মিঞা মোঃ বেহার বর্তমান জমি ১৴৷৴০ খুর জমা ১০।০ সিট নং ৪ দাগ নং ১০৫, ১০৬ গৃহীত জমি ১৷৴০ খুর জমা ১০।০ আনা

৩। পঃ তাং তথা ৩৩৬ নং তৌঃ ৩০৪ নং খং দখলিস্বত্ব নিখিলচন্দ্র সিংহ পিং প্রসন্নকুমার সিংহ মোঃ বেহার বর্তমান জমি ১৷০।০ খুর জমা ২৪৷০ সিট নং ৪ দাগ নং ১০৭, ১০৮ গৃহীত জমি ১৷০।০ খুর জমা ২৪৷০ আনা

৪। পঃ তাং তথা ৩৩৫ নং তৌঃ ৩০৫ নং খং দখলি স্বত্ব মহম্মদ দুলাই মিঞা ৴০ আব্দুল হাকিম মিঞা ৴০ পিং জোনাব মিঞা বসরত আলি মিঞা ৴০ পিং ববরুল মিঞা আব্দুল হাকিম মিঞা ৴০ পিং সুবন মিঞা মোঃ বেহার বর্তমান জমি ২৴৪৷৴০ খুর জমা ২২৷৴০ সিট নং ৪ দাগ নং ১১০, ১১২, ১১৩ গৃহীত জমি ২৴৪৷৴০ খুর জমা ২২৷৷০ আনা।

৫। পঃ ৯১৪ নং থাক তাং তথা ৮২৩ নং তৌঃ ৩০৬ নং খং দখলি স্বত্ব শিবরতন কাহার ।৴৩= রামচরিত কাহার ।৴৪= পিং সুমর কাহার গণপত কাহার ।৴৩= পিং রামকিশোর কাহার মোঃ বেহার বর্তমান জমি ৮১৷৴০ খুর জমা ৮৷০ আনা সিট নং ৪ দাগ নং ১১৪ গৃহীত জমি ৮১৷৴০ খুর জমা ৮৷০ আনা।

৬ পঃ থাক তাং তথা ৮২৮ নং তৌঃ ৩০৭ নং খং দখলীস্বত্ব শিবু কাহার পিং সুমর কাহার মোঃ বেহার বর্তমান জমি ।১৴০ খুর জমা ৩৲ সিট নং ৪ দাগ নং ১১৫ গৃহীত জমি ।১৴০ জমা ৩৲ টাকা।

৭। পঃ থাক তাং তথা ৮২৯ নং তৌঃ ৩০৮ নং খং দখলি স্বত্ব প্রেমচন্দ্র অগোয়াল পিং সরবাজমল অগোয়াল মোঃ বেহার বর্তমান জমি ।১৷৴০ জমা ৩৴০ আনা সিট নং ৪ দাগ নং ১১৬ গৃহীত জমি ।১৷৴০ খুর জমা ৩৴০ আনা

চৌহদ্দী—উঃ সিং তাং নিজ নৃপেন্দ্রনারায়ণ রোড দং সিং তাং নিজ সরকারী খাস রাস্তা বাবদ ভূমি পূঃ সিং তাং নিজ গার্ডস্ রোড ও ১৯৪৪।৪৫ ইং সনের ২০ নং ভূমি গ্রহণ বাবদ সরকারী খাস ভূমি পঃ সিং তাং নিজ ১৯৪৪।৪৫ ইং সনের ১০ নং ভূমি গ্রহণ বাবদ সরকারী খাস ভূমি।

ইস্তাহারনামা কাছারী মাল মোতালকে নিজবেহার, সন ১৯৪৭ তারিখ ২৩শে মে মোতাবেক বাঙ্গালা ১৩৫৪ সন তারিখ ৯ই জ্যৈষ্ঠ

সরগণে কোচবিহার এলাকাধীন ৯৫৩ নং থাক তালুক গুড়িয়াহাটী অন্তর্গত এগ্রিকালচার ফার্মের নালার জন্য অত্র আদালতের ১৯৪৭।৪৮ ইং সনের ২ নং ভূমিগ্রহণের মোকদ্দমায় ৭।৫।৪৭ ইং তারিখের আদেশ সূত্রে নিম্নলিখিত বিবরণযুক্ত ভূমি ১৩৫৩ সনের শেষ ৩ মাস হইতে সরকারে গৃহীত হওয়ায় সর্ব্বসাধারণের অবগতির জন্য এই ইস্তাহার প্রচারিত হইল। ইতি

১। পঃ কোচবিহার ৯৫৩ নং থাক তাং গুড়িয়াহাটি মধ্যে ৩৩ নং বন্দোবস্ত ২১০৯ নং তৌঃ ১১৮ নং জমাবন্দী জোত ললিতমোহন পোদ্দার পিং ইন্দ্রমোহন পোদ্দার মোঃ বেহার বং জমি ১৩৪৴০৴০ খুর জমা ২২০৷৴০ ২ নং সিট গৃঃ জমি ৴০৷৴০ খুর জমা ৴৮ পাই।

১৮০ নং খং চুকানী ছুংগু পিং ভেটু মিঞা সাং খড়িমালা খাগড়াবাড়ী বং জমি ৯।৪।৴০ খুর জমা ১৩৷৴০ ২ নং সিট ১৭৩/১ নং দাগ গৃঃ জমি ৴০৷৴০ খুর জমা ৴২ পাই।

চৌঃ—উঃ সিং ১১৪ নং দাগ পুঃ পঃ সিং ১১৮ নং দাগ দঃ সিং সরকারী খাস।

K C GANGULI,
Revenue Minister of the
Cooch Behar State.

দেওয়ানী কার্য্যবিধি আইনের ২১ হুকুম, ৬৬ নিয়মের ঘোষণাপত্র।

রাজ্য কোচবিহারের সিঃ জজ আদালত।

এতদ্বারা সর্ব্বসাধারণকে জানান যাইতেছে যে, দায়ীকগণের নিম্নলিখিত সম্পত্তি আগামী ১৯৪৭ সনের ৪ঠা আগষ্ট মোঃ ১৩৫৪ সনের ১৮ই শ্রাবণ তারিখে দিবা ১ ঘটিকার সময় প্রকাশ্য নিলাম আরম্ভ হইবে।

১ নং ১৯৪৭।৪৮ ইং। বাঃ ডিঃ ১১২৯৵৩ মোঃ।

ডিঃ—ভীমরাজ শেঠিয়া গঃ।

দেঃ—লক্ষ্মীপ্রসাদ সাহা গঃ সাং খাগড়াবাড়ী।

তপশিল সম্পত্তি।

১। পং বেহার ১০১৩ নং থাক তাং কালজানী মধ্যে ৯২ নং তৌঃ লিঃ ৪৫৯৷০৷৴০ খুব জমির কাত বাঃ ৪০০৷৴০ আনা জমার জোত খব।

২। পং তথা ১০২০ নং থাক তাং ভাটিবাগুড়ি মধ্যে ১১ নং তৌঃ লিঃ ৩২৯৸৫৶০ খুব জমির কাত বাঃ ৩৪৫৷০ আনা জমার জোত খব।

৩। পং তথা ১০১৩ নং থাক তাং কালজানী মধ্যে ৩১৪৭ নং তৌঃ লিঃ ২৫৴৩৶০ খুব জমির কাত বাঃ ২৮৷৶০ আনা জমার জোত খব।

৪। পং তথা ১০৭৩ নং থাক তাং শকুনীবালা মধ্যে ৮২৫ নং তৌঃ লিঃ ৭৮৭৴৫৷৶০ খুব জমির কাত বাঃ ৪৭৫৸৶০ আনা জমার জোত খব।

BAZLEY RAHMAN SARKAR *Civil Judge.*

ইং ১৯১০ সালের ৫ আইনের ৫৩ ধারার ২ প্রকরণ মতে নিলামী ইস্তাহার।

আদীন মহকুমা দিনহাটার মাল আদালত।

এতদ্বারা সর্ব্বসাধারণকে জানান যাইতেছে যে, প্রতিবাদীর দাবীর বাকী খাজানা আদায় না করায় তাহার নিম্নলিখিত ক্রোকী সম্পত্তি আগামী ১৩৫৪ সনের ১৮ই শ্রাবণ মোতাবেক ১৯৪৭ সনের ৪ঠা আগষ্ট তারিখে বেলা ১ ঘটিকার সময় প্রকাশ্য নিলাম আরম্ভ হইবে।

৩৭৫ নং ১৯৪৬।৪৭ ইং। বাঃ খাঃ ৬৮৶/৪ মোঃ।

ডিঃ—মৌলভী জমির উদ্দিন

দেঃ—মালখী নেছা

তপশিল সম্পত্তি।

পং দিনহাটা তাং বড়নাচিনা মধ্যে ৩৸৴১৷৶০ খুব জমির কাত বাঃ ৫৫৷৶০ আনা জমার আং চুঃ খব।

৩০৮ নং ১৯৪৬।৪৭ ইং। বাঃ খাঃ ১৭৷৯ মোঃ।

ডিঃ—সাদি মহম্মদ মিঞা

দেঃ—সতীশ বর্ম্মণ গং

তপশিল সম্পত্তি।

পং লালবাজার ৪৯৯ নং থাক তাং খুদেরখাতা মধ্যে ১৮ নং বেঝেটারী লিঃ ২৩।১৸৶০ খুব জমির কাত বাঃ ২১৷৴০ আনা জমার জোত।

AHAMED HOSAIN PRODHAN, *Naib Ahilkar.*

ইস্তাহারনামা। সিভিলজজ আদালত, মোতাবেক নিজ বেহার সন ১৯৪৭ ইং তারিখ ৬ই জুন।

এতদ্বারা সর্ব্বসাধারণকে জানান যাইতেছে যে সমস্ত খাজনাবাকী এবং দেওয়ানী মোকদ্দমার নথিসমূহ এযাবৎ কাল চিররক্ষণীয় ছিল; মহামান্য State Council এর ১৯৩১ ইং সনের ১৩ই ফেব্রুয়ারী তারিখের Notification সূত্রে স্বত্ব সাব্যস্ত মোকদ্দমার নথী সমূহ চিররক্ষণীয় এবং অন্যান্য দেওয়ানী মোকদ্দমার নথী ও খাজনাবাকী মোকদ্দমার নথি সমূহ ২০ বৎসর কাল, রক্ষণীয়বলিয়া আদেশ হইয়াছে, এবং উক্ত Notification এর মর্ম্মানুযায়ী সিভিলজজ আদালতের মহাফেজখানায় রক্ষিত কাগজাৎ মধ্যে দিনহাটা, মাথাভাঙ্গা, মেখলীগঞ্জ, তুফানগঞ্জ ও সদর মহকুমার আদালত সমূহের খাজনাবাকী মোকদ্দমার নথী সমূহ ১৯৩৩ ইং সনের মার্চ্চ এবং দেওয়ানী মোকদ্দমার নথী সমূহের ১৯২৬ সনের মার্চ্চ মাস পর্য্যন্ত বাছনী হইয়া মোট ১৭,৩৫৫ নথী নষ্ট যোগ্য নির্দ্দিষ্ট হইয়াছে; উক্ত নথী সমূহের [illegible] কার্য্য আগামী ১৯৪৭ ইং সনের ২রা সেপ্টেম্বর তারিখ মোতাবেক ১৬ই ভাদ্র মঙ্গলবার সম্পাদিত হইবেক।

অতএব নষ্টযোগ্য নির্দ্দিষ্ট উক্ত নথী সমূহ হইতে কাহারও কোন দাখিলী দলিলাদি ওয়াপোষ অথবা নকল বা সংবাদ গ্রহণের প্রয়োজন থাকিলে নষ্টের ৭দিন পূর্ব্বে দরখাস্ত দাখিল করিবে, অন্যথায় আর কোন নকল বা ওয়াপোষ আদি দেওয়া হইবে না। সর্ব্বসাধারণের অবগতির জন্য এই বিজ্ঞাপন দেওয়া গেল। ইতি—

সিভিল জজ আদালতের মহাফেজখানায় নাশোপযোগী কাগজের লিষ্ট।

আদালতের নাম	নথির প্রকার	যেসময়ের নথী	নথীর সংখ্যা
মাথাভাঙ্গা এঃ ডিঃ নাঃ আঃ আঃ	দেওয়ানী সরণও	এপ্রিল ১৯২৫—মার্চ্চ ১৯২৬	১৬৭
ঐ	দেওয়ানী ডিক্রীজারী	ঐ	১১৮
ঐ	দেওয়ানী মোৎফর্কা বিঃ	ঐ	২৬
দিনহাটা নাঃ আঃ আদালত	খাজনাবাকি সরণও	এপ্রিল ১৯৩৩—মার্চ্চ ১৯৩৪ ও এপ্রিল ১৯২৫—মার্চ্চ ১৯২৬	৯১৪
ঐ	খাজনাবাকি ডিক্রীজারী	ঐ	৫৮৬
ঐ	খাজনাবাকি মোৎফর্কা বিঃ	ঐ	১০৭
দিনহাটা এঃ ডিঃ নাঃ আঃ আঃ	খাজনাবাকি সরণও	ঐ	১৫২১
ঐ	খাজনাবাকি ডিক্রীজারী	ঐ	৭৫৩
ঐ	খাজনাবাকি মোৎফর্কা বিঃ	ঐ	২০
দিনহাটা নাঃ আঃ আদালত	দেওয়ানী সরণও	এপ্রিল ১৯২৫—মার্চ্চ ১৯২৬	১৩৫
ঐ	দেওয়ানী ডিক্রীজারী	ঐ	১৭০
ঐ	দেওয়ানী মোৎফর্কা বিঃ	ঐ	২১
দিনহাটা এঃ ডিঃ নাঃ আঃ আঃ	দেওয়ানী সরণও	এপ্রিল ১৯২৫—মার্চ্চ ১৯২৬	৭৭
ঐ	দেওয়ানী ডিক্রীজারী	ঐ	৪৮
ঐ	দেওয়ানী মোৎফর্কা বিঃ	ঐ	১৪
তুফানগঞ্জ নাঃ আঃ আঃ	খাজনাবাকী সরণও	এপ্রিল ১৯৩৩—মার্চ্চ ১৯৩৪ ও এপ্রিল ১৯২৫—মার্চ্চ ১৯২৬	৮০৭
ঐ	খাজনাবাকী ডিক্রীজারী	ঐ	৫০৫
ঐ	খাজনাবাকী মোৎফর্কা বিঃ	ঐ	৫৭
ঐ	দেওয়ানী সরণও	এপ্রিল ১৯২৫—মার্চ্চ ১৯২৬	৫৫৩
ঐ	দেওয়ানী ডিক্রীজারী	ঐ	২৫৯
ঐ	দেওয়ানী মোৎফর্কা বিঃ	ঐ	২৩
মেখলীগঞ্জ নাঃ আঃ আঃ	খাজনাবাকী সরণও	এপ্রিল ১৯৩৩—মার্চ্চ ১৯৩৪ ও এপ্রিল ১৯২৫—১৯২৬ মার্চ্চ	১০৬৫
ঐ	খাজনাবাকী ডিক্রীজারী	ঐ	৭৬৭
ঐ	খাজনাবাকী মোৎফর্কা বি	ঐ	৮৯
মেখলীগঞ্জ নাঃ আঃ আদালত	দেওয়ানী সরণও	এপ্রিল ১৯২৫—মার্চ্চ ১৯২৬	১৪৪
ঐ	দেওয়ানী ডিক্রিজারী	ঐ	১১৫
ঐ	দেওয়ানী মোৎফর্কা (বিঃ)	ঐ	২৭
এসিষ্টান্ট সিঃ জজ আদালত	খাজনাবাকী সরণও	এপ্রিল ১৯২৫—মার্চ্চ ১৯২৬	১৩
ঐ	খাজনাবাকী ডিক্রিজারী	ঐ	২৯০
ঐ	খাজনাবাকী মোৎফর্কা বিঃ	ঐ	৮৩
ঐ	দেওয়ানী সরণও	ঐ	২৫৭
ঐ	দেওয়ানী ডিক্রিজারী	ঐ	২৫২
ঐ	দেওয়ানী মোৎফর্কা বিঃ	ঐ	২১

আদালতের নাম	নথীর প্রকার	যে সময়ের নথী	নথীর সংখ্যা
ট্রেজারী নাঃ আঃ আদালত	খাজনাবাকী ডিক্রিজারী	এপ্রিল ১৯২২—মার্চ ১৯২৬	১২
ঐ	খাজনাবাকী মোৎফর্কা বিঃ	ঐ	৩
ঐ	দেওয়ানী সরনও	ঐ	১
ঐ	দেওয়ানী ডিক্রিজারী	ঐ	২
ঐ	দেওয়ানী মোৎফর্কা বিঃ	ঐ	২
সঃ সব ডিঃ নাঃ আঃ আদালত	খাজনাবাকী সরনও	এপ্রিল ১৯৩১—ফেব্রুয়ারী ১৯৩৪	৮৪৭
ঐ	খাজনাবাকী ডিক্রিজারী	ঐ	৪৮৭
ঐ	খাজনাবাকী মোৎফর্কা বিঃ	ঐ	৩১
সদর সব ডিঃ অফিঃ আদালত	খাজনাবাকী সরনও	ফেব্রুয়ারী ১৯৩০—মার্চ ১৯৩১	৭০
ঐ	খাজনাবাকী ডিক্রিজারী	ঐ	১১৫
ঐ	খাজনাবাকী মোৎফর্কা বিঃ	ঐ	১৩
সদর নাঃ আঃ আদালত	খাজনাবাকী সরনও	মে ১৯৩০—মার্চ ১৯৩৪	৬২৯
ঐ	খাজনাবাকী ডিক্রিজারী	ঐ	৩২৭
ঐ	খাজনাবাকী মোৎফর্কা বিঃ	ঐ	২৮
মাথাভাঙ্গা নাঃ আঃ আঃ	খাজনাবাকী সরনও	এপ্রিল ১৯৩৩—মার্চ ১৯৩৪ ও এপ্রিল ১৯২৫—মার্চ ১৯২৬।	৮৯৪
ঐ	খাঃ বাকী ডিক্রীজারী	ঐ	৬৭৭
ঐ	খাঃ বাঃ মোৎফর্কা (বিঃ)	ঐ	১৪০
মাথাভাঙ্গা এঃ নাঃ আঃ আঃ	খাঃ বাকী সরনও	ঐ	১০৮৪
ঐ	খাঃ বাঃ ডিক্রীজারী	ঐ	৯৪২
ঐ	খাঃ বাঃ মোৎফর্কা (বিঃ)	ঐ	১৫৭
মাথাভাঙ্গা নাঃ আঃ আঃ	দেওয়ানী সরনও	১৯২৫ এপ্রিল হইতে ১৯২৬ মার্চ মাস পর্য্যন্ত	১২৮
ঐ	দেওয়ানী ডিক্রীজারী	ঐ	১০৯
ঐ	দেঃ মোৎফর্কা (বিঃ)	ঐ	৪৫
সদর এঃ নাঃ আঃ আঃ	খাজনাবাকী সরনও	১৯৩৩ সনের এপ্রিল হইতে ১৯৩৪ সনের মার্চ পর্য্যন্ত	১৪৫
ঐ	খাঃ বাঃ ডিক্রীজারী	ঐ	১০০
ঐ	খাঃ বাঃ মোৎফর্কা বিঃ)	ঐ	১৩
মেখলিগঞ্জ নাঃ আঃ আঃ	খাঃ বাকী ডিক্রীজারী	১৯২৫ সনের এপ্রিল হইতে ১৯২৬ সনের মার্চ পর্য্যন্ত	১৫
ঐ	খাঃ বাকী মোৎফর্কা (বিঃ)	ঐ	১১
ঐ	দেওয়ানী ডিক্রীজারী	ঐ	৪
সিভিল জজ আদালত	খাজনাবাকী সরনও	১৯২৫ সনের এপ্রিল হইতে ১৯২৬ সনের মার্চ ও ১৯৩৩ সনের মে হইতে ১৯৩৩ সনের ডিসেম্বর পর্য্যন্ত	১৮
ঐ	খাঃ বাঃ ডিক্রীজারী	এপ্রিল ১৯৩০—মার্চ ১৯৩১	১৩
ঐ	খাঃ বাঃ মোঃ (বিঃ)	এপ্রিল ১৯২৫—মার্চ ১৯২৬	৫
ঐ	খাঃ বাকী আপীল	ঐ	৩৩
ঐ	দেওয়ানী সরনও	ঐ	৩৩
সিভিল জজ আদালত	দেওয়ানী ডিক্রীজারী	১৯২৫ সনের এপ্রিল হইতে ১৯২৬ সনের মার্চ পর্য্যন্ত	৫৮
ঐ	দেওয়ানী আপীল	ঐ	৪৭
ঐ	দেওয়ানী মোৎফর্কা	ঐ	৯২

BASIRUR RAHMAN SARKAR, *Civil Judge.*

MALCUCHERY NOTICE.

ইস্তাহারনামা কাছারী মাল দেওয়ানকে নিজ বেহার, সন ১৯৪৭ তারিখ ২৬শে মে
মোতাবেক বাঙ্গালা ১৩৫৪ সন তারিখ ১১ই জ্যৈষ্ঠ।

পরগণে কোচবিহার এলাকাধীন ৯১৪ নং থাক তালুক সহর কোচবিহার অন্তর্গত রাস্তার জন্য অত্র আদালতের ১৯৪৭।৪৮ ইং সনের ৫ নং ভূমি গ্রহণের মোকদ্দমার ২১।৫।৪৭ তারিখের আদেশক্রমে নিম্নলিখিত বিবরণযুক্ত ভূমি ১৩৫২ সনের শেষ ৬ মাস হইতে সরকারে গৃহীত হওয়ায় সর্ব্বসাধারণের অবগতির জন্য এই ইস্তাহার প্রচারিত হইল। ইতি

১। পং কোচবিহার ৯১৪ নং থাক তাং সহর কোচবিহার ৪৬৭ নং তৌঃ ১১৮৮ নং স্বত্ব দখলি স্বত্ব উমানন্দ ৵৪ নিত্যানন্দ ৵৪ হরিকান্ত ৵৪ হরেন্দ্র ৵৪ নরেন্দ্র ৵৪ পিং বোন্দরু মাঝি ওঃ পরমানন্দ দাস মোঃ বেহার বর্ত্তমান জমি ১/২৸৶০ খুরজমা ১১॥০ আনা সিট নং ১১ দাগ নং ৫৭/২ গৃহীত জমি /৪৮৶০ খুর জমা ২।৶১০ পাই।

২। পং থাক তাং তথা ১১০ নং তৌঃ ১২৮৯ নং স্বত্ব জোত স্বত্ব চন্দ্রমোহন চৌধুরী পিং প্যারীমোহন চৌধুরী মোঃ বেহার বর্ত্তমান জমি ১১২৸/০ খুর জমা ১৯০৮৶০ আনা গৃহীত জমি ৮৩॥৶০ খুর জমা ৯।/৭ পাই।

বিতং

১৩০৭ নং স্বত্ব চুকানী বীরেন্দ্রকুমার পিং বিজয়চন্দ্র দাস বিনোদিনীবালা দেবী জঃ চিন্তাহরণ রায় মোঃ বেহার (অংশ দখল মোতাবেক) বর্ত্তমান জমি ১/১৸০ খুর জমা ১৪॥৶০ আনা সিট নং ৮ দাগ নং ১০০৩/১১ গৃহীত জমি /৪৸৶০ খুর জমা ৩৫ পাই।

১৩০৮ নং স্বত্ব চুকানী শুক্রমী মাহুয়ানী জঃ নব মাঝি মোঃ বেহার বর্ত্তমান জমি ।১/০ খুর জমা ৪/০ আনা গৃহীত জমি /১৮/০ খুর জমা ১৶৩ পাই।

বিতং

পং থাক তাং তথা ১১০ নং তৌঃ ১৩০৯ নং স্বত্ব দরচুঃ উমাকান্ত পিং নন্দ নমঃদাস বর্ত্তমান জমি ।১/০ খুর জমা ৪৮৶০ সিট নং ৮ দাগ নং ১০০৪/৯ গৃহীত জমি /১৸/০ খুর জমা ১।৶১ পাই।

১৩১০ নং স্বত্ব চুকানী চন্দ্রমোহন পিং প্যারীমোহন চৌধুরী মোঃ বেহার বর্ত্তমান জমি ১৮৩॥৶০ খুর জমা ২৬/০ আনা গৃহীত জমি /৩০৸/০ খুর জমা ২।৶১১ পাই।

বিতং

নিজ দখল সিট নং ৮ দাগ নং ১০১২/৭ গৃহীত জমি /১৶০ খুর।

১৩১১ নং স্বত্ব কুঞ্জিপ্রভা অন্ন মাহুয়ানী জঃ বলহরি মাঝি মোঃ বেহার বর্ত্তমান জমি /২৶০ খুর জমা ১৸৶০ আনা সিট নং ৮ দাগ নং ১০১১/৩ গৃহীত জমি /১৶০ খুর জমা ৸৶। পাই।

১৩১৩ নং স্বত্ব দরচুঃ টৈরা ॥০ সুরেন্দ্র ॥০ পিং গঙ্গাচরণ দাস মোঃ বেহার বর্ত্তমান জমি ।২।০ খুর জমা ৫৸/০ সিট নং ৮ দাগ নং ১০২১/১০ গৃহীত জমি /১৶০ খুর জমা ৸৶৪ পাই।

১৩১৪ নং স্বত্ব দরচুঃ সুখেশ্বরী মাহুয়ানী জঃ ঢুড়ু মাঝি মোঃ বেহার বর্ত্তমান জমি /৩॥৶০ খুর জমা ২৫৸৶০ আনা সিট নং ৮ দাগ নং ১০,৪.৮ গৃহীত জমি /১৶০ খুর জমা ৸৶৪ পাই।

১৩.৬ নং স্বত্ব চুকানী চন্দ্রমোহন চৌধুরী পিং প্যারীমোহন চৌধুরী মোঃ বেহার বর্ত্তমান জমি ১/॥/০ খুর জমা ১৩৸৶০ আনা গৃহীত জমি ।০।৶০ খুর জমা ৫॥৶১০ পাই।

বিতং

১৩১৭ নং স্বত্ব দরচুঃ সুখেশ্বরী মাহুয়ানী জঃ ঢুড়ু মাঝি মোঃ বেহার বর্ত্তমান জমি /১৸/০ খুর জমা ১৶০ আনা সিট নং ৮ দাগ নং ১০১৩ গৃহীত জমি /১৸/০ খুর জমা ১।৶০ আনা

১৩০৫ নং স্বত্ব চুকানী চন্দ্রমোহন পিং প্যারীমোহন চৌধুরী মোঃ বেহার বর্ত্তমান জমি ।০/০ খুর জমা ৩৸৶০ আনা গৃহীত জমি /১৶০ খুর জমা ৸১১ পাই।

১৩০৬ নং স্বত্ব দরচুঃ বীরেন্দ্রকুমার পিং বিজয়চন্দ্র দাস মোঃ বেহার বর্ত্তমান জমি ॥০/০ খুর জমা ৮।০ আনা সিট নং ৮ দাগ নং ১০০৭/১০ গৃহীত জমি /১৶০ খুর জমা ৸৶৪ পাই।

পং থাক তাং তথা ১৩১৮ নং স্বত্ব দরচুঃ সুখেন্দ্রনাথ পিং সুরেন্দ্রনাথ ঘোষ মোঃ বেহার বর্ত্তমান জমি ৸০৶০ খুর জমা ১২/০ আনা সিট নং ৮ দাগ নং ১০১০/৫ গৃহীত জমি /৩॥৶০ খুর জমা ২৸৶৮ পাই।

১৩১৯ নং স্বত্ব চুকানী রাজেন্দ্রনাথ ।০ নগেন্দ্রনাথ ।০ হরেন্দ্রনাথ ।০ নরেন্দ্রনাথ পিং রামচন্দ্র নমঃদাস মোঃ বেহার বর্ত্তমান জমি ৸৩৸০ খুর জমা ১২॥৶০ আনা সিট নং ৮ দাগ নং ১০১৩/১২, ১০১২/১৩ গৃহীত জমি /১৸/০ খুর জমা ১৶৩ পাই।

। পং থাক তাং তথা মধ্যে ৪০৫ নং তৌঃ ১৩৫৮ নং স্বত্ব দখলি স্বত্ব তৌঃ মধ্যে বিপিনচন্দ্র দাস বেহারা নৃপেন্দ্রচন্দ্র দাস বেহারা নাঃ হরেন্দ্রনাথ দাস বেহারা নাঃ উক্ত নাঃ দ্বয় পক্ষে উহি মাতা নিজ মাতা জঃ মৃত হরবোল বেহারা সাং সহর কোচবিহার বর্ত্তমান জমি ৩৷২॥/০ খুর জমা ৩৬।০ সিট নং ১১ দাগ নং ৫৫/৩ গৃহীত জমি /৪।০ খুর জমা ২।/০ আনা।

। পং থাক তাং তথা ১৩৩৪ নং স্বত্ব নিষ্কর কুমার যোগেন্দ্র নারায়ণ ॥০ কুমার চারু নারায়ণ ॥০ পিং মহিলনারায়ণ সাহেব মোঃ বেহার বর্ত্তমান জমি ১১৮১॥০ খুর সিট নং ৮ দাগ নং ১০৩৩/১, ১০৩০/৩, ১০৩১/৪ গৃহীত জমি ৸১।৶০ খুর।

৫। পঃ থাক তাং তথা ১৫৬০ নং তৌঃ ২০১ নং স্বত্ব দখলি স্বত্ব কুমার যোগেন্দ্রনারায়ণ পিং কুমারগজিন নারায়ণ মোঃ বেহার বর্ত্তমান জমি ১/৪৫/০ ধুর জমা ১২৬/০ আনা সিট নং ৮ দাগ নং ১০২৯/২ গৃহীতজমি ।১/০ ধুর জমা ৩৫ পাই।

৬। পঃ থাক তাং তথা ১৫৬১ নং তৌঃ ২০২৭ নং স্বত্ব দখলি স্বত্ব যোগেন্দ্রনাথ রায় পিং জগন্নাথ রায় বর্ত্তমান জমি ৪।৩৬০/০ ধুর জমা ৯৪০০ আনা সিট নং ১১ দাগ নং ৬৮/১ গৃহীত জমি /৪।০ ধুর জমা ২০/০ আনা।

চৌঃ—উঃ সীঃ ৮ নং সিটের ৯৯৯, ১০০২, ১০০১, ১০১৪, ১০১৫, ১০১৬ ১০১৭ নং দাগ ও সরকারী রাস্তা বাবদ ভূমি। দঃ সীঃ ৮ নং সিটের ১০০৩—১০০৫, ১০১১—১০১২ ১০১০নং দাগ ও ১১ নং সিট অন্তর্গত সরকারী খাস রাস্তা বাবদ ভূমি। পূঃ সীঃ ৮ নং সিটের ১০২৯—১০৩১, ১০৩০ নং দাগের পূর্ব্বাংশ ও ১১ নং সিটের ৬৬, ৫৭ ও ৫৫ নং দাগের পূর্ব্বাংশ। পঃ সীঃ ৮ নং সিটের ১০৩৩, ১০২৯—১০৩, নং দাগের পশ্চিমাংশ ও ১১ নং সিটের ৬৬, ৫৭ ও ৫৫ নং দাগের পূর্ব্বাংশ পঃ সীঃ ৮ নং সিটের ১০৩৩, ১০২৯—১০৩১ নং দাগের পশ্চিমাংশ ও ১১ নং সিটের ৬৬, ৫৭, ৫৫ নং দাগের পশ্চিমাংশ।

ইস্তাহারনামা কাছারী মাল মোতালকে নিজবেহার, সন ১৯৪৭ তারিখ ২৬।৫
মোতাবেক বাঙ্গলা ১৩৫৪ সন তারিখ ১১ই জ্যৈষ্ঠ

পরগণে কোচবিহার এলাকাধিন ৯৯৭ নং থাক তালুক চক চকা অন্তরগত মহারাজকুমারের বাসগৃহ নির্ম্মানের জন্য অত্র আদালতের ১৯৪৭।৪৮ ইং সনের ৭ নং ভূমিগ্রহণের মোকদ্দমায় ২৪।৫।৪৭ ইংতারিখের আদেশ সূত্রে নিম্নলিখিত বিবরণযুক্ত—ভূমি ১৩৫৪ সনের সুরু হইতে সরকারের গৃহীত হওয়ায় সর্ব্বসাধারণের অবগতির জন্য এই ইস্তাহার প্রচারিত হইল। ইতি

১। পঃ কোচবিহার ৯৯৭নং থাক তাং চকচকা বন্দবস্ত নং ৪৩ তৌঃ নং ৩৩৫০ স্বত্ব নং ২০১ জোত সরলা বালা দাস্যা অং ধীরেন্দ্রনাথ দাস পক্ষে কোর্টঅবওয়ার্ডস ম্যানেজার মোং বেহার তৌং সূত্রে মনমোহন দাস বর্ত্তমান জমি ৬৯।১০/ ধুর বর্ত্তমান জমা ২৯৮/০ আনা, গৃহীত জমি ২৮।৪৮৫/ ধুর জমা ১১/১০ পাই

বিতং

২০২ নং স্বত্ব চুকানী বরদা কুমার পিং আনন্দ মোহন বসু মোং বেহার বর্ত্তমান জমি৪৮৫২।।/ধুর বর্ত্তমান জমা ৩৪৲ টাকা সিট নং ২ দাগ নং ৭৩/১, ৭৩/৪৪৮ গৃহীত জমি ১৯৷২৫/ধুর জমা ৮।৫ পাই

২০৩ নং স্বত্ব চুকানী শ্রীশচন্দ্র পিং কালীপ্রসাদ সেন মোং বেহার বর্ত্তমান জমি ১২॥৩ ধুর জমা ১০৮০/আনা সিট নং ২ দাগ নং ৭৪/২ গৃহীত জমি৮৫২।ধুর জমা৩॥/ আনা।

চৌঃ—উঃ সিং তাং নিজ ৭১, ৭২ নং দাগ বাবদ ভূমি, দঃ সিং তাং খড়িমালা খাগড়া বাড়ী ৭৭২, ৫৯৯,৬০০ নং দাগ বাবদ ভূমি পূং সিং ৭৩, ৭৪ নং দাগ বাবদ ভূমি পং সিং বুড়া তোর্ষা নদী

ইস্তাহারনামা কাছারী মাল মোতালকে নিজবেহার, সন ১৯৪৭ তারিখ ২৬শে মে
মোতাবেক বাঙ্গলা ১৩৫৪ সন তারিখ ১১ই জ্যৈষ্ঠ

পরগণে কোচবিহার এলাকাধীন ৯৫৪ নং থাক তালুক খড়িমালা খাগড়াবাড়ী মধ্যে মহারাজকুমারের বাসগৃহ নির্ম্মাণের জন্য অত্র আদালতের ১৯৪৭।৪৮ ইং সনের ৭নং ভূমিগ্রহণের মোকদ্দমায় ২৪.৫।৪৭ ইং তারিখের আদেশ সূত্রে নিম্নলিখিত বিবরণযুক্ত ভূমি ১৩৫৪ সনের সুরু হইতে সরকারে গৃহীত হওয়ায় সর্ব্বসাধারণের অবগতি জন্য এই ইস্তাহার প্রচারিত হইল। ইতি

১। পরগণে কোচবিহার থাক ৯৫৪নং তাং খড়িমালা খাগড়াবাড়ী বঃ ২ নং তৌঃ ১৭১ নং স্বত্ব ২৩৯ নং জোত—সাহের মহম্মদ পিং হায়াৎ মহম্মদ সাং রাশিডাঙ্গা, বর্ত্তমান জমি ৭৬।০/০ ধুর জমা ৫২৬/০ আনা গৃহীত জমি ৩।/১৮/ ধুর জমা ২২।৫/৭ পাই।

বিতং

স্বত্ব ২৪১ নং চুকানি—সাদিমহম্মদ ৷৷০ সাহের মহম্মদ ৷৷০ পিং হায়াৎ মামুদ সাং রাশিডাঙ্গা, বর্ত্তমান জমি ১৫৷১।/ ধুর জমা ১৫৲ গৃহীত জমি ১৪।৩৷/ ধুর জমা ১৪।/২ পাই। বিতং স্বত্ব ২৪২ নং দরচুকানি—জগমোহন নাঃ পক্ষে উচ্ছিমাতা বুধিয়া হুনিয়ানী অঃ সাধু হুনিয়া বর্ত্তমান জমি ১৫৷১৫/ ধুর জমা ১৭৮০ আনা সিট ২ নং দাগ নং ৫৮৫—৫৯৬, ৬০৪—৬১০ গৃহীত ভূমি ১৪।৩৷/ ধুর জমা ১৩৮/৭ পাই।

পঃ কোচবিহার ৯৫৪ নং থাক তাং খড়িমালা খাগড়াবাড়ী বঃ ২ নং তৌঃ ১২৮ নং স্বত্ব ২৪৩ চুকানি মুনশি গোয়ালিনী অঃ কেশব গোয়ালা বর্ত্তমান জমি ২২।০৮/০ ধুর জমা ১৭৷/ সিট ২ নং দাগ নং ৫৯৭—৬০৩ গৃহীত জমি ২০৷৷৩। ধুর জমা ১৩৲৩ পাই।

চৌহদ্দি—উত্তর সীমানা তাং চকচকা দক্ষিণ সীমানা সরকারী খাস রাস্তা পূর্ব্ব সীঃ তাং খড়িমালা খাগড়াবাড়ী সিট ২ নং, ৬১১, ৬১২, নং দাগ বাবদ ভূমি পশ্চিম সীমানা বুড়া তোর্ষা নদী

K C GANGULI,
Revenue Minister of the
Cooch Behar State.

দেওয়ানী কার্য্যবিধি আইনের ২১ হুকুম, ৬৬ নিয়মের ঘোষণাপত্র।

রাজ্য কোচবিহারের এঃ সিঃ জজ আদালত।

এতদ্দ্বারা সর্ব্বসাধারণকে জানান যাইতেছে যে, দায়ীকগণের নিম্নলিখিত সম্পত্তি আগামী ১৯৪৭ সনের ৪ঠা আগষ্ট মোঃ ১৩৫৪ সনের ১৮ই শ্রাবণ তারিখে দিবা ১ ঘটিকার সময় প্রকাশ্য নিলাম আরম্ভ হইবে।

৩ নং ১৯৪৭।৪৮ ইং। বাঃ ডিঃ ১১২১৮৯ মোঃ।

ডিঃ—শ্রী সুধীর কুমার বিশ্বাস গং সোঃ বেহার।

দেঃ—কালিয়া প্রসাদ মহতো মুনিয়া নাঃ গং মোঃ বেহার।

তপশিল সম্পত্তি।

১। পঃ বেহার ৯১৪ নং থাক তাং সহর কুচবিহার মধ্যে ১৪৮৪ নং তৌঃ লিঃ ।৪৷৷৴ ধুর] জমির কাত বাঃ ৪৸৴০ জমার জোত।

২। পঃ বেহার ৯১৪ নং থাক তাং সহর কুচবেহার মধ্যে ১৪৫৩ নং তৌ লিঃ ।২৷৷৴০ ধুর জমির বাঃ কাত ৩৴০ জমার জোত।

F. AHMED, *Asst. Civil Judge.*

ইং ১৯১০ সালের ৫ আইনের ৫৩ ধারার ২ প্রকরণ মতে নিলামী ইস্তাহার।

জারির মহকুমা মাথাভাঙ্গা এ ডিঃ মাল আদালত।

এতদ্দ্বারা সর্ব্বসাধারণকে জানান যাইতেছে যে, প্রতিবাদীর দাবীর বাকী খাজনা আদায় না করায় তাহার নিম্নলিখিত ক্রোকী সম্পত্তি আগামী ১৩৫৪ সনের ২২শে আষাঢ় মোতাবেক ১৯৪৭ সনের ৭ই জুলাই তারিখে বেলা ১ ঘটিকার সময় প্রকাশ্য নীলাম আরম্ভ হইবে।

২২ নং। ১৯৪৭।৪৮ বাঃ খাঃ ১৭৸৴০ মোঃ।

ডিঃ—ভবানীপ্রসন্ন তালুকদার মোঃ মাথাভাঙ্গা।

দেঃ—পিশু বর্ম্মণ নাঃ গঃ সাং বড় গদাইখোড়া।

তপশিল সম্পত্তি।

পঃ লালবাজার ৪৩৫ নং থাক তাং গাঙ্গধর মধ্যে ৮১৸৴০ ধুর জমির কাত বাঃ ৬০ আনা জমার চুকানী স্বত্ব।

২১ নং ১৯৪৭।৪৮ ইং। বাঃ খাঃ ১১২৸০ মোঃ।

ডিঃ—ভবানীপ্রসন্ন তালুকদার মোঃ মাথাভাঙ্গা।

দেঃ—ধনর উদ্দিন মিঞা গং সাং ছোট মধুসুদন।

তপশীল সম্পত্তি।

পঃ লালবাজার ৫১৯ নং থাক তাং ছোট মধুসুদন মধ্যে ২৭।১৷৷০ ধুর জমির কাত বাঃ ৩৮৴০ আনা জমার দরচুকানী স্বত্ব

২০ নং ১৯৪৭।৪৮ ইং বাঃ খাঃ ৫৫৷৴০ মোঃ

ডিঃ—ভবানীপ্রসন্ন তালুকদার মোঃ মাথাভাঙ্গা।

দেঃ—হেমেন্দ্রনাথ বর্ম্মণ সাং কেদারকুঠী খলিশামারী।

তপশিল সম্পত্তি

পঃ লালবাজার ৬১৬ নং থাক তাং খাসরেশ খলিশাবাড়ী মধ্যে ২০।৩।০ ধুর জমির কাত বাঃ ২৭৸৴০ আনা জমার চুঃ স্বত্ব।

১৯ নং ১৯৪৭।৪৮ ইং। বাঃ খাঃ ৫১৷৴০ মোঃ।

ডিঃ—ভবানীপ্রসন্ন তালুকদার মোঃ মাথাভাঙ্গা।

দেঃ—রুকমণী বর্ম্মাণী গঃ সাং তেকুনিয়া।

তপশিল সম্পত্তি।

পঃ মাথাভাঙ্গা ২৫৯ নং থাক তাং তেকুনিয়া মধ্যে ১৫।৩ কাঠা জমির কাত বাঃ ১৮৸৴০ আনা জমার চুকানী স্বত্ব।

১৮ নং ১৯৪৭।৪৮ ইং। বাঃ খাঃ ৫৭৴০ মোঃ।

ডিঃ—ভবানীপ্রসন্ন তালুকদার মোঃ মাথাভাঙ্গা।

দেঃ—রহমউদ্দিন মিঞা সাং শিবরাম জেঃ জলপাইগুড়ী।

তপশিল সম্পত্তি

পঃ লালবাজার ৪১৯ নং থাক তাং ছোট মধুসুদন মধ্যে ৯।১৷০ ধুর জমির কাত বাঃ ৯৭০ আনা জমার চুকানী স্বত্ব।

১৩ নং ১৯৪৭।৪৮ ইং। বাঃ খাঃ ১১১৸০ মোঃ।

ডিঃ—জয়চাঁদলাল বথেরা মোঃ মাথাভাঙ্গা।

দেঃ—শ্রীমন্ত বর্ম্মণ সাং ধলারপাড়।

তপশিল সম্পত্তি

পঃ লালবাজার ৪৪১ নং থাক তাং বড় শিকারপুরখাতা মধ্যে ১৩।২৸৴০ ধুর জমির কাত বাঃ ১৮।০ আনা জমার চুঃ স্বত্ব।

৪৭ নং ১৯৪৭।৫৮ ইং। বাঃ খাঃ ৯৩৸৹ দোঃ।

দিঃ—শ্রীরমানাথ তরফদার মোঃ মাথাভাঙ্গা।

মোঃ—নসির উদ্দিন মিঞা পঃ নাং গোলেনাওহাটী।

তপশিল সম্পত্তি।

পঃ লালবাজার ৪৬৬ নং খাক তাং গোলেনাওহাটী মধ্যে ৬৮৪৪৶৹ ধুর জমির কাত বাঃ ১৯৮/০ আনা জমার হঃ চুঃ স্বত্ব

TINKARI MOHAN MUKERJEE, *Addl. Naib Ahilkar.*

NOTICE.

It is notified for general information that persons who require a Jeep car should furnish with their requisition with the particulars noted below :—

(1) If the Jeep is wanted for tour on official works or for private purpose.
(2) Date and hour of starting of the outward journey.
(3) Date and expected hour of return.
(4) Destination.
(5) Approximate mileage of the proposed journey.

L. M. BAKSI,
Development Commissioner, Cooch Behar.

সিভিল সাপ্লাইজ কমিশনার ও কন্ট্রোলার অব প্রাইসেস আফিস, কুচবিহার

বিজ্ঞাপন।

(মূল্য নিয়ন্ত্রণ)

সিভিল সাপ্লাইজ কমিশনারের উপর প্রদত্ত এবং ন্যস্ত ক্ষমতাবলে কোচবিহার Essential Supplies (Temporary Powers) Act 1946 এর ৩ ধারার অন্তর্গত ২ উপধারার সি ক্লজ অনুযায়ী নিম্নলিখিত দ্রব্যগুলির সর্ব্বোচ্চ মূল্য নিম্নলিখিতরূপে ধার্য্য করা হইল এবং তাহা কুচবিহার গেজেটে প্রকাশিত হওয়ার তারিখ হইতে পুনরাদেশ না হওয়া পর্য্যন্ত বলবৎ থাকিবে। এতদ্বিষয়ক পূর্ব্ব বিজ্ঞপ্তি বাতিল করা হইল। কোন ব্যক্তি নির্দ্ধারিত মূল্যের অতিরিক্ত মূল্যে বিক্রয় করিলে বা দ্রব্যাদি বিক্রয়ার্থ আনিয়া নির্দ্ধারিত মূল্যে বিক্রয় করিতে অস্বীকার করিলে উপরোক্ত আইনের ৭ ধারা অনুযায়ী দণ্ডনীয় হইবে। ইতি ২৬শে জুন ১৯৪৭।

বিশেষ দ্রষ্টব্য ঃ—সরিষা ও পাটের দর রাজ্যের হাটে, তহবাজারে, মিলে ও খুচরা দোকানে ও বন্দরে প্রযোজ্য। রাজ্যের অন্যান্য স্থানের দর উহা অপেক্ষা।০ চারি আনা হিসাবে কম হইবে। ময়দা, লবণ ও চিনির দর রাজ্যের সর্ব্বত্র এক।

কেরাসিন—হলদিবাড়ী বন্দরের দর—

লাল কেরোসিন প্রতি টিন ৪৸৶ টিন সমেত প্রতি সের ৶১০

সাদা কেরোসিন প্রতি টিন ৫৶০ (ঐ) প্রতি সের ।০

কয়লা—কয়লার দর মাত্র কুচবিহার শহরের জন্য নির্দ্ধারিত হইল।

মফঃস্বলের দর—কোচবিহার টাউন, দিনহাটা বন্দর, হলদিবাড়ী বন্দর, মাথাভাঙ্গা বন্দর ব্যতীত অন্যান্য স্থানের দর নিম্নলিখিত দর অপেক্ষা (ধান্য, চাউল, সরিষা ও পাট ব্যতীত) মণ প্রতি এক টাকা চারি আনা অর্থাৎ সের প্রতি দুই পয়সা বেশী হইবে। কিন্তু যে সকল ক্ষেত্রে রাজ্যের অন্যান্য স্থানের দর পৃথক ভাবে ধার্য্য আছে সেই সব ক্ষেত্রে ঐ নির্দ্ধারিত দরই প্রযোজ্য হইবে।

পাইকারী দর—মণ সেরের নীচে আড়াই সের পর্য্যন্ত খরিদ বিক্রী হইলে মণ প্রতি ৷০ চারি আনা বেশী হইবে। কিন্তু এই নিয়ম, চাউল, সরিষা, গম, সম্বন্ধে প্রযোজ্য হইবে না এবং রেশন দোকানে ইহা প্রযোজ্য হইবে যথায় কেবলমাত্র নির্দ্ধারিত খুচরা দরে কেনা বেচা হইবে।

ষ্ট্যাণ্ডার্ড বস্তা—লবণ ১৮৯ সের বস্তা সহ।
চিনি ২৮১ সের বস্তা সহ।

পণ্য দ্রব্যের নাম	প্রতি সের	প্রতি মণ	প্রতি ষ্ট্যাণ্ডার্ড বস্তা	মন্তব্য
১। গম—দেশী জাতের	৶০	৯৲		
ঐ বড়দানা পাঞ্জাবী জাতের		১৫৲		
২। চিনি	৸৶০	২৪৷৷০	৬৭৷৵০ (কোচবিহার সহর, দিনহাটা বন্দর, চাংরাবান্ধা বন্দর, হলদিবাড়ী বন্দরের জন্য) প্রতি ষ্ট্যাণ্ডার্ড বস্তা ৭০৸৵০ আনা	
ঐ	৸৶০	২৭৲	(রাজ্যের অন্যান্য স্থানের দর)	
বাতাসা, কদমা, তিলুয়া	৸৵	৩১৲		
মিস্ত্রী	৸৵১০	৩২৷০		
রসগোল্লা	১৷০	×		
সন্দেশ (উৎকৃষ্ট)	২৷০	×		
ঐ (সাধারণ)	১৸০	×		
৩। আটা	৷৶৹	১৫৸০		
৪। ময়দা	৷৵৹	১৮৷০		
ঐ	৷৷৯	২০৸০	(রাজ্যের অন্যান্য স্থানের দর)	
৫। নারিকেল তৈল	২৲	৭৭৷৷০		
৬। কয়লা		১৷৷৵০		
৭। লবণ ঐ (করকচ)	৵৹			
৮। কেরোসিন তৈল (সাদা)	৷০ প্রতি বোতল	৫৷৵৹ প্রতি টিন (টিন সমেত) ৪৷৷৵৹ (৪ গ্যালন) টিন ছাড়া।		
ঐ (লাল)	৶৯	৪৸৵৹ প্রতি টিন (টিন সমেত)। ৪৷৯ (৪ গ্যালন) টিন ছাড়া।		
৯। মাখন (পার্শী খানী)	১৸০ প্রতি সের			
১০। পাউরুটী পাউণ্ড	৷৷৵৹			
ঐ ৫ ছটাক	৷৵৹			
১১। দুধ	তিন সের প্রতি টাকা (এই দর ষ্টেট মডেল ডেইরি ফার্মে প্রযোজ্য নহে)			
১২। গুড় চট মোড়াই চাকি		২০৸৵৹		
ঐ খোলা গুড়	৷৵৹			

শ্রীহিমাদ্রিবল্লভ বিশ্বাস,
সিভিল সাপ্লাইজ কমিশনার, কণ্ট্রোলার অব প্রাইসেস্ কুচবিহার

Notice.

It is notified for information of those to whom it may concern that for facility of works the registered Contractors of the P. W. D. have been classified into three groups, *viz.* A, B and C. All A class Contractors will be entrusted with works upto Rs. 1 lakh. All B class Contractors will be entrusted with works upto Rs. 50,000. All C class Contractors will be entrusted with minor works under Rs. 10,000. A list of recognised Contractors under each classification is appended below. The list will stand for the current financial year, but additions and alterations may be made at any time at the discretion of the Chief Engineer. In future only Contractors who are in the P. W. D. Register may reply to local tenders in the State.

G. NARAYAN,
MAJOR,
Deputy Chief Engineer, P. W. D., Cooch Behar.

List of Recognised Contractors.

1947-48.

CLASS—A.

1. Seth Ottenmal.
2. Babu Arjun Singh.
3. Babu Bhulai Singh.
4. Babu Sawarat Singh,
5. Messrs. S. N. Maitra & Co.
6. Messrs. Structural Engineering & Construction Co.
7. Ajmat Mistry.
8. Sjt. Bhuban Mohan Das Gupta.
9. Jnani Mistry (Darjeeling).

CLASS—B.

1. Jogdeo Singh.
2. Sjt. Haridas Lahiri.
3. ,, Kamakhya Ch. Roy Chowdhury.
4. Nabi Mahammed.

CLASS—C.

1. Sjt. J. Maitra.
2. Messrs. G. S. Emporium Ltd.
3. Basanta Mistry.
4. Ghuran Meah,
5. Harilal Mistry.
6. Julum Routh.
7. Sjt. Lakshmi Kanta Das.
8. Messrs. Young Builders.
9. Sjt. Ananda Mohan Banerjee.
10. Asturni Dafadarni.
11. Sjt. Bhupati Charan Sen.
12. ,, Biseswar Guha.
13. ,, Barada Kanta Barma.
14. ,, Dharani Mohan Chakravarti.
15. ,, Lakshmi Kanta Barma.
16. Kalu Mistry.
17. Kerketu Meah.
18. Maniruddin Ahmed.

CLASS—C.

19. Sjt. Pramatha Nath Lahiri.
20. Ramayan Singh.
21. Sjt. Sudhir Chandra Chakravarti.
22. Ful Mahammed.
23. Chirkut Mahato.
24. Chaneswar Mahato.
25. Chandrama Mahato.
26. Chait Mahato.
27. Bitori Mahato.
28. Balgobind Mahato.
29. Gouri Mahato.
30. Gokul Nunia.
31. Lal Bahadur Mahato.
32. Motor Sohani.
33. Nathoni Mahato.
34. Nihora Mahato.
35. Rambachan Mahato.
36. Ramfal Mahato.
37. Ram Lakshman Mahato.
38. Saraju Mahato.
39. Saran Mahato.
40. Sukdeo Routh.
41. Brahmo Prosad Mahato.
42. Balam Mahato.
43. Chowdhury Mahato.
44. Gohari Nunia.
45. Jognarayan Chowdhury.
46. Kukhan Mistry.
47. Lakshman Mistry.
48. Omprokash Chowdhury.
49. Rajendra Prosad.
50. Ramsebak Chowdhury.
51. Md. Siddik Mistry.
52. Tarash Mahato.
53. Sjt. Satish Chandra Roy Singh.
54. ,, Nandalal Banerjee (Mekliganj).
55. ,, Satyendra Mohan Chakravarti.

The Cooch Behar Gazette.

৩ শে আষাঢ়, বুধবার ; WEDNESDAY, JULY 16, 1947 [১৩৫৪ সাল ৪৩৮ রাজশক]

PART II.

NOTICES.

ইং ১৯১০ সালের ৫ আইনের ৫৩ ধারার ২ প্রকরণ মতে নিলামী ইস্তাহার।

জারীর মহকুমা মেখলীগঞ্জের মাল আদালত।

এতদ্দ্বারা সর্ব্বসাধারণকে জানান যাইতেছে যে, প্রতিবাদীর দাবীর বাকী খাজানা আদায় না করায় তাহার নিম্নলিখিত ক্রোকী সম্পত্তি আগামী ১৩৫৪ সনের ১৮ই শ্রাবণ মোতাবেক ১৯৪৭ সনের ৪ঠা আগষ্ট তারিখে বেলা ১ ঘটিকার সময় প্রকাশ্য নিলাম আরম্ভ হইবে।

৬ নং ১৯৪৭।৪৮ ইং। বাঃ খাঃ ২৭।৯ মোঃ।

ডিঃ—মহরমল মহেশ্বরী মোঃ চ্যাংরাবান্ধা

দেঃ—বিন্দেশ্বরী বর্ম্মণী সাং পানিকা।

তপশিল সম্পত্তি।

পঃ মেখলীগঞ্জ ৭৭নং থাক তাং নিজ ৬৭১ নং জোঃ লিখিত ১০১ কাঠা জমির কাত বাঃ ৩৲ টাকা জমার চুকানি স্বত্ব।

১৫নং ১৯৪৭।৪৮ ইং। বাঃ খাঃ ৩৪৮।১০ মোঃ।

ডিঃ—নরেন্দ্র নারায়ণ রায় সরকার গং

দেঃ—মনিরুদ্দিন মহাম্মদ সাং পাঃ মেখলীগঞ্জ হেঃ রসিবাড়ী।

তপশিল সম্পত্তি।

পঃ মেখলীগঞ্জ ৬৫ নং থাক তাং দক্ষিণখড়ী মধ্যে ১ নং জোঃ লিখিত ৮০৪৶২৸০ ধুর জমির কাত বাঃ ২৮৴০ আনা জমার জোত।

K UMAR P. NARAYAN, *Naib Ahilkar.*

MALCUCHERY NOTICE.

ইস্তাহারনামা কাছারী মাল মোতালকে কিচবেহার, সন ১৩৪৭ তারিখ ৭ই জুলাই
মোতাবেক বাঙ্গালা ১৩৫৩ সন তারিখ ২২শে আষাঢ়।

পং মেখলীগঞ্জ এলাকাধীন ৫৪ নং থাক তাং নগরসাহেবগঞ্জ অন্তর্গত দেওয়ানগঞ্জ হইতে পানেরহাট রাস্তা তাই-ভার্সনের জন্য অত্র আদালতের ১৯৪৭।৪৮ ইং সনের ৯ নং ভূমিগ্রহণের মোকদ্দমায় ২৩।৬।৪৭ইং তারিখের আদেশ সূত্রে নিম্নলিখিত বিবরণযুক্ত—ভূমি ১৩১৪ সনের শুরু হইতে সরকারে গৃহীত হওয়ায় সর্ব্ব সাধারণের অবগতির জন্য এই ইস্তাহার প্রচারিত হইল। ইতি

পং মেখলীগঞ্জ ৫৪ নং থাক তাং নগরসাহেবগঞ্জ ৩৫ নং বন্দোবস্ত ৩৬৮/৪২৭ নং তৌঃ ১৩৩ নং স্বত্ব জোত পূর্ণ চন্দ্র, প্রতাপ চন্দ্র, বীরেন্দ্র চন্দ্র পিং গোলক চন্দ্র মিত্র বর্ত্তমান জমি ৬৪।১৩৮/০ ধুর জমা ২৭২৷৵০ আনা ২ নং সিট গৃহীত জমি ২।০।৶০ ধুর জমা ১।৯ পাই।

বিতং

১৩৪ নং চুকানী স্বত্ব শিবদয়াল, কমলাকান্ত বাবুরাম, নন্দমোহন, রূপকান্ত পিং ভোগনাথ বর্ম্মণ রূপেশ্বরী বর্ম্মণী জঃ শিবদয়াল বর্ত্তমান জমি ৭২।৩৵০ ধুর জমা ২৫৶০ আনা ২নং সিট ৯১৬/২ ৯১৭/১, ৯২৯/৯, ৯৩০/৫ নং দাগ গৃহীত জমি ।/১৶০ধুর জমা ।৭ পাই।

১৩৫ নং চুকানী স্বত্ব শিবদয়াল, কমলাকান্ত রূপদয়াল, নন্দমোহন, বাবুরাম রূপকান্ত পিং ভোগনাথ বর্ম্মণ বর্ত্তমান জমি ২১৮।৶০ ধুর জমা ২০৷৵০ আনা সিট নং ২ দাগ নং ৯২৬/৩, ৯২৭/৪, ৯৩৭/৮, গৃহীত জমি ৷৩৮৶০ ধুর জমা ৷/৯ পাই।

১৩৭ নং চুকানী স্বত্ব পূর্ণ চন্দ্র, প্রতাপ চন্দ্র, বীরেন্দ্র চন্দ্র পিং গোলক চন্দ্র মিত্র—সাং শৌলমারী বর্ত্তমান জমি ২৪৷৪৮৶০ ধুর জমা ২১৷৵০ আনা সিট নং ২ গৃহীত জমি ৷০।/০ ধুর জমা ৷৭ পাই।

বিতং

৩৫ নং বন্দোবস্ত ৪২৭ নং তৌঃ ১৩৯ নং দরচুকানী স্বত্ব দৌলত মহম্মদ পিং তাজ মহম্মদ বর্ত্তমান জমি ২।২৮/০ ধুর জমা ২।৵০ আনা সিট নং ২ দাগ নং ৯১৮/১১ গৃহীত জমি /১৶০ ধুর জমা ৫১১ পাই।

১৪১ নং দরচুকানী স্বত্ব কেষ্মেন্দু পিং বুচু দাস ধনেশ্বরী জঃ কেষ্মেন্দু দাস বর্ত্তমান জমি ৩।৷৶০ ধুর জমা ৩০ আনা সিট নং ২ দাগ নং ৯২৪-১০ গৃহীত জমি /।৶০ ধুর জমা ৫৭ পাই।

১৪২ নং দরচুকানী স্বত্ব শিবদয়াল, কমলাকান্ত, রূপদয়াল, নন্দমোহন, বাবুরাম, রূপকান্ত পিং ভোগনাথ বর্ম্মণ বর্ত্তমান জমি ২১৫৮৵০ ধুর জমা ৪৮০ আনা সিট নং ২ দাগ নং ৯৩১/৬ গৃহীত জমি /৪।০ ধুর জমা ।৫ পাই

১৪৩ নং দরচুকানী স্বত্ব শিবদয়াল, কমলাকান্ত রূপদয়াল, নন্দমোহন বাবুরাম, রূপকান্ত পিং ভোগনাথ বর্ম্মণ বর্ত্তমান জমি ৩৮২৷৶০ ধুর জমা ৪৷৹০ আনা সিট-নং ২ দাগ নং ৯৩৬/৭ গৃহীত জমি /৪।০ ধুর জমা ।৫ পাই

চৌহদ্দী—পূর্ব্ব উত্তর নিজ জোত দক্ষিণ পশ্চিম সরকারী খাস রাস্তা

ইস্তাহারনামা কাছারী মাল মোতালকে কিচবেহার সন ১৯৪৭ তারিখ ১০ই জুলাই
মোতাবেক বাঙ্গালা ১৩৫৩ সন তারিখ ২৫শে আষাঢ়

পং লালবাজার এলাকাধীন ৫০২ নং থাক তালুক বরগড় অন্তর্গত রেঞ্জ অফিস নির্ম্মাণের জন্য অত্র আদালতের ১৯৪৭।৪৮ ইং সনের ১১ নং ভূমিগ্রহণের মোকদ্দমায় ২৮।৬।৪৭ ইং তারিখের আদেশ সূত্রে নিম্নলিখিত বিবরণযুক্ত ১।০।৶০ ভূমি ১৩৫৩ সনের শেষ ৬ মাস হইতে সরকারে গৃহীত হওয়ায় সর্ব্বসাধারণের অবগতির জন্য এই ইস্তাহার প্রচারিত হইল। ইতি

১। পং লালবাজার ৫০২ নং থাক তাং বরগড় ৮ নং বন্দোবস্ত ৯৪১ নং হাঃ তৌঃ ২৪৪ নং জোত স্বত্ব উমানন্দ পিতা দুর্গানন্দ রায় মোঃ বেহার বর্ত্তমান জমি ৩৫৯৲১৮৶০ ধুর জমা ৩১৫।০ আনা গৃহীত জমি ১।০।৶০ ধুর জমা ১৮৶০ আনা।

বিতং

২৭১ নং চুকানী স্বত্ব গণপতি ৷০ ভগৎ চন্দ্র ৷০ পিতা যাদব চন্দ্র ভট্ট মোঃ বেহার বর্ত্তমান জমি ৯৯৮।০ ধুর জমা ১১৭৷৵০ আনা গৃহীত জমি ১০৶০ ধুর জমা ২৶১০ পাই।

বিতং

২৭২ নং দরচুকানী স্বত্ব মাইও দাসী ৷০ জ পচাদাস মোক্তাই ৷০ পিতা বিরসিং দাস বর্ত্তমান জমি ২৪/৪৪।০ ধুর জমা ৩১৮৶০ আনা গৃহীত জমি ১।০।৵০ ধুর জমা ২৮৶১০ পাই।

বিতং

নিজ দখল সিট নং ২ দাগ নং ১১৪ গৃহীত জমি ৷।৮/০ ধুর সিট নং ১ দাগ নং ৮৩৮/২ গৃহীত জমি /৷৮/০ ধুর মোট ৷০৮৶০ ধুর।

২৭৩ নং কুর্ফাস্বত্ব নন্দাই পিতা বিরসিং দাস বর্ত্তমান জমি ৪/৩৷০ ধুর জমা ৫।০ আনা সিট নং ২ দাগ নং ৯০/১ গৃহীত জমি ৷৪।০ ধুর জমা ১৮১০ পাই।

চৌঃ—উত্তর সীমানা ১১৩, ৮৫৮ দাগ জোত উমানন্দ রায় পূর্ব্ব সীমানা ১১৫ দাগ রাস্তা দক্ষিণ সীমানা ১১১ দাগ রাজসড়ক পশ্চিম সীমানা ১১২, ৮৩৩ দাগ জোত উমানন্দ রায়।

ইস্তাহারনামা কাছারী নাএব মোক্তারকে বিজ্ঞাপন, সন ১৯৪৭ তারিখ ১০ই জুলাই মোতাবেক বাঙ্গলা ১৩৫৪ সন তারিখ ২৫শে আষাঢ়।

পরগনে কোচবিহার এলাকাধীন ১৫৪ নং খাক তাং খড়িমালা খাগড়াবাড়ী অন্তর্গত একটী রাস্তার জন্য অত্রাদালতে ১৯৪৭।৪৮ ইং সনের ১০ নং ভূমিগ্রহণের মোকদ্দমায় ২৮।৬।৪৭ ইং তারিখের আদেশসূত্রে নিম্নলিখিত বিবরণযুক্ত ভূমি ১৩৫৪ সনের সুরু সন হইতে সরকারে গৃহীত হওয়ায় সর্ব্বসাধারণের অবগতি জন্য এই ইস্তাহার প্রচারিত হইল। ইতি।

১। পঃ কোচবিহার ১৫৪ নং খড়িমালা খাগড়াবাড়ী ২ নং বঃ ১৭১ নং তৌঃ ২৩১ নং স্বত্ব জোত সাহার মহম্মদ পিং হযরত মহম্মদ সাং রাণীডাঙ্গা বর্ত্তমান জমি৭৬।২ কাঠা জমা ৫২৸/০ আনা ২ নং সিট ৬১৪/১ নং দাগ গৃহীত জমী ।৩।/০ মূল জমা ।৶ পাই।

চৌহদ্দী — উঃ সীঃ সরকারী রাস্তা, দঃ সীঃ সরকারী খাস ভূমী, পূ সীঃ সরকারী গো রাস্তা, প সী ৬১৪ নং দাগের ভূমি।

K C GANGULI,
Revenue Minister of the
Cooch Behar State.

সিভিল সাপ্লাইজ কমিশনার ও কণ্ট্রোলার অব প্রাইসেস্ আফিস, কুচবিহার।

বিজ্ঞাপন ঃ

(মূল্য নিয়ন্ত্রণ)

সিভিল সাপ্লাইজ কমিশনারের উপর প্রদত্ত এবং ন্যস্ত ক্ষমতাবলে কোচবিহার Essential Supplies (Temporary Powers) Act 1946 এর ৩ ধারার অন্তর্গত ২ উপধারার সি রুল অনুযায়ী নিম্নলিখিত দ্রব্যগুলির সর্ব্বোচ্চ মূল্য নিম্নলিখিতরূপে ধার্য্য করা হইল এবং তাহা কুচবিহার গেজেটে প্রকাশিত হওয়ার তারিখ হইতে পুনরাদেশ না হওয়া পর্য্যন্ত বলবৎ থাকিবে। এতৎসম্পর্কে পূর্ব্ব বিজ্ঞপ্তি বাতিল করা হইল। কোন ব্যক্তি নির্দ্ধারিত মূল্যের অতিরিক্ত মূল্যে বিক্রয় করিলে বা দ্রব্যাদি বিক্রয়ার্থ আনিয়া নির্দ্ধারিত মূল্যে বিক্রয় করিতে অস্বীকার করিলে উপরোক্ত আইনের ৭ ধারা অনুযায়ী দণ্ডনীয় হইবে। ইতি ৭ই জুলাই ১৯৪৭।

বিশেষ দ্রষ্টব্য ঃ—সরিষা ও গমের দর রাজ্যের হাটে, গঞ্জবাজারে, মিলে ও খুচরা দোকানে ও বন্দরে প্রযোজ্য। রাজ্যের অন্যান্য স্থানের দর উহা অপেক্ষা ।০ চারি আনা হিসাবে কম হইবে। রসগোল্লা, সন্দেশ ও চিড়ার দর রাজ্যের সর্ব্বত্র এক।

কেরোসিন—হলদিবাড়ী বন্দরের দর—

লাল কেরোসিন প্রতি টিন ৪৸৬ টিন সমেত প্রতি সের ৶৯

সাদা কেরোসিন প্রতি টিন ৫৶০ (ঐ) প্রতি সের ।০

কয়লা—কয়লার দর মাত্র কুচবিহার সহরের জন্য নির্দ্ধারিত হইল।

মফঃস্বলের দর—কোচবিহার টাউন, দিনহাটা বন্দর, হলদিবাড়ী বন্দর, চাংরাবান্ধা বন্দর ব্যতীত অন্যান্য স্থানের দর নিম্নলিখিত দর অপেক্ষা (ধান্য, চাউল, সরিষা ও গম ব্যতীত) মণ প্রতি এক টাকা চারি আনা অর্থাৎ সের প্রতি দুই পয়সা বেশী হইবে। কিন্তু যে সকল ক্ষেত্রে রাজ্যের অন্যান্য স্থানের দর পৃথক ভাবে ধার্য্য আছে সেই সব ক্ষেত্রে ঐ নির্দ্ধারিত দরই প্রযোজ্য হইবে।

পাইকারী দর—মণ সেরের নীচে আড়াই সের পর্য্যন্ত খরিদ বিক্রী হইলে মণ প্রতি ।০ চারি আনা বেশী হইবে। কিন্তু এই নিয়ম, চাউল, সরিষা, গম, সম্বন্ধে প্রযোজ্য হইবে না এবং যেখানে দোকানে ইহা প্রযোজ্য হইবে তথায় কেবলমাত্র নির্দ্ধারিত মূল্যে দরে কেনা বেচা হইবে।

ষ্ট্যাণ্ডার্ড বস্তা—লবণ ১৮৯ সের বস্তা সহ।
চিনি ২৮১ সের বস্তা সহ।

পণ্য দ্রব্যের নাম	প্রতি সের	প্রতি মণ	প্রতি ষ্ট্যাণ্ডার্ড বস্তা	মন্তব্য
১। গম—দেশী জাতের	৶০	৯৲		
ঐ বড়দানা পাঞ্জাবী জাতের		১৫৲		
২। চিনি	৷৵০	২৪৷৷০	৬৭৷৶০ (কোচবিহার সহর, দিনহাটা বন্দর, চ্যাংরাবান্ধা বন্দর, হলদিবাড়ী বন্দরের জন্য) প্রতি ষ্ট্যাণ্ডার্ড বস্তা ৭০৸৵০ আনা	
ঐ	৷৷৶০	২৭৲	(রাজ্যের অন্যান্য স্থানের দর)	
বাতাসা, কদমা, তিলুয়া	৸৵	৩১৲		
মিশ্রী	৸৴১০	৩২৷০		
রসগোল্লা	১৷০	×		
সন্দেশ (উৎকৃষ্ট)	২৷০	×		
ঐ (সাধারণ)	১৸০	×		
৩। আটা	৷৵৯	১৫৸০		
৪। ময়দা	৷৶৯	১৮৷০		
ঐ	৷৷৹	২০৸০	(রাজ্যের অন্যান্য স্থানের দর)	
৫। নারিকেল তৈল	২৲	৭৭৷৷০		
৬। কয়লা		১৷৶০		
৭। লবণ }	৵৹			
ঐ (করকচ) }				
৮। কেরোসিন তৈল (সাদা)	।৩ প্রতি বোতল	৫৪০ প্রতি টিন (টিন সমেত) ৪৸৶০ (৪ গ্যালন) টিন ছাড়া।		
ঐ (লাল)	।০	৫৴০ প্রতি টিন (টিন সমেত)। ৪৷৶০ (৪ গ্যালন) টিন ছাড়া।		
৯। মাংস (পাঁঠা খাসী)	১৸০ প্রতি সের			
১০। পাউরুটী পাউণ্ড	৷৶৹			
ঐ ৫ ছটাক	৷৵৹			
১১। দুধ	তিন সের প্রতি টাকা (এই দর ষ্টেট ডেয়ারী ফার্ম্মে প্রযোজ্য নহে)			
১২। গুড় চট মোড়াই চাকি		২০৸৵৹		
ঐ খোলা গুড়	৷৵৹			

শ্রীহিমাদ্রিবল্লভ বিশ্বাস,
সিভিল সাপ্লাইজ কমিশনার, কন্ট্রোলার অব প্রাইসেস কুচবিহার

NOTIFICATION.

CIVIL SUPPLIES DEPARTMENT

Cooch Behar, the 15th July, 1947.

It is notified for general information that distribution of cloth for April-June quarter for the Sadar subdivision, will continue upto 2nd August 1947 in extension of the time as announced in the previous Notification dated 13th June, 1947.

H. BISWAS,
Civil Supplies Commissioner, Cooch Behar.

The Cooch Behar Gazette.

১৫ই শ্রাবণ, শুক্রবার ; FRIDAY, AUGUST 1, 1947 [১৩৫৪ সাল ৪৩৮ রাজশক]

PART II.

NOTICES.

MALCUCHERY NOTICE.

ইস্তাহারনামা কাছারী মাল মোতালকে নিজ বেহার, সন ১৯৪৭ তারিখ ১২ই জুলাই
মোতাবেক বাঙ্গালা ১৩৫৪ সন তারিখ ২৭শে আষাঢ় ।

পরগণে কুচবিহার এলাকাধীন ১০৩৯ নং থাক তাং কালপানী অন্তর্গত ভাই তার্সন রাস্তার জন্য অত্র আদালতের ১৯৪৭।৪৮ ইং সনের ১২ নং ভূমিগ্রহণের মোকদ্দমায় ২৮।৬।৪৭ ইং তারিখের আদেশ সূত্রে নিম্নলিখিত বিবরণযুক্ত ভূমি ১৩৫৩ সনের শুরু হইতে সরকারে গৃহীত হওয়ার সর্ব্বসাধারণের অবগতি জন্য এই ইস্তাহার প্রচারিত হইল। ইতি

১। পঃ কোচবিহার ১০৩৯ নং থাক তাং কালপানী ১৮৫৫ নং জোৎ ২০৬ নং পঃ স্বত্ব কিয়ত আকন্দ ॥০ পিং ইমান আকন্দ, সবুমুন্সি ৷৵৩॥— পিং গবুমোল্লা, হামেদ আলী ৵॥ হামছায়া /৩॥— পিং আলে আকন্দ সাং নিজ বর্ত্তমান জমি ১১৪/১।৶০ খুব জমা ৯৬/০ আঃ ৩ নং সিট ১০৩২/২৭, ২৪৪/২৯, ১০৭৬/৩১ নং দাগ গৃহীত জমি ০৵০ জমা ৶৩ পাই।

২। পঃ কোচবিহার থাক তাং তথা মধ্যে ১৮৫৮ নং জোৎ ২০৯ নং পঃ স্বত্ব আবদুল হামিদ মুন্সি ।৵৩॥— এনাহি বকস ।/৩॥— মফিজ উদ্দিন ।/৩॥— পিং আয়ন উদ্দিন মুন্সি সাং নিজ বর্ত্তমান জমি ৩/১॥৶০ খুব জমা ১৵৶০ ৩ নং সিট ১০৫/৫২৫/২৫, ৫২৫/১০৫৭/২৪ নং দাগ গৃহীত জমি ৮৩৶০ খুব জমা ॥/৮ পাই।

৩। পঃ কোচবিহার ১০৩৯ নং থাক তাং কালজানী ১৯০৩ নং জোৎ ৩৪১ নং পত্তনি স্বত্ব বর্ত্তমান জমি ৫৬।২৷৶ খুব জমা ৬৩॥৶০ আনা ৩ নং সিট ৯৫/২, ৮১৯/৩, ৫০৭/৪, ৯৩ ৫, ৮৫৫/৭, ৮২৩/৮, ৮৮৫/৯, ৮৫৭/১০, ৮৫৯/১১, ৮৭৫/১২, ৮৩১/১৩, ৮৭৪/১৪, ৮৭৩/১৫, ৮৫৫/৬ নং দাগ গৃহীত জমি ৩৮৩॥৶ খুব জমা ৫৮২

৪। পঃ কোচবিহার থাক তাং তথা মধ্যে ১৯৩১ নং জোৎ ৫৫৯ নং পঃ স্বত্ব উমেশচন্দ্র ।০ রাজচন্দ্র ।০ রাজেন্দ্রচন্দ্র ।০ ভুবনচন্দ্র ।০ পিং নারায়ণ দাস সাং নিজ বর্ত্তমান জমি ৬৩.০ খুব জমা ৪৯৶০ আঃ ৩ নং সিট ৮৭০/১৬, ৮৭১/১৭, ২৪১/২৬, ২৪২/২৮ নং দাগ গৃহীত জমি ২৮০।৶০ খুব জমা ১।০ আনা।

৫। পঃ কোচবিহার থাক তাং তথা মধ্যে ৩২৮৪ নং জোৎ ৫:৪ নং স্বত্ব কামদেবকুমার দাস পিং ছিনাবু দাস সাং নিজ বঃ জমি ৩৩.০।০ খুব জমা ৪৫৸০ ৩ নং সিট ৯০/১ নং দাগ গৃহীত জমি ৵৪২৶ খুব জমা ।৮২ পাই।

K C GANGULI,
Revenue Minister of the
Cooch Behar State.

দেওয়ানী কার্য্যবিধি আইনের ২১ হুকুম, ৬৬ নিয়মের ঘোষণাপত্র ।

কাইার মহকুমা মেখলীগঞ্জের মাল কাছারী আদালত ।

এতদ্দ্বারা সর্ব্বসাধারণকে জানান যাইতেছে যে, দাবীকগণের নিম্নলিখিত সম্পত্তি আগামী ১৯৪৭ সনের ১লা সেপ্টেম্বর মোঃ ১৩৫৪ সনের ১৫ই ভাদ্র তারিখে দিবা ১ ঘটিকার সময় প্রকাশ্য নিলাম আরম্ভ হইবে ।

নং ১১৯ ।৪ ইং । বাঃ ডিঃ মোঃ ।

সরকার বাহাদুর বঃ করিম মহম্মদ সাং ঝাড় সিংহেশ্বর ।

তপশিল সম্পত্তি

পঃ মেখলীগঞ্জ ৮৭ নং থাক তাং ঝাড় সিংহেশ্বর মধ্যে ১৬৭৮ নং তৌঃ লিঃ ২৮।০ কাঠা জমির কাত বাঃ ।০।/০ আনা জমার আং চুকানী জমি ।

KUMAR P. NARAYAN, *Naib Ahilkar.*

রাজকীয় প্রাপ্য আদায় বিষয়ক ১৯৪৩ ইং সনের ১০ আইনের ২ সিডিউলের ৪৬ নিয়মের ঘোষণাপত্র ।

রাজ্য কোচবিহারের সদর খাষ মহাল আদালত ।

এতদ্দ্বারা সর্ব্বসাধারণকে জানান যাইতেছে যে দাবীকগণের নিম্নলিখিত সম্পত্তি আগামী ১৯৪৭ ইং সনের ৪ঠা আগষ্ট মোঃ ১৩৫৪ সনের ১৮ই শ্রাবণ তারিখে দিবা ১ ঘটিকার সময় দিনহাটা খাষ মহাল আফিসে খাষ মহাল আফিসার কর্ত্তৃক প্রকাশ্য নিলাম আরম্ভ হইবে ।

৬৮৭ নং সার্ট্ট ১৯৪৬।৪৭ ইং । বাঃ ডিঃ ৯৲ মোঃ ।

সরকার বাহাদুর বঃ হারাধন ব্যাধ ।

তপশিল সম্পত্তি ।

পঃ দিনহাটা ৫৬ নং থাক তাং বোরডাঙ্গা মধ্যে ৩৫৬ নং তৌঃ লিঃ ২।/০ ধুর জমির কাত বাঃ ১৷৹ আনা জমার পঃ স্বত্ব ।

৭৪৯ নং সার্ট্ট ১৯৪৬।৪৭ ইং । বাঃ ডিঃ ৫৮৷৴০ মোঃ ।

সরকার বাহাদুর বঃ ভেরবেন্দ্র বর্ম্মণ গঃ ।

তপশিল সম্পত্তি ।

পঃ দিনহাটা ৭৭২ নং থাক তাং টিয়াদহ মধ্যে ৪২০৫ নং তৌঃ লিঃ ১৮৸৴৹ ধুর জমির কাত বাঃ ১৯৷০ আনা জমার পঃ স্বত্ব ।

৭৯৬ নং সার্ট্ট ১৯৪৬।৪৭ ইং । বাঃ ডিঃ ২৩।/৯ মোঃ ।

সরকার বাহাদুর বঃ সমসের উদ্দীন গঃ ।

তপশিল সম্পত্তি ।

পঃ দিনহাটা ৫১৮ নং থাক তাং বড় নাচিনা মধ্যে ১২৫৪৮ নং তৌঃ লিঃ ১১৷২।৴০ ধুর জমির কাত বাঃ ৷৴০ আনা জমার পঃ স্বত্ব ।

৮০৪ নং ১৯৪৬।৪৭ ইং । বাঃ ডি. ৩২৸৴৯ মোঃ ।

সরকার বাহাদুর বঃ নগেন্দ্রনাথ ।

তপশিল সম্পত্তি ।

পঃ দিনহাটা ৫১৮ নং থাক তাং বড় নাচিনা মধ্যে ১৮৭২৯ নং তৌঃ লিঃ ১৩৸১৷৴০ ধুর জমির কাত বাঃ ১০৴০ আনা জমার পঃ স্বত্ব ।

৮৪২ নং সার্ট্ট ১৯৪৬।৪৭ ইং । বাঃ ডিঃ ৫১৶৯ মোঃ ।

সরকার বাহাদুর বঃ সুরেন্দ্রনাথ রায় গঃ ।

তপশিল ।

পঃ দিনহাটা তাং পক্ষিহাগা মধ্যে ২০১৪৪ নং তৌঃ লিঃ ৮।১।৶০ ধুর জমির কাত বাঃ ১০৮৴০ আনা জমার পঃ স্বত্ব ।

৫৮০ নং সার্ট্ট ১৯৪৬।৪৭ ইং । বাঃ ডিঃ ৫৭।/৩ মোঃ ।

সরকার বাহাদুর বঃ চন্দ্রকান্ত বর্ম্মণ গঃ ।

তপশিল সম্পত্তি ।

পঃ দিনহাটা তাং ১ম খণ্ড চকিয়ারপাড়া মধ্যে ২১৯১০ নং তৌঃ লিঃ ২৩।৫।/০ ধুর জমির কাত বাঃ ২৩৸৴০ আনা জমার পঃ স্বত্ব ।

১৪২০ নং সার্ট্ট ১৯৪৬।৪৭ ইং । বাঃ ডিঃ ৫৯/৯ মোঃ ।

সরকার বাহাদুর বঃ খরুসেখ বাদে দখল জাফর আলী ।

তপশিল সম্পত্তি ।

পঃ দিনহাটা ৭২০ নং থাক তাং ২য় খণ্ড ভাংনী মধ্যে ১৬৯৮ নং তৌঃ লিঃ ৩।৸০৸৶০ ধুর জমির কাত বাঃ ১০/০ আনা জমার পঃ স্বত্ব ।

৮৯১ নং ১৯৪৬।৪৭ ইং । বাঃ ডিঃ ১৪৫৩ মোঃ ।

সরকার বাহাদুর বঃ শিত বর্ম্মণ গঃ ।

তপশিল সম্পত্তি ।

পঃ দিনহাটা ৫৫৩ নং থাক তাং সিঙ্গীমারী মদনকুড়া মধ্যে ১২৫২ নং তৌঃ লিঃ ৪৮।০৷৶০ ধুর জমির কাত বাঃ ৪৷৴ আনা জমার পঃ স্বত্ব ।

৯১৪ নং সাট্ট ১৯৪৬।৪৭ ইং। বাঃ ডিঃ ৮।৶৯ মোঃ।

সরকার বাহাদুর বঃ যতীন্দ্রনাথ রায় গঃ।

তপশিল সম্পত্তি।

পঃ দিনহাটা তাং বজিগাছ মধ্যে ১৫৭১১ নং তৌঃ লিঃ ২॥২ কাঠা জমির কাত বাঃ ৩/০ আনা জমার অং পং স্বত্ব।

৯২১ নং সাট্ট ১৯৪৬।৪৭ ইং। বাঃ ডিঃ ৫০৶০ মোঃ।

সরকার বাহাদুর বঃ যোগেন্দ্র বর্মণ গঃ।

তপশিল সম্পত্তি।

পঃ দিনহাটা ৫৫০ নং থাক তাং জামাদারের বশ মধ্যে ৫১২২ নং তৌঃ লি ১৮/১।৶০ ধুর জমির কাত বাঃ ১০৮০ আনা জমার পঃ স্বত্ব।

৯১০ নং সাট্ট ১৯৪৬।৪৭ ইং। বাঃ ডিঃ ১৩/০ মোঃ।

সরকার বাহাদুর বঃ ছবিল সেখ গঃ।

তপশিল সম্পত্তি।

পঃ দিনহাটা ৬০৮ নং থাক তাং বড় আটিয়াবাড়ী মধ্যে ১৬৯৫২ নং তৌঃ লিঃ ৩৯৸৩ কাঠা জমির কাত বাঃ ৫৩/০ আনা জমার পঃ স্বত্ব।

১০৮১ নং সাট্ট ১৯৪৬।৪৭ ইং। বাঃ ডিঃ ২৪৶৯ মোঃ।

সরকার বাহাদুর বঃ তালে মামুদ।

তপশিল সম্পত্তি।

পঃ দিনহাটা ৫৩৩ নং থাক তাং পেটলাগুড়ী মধ্যে ৬৪৬২ নং তৌঃ লিঃ ১৩।১৮৶০ ধুর জমির কাত বাঃ ২০।০ আনা জমার অং পঃ স্বত্ব।

১২৮ নং সাট্ট ১৯৪৬।৪৭ ইং। বাঃ ডিঃ ২৭।৶৩ মোঃ।

সরকার বাহাদুর বঃ আয়েমন বিবি।

তপশিল সম্পত্তি।

পঃ দিনহাটা ৬৫২ নং থাক তাং কোনামুক্তা রতিনন্দন মধ্যে ১৮৮৬০ নং তৌঃ লিঃ ৭/৪ কাঠা জমির কাত বাঃ ৮৸/০ আনা জমার পঃ স্বত্ব।

১২১৭ নং সাট্ট ১৯৪৬।৪৭ ইং। বাঃ ডিঃ ২১॥৶৯ মোঃ।

সরকার বাহাদুর বঃ বাহার উদ্দীন গঃ।

তপশিল সম্পত্তি।

পঃ দিনহাটা ৭১৮ নং থাক তাং গীতালদহ আটিয়াবাড়ী মধ্যে ৬১৫৬ নং তৌঃ লিঃ ৬৸২।/০ ধুর জমির কাত বাঃ ৯।/০ আনা জমার পঃ স্বত্ব।

১১৪০ নং সাট্ট ১৯৪৬।৪৭ ইং। বাঃ ডিঃ ৯॥/০ মোঃ।

সরকার বাহাদুর বঃ শশীমোহন গঃ।

তপশিল সম্পত্তি

পঃ দিনহাটা ৫৫৩ নং থাক তাং সিঙ্গীমারী মদ কুড়া মধ্যে ৪১৯১ নং তৌঃ লিঃ ১/৪৶০ ধুর জমির কাত বাঃ ৩৶০ আনা জমার পঃ স্বত্ব।

৮৭৮ নং সাট্ট ১৯৪৬।৪৭ ইং। বাঃ ডিঃ ১৪৸৩ মোঃ।

সরকার বাহাদুর বঃ বিদা দাস গঃ।

তপশিল সম্পত্তি।

পঃ লালবাজার ৪৮৯ নং থাক তাং ডাউয়া বাড়ী ১৭৬৯ নং তৌঃ লিঃ ১।৪।৶০ ধুর জমির কাত বাঃ ৩৮০ আনা জমার পঃ স্বত্ব।

১২৫৮ নং ১৯৪৬।৪৭ ইং। বাঃ ডিঃ ৫৫॥০ মোঃ।

সরকার বাহাদুর বঃ হিঙ্গেশ্বরী বর্মাণী।

তপশিল সম্পত্তি।

পঃ লালবাজার ৪৯৮ নং থাক তাং কেশরীবাড়ী মধ্যে ১৮৭ নং তৌঃ লিঃ ৭॥৩ কাঠা জমির কাত বাঃ ১১।০ আনা জমার পঃ স্বত্ব।

১২৭১ নং ১৯৪৬।৪৭ ইং। বাঃ ডিঃ ১৩৬৶৩ মোঃ

সরকার বাহাদুর বঃ বাকের সেখ গঃ।

তপশিল সম্পত্তি।

পঃ লালবাজার ৫০৩ নং থাক তাং কায়েতেরবাড়ী মধ্যে ২৩৯১ নং তৌঃ লিঃ ২৯/২ কাঠা জমির কাত বাঃ ৩৬৸৶০ আনা জমার পঃ স্বত্ব।

১২৭২ নং সাট্ট ১৯৪৬।৪৭ ইং। বাঃ ডিঃ ৭৪।৶৯ মোঃ।

সরকার বাহাদুর বঃ বাকের সেখ গঃ।

তপশিল সম্পত্তি।

পঃ লালবাজার ৫০৩ নং থাক তাং কায়েতেরবাড়ী মধ্যে ২৩৯২ নং তৌঃ লিঃ ১৬।৩॥/০ ধুর জমির কাত বাঃ ২০।০ আনা জমার পঃ স্বত্ব।

১২৭৩ নং ১৯৪৬।৪৭ ইং। বাঃ ডিঃ ৩২৬৩ মোঃ।

সরকার বাহাদুর বঃ কাকেজ সেখ গঃ।

তপশিল।

পঃ লালবাজার ৫০৩ নং থাক তাং কান্তেশ্বরবাড়ী মধ্যে ২৯৯৩ নং তৌঃ লিঃ ১৯৮৭।৶০ ধুর জমির কাত বাঃ ১২৶০ আনা জমার পঃ স্বত্ব।

১৩০৩ নং সাটিঃ ১৯৪৬।৪৭ ইং। বাঃ ডিঃ ৫১৫১ মোঃ।

সরকার বাহাদুর বঃ আফছার সেখ গঃ।

তপশীল সম্পত্তি।

পঃ লালবাজার ৫২৮ নং থাক তাং আঠারবানী মধ্যে ৫৫০ নং তৌঃ লিঃ ২৫।০৸৶০ ধুর জমির কাত বাঃ ১৩৸৶০ আনা জমার পঃ স্বত্ব।

১৩৩৫ নং ১৯৪৬।৪৭ ইং। বাঃ ডিঃ ১০৸০ মোঃ।

সরকার বাহাদুর বঃ আবছার সেখ গঃ।

তপশিল সম্পত্তি।

পঃ লালবাজার ৫২৮ নং থাক তাং আঠারবানী মধ্যে ১৯৮৩ নং তৌঃ লিঃ ৮।৩।০ ধুর জমির কাত বাঃ ২৸৶০ আনা জমার পঃ স্বত্ব।

১৩৫৪ নং সাটি ১৯৪৬।৪৭ ইং। বাঃ ডিঃ ২২৷৶৩ মোঃ।

সরকার বাহাদুর বঃ নিত্যময়ী বর্ম্মণী।

তপশিল সম্পত্তি

পঃ লালবাজার ৫১১ নং থাক তাং পানীখাওয়া মধ্যে ১০৪৬ নং তৌঃ লিঃ ৪৴২৷৶০ ধুর জমির কাত বাঃ ৬৷০ আনা জমার পঃ স্বত্ব।

১৩৬৩ নং ১৯৪৬।৪৭ ইং। বাঃ ডিঃ ৩৩৷৶৯ মোঃ।

সরকার বাহাদুর বঃ মহেশচন্দ্র রায় প্রামানিক গঃ।

তপশীল সম্পত্তি।

পঃ লালবাজার ৫১৩ নং থাক তাং গাবুয়া মধ্যে ২১৭৬ নং তৌঃ লিঃ ৭৸৩৸০ ধুর জমির কাত বাঃ ১০৴০ আনা জমার পঃ স্বত্ব।

১৩৬৬ নং ১৯৪৬।৪৭ ইং। বাঃ ডিঃ ১৫।৴৯ মোঃ।

সরকার বাহাদুর বঃ বাচ্চানী বেওয়া

তপশীল সম্পত্তি।

পঃ লালবাজার ৫২০ নং থাক তাং বারবাংলা মধ্যে ৪৩১ নং তৌঃ লিখিত ১।১৸৶০ ধুর জমির কাত বাঃ ১৶০ আনা জমার পঃ স্বত্ব।

১৩৬৭ নং ১৯৪৬।৪৭ ইং। বাঃ ডিঃ ২৪৷ ৭ মোঃ।

সরকার বাহাদুর বঃ বাচ্চানী বেওয়া

তপশিল সম্পত্তি।

পঃ লালবাজার ৫২০ নং থাক তাং বারবাংলা মধ্যে ৪৩২ নং তৌঃ লিখিত ৩৸৩ কাঠা জমির কাত বাঃ ৩১৶০ আনা জমার পঃ স্বত্ব।

১৩৮৪ নং ১৯৪৬।৪৭ ইং। বাঃ ডিঃ ২৭৸৶০ মোঃ।

সরকার বাহাদুর বঃ তমিজ উদ্দিন গঃ

তপশীল সম্পত্তি।

পঃ লালবাজার ৫৩৩ নং থাক তাং শিজিমারী মধ্যে ৬৩৩ নং তৌঃ লিখিত ১৩।০ কাঠা জমির কাত বাঃ ২০৴০ আনা জমার পঃ স্বত্ব।

১৩৮৫ নং ১৯৪৬।৪৭ ইং। বাঃ ডিঃ ২০।০ মোঃ।

সরকার বাহাদুর বঃ টাবুকা সেখ

তপশিল সম্পত্তি।

পঃ লালবাজার ৫৩৩ নং থাক তাং শিজিমারী মধ্যে ৬৩৪ নং তৌঃ লিঃ ২৷২৴০ ধুর জমির কাত বাঃ ৫৷৶০ আনা জমার পঃ স্বত্ব।

১৪১৪ নং ১৯৪৬।৪৭ ইং। বাঃ ডিঃ ৫৪৸৶৩ মোঃ।

সরকার বাহাদুর বঃ মনসের আলি সরকার গঃ

তপশিল সম্পত্তি।

পঃ লালবাজার ৫৩২ নং থাক তাং বরবর মধ্যে ১২৮৭ নং তৌঃ লিখিত ৪৸৴১৸৶০ ধুর জমির কাত বাঃ ৫৯৸৶০ আনা জমার জমি মধ্যে ২।৩ নং দেনদারগণের ৷০ আনা অংশ।

৪২৮ নং ১৯৪৬।৪৭ ইং। বাঃ ডিঃ ৫২৴৯ মোঃ।

সরকার বাহাদুর বঃ শিও দাস গঃ

তপশিল সম্পত্তি।

পঃ দিনহাটা ৬৮৫ নং থাক তাং কিংকরলা মধ্যে ২২২৭১ নং তৌঃ লিঃ ৯৸২১০ ধুর জমির কাত বাঃ ১৪৷৶০ আনা জমার পঃ স্বত্ব।

DWIJENDRA CHANDRA SEN, *Certificate Officer.*

রাজকীয় প্রাপ্য আদায় বিষয়ক ১৯৪৩ ইং সনের ১০ আইনের ২ সিডিউলের ৪৬ নিয়মের ঘোষণাপত্র।

রাজ্য কোচবিহারের সদর খাস মহাল আদালত।

এতদ্দ্বারা সর্ব্বসাধারণকে জানান যাইতেছে যে, দাবীকগণের নিম্নলিখিত সম্পত্তি আগামী ১৯৪৭ সনের ৭ই আগষ্ট মোঃ ১৩৫৪ সনের ২১শে শ্রাবণ তারিখে দিবা ১ ঘটিকার সময় সদর খাসমহাল আদালতে প্রকাশ্য নিলাম আরম্ভ হইবে।

১৮ নং ১৯৪৬।৪৭ ইং। বাঃ ডিঃ ১১৷৶৹ মোঃ

সরকার বাহাদুর বঃ বীরেন রায়।

তপশিল সম্পত্তি।

পঃ বেহার ১০৭৮ নং থাক তাং ছাট সিঙ্গীমারী মধ্যে ৩১০৪ নং তৌঃ লিঃ ৮/২৶৹ ধুর জমির কাত বাঃ ৭৶৹ আনা জমার পঃ স্বত্ব।

১৯ নং ১৯৪৬।৪৭ ইং। বাঃ ডিঃ ৫৮৹ মোঃ।

সরকার বাহাদুর বঃ বীরেন রায়।

তপশিল সম্পত্তি।

পঃ বেহার ১০৭৮ নং থাক তাং ছাট সিঙ্গীমারী মধ্যে ৩১০৫ নং পঃ তৌঃ লিঃ ১৮২৷৹ ধুর জমির কাত বাঃ ২৮৶৹ আনা জমার পঃ স্বত্ব।

২৫৮ নং ১৯৪৬।৪৭ ইং। বাঃ ডিঃ ১৩৸৶৬ মোঃ।

সরকার বাহাদুর বঃ রাজেন্দ্র নাথ গুহ।

তপশিল সম্পত্তি।

পঃ বেহার ১০৮৩ নং থাক তাং কালজানী মধ্যে ৩৫৩১ নং পঃ তৌঃ লিঃ ৫৪৮৹ কাঠা জমির কাত বাঃ ৩১৶৹ আনা জমার পঃ স্বত্ব।

৫৪৪ নং ১৯৪৬।৪৭ ইং। বাঃ ডিঃ ৭৬৷৹ মোঃ।

সরকার বাহাদুর বঃ থাকুড়া পঃ।

তপশিল সম্পত্তি।

পঃ বেহার ৮৫৪ নং থাক তাং খারিজা বলদেশ্বরা মধ্যে ৫২০৮ নং পঃ তৌঃ লিখিত ১৭/৪৶৹ ধুর জমির কাত বাঃ ১৯৷/৹ আনা জমার পঃ স্বত্ব।

৪৮২ নং ১৯৪৫।৪৬ ইং বাঃ ডিঃ ১০২৷৯ মোঃ।

সরকার বাহাদুর বঃ কতিজা নেছা পঃ।

তপশিল সম্পত্তি।

পঃ বেহার ৮৫৬ নং থাক তাং বলরামী মধ্যে ৫৪৬৹ নং পঃ তৌঃ লিঃ ২৩/২৷৶৹ ধুর জমির কাত বাঃ ১২৮/৹ আনা জমার পঃ স্বত্ব।

১০০৩ নং ১৯৪৫।৪৬ ইং। বাঃ ডিঃ ১০৮/৹ মোঃ।

সরকার বাহাদুর বঃ সমতুল্যা মিঞা পঃ।

তপশিল সম্পত্তি।

পঃ বেহার ৮৭১ নং থাক তাং একমুখা মধ্যে ৪১৪ নং পঃ তৌঃ লিঃ ৯।২৷৶৹ ধুর জমির কাত বাঃ ১২৸৶৹ আনা জমার পঃ স্বত্ব।

৫৬৩ নং ১৯৪৫।৪৬ ইং। বাঃ ডিঃ ৩৪৸/৹ মোঃ।

সরকার বাহাদুর বঃ অভয়া দাস।

তপশিল সম্পত্তি।

পঃ বেহার ৮৩০ নং থাক তাং কাশীরাবাড়ী মধ্যে ৩৯৯২ নং পঃ তৌঃ লিঃ।১/৹ ধুর জমির কাত বাঃ।৹ আনা জমার পঃ স্বত্ব।

৬৯৯ নং ১৯৪৫।৪৬ ইং। বাঃ ডিঃ ৮৲ মোঃ।

সরকার বাহাদুর বঃ অজনআলী পঃ।

তপশীল সম্পত্তি।

পঃ বেহার ৯০৮ নং থাক তাং পানিগ্রাম ঘুঘুমারী মধ্যে ১০৪২৯ নং পঃ তৌঃ লিঃ ১৩/১৸৶৹ ধুর জমির কাত বাঃ ১৭৷৹ আনা জমার পঃ স্বত্ব।

৭০৫ নং ১৯৪৫।৪৬ ইং। বাঃ ডিঃ ২০।৶৬ মোঃ।

সরকার বাহাদুর বঃ হামিদা খাতুন পঃ।

তপশিল সম্পত্তি।

পঃ বেহার ৯১০ নং থাক তাং ঘুঘুমারী মধ্যে ১০২২০ নং তৌঃ লিঃ ৫৮০৷/৹ ধুর জমির কাত বাঃ ৬৸/৹ আনা জমার পঃ স্বত্ব।

৭৪৪ নং ১৯৪৫।৪৬ ইং বাঃ ডিঃ ১০৷/৩ মোঃ।

সরকার বাহাদুর বঃ বাবুজানী সরকার।

তপশীল সম্পত্তি।

পঃ বেহার ১০১২ নং থাক তাং পৌনটুকনী বড়পাত মধ্যে ২৬৬৩ নং পঃ তৌঃ লিঃ ৮/৸৶৹ ধুর জমির কাত বাঃ ১৷৶৹ [illegible]

৮১৭ নং ১৯৪৫।৪৬ ইং। বাঃ ডিঃ ৯. মোঃ।

সরকার বাহাদুর বঃ পচা মুরুজিয়া গং।

তপশিল সম্পত্তি

পঃ বেহার ১০০৯ নং থাক তাং কালাপানী মধ্যে ৮৪৮৭ নং পঃ তৌঃ লিঃ ২।৪ কাঠা জমির কাত বাঃ ৩৲ টাকা জমার পঃ স্বত্ব।

৮৮০ নং ১৯৪৫।৪৬ ইং। বাঃ ডিঃ ১২॥৯ মোঃ।

সরকার বাহাদুর বঃ খটু শিকারী গং।

তপশিল সম্পত্তি।

পঃ বেহার ১০৩৯ নং থাক তাং কালপানী মধ্যে ৮৪৮২ নং পঃ তৌঃ লিঃ ॥৩/০ ধুর জমির কাত বাঃ ১৸/০ আনা জমার পঃ স্বত্ব।

১০০১ নং ১৯৪৫।৪৬ ইং। বাঃ ডিঃ ৩১।০ মোঃ।

সরকার বাহাদুর বঃ ধওলা দাস গং।

তপশিল সম্পত্তি।

পঃ বেহার ৮১৬ নং থাক তাং একমূখা মধ্যে ৩৯৪ নং পঃ তৌঃ লিঃ ১৷৴২৸৶০ ধুর জমির কাত বাঃ ১৬/০ আনা জমার পঃ স্বত্ব।

৩০৩ নং ১৯৪৪।৪৫ ইং বাঃ ডিঃ ১৪৸৶৯ মোঃ।

সরকার বাহাদুর বঃ বাহার নস্ত গং।

তপশিল সম্পত্তি।

পঃ বেহার ৮২৪ নং থাক তাং ভোটের হাট মধ্যে ২২ নং পঃ তৌঃ লিঃ ৩॥১॥/০ ধুর জমির কাত বাঃ ৪।৷০ আনা জমার পঃ স্বত্ব।

৩৩৭ নং ১৯৪৪।৪৫ ইং। বাঃ ডিঃ ১৩৸/৬ মোঃ।

সরকার বাহাদুর বঃ রহমান হোসেন গং।

তপশীল সম্পত্তি।

পঃ বেহার ৮৭২ নং থাক তাং ভোগডাবরী কেশরীবাড়ী মধ্যে ৪৭৬০ নং পঃ তৌঃ লিঃ ১/॥/০ ধুর জমির কাত বাঃ ১॥৶০ আনা জমার পঃ স্বত্ব।

৪৪৯ নং ১৯৪৪।৪৫ ইং। বাঃ ডিঃ ৫২৸৬ মোঃ।

সরকার বাহাদুর বঃ পূর্ণানন্দ দাস গং।

তপশিল সম্পত্তি

পঃ বেহার ৮২৫ নং থাক তাং ফলীমারী মধ্যে ৮৯০২ নং পঃ তৌঃ লিঃ ১০।৪৸/০ ধুর জমির কাত বাঃ ১০৷০ আনা জমার পঃ স্বত্ব।

১৪১৫ নং ১৯৪২।৪৩ ইং। বাঃ ডিঃ ১২৸৷৯ মোঃ।

সরকার বাহাদুর বঃ মন্তেশ্বর দাস গং।

তপশিল সম্পত্তি।

পঃ বেহার ১০৬৯ নং থাক তাং সাঁজেরপাড় কাঠালবাড়ী মধ্যে ৮৭১১ নং পঃ তৌঃ লিঃ ৩॥২৷৶০ ধুর জমির কাত বাঃ ৩৶০ আনা জমার পঃ স্বত্ব।

DWIJENDRA CHANDRA SEN, *Certificate Officer.*

রাজকীয় প্রাপ্য আদায় বিষয়ক ১৯৪৩ ইং সনের ১০ আইনের ২ সিডিউলের ৪৬ নিয়মের ঘোষণাপত্র।

রাজ্য কোচবিহারের সদর খাস মহাল আদালত।

এতদ্বারা সর্ব্বসাধারণকে জানান যাইতেছে যে, বাকীদারগণের নিম্নলিখিত সম্পত্তি আগামী ১৯৪৭ সনের ১২ই আগষ্ট মোঃ ১৩৫৪ সনের ২৬শে শ্রাবণ তারিখে দিবা ১ ঘটিকার সময় হলদিবাড়ী খাসমহাল অফিসে খাসমহাল অফিসার কর্ত্তৃক প্রকাশ্য নীলাম আরম্ভ হইবে।

১৭২ নং ১৯৪৬।৪৭ ইং। বাঃ ডিঃ ৪২।৶৩ মোঃ।

সরকার বাহাদুর বঃ মন্থেশ্বরী বর্ম্মণী গং।

তপশিল সম্পত্তি।

পঃ মেখলীগঞ্জ ৯ নং থাক তাং বকসীগঞ্জ মধ্যে ২০৩ নং তৌঃ লিখিত ৪৪৪ ধুর জমির কাত বাঃ ১৪।৶ আনা জমার পঃ স্বত্ব।

২৭০ নং ১৯৪৪।৪৫ ইং। বাঃ ডিঃ ১১।৵ মোঃ।

সরকার বাহাদুর বঃ ভোলানাথ রায় গং।

তপশিল সম্পত্তি।

পঃ মেখলীগঞ্জ ৩ নং ছিট তাং বালাপাড়া খাগড়াবাড়ী মধ্যে ২১৩৩ নং তৌঃ লিখিত ১৮/৩৷০ ধুর জমির কাত বাঃ ২৩৸৶০ আনা জমার পঃ স্বত্ব

১১১ নং। ১৯৪৬।৪৭ বাঃ ডিঃ ২৮৸৶৬ মোঃ।

সরকার বাহাদুর বঃ তাজিমউদ্দিন গঃ।

তপশিল সম্পত্তি।

পং মেখলিগঞ্জ ১ নং থাক তাং বড় হলদিবাড়ী মধ্যে ১২০৫ নং তৌঃ লিখিত ৩৮।০৸৶০ ধুর জমির কাত বাঃ ৩৬৸৶০ আনা জমার পং স্বত্ব।

DWIJENDRA CHANDRA SEN, *Certificate Officer.*

রাজকীয় প্রাপ্য আদায় বিষয়ক ১৯৪৩ ইং সনের ১০ আইনের ২ সিডিউলের ৪৬ নিয়মের ঘোষণাপত্র।

রাজ্য কোচবিহারের সদর খাস মহাল আদালত।

এতদ্বারা সর্ব্বসাধারণকে জানান যাইতেছে যে দাবীকগণের নিম্নলিখিত সম্পত্তি আগামী ১৯৪৭ ইং সনের ১৫ই আগষ্ট মোঃ ১৩৫৪ সনের ২৯শে শ্রাবণ তারিখে দিবা ১ ঘটিকার সময় তুফানগঞ্জ খাস মহাল অফিসে খাস মহাল অফিসার কর্তৃক প্রকাশ্য নিলাম আরম্ভ হইবে।

১৯ নং সার্ট ১৯৪৬।৪৭ ইং। বাঃ ডিঃ ১০৮৶৩ মোঃ।

সরকার বাহাদুর বঃ আলের আকন্দ গঃ।

তপশিল সম্পত্তি।

পং তুফানগঞ্জ ৯৫৫ নং থাক তাং বলরামপুর মধ্যে ৩৮ নং তৌঃ লিখিত ৫০।৩।৶০ধুর জমির কাত বাঃ ৪৩৶০ আনা জমার পং স্বত্ব।

১৫৮ নং ১৯৪৬।৪৭ ইং। বাঃ ডিঃ ৩৬৸৶৩ মোঃ।

সরকারবাহাদুর বঃ তারাং দাস গঃ।

তপশিল সম্পত্তি।

পং তুফানগঞ্জ ১১৮৮ নং থাক তাং ছাট ভলকা মধ্যে ২০১৭ নং তৌ লিখিত ৫৮৸০৸৶০ ধুর জমির কাত বাঃ ৫০।৶০ আনা জমার পং স্বত্ব

DWIJENDRA CHANDRA SEN, *Certificate Officer.*

ইং ১৯১০ সালের ৫ আইনের ৫৩ ধারার ২ প্রকরণ মতে নিলামী ইস্তাহার।

জারীর মহকুমা মাথাভাঙ্গার নাঃ আঃ মাল আদালত।

এতদ্বারা সর্ব্বসাধারণকে জানান যাইতেছে যে, প্রতিবাদীর দাবীর বাকী খাজানা আদায় না করায় তাহার নিম্নলিখিত ক্রোকী সম্পত্তি আগামী ১৩৫৪ সনের ১৮ই শ্রাবণ মোতাবেক ১৯৪৭ সনের ৪ঠা আগষ্ট তারিখে বেলা ১ ঘটিকার সময় প্রকাশ্য নিলাম আরম্ভ হইবে।

৮২ নং ১৯৪।৪ ইং। বাঃ খাঃ ২৬৯৷০ মোঃ।

ডিঃ—মোহনলাল বয়েদ গঃ।

দেঃ—ইন্দ্রমণী বর্ম্মাণী অওজে দয়ারাম বর্ম্মণ।

তপশিল সম্পত্তি

পঃ মাথাভাঙ্গা ৩৮৯ নং থাক তাং গোজ পোতা মধ্যে ২৪০০ নং তৌঃ লিঃ ৫২৶৪৷৶০ ধুর জমির কাত বাঃ ৫৭৲ টাকা জমার চুঃ স্বত্ব।

৮১ নং ১৯৪৭।৪৮ ই বাঃ খাঃ ৭৪৶০ মোঃ

ডিঃ—প্রিয়নাথ তরফদার।

দেঃ—নোহার উদ্দিন মিঞা।

তপশিল সম্পত্তি

পঃ লালবাজার ৪৩৬ নং থাক তাং গোলেনও হাটী মধ্যে ২২ নং তৌ লিঃ ১০৸১৷৶০ ধুর জমির কাত বাং ১৮৶০ আনা জমার দঃ চুঃ স্বত্ব।

৮৫ নং ১৯৪৭।৪৮ ইং। বাঃ খাঃ ১০৸৶০ মোঃ।

ডিঃ—আরতি তরফদার অওজে প্রিয়নাথ তরফদার।

দেঃ—হুকম উদ্দিন মিঞা গঃ।

তপশিল সম্পত্তি

পঃ লালবাজার থাক নং ৪৩৬ তাং গোলেনও হাটী মধ্যে ৭২৩ নং তৌঃ লিঃ ২০৷০ কাঠা জমির কাত বাঃ ৩৭৲ টাকা জমার দঃ চুঃ স্বত্ব।

৮৭ নং ১২৪৭।৪৮ ইং ; বাঃ খাঃ ১১৮।৴০ আঃ ।

ডিঃ—প্রিয়নাথ তরফদার ।
দেঃ—আজেমুদ্দিন মিঞা ।

তপশীল সম্পত্তি

পঃ লালবাজার ৪১৫ নং খাক তাং চেংড়াকুটি [illegible] মধ্যে ১০২ [illegible] লিঃ [illegible] মধ্যে [illegible] বাঃ ৫৫।৴০ আনা জমার দঃ চুঃ স্বত্ব ।

MANABENDRA NATH BHATTACHARJEE, *Naib Ahilkar*

NOTICE.

The following persons are enlisted as recognised contractors of Cooch Behar P. W. D for the current financial year. All these are "C" class Controctors and will be entrusted with minor works, the value of which must not exceed Rs. 10,000.

1. Sjt. Dhirendra Kumar Dutta (Haldibari).
2. ,, Adhir Chandra Bhattabharjee Do
3. Lovi Dafadar ... Do
4. Brij Behari Singh ... Do
5. Lachman Mistry ... Cooch Behar.

G. NARAYAN,
MAJOR,
Deputy Chief Engineer, Cooch Behar

The Cooch Behar Gazette.

৩০শে শ্রাবণ, শনিবার ; SATURDAY, AUGUST 1[illegible], 1947 [১৩৫৪ সাল ৪৩৮ রাজশক

PART II.

NOTICES.

রাজকীয় প্রাপ্য আদায় বিষয়ক ১৯৪৩ ইং সনের ১০ আইনের ২ সিডিউলের ৪৬ নিয়মের ঘোষণাপত্র।

রাজ্য কোচবিহারের সদর খাস মহাল আদালত।

এতদ্দ্বারা সর্ব্বসাধারণকে জানান যাইতেছে যে, দায়ীকগণের নিম্নলিখিত সম্পত্তি আগামী ১৯৪৭ সনের ২১শে আগষ্ট মোঃ ১৩৫৪ সনের ৪ঠা ভাদ্র তারিখে দিবা ১ ঘটিকার সময় মাথাভাঙ্গা খাসমহাল আদালতে প্রকাশ্য নিলাম আরম্ভ হইবে।

২০৯ নং ১৯৪২।৪৩ ইং। বাঃ ডিঃ ৫।৬ বে।

সরকার বাহাদুর বঃ টরয়া বর্ম্মণ।

তপশীল সম্পত্তি।

পং মাথাভাঙ্গা তাং আটিয়াবাড়ী মধ্যে ১১৫৫ পাঃ তৌঃ লিঃ ১১।০ আনা জমার পাঃস্বত্বের জমি।

২২৯ নং ১৯৪২।৪৩ ইং বাঃ ডিঃ ৬০।৫/৩ মোঃ।

সরকার বাহাদুর বঃ বুধেশ্বর বর্ম্মণ।

তপশিল সম্পত্তি।

পং মাথাভাঙ্গা তাং নগরশোভাগঞ্জ মধ্যে ১১৭৯ পাঃ তৌঃ লিঃ ১৩৮২।০ বুঃ জমির কাত বাঃ ১৫৸৶০ আনা জমার পাঃ স্বত্ব।

৪৫৬ নং ১৯৪৩।৪৪ ইং। বাঃ ডিঃ ২৭৸/৩ মোঃ।

সরকার বাহাদুর বঃ বিবাহু বর্ম্মণ বাঃ পং

তপশীল সম্পত্তি।

পং মাথাভাঙ্গা ২৮১ নং খাস তাং কেদারহাটী মানাবাড়ী মধ্যে ১৫০৭ পাঃ তৌঃ ২৮২।৶০ বুঃ জমি ও ৩।৶০ আনা জমার মধ্যে ১৬৪।/০ বুঃ জমির কাত বাঃ ২০০ আনা জমার জমি নিলাম।

৮৭৫ নং ১৯৪৪।৪৫ ইং। বাঃ ডিঃ ১৩৸/০ মোঃ।

সরকার বাহাদুর বঃ ও;রবান বর্ম্মণ।

তপশিল সম্পত্তি।

পং মাথাভাঙ্গা ৬৯২ নং খাস তাং কেদারহাটী মধ্যে ৫১৮০ পাঃ তৌঃ লিঃ ২/৪৸/০ বুঃ জমির কাত বাঃ ২।০ আনা জমার পাঃ স্বত্বের জমি নিলাম।

৬৪ নং-১৯৪৫।৪৬ ইং। বাঃ ডিঃ ৪৮/৬ মোঃ।

সরকার বাহাদুর বঃ আব্বাছ আলী গং

তপশিল সম্পত্তি।

পং মাথাভাঙ্গা ৫০৩ নং খাস তাং কইমারী মধ্যে ১৬৬২ নং পাঃ তৌঃ লিঃ ১০/৸০ বুঃ জমির কাত বাঃ ১৪।৶০ আনা জমার জমি নিলাম।

২৯৭ নং। ১৩৫৪।৪৬ ইং। বাঃ ডিঃ ১০॥/০ মোঃ।

সরকার বাহাদুর বঃ জুলুন মুচী গং

তপশিল সম্পত্তি

পং মাথাভাঙ্গা ৪৬৩ নং থাক তাং গড়খোলা মধ্যে ৩২৩৫ নং পাঃ তৌঃ লিঃ ১৩৮৩।৮/০ যুক্ত জমির কাত বাঃ ১০॥/০ আনা জমার পঃ স্বত্বের জমি নিলাম।

৬৩১ নং ১৩৫৪।৪৬ ইং বাঃ ডিঃ ৩৫।/০ মোঃ।

সরকার বাহাদুর বঃ সাবুদ্দি সেখ গং

তপশিল সম্পত্তি।

পং মাথাভাঙ্গা ৪৬৩ নং থাক তাং গড়খোলা মধ্যে ৩৪৬৩ নং পাঃ তৌঃ লিঃ ২৯/৩।০ যুক্ত জমির কাত বাঃ ২৯৬/০ আনা জমার মধ্যে দেনদার মেহের সেখের ৪০ আনা অংশের জমি নিলাম।

৬৩২ নং ১৩৫৪।৪৬ ইং। বাঃ ডিঃ ২৬৶/৭ মোঃ।

সরকার বাহাদুর বঃ সাবুদ্দি সেখ গং

তপশিল সম্পত্তি।

পং মাথাভাঙ্গা ৪৬৩ নং থাক তাং গড়খোলা মধ্যে ৩৪৬২ নং পাঃ তৌঃ লিঃ ৭৯৩৪/০ যুক্ত জমির ও ১০৪/০ আনা জমার মধ্যে দেনদার মেহের সেখের ৪০ আনা অংশের জমি নিলাম।

৬৩৩ নং ১৩৫৪।৪৬ ইং। বাঃ ডিঃ ৪৩॥/০ মোঃ।

সরকার বাহাদুর বঃ সাবুদ্দি সেখ গং

তপশিল সম্পত্তি।

পং মাথাভাঙ্গা ৪৬৩ নং থাক তাং গড়খোলা মধ্যে ৩৪৬৩ নং পাঃ তৌঃ লিঃ ৭৫॥২৶/০ যুক্ত জমির কাত বাঃ ৬৩।/০ আনা জমার আং পঃ স্বত্ব।

৯২০ নং ১৩৫৪।৪৬ ইং। বাঃ ডিঃ ২৫/৩ মোঃ।

সরকার বাহাদুর ব আমিরহোসেন মহম্মদ

তপশিল সম্পত্তি

পং মাথাভাঙ্গা ২৩৫ নং থাক তাং ক্ষেতি মধ্যে ৪১৩১ নং পাঃ তৌঃ লিঃ ১১/৩৮৶/০ যুক্ত জমির কাত বাঃ ৩, টাকা জমার পঃ স্বত্বের জমি নিলাম।

৬১ নং ১৩৫৬।৪৭ ইং বাঃ ডিঃ ২০৪/১ মোঃ।

সরকার বাহাদুর বঃ আমরাও জুমারিনী

তপশিল সম্পত্তি।

পং মাথাভাঙ্গা ২৮৭ নং থাক তাং কেরেঙ্গেরী মামাবাড়ী মধ্যে ১৫৪১ নং পাঃ তৌঃ লিঃ ৮। ৯০ যুক্ত জমির কাত বাঃ ৯৶০ আনা জমার পঃ স্বত্বের জমি নিলাম।

১০০ নং ১৩৫৬।৪৭ ইং। বাঃ ডিঃ ১৫৬০ মোঃ।

সরকার বাহাদুর বঃ যোগেশচন্দ্র বর্ম্মণ গং

তপশিল সম্পত্তি।

পং মাথাভাঙ্গা ৩১২ নং থাক তাং পুটীমারী মধ্যে ১৫৭০ নং পাঃ তৌঃ লিঃ ৯।৫৶/০ যুক্ত জমির কাত বাঃ ১২৬০ আনা জমার পঃ স্বত্বের জমি নিলাম।

১২৫ নং ১৩৫৬।৪৭ ইং। বাঃ ডিঃ ৬৮।৶/০ মোঃ।

সরকার বাহাদুর বঃ উম্রু মহম্মদ গং

তপশিল সম্পত্তি।

পং মাথাভাঙ্গা ২৯৫ নং থাক তাং বালাসী মধ্যে ৩১৮৮ নং পাঃ তৌঃ লিঃ ৫৬।০৮/০ যুক্ত জমির ও ৫১।০ আনা জমার মধ্যে দেনদার উম্রু মহম্মদ ৯০৮ পাই অংশ বাদ আর দেনদার ১/৪ পাই অংশের জমি নিলাম।

১২৮ নং ১৩৫৬।৪৭ ইং। বাঃ ডিঃ ৯০৬০/০ মোঃ।

সরকার বাহাদুর বঃ মহিমচন্দ্র বর্ম্মণ গং

তপশিল সম্পত্তি

পং মাথাভাঙ্গা ২৯৫ নং থাক তাং বালাসী মধ্যে ৩২২৫ নং পাঃ তৌঃ লিঃ ৬৩/৫৯/০ যুক্ত জমির কাত বাঃ ৩৯৬/০ আনা জমার পঃ স্বত্বের জমি নিলাম।

১৫৯ নং সাং ১৩৫৬।৪৭ ইং। বাঃ ডিঃ ২৭/০ মোঃ।

সরকার বাহাদুর বঃ হরেন্দ্রনাথ বর্ম্মণ নাঃ

তপশিল সম্পত্তি।

পং মাথাভাঙ্গা ৩২৪ নং থাক তাং মুকুলডাঙ্গা মধ্যে ২২৪২ নং পাঃ তৌঃ লিঃ ৪৪৪।৶/০ যুক্ত জমির কাত বাঃ ৯৶/০ আনা জমার পঃ স্বত্বের জমি নিলাম।

১৬২ নং সাট্ট ১৯১৩।১৭ ইং। বাঃ ডিঃ ৩৸/০ মো।

সরকার বাহাদুর বঃ মাইজান বিবি গং

তপশিল সম্পত্তি।

পং মাথাভাঙ্গা ৪০০ নং থাক তাং ডাউয়াগুড়ী মধ্যে ৬৩৮ নং পঃ তৌঃ লিঃ ৮৩৶/০ দুর জমির কাত বাঃ ৷৫/০ আনা জমার পঃ বদের জমি নিলাম।

১৭০ নং সাট্ট ১৯১৪।১৭ ইং। বাঃ ডিঃ ২৫৴১১ মোঃ।

সরকার বাহাদুর বঃ ইউছুব উজিন মিঞা।

তপশিল সম্পত্তি।

পং মাথাভাঙ্গা ৪০০ নং থাক তাং ডাউয়াগুড়ী মধ্যে ৬৭৮ নং পঃ তৌঃ লিঃ ১২৷২।০ দুর জমির কাত বাঃ ১২৸৵০ আনা জমার পঃ খং।

৩৫৭ নং ১৯১৪।১৭ ইং। বাঃ ডিঃ ৬৮৬ মোঃ।

সরকার বাহাদুর বঃ আহাদি মিঞা বাঃ গং

তপশিল সম্পত্তি

পং মাথাভাঙ্গা ৪৫৯ নং থাক তাং শীতলখুচী মধ্যে ৬১২ নং পঃ তৌঃ লিঃ ২৮৴৪৷০ দুর জমির কাত বাঃ ৩৫।০ আনা জমার পঃ অংশবদ।

৫৭৬ নং সা ১৯১৪।১৭ ইং। বাঃ ডিঃ ৩২৩৸/৬ মোঃ।

সরকার বাহাদুর বঃ ব্রজগোপাল ভদ্র গং

তপশিল সম্পত্তি।

পং মাথাভাঙ্গা ৪৫০ নং থাক তাং খারিজাখাগেরচাত্রা ১১৩১ নং পঃ তৌঃ লিঃ ৬১৴।৴০ দুর জমির কাত বাঃ ৫৬৸০ আনা জমার পঃ খদ।

৬১৪ নং সাট্ট ১৯১৪।১৭ ইং। বাঃ ডিঃ ৪২৶৬ মোঃ।

সরকার বাহাদুর বঃ হরেশ্বর বর্ম্মণ গং

তপশিল সম্পত্তি।

পং মাথাভাঙ্গা ৪৪৬ নং থাক তাং গাদাপোতা মধ্যে ২৪৪ নং পঃ তৌঃ লিঃ ১৯৴৪৶০ দুর জমির কাত বাঃ ১৭৸০ আনা জমার পঃ খদ।

৬১৬ নং সাট্ট ১৯১৪।১৭ ইং। বাঃ ডিঃ ৬১৮৩ মোঃ।

সরকার বাহাদুর বঃ টোনেয়া মিঞা গং

তপশিল সম্পত্তি

পং মাথাভাঙ্গা ৪৪৬ নং থাক তাং গাদাপোতা মধ্যে ২৭৭৫ নং পঃ তৌঃ লিঃ ৪৫৴৪৷০ দুর জমির কাত বাঃ ৩৭৷৶০ আনা জমার পঃ খদ।

৬৩১ নং সাট্ট ১৯১৪।১৭ ইং। বাঃ ডিঃ ৯৶৭ মোঃ।

সরকার বাহাদুর বঃ ইব্রাহিম গং

তপশিল সম্পত্তি।

পং মাথাভাঙ্গা ৪৪৬ নং থাক তাং গাদাপোতা মধ্যে ২৬২ নং পঃ তৌঃ লিঃ ১৴৪৶০ দুর জমির কাত বাঃ ১৶০ আনা জমার পঃ খদ।

৬৪৩ নং ১৯১৪।১৭ ইং। বাঃ ডিঃ ৮১।৴১ মোঃ।

সরকার বাহাদুর বঃ গহুরণনেছা বিবি

তপশিল সম্পত্তি।

পং মাথাভাঙ্গা ৪৩২ নং থাক তাং শিবপুর মধ্যে ২০৬ নং পঃ তৌঃ লিঃ ১৭৪০।৶০ দুর জমির কাত বাঃ ২১৷৴০ আনা জমার পঃ খদ।

৬৪৮ নং ১৯১৪।১৭ ইং। বাঃ ডিঃ ১১০।৵৩ মোঃ

সরকার বাহাদুর বঃ নন্দু বর্ম্মণ।

তপশিল সম্পত্তি।

পং মাথাভাঙ্গা ৪৩৪ নং থাক তাং জোনডাবরী মধ্যে ৮৩৭ নং পঃ তৌঃ লিঃ ২৫৷৪৸৶০ দুর জমির কাত বাঃ ২৯৶০ আনা জমার পঃ খদ।

৬৪৯ নং সাট্ট ১৯১৪।১৭ ইং। বাঃ ডিঃ ৩১।৶০ মোঃ।

সরকার বাহাদুর বঃ চন্দ্রমোহন চৌধুরী

তপশিল সম্পত্তি।

পং মাথাভাঙ্গা ৪৩৪ নং থাক তাং জোনডাবরী মধ্যে ৮৬৬ নং পঃ তৌঃ লিঃ ৩৴১৷৶০ দুর জমির কাত বাঃ ২।৴০ আনা জমার পঃ খদ।

৬৫০ নং সাট্ট ১৯১৪।১৭ ইং। বাঃ ডিঃ ১৪২৶৩ মোঃ।

সরকার বাহাদুর বঃ চন্দ্রমোহন চৌধুরী।

তপশিল সম্পত্তি

পং মাথাভাঙ্গা ৪৩৪ নং থাক তাং জোনডাবরী মধ্যে ৮৬৯ নং পঃ তৌঃ লিঃ ৫৭৪০৶০ দুর জমির কাত বাঃ ৩৬৶০ আনা জমার পঃ খদ।

৬৫১ নং ১৩৪৬।১৭ বাঃ জিঃ ৪৬।/০ ।

সরকার বাহাদুর বঃ চন্দ্রমোহন চৌধুরী ।

তপশীল সম্পত্তি।

পঃ মাথাভাঙ্গা ৪০৭ নং থাক তাং ভোগডাবরী মধ্যে ২৯৪৫ নং পৌঃ লিঃ ৩৯/২৯৫/০ খুর জমির কাত বাঃ ১৯।০ আনা জমার পঃ স্বত্ব ।

৬৮৯ নং ১৩৪৬।১৭ ইং। বাঃ জিঃ ৩২৫/৯ মোঃ ।

সরকার বাহাদুর বঃ একাব্বর সেখ গং

তপশিল সম্পত্তি ।

পঃ মাথাভাঙ্গা ৪৫৯ নং থাক তাং গয়াইখোড়া মধ্যে ৩২০৪ নং পঃ পৌঃ লিঃ ১২।৩৶০ খুর জমির কাত বাঃ ১৫৶০ আনা জমার পঃ স্বত্ব ।

৬৭৩ নং ১৩৪৬।১৭ ইং । বাঃ জিঃ ৪৩।৶৯ মোঃ ।

সরকার বাহাদুর বঃ কলিম উদ্দিন মিঞা ।

তপশিল সম্পত্তি ।

পঃ মাথাভাঙ্গা ৪১৩ নং থাক তাং মহিষখুচী মধ্যে ১০৯৯ নং পঃ পৌঃ লিঃ ১০৪১/০ খুর জমির কাত বাঃ ৯।০ আনা জমার পঃ স্বত্ব।

৫৮১ নং সাট্টি ১৩৪৬।৪৭ ইং । বাঃ জিঃ ১২৭৸৶০ মোঃ ।

সরকার বাহাদুর বঃ হেমেন্দ্রনাথ বর্ম্মণ গং

তপশীল সম্পত্তি ।

পঃ মাথাভাঙ্গা ৪১৬ নং থাক তাং খারবন্দ খলিশামারী মধ্যে ১৬০১ নং পঃ পৌঃ লিঃ ১৪।৫৪/০ খুর জমির কাত বাঃ ২৯।/০ আনা জমার পঃ স্বত্ব ।

৭১৪ নং ১৩৪৬।৪৭ ইং । বাঃ জিঃ ১০১৶৩ মোঃ ।

সরকার বাহাদুর বঃ হরিনাথ অধিকারী গং

তপশিল সম্পত্তি

পঃ মাথাভাঙ্গা ৩৪২ নং থাক তাং কেরকেরী মধ্যে ৫৪২ নং পঃ পৌঃ লিঃ ১৫৸৪।৶০ খুর জমির কাত বাঃ ২৭।৶০ আনা জমার পঃ স্বত্ব ।

৭১৫ নং ১৩৪৬।৪৭ ইং । বাঃ জিঃ ২৯৸৶১০ মোঃ ।

সরকার বাহাদুর বঃ বৈকুণ্ঠ নায়েক গং

তপশিল সম্পত্তি ।

পঃ মাথাভাঙ্গা ৫৪৫ নং থাক তাং ভোগমারা মধ্যে ৩৬৪ নং পঃ পৌঃ লিঃ ৬/১৪৶০ খুর জমির কাত বাঃ ৯।/০ আনা জমার পঃ স্বত্ব ।

৭২৬ নং সা [illegible] ৬।৪৭ ইং । বাঃ জিঃ ৫৸৶০ মোঃ ।

সরকার বাহাদুর বঃ হরকান্ত নায়েক গং

তপশিল সম্পত্তি ।

পঃ মাথাভাঙ্গা ৩৪৫ নং থাক তাং ভোগমারা মধ্যে ৩৫৫ নং পঃ পৌঃ লিঃ ৬৩২/০ খু[illegible] কাত বাঃ ১ [illegible] টাকা জমার ॥৵ আনা অংশের পঃ স্বত্ব ।

৭৩৮ নং সাট্টি ১৩৪৬।৪৭ ইং । বাঃ জিঃ ৪৮৸৶৯ মোঃ ।

সরকার বাহাদুর বঃ দসাই বৈরাগী ।

তপশীল সম্পত্তি ।

পঃ মাথাভাঙ্গা ৩৮৮ নং থাক তাং উনিশবিশা মধ্যে ১২২৪ নং পঃ পৌঃ লিঃ ২৭।০৶ খুর জমির কাত বাঃ ৪১/০ আনা জমার পঃ স্বত্ব ।

৭৪১ নং ১৩৪৬।৪৭ ইং । বাঃ জিঃ ১৬০।০ মোঃ ।

সরকার বাহাদুর বঃ চেংরু নারায়ণ সাউদ

তপশিল সম্পত্তি ।

পঃ মাথাভাঙ্গা ৩৪৮ নং থাক তাং ফেরসামারী মধ্যে ৪০৯ নং পঃ পৌঃ লিঃ ১৮/৪৸/০ খুর জমির কাত বাঃ ১৬৶০ আনা জমার পঃ স্বত্ব।

৭৬২ নং সাট্টি ১৩৪৬।৪৭ ইং । বাঃ জিঃ ১২৩৶১১ মোঃ ।

সরকার বাহাদুর বঃ নরেন্দ্র বর্ম্মণ ।

তপশিল ।

পঃ মাথাভাঙ্গা ৩৭৮ নং থাক তাং উনিশবিশা মধ্যে ৪৯০ নং পঃ পৌঃ লিঃ ১১৬৩/০ খুর জমির কাত বাঃ ১৩৯৶০ আনা জমার পঃ স্বত্ব ।

৭৬৩ নং সাট্টি ১৩৪৬।৪৭ ইং । বাঃ জিঃ ১৬২৶১ মোঃ ।

সরকার বাহাদুর বঃ দুলাল বর্ম্মণ গং

তপশিল ।

পঃ মাথাভাঙ্গা ৩৭৮ নং থাক তাং উনিশবিশা মধ্যে ৪৪০ নং পঃ পৌঃ লিঃ ১১।৵০ খুর জমির কাত বাঃ ১৩৯৶০ আনা জমার পঃ স্বত্ব ।

৭৩৩ নং ১৯৪৬,৪৭ ইং। বাঃ ডিঃ ২৩/১১ মোঃ।

সরকার বাহাদুর বঃ রমেশ বর্ম্মণ।

তপশিল সম্পত্তি।

পং মাথাভাঙ্গা ৩০৮ নং খাক তাং উনিশবিশা মধ্যে ৪৪০ নং পাঃ তৌঃ লিঃ ১১।০৶০ পুর জমির কাত বাঃ ১৫।৶০ আনা জমার পাঃ স্বত্ব।

৭৩৭ নং ১৯৪৬।৪৭ ইং। বাঃ ডিঃ ২৬৶/১ মোঃ।

সরকার বাহাদুর বঃ নরেন্দ্র বর্ম্মণ।

তপশিল সম্পত্তি।

পং মাথাভাঙ্গা ৩০৮ নং খাক তাং উনিশবিশা মধ্যে ৪৪৬ নং পাঃ তৌঃ লিঃ ৬২।।০ পুর জমির কাত বাঃ ২/০ আনা জমার পাঃ স্বত্ব।

৭৬৮ নং ১৯৪৬।৪৭ ইং। বাঃ ডিঃ ১৩।৶/১১ মোঃ।

সরকার বাহাদুর বঃ দয়াল বর্ম্মণ গং

তপশিল সম্পত্তি।

পং মাথাভাঙ্গা ৩০৮ নং খাক তাং উনিশবিশা মধ্যে ৪৩০ নং পাঃ তৌঃ লিঃ ১১।৩৶০ পুর জমির কাত বাঃ ১৩।৶০ আনা জমার পাঃ স্বত্ব।

DWIJENDRA CHANDRA SEN, *Certificate Officer.*

দেওয়ানী কার্য্যবিধি আইনের ২১ হুকুম, ৬৬ নিয়মের ঘোষণাপত্র।

রাজ্য কোচবিহারের সদর খাস কাছারী নাঃ আঃ আদালত।

এতদ্দ্বারা সর্ব্বসাধারণকে জানান যাইতেছে যে, দায়ীকগণের নিম্নলিখিত সম্পত্তি আগামী ১৯৪৭ সনের ১৫ই সেপ্টেম্বর মোঃ ১৩৫৪ সনের ২৯শে ভাদ্র তারিখে দিবা ১ ঘটিকার সময় প্রকাশ্য নিলাম আরম্ভ হইবে।

৩ নং misc ১৯৪৭।৪৮ ইং। বাঃ ডিঃ ১০৭।১ মোঃ।

সরকার বাহাদুর বঃ যোগেন্দ্রনাথ দে মোঃ বেহার।

তপশিল সম্পত্তি।

১। তাংগুড়িয়াহাটী কুচেখরী মধ্যে ৪৭৩৩ নং পাঃ তৌঃ লিঃ ২/১৶৶০ পুর জমির কাত বাঃ ২৮০ আনা জমার জোত।

২। তাং তথা মধ্যে ৭৫১২ নং পাঃ তৌঃ লিঃ ৩৮৬৶০ পুর জমির কাত বাঃ ৪৮।৶০ আনা জমার জোত।

৩। তাং তথা মধ্যে ৪১৭৭ নং পাঃ তৌঃ লিঃ ৫৪০/০ পুর জমির কাত বাঃ ৩৶০ আনা জমার জমি।

NAGENDRA NATH ROY, *S. S. Naib Ahilkar.*

দেওয়ানী কার্য্যবিধি আইনের ২১ হুকুম, ৬৬ নিয়মের ঘোষণাপত্র।

রাজ্য কোচবিহারের এঃ সিঃ জজ আদালত।

এতদ্দ্বারা সর্ব্বসাধারণকে জানান যাইতেছে যে, দায়ীকগণের নিম্নলিখিত সম্পত্তি আগামী ১৯৪৭ সনের ৪ই অক্টোবর মোঃ ১৩৫৪ সনের ১৭শে আশ্বিন তারিখে দিবা ১২ ঘটিকার সময় প্রকাশ্য নিলাম আরম্ভ হইবে।

২৯ নং ১৯৪৭।৪৮ ইং। বাঃ ডিঃ ৪৫/৩ মোঃ।

ডিঃ—রজনীমোহন শীল মোঃ বেহার।

দেঃ—বিধুভূষণ দে মোঃ বেহার।

তপশিল সম্পত্তি।

পাঃ বেহার ২১৪ নং খাক তাং সহর কোচবিহার মধ্যে চাত দেয় দাঃ ভিটার উপর করগেট ১০ ফুট ১০ খানা টীনের চাপড়া ১ খানা লম্বা অনুমান ৯। হাত প্রস্থ অনুমান ৪। হাত কাদনার বেড়া বাঁশের খুটী যাবৎ সরঞ্জাম সহ।

F. AHMED, *Asst. Civil Judge.*

সরকারী খাস নাজরানা পত্তনী স্বত্বের ভূমির নিলামী ইস্তাহার।

ইস্তাহার জারী কাছারী খাস মাথাভাঙ্গা সবডিভিসন মাথাভাঙ্গা মোতাবেক নিজ বেহার, সন ৪৩৮ শকা মোঃ ১৩৫৪। ১৯৪৭ ইং তাং ৫ই আগষ্ট।

নং ৬১৩ নামজারী (খাস মহাল)

৪৬৪৭ নাজরানা

যেহেতু নিম্নলিখিত নাজরানা পত্তনী স্বত্বের ভূমি ডাক বন্দোবস্ত করার আদেশ হইয়াছে মতে এতদ্দ্বারা সর্ব্ব সাধারণকে জানান যাইতেছে নিম্নলিখিত সরকারী খাস পত্তনী স্বত্বের ভূমি আগামী ২০।৮।৪৭ ইং মোতাবেক ভূক্ষণ তি বার ৪ঠা ভাদ্র তারিখে বেলা ১২ ঘটিকার সময় অত্রাদালতে নিলাম করা যাইবে। খরিদ করণেচ্ছুক ব্যক্তিগণ নির্দ্ধারিত দিবসে নির্দ্দিষ্ট সময়ে অত্রাদালতে উপস্থিত হইয়া রীতিমত ডাক করে।

তপশিল সম্পত্তি

মহাল খাস পঃ খাস মাথাভাঙ্গার অন্তর্গত ৬০০০ নং পত্তনী তৌজির লিখিত তালুক পাটাকামরী মধ্যে ২৮/১।৶০ পুর ভূমির কাত বার্ষিক ২০৶০ আনা জমার জোত গোপাল বর্ম্মণ নামীয় ১০/০ আনা জমার ভূমি।

MANABENDRA NATH BHATTACHARJEE, *Naib Ahilkar.*

ইং ১৯১০ সালের ৫ আইনের ৫৩ ধারার ২ প্রকরণ মতে নিলামী ইস্তাহার।

জমির মহকুমা মেখলীগঞ্জের মাল আদালত।

এতদ্বারা সর্ব্বসাধারণকে জানান যাইতেছে যে, প্রতিবাদীর রাজস্ব বাকী খাজনা আদায় না করায় তাহার নিম্নলিখিত ক্রোকী সম্পত্তি আগামী ১৩৫৪ সনের ১৫ই ভাদ্র মোতাবেক ১৯৪৭ সনের ১লা সেপ্টেম্বর তারিখে বেলা ১ ঘটিকার সময় প্রকাশ্য নীলাম আরম্ভ হইবে।

২০ নং ১৯৪৭।৪৮ বাঃ খাঃ ১০১।/৯।

ডিঃ—জয়ন্তি রায় সাং উপকণ্ঠী কুচলীবাড়ী থাঃ মেখলীগঞ্জ।

দেঃ—ডাক্তারচন্দ্র অধিকারী সাং জামালদহ বালাপুখরী থাঃ মেখলীগঞ্জ।

তপশিল সম্পত্তি।

পঃ মেখলীগঞ্জ ১২০ নং খাক তাং জামালদহ বালাপুখরী মধ্যে ১ নং তৌঃ লিঃ ৫৫৷১৪ কাঠা জমির কাত বাঃ ৩৫৸৵ আনা জমার আং চুঃ জমি।

৩১ নং ১৯৪৭।৪৮ ইং। বাঃ খাঃ ১৩৫৭ মোঃ।

ডিঃ—মশারফ হোসেন প্রধান গং।

দেঃ—ছহিমুদ্দিন ওঃ চৌধুরী গং সাং ছোট হলদীবাড়ী।

তপশিল।

পঃ মেখলীগঞ্জ ২৮ নং খাক তাং ছোট হলদীবাড়ী মধ্যে ৬৪৯ নং তৌঃ লিঃ ২৮২।৶০ খুর জমির কাত বাঃ ৪৸/০ আনা জমার আং চুঃ।

৩০ নং ১৯৪৭।৪৮ ইং। বাঃ খাঃ ১০৪/১ মোঃ।

ডিঃ—বেগম কাতেমা খাতুন সাং কিঃ ফতেমামুদ থাঃ হলদিবাড়ী।

দেঃ—আনন্দ লাল গং সাং বড় হলদিবাড়ী থাঃ হলদিবাড়ী।

তপশিল।

পঃ মেখলীগঞ্জ ১ নং খাক তাং বড় হলদিবাড়ী মধ্যে ৭৮ নং তৌঃ লিঃ ।৪/০ খুর জমির কাত বাঃ ।৶০ আনা জমার কৃষিপ্রজা।

৩৮ নং ১৯৪৭।৪৮ ইং। বাঃ খাঃ ৩২।৶০ মোঃ।

ডিঃ—ভবানীপ্রসন্ন তালুকদার মোঃ মেখলীগঞ্জ।

দেঃ—হালিমন নেছা বেওয়া সাং ভোটবাড়ী পোঃ চাংরাবান্ধা।

তপশিল সম্পত্তি।

পঃ মেখলীগঞ্জ ১৫৭ নং খাক তাং ভোটবাড়ী মধ্যে ১৭৯১ নং তৌঃ লিঃ ২৬/২।০ খুর জমির কাত বাঃ ২৬৶০ আনা জমার চুঃ।

৩৯ নং ১৯৪৭।৪৮ ইং। বাঃ খাঃ ১৮৶৩ মোঃ।

ডিঃ—আনন্দমোহন সিংহ মোঃ মেখলীগঞ্জ।

দেঃ—বিন্ধ্যাচলপ্রসাদ চৌবে গং সাং হেমকুমারী।

তপশিল সম্পত্তি

পঃ মেখলীগঞ্জ ৩৯ নং খাক তাং নিজ তরফ মধ্যে ৭৬৭ নং তৌঃ লিঃ ৬৬৪২৷/০ খুর জমির কাত বাঃ ১০২৪৴০ আনা জমার চুঃ।

৪০ নং ১৯৪৭।৪৮ ইং। বাঃ খাঃ ২৮২৸৶০ মোঃ।

ডিঃ—জীবপ্রসাদ কাহু মোঃ মেখলীগঞ্জ।

দেঃ—বারাবকস মণ্ডল গং সাং উকারমারা থাঃ পাটগ্রাম জেঃ জলপাইগুড়ী।

তপশীল সম্পত্তি।

পঃ মেখলীগঞ্জ ১০১ নং খাক তাং কুচলীবাড়ী মধ্যে ১৫৭৬ নং তৌঃ লিঃ ৬৬৭১৶০ খুর জমির কাত বাঃ ১০।৶০ আনা জমার চুঃ।

৪১ নং ১৯৪৭।৪৮ ইং। বাঃ খাঃ ১৫৸৶৩ মোঃ।

ডিঃ—জীবপ্রসাদ কাহু মোঃ মেখলীগঞ্জ।

দেঃ—বারাবকস মণ্ডল গং সাং উকারমারা থাঃ পাটগ্রাম জেঃ জলপাইগুড়ী।

তপশিল সম্পত্তি।

পঃ মেখলীগঞ্জ ১০১ নং খাক তাং কুচলীবাড়ী মধ্যে ১৫৭৬ নং তৌঃ লিঃ ৬৬/২।০ খুর জমির কাত বাঃ ৬৫/০ আনা জমার চুঃ।

৪২ নং ১৩৫৭।৪৮ ইং। বাঃ বাঃ ৪০৶১০ বোঃ।

ডিঃ—উপানন্দ সিংহ সরকার পং সো মেখলীগঞ্জ।

দেঃ—সোনাবালা বসাক নাঃ প সাং মোহাম্মদপুর ষ্টেঃ পাটগ্রাম।

তপশিল সম্পত্তি।

পঃ মেখলীগঞ্জ ১৩৭ নং খাক তাং কোটবাড়ী মধ্যে ১ নং চৌ. লিঃ ৭।১।৶০ খুব জমির কাত নাং ২৸৵০ আনা জমার কৃষিপ্রজা।

৪৩ নং ১৩৫৭।৪৮ ইং। বাঃ বাঃ ২২১৶০ বোঃ।

ডিঃ—মোহাম্মদ নালু সাং বগরাজবালা ষ্টেঃ হলদিবাড়ী।

দেঃ—মৌঃ মজাফর হোসেন প্রধান পং সাং কিঃ ফতেমামুদ ষ্টেঃ হলদিবাড়ী।

তপশীল সম্পত্তি।

পাঃ মেখলীগঞ্জ ৩২ নং খাক তাং বগরাজবালা মধ্যে ১৪৮৯ নং চৌঃ লিঃ ১/৩৸৶০ খুব জমির কাত বাঃ ৩৶০ আনা জমার দখলদার।

KUMAR P. NARAYAN, *Naib Ahilkar.*

সিভিল সাপ্লাইজ কমিশনার ও কণ্ট্রোলার অব প্রাইসেস্ আফিস, কুচবিহার।

বিজ্ঞাপন।

(মূল্য নিয়ন্ত্রণ)

সিভিল সাপ্লাইজ কমিশনারের উপর প্রদত্ত এবং ন্যস্ত ক্ষমতাবলে কোচবিহার Essential Supplies (Temporary Powers) Act 1946 এর ৩ ধারার অন্তর্গত ২ উপধারার সি ক্লজ অনুযায়ী নিম্নলিখিত দ্রব্যগুলির সর্বোচ্চ মূল্য নিম্নলিখিতরূপে ধার্য্য করা হইল এবং তাহা কুচবিহার গেজেটে প্রকাশিত হওয়ার তারিখ হইতে পুনরাদেশ না হওয়া পর্য্যন্ত বলবৎ থাকিবে। এতদ্বিষয়ক পূর্ব বিজ্ঞপ্তি বাতিল করা হইল। কোন ব্যক্তি নির্দ্ধারিত মূল্যের অতিরিক্ত মূল্যে বিক্রয় করিলে বা দ্রব্যাদি বিক্রয়ার্থ আনিয়া নির্দ্ধারিত মূল্যে বিক্রয় করিতে অস্বীকার করিলে উপরোক্ত আইনের ৭ ধারা অনুযায়ী দণ্ডনীয় হইবে। ইতি ১২ আগষ্ট ১৯৪৭।

বিশেষ দ্রষ্টব্য ঃ—সরিষা ও ধানের দর রাজ্যের হাটে, গঞ্জবাজারে, মিলে ও খুচরা দোকানে ও বন্দরে প্রযোজ্য। রাজ্যের অন্যান্য স্থানের দর উহা অপেক্ষা ।০ চারি আনা হিসাবে কম হইবে। রসগোল্লা, সন্দেশ ও চিড়ার দর রাজ্যের সর্বত্র এক।

কেরোসিন—হলদিবাড়ী বন্দরের দর—

লাল কেরোসিন প্রতি টিন ৬৸০ টিন সমেত প্রতি সের ৶৩

সাদা কেরোসিন প্রতি টিন ৫৸৵০ (ঐ) প্রতি সের ।০

কয়লা—কয়লার দর মাত্র কুচবিহার সহরের জন্য নির্দ্ধারিত হইল।

মফঃস্বলের দর—কোচবিহার টাউন, দিনহাটা বন্দর, হলদিবাড়ী বন্দর, মেখলীগঞ্জ বন্দর ব্যতীত অন্যান্য স্থানের দর নিম্নলিখিত দর অপেক্ষা (ধান্য, চাউল, সরিষা ও ধান ব্যতীত) মণ প্রতি এক টাকা চারি আনা অর্থাৎ সের প্রতি দুই পয়সা বেশী হইবে। কিন্তু যে সকল জেলে রাজ্যের অন্যান্য স্থানের দর পৃথক ভাবে ধার্য্য আছে সেই সব জেলে ঐ নির্দ্ধারিত দরই প্রযোজ্য হইবে।

পাইকারী দর—মণ সেরের নীচে আড়াই সের পর্য্যন্ত খরিদ বিক্রী হইলে মণ প্রতি ।০ চারি আনা বেশী হইবে। কিন্তু এই নিয়ম, চাউল, সরিষা, গম, সম্বন্ধে প্রযোজ্য হইবে না এবং যেখন দোকানে ইহা প্রযোজ্য হইবে তথায় কেবলমাত্র নির্দ্ধারিত খুচরা দরে কেনা বেচা হইবে।

ষ্ট্যাণ্ডার্ড বস্তা—লবণ ১৮৩ সের বস্তা সহ।
চিনি ২৮১ সের বস্তা সহ।

পণ্য দ্রব্যের নাম	প্রতি সের	প্রতি মণ	প্রতি ষ্ট্যাণ্ডার্ড বস্তা	মন্তব্য
১। গম—দেশী জাতের	৶৭	১৲		
ঐ বড়দানা পাঞ্জাবী জাতের		১৫৲		
২। চিনি	৸৶০	২৪॥০	৬৭৸৶০ (কোচবিহার সদর, দিনহাটা বন্দর, মাথাভাঙ্গা বন্দর, হলদিবাড়ী বন্দরের জন্য) প্রতি ষ্ট্যাণ্ডার্ড বস্তা ৭০৸৶০ আনা	
ঐ	৸৶০	২৭৲	(রাজ্যের অন্যান্য স্থানের দর)	
বাতাসা, কদমা, তিলুয়া	৸৵	৩১৲		
মিশ্রী	৸৴১০	৩৫।০		
রসগোল্লা	১।০	×		
সন্দেশ (উৎকৃষ্ট)	২।০	×		
ঐ (সাধারণ)	১৸০	×		
৩। আটা	।৶৬	১৫৸০		
৪। ময়দা	।৵৬	১৮।০		
ঐ	॥৵	২০৸০	(রাজ্যের অন্যান্য স্থানের দর)	
৫। নারিকেল তৈল	২৲	৭৭॥০		
৬। কয়লা		১৸৶০		
৭। লবণ ঐ (করকচ)	৵৬			
৮। কেরোসিন তৈল (সাদা)	।৶ প্রতি বোতল	৫৸৶০ প্রতি টিন (টিন সমেত) ৫৵০ (৪ গ্যালন) টিন ছাড়া।		
ঐ (লাল)	।৶	৫।৶০ প্রতি টিন (টিন সমেত)। ৪৸০ (৪ গ্যালন) টিন ছাড়া।		
৯। মাংস (পাঁঠা খাসী)	১৸০ প্রতি সের			
১০। পাউরুটি পাউণ্ড	॥৶৬			
ঐ ৫ ছটাক	।৵৩			
১১। দুধ	তিন সের প্রতি টাকা (এই দর ষ্টেট মডেল ডেইরি ফার্মে প্রযোজ্য নহে)			
১২। গুড় চট মোড়াই পাকি		২২॥৶৬		
ঐ খোলা গুড়	॥৶৩			

শ্রীহিমাদ্রিচন্দ্র বিশ্বাস,
সিভিল সাপ্লাইজ কমিশনার, কোচবিহার ষ্টেট, কুচবিহার।

NOTICE.

It is notified for general information that the distribution of cloth for the July—September, 1947 quarter commences from the 11th August, 1947 and shall continue upto the 7th September, 1947.

The allotted yardage of distribution for the Urban population in the Sudder Sub-Division is 3½ yards of Dhuti, Saree and 4½ yards of other cloth per head, while the Rural people of this Sub-Division will get 2 yards of Dhuti, Saree and 3 yards of other cloth.

H. B. BISWAS,
Civil Supplies Commissioner, Cooch Behar.

The Cooch Behar Gazette.

SUPPLEMENTARY.

২রা ভাদ্র, মঙ্গলবার ; TUESDAY, AUGUST 19, 1947 [১৩৫৪ সাল ৪৩৮ রাজশক

PART II.

NOTICES.

সং ১৯১০ সালের ৫ আইনের ৫৩ ধারার ২ প্রকরণ মতে নিলামী ইস্তাহার।

জারীর মহকুমা মাথাভাঙ্গার নাঃ আঃ মাল আদালত।

এতদ্বারা সর্ব্বসাধারণকে জানান যাইতেছে যে, প্রতিবাদীর দাবীর বাকী খাজানা আদায় না করায় তাহার নিম্নলিখিত ক্রোকী সম্পত্তি আগামী ১৩৫৪ সনের ১৫ই ভাদ্র মোতাবেক ১৯৪৭ সনের ১লা সেপ্টেম্বর তারিখে বেলা ১ ঘটিকার সময় প্রকাশ্য নিলাম আরম্ভ হইবে।

১,৬৭ নং ১৯৪৭ '৪৮ ইং। বাঃ খাঃ ৩২।৶০ মোঃ।

ডি — ভবানীপ্রসন্ন তালুকদার মোঃ মাথাভাঙ্গা।

দেঃ— উকিল অধিকারী বাঃ কং সাং ভেকডেরী।

তপশীল সম্পত্তি

পঃ মাথাভাঙ্গা ২৮৭ নং থাক ৩১২ ভেকডেরী আনাবাড়ী মধ্যে ১৮০ নং খত লিঃ ২৸৩৶০ খুব জমির কাত বাঃ ৫৵০ আনা জমার কৃষিপ্রজা স্বত্ব।

১১৫ নং ১৩৪৭।৪৮ ই বাঃ খাঃ ১০৮৴০ মোঃ

ডিঃ—ভবানীপ্রসন্ন তালুকদার সাং মাথাভাঙ্গা।

দেঃ—উকিল অধিকারী নাঃ গঃ সাং ভেরভেরী মানাবাড়ী।

তপশিল সম্পত্তি।

পঃ মাথাভাঙ্গা ২৮৭ নং খাক তাং ভেরভেরী মানাবাড়ী মধ্যে ১৩২ নং খতের লিঃ ১।১৪০ ধুর জমির কাত বাঃ ।০ আনা জমার দরচুকানী স্বত্ব।

১১৩ নং ১৩৪৭।৪৮ ইং। বাঃ খাঃ ২২।৴

ডিঃ—ভবানীপ্রসন্ন তালুকদার মোঃ মাথাভাঙ্গা।

দেঃ—আছা উদ্দিন মিঞা গঃ সাং ছোট মধুসুদন।

তপশিল সম্পত্তি।

পঃ লালবাজার ৪১৯ নং খাক তাং ছোট মধুসুদন মধ্যে ৮৮ নং খতের লি. ২৴১৶০ ধুর জমির কাত বাঃ ২।০ আনা জমার দরচুকানী স্বত্ব।

৩১ নং ১৩৪৭।৪৮ ইং। বাঃ খাঃ ২০৩৶ মোঃ।

ডিঃ—ইন্দ্রনারায়ণ প্রামানিক সাং শীতলখুচী।

দেঃ—হরেন্দ্র বর্ম্মণ গঃ সাং শীতলখুচী।

তপাশিল।

পঃ লালবাজার ৪৪৯ নং খাক তাং শীতলখুচী মধ্যে ৪১৫ নং তৌঃ লিঃ ২৭।৩।৴০ ধুর জমির কাত বাঃ ৪২৲ টাকা জমার দরচুকানী স্বত্ব।

৭২ নং ১৩৪৭।৪৮ ইং। বাঃ খাঃ ২৮৲ মোঃ।

ডিঃ—প্রিয়নাথ তরফদার মোঃ মাথাভাঙ্গা।

দেঃ—সজনীমোহন বর্ম্মণ সাং শীতলখুচী।

তপশিল।

পঃ লালবাজার ৪৬৩ নং খাক তাং গোলেনওহাটী মধ্যে ১১৮৯ নং তৌঃ লিঃ ১।২৮/০ ধুর জমির কাত বাঃ ৩।০ আনা জমার দরচুকানী স্বত্ব।

৯৬ নং ১৩৪৭।৪৮ ইং। বাঃ খাঃ ১০৯৸/০ মোঃ।

ডিঃ—প্রয়াগ দত্ত গুকুল গঃ মোঃ মাথাভাঙ্গা।

দেঃ—মরালী বর্ম্মাণী সাং বড় শিমুলগুড়ী।

তপশিল সম্পত্তি।

পঃ মাথাভাঙ্গা ৩৮০ নং খাক তাং বড় শিমুলগুড়ী মধ্যে ২৪।১৶০ ধুর জমির কাত বাঃ ৩৭৸/০ আনা জমার করের চুকানী স্বত্ব।

MANABENDRA NATH BHATTACHARJEE, *Naib Ahilkar.*

ইং ১৯১০ সালের ৫ আইনের ৫৩ ধারার ২ প্রকরণ মতে নিলামী ইস্তাহার।

জমির মহকুমা মাথাভাঙ্গা এঃ সাঃ আদালত।

এতদ্বারা সর্ব্বসাধারণকে জানান যাইতেছে যে, প্রতিবাদীর দাবীর বাকী খাজনা আদায় না করায় তাহার নিম্নলিখিত ক্রোকী সম্পত্তি আগামী ১৩৫৪ সনের ১৫ই ভাদ্র মোতাবেক ১৯৪৭ সনের ১লা সেপ্টেম্বর তারিখে বেলা ১ ঘটিকার সময় প্রকাশ্য নীলাম আরম্ভ হইবে।

৩০ নং ১৩৪৭।৪৮ বাঃ খাঃ ৩৮৷৶।

ডিঃ—ভবানীপ্রসন্ন তালুকদার মোঃ মাথাভাঙ্গা।

দেঃ—সমিরুন নেছা বিবি গঃ সাং শিবপুর।

তপশিল সম্পত্তি

পঃ লালবাজার ৪৩১ নং খাক তাং পানাগুড়ী মধ্যে ১৩ নং খতের লিঃ ১৭।০।৶০ ধুর জমির কাত বাঃ ১১৸/০ আনা জমার চুকানী আং স্বত্ব।

৩২ নং ১৯৪৭।৪৮ ইং। বাঃ খাঃ ৫৩।० মোঃ।

ডিঃ—ভবানীপ্রসন্ন তালুকদার মোঃ মাথাভাঙ্গা।

দেঃ—সরিকন নেছা বিবি গঃ সাং শিবপুর।

তপশীল সম্পত্তি।

পঃ লালবাজার ৪৩১ নং থাক তাং পানাগুড়ী মধ্যে ১৯ নং খত্বের লিঃ ২২৷১/০ ধুর জমির কাত বাঃ ১৪৷৷৵০ আনা জমার চুকানী আং খত্ব।

৩১ নং ১৯৪৭।৪৮ ইং। বাঃ খাঃ ৪৩৷৵০ মোঃ।

ডিঃ—ভবানীপ্রসন্ন তালুকদার মোঃ মাথাভাঙ্গা।

দেঃ—সরিকন নেছা বিবি গঃ সাং শিবপুর।

তপশিল সম্পত্তি।

পঃ লালবাজার ৪৩১ নং থাক তাং পানাগুড়ী মধ্যে ১৩ নং খত্বের লিঃ ৭৷৩/০ ধুর জমির কাত বাঃ ১০৲ টাকা জমার চুকানী আং খত্ব।

TINKARI MOHAN MUKERJEE, *Addl. Naib Ahilkar.*

দেওয়ানী কার্য্যবিধি আইনের ২১ হুকুম, ৬৬ নিয়মের ঘোষণাপত্র।

রাজ্য কোচবিহারের সদর মাল কাছারী নাঃ আঃ আদালত।

এতদ্বারা সর্ব্বসাধারণকে জানান যাইতেছে যে, দাবীকগণের নিম্নলিখিত সম্পত্তি আগামী ১৯৪৭ সনের ২২শে সেপ্টেম্বর মোঃ ১৩৫৪ সনের ৫ই আশ্বিন তারিখে দিবা ১ ঘটিকার সময় প্রকাশ্য নিলাম আরম্ভ হইবে।

৩ নং misc ১৯৪৭।৪৮ ইং। বাঃ ডিঃ ১০৭৷১ মোঃ।

সরকার বাহাদুর বঃ যোগেন্দ্র নাথ দে।

তপশীল সম্পত্তি।

(১) তাং পুটিমারী ফুলেশ্বরী মধ্যে ৪১৬৬ নং পঃ তৌঃ লিঃ ২/২৸৶ ধুর জমির কাত বাঃ ২৸০ আনা জমার জমি।
(২) তাং পুটিমারী ফুলেশ্বরী মধ্যে ৭৫২৯ নং পঃ তৌঃ লিঃ ৩৸০৶ ধুর জমি কাত বাঃ ৪৮৶ আনা জমার জমি।
(৩) তাং পুটিমারী ফুলেশ্বরী মধ্যে ৪১৭৭ নং পঃ তৌঃ লিঃ ৫৷০/০ ধুর জমির কাত বাঃ ৬৵০ আনা জমার জমি।

NAGENDRA NATH ROY, *S. S, Naib Ahilkar.*

রাজ্য কোচবিহার।

মহকুমা মেখলীগঞ্জ।

এতদ্দ্বারা সর্বসাধারণকে জানান যাইতেছে যে, ১৮৯৭ সালের কোচবিহার রাজস্বক্রান্ত নীলাম বিষয়ক আইনের ৬ ধারা (অথবা ১১ ধারা) অনুসারে রাজ্য কোচবিহারের অন্তর্গত মহকুমা মেখলীগঞ্জের এলাকাধীন নিম্নলিখিত জোত (বা জোতের অংশগুলি) বাকী রাজস্বের জন্য আগামী ইং ১৯৪৭ সনের ৪ঠা সেপ্টেম্বর, মোতাবেক ১৩৫৪ সনের ১৮ই ভাদ্র তারিখে কোচবিহার রাজ্যের উক্ত মহকুমার খাস কাছারীতে প্রকাশ্য নিলামে বিক্রয় করা হইবে।

এই সকল জোতের (বা জোতের অংশের) রাইয়ত বা অধীন প্রজাদিগকে এতদ্দ্বারা নিষেধ করা যাইতেছে যে তাহারা বাকী রাজস্ব দিবার অবধারিত শেষ দিনের পর যে খাজানা দেয় হইয়াছে তাহা বাকীদার মালিককে না দেয়; যদি দেয় তাহা হইলে এই প্রকার যে টাকা দেওয়া হইবে তাহা ক্রেতার সহিত হিসাবে তাহারা জমা পাইবার অধিকারী হইবে না। ইতি—

তৌজি নম্বর	তালুকের নাম	পরগণা ও নাম		সম্পূর্ণ জোতের জমা।	সম্পূর্ণ জোত নীলাম হইবে কিনা	কেবল মাত্র অংশ নীলাম হইলে ঐ অংশের বিবরণ।	কোন অংশ মাত্র নীলাম হইলে ঐ অংশের জমা।	সম্পূর্ণ জোত নীলাম হইলে তাহার বাকী খাজনা।	কোন অংশ মাত্র নীলাম হইলে ঐ অংশে দায়ী বাকী।
যে ৯	অমরান বরবরিয়া	যামিনীমোহন সিংহ	...	২১৯৯৶০	সমস্ত	......	.....	৮২৷৶৩	......
১০	ভোটবাড়ী	সাহাজাউদ্দিন গং	...	৪৭৮৲	অংশ	......	৩৩৫৷৶৫	...	৪৭৷/০
যা ১	বড় হলদিবাড়ী	সতীশচন্দ্র বিশ্বাস গং	...	১৩৩৬৶০	সমস্ত		.....	৩৩২৷৶৩	.....
১ক	,,	কলিমদ্দিন গং	...	৫৭৩৶০	অংশ	.....	৫৫৷১	...	২০৷৶৬
১৩	,,	এতিমন বিবি	...	১৭৭৸০	সমস্ত	.....	......	৫৪৷/০	...
১৭ব	,,	আমিউদ্দিন প্রামানিক	...	১৩৯৷/০	অংশ	......	১৩৶১	.....	৬৯
১৭গ	,,	রহিমদ্দিন গং	...	১৩১৷/০	..	.....	৬৪৷৵	......	২৪৷৶৩
২৫	,,	বছিরউদ্দিন প্রাঃ	...	১২১৶০	সমস্ত	.....	.....	৪৫৷৶০	.....
৪৫ক	,,	জহিমদ্দিন সরকার গং	...	১০৭৸০	অংশ	.....	৫৩৸/৬	......	২০৶০
৪৮	,,	আকেরবামুর সরকার গং	...	৩৩২৷/০	সমস্ত	......	......	৮৮৸০	...
৬৭	,,	সালেহা খাতুন	...	১৪৩৷৶০	অংশ	.....	৬৪৷৵	....	২৪৶৬
৬৭ক	,,	আমজেদর রহমন প্রধান	...	১৪৩৷৶০	,,	.....	৭৮৸/৪	.....	২৯৷/০

৮৭	ঐ	আ?াস্বর হোসেন প্রধান গং ...	৩১২৸৶০	সমস্ত	......	......	১৫৭৷৵	......
৮৮খ	ঐ	আফতাফউদ্দিন আহম্মদ ...	৪৩৷৶০	অংশ	......	১৮৬৷১১	......	৩৯৸/১১
৯২	ঐ	আবদুল রহমান গং ...	১৫৮৷০	ঐ	......	৭৫৶০	......	২৯৸৩
৯৫	ঐ	আবদুল রহমান ...	১৩৭৸৶০	সমস্ত	......	......	৩২৸৶০	......
১০৩	বড় বলাবিবাড়ী	বশির উদ্দিন সরকার ...	১১২৶০	সমস্ত	......	......	৫২/০	......৪
১০৭	ঐ	কছির উদ্দিন মহম্মদ গং ...	২১৫৶০	অংশ	......	১৪৮৸৶৩	......	৬০৸৶৩
১১১	ঐ	নাবর উদ্দিন গং ...	১৯১/০	ঐ	......	১৩২৵০	......	৮৸৶০
১১১ক	ঐ	অহেজুল্যা প্রামাণিক গং ...	১৩১৷/০	ঐ	......	৫৯৶০	......	২২৶০
১২৪	ঐ	আফসরউদ্দিন আহম্মদ গং ...	১১৯৶০	সমস্ত	......	......	১১৯৶৩	......
১৩১	ঐ	আমজুল রহমান ...	১২৯৲	ঐ	......	......	৪৮৷৶০	......
১৩২	ঐ	আব্বেকর রহমান প্রধান গং ...	১৮৮৲	অংশ	......	৯৩৲	......	৩৫৷০
১৪৭	বড়গৌগর	জালাল উদ্দিন মহম্মদ গং ...	২০২৸৶০	ঐ	......	৫৪৮/১১	......	১৫৷০
১৪৭খ	ঐ	মইছন বিবি গং ...	২০২৸৶০	ঐ	......	৩৶/৫	......	১৶০
১৪৭ক	ঐ	জালাল উদ্দিন মহম্মদ ...	২০২৸৶০	ঐ	......	১০৲	......	২৸৪
১৪৫	ঐ	আহার উদ্দিন আহাম্মদ ...	৩২২৸৶০	সমস্ত	......	......	১২৫৷৶৩	......
১৬০	ঐ	মোস্তফিজর রহমান বসুনীয়া ...	১৬৭৷০	ঐ	......	......	৩২৸৶৩	......
১৭০	ঐ	নিজার উদ্দিন বসুনীয়া গং ...	২৭৩৸০	ঐ	......	......	১০২৸৶৩	......
১৭১	ঐ	হবিবর রহমান বসুনীয়া গং ...	২৬৮৸/০	ঐ	......	......	১০০৸/০	......
১৭৯	ঐ	আছির উদ্দিন গং ...	১০২০	ঐ	......	......	৩৮৷৩	......
২০০	ঐ	তোজমদ্দিন পাটোয়ারী গং ...	১১৪৷৶০	ঐ	......	......	৪২৸৶৩	......
২২২	ঐ	ককর উদ্দিন মহম্মদ গং ...	১৭৫৸৶০	ঐ	......	......	৪৵৶৩	......
২৫৫	হলুদডাঙ্গা	আজিমুদ্দীন গং ...	১১৩৷০	অংশ	......	৫৫৷০	......	২০৷৶৩
২৭৬	ঐ	একাম'দ্দন গং ...	১২৫৸৶০	সমস্ত	......	......	২৩৷/০	......
৩২৩	ঐ	কৃষ্ণকুমার বসুনীয়া গং ...	১১৩/০	ঐ	......	......	৪২৷৶	......

জোতনম্বর	তালুকের নাম।	পরগণা ও নাম।	সম্পূর্ণ জোতের জমা।	সম্পূর্ণ জোত নীলাম হইবে কি না।	কেবল মাত্র অংশ নীলাম হইলে ঐ অংশের বিবরণ।	কোন অংশ মাত্র নীলাম হইলে ঐ অংশের জমা।	সম্পূর্ণ জোত নীলাম হইলে তাহার বাকী বাকী	কোন অংশ মাত্র নিলাম হইলে ঐ অংশের বাকী
৩৩৩	চুড়ইভাঙ্গা	জাফেরমামুদ সরকার গং ...	১১২৷৷০	অংশ	......	৭১৻৯	......	২৪'৵০
৩৬১ক	জ্ঞানদাস	মনসুজ্জমান প্রধান ...	১৭১৸৵০	ঐ	......	৯২৸৶৩	......	৩৭৷৶৩
৩৬০ক	”	আহাম্মদ হোসেন প্রধান গং ...	১৫৫৫৵০	”	......	২২৸৶৯	......	৮৷৶৯
৩১১ক	জ্ঞানদাস	আহাম্মদ হোসেন গং ...	১৫২৸৶০	অংশ	......	৪৩৲	......	৮৷৷৵০
৩২১ক	”	মৌঃ মোশায়েফ হোসেন প্রধান গং	১৫৫৮৶০	”	......	২৮৻৶৩	......	১০৸৶৩
৪২৮	সাবিলাবশ	সঁপরথনেছা ...	১১১৷৵০	সম্পূর্ণ	......	......	৪৭৸০	......
৩০০ক	”	আহাম্মদ হোসেন প্রধান ...	২২৩৷০	অংশ	......	১১২৷৶০	......	৪১৸৶০
৬৫১	ছোটকলিবাড়ী	ঐ গং	১০৪৷৶০	সমস্ত	......	......	১৯৸৵০	......
৬৫০	”	বকারউদ্দিন সরকার গং ...	১১৪৷৶০	”	......	......	২১৷৶৩	......
৬৬৩	”	সাবরউদ্দিন গং ...	১২৩৲	”	......	......	৪৭৷০	......
৭০১	বানীকান্ত	আছাদউদ্দিন আহাম্মদ গং ...	১৮২৷৵০	”	......	......	৬৮৷৶৩	......
৭১৮	বর্ণাজলাখালা	এরাজউদ্দিন সরকার ...	১৫১৷০	অংশ	......	৭৩৸৶৩	......	২৭৷৶৩
৭১৮ক	”	বেজু মহম্মদ গং ...	১৫৩৷০	”	......	৭৭৸৶৩	......	২৫৶৩

Kumar P. Narayan, *Naib Ahilkar.*

রাজ্য কোচবিহার।

মহকুমা মেখলীগঞ্জ।

এতদ্বারা সর্ব্বসাধারণকে জানান যাইতেছে যে, ১৮৯৭ সালের কোচবিহার রাজস্বসংক্রান্ত নীলাম বিক্রয় আইনের ৬ ধারা (অথবা ১১ ধারা) অনুসারে রাজ্য কোচবিহারের অন্তর্গত মহকুমা মেখলীগঞ্জের এলাকাধীন নিম্নলিখিত জোত (বা জোতের অংশগুলি) বাকী রাজস্বের জন্য আগামী ইং ১৯৪৭ সনের ৫ই সেপ্টেম্বর, মোতাবেক ১৩৫৪ সনের ১৯শে ভাদ্র তারিখে কোচবিহার রাজ্যের উক্ত মহকুমার খাস তহশীলের প্রকাশ্য নিলামে বিক্রয় করা হইবে।

এই সকল জোতের (বা জোতের অংশের) স্বত্বাধিকারী ও অধীন প্রজাদিগকে এতদ্বারা নিষেধ করা যাইতেছে যে, তাহারা বাকী রাজস্ব দিবার অব্যবহিত শেষ দিনের পর যে খাজানা দেয় হইয়াছে তাহা বাকীদার মালিককে না দেয়; যদি দেয় তাহা হইলে এই প্রকারে যে টাকা দেওয়া হইবে তাহা ক্রেতার সহিত হিসাবে তাহারা জমা পাইবার স্বত্ববান হইবে না।

তৌজির নং	তালুকের নাম	সরবরা ও নাম।	সম্পূর্ণ জোতের জমা।	সম্পূর্ণ জোত নীলাম হইবে কি না।	কেবল মাত্র অংশ নীলাম হইলে অংশের বিবরণ।	কোন অংশ মাত্র নিলাম হইলে ঐ অংশের জমা।	সম্পূর্ণ জোত নীলাম হইলে তাহার বাবদ বাকী।	কোন অংশ মাত্র নীলাম হইলে ঐ বাবদ বাকী।
৭৪১	খাবরণ	কফিলুলকরিম প্রধান গং ...	২৯৮/০	অংশ	......	১৪৯২৬	......	২২।/৯
৭৪৫	,,	কারাম উদ্দিন গং ...	৪০৪৸৶০	সমস্ত	......	......	১৫১৸০	......
৭৭৯	নিজতরফ	বৈদ্যনাথ মিছির গং ...	৩৬৯।০	,,	......	......	৮৷৶৩	......
৭৮৩ খ	বাজেজমা	শ্যামাচরণ গোপ ...	৩৩৩৸৶০	অংশ	......	৮১৸৶২	......	৩০॥৶৬
৭৯০	প্রাণমজুমদার	ঠাকুর সিংহমঙ্গলপ্রসাদ সিংহ ...	১৩৩২॥০	সমস্ত	......	......	৫০৫।৶০	......
৮০৩	কিসামত কতে খাঁ	আকবর উদ্দিন প্রধান ...	৫২১।৶০	অংশ	......	১৩০/৯	......	৪৮৸০৩
৮০৪	কিসামতকতেখাঁ	বছিরউদ্দিন সরকার গং ...	১৪৮।/০	সমস্ত	......	......	৩১।৶০	......
৮০৫	,,	আহমদউদ্দিন প্রধান গং ...	১২৩।/০	,,	......	......	৫৩৸০	......
৮০৭	,,	হনুমান দাস ভগৎ ...	৪৬৪/০	অংশ	......	২০৶১১	......	৭॥২
৯৩ক	হেমকুমারী	আকবরউদ্দিন সরকার গং ...	১৫৪॥/০	,,	......	৩৬৸৭	......	৯৷/৬
৯৩২	,,	কাদেচোনউদ্দিন আহাম্মদ ...	১০২॥/০	সমস্ত	......	......	৪৯॥৶৬	......
৯৩৫	,,	অজমুদ্দিন সরকার গং ...	১৭৫৶০	,,	......	......	১৭।০	......
৯৩৬	,,	মছিরউদ্দিন প্রামানিক গং ...	১৩৪৸৶০	,,	......	......	৫০॥৶০	......

জোত নং	তালুকের নাম	নাম ও পরগণা	সম্পূর্ণ জোতের জমা	সম্পূর্ণ জোত নীলাম হইল কি না	কেবল মাত্র অংশ নীলাম হইলে ঐ অংশের বিবরণ	কোন অংশ মাত্র নীলাম হইলে ঐ অংশের জমা	সম্পূর্ণ জোত নীলাম হইলে তাহার বাকী বাকী	কেবল অংশ মাত্র নীলাম হইলে ঐ অংশের বাকী বাকী
৯৯১৪	বেহুকুমারী	সাবুদ্দিন মহম্মদ প্রং ...	১১৯৬৶০	অংশ	......	৭৮৸৩	......	২১৭৶৩
২৭১৪ক	”	আলমাউদ্দিন সরকার প্রং ...	১১৯৸৵০	”	......	১২১৲৩	......	৪৫।৶৩
৯৮৭	”	জনরুদ্দিন সরকার প্রং ...	১১৮।০	সমস্ত	......	......	৪৪।৶৩	......
৯১৪	”	শুকিমউদ্দিন প্রং ...	১৪২।০	সমস্ত	......	......	১৪।৶০	......
১১৮০	”	মহিরণ নেছা বিবি ...	৬৬০।৵০	অংশ	......	৫১০৵০	......	১২৩৬০
৯৫০০ক	”	আজিজুল এসলাম চৌধুরী ...	৬৬০।৵০	”	......	৫৩০৵০	......	১২৬৬০
১৫০৪ক	”	খলিলর রহমান প্রং ...	১১১৵০	”	......	৫৫।৬	......	২৭৸৵০
১৬০১ক	”	আবু নসির আহাম্মদ প্রং ...	১১১।০	”	......	৫৫।৬	......	২০।৶০
২৬০৭	”	শেখ প্যারীকুমারী বেওয়া ...	২৪১।০	সমস্ত	......	......	৯।৶৩	......
১০০৯	”	কমিরউদ্দিন সরকার প্রং ...	৫৮১৬৵০	অংশ	......	২১৬৸৵০	......	৮১।৩
১০০৩	”	খানকুল্যা মহম্মদ প্রং ...	১০৭৶০	সমস্ত	......	......	৫১।৶০	......
৩০১০	”	মোবারকউদ্দিন প্রধান প্রং ...	৪০৮৲	অংশ	......	১৯১৵৩	......	৫৫৶
১০১০ক	”	মহরুল্যা সরকার প্রং ...	৪০৮৲	”	......	১০১৲	......	৫৯৵০
১৬১০খ	”	আজিজুল বর্মণ প্রং ...	৪০৮৲	”	......	৩১৸৵৩	......	১৪৸৶০
১০১০খ	”	বিনাক বর্মণ প্রং ...	৪০৮৲	”	......	৫৫৲	......	১৬৵০
১১১৭	”	আসমতুল্যা প্রাং ...	১১৫৬৵০	সমস্ত	......	......	৪০।৶০	......
১১২০	”	আকবরউদ্দিন প্রং ...	৩৫৮।৵০	অংশ	......	১৬৯৸৵৭	......	৫৩৮
১১২০ক	”	হকিম উদ্দিন প্রাং ...	৩৫৮৵০	”	......	৪১।৶৫	......	১৮।৯
১১২০খ,গ	”	হাসমউদ্দিন প্রং ...	৩৫৮৵০	”	......	২৬৬৵৩	......	৩৬৵০
১১২০ঘ	”	পি চাঁদমামুদ প্রং ...	৩৫০।৵০	”	......	১৮।৬	......	৭৵৩
১১৪১	”	ঠাঃ শিউরতন প্রসাদ সিংহ ...	১০২৯৶০	সমস্ত	......	......	৩৮৭৶০	......

১১৪২	,,	জিয়াবুদ্দিন গং	...	১৭১।৶০	অংশ	......	৮৩৬	......	৩১।/৬
১১৪২ক	,,	কেরামতুল্যা প্রাঃ	...	১৭২।৶০	,,	......	৬৬।/০	......	২৪৸/৬
১১৪২খ	,,	গিরধারী গং	...	১৭২৷।/০	,,	......	২২৸/০	......	৮৷।/০
১১৪৪ক	,,	নসিরউদ্দিন সরকার গং	...	১৭৭৷৶০	,,	......	৩৪৫	......	১২৮০
১১৪৪খ	,,	ঐ	...	১৭৭৸৶০	,,	......	৩৪৫	......	১২৮০
১১৪৪গ	,,	আমিনউদ্দিন মন্ডল গং	...	১৭৭৸৶	,,	......	৩৪৫	......	১২৮০
১১৪৫	,,	মনসুরউদ্দিন গং	...	১২১৶০	সমস্ত	......	......	৪৪৫০	......
১১৪৬	,,	ঠাঃ শিউনন্দন প্রসাদ সিংহ	...	৮৭৭৷০	,,	......	......	৩২১।৬	......
১১৪৪	মধুরাম	কলিমউদ্দিন গং	...	১৬৭৶০	অংশ	......	১১১৷৮	......	৫২৷/০
১১৪৩	দক্ষিণ	কৃষ্ণমোহন সিংহ গং	...	৩১৮৮/০	সম্পূর্ণ	...		১৪৩৸৬	...

Kumar P Narayan, *Naib Ahilkar.*

রাজ্য কোচবিহার

মহকুমা মেখলীগঞ্জ।

এতদ্বারা সর্বসাধারণকে জানান যাইতেছে যে, ১৮৯১ সনের কোচবিহার রাজস্ব-সংক্রান্ত নীলাম বিষয়ক আইনের ৩ ধারা (অথবা ১১ ধারা) অনুসারে রাজ্য কোচবিহারের অন্তর্গত মহকুমা মেখলীগঞ্জের এলাকাধীন নিম্নলিখিত জোত (বা জোতের অংশগুলি) বাকী রাজস্বের জন্য আগামী ইং ১৯৪৭ সনের ৩ই সেপ্টেম্বর, মোতাবেক ১৩৫৪ সনের ২০শে ভাদ্র তারিখে কোচবিহার রাজ্যের উক্ত মহকুমার মাল কাছারীতে প্রকাশ্য নিলাম বিক্রয় করা হইবে।

এই সকল জোতের (বা জোতের অংশের) রাইয়ত বা অধীন প্রজাদিগকে এতদ্বারা নিষেধ করা যাইতেছে যে তাহারা বাকী রাজস্ব বিষয় অব্যবহিত শেষ কিস্তির পর যে খাজানা দেয় হইয়াছে তাহা বাকীদার মালিককে না দেয়; যদি দেয় তাহা হইলে এই প্রকার যে টাকা দেওয়া হইবে তাহা ক্রেতার সহিত হিসাবে তাহারা জমা পাইবার হকদার হইবে না। ইতি—

জোতের নম্বর	তালুকের নাম	মালগুজার ও নাম	সম্পূর্ণ জোতের জমা।	সম্পূর্ণ জোত নীলাম হইবে কি না	কেবল মাত্র অংশ নীলাম হইলে ঐ অংশের বয়ান।	কোন অংশ মাত্র নীলাম হইলে ঐ অংশের জমা।	সম্পূর্ণ জোত নীলাম হইলে তাহার বাকী রাজস্ব।	কোন অংশ মাত্র নীলাম হইলে ঐ অংশে বাকী রাজস্ব।
১১৩৪	হরিবন	পরশ বর্মণ গং ...	১০২৵০	সমস্ত	......	......	৪৪৸৬	......
১১৩৫	"	পরমানন্দ গীর সন্ন্যাসী গং ...	২২৪।০	"	......	......	৬৩৶৬	......
১২২৫	হরিণচরা	সুরসুন্দরী চৌধুরাণী গং ...	১১১।০	"	......	......	৫১৵৬	......
১২২৬	নিজ মেখলীগঞ্জ	মোঃ বেগম সফিউন্নিছা ...	২৮৮৶০	অংশ	......	১৩৪৷৵৬	......	২৭৵৬
১২২৬ক	"	যোগেন্দ্রনাথ রায় ...	২৮০৶০	"	......	১৩৪৷৴৮	......	২৭।০
১৩০২	"	রুক্মিণীমোহন সিংহ সরকার গং ...	১১০০০	সম্পূর্ণ	......	......	৩৪৷৵০	......
১৩০৩	"	কিশোরীমোহন রায় সরকার গং	২০৪৸৶০	"	......	......	৬৮৸৶৬	......
১২৩৭	"	লোথা মহম্মদ গং ...	১৫০।০	"	......	......	৪৩৸০	......
১২৪১	"	সদানন্দ প্রামাণিক গং ...	১৭৩।০	"	......	......	৫২।৶৬	......
১২৪০ক	"	সুরসুন্দরী চৌধুরাণী গং ...	১১৪৸০	অংশ	......	৭০৶৬	......	২৭৸৶৬
১৩৪৭	"	ত্রৈলোক্যনাথ সিংহ সরকার গং	১৩১।০	সম্পূর্ণ	......	......	২৬৸৶৬	......
১২১২	মেখলীগঞ্জ	ইব্রাহেম ওস্তা ...	২৪৪৸৶০	"	......	......	৬৪৸৶৬	......

১২৩৩ক	,,	হেমেন্দ্র সিংহ সরকার গং ...	১৭১.০	অংশ	......	৫৩।/৬	......	২০.৬
১২৯৬	,,	রামকিশোর অধিকারী গং	২০২।৵০	,,	...	১০১।৵৩	......	৪।৩
১২৯৬ক	,,	প্রমথনাথ অধিকারী গং ...	২০২॥০	,,	......	২৭৶০	......	১০।৮
১২৯৬খ	,,	অ:তারণ অধিকারী গং ...	২০২৸/০	,,	......	২২৬	......	৮৶০
১২৯৬গ	,,	তরুবালা দত্ত ...	২০২৸৶০	,,	......	১৮।০	......	৬৸০
১৩১৮	নিজ হস্তক	ব্রজকিশোর সেন গং ...	১০:॥০	সমস্ত	......	......	২৬৸০	......
১৩২২	,,	চন্দ্র বর্ম্মণ গং ...	১১০॥০	অংশ	......	১৫৭৸৭	......	৫৫৫৩
১৩২৫খ	,,	দিগেন্দ্র বর্ম্মণ গং ...	৩১০॥০	,,	......	৩২।/৬	......	১৯৶০
১৩২৫গ	,,	কেওয়ানশরী বর্ম্মণী গং ...	৩১০॥০	,,	......	৬৪।৶০	......	২৪।০
১৩২৬	,,	সোমল ডাগা গং ...	১২১৮৲০	সমস্ত	......	......	৪৪॥৶৬	......
১৩৫৩	,,	রমণীমোহন বর্ম্মণ গং ...	১৪০৲০	,,	......	......	৫০৶০	......
১৩৬১	,,	গঙ্গামোহন বর্ম্মণ গং ...	১০২৸৶০	,,	......	......	২৪৸৬	......
১৩৬২ক	,,	ত্রৈলোক্যনাথ সিংহ গং ...	৬৮৩॥০	অংশ	......	৪৭৸৶০	......	১৭৸/৬
১৩৬৪	নিজতরফ	কৃষ্ণমোহন সিংহ গং ...	৪৬৪।/০	সমস্ত	......	......	১৪৫৸/৬	......
১৩৬৬	,,	রমেন্দ্রনারায়ণ সিংহ ...	২০৬॥০	,,	......	......	৭২৵৩	......
১৩৬৮ক	,,	কৃষ্ণমোহন সিংহ গং ...	২১৮৸৶০	অংশ	......	১২৪৶০	......	২৬।০
১৩৭২	,,	ঐ	৫২৩৮০	সমস্ত	......	......	১৮২।৶৬	......
১৩৭৩	,,	বিশ্বনাথ সিংহ গং ...	২৩৮৸৶০	,,	......	......	৮২৸/৬	......
১৩৭৬	,,	অজিতকুমার সাহা গং ...	২৬৫।/০	,,	......	......	৪৪৵৬	......
৬৮৩	,,	বানী দাস গং ...	২৬৬৲/০	,,	......	......	৩৩৶৬	......
১৩৯০	,,	ইন্দ্রদেব ওঝা ...	২৩৫৲/০	,,	......	......	৬৪/৬	......
১৩৯৫	,,	অম্বিকাচন্দ্র দাস গং ...	১৩৮॥০	,,	......	......	৭॥৶১	......
১৩৯৭	,,	রাজমোহন বর্ম্মণ গং ...	১৪১৮০	,,	......	......	১৪।৵৬	......
১৩৯৮	,,	ন.দাস গং ...	১২৪॥৶০	,,	......	......	৩৮৲	......

জোতের নং	তালুকের নাম।	নাম ও পরগণা।	সম্পূর্ণ জোতের জমা।	সম্পূর্ণ জোত নীলাম হইবে কি না।	কেবল মাত্র অংশ নীলাম হইলে ঐ অংশের বিবরণ।	যে যে অংশ মাত্র নীলাম হইলে ঐ অংশের জমা।	সম্পূর্ণ জোত নীলাম হই তাহার বাবদ বাকী।	কোন অংশ মাত্র নীলাম হইলে ঐ অংশের বাবদ বাকী।
১০৯৯	নিজতরফ	বসন্ত নাই গং ...	২০১৮/০	,,	......	......	৯৮০/১	......
১৪০২ক	,,	কৃষ্ণমোহন সিংহ গং ...	২১৩৮০/০	অংশ	......	১০১৮/০	......	২৯৪/৬
১৪০৬	,,	সাহাবউদ্দিন সরকার গং ...	১৫০৮০/০	সমস্ত	......	......	৫৬১/৯	......
১৪০৮	,,	পরমানন্দগীর সন্ন্যাসী গং	৩০৪০/০	,,	......	......	১১৪৫৬	......
১৪১৫	,,	ছৈয়দ রহমান গং ...	২১১১/০	,,	......	......	১০৫৮	......
১৪১৯ক	জানকাটা অধিকারী	রাধে ব্রজনাথ রায় গং ...	২০৩৲	অংশ	......	৩৭৪/০	......	২৪৫/০
১৪৫৩	বাড়সিংহেশ্বর	চন্দ্রমোহন রায় গং ...	১৮০।০	সমস্ত	......	......	৩৭৪/০	......
১৪৭৮	,,	জগন্মোহন বর্ম্মণ গং ...	১৭৭।/০	,,	......	......	৪৫০/৬	......
১৪৩৮	কুমপাড়াবরী	রাধেশ্বরপ্রসাদ সিংহ ...	৩।৯৫০	অংশ	......	২৪৪।০	......	২৫৫/০
১৪৪০	,,	কামিনী দুলাল ...	২৫১১/০	সমস্ত	......	......	৩৫০/৬	......
১৪৪১	ঐ	মুকুন্দমোহন সিংহ সরকার গং ...	১২৩/০	,,	......	......	১৪০/৭	......
১৫০৩ক	কুমপাড়াবরী	যামিনীসুন্দরী ঘোষ	১৩৪১/০	অংশ	......	৪১।/০	......	১৫৪৭
১৫০৭	,,	রূপনাথ বর্ম্মণ গং ...	১০৫৯০	,,	......	৭২৯০/০	......	৭৯০৩
১৫০৭ক	,,	বেহারা কর্ম্মা গং ...	১০৫৯০	,,	......	১৩৭০	......	৫১০/৬
১৫৩৮	,,	করিমউদ্দিন গং ...	১৩৫৪।০	,,	......	৩৬৯৬	......	২৯০/৬
১৫৭৮	,,	হরকান্ত সরকার ...	১২১৯০/০	সমস্ত	......	......	৭১৯০/৬	......
১৫৮৭	,,	মুকুন্দমোহন সিংহ সরকার গং ...	৩১১৪/০	,,	......	......	১১৯০০/০	......
১৫৯২	কুমপাড়াবরী কালীরাবাড়ী	ব্রজনাথ বর্ম্মণ ...	১৬৭৫০/০	,,	......	......	১৪।০৮	......
১৫৯৩	বড় কুচলীবাড়ী	মেহরা রায় গং ...	১৫২৯/০	সমস্ত	......	......	৫৬/৬	......
১৬০৫	,,	সতীশচন্দ্র বিশ্বাস গং ...	২৫২৲	,,	......	......	২০৭০	......
১৬১৮	উ. কুচলীবাড়ী	সাহাবউদ্দিন মহম্মদ ...	১৫০১/০	,,	......	......	৪৯০/০	......

১৬৫১	”	মনজারি বিবি গং ...	১৫০৲	অংশ	......	১১৫৸/৩	......	৪৩৸/০
১৬৫৪	”	নৈমুদ্দিন মোক্তাজোর ...	১৩৩।৶/০	সমস্ত	......	......	৩৪৪৸	......
১৬৫৭	”	আদরিনী সরকার ...	১০৯।/০	অংশ	......	৫৪৪৸/৩	......	২০।০
১৬৬৮	”	নিয়ামতুল্যা মহম্মদ গং ...	১৩০।৸/০	”	......	৬৫।/০	......	৩২।০
১৬৬৯	”	বাদশাজাদি বিবি ...	১৩২৪৸/০	সমস্ত	......	......	৪৩৸৶	......
১৬৯০	”	প্রতাপচন্দ্র মিশ্র গং ...	৩১১৯৸/০	”	......	......	৫৩৯৸/৩	......
১৬৯৭	অং কুশলীবাড়ী	রহমানআলী বসুনীয়া ...	১২৩৸/০	”	......	......	৪৩৸/০	......
১৭০৪	বড়খড়িয়া	বাণেশ্বর ওঝা ...	৩৫১৶/০	”	......	......	১৩১।৶/৩	......
১৭০৭	”	অনু:সুন্দরী দাস্যা গং ...	৪২.৸/০	”	......	......	১৫৮৶/৩	......
১৭০৮	”	লাল বাহাদুর ওঝা গং ...	৩৪৭৸/০	”	......	......	১৩০৲৩	......
১৭৪৭	”	পঙ্কজকুমার সিংহ গং ...	১৪৮৸/০	”	......	......	২৭৸/০	......
১৭৫২	ভোটবাড়ী	গোবিন্দচন্দ্র অধিকারী ...	১২১৶/০	”	......	......	৫৪।৶/৩	......
১৭৫৩	”	মুকুন্দমোহন সিংহ সরকার গং ...	৫০০/০	”	......	......	১৮৭॥৩	......
১৭৫৭	”	যতীন্দ্রনাথ সরকার ...	১৩৪৸/০	অংশ	......	৩১/৩	......	১১।৶/৩
১৭৫৭	”	মুক্তামোহন সরকার ...	১৩৪৸/০	”	......	৮২৶/৩	......	৫৸/৩
১৭৮৩	বোক্সনাবান্ধা	সতীশচন্দ্র গুহ ...	২৫২।৶/০	সমস্ত	......	......	৯৪॥৶/০	......
১৭৯২	ভোটবাড়ী	ভোলা মহম্মদ গং ...	১৭ ।০	”	......	......	৬৯৶/০	......
১৭৯৫	”	কৃষ্ণমোহন সিংহ ...	১১৮৲	”	......	......	২৪॥/০	......
১৭৯৭	”	গোবর্দ্ধন ওঝা গং ...	১৭২।৶/০	”	......	......	৬৪॥৶/০	......
১৮০৩	”	ঐ ...	২২২।৶/০	”	......	......	৮৭॥৩	......
১৮০৫	”	কৃষ্ণমোহন সিংহ গং ...	২১১।৶/০	”	......	......	৫৯৲৩	......
১৮০৬	”	বেদান্ত দাস গং ...	১৬৭॥/০	”	......	......	৫৸৩	......
১৮০৯	”	বৈজনাথ ওঝা গং ...	১৭৫৶/০	”	......	......	৩।৸/০	......
১৮১১	”	মালুয়া মহম্মদ গং ...	১১৪৸০	”	......	......	৪৩৲৩	......
১৮১৭	”	দেবকুমার সিংহ গং ...	২৪২৲	”	......	......	২৩।/:১	......
১৮১৮	”	কৃষ্ণমোহন সিংহ গং ...	২০৯৸/০		......	......	২১৶/৩	

KUMAR P. NARAYAN, *Naib Ahilkar.*

রাজ্য কোচবিহার

মহকুমা মেখলীগঞ্জ।

এতদ্বারা সর্বসাধারণকে জানান যাইতেছে যে, ১৮৯৭ সালের কোচবিহার রাজস্ব সংক্রান্ত নীলামবিষয়ক আইনের ৬ ধারা (অথবা ১১ ধারা) অনুসারে রাজ্য কোচবিহারের অন্তর্গত মহকুমা মেখলীগঞ্জের এলাকাধীন নিম্নলিখিত জোত (বা জোতের অংশগুলি) বাকী রাজস্বের জন্য আগামী ১৩২৪ সনের ৮ই সেপ্টেম্বর মোতাবেক ১৩২৪ সনের ২২শে ভাদ্র তারিখে উক্ত মহকুমার মালকাছারীতে প্রকাশ্য নিলামে বিক্রয় হইবে।

এই সকল জোতের (বা জোতের অংশের) মালিক বা অধীন প্রজাদিগকে এতদ্বারা নিষেধ করা যাইতেছে তাহারা বাকী রাজস্ব দিবার অব্যবহিত শেষ দিনের পর যে খাজানা দেয় হইয়াছে তাহা বাকীদার মালিককে না দেন; যদি দেন তাহা হইলে এই প্রকার যে টাকা দেওয়া হইবে তাহা ক্রেতার সহিত হিসাবে তাহারা জমা পাইবার হকদার হইবে না। ইতি—

তৌজীর নম্বর।	তালুকের নাম।	[illegible] ও নাম।	সম্পূর্ণ জোতের জমা।	সম্পূর্ণ জোত নীলাম হইবে কি না।	কেবল মাত্র অংশ নীলাম হইলে ঐ অংশের বিবরণ	কোন অংশ মাত্র নীলাম হইলে ঐ অংশের জমা।	সম্পূর্ণ জোত নীলাম হইলে তাহার বাকী রাজস্ব	কোন অংশ মাত্র নীলাম হইলে ঐ অংশের বাকী রাজস্ব
১৮২৩	জোড়াবাড়ী	কিশোরীমোহন রায় সরকার ...	৩০৯৸০	সমস্ত	......	......	১১৷৶০	......
১৮৯১	"	আনন্দমোহন সিংহ প্রঃ	২৩৮৸৶০	অংশ	......	২০৬৶১	......	৩৬৷০
১৬৩২	পাঠানপাড়া	কিশোরীমোহন রায় সরকার ...	১৭১১৶০	সমস্ত	......	......	৬০৷৶০	......
১৯০৪	ধুঁপিয়া খলিশা	[illegible] প্রঃ ..	৩৪৮৶০	"	......	......	৷৶০	......
১৯১৭	[illegible]	[illegible] রায় ...	১৮১১৶০	অংশ	......	২০৮৶০	......	২৪১০
[illegible]	বাউ সারিষা	[illegible] রায় সরকার ...	২১০৶০	সমস্ত	......	......	৪১।৶০	......
[illegible]	বালিকা গোপালপুর	[illegible] প্রঃ ...	৩৪১৸০	"	......	......	১২৮৶০	......
[illegible]	বালিকাবাড়ী হসজপুর	[illegible] সিংহ ...	১১৬৩৶০	"	......	......	২০৷৶০	......
[illegible]	ধবলা [illegible]বাড়ী	[illegible] দেবী প্রঃ ...	১৪১৲	অংশ	......	১২৭৶৪	......	৪৪৸০
[illegible]	"	[illegible] রায় ...	৪৪২৷৶০	সমস্ত	......	......	১১৪৷৶০	......
[illegible]	"	মাঃ চৌঃ [illegible] প্রঃ	৮৪৩৷০	"	......	......	৩১২৶০	......
১০১৬	"	দুর্গাচরণ আগড়ওয়ালা ...	৪৫৯৸০	"	......	......	১৭৪।৶০	......
১০১৮	"	[illegible] আগড়ওয়ালা ...	২৩৶০	"	......	......	১০২৷৶০	......

২০১১	,,	মহির উদ্দিন মহম্মদ গং ...	১০২৶০	অংশ	......	৩২৸৵৩	......	৫৩
২০১১ক	,,	আহম্মদ আলী সরকার গং ...	১০৫৶০	,,	......	৬৩৸৵৩	......	২৯৶
২১০১	,,	মহির উদ্দিন সরকার ...	১৮৷০	সমগ্র	......	......	৪০৸৵০	......
২১৬৮	কোটভাজনী	বিবি জরিমন নেছা ...	২১৭৸৵০	,,	......	......	১০০৵৬	......
২১৬০	বাগাপাড়া বাগডাবাড়ী	হরপ্রসাদ চক্রবর্ত্তী গং ...	১০৫৸৵০	,,	......	......	৫৯৵৩	......
২২১৮	বেউগাড়াঙ্গা	মদনমোহন বক্সী ...	৯০১৵০	,,	......	......	৫৫৮৶৵৬	......
২২২২	,,	মনমোহন রায় গং ...	১০৪৩৶৵০	,,	......	......	৩১৷৬	......
২২৪২	কাকলদিঘী	হেমন্তকুমার রায় ...	২৮৪৷৶০	,,	......	......	১০৩৸৶৬	......
২৪৮১	শালবাড়ী	মদনমোহন বক্সী ...	৩৬২৲	,,	......	......	১৪৫৸০	......
২২৮৪	,,	রামচাঁদ দাস ...	১২২৸০	,,	......	......	৪৫৶৵০	......
২৩৩০	দৈখাতা	আবদুল কাদের মন্ডল গং ...	১১৪৷৵০	,,	......	......	৪২৸৶৬	......
২৩৫১	শিবাবাড়ী	আবদুল গফুর গং ...	৫২৬৶০	,,	......	......	১৪৮৸৬	......
২৩৯৫	২য় খণ্ড শিবাবাড়ী	ঠাঃ শিউমঙ্গল প্রসাদ সিংহ ...	১১৫৪৷৵০	,,	......	......	৪৩২৸৵৩	......
২৪১১	ডিঙ্গাদহের গরজী	মুকুন্দমোহন সিংহ সরকার গং	১৬৭৸৶০	,,	......	......	৩৫,০	......
২৫১৭	অমরাজন জুজলীবাড়ী	হাকিম উদ্দিন মোক্তার গং ...	১৩২৸৵০	,,	......	......	৩১৶৬	......
৪৩৭৮	চাংরাবান্ধা বন্দর	সফিরণ বিবি ...	১০৪৸৶০	,,	......	......	৩৯৶৬	......
৯৪২	,,	চাংরাবান্ধা রাইস মিল ...	৫২৩৸৵০	,,	......	......	১১৯৷৶০	......

KUMAR P. NHRAYAN, *Naib Ahilkar*.

ইং ১৯১০ সালের ৫ আইনের ৫৩ ধারার ২ প্রকরণ মতে নিলামী ইস্তাহার।

রাজ্য কোচবিহারের এঃ সিঃ জজ আদালত।

এতদ্বারা সর্ব্বসাধারণকে জানান যাইতেছে যে, প্রতিবাদীর দাবীর বাকী থাকা আদায় না করায় তাহার নিম্নলিখিত ক্রোকী সম্পত্তি আগামী ১৩৫৪ সনের ১৯শে আশ্বিন মোতাবেক ১৯৪৭ সনের ৬ই অক্টোবর, তারিখে বেলা ১ ঘটিকার সময় প্রকাশ্য নীলাম আরম্ভ হইবে।

৯১ নং ১৯৪৭।৪৮ ইং। ম্যাঃ খাঃ ২২৪৵০ মোঃ।

ডিঃ—দি কুচবিহার ব্যাঙ্কিং কর্পোরেশন লিঃ মোঃ রেহায়।

দেঃ—রামকুমার দাস সাং ব্রহ্মত্তর কশালডাঙ্গা।

তপশিল সম্পত্তি।

১নং বেহার ৮২৮নং থাক তাং ব্রহ্মত্তর কশালডাঙ্গা ১০১নং খত ৪৭।৵ দুর জমির জাত বার্ষিক ২৷৵০ আনা জমার কৃষি প্রজা স্বত্ব।

F. AHMED, *offg. Ass., Civil Judge.*

৺জয়নী ধর্ম্ম স্তলী জয়

The Cooch Behar Gazette.

১৫ই ভাদ্র, সোমবার ; MONDAY, SEPTEMBER 1, 1947 [১৩৫৪ সাল ৪৩৮ রাজশক

PART II.

NOTICES.

ইং ১৯১০ সালের ৫ আইনের ৫৩ ধারার ২ প্রকরণ মতে নিলামী ইস্তাহার

রাজ্য কোচবিহারের এঃ সিঃ জং আদালত।

এতদ্বারা সর্ব্বসাধারণকে জানান যাইতেছে যে, প্রাপ্তব্যের দাবীর বাকী খাজানা আদায় না হওয়ায় তাহার নিম্নলিখিত ক্রোকী সম্পত্তি আগামী ১৩৫৪ সনের ১৯শে আশ্বিন মোতাবেক ১৯৪৭ সনের ৬ই অক্টোবর তারিখে বেলা ১ ঘটিকার সময় প্রকাশ্য নিলাম আরম্ভ হইবে।

৯১ নং ১৯৪৭।৪৮ ইং। বাঃ খাঃ ২২৮/০ মোঃ।

ডিঃ—দি কুচবিহার ব্যাঙ্কিং করপোরেশন লিমিটেড, মোঃ মেখলীগঞ্জ।

দেঃ—রামকুমার দাস সাং ব্রঃ কশালডাঙ্গা।

তপশিল সম্পত্তি।

পঃ মেখলীগঞ্জ ৮২৮ নং খাক তাং ব্রহ্মত্তর কশালডাঙ্গা মধ্যে ৪২।/০ খুব জমির কাত বাঃ ২৵০ আনা জমার প্রজা স্বত্ব জমি।

F. AHMED, *Offg. Asst. Civil Judge.*

দেওয়ানী কার্য্যবিধি আইনের ২১ হুকুম, ৬৬ নিয়মের ঘোষণাপত্র।

রাজ্য কোচবিহারের এঃ সিঃ জজ আদালত।

এতদ্বারা সর্ব্বসাধারণকে জানান যাইতেছে যে, দাবীকগণের নিম্নলিখিত সম্পত্তি আগামী ১৯৪৭ সনের ৬ই অক্টোবর মোঃ ১৩৫৪ সনের ১৯শে আশ্বিন তারিখে দিবা ১২ ঘটিকার সময় প্রকাশ্য নিলাম আরম্ভ হইবে।

১২ নং ১৯৪৭।৪৮ ইং। বাঃ ডিঃ ১২৫৭।৶০ মোঃ।

ডিঃ—বীরেন্দ্রচন্দ্র মিত্র সাং কলিকাতা।

দেঃ—মদন মোহন সাং গোপালপুর।

তপশিল সম্পত্তি।

১। পঃ মেখলীগঞ্জ ১৮৮ নং খাক তাং খাজিনা গোপালপুর মধ্যে ১৯৭৮ নং তৌঃ সিঃ ৫৯।১৪৵০ খুব জমির কাত বাঃ ৭০।৶০ আনা জমার চুকানা স্বত্ব।

২। পঃ মেখলীগঞ্জ ১৮৮ নং খাক তাং গোপালপুর মধ্যে ৯১২ নং তৌঃ সিঃ ৩৬।১৬৵০ খুব জমির কাত বাঃ ১৮।৶০ আনা জমার চুকানী স্বত্ব।

৩। পঃ মেখলীগঞ্জ ১৮৮ নং খাক তাং গোপালপুর মধ্যে ১২৫৫ নং তৌঃ সিঃ ৭১/০১৵০ খুব জমির কাত বাঃ ২৫।০ আনা জমার চুকানী স্বত্ব।

F. AHMED, *Asst. Civil Judge.*

রাজ্য কোচবিহার।

মহকুমা তুফানগঞ্জ।

এতদ্দ্বারা সর্ব্বসাধারণকে জানান যাইতেছে যে, ১৮৯৭ সালের কোচবিহার রাজস্ব সংক্রান্ত নীলাম বিষয়ক আইনের ৬ ধারা (অথবা ১১ ধারা) অনুসারে রাজ্য কোচবিহারের অন্তর্গত মহকুমা তুফানগঞ্জের এলাকাধীন নিম্নলিখিত জোত (বা জোতের অংশগুলি) বাকী রাজস্বের জন্য আগামী ইং ১৯৪৭ সনের ৩রা সেপ্টেম্বর মোতাবেক ১৩৫৪ সনের ১৭ই ভাদ্র তারিখে কোচবিহার রাজ্যের উক্ত মহকুমার মাল কাছারীতে প্রকাশ্য নিলামে বিক্রয় করা হইবে।

ঐ সকল জোতের (বা জোতের অংশের) রায়ত ও অধীন প্রজাদিগকে এতদ্দ্বারা নিষেধ করা যাইতেছে যে, তাহারা বাকী রাজস্ব দিবার অব্যবহিত শেষ দিনের পর যে খাজানা দেয় হইয়াছে তাহা বাকীদার মালিককে না দেয়; যদি দেয় তাহা হইলে ঐ প্রকারে যে টাকা দেওয়া হইবে তাহা ক্রেতার প্রতি হিসাবে তাহারা জমা পাইবার হকদার হইবে না।

ক্রমিক নং	তালুকের নাম	প্রজার নাম।		সম্পূর্ণ জোতের জমা।	সম্পূর্ণ জোত নিলামে বিক্রয় হইবে কি না।	কেবল মাত্র অংশ বিক্রয় হইলে ঐ অংশের পরিমাণ।	কেবল মাত্র অংশ বিক্রয় হইলে ঐ অংশের জমা।	সম্পূর্ণ জোত বিক্রয় হইলে তাহার বাকী।	কেবল অংশ বিক্রয় হইলে ঐ অংশের বাকী।
১ ষোঃ	ভুরকুম	আবদুল রহিম মিঞা	...	১০৮৸/৪	সমস্ত	...	....	৪০৸/৩	
৭ নেং	বড়াডাঙ্গা	প্রফুল্লকুমার সরকার গং	...	১৬৩/০	"	...		৬৬৸/৫	...
১৭	চং খং ভেলাকোবা	মানীকচাঁদ ওসোয়াল	...	২২৪৷০	"			৮৪৶০	......
১৭	যোগারকুঠী	হেমেন্দ্র নারায়ণ মণ্ডল	...	১৯৮৸০	"			৭৪৷০	
৯৬	বিলদহালা	মাতাদিন দাস গং	...	১১৫৷০	"	......		৪০৷/০	
৯৭	ঐ	ইউছুফ উদ্দিন গং	...	১৭৮৶০	"	...	....	৬৬৸/২	......
১৩৩ নেং	মাজারকুঠী	কালু দাস	...	১১২৷/০	"	..	.....	৪২৶৩	......
৭১৫	ঐ	প্রফুল্লকুমার সরকার গং	...	১৪৮৸/০	"	...	......	৫৫৷৶৪	
১৬০	মাকলাই	মঙ্গলদাস ব্যাপারী গং	...	১২০৸০	"	.....		৭১৷০	
১৭১	চোপগুড়ী	ঈশ্বরচাঁদ মণ্ডল	...	১৫৪৷৶০	"	.. ....	......	৫৭৸/৩	...
১৮০	বেঃ চান্ডালবারী	সতীশচন্দ্র দাস গং	...	২৫৫৸৶০	"	... .	...	১৫৸৶৪	......
২১৭	বালাকুঠী	জলধর মিত্র	...	১৫৬৬৸/০	"		.....	৫৮৸৶৩	......
১০ খাঃ	বড়াডাঙ্গা	বালচাঁদ ভাদানী গং	...	২৪৫৫৷/০	"	....	......	৯২০৸৩	...

৪১	৫: খ: ভেলাকোবা	আছানউল্লা আকান্দ ...	১৭৪।৶০	..		—	৩৫।৶	......
৩৭৪	বলরামপুর	বোনা শেখ গং ..	১২৬৲	.		... ..	৪৭৷১০	......
৩৮১	ঐ	বৃন্দাবন দাস গং ...	১৫৫/০	.		.. ..	৫৮৵৫	.. .
৩৯১	ঐ	শ্যামাচরণ দাস গং ...	১২১।৶০				৪৫।৶	

H. BARMA, *Naib Ahilkar*.

রাজ্য কোচবিহার।

মহকুমা তুফানগঞ্জ।

এতদ্বারা সর্বসাধারণকে জানান যাইতেছে যে, ১৮৯৭ সালের কোচবিহার রাজস্বসংক্রান্ত নীলাম বিষয়ক আইনের ৭ ধারা (অথবা ১১ ধারা) অনুসারে রাজ্য কোচবিহারের অন্তর্গত মহকুমা তুফানগঞ্জের [illegible] তালুকের নিম্নলিখিত জোত (বা জোতের অংশগুলি) ১৫১ রাজস্বের জন্য আগামী ইং ১৯৪৭ সনের ৪ঠা সেপ্টেম্বর, মোতাবেক ১৩৫৪ সালের ১৮ই ভাদ্র তারিখে কোচবিহার রাজ্যের উক্ত মহকুমার [illegible] কাছারীতে প্রকাশ্য নীলামে বিক্রয় হইবে।

এই সকল জোতের (বা জোতের অংশের) রাইয়ত ও অধীন প্রজাদিগকে এতদ্বারা নিষেধ করা যাইতেছে যে, তাহারা বাকী রাজস্ব দিবার অব্যবহিত শেষ দিনের পর যে খাজানা দেয় হইবে তাহা বাকীদার মালিককে না দেয়: যদি দেয় তাহা হইলে এই প্রকারের যে টাকা দেওয়া হইবে তাহা ক্রেতার দাবীর বিরুদ্ধে হিসাবে তাহারা জমা পাইবার হকদার হইবে না। ইতি—

জোত নং	তালুকের নাম	মালিকের নাম	সম্পূর্ণ জোতের জমা	সম্পূর্ণ জোত নীলাম হইবে কি না	কেবল মাত্র অংশ নীলাম হইলে ঐ অংশের বিশেষ বিবরণ।	কোন অংশ মাত্র নীলাম হইলে ঐ অংশের জমা।	সম্পূর্ণ জোত নীলাম হইলে বাকী	কোন অংশ মাত্র নীলাম হইলে ঐ অংশের বাবদ বাকী
৩০৪৪	সোনাখুলী	শরৎচন্দ্র মণ্ডল ...	১৭৯৶	সমস্ত	...	...	১৩৸৹	...
৪৭	দেওচড়াই	সর্বানন্দ ব্যাপারী ...	৩৩৩৶৹	,,	...	...	১২৫/৫	...
৭০	,, ...	হরকান্ত ব্যাপারী ...	১৪৭৸৹	,,	...	...	৫৫।৶২	...
৯৯	মহাভারপুর	সর্বানন্দ ব্যাপারী ...	১৫১৸৹	,,	...	...	৫৩৸৶৩	...
১০৮	বলরামী	মহানন্দ পাল গং ...	২০০৶৹	,,	...	...	৩৭৸১১	...
১০৯	,, ...	সুশীলকুমার সান্যাল	১০১৸৶৹	,,	...	...	৪৯।৮	...
১১৩ক	,,	মহিকান্ত দেবশর্মা গং ...	১৭৮৶৹	অংশ	...	১১৬৩৸৶৹	...	৪৪৶৩
১১৭	,, ...	হরকান্ত ব্যাপারী ...	২২৩৸৶৹	সমস্ত	...	...	৪১৸৶১১	...
৭৭৮	বালিবাদ	সরৎবাবু বাদ গং ...	২৩৩৸৶৹	,,	...	...	৩৫৩৸৶৹	...
১৮৭	,, ...	সতীশচন্দ্র রায় সিংহ গং ...	৩৬২৸৶৹	,,	...	...	১০৭৶৩	...
১৮৩খাঃ	বালিবাদ	শ্রীকান্ত ব্যাপারী ...	১৩০৸৹	,,	...	...	৭১৸৹	...
১৯২	,, ...	কার্ত্তিকচন্দ্র চক্রবর্ত্তী ...	১৫৮৶	,,	...	...	৯২।৶৮	...
৩৮৫	হরিপুর	ঐ	১১৩৸৶৹	,,	...	...	৫৪৸৶১১	...

৪৪০	বিপরপার	গিরিজাকুমার চক্রবর্ত্তী	...	২৭৭৸৶০		...	...	১০৪৵২	...
৪৮৬	বালাভূত	খড়্গনারায়ণ সিংহ গং	...	১৮৭৸৶০		...	...	৭০৷৶৪	...
৪৮৯	„	রাজচন্দ্র দাস	...	১২৪।০		...	...	৪৬৷/১	...
৪৯২	„	হরিমোহন দাস গং	...	১১৯৷৶০	„	...	...	৪৪৷৮	...
৪৯৮	„	শ্রীকান্ত ব্যাপারী	...	১৩০৷৶০	„	...	...	৪৮৸৵৮	...
৫০৪	„	সতীশচন্দ্র ব্যাপারী	...	২৫২৸৶০	„		...	৪৯৸/৪	...
৫০৭	„	সদর সেখ গং	...	১২৮৴০	„	...	...	৪৮/১১	...
৫১২	„	মদন দাস ব্যাপারী	...	২২৪।০	„	...	...	৮৪/৫	...
৫৫৩ খাঃ	বালাভূত	বাবুমামুদ সেখ গং	...	১২৪৸৶০	„	...	...	৪৬৸০	...
৫৭৮	„	খয়রউদ্দিন ব্যাপারী	...	৩২১৷৶০	অংশ	।০	১৩০।৶৬	...	৬০।৪
৫৭৮ ক	„	ঐ	...	৩২১৷৶০	„		১৬০৶৬	...	৬০।৪
৬৫৪খাঃ	খাউকুঠী	মানিরউদ্দিন সরকার	...	২০২৸৶০	সম্পূর্ণ	...	...	৮৭।০	...
৬৫৬	„	শুকচন্দ দাস গং	...	৭১২৷০	„	...	...	২৪৭/৬	...
৬৬৫	„	হবিরউদ্দিন সরকার	...	২২০৷৶০	„	...		৮২৷০৭	...
৬৬৮	„	যতীন্দ্রনাথ চক্রবর্ত্তী	...	১১৩৷০	„	...	...	৪২৷/০	...
৬৬৯	„	শ্রীমন্ত দাস গং	...	১০৪৸৴০	„	...	...	৩৬৶৪	...
৬৭৮ ক	„	শুকচাঁদ দাস	...	৪০৯৷০	অংশ	...	১০৯।৶০	...	৩৬৷৶৩
৬৮৯	গোপালেরকুঠী	বাসকমামুদ ব্যাপারী	...	১৩০৷৸৶০	সম্পূর্ণ	...	...	৪৯৵২	...
৭০২	„	যুধিষ্ঠিরচন্দ্র চক্রবর্ত্তী	...	১৯১৷৸৶০	„	...	...	৭১৸/৬	...
৭০৩	„	রায়চৌঃ সুরেশচন্দ্র মুস্তফি গং	...	১০৫৮৵০	„	...	...	৩৬৷৸২	...
৭২৩ খাঃ	মেখগ্রাম	কার্ত্তিকচন্দ্র চক্রবর্ত্তী	...	১১৬৶০		...	...	৪৩৷/০	...
৭৯১ খাঃ	মানসাই	রায়চৌঃ সুরেশচন্দ্র মুস্তফি গং	...	১৪৯৴০			...	৫৫৮৶৪	...
৭৯৫	ডাঙ্গো	ঐ	...	১৫৮৶০	„	...	...	৫৩৷/১	...
৮০৭	বাজকোদালী	ঐ	...	১১৪৷৶০	„	...	...	৭২৸৶৩	...

জোত নং	তালুকের নাম	নাম ও পরগণা	সম্পূর্ণ জোতের জমা	সম্পূর্ণ জোত নীলাম হইবে কি না	কেবল মাত্র অংশ নীলাম হইলে ঐ অংশের বিশেষ বিবরণ	কোন অংশ মাত্র নীলাম হইলে ঐ অংশের জমা	সম্পূর্ণ জোত নীলাম হইলে তাহার রাজস্ব বাকী	কেবল অংশ মাত্র নীলাম হইলে ঐ অংশের রাজস্ব বাকী
৮১৪	বাড়কোদালী	রমণীমোহন সরকার গং ...	১১৬৶০	সমস্ত	......	......	৪৩৷১০	...
৯০৭	চোপগুড়ী	উমাকান্ত অধিকারী ...	২৪৯৶০	"	......	......	৯৫৶২	...
৯৯৫	গ্রঃ খঃ বাজেকমা চিলাখানা	রায়চৌঃ সুরেশচন্দ্র মুস্তফি গং	৪৪৪৸৶০	"	.....		১৬৬৸১০	...
১০১৮	ভেলাপেটা	সাদারাম দাস গং ...	১১০।৶০	"	.....	..	৭১৸৶৩	.....
১০৭৩	খাঃ চিলাখানা	বাদ্রা শেখ গং ...	১৩১, ০	"	....	...	৬৯৶২	
১০৭৮	"	দুলাল নস্ত গং ...	১০৭৶০	"	......	.....	৪০৶২	......
১০৯০ খাঃ	"	কুদ্দুসউদ্দিন গং ...	১২২৸৶০	"	...	......	৪৫৮৶২	......
১০৯৫	"	প্রাণনাথ দাস ...	১৩৩।৶০	"	......	......	[illegible] ২	
১১০২	"	প্রফুল্লচন্দ্র মুস্তফি গং ...	১৬৪।৶০	"	.....	.....	৬১[illegible]	......
১১৬০	গ্রঃ খঃ কিশলী	রাজেশ্বরী দাস ...	১০৮৸৶০	"	.....		৪০ ৸৶৩	...

H. BARMA, *Naib Ahilkar*.

রাজ্য কোচবিহার

মহকুমা তুফানগঞ্জ।

সর্বসাধারণকে জানান যাইতেছে যে, ১৮৯৭ সালের কোচবিহার রাজস্বসংক্রান্ত নীলাম বিষয়ক আইনের ৩ ধারা (অথবা ১১ ধারা) অনুসারে রাজ্য কোচবিহারের অন্তর্গত মহকুমা তুফানগঞ্জের এলাকাধীন নিম্নলিখিত জোত (বা জোতের অংশগুলি) বাকী রাজস্বের জন্য আগামী ইং ১৯৪৭ সনের ৫ই সেপ্টেম্বর মোতাবেক ১৩৫৪ সালের ১৯শে ভাদ্র তারিখে কোচবিহার রাজ্যের উক্ত মহকুমার মাল কাছারীতে প্রকাশ্য নীলামে বিক্রয় হইবে।

এই সকল জোতের (বা জোতের অংশের) রাইয়ত ও অধীন প্রজাদিগকে এতদ্বারা নিষেধ করা যাইতেছে যে, তাহারা বাকী রাজস্ব দিবার অবধারিত শেষ দিনের পর যে খাজানা দেয় হইয়াছে তাহা বাকীদার মালিককে না দেয় যদি দেয় তাহা হইলে এই প্রকারের যে টাকা দেওয়া হইবে তাহা ক্রেতার সহিত হিসাবে তাহারা জমা পাইবার স্বত্ববান হইবে না। ইতি—

তৌজির নং	তালুকের নাম	নাম ও পরগণা	সম্পূর্ণ জোতের জমা	সম্পূর্ণ জোত নীলাম হইবে কি না	কেবল মাত্র অংশ নীলাম হইলে ঐ অংশের বিশেষ বরণ	কোন অংশ মাত্র নীলাম হইলে ঐ অংশের জমা	সম্পূর্ণ জোত নীলাম হইলে তাহার দেয় বাকী	কোন অংশ মাত্র নীলাম হইলে ঐ অংশের বাবদ বাকী
১২৩১	২য় খঃ ছাটরামপুর	আছানউল্যা আহাম্মদ ...	২৭৭।৶০	সমস্ত	...	......	১০।৮	......
১২৩২	১ম খঃ চিকলীগুড়ী	ঐ	১১৬৮৴০	,,	...	......	৪৫.	......
১২৩৩	,,	আহাম্মদ হোসেন গঃ ...	৩১৭৲	,,	......	......	১৩৩৶০	...
১২৩৬	,,	প্রফুল্লকুমার সরকার গঃ ...	১২ ৷/০	,,	......	......	৫৬৷৴৪	...
১২৭৪	২য় খঃ চিকলীগুড়ী	কেরামতআলী মিঞা গঃ ...	২৮৯৶০	,,	......	......	১০৮৷৶৯	
১২৮১	,,	আ ছানউল্যা আহাম্মদ ...	১১৭৷৴০	,,	...	......	৭১৸/৫	......
১২৯৫	শিকদারের খাতা	নমলচাঁদ মণ্ডল গঃ ...	১২৩৷৷০	,,	...	......	৪৯৷৴০	..
১৩৪৮	শালবাড়ী	প্রফুল্লকুমার সরকার গঃ	১২৯৷৶০	,,	..	..	৪৮৷৷৮	
১৩৫৫	,,	ইন্দুকুমারী ঈশ্বরী	১৯৫৶০		..		৭৩,২	..
১৫৮০	গুড়িয়ারপার	বরেশ্বর দাস গঃ ...	১২১৶০	,,	..		৪৫৷৶২	......
১৭০০	বালাপুখরী	গোড়াচাঁদ মণ্ডল গঃ ...	৪৬০৷৶০	অংশ	...	১৫০/৯	......	৪৩৶০
১৬৩১	অন্দরান ফুলবাড়	রাজেশ্বরী পাল ...	২০৭৮৶০			১০৩৸/৬		৩৮৸/১০

হাঁট নং	তালুকের নাম।	পত্তনীদার নাম।	সম্পূর্ণ জোতের জমা।	সম্পূর্ণ জোত নীলাম হইবে কি না।	যদি আংশিক হয় তবে নীলাম হইলে ঐ অংশের বিবরণ।	কোন অংশ মাত্র নীলাম হইলে ঐ অংশের জমা।	সম্পূর্ণ জোতের বাকী সমস্ত বা	কোন অংশ মাত্র নীলাম হইলে ঐ অংশের বাকী
১৬৩৪	অন্তরান ফুলবাড়ী	পঞ্চমা দাস পঃ ...	১০৩।০	সমস্ত	...	...	৫২৶৩	...
১৬৩৮	,,	প্রফুল্লকুমার সরকার পঃ ...	১৩২৸০	,,	...	...	৪৯৸৩	...
১৬৩৯	,,	নরেশ্বর দাস পঃ ...	১২৫।০	,,	...	...	৪০৸৶৩	...
১৭০৫	বিন্নাপুনী	মহেন্দ্রনাথ সিং ...	১১৪৸/০	,,	...	...	৪২৸: ৫	...
১৮১৩	শিলবাধরী	আব্দু লতফ পঃ ...	১৩৬৶/০	,,	...	...	৪৭।১০	...
১৮১৬	,,	লক্ষ্মণচন্দ্র দাস পঃ ...	১০৫৸৶/০	,,	...	...	৮৷/৩	...
১৮৪০ খাস	বাকারবান্না	নরেশ্বরী দাস্যা ...	২৮৫৸/০	সমস্ত	...	...	১০৭৶/১১	...
১৮৪৯	,,	প্রফুল্লকুমার সরকার পঃ ...	১১৯৸৶০	,,	...	...	৪৪৸৶৩	...
১৮৫০	,,	গিরিন্দ্রকুমার চক্রবর্ত্তী ...	১৯৩।/০	,,	...		৭১৷৶৩	...
১৮৫১	,,	প্রফুল্লকুমার সরকার পঃ ...	১৫১৵০	,,	...	...	৪৭৷/০	
১৯৯১	টাটেরকুঠী	মহেন্দ্রনাথ সিংহ সরকার পঃ ...	১০৯৸/০	,,	...		৪১৶/১১	...
১৯৯৪	,,	সোনাউল্লা আহাম্মদ ...	১৪২/০		...	...	৫৩/৫	...
১৯৯৬	,,	ঐ ...	১৮৯৸৶/০	,,	...	...	৭১৶৩	
২০০১	বড় শালবাড়ী	প্রফুল্লকুমার সরকার পঃ	১০৯/০	,,	...		৪১/৪	
২০০৮	,,	ঐ ...	১৫৪৸৶/০		...	...	৫৭৸৶/৩	...
২০১০	,,	যতীন্দ্রনাথ ভট্টাচার্য্য ...	২৫২৸৶/০	,,	...	...	১৪৯৶/৮	...
২০১১	,,	যোগেশ্বর সরকার পঃ ...	২০৩২৷/০	,,	...	...	৮৭৶/৩	...
২০১৭	,,	মহেন্দ্রনাথ দাস পঃ ...	২৪১৸০	,,	...		১০৮৶৩	...
২০৬৯	রসিকবিল	জিতনরাম সুখা ...	১৭৫৸০	,,	...	...	৬৫৸৶	...
২০৭৯	বাক্সা	সোনাউল্লা আহাম্মদ ...	১২৫।০	,,		...	৪৭/০	...
২২১০	ইংরেজবাসামারী	সোনাউদ্দিন আহাম্মদ ...	১২৪৸৶/০		...	...	৪৬৸৶/৪	...

২২৯২	জালঘোরা	আবদুল হক গং	...	৩২৮৸৶০		...	...	১২৩/৪	...
২২৯৩	”	প্রফুল্লকুমার সরকার গং	...	১১৪৸৶০	”	...	...	৪৩৬	...
২২৯৮	”	শারেশ্বর কুমার গং	...	১০৩/০	”	.	.	৩৮৷৶৫	...
২৩৩১	বহিরখুচি	মেঘরাজ ওশোয়াল	...	১২২৷৶০	”	...	...	৬১৫২	...
২৩৩৪	”	লক্ষ্মীরাম ব্যাপারী	...	১২৮৷৶০	”	...	...	৫১৸৶৩	...
২৩৩৫	”	খীমরাম ব্যাপারী		১৩৭৷৶০		...	...	৫০৷৶৩	.
২৩৬০	কলিমারী	যতীন্দ্রনাথ ঘোষ	..	২৬.৷৫০	”	...	...	৯৮৷২	..
২৩৬২	”	ঐ	..	১৪৩৷/০	”		...	৫৪৸৶৫	..
২৩৬৪		ঐ	..	১১০৸৶০	”	.	...	৪১৷৶৮	..
২৩৭২	”	প্রফুল্লকুমার সরকার গং		১২ ৷/০	”	...	.	১৫৷৶১১	...
২৩৭৬	”	যতীন্দ্রনাথ ঘোষ	...	২১৬৸৶০	”	...	..	৮১ /১	

H. BARMA, *Naib Ahilkar.*

রাজ্য কোচবিহার।

মহকুমা সদর।

এতদ্বারা সর্ব্বসাধারণকে জানান যাইতেছে যে, ১৮৯১ সালের কোচবিহার রাজস্বক্রান্ত নীলাম বিষয়ক আইনের ৬ ধারা (অথবা ১১ ধারা) অনুসারে রাজ্য কোচবিহারের অন্তর্গত মহকুমা সদরের এলাকাধীন নিম্নলিখিত জোত (বা জোতের অংশগুলি) বাকী রাজস্বের জন্য আগামী ইং ১৯৪৭ সনের ১১ই সেপ্টেম্বর, মোতাবেক ১৩৫৪ সনের ২৫শে ভাদ্র তারিখে কোচবিহার রাজ্যের উক্ত মহকুমার মাল কাছারীতে প্রকাশ্য নিলাম বিক্রয় করা হইবে।

এই সকল জোতের (বা জোতের অংশের) রাইয়ত বা অধীন প্রজাদিগকে এতদ্বারা নিষেধ করা যাইতেছে যে তাহারা বাকী রাজস্ব দিবার অবধারিত শেষ দিনের পর যে খাজানা দেয় হইয়াছে তাহা বাকীদার মালিককে না দেয়; যদি দেয় তাহা হইলে এই প্রকার যে টাকা দেওয়া হইবে তাহা ক্রেতার সহিত হিসাবে তাহারা জমা পাইবার স্বত্ববান হইবে না। ইতি—

জোতের নম্বর	[illegible]	[illegible]	সম্পূর্ণ জোতের জমা।	সম্পূর্ণ জোত নীলাম হইবে কিনা	কেবল মাত্র অংশ নীলাম হইলে ঐ অংশের [illegible]	জোতের অংশ মাত্র নীলাম [illegible] ঐ অংশের [illegible]	সম্পূর্ণ জোত [illegible] হইলে তাহার [illegible]	[illegible] ঐ অংশে [illegible]
২৮ সদর	সহর কোচবিহার	আতাহর উদ্দিন আহাম্মদ গং ...	১০৬।০	অংশ	হি ।/৪	৩৫।।৶	...	১৭।
৩০ ছেঃ	মরিচবাড়ী	কনকলতা দেবী	১১৫৪৶০	সমস্ত	...	.....	১৭৩।/৪	..
৫১	২য় খণ্ড-গুড়িয়াহাটি	করুণাময়ী দাস্যা ...	২১০/০	,,	...		৭৮৸৪	...
১৯২ ছেঃ	ডাউয়াগুড়ী	রাজেন্দ্রনাথ দাস সরকার ...	১৩৩৸৶০	,,	......	...	৫২৶০	.....
১৯৮	ঐ	পির বকস গং ...	১১৭৸/০	,,	......	......	৪৪৶০	....
১৯৯	২য় খণ্ড ঘুঘুমারি	গোপালচন্দ্র মিত্র ...	২৫৩৸/০	,,		......	৯৫৶১১	......
১৮৮ ছেঃ	চান্দামারি	করুণাময়ী দাস্যা	১৩১।৶০	,,	...	......	৫২।২	...
২০৩	ইকরচালা	ঐ	৩১৬৸০	,,	হিঃ ।০	১২৮৶৩		৫ ।/৩
২৮২	শিঙ্গিমারী	সত্যেন্দ্রমোহন চক্রবর্ত্তী ..	১৭১৸০	সমস্ত		....	৬৪।/৯	.....
৩২৮	খেটটিবাড়ী	করুণাময়ী দাস্যা ..	১২১।৶০	,,	......	.....	৪৫।৩	....
৫ মাল	গোপালপুর	ঐ ...	১৫৮/০	,,	......	....	৫১৸৩	......
১১৩	হাওয়াগাড়া	ঐ	৬৬৩৸০	,,			২৪৮৸৶৩	....

১৭৪	বড়শগুড়ি	ঐ	...	১০৭৸৶০		..	...	৪০৸৶৭	..
২৭৪	কুচীপাড়া	ঐ	..	১০২৷/০		...	অংশ	৩৸/১০	...
৩২৩	হলগুড়ী	সুরেন্দ্রনাথ ভট্টাচার্য্য	...	১২৭৷৶০				৪৭৸৪	...
৫৪৮	বোকালীমঠ	করুণাময়ী দাস্তা	...	১২০৸৶০			..	৪৩৷/০	
৪০৮ খাঃ	আমবাড়ী	রামস্বরূপসোনা		১৫৬৸০	সমস্ত	...		৩৮৷৩	...
৫০০	,,	বুদ্ধিনাথ দাস		১০৮৷/০	সমস্ত	......	...	৪০৸৶৩	.....
৬৬৬	ফোলোমেরকুঠী	নবীনচন্দ্র সরকার	...	১১৫৷৶০	[illegible]	....	...	৪৫৷	..
৭০৭	হোকলাবাড়ী	করুণাময়ী দাস্তা	...	১১৮৸০	সমস্ত		......	৪৪৷/১	
৭০৮	,,	,,		১০৩৸৶০	সমস্ত			৩৮ ৮	..
৭২৩	কালারায়েরকুঠী	,,		২০৩৸০	সমস্ত	......		৮৭৸৶৬	
৭৪৯ক	,,	রাজবর রহমান	...	২৭৫৸৶০	অংশ	৷০	৩০৶৬		৫১৸৶৯
৭৭৩	সাজেরপার খোড়াবাড়া	করুণাময়ী দাস্তা	...	৪১২৷৶০	সমস্ত		......	১৬৭৻৯	...
৮১৭	আটিয়ালীগুড়ী	,,		৯১৭	সমস্ত	...	...	৩৪১৷০	.....
৮১৮	,,	,,		১১৪৶০	অংশ	...	...	৪৪৸৶২	
৮১৯ খাঃ	আটিয়ালীগুড়ী	করুণাময়ী দাস্তা	...	২৩৷৶০	সমস্ত	...	...	৮৩৸৶৩	..
৮২৭	শুলীবাড়া	আছরুদ্দিন মিঞা	...	১৮৫৷/০	অংশ	৷০	৯২৸৶৩	..	৩৪৸/১০
৮২৯	,,	যোগেশচন্দ্র মজুমদার	...	১৫৫৸০	সমস্ত	......	...	৫৮৷৶৩	...
৮৪৪	,,	বছিরুদ্দিন মিঞা গং	...	১০১৶০	অংশ	৴৪	৩৫৸৶৪	..	১১৸৶২
৮৫৩	শুকদেবেরকুঠী	নবিরুদ্দিন প্রধান	...	২৫৭৷০	সমস্ত	...		৯৩৸/০	...
৮৬০	,,	সেখ আনোয়ার উদ্দিন গং	...	১১৫/০	,,	......	...	৪৩৬৫	
৮৮০	খাগড়াবাড়ী	দেবনাথ সরকার	...	১৪২৷৶০			...	৫০৶৮	..

NAGENDRA NATH ROY, *S. S. Naib Ahilkar.*

রাজ্য কোচবিহার।

মহকুমা সদর।

এতদ্বারা সর্বসাধারণকে জানান যাইতেছে যে, ১৮৯৭ সালের কোচবিহার রাজস্ব সংক্রান্ত নীলামবিষয়ক আইনের ৬ ধারা (অথবা ১১ ধারা) অনুসারে রাজ্য কোচবিহারের অন্তর্গত মহকুমা সদরের এলাকাধীন নিম্নলিখিত জোত (বা জোতের অংশ) বাকী রাজস্বের জন্য আগামী ১৯১৭ সনের ১২ই সেপ্টেম্বর মোতাবেক ১৩২৪ সনের ২৭শে ভাদ্র তারিখে উক্ত মহকুমার নায়েব আহিলকারের কাছারীতে প্রকাশ্য নিলামে বিক্রয় হইবে।

এই সকল জোতের (বা জোতের অংশের) মালিক ও দাবীদারগণকে এতদ্বারা নিষেধ করা যাইতেছে যে, তাহারা বাকী রাজস্ব দিবার অব্যবহিত শেষ দিনের পর যে খাজানা দেয় হইয়াছে তাহা বাকীদার মালিককে না দেন, যদি কেহ তাহা দেন তবে এই প্রকারে যে টাকা দেওয়া হইবে তাহা ক্রেতার সহিত হিসাবে তাহারা জমা পাইবার হকদার হইবেন না। ইতি—

তৌজির নম্বর	মৌজার নাম	মালিকের নাম		সম্পূর্ণ জোতের জমা	পূর্ণ জোত নীলাম হইবে কি না	কোন অংশ মাত্র নীলাম হইলে ঐ অংশের বিবরণ	কোন অংশ মাত্র নীলাম হইলে ঐ অংশের জমা	সম্পূর্ণ জোত নীলাম হইলে তাহার বাকী	কোন অংশ মাত্র নীলাম হইলে ঐ অংশের বাবত বাকী
১৮৩ক খাস	মাথপালা	প্রফুল্লকুমার সরকার গং	...	৫৫৩৸/০	অংশ	৮০ অংশ	৪১৮৩	...	১৫৩৸৫
৩৭০	চান্দামারী	রমণীমোহন মিত্রা গং	...	৩০১৷৶০	সমস্ত	......	......	১১৩৻১	......
৪০৭	[illegible] কলাপাতা	প্রফুল্লকুমার সরকার গং	...	২৮৮৸/০	সমস্ত	....		১০৮৷০	....
৭০৫	পাটছড়া	সতীশচন্দ্র রায়	...	১১৬৶/০	সমস্ত	.....		৪৩৷/২	....
৮৮১	১ম খণ্ড শিমুলী	অম্বিকাচরণ রায়	...	১৮০৷/০	সমস্ত	...	...	৬৮৷/৪	....
৯৫৪	•গড়ীভাঙ্গা	প্রমথনাথ লাহিড়ী গং	...	৬৬৫৷০	সমস্ত	...	.....	৩২৲	...
২২৭১	গোসাইগঞ্জ	মফিজউদ্দিন মিঞা	...	১৪৮৷৶০	সমস্ত	...		৫৫৸/০	...
২৪৩৩	পানীশালা	গোপালচন্দ্র মিত্র	...	২০৪৶/০	সমস্ত	...	.....	৭৬৷১	.....
২৮১৫	পশ্চিম খাগড়াবাড়ী	কমলা ব্যাঙ্ক লিঃ	...	১৬৫৸৶০	সমস্ত	...	....	৫৪৸৶০	
৩১২১	ইকড়াকালা	কমলাপতী রাজা	...	২০৭৸৶০	সমস্ত			৭৭৸/৩	
৩১২৪	"	ঐ	...	১৮৩৸৶০	সমস্ত	..	...	৬৩৸/৩	.
৩১৫৪	হাড়িভুবা	ঐ	...	১৭৫৷/০	সমস্ত			৬৫৸৶১১	...
৩২১৪	খাপাইডাঙ্গা	মনসুর আলী মিঞা গং	...	১১২৶/০	সমস্ত	...	...	৪১৸/০	.....

৩৩২৬	চকচকা	মদনমোহন সরকার	...	১৩২৲	সমস্ত	......	......	৪৮৸৹	.....
৩৬৭৬	কালজানী	করুণাময়ী দাসা	...	১৩৩৸৴৹	সমস্ত	...	......	৫০৶/২	...
৪১৭৬	চান্দচৌকা	দীনেন্দ্রনাথ ভট্টাচার্য্য গং	...	৩১৩৸৶৹	সমস্ত	... .	......	৭৩৲	......
৪২৩১	বাবজাওয়ার	উমাকান্ত চক্রবর্ত্তী	...	৪২৯৸৶৹	সমস্ত	.....	....	১৬১৶/৭	

NAGENDRA NATH ROY, *S. g. Naib Ahilkar.*

রাজ্য কোচবিহার

মহকুমা মাথাভাঙ্গা।

এতদ্বারা সর্বসাধারণকে জানান যাইতেছে যে, ১৮৯৭ সালের কোচবিহার রাজস্বসংক্রান্ত নীলাম বিষয়ক আইনের ৬ ধারা (অথবা ১১ ধারা) অনুসারে রাজ্য কোচবিহারের অন্তর্গত মহকুমা মাথাভাঙ্গার এলাকাধীন নিম্নলিখিত জোত (বা জোতের অংশগুলি) বাকী রাজস্বের জন্য আগামী ইং ১৯৪৭ সনের ৯ই সেপ্টেম্বর, মোতাবেক ১৩৫৪ সনের ২৩শে ভাদ্র তারিখে কোচবিহার রাজ্যের উক্ত মহকুমার মাল কাছারীতে প্রকাশ্য নিলামে বিক্রয় করা হইবে।

এই সকল জোতের (বা জোতের অংশের) রাইয়ত ও অধীন প্রজাদিগকে এতদ্বারা নিষেধ করা যাইতেছে যে, তাহারা বাকী রাজস্ব দিবার অবধারিত শেষ দিনের পর যে খাজানা দেয় হইয়াছে তাহা বাকীদার মালিককে না দেয়; যদি দেয় তাহা হইলে এই প্রকারে যে টাকা দেওয়া হইবে তাহা ক্রেতার সহিত হিসাবে তাহারা জমা পাইবার স্বত্ববান হইবে না।

[illegible]	[illegible]	[illegible]	সম্পূর্ণ [illegible]	[illegible]	[illegible]	[illegible]	[illegible]	[illegible] নিলাম হইবে [illegible] বাকী।
১১৫ে	জোড় শিমুলী	হৃদয়লাল ভৌমিক	১২০৸৶০	সমস্ত	......	......	৪৫।০	
১২১মা	ক্ষেতী	জগমোহন রায় কায়েত ...	২২৮৶০	,,	......		২৬৬৶৩	
৩০৩	ছাতলক্ষীপুর	কাউয়া দাস গং ...	১২৮৸০	অংশ		১১২॥৵৭	...	৪২৸৶০
৩১৭	ফুলবাড়ী হরিবংশ	চন্দ্রমোহন সরকার ...	৩২১৸০	,,	...	৩১০॥৶০		১১৬৸৶০
৩৩৩	বলদিয়াহাটি বালাসি	রূপা মহম্মদ গং ...	৩৪৩৶০	,,	.....	১৭১॥৶০		৬৪।৶০
৩৩৩ক	,,	নলজিন গং ...	৩৪৩৶০	,,	...	৮৫৸		৩২৴৬
৩৩৩খ	,,	ঐ	৩৪৩৶০	,,		৪২৸৶৫	...	১৬৶০
৩৩৩গ	,,	ঐ ...	৩৪৩৶০	,,	..	৪২৸৶৫	......	১৬৶০
৩৫৮	মহিস্কুচ	কৃষ্ণমোহন সিংহ ...	৩৫১৶০	সমস্ত		......	১৩১॥৶০	...
৭২৪	কানকাটা	গং জনারায়ণ রায় বসুনীয়া গং...	২২১৶০	,,	......	......	৮২৸৶৩	...
৭২৭	,,	ঐ	১৭৬।০	,,	......	..	৩৪।৶৩	...
৭৩৩	,,	ঐ	১০১৸৶০	,,		......	৩৮৶৬	
১০৮০	গেন্দুগুড়ি	রাজা কুমারী ..	২০০৸৴০	,,	..	...	৭৫।৶০	...

১০৮১		গজেন্দ্রনারায়ণ রায় বসুনীয়া প...	১১৫৸৶/০	,,		...	৮৪॥৶০	......
১১৭৬	কুজিকাটা	রূপেশ্বরী বর্ম্মাণী ...	১৫২॥৶০	,,	......	....	৪৭॥৵৬	....
১১৬২	চোদারখাত' খাগরীবাড়ী	চন্দ্রভাগ দুবে	১৪৫॥/০	,,	...		৫৪॥৩	...
১৩৭৫	ইন্দ্রেশকুঠি	উমাচরণ বর্ম্মণ গঃ ...	১২৩৷৶০	,,	......	...	৪৩৷৬	...
১৭২৬	ছোট কেশরীবাড়ী	তিলকচন্দ্র বর্ম্মণ গঃ ...	২৩০৸/০	,,	....	......	৮৯৶৯	... ..
১৪৮৪	ভোগরামগুড়ি	আলাজউদ্দিন ...	১২৮৷৶০	অংশ	.. ..	৬৪৶০	...	২৪/০
১৪৮৪ক	,,	ঐ ...	১২৮৷৵০	,,	......	৬৪৶০		২৪/০
১৫৬০	বুড়াবুড়ি	উজিরমামুদ গঃ ..	১৬১॥/০	,,	......	৮০৸৬		৩০৷৩
১৫৬০ক		বছিরউদ্দিন ..	১৬১॥/০	,,	..	৮০৵৬		৩০৷৭
১৭২৮	ভোগমারা	পদ্মনাথ মাঝি ...	১২১৸০	সমস্ত			৩৮৻২	.
১১৪৬	শিলডাঙ্গা	লক্ষ্মী বর্ম্মাণী	১১২৸/০	,,		...	৪৷৬	..

MANABENDRA NATH BHATTACHARJEE, *Naib Ahilkar.*

রাজ্য কোচবিহার।

মহকুমা মাথাভাঙ্গা।

এতদ্বারা সর্বসাধারণকে জানান যাইতেছে যে, ১৮৯৭ সালের কোচবিহার রাজস্বসংক্রান্ত নীলাম বিক্রয় আইনের ৭ ধারা (অথবা ১১ ধারা) অনুসারে রাজ্য কোচবিহারের অন্তর্গত মহকুমা মাথাভাঙ্গার এলাকাধীন নিম্নলিখিত জোত (বা জোতের অংশগুলি) বাকী রাজস্বের জন্য আগামী ইং ১৯৪৭ সনের ১০ই সেপ্টেম্বর, মোতাবেক ১৩৫৪ সালের ২৪শে ভাদ্র তারিখে কোচবিহার রাজ্যের উক্ত মহকুমার খাস কাছারিতে প্রকাশ্য নীলামে বিক্রয় হইবে।

ঐ সকল জোতের (বা জোতের অংশের) রাইয়ত ও অধীন প্রজাদিগকে এতদ্বারা নিষেধ করা যাইতেছে যে, তাহারা বাকী রাজস্ব দিবার অব্যবহিত শেষ দিনের পর যে খাজানা দেয় হইবে তাহা বাকীদার মালিককে না দেন। যদি দেন তাহা হইলে এই প্রকারের যে টাকা দেওয়া হইবে তাহা ক্রেতার সহিত হিসাবে তাহারা জমা পাইবার স্বত্ববান হইবে না। ইতি—

তৌজি নং	তালুকের নাম	মালিকের নাম।	সম্পূর্ণ জোতের জমা	সম্পূর্ণ জোত বা অংশ নীলাম হইবে কিনা	কেবল মাত্র অংশ নীলাম হইলে ঐ অংশের বিশেষ বিবরণ	কোন অংশ মাত্র নীলাম হইলে ঐ অংশের জমা	সম্পূর্ণ জোত নীলাম হইলে বাকী [illegible]	কোন অংশ নীলাম হইলে ঐ অংশের [illegible] বাকী
১৩ খাঃ	জোড়পাটকী	প্রসাদিরাম চক্রবর্তী গং ...	১৮০৶০	অংশ	...	১২০৶০	...	৩৩৸১
৩০	ঐ	সোবহান আলী ...	১৪২৫৷৶০	সম্পূর্ণ	...	...	৯৫৩৩/১১	...
৩২০	[illegible]	[illegible] ...	৪৫৯৸/০	ঐ	...	...	১১২৷/৯	...
১১৮৭	ছোটশালবাড়ী	দেবেন্দ্রনাথ ভট্ট	২৯৩৸০	ঐ	...		১১১৷৬	...
১৬১৭	[illegible]	মোহিনী মোহন বক্সী ...	২১৮/০	ঐ	...	...	১১১৶৬	...
১৭৫৩	[illegible]	[illegible] ...	১৮৮৷০	ঐ	...	...	৭০৪/৬	...

MANABENDRA NATH BHATTACHARJEE, *Naib Ahilkar.*

ORDER.

Sjt. Ramesh Narayan Chowdhuri, B.L., Advocate, Cooch Behar, is appointed liquidator in the matter of winding up of the Cooch Behar Loan office Ltd. a company registered under the Cooch Behar companies Act and located in Cooch Behar with all powers as defined in Section 179 companies Act.

COOCH BEHAR, *the 28th August, 1947.*

N. SENGUPTA, *Additional Civil Judge.*

নোটিশ

এতদ্দ্বারা সর্ব্বসাধারণকে জানান যাইতেছে যে মৎস্য চাষের জন্য কুচবিহার সহরস্থ সাঁওতাল দিঘী প্রকাশ্য নিলামে ৫ বৎসর মেয়াদে নিম্নলিখিত সর্ত্তে বন্দোবস্ত করা হইবে :—

১। পুষ্করিণীর পাড় ভাল করিতে হইবে।

২। পুষ্করিণী সর্ব্বদা পরিষ্কার রাখিতে হইবে।

৩। ইহাতে যথেষ্ট পরিমাণে মাছের চাষ করিতে হইবে।

উপরোক্ত সর্ত্ত না মানিলে লীজ বাতিল হইবে। বাৎসরিক জমার টাকা বৎসরের পূর্ব্বে অগ্রিম দিতে হইবে এবং প্রথম বৎসরের টাকা ডাক কতন হইবার সঙ্গেই জমা দিতে হইবে।

বন্দোবস্ত গ্রহণেচ্ছু ব্যক্তিগণ আগামী ৮ই সেপ্টেম্বর সোমবার ডেভেলাপমেন্ট অফিসে নিলামে ডাকিবার জন্য উপস্থিত থাকিবেন। বেলা ৩ ঘটিকায় ডাক সুরু হইবে। ইতি তাং ২৯.৮.৪৭

শ্রীললিতমোহন বক্সী
ডেভেলপমেন্ট কমিশনার, কুচবিহার ষ্টেট।

সিভিল সাপ্লাইজ কমিশনার ও কন্ট্রোলার অব প্রাইসেস্ অফিস, কুচবিহার।

বিজ্ঞাপন।

(মূল্য নিয়ন্ত্রণ)

সিভিল সাপ্লাইজ কমিশনারের উপর প্রদত্ত এবং ন্যস্ত ক্ষমতাবলে কোচবিহার Essential Supplies (Temporary Powers) Act 1946 এর ৩ ধারার অন্তর্গত ২ উপধারার সি ক্লজ অনুযায়ী নিম্নলিখিত দ্রব্যগুলির সর্ব্বোচ্চ মূল্য নিম্নলিখিতরূপে ধার্য্য করা হইল এবং তাহা কুচবিহার গেজেটে প্রকাশিত হওয়ার তারিখ হইতে পুনরাদেশ না হওয়া পর্য্যন্ত বলবৎ থাকিবে। এতদ্বিষয়ক পূর্ব্ব বিজ্ঞপ্তি বাতিল করা হইল। কোন ব্যক্তি নির্দ্ধারিত মূল্যের অতিরিক্ত মূল্যে বিক্রয় করিলে বা দ্রব্যাদি বিক্রয়ার্থ আনিয়া নির্দ্ধারিত মূল্যে বিক্রয় করিতে অস্বীকার করিলে উপরোক্ত আইনের ৭ ধারা অনুযায়ী দণ্ডনীয় হইবে। ইতি ২৮শে আগষ্ট ১৯৪৭।

বিশেষ দ্রষ্টব্য :—সরিষা ও গমের দর রাজ্যের হাটে, তহবাজারে, মিলে ও খুচরা দোকানে ও বন্দরে প্রযোজ্য / রাজ্যের অন্যান্য স্থানের দর উহা অপেক্ষা ।০ চারি আনা হিসাবে কম হইবে। রসগোল্লা, সন্দেশ ও চিড়ার দর রাজ্যের সর্ব্বত্র এক।

কেরাসিন—হলদিবাড়ী বন্দরের দর—

লাল কেরোসিন প্রতি টিন ৪৸৬ টিন সমেত প্রতি সের ৵১

সাদা কেরোসিন প্রতি টিন ৫৵০ (ঐ) প্রতি সের ।০

কয়লা—কয়লার দর মাত্র কুচবিহার সহরের জন্য নির্দ্ধারিত হইল।

মফঃস্বলের দর—কোচবিহার টাউন, দিনহাটা বন্দর, হলদিবাড়ী বন্দর, চাংরাবান্ধা বন্দর ব্যতীত অন্যান্য স্থানের দর নিম্নলিখিত দর অপেক্ষা (ধান্য, চাউল, সরিষা ও গম ব্যতীত) মণ প্রতি এক টাকা চারি আনা অর্থাৎ সের প্রতি দুই পয়সা বেশী হইবে। কিন্তু যে সকল ক্ষেত্রে রাজ্যের অন্যান্য স্থানের দর পৃথক ভাবে ধার্য্য আছে সেই সব ক্ষেত্রে ঐ নির্দ্ধারিত দরই প্রযোজ্য হইবে।

পাইকারী দর—মণ সেরের নীচে আড়াই সের পর্য্যন্ত খরিদ বিক্রী হইলে মণ প্রতি ।০ চারি আনা বেশী হইবে। কিন্তু এই নিয়ম, চাউল, সরিষা, গম, সম্বন্ধে প্রযোজ্য হইবে না এবং রেশন দোকানে ইহা প্রযোজ্য হইবে না। তথায় কেবলমাত্র নির্দ্ধারিত খুচরা দরে কেনা বেচা হইবে।

ষ্ট্যাণ্ডার্ড বস্তা—লবণ ১৮৯ সের বস্তা সহ।
চিনি ২৮১ সের বস্তা সহ।

পণ্য দ্রব্যের নাম	প্রতি সের	প্রতি মণ	প্রতি ষ্ট্যাণ্ডার্ড বস্তা	মন্তব্য
১। গম—দেশী জাতের	৶০	৯৲		
ঐ বড়দানা পাঞ্জাবী জাতের		১৫৲		
২। চিনি	৷৶০	২৪৷৷০	৬৭।৶০ (কোচবিহার সহর, দিনহাটা বন্দর, চাংরাবান্ধা বন্দর, হলদিবাড়ী বন্দরের জন্য) প্রতি ষ্ট্যাণ্ডার্ড বস্তা ৭০৸৶০ আনা	
ঐ	৸৶০	২৭৲	(রাজ্যের অন্যান্য স্থানের দর)	
বাতাসা, কদমা, তিলুয়া	৸৴	৩১৲		
মিশ্রী	৸৵১০	৩২।০		
রসগোল্লা	১।০	×		
সন্দেশ (উৎকৃষ্ট)	২।০	×		
ঐ (সাধারণ)	১৸০	×		
৩। আটা	।৵৩	১৫৸০		
৪। ময়দা	।৶৩	১৮।০		
ঐ	৷৬	২০৸০	(রাজ্যের অন্যান্য স্থানের দর)	
৫। নারিকেল তৈল	২৲	৭৭৷৷০		
৬। কয়লা		১৷৷৶০		
৭। লবণ ঐ (করকচ)	৶৩			
৮। কেরোসিন তৈল (সাদা)	।৩ প্রতি বোতল	৫৸৵০ প্রতি টিন (টিন সমেত) ৫৶০ (৪ গ্যালন) টিন ছাড়া।		
ঐ (লাল)	।৩	৫।৶০ প্রতি টিন (টিন সমেত)। ৪৸০ (৪ গ্যালন) টিন ছাড়া।		
৯। মাংস (পাঁঠা খাসী)	১৸০ প্রতি সের			
১০। পাউরুটি পাউণ্ড	৷৶৩			
ঐ ৫ ছটাক	।৵৩			
১১। দুধ	তিন সের প্রতি টাকা (এই দর ষ্টেট মডেল ডেইরি সম্বন্ধে প্রযোজ্য নহে)			
১২। গুড় চট মোড়াই চাকি		২২৷৷৶৩		
ঐ খোলা গুড়	৷৶৩			
১৩। অরহর ডাল (বড়দানা)	৸৶০ খুচরা প্রতি সের	৩২৷৷০ পাইকারী প্রতিমণ		
ঐ (ছোটদানা)	৸০ "	২৮৶০ " "		
১৪। চালানি ছাটা মসুর	৸৯ পাই "	২৯৶০ " "		

শ্রীহিমাদ্রিপ্রসাদ বিশ্বাস,
সিভিল সাপ্লাইজ কমিশনার, কণ্ট্রোলার অব প্রাইসেস্ কুচবিহার।

The Cooch Behar Gazette.

৩০শে ভাদ্র, মঙ্গলবার ; TUESDAY, SEPTEMBER 16, 1947 [১৩৫৪ সাল ৪৩৮ রাজশক

PART II.

NOTICES.

ইং ১৯১০ সালের ৫ আইনের ৫৩ ধারার ২ প্রকরণ মতে নিলামী ইস্তাহার।

জারীর মহকুমা দিনহাটার এঃ ডিঃ নাঃ আঃ মাল আদালত।

এতদ্বারা সর্ব্বসাধারণকে জানান যাইতেছে যে, প্রতিবাদীর দাবীর বাকী খাজনা আদায় না করায় তাহার নিম্নলিখিত ক্রোকী সম্পত্তি আগামী ১৩৫৪ সনের ১৯শে আশ্বিন মোতাবেক ১৯৪৭ সনের ৬ই অক্টোবর, তারিখে বেলা ১ ঘটিকার সময় প্রকাশ্য নীলাম আরম্ভ হইবে।

৩৭নং ১৯৪৭।৪৮ ইং। বাঃ খাঃ মোঃ ৮৩৵৩।

ডিঃ—মহাম্মদ ফজলে হক সাং জাটীয়াবাড়ী।

দেঃ—বৈশাখ উদ্দীন গং সাং শিকদাধরা।

তপশিল সম্পত্তি।

পঃ দীনহাটা ৩৫৮ নং খাক তাং শিকনাধরা মধ্যে ১৭৮৪।৹ খুর জমির কাত বাঃ ২৪৷/৹ আনা জমার চুকানী স্বত্ব।

GIRISH CHANDRA LAHIRI, *Addl. Naib Ahilkar.*

দেওয়ানী কার্য্যবিধি আইনের ২১ হুকুম, ৬৬ নিয়মের ঘোষণাপত্র।

জারীর মহকুমা তুফানগঞ্জের দেঃ আদালত।

এতদ্বারা সর্ব্বসাধারণকে জানান যাইতেছে যে, দাবীকগণের নিম্নলিখিত সম্পত্তি আগামী ১৯৪৭ সনের ৬ই অক্টোবর মোঃ ১৩৫৪ সনের ১৯শে আশ্বিন তারিখে দিবা ১ ঘটিকায় সময় প্রকাশ্য নিলাম আরম্ভ হইবে।

৫ নং ১৯৪৭।৪৮ ইং। বাঃ ডিঃ ৫০৶৩ মোঃ।

ডিঃ—বাল্কটার ওসোয়াল সাং ফুলবাড়ী।

দেঃ—তজ্র দাস গং সাং দোয়কো।

তপশীল সম্পত্তি।

১। পঃ তুফানগঞ্জ ১১৩৪ নং খাক তাং দোয়কো মধ্যে ১৩৩ নং তৌঃ কিঃ ৫০।১।৴ খুর জমির কাত বাঃ ৪৩৷৴৹ আনা জমার চুকানী স্বত্ব।

২। পঃ খাক তাং [illegible] মধ্যে ৫৫৯ নং তৌঃ কিঃ ২৩.০৮৵৹ জমির কাত বাঃ ২৫৸৶৹ আনা জমার চুকানী স্বত্ব।

H. BARMA, *Naib Ahilkar.*

রাজ্য কোচবিহার।

মহকুমা দিনহাটা।

এতদ্দ্বারা সর্ব্বসাধারণকে জানান যাইতেছে যে, ১৮৯৭ সালের কোচবিহার রাজস্বক্রান্ত নীলাম বিষয়ক আইনের ৬ ধারা (অথবা ১১ ধারা) অনুসারে রাজ্য কোচবিহারের অন্তর্গত মহকুমা দিনহাটার এলাকাধীন নিম্নলিখিত জোত (বা জোতের অংশগুলি) বাকী রাজস্বের জন্য আগামী ইং ১৯৪৭ সনের ২২শে সেপ্টেম্বর, মোতাবেক ১৩৫৪ সনের ৫ই আশ্বিন তারিখে কোচবিহার রাজ্যের উক্ত মহকুমার মাল কাছারীতে প্রকাশ্য নিলামে বিক্রয় করা হইবে।

এই সকল জোতের (বা জোতের অংশের) রাইয়ত বা অধীন প্রজাদিগকে এতদ্দ্বারা নিষেধ করা যাইতেছে যে তাহারা যাহা রাজস্ব দিবার অবধারিত শেষ দিনের পর যে খাজানা দেয় হইয়াছে তাহা বাকীদার মালিককে না দেয়; যদি দেয় তাহা হইলে এই প্রকার যে টাকা দেওয়া হইবে তাহা ক্রেতার সহিত হিসাবে তাহারা জমা পাইবার হকদার হইবে না। ইতি—

জোতের নম্বর	তালুকের নাম	মালিকের নাম।	সম্পূর্ণ জোতের জমা।	সম্পূর্ণ জোত নীলাম হইবে কিনা	কেবল মাত্র অংশ নীলাম হইলে ঐ অংশের বিবরণ।	কোন অংশ মাত্র নীলাম হইলে ঐ অংশের জমা।	সম্পূর্ণ জোত নীলাম হইলে তাহার বাকী।	কোন অংশ মাত্র নীলাম হইলে ঐ অংশে বাকী রাজস্ব।
১১৪ ছে	পেটলা	বসিরউদ্দীন পাটোয়ারী ...	১৭২৷৷০	সমস্ত	......	......	৬৪৷৷৴০	......
১৪৪	কোদালকুটা	গোপালচন্দ্র মিত্র ...	২১১৯৷৵০	,,	......	......	৭১৷৷৴২	......
৩. খঃ	কাবরাপুর	মহারাজ বাহাদুর সিংহ ...	৩২৬৷৷০	,,	......	......	১২২৷৵৮	......
৩৩	খঃ গোলানীমারী	ঐ ...	১৩০৷৷০	,,	......	......	২৭৩৷৵৭	......
২৯০	শিমুলবাড়ী	মঃ মহামলুল্লা বেপারী ...	১৩৩৷৵০	,,	......	......	[illegible]	......
৩৩৬	বালিগাছ	মঃ ছমিরউদ্দীন বেপারী গং ...	২৮৮৷৵০	,,	......	......	১০৮৴০	......
৩০৭	,,	মঃ নবিবকস বেপারী গং ...	১০৩/০	,,	......	......	৩৮৷৴১০	......
৩১৭	ছোট গৌলমারী	বীরনারায়ণ সিংহ গং ...	১৭৯৷৴০	,,	......	......	৩৭.৪	......
৩৭০	বোড়তাথা	রামগোবিন্দ রায়াউৎ ...	১২২৲	,,	......	......	৪৫৸০	......
৪১৪	দিনারাই	পোষকবিকা বেপারী ...	২৫৫৷০	,,	......	......	৯৫৷৴১	......
৪৪৩	চাউলের কুটী	আবুলকাসিম আহাম্মদ ...	১১৫৷০	,,	......	......	৪৩/০	......
৬০২	খাবরণ	প্রসন্নকুমারী রায় ...	৩৭৩/০	,,	......	......	১২৸/৪	......

৬৯৭	কুড়কুড়া	মোহিনীমোহন বকসী	..	২৯০৶০	"	......	......	১০৮৸/২	......
৮০০	ডক্সা	শ্যামাচরণ রায় মণ্ডল	...	১৫২।/০	"	......	......	৫৭৶৪	......
৮০৩	বড় আছিনা	মঃ আবু মোজাফর মুন্সী গং	...	২১২।০	"	......	......	৫৩,১১	......
৯৫৪	তারিকাবাড়ী	তালুকমামুদ বেপারী	...	১১৭।৶০	"	......	......	৬৯৸৪	......
১০৭৫	আঠারবাড়ী	দেবেন্দ্রনাথ ভট্ট	...	১২৮৷৶০	"	......	......	৪৮৶৴	......
১০৭৯	বড় আঠারবাড়ী	পরিমলনেছা বিবি গং	...	২১৮৲	"	......	......	৮২৸০	......
১২২৫	চন্দ্রনারায়ণ	ফুলীচাদ শেঠিয়া গং	...	১৫৫।৶০	"	......	......	৫৮।৪	......
১২৪৭	ইন্দ্রনারা.৭	শাহারণ নেছা গং	...	১৮৪৸৵০	"	......	......	৩০।৶৮	......
১৫২৭	কিংশুগ্রাম	বছিরউদ্দীন পাটয়ারী	...	৬১৩৶০	"	......	......	৩৫৪,৫৶	......
১৫৫৯	"	সত্যেন্দ্রেশ্বর দে সরকার	...	১৪৫৲	"	......	......	১৪৬২৻১০	......

AHAMID HOSAIN PRADHAN, *Naib Ahilkar*.

রাজ্য কোচবিহার।

মহকুমা দিনহাটা।

এতদ্বারা সর্বসাধারণকে জানান যাইতেছে যে, ১৮৯৭ সালের কোচবিহার রাজস্বসংক্রান্ত নীলাম বিষয়ক আইনের ৬ ধারা অথবা ১১ ধারা) অনুসারে রাজ্য কোচবিহারের অন্তর্গত মহকুমা দিনহাটার এলাকাধীন নিম্নলিখিত জোত (বা জোতের অংশগুলি) বাকী রাজস্বের জন্য আগামী ইং ১৯৪৭ সনের ২৩শে সেপ্টেম্বর, মোতাবেক ১৩৫৪ সনের ৬ই আশ্বিন তারিখে কোচবিহার রাজ্যের উক্ত মহকুমার মাল কাছারীতে প্রকাশ্য নিলামে বিক্রয় করা হইবে।

এই সকল জোতের (বা জোতের অংশের) মালিক ও অধীন প্রজাদিগকে এতদ্বারা নিষেধ করা যাইতেছে যে, তাহারা বাকী রাজস্ব দিবার অবধারিত শেষ দিনের পর যে খাজানা দেয় হইয়াছে তাহা বাকীদার মালিককে না দেয়, যদি দেয় তাহা হইলে এই প্রকারে যে টাকা দেওয়া হইবে তাহা ক্রেতার সহিত হিসাবে তাহারা জমা পাইবার হকদার হইবে না।

তৌজির নং	তালুকের নাম	পরগণা ও নাম।	সম্পূর্ণ জোতের জমা।	সম্পূর্ণ জোত নীলাম হইবে কি না।	কেবল মাত্র অংশ নীলাম হইলে অংশের বিবরণ।	কোন অংশ মাত্র নিলাম হইলে ঐ অংশের জমা।	সম্পূর্ণ জোত নীলাম হইলে তাহার বাবদ বাকী।	কোন অংশ মাত্র নীলাম হইলে ঐ বাবদ বাকী।
৮০২	২য় হরিণ	আছের মামুদ সেক ...	১১৪৮/০	সমস্ত	......	......	৪৩৻১০	......
১৫৪৫	ঐ	আকবর আলী থন্দকার গং ...	১০২৲	ঐ	......	......	৪০৸/০	......
১৭০৪	করলা	কছিমুদ্দীন বেপারী ...	১৮৮৸/০	ঐ	......	......	৭০৸/৮	......
১৮৫১	বাগডোবাড়ী	মোহিনীমোহন বক্সী ..	৪২৭৸/০	ঐ	......	......	১৩০।/৪	......
১৮৫৩	ঐ	বহরউদ্দীন মিঞা ...	৫৪৸০	ঐ	......	......	২০৫।৶১০	......
১৮৬৮	চান্দেরকুটী	মৃত্যুঞ্জয় ওয়োয়াল ...	২১৯৸/০	ঐ	......	......	৮২।৶২	......
১৯২৬	দেবনারায়ণের কুটী	রায় চৌঃ ঈশানচন্দ্র লাহিড়ী ...	১৪৩।০	ঐ	......	......	৫৫।৶৩	......
২০৫১	১ম খঃ সেউটী	এরছান আলী মিঞা গং ...	৩২৮৶০	ঐ	......	......	৬৭৸/৮	......
২০৮৩	তুফানকুটী	মোহিনীমোহন বক্সী ...	২৬৬৸০	ঐ	......	......	১১১।৩	......
২১৩৩	কাউচাপড়া	মঃ নিয়ামতুল্যা গং ...	৪৪৮৸০	ঐ	......	......	১৬৬।৩	......
২১৭৩	ঐ	রুক্মিণীসুন্দরী দাস্যা ...	২০০৸০	ঐ	......	......	৭৪।৩	......
২২৩৩	বামনীর বালাবাড়ী	গোপালচন্দ্র মিত্র ...	৩৩৮।৶০	ঐ	......	......	১৪৯।৶৩	......

২২৪৮	বাবলগীর	মহারাজ বাহাদুর সিংহ ...	২৭২।৶০	"	......	......	১০২৸৶৮	......
২২৪৯	আটিয়ালডাঙ্গা	দয়ারাম বর্ম্মণ গং ...	১৪০।৶০	"	......	......	৫২॥৵৮	......
২২৫০	"	ঐ ...	১৩১৸০	"	......	......	৪১।/৯	......
২২৫৪	"	কালীপদ চট্টোপাধ্যায় ...	৫৩৮৷৶০	অংশ	......	১২৪॥/০	......	৩৯৸/৪
২২৬১	কাশমারি	মঃ নিয়াশা চৌঃ ...	১৮৩৶০	সমস্ত	......	......	৭৩৪৲৯	......
২২৬৬	"	জগমোহন বর্ম্মণ ...	১৬৭৸০	"	......	......	৬৩৸০	......
২২৭০	"	মঃ নিয়ামত উল্যা ...	৭১৮৶০	"	......	......	৫২৩৮।৶৮	......
২২৮২	"	মহারাজ বাহাদুর সিংহ ...	১৮৭৶০	"	......	......	৭৫৶২	......
২৩২৩	"	যোগগোবিন্দ সরকার ...	১১২৴০	"	......	......	২৮৩	......
২৩২৮	দুরাকহাটা	টয়রা বর্ম্মণ গং ...	১৭৸০	"	......	......	৬৬/৩	......
২৩১৯	"	যোগেশচন্দ্র ভাদুড়ী গং ...	২৪০৵০	অংশ	......	১২০৴০	......	৪৫৲৪
২৩১৯ ক	"	অবেশচন্দ্র ভাদুড়ী ...	২৪০৶০	"	......	১২০/০	......	৪৫৲৯
২৩৫৪	দুর্গানগর	মঃ এনায়েত উল্যা ...	২৪০॥০	সমস্ত	......	......	১২৭০৶১	......
২৩৬০	"	মঃ নিয়াশা চৌঃ ...	১০৩৸৶০	"	......	......	৩৮৸৶০	......
২৩৬৮	চৌপরাই	মঃ নিয়াদৎ উল্যা ...	৪৩৫।৶০	সমস্ত	......	......	১৩৫৩॥১	......
২৪০৭	হোকদহ	মোহিনীমোহন বক্সী ...	৭৫৫।০	"	......	......	২৮২॥/০	......
২৪১২	পাথরসন	আলাবউদ্দীন বেপারী ...	১৭১৷৶০	"	......	......	৬৫॥২	......
২৪১৯	"	সাহিদ রহমান সরকার ...	২৫৭৸৶০	"	......	......	৪৮।/৯	......
২৪২২	"	রায় চৌঃ ঈশানচন্দ্র লাহিড়ী গং ...	৬৬১৸০	"	......	......	৫৩৵৮	......
২৪৪১	২য় দুর্গানগর	মঃ নিশাবুদ্দীন চৌধুরী ...	১৪৫৲৶০	"	......	......	৫৪॥৪	......
২৪৪৪	"	মঃ নিয়াসা চৌধুরী ...	২৭৩৸/০	"	......	......	৫৮৬॥৴০	......
২৪৬৮	ভেটাগুড়ী সিংজানী	ভবনাথ অধিকারী ...	১১৭।০	"	......	......	৪৩৸৶৪	......
২৫০২	দিনহাটা	ফুলশীরাম ডাগা ...	৪০৫৸৶০	"	......	......	১৫২।৭	......
২৫৮২	গিতালদহ আটিয়াবাড়ী	সূর্য্যকান্ত মণ্ডল ...	১২৫৶০	"	......	......	৪৪৸৶১১	......

জোত নং	তালুকের নাম।	প্রজা ও নাম।	সম্পূর্ণ জোতের জমা।	সম্পূর্ণ জোত নীলাম হইবে কি না।	কেবল মাত্র অংশ নীলাম হইলে ঐ অংশের বিবরণ।	কোন অংশ মাত্র নীলাম হইলে ঐ অংশের জমা।	সম্পূর্ণ জোত নীলাম হইলে তাহার বাবৎ বাকী।	কোন অংশ মাত্র নিলাম হইলে ঐ অংশের বাকী
২৭০৮	ছোট আটিয়াবাড়ী	বিজলাল অপোয়াল ...	৫৩২।৶০	সমস্ত	......	......	১০৸৵২	......
২৭৮১	২য় খঃ ডাঙ্গনী	অনিরুদ্দিন মিছির ...	১০৫২৷.০	,,	......	......	৫৬১৸৶৪	......
২৭৬৪	,,	কোবাজত্র ছুড়ি ...	২১৪।০	অংশ	......	১৮৸৶০	......	৩৭৲
২৭৭০	খাঃ খাখামারী	আমিরউদ্দীন সরকার ...	১২৫৷৵০	সমস্ত	......	......	৪৭৶৵৩	......
২৭৭১	,,	আকাজউদ্দীন ...	১১১৵০	,,	......	......	৭২৲৬	......
২৮০১	কোয়ারীর	সমসুল হক ...	১২৭৸৶০	,,	......	......	৪৭৸৵২	......
২৮১০	,,	নিজামুদ্দীন বেপারী ...	১১৮।০	,,	......	......	৪৪।৶৬	......
২৩১৯	খাং বালাসুকা	অং-কফুরুদ্দীন মিছির ...	৪০৮৲	,,	......	......	১৫৭৲	......
২৯২০	,,	গজেন্দ্র বর্মণ ...	১২৪।০	,,	......	......	৪৫৷৶০	......
২৩২৪	খাং বালাডাঙ্গা	রাজমণী বর্মণী ...	১৮৫৷০	,,	......	......	৩৲।৵৩	......
২৩৪৪	,,	মহেশ্বর বিলাখিয়া ...	১৭৪৸৵০	,,	......	......	২৫৲	......
২৯৩৭	রুদ্রাপুনী	কালানারায়ণ সরকার ...	১০১৸৵০	,,	......	......	৪১।৶৴	......

AHAMED HOSAIN PRODHAN, *Naib Ahilkar.*

রাজ্য কোচবিহার।

মহকুমা দিনহাটা।

এতদ্বারা সর্বসাধারণকে জানান যাইতেছে যে, ১৯৩৭ সালের কোচবিহার রাজস্ব সংক্রান্ত নীলামবিষয়ক আইনের ৬ ধারা (অথবা ১১ ধারা) অনুসারে রাজ্য কোচবিহারের অন্তর্গত মহকুমা দিনহাটার প্রজাকারীর নিম্নলিখিত জোত (বা জোতের অংশগুলি) বাকী রাজস্বের জন্য আগামী ১৯৪৭ সনের ২৩শে সেপ্টেম্বর মোতাবেক ১৩৫৪ সনের ৭ই আশ্বিন তারিখে উক্ত মহকুমার মালকাছারীতে প্রকাশ্য নিলামে বিক্রয় হইবে।

এই সকল জোতের (বা জোতের অংশের) মালিক বা অধীন প্রজাদিগকে এতদ্বারা নিষেধ করা যাইতেছে যে, তাহারা বাকী রাজস্ব দিবার অব্যবহিত শেষ দিনের পর যে খাজানা দেয় হইয়াছে তাহা বাকীদার মালিককে না দেয়; যদি দেয় তাহা হইলে ঐ প্রকার যে টাকা দেওয়া হইবে তাহা ক্রেতার সহিত হিসাবে তাহারা জমা পাইবার হকদার হইবে না। ইতি—

জোতের নম্বর	তালুকের নাম।	প্রজাগণের নাম।		সম্পূর্ণ জোতের জমা।	সম্পূর্ণ জোত নীলামে হইবে কি না।	কেবল মাত্র অংশ নীলাম হইলে ঐ অংশের বিবরণ।	কোন অংশ মাত্র নীলাম হইলে ঐ অংশের জমা।	সম্পূর্ণ জোত নীলাম হইলে তাহার বাকী খাজানা।	কোন অংশ মাত্র নীলাম হইলে ঐ অংশের বাকী খাজানা।
৩০১৭	কুইয়ারকুঠী	মহেশচন্দ্র চক্রবর্ত্তী	...	১১৯৬/০	সমস্ত	......	.....	৫৯৸৵২	......
৩০৬৫	ভূলকী	মধুসূদন চক্রবর্ত্তী	...	২৪৩/০	ঐ	......	......	৪১৵৪	......
৩১৩৬	খুটামারা	গিরিধারীমল বয়েদ	...	১১২৶০	ঐ	......	......	৭২৴২	......
৩১৫৯	বাজেখরা দেওয়াগুড়ী	যামিনী সুন্দরী দাস্যা	...	৬৪২৶০	ঐ	......	......	২৪০৸৴২	......
৩১৬৪	ঐ	নবীনচন্দ্র দে	...	১২৫৶০	ঐ	......	......	৪৬৸৴০	......
৩২১৭	মনমথসেওড়াগুড়ী	যজ্ঞচন্দ্র সরখেল	...	১০২৸/০	ঐ	......	......	৪২৸৴৩	......
৩২১৯	ঐ	গিরিধারী মলবয়েদ	...	১৯৭/০	ঐ	......	......	৩৬৸৴৪	......
৩২২০	ঐ	গঙ্গানারায়ণ রায়সিংহ	...	১০২৶০	ঐ	......	......	৩০৸৩	......
৩২৩৬	ঐ	প্রসন্নেশ্বর দে সরকার	...	১১৫৶০	ঐ	......	......	৮৫৷৴৭	......
৩৩১২	ছোটপাড়ালবোড়া	আমির উদ্দিন সরকার	...	১৫৫।০	ঐ	......	......	৪৭৲	......
৩৩০৭	ঝিকরটারী	বনবিহারী রুদ্র	...	১৫০৶০	ঐ	......	......	৫৩৸৴২	......
৩৩৪৪	ঐ	গুরুপ্রসাদ রায়সিংহ	...	২৪।০	ঐ	......	......	৭১৸৴০	......
৩৩১৫	ঐ	গঙ্গানারায়ণ রায়সিংহ গং	...	৩২৫৸/০	ঐ	......	......	২০৪৸৴৩	......

জোত নং	তালুকের নাম	জোতদারের নাম।	সম্পূর্ণ জোতের জমা।	সম্পূর্ণ জোত নীলাম হইবে কি না	কেবল মাত্র অংশ নীলাম হইলে ঐ অংশের বিশেষ বিবরণ।	কোন অংশ মাত্র নীলাম হইলে ঐ অংশের জমা।	সম্পূর্ণ জোত নীলাম হইলে [illegible] খাজনা বাকী।	কোন অংশ মাত্র নীলাম হইলে ঐ অংশের খাজনা বাকী
৩০৩৬	ভিসাগুড়ী	যোবাজিয়া সিংহ গং ...	১০৭/০	সমস্ত	......	......	৪০৶৯	......
৩৩৪৭	,,	খুরানাথ রায় সিংহ গং ...	১৬১৷৴০	,,	......	......	৬০॥০	......
৩০৩৮	,,	মহারাজ বাহাদুর সিংহ গং ...	২৭২॥০	,,	......	......	৮৫৶৯	......
৩০৪০	,,	আমিরউদ্দিন সরকার ...	১১৮৲	,,	......	......	৪৪ ০	......
৩০৫৮	খাকচুকা	,,	২০৪৸৴০	,,	......	......	৭১৸৴৩	......
৩০৭১	পুরুলীয়া	মৌঃ অ কির উদ্দিন বক্সী ...	২৯০।০	,,	......	......	১০৮৸৴৮	......
৩০৭৫	গৌসাইগী	জ্যোৎস্নারাণী দেবী ...	২৬৩॥৴০	,,	......	......	৯৮৸৴৯	......
৩০৭৮	,,	,,	১০৫॥০	,,	......	......	৫০ /০	......
[illegible]	শিকারপুর	জলধর মিত্র ...	৩৯০/০	,,	......	......	১৪৬৫	......
[illegible]	,,	জ্যোৎস্নারাণী দেবী ...	১৫৩৲	,,	......	......	৪৯৲	......
[illegible]	[illegible]	অনিলকুমার মিত্র ...	১৮৩৶০	,,	......	......	[illegible]/১০	......
[illegible]	[illegible]	[illegible]	১৫০/০	সমস্ত	......	......	[illegible]	......
[illegible]	,,	মঃ আলম হোসেন ...	১২৩/০	সমস্ত	......	......	[illegible]	......
[illegible]	,,	[illegible] দাস ...	১০৩৸০	সমস্ত	......	......	[illegible]	......
[illegible]	[illegible]	[illegible] ও মিত্র ...	[illegible]	সমস্ত	......	......	[illegible]	......
[illegible]	,,	[illegible] রায় সরকার ...	১১১৸৴০	সমস্ত	......	......	[illegible]	......
[illegible]	[illegible]	[illegible] রায় ...	২২৩৸৴০	সমস্ত	......	......	[illegible]/১০	......
[illegible]	,,	[illegible] বর্ম্মণ ...	২১১৶০	সমস্ত	......	......	২৯৸০	......
[illegible]	২য় [illegible]	চন্দ্রকান্ত হিসাবিয়া ...	১৯২৴০	সমস্ত	......	......	[illegible]	......
[illegible]	১ম জিতপুর	শ্যামাচরণ হিসাবিয়া ...	১৩৮৷৶০	সমস্ত	......	......	[illegible]	......
[illegible]	২য় জিতপুর	চক্রপতি সরকার ...	৩৮৭৶০	অংশ	......	১২৩৸৶০	......	৭২॥৴৭

৩৫৩২	কুচগ্রী	ভাবাচরণ সিংহ বিশ্বা	...	১৬৩৮৵০	সম্পূর্ণ	......	......	৩৭।৵৩	......
৩৭৬৩	রাধাদমারী	অনিরুদ্ধকুমার মিহির	...	৩৫৩।০	সম্পূর্ণ	......	......	১৩২।৶	......
৩৭৯৭	"	কুমারস্বরেন্দ্র নারায়ণ	...	১৭৭॥০	সমস্ত	......	......	৩৩।৩	......
৩৮০১	"	মঃ নিয়ামা চৌধুরী	...	১৩১॥৵০	সমস্ত	......	......	২১০৸২	......
৩৮৫১	কুটিশাকমল	ঐ	...	১৪৩৮৶০	সমস্ত	......	......	১২২৩৸৵০	......
৩৮৭৮	নাবেবগঞ্জ	ঐ	...	১৫৬৸৵০	সমস্ত	......	......	৫৬৸৴১০	......
৩৯০০	কুর্ডাঙ্গা	ঐ	...	২০২।০	সমস্ত	......	......	৫১৭॥২	......
৩৯০৪	"	ঐ	...	১৯০॥০	সমস্ত	......	......	৭৩॥৵০	......
৩৯০৮	"	ঐ	...	৫১১৴০	সমস্ত	......	......	১৭৭২৶৯	......
৩০২১	খোচাবাড়ী	ঐ	.	১৮৯	সমস্ত	......	......	১০৮ ২৮	......
৩ ২৪	"	ঐ	...	১০৩॥০	অংশ	......	......	৭৭৩॥৩	......
৩১২৭	"	ঐ	...	২৬৭।৴০	সমস্ত	......	......	১১৫৫৸৵১০	...
৩১২৮	"	ঐ	...	১২২৸৵০	অংশ	......	৩২৸৵৩	......	২৩॥৵১০
৩১২৮ক	"	ঐ	...	১২২৸৵০	অংশ	......	৩২৭৴৩	......	১৬৩৸৵৭
৩১৩৪	"	ম নিয়ামতুল্লা গঃ	...	২৮৪।৶০	সমস্ত	......	...	৭৩৯৶৮	......
৩১৩৫	২য় খঃ ছাট খোচাবাড়ী	হরেন্দ্রনাথ চক্রবর্তী	...	১০৩৴৵০	সমস্ত	......	......	৩৭৸৵২	......
৩১৪১	শ চন্দন	ম নিয়াসা চৌধুরী	...	২৬৫৸৵০	সমস্ত	......	......	১১২।৯	......
৩১৪৪	বিল কালাইঘাটি	ঐ	...	২৩১।০	সমস্ত	......	......	১২৭৯৸৭	......
৩১৪৯	খাং কালাইঘাটি	মঃ নিয়ামতুল্লা গঃ	...	৪১৫৮৵০	সমস্ত	......	......	১৭ ৮॥১০	......
৩১৫১	কুমরগঞ্জ	দুলীচাঁদ মহেশ্বরী	...	১৬২৸৵০	সমস্ত	......	......	৬১/৪	......
৩১৬৪	"	মঃ নিশাবুদ্দী চৌধুরী	...	২৪১৶০	সমস্ত	......	......	৬৪৭৶৮	......
৪০০২	দাসিয়ার ছড়া	ওসমান আলি মিয়া	...	৬৭০॥৶০	সমস্ত	......	......	২৫১।০	......
৪০০৩	"	ঐ	...	২২১॥৶০	সমস্ত	......	......	৮৩/৯	......
৪০১৯	"	বিষ্ণুনাথ রামাউৎ	...	১০৭।৶০	সমস্ত	......	......	৪০।৵	......
[illegible]	দিনহাটা টাউন	লুইসা আপকার	...	২৮৬৵০	অংশ	......	১১৮।০	......	২৭।৵
৩৫৭		সতীশচন্দ্র পাল গঃ	.	১৭৫৸৵০	সমস্ত	......	...	৬৫৸৵০	......

AHAMED HOSAIN PRODHAN, *Naib Ahilkar.*

রাজ্য কোচবিহার।

মহকুমা দিনহাটা।

এতদ্দ্বারা সর্বসাধারণকে জানান যাইতেছে যে, ১৮৯৭ সালের কোচবিহার রাজস্বসংক্রান্ত নালাম বিষয়ক আইনের ৬ ধারা (অথবা ১১ ধারা) অনুসারে রাজ্য কোচবিহারের অন্তর্গত মহকুমা দিনহাটার এলাকাধীন নিম্নলিখিত জোত, (বা জোতের অংশবিশেষ) বাকী রাজস্বের জন্য আগামী ইং ১৯৪৭ সনের ২৫শে সেপ্টেম্বর, মোতাবেক ১৩৫৪ সনের ৮ই আশ্বিন তারিখে কোচবিহার রাজ্যের উক্ত মহকুমার মাল কাছারীতে প্রকাশ্য নিলামে বিক্রয় করা হইবে।

এই সকল জোতের (বা জোতের অংশের) রাইয়ত ও অধীন প্রজাদিগকে এতদ্বারা নিষেধ করা যাইতেছে যে, তাহারা বাকী রাজস্ব দিবার অবধারিত শেষ দিনের পর যে খাজানা দেয় হইয়াছে তাহা জোতদারকে না দেয়; যদি দেয় তাহা হইলে এই প্রকারে যে টাকা দেওয়া হইবে তাহা ক্রেতার সহিত হিসাবে তাহারা জমা পাইবার হকদার হইবে না।

তৌজি নং	তালুকের নাম।	নাম ও পরিচয়।		সম্পূর্ণ জোতের জমা।	সম্পূর্ণ জোত নীলাম হইবে কি না।	কেবল মাত্র অংশ নীলাম হইলে ঐ অংশের বিবরণ।	কোন অংশ মাত্র নীলাম হইলে ঐ অংশের জমা।	সম্পূর্ণ জোত নীলাম হইলে তাহার বাকী টাকা।	কোন অংশ মাত্র নিলাম হইলে ঐ অংশের বাকী।
৩১ খাস	পেটলা আধাবাড়ী	ভূপাল বাহাদুর সিংহ	...	২১৫।৵০	সমস্ত	......	......	৮০/৮	......
৩২	ঐ	বদরুদ্দীন মহম্মদ	...	১৫২৵০	ঐ	......	......	৫০/২	......
৩৩	ঐ	সতীশচন্দ্র ভট্টাচার্য্য	...	২০১।/০	ঐ	......	......	৭৫।৪	......
৭৭	কিং আধাবাড়ী	ভূপাল বাহাদুর সিংহ	...	২০০৲	ঐ	......	......	৭৫৲	......
১৩৩	ছাট বালাসিয়া	পানসাযুর প্রামানিক গং	...	১২৭।৵০	ঐ	......	......	৪৭৸	......
৩২০	বেখরীবাড়ী	মাদেশ্বর প্রামানিক গং	...	১২৩৵০	ঐ	......	......	২৬৲	......
৪১১	আড়িয়াবাড়ী গেন্দ আধাবাড়ী	ভূপাল বাহাদুর সিংহ	...	২২১৸৵০	ঐ	......	......	৮৩/১০	......
৪৫২	ভারালী	ঐ	...	২৭৪।/০	ঐ	......	......	১০২৸/১০	......
৪৮৫	ঐ	এছাহিন হোসেন	...	১১৪৵০	ঐ	......	......	২১৸৵০	......
৫৩৩	সীতাই	কৃষ্ণচরণ দাস গং	...	১১২৸৵০	ঐ	......	......	৫২৵৩	......
৬৩৭	চৌকিয়াধান	সিদ্ধিনাথ সরকার গং	...	১১১।/০	ঐ	......	......	৪৩৸৵৮	......
৬৩১	ঐ	হরকান্ত ভাদানী	...	২৮০/০	ঐ	......	......	১০৪/১	......
৬২৪	ঐ	বিন্দুবাসিনী দাসী	...	১৩২৵০	ঐ	......	......	৪৯৸/২	......

৬২৫	,,	হরকান্ত সরকার	...	১৭০।৶০	,,	......	......	৬৪৪৶	......
৬৭৪	সাগরদিঘি	ঐ	...	১২২।০	অংশ	......	১০১৶১০	......	৫৭৸৶৪
৬৭৪ ক	,,	ঐ	...	১২২।০	,,	......	২১৲২	......	৭৸৶২
৬৮৪	,,	দেবেন্দ্রনাথ ভট্ট	...	১৪০৷/০	সমস্ত	......	......	৫২৸৶৪	......
৬৮৬	,,	সরযূবালা গুহ গং	...	১২৫৶০	,,	......	......	২২।১১	......
৭২০	বার বাঙ্গলা	পরশুরাম সরকার	...	১৪৪৸/০	,,	......	......	৫৭।১১	......
৭৫৮	জামাগুড়ী	গোপালচন্দ্র মিত্র	...	২৮৭।০	,,	......	......	১০৭৸৶০	......
৭৬৩	,,	বিশেশ্বর সরকার গং	...	১২৪৲	,,	......	......	৪৬৸০	......
৭৭২	ছাট সিঙ্গিমারী	নবিকস বেপারী	...	১০৪৮৶০	,,	......	......	১০৪।৫২	......
৭৭৭	,,	সন্তানাথ মণ্ডল	...	১২২৷/০	,,	......	......	৪৫৸/৪	......
৭৮১	,,	পদ্মনাথ দাস	...	২০৸৶০	,,	......	......	৭৭।৶২	......
৭৮৮	নাকারগান	হলহরি দাস	...	১৪৮৷/০	,,	......	......	৫৫৮৶৮	......
৭৯২	,,	বিশ্বেশ্বর সরকার	...	১৪৮/০	,,	......	......	৬৫।	......
৭৯৮	,,	ঐ	...	১৬৭৶০	,,	......	......	৬২৶২	......
৮৩৯	চামটা	নেকমামুদ বেপারী	...	২৩২৶০	,,	......	......	৮৭৶৫	......
৮৭৩	,,	বেগম মোহাম্মৎ নুরজাহান	...	৫৫০৶০	,,	......	......	১৬৮৸৯	......
৯০৬	,,	সহরউদ্দীন সেক	...	১৪০৷/০	,,	......	......	৫৫।/৩	......
৯১৫	,,	কুজিরণ নেছা	...	৬৫৫৲	,,	......	......	২১২২।৶৮	......
৯৩০	২য় কৈমারী	বিলাতু দাস গং	...	১৬৯৶০	,,	......	......	৬।৶২	......
৯৩১	,,	কমলাকান্ত সরকার	...	১৫৯৶০	অংশ	......	৮৯৶৮	......	৩৩৶৮

AHAMED HUS.

A.S., Naib Ahilkar.

ইং ১৯১০ সালের ৫ আইনের ৫৩ ধারার ২ প্রকরণ মতে নিলামী ইস্তাহার।

নায়েব মহকুমা তুফানগঞ্জের মাল আদালত।

এতদ্দ্বারা সর্ব্বসাধারণকে জানান যাইতেছে যে, নিম্নলিখিত বাবদ বাকী থাকায় আদায় না হওয়ায় নিম্নলিখিত ক্রোকী সম্পত্তি আগামী ১৩৫৪ সনের ১২শে আশ্বিন মোতাবেক ১৯৪৭ সনের ৬ই অক্টোবর তারিখে বেলা ১ ঘটিকার সময় প্রকাশ্য নিলাম আরম্ভ হইবে।

১০ নং ১৯৪৭।৪৮ ইং। বাঃ খাঃ ৭২৶৩ মোঃ।

ডিঃ—শিরোমণিমোহন সরকার মোং হেবার।

দেঃ—অমূল্যচন্দ্র ঈশ্বর সাং মানসাই।

তপশিল সম্পত্তি।

পঃ তুফানগঞ্জ ১১১ নং খাস তাং মানসাই মধ্যে ৫১৮ দাগ ৮০ খুব জমির কাত বাঃ ৪৫৶০ আনা জমার জোত স্বত্ব।

H. BARMA, *Naib Ahilkar.*

রাজকীয় প্রাপ্য আদায় বিষয়ক ১৯৪৩ ইং সনের ১০ আইনের ২ সিডিউলের ৪৬ নিয়মের ঘোষণাপত্র।

রাজ্য কোচবিহারের সদর খাস মহাল আদালত।

এতদ্দ্বারা সর্ব্বসাধারণকে জানান যাইতেছে যে দায়ীকগণের নিম্নলিখিত সম্পত্তি আগামী ১৯৪৭ ইং সনের ২৯শে সেপ্টেম্বর মোঃ ১৩৫৪ সনের ১ই আশ্বিন তারিখে দিবা ১ ঘটিকার সময় হলদিবাড়ী খাস মহাল অফিসে খাস মহাল অফিসার কর্তৃক প্রকাশ্য নিলাম আরম্ভ হইবে।

৭৩ নং সার্ট ১৯৪৬।৪৭ ইং। বাঃ ডিঃ ৮৭৩ মোঃ।

সরকার বাহাদুর বঃ দীনেশচন্দ্র বর্ম্মণ।

তপশিল সম্পত্তি।

পঃ মেখলীগঞ্জ ১ নং খাস তাং ধবলীগঞ্জ মধ্যে ২১০ নং পঃ তৌঃ লিঃ ৩২/৬৷৶০ খুব জমির কাত বাঃ ৪৭৷৴০ আনা জমার পঃ স্বঃ।

১৭৮ নং ১৯৪৬।৪৭ ইং। বাঃ ডিঃ ১৯/৬ মোঃ।

সরকার বাহাদুর বঃ লক্ষেশ্বরী বর্ম্মণী।

তপশিল সম্পত্তি।

পঃ মেখলীগঞ্জ ৭৪ নং খাস তাং নিজতরফ মধ্যে ৪৬৬ নং পঃ তৌঃ লিঃ ১০।৪৮৶০ খুব জমির কাত বাঃ ৪/০ আনা জমার পঃ স্বঃ।

২৩৮ নং ১৯৪৬।৪৭ ইং। বাঃ ডিঃ ১৭.৬ মোঃ।

সরকার বাহাদুর বঃ আফিরুদ্দিন সরকার গং।

তপশিল সম্পত্তি।

পঃ মেখলীগঞ্জ ৩ নং ছিট তাং বালাপাড়া খাগড়াবাড়ী মধ্যে ৩৭৬ নং পঃ তৌঃ লিঃ ২২।৩/০ খুব জমির কাত বাঃ ২২৮৶০ আনা জমার পঃ স্বঃ।

৯৮ নং ১৯৪৫।৪৬ ইং। বাঃ ডিঃ ২৶০ মোঃ।

সরকার বাহাদুর বঃ সাপোই মহম্মদ।

তপশিল সম্পত্তি।

পঃ মেখলীগঞ্জ ১ নং ছিট তাং কোটভাজনী মধ্যে ৫৫২ নং তৌঃ লিঃ /৪।০ খুব জমির কাত বাঃ ।৶০ আনা জমার পঃ স্বঃ।

১১২ নং ১৯৪৫।৪৬ ইং বাঃ ডিঃ ৩০।০ মোঃ।

সরকার বাহাদুর বঃ হজরত উদ্দিন গং।

তপশিল সম্পত্তি।

পঃ মেখলীগঞ্জ তাং কোটভাজনী মধ্যে ২৫৮৪ নং পঃ তৌঃ লিখিত ১৩/১৶ খুব জমির কাত বাঃ ২৯/০ আনা জমার পঃ স্বঃ।

DWIJENDRA CHANDRA SEN, *Certificate Officer.*

দেওয়ানী কার্য্যবিধি আইনের ২১ হুকুম, ৬৬ নিয়মের ঘোষণাপত্র।

রাজ্য কোচবিহারের সিভিল জজ আদালত।

এতদ্বারা সর্ব্বসাধারণকে জানান যাইতেছে যে, দায়ীকগণের নিম্নলিখিত সম্পত্তি আগামী ১৯৪৭ সনের ৫ই অক্টোবর মোঃ ১৩৫৪ সনের ১৯শে আশ্বিন তারিখে দিবা ১ ঘটিকার সময় প্রকাশ্য নিলাম আরম্ভ হইবে।

৪ নং ১৯৪৭।৪৮ হং। বাঃ ডিঃ ৩১৩৯৮/০ মোঃ।

ডিঃ—প্রিয়নাথ অধিকার সাং মাথাভাঙ্গা।

দেঃ—জানারাম বর্ম্মণ সাং চোরাখাতা খাগড়ীবাড়ী।

তপশিল সম্পত্তি।

২। পঃ মাথাভাঙ্গা ৩০৯ নং থাক তাং চোরাখাতা খাগড়ীবাড়ী মধ্যে ২২৫৬ নং তৌঃ লিঃ ২৭।৪৮/০ ধুর জমির কাত বাঃ ৩৭৶০ আনা জমার কৃষিপ্রজা।

৯। পঃ, থাক, তাং তথা মধ্যে ৭৪৪ নং তৌঃ লিঃ ৩০/১০।০ ধুর জমির কাত বাঃ ৪৫৸/০ আনা জমার দরচু।

১০। পঃ, থাক, তাং, তৌঃ তথা মধ্যে ১১॥০॥০ ধুর জমির কাত বাঃ ২১।০ আনা জমার দরচুঃ।

B**AZLEY RAHMAN SARKAR**, *Civil Judge.*

দেওয়ানী কার্য্যবিধি আইনের ২১ হুকুম, ৬৬ নিয়মের ঘোষণাপত্র।

রাজ্য কোচবিহারের এঃ সিঃ জজ আদালত।

এতদ্বারা সর্ব্বসাধারণকে জানান যাইতেছে যে, দায়ীকগণের নিম্নলিখিত সম্পত্তি আগামী ১৯৪৭ সনের ৫ই অক্টোবর মোঃ ১৩৫৪ সনের ১৯শে আশ্বিন তারিখে দিবা ১ ঘটিকার সময় প্রকাশ্য নিলাম আরম্ভ হইবে।

২৭ নং ১৯৪৭।৪৮ ইং। বাঃ ডিঃ ১৮৬৸/০ মোঃ।

ডিঃ—হারচাঁদ সা মাং মোঃ কোচবিহার।

দেঃ—ছায়দউল্লা মুন্সী সাং ডাউয়াগুড়ী।

তপশিল সম্পত্তি।

১। পঃ বেহার ২৩০ নং থাক তাং ডাউয়াগুড়ি মধ্যে ৮৫২ নং তৌঃ লিখিত ২২।২৶০ ধুর জমির কাত বাঃ ২২।০ আনা জমার চুকানী স্বত্ব।

২। পঃ থাক তাং তথা মধ্যে ৮৫২ নং তৌঃ লিঃ ১৫।২৸/০ ধুর জমির কাত বাঃ ২০৶০ আনা জমার চুকানী স্বত্ব।

৩৭ নং। ১৯৪৭।৪৮ ইং। বাঃ ডিঃ ১১২৯৶৬ মোঃ।

ডিঃ—ব্রজমোহন গুহ মোঃ বেহার।

দেঃ—প্রবোধচন্দ্র সেন মোঃ বেহার।

তপশিল সম্পত্তি

১। পঃ বেহার ৯১৪ নং থাক তাং সহর কোচবিহার মধ্যে ১৮২২ নং তৌঃ লিঃ ১/১।৶০ ধুর জমির কাত বাঃ ১১৶০ আনা জমার ।০ আনা জোত স্বত্ব।

২। উপরোক্ত ১ নং তপশীলের লিঃ জোত স্বত্বের উপরিস্থিত অনুমান দৈর্ঘ্য ১৮ ফুট প্রস্থ ৪ ফুট তিন পাকা কাঠের পার্টিসন করা করগেট টিনের ঘর ধারার বেড়া ছাদ বারান্দা পাকা এই ঘরের জানালা ও কপাট সহ ॥০ অংশ

৩। উপরোক্ত ১ নং তপশীলের লিঃ জোত স্বত্বের উপরিস্থিত অনুমান দৈর্ঘ্য ২৭ ফুট প্রস্থ ৪ ফুট ৫ ফুট দেওয়াল করগেট টিনের পাকা ঘর বারান্দা পাকা জানালা ও কপাট ইঃ সহ ॥০ অংশ।

৪। উক্ত ১ নং তপশীলের লিঃ জোত স্বত্বের উপরিস্থিত অনুমান ১৭ × ১৩ হাত করগেট টিনের ঘর ধারার বেড়া এই ঘরের জানালা ও কপাট ও খুটি ইঃ সহ ॥০ অংশ।

৫। উক্ত ১ নং তপশীলের লিঃ জোত স্বত্বের উপরিস্থিত অনুমান ১৮ × ৮ ফুট করগেট টিনের ঘর পাকা মেঝে হাদলার বেড়া এই ঘরের জানালা কপাট ও খুটী ইঃ সহ ॥০ অংশ।

৬। উক্ত ১ নং তপশীলের লিঃ জোত স্বত্বের উপরিস্থিত অনুমান ১০ × ৯ করগেট টিনের ঘর মেঝে পাকা হাদলার বেড়া এই ঘরের জানালা ও কপাট ইঃ সহ ॥০ অংশ।

F. **AHMED**, *Asst. Civil Judge.*

দেওয়ানী কার্য্যবিধি আইনের ২১ হুকুম, ৬৬ নিয়মের ঘোষণাপত্র।

কাটৌর মহকুমা মাথাভাঙ্গার এঃ ডিঃ নাজের আদালত।

এতদ্দ্বারা সর্ব্বসাধারণকে জানান যাইতেছে যে, দাবীকগণের নিম্নলিখিত সম্পত্তি আগামী ১৯৪৭ সনের ৬ই অক্টোবর মোঃ ১৩৫৪ সনের ১৯শে আশ্বিন তারিখে দিবা ১২ ঘটিকার সময় প্রকাশ্য নিলাম আরম্ভ হইবে।

১২ নং ১৯৪৭।৪৮ ইং। বাঃ ডিঃ ৬৮২॥৶০ মোঃ।

ডিঃ—শিবরাণী দেব্যা মোঃ মাথাভাঙ্গা।

দেঃ—সিদ্ধেশ্বর বর্ম্মণ পঃ সাং লোতাপোতা।

তপশিল সম্পত্তি।

পঃ মাথাভাঙ্গা ৩৮৯ নং থাক ১৩০৩ নং তৌঃ তাং লোতাপোতা মধ্যে ১৮৪১/৶০ খুদ জমির কাত বাঃ ২৫।৶০ আনা জমার দঃ চুঃ।

TINKARI MOHAN MUKHERJEE, *Addl. Naib Ahilkar.*

রাজকীয় প্রাপ্য আদায় বিষয়ক ১৯৪৩ ইং সনের ১০ আইনের ২ সিডিউলের ৪৬ নিয়মের ঘোষণাপত্র।

রাজ্য কোচবিহারের সদর খাস মহাল আদালত।

এতদ্দ্বারা সর্ব্বসাধারণকে জানান যাইতেছে যে, দাবীকগণের নিম্নলিখিত সম্পত্তি আগামী ১৯৪৭ সনের ২৯শে সেপ্টেম্বর মোঃ ১৩৫৪ সনের ১২ই আশ্বিন তারিখে দিবা ৯ ঘটিকার সময় দিনহাটা খাসমহাল আদালতে প্রকাশ্য নিলাম আরম্ভ হইবে।

৩২৭ নং ১৯৪৬।৪৭ ইং। বাঃ ডিঃ ৭॥/১ মোঃ।

সরকার বঃ জানাই মুচি পঃ।

তপশিল সম্পত্তি।

পঃ দিনহাটা ৭৫৬ নং থাক তাং পৌলমারী মধ্যে ৮৯২ নং পঃ তৌঃ লিঃ ১/১৶০ খুদ জমির কাত বাঃ ২৶০ আনা জমার পঃ স্বত্ব।

৪৮২ নং সাট ১৯৪৬।৪৭ ইং। বাঃ ডিঃ ২১৯/০ মোঃ।

সরকার বাহাদুর বঃ ডুবকুটু পাল পঃ।

তপশিল সম্পত্তি।

পঃ দিনহাটা ৬৩৮ নং থাক তাং বানিয়াদহ মধ্যে ৪৩০১ নং তৌঃ লিঃ ১১৯৶০ খুদ জমির কাত বাঃ ৪।/০ আনা জমার পঃ স্বত্ব।

১২২২ নং ১৯৪৪।৪৫ ইং। বাঃ ডিঃ ১০৫॥৶০ মোঃ।

সরকার বাহাদুর বঃ মহরউদ্দিন মুনসী পঃ।

তপশিল সম্পত্তি

পঃ দিনহাটা ৬৬২ নং থাক তাং কামাত আবুতারা মধ্যে ১৬১৩ নং পঃ তৌঃ লিঃ ২০/১/০ খুদ জমির কাত বাঃ ১৪।০ আনা জমার পঃ স্বত্ব।

৯৩৬ নং ১৯৪৬।৪৭ ইং বাঃ ডি ৪০৯/১ মোঃ।

সরকার বাহাদুর বঃ আব্বাস সেখ পঃ।

তপশিল সম্পত্তি।

পঃ দিনহাটা ৫৩৮ নং থাক তাং সিঙ্গিমারী মধ্যে ২৮২৮ নং পঃ তৌঃ লিঃ ৪৯২।৶০ খুদ জমির কাত বাঃ ১৭৶০ আনা জমার পঃ স্বত্ব।

৯৮০ নং ১৯৪৬।৪৭ ইং। বাঃ ডিঃ ১৩৯০ মোঃ।

সরকার বাহাদুর বঃ রোহিনীকান্ত দেব সিংহ।

তপশিল সম্পত্তি।

পঃ দিনহাটা ৬০৫ নং থাক তাং ডাঙ্গা মধ্যে ২২৭০৬ নং পঃ তৌঃ লিঃ ২৩১১৶০ খুদ জমির কাত বাঃ ৩।০ আনা জমার পঃ স্বত্ব।

১০-১ নং ১৯৪৬।৪৭ ইং। বাঃ ডিঃ ২৮৷৶০ মোঃ।

সরকার বাহাদুর বঃ পৈরবউদ্দিন গং।

তপশিল সম্পত্তি।

পঃ দিনহাটা ৬৫৭ নং থাক তাং তুতীয়ার কুঠী মধ্যে ১৭৫৯৭ নং পঃ তৌঃ লিঃ ৭৷৩৷৶০ ধুর জমির কাত বাঃ ৮৷৶০ আনা জমার পঃ স্বত্ব।

১১৫০ নং ১৯৪৬।৪৭ ইং। বাঃ ডিঃ ৩৫৷/৩ মোঃ।

সরকার বাহাদুর বঃ ছপির সেখ গং।

তপশিল সম্পত্তি

পঃ দিনহাটা ৬৭৭ নং থাক তাং জারি ধরলা মধ্যে ১৯০৪৮ নং তৌঃ লিঃ ৯৷৩৮০ ধুর জমির কাত বাঃ ১০৶০ আনা জমার পঃ স্বত্ব।

১১৭৯ নং সাট্ট ১৯৪৬।৪৭ ইং।. বাঃ ডিঃ ১২৮০ মোঃ।

সরকার বাহাদুর ব. মানিক মণ্ডল

তপশিল সম্পত্তি।

পঃ দিনহাটা ৬২০ নং থাক তাং বরিবশ মধ্যে ২০৪৭৯ নং তৌঃ লিঃ ৯১৩৶০ ধুর জমির কাত বাঃ ৩৸৶০ আনা জমার পঃ স্বঃ।

১২৪৭ নং ১৯৪৬।৪৭ ইং। বাঃ ডিঃ ২৪৷০ মোঃ।

সরকার বাহাদুর বঃ পৈরবউদ্দিন সেখ গং

তপশিল সম্পত্তি।

পঃ দিনহাটা ৬৫৭ নং থাক তাং তুতীয়ার কুঠী মধ্যে ৬৯১১ নং তৌঃ লিঃ ৮৷২৷/০ ধুর জমির কাত বাঃ ১০৷/০ আনা জমার পঃ স্বত্ব।

১২৩ নং ১৯৪৬।৪৭ ইং। বাঃ ডিঃ ৪৷৶৯ মোঃ।

সরকার বাহাদুর বঃ তরনী বর্ম্মণ গং

তপশীল সম্পত্তি।

পঃ দিনহাটা ৫৭৭ নং থাক তাং ১ খণ্ড চকিয়ার পাড়া মধ্যে ২৭৪০ নং তৌঃ লিঃ ৭৮৷৶০ ধুর জমির কাত বাঃ ৸৶ আনা জমার পঃ স্বত্ব।

৭৩০ নং ১৯৪৬।৪৭ ইং। বাঃ ডিঃ ৫৷৩ মোঃ।

সরকার বাহাদুর বঃ মেম্বুনান্নেছানী বঃ মৃত—যোগেশচন্দ্র নমদাস

তপশিল সম্পত্তি।

পঃ দিনহাটা ৭২০ নং থাক তাং ২য়খণ্ড ভাংনী মধ্যে ১৫৮১৯ নং তৌঃ লিঃ ।২। /০ ধুর জমির কাত বাঃ ১০ আনা জমার পঃ স্বত্ব। ও তাং তথা মধ্যে ১৫৮১৩ নং তৌঃ লিঃ ৪২।৪ /০ ধুর জমির কাত বাঃ ৪৮৸/০ আনা জমার পঃ স্বত্ব।

৭৬৪ নং সাট্ট ১৯৪৬।৪৭ ইং। বাঃ ডিঃ ১৸৶০ মোঃ।

সরকার বাহাদুর বঃ সিরাজ আলি গং

তপশিল সম্পত্তি

পঃ দিনহাটা ৭৭২ নং থাক তাং টিয়াদহ মধ্যে ২০০৯৩ নং তৌঃ লিঃ ১/৩ কাঠা জমির কাত বাঃ ১৷০ আনা জমার পঃ স্বত্ব।

৭৩৬ নং ১৯৪৬।৪৭ ইং। বাঃ ডিঃ ২৫।৶৬ মোঃ।

সরকার বাহাদুর বঃ বরনী বর্ম্মণ গং

তপশীল সম্পত্তি।

পঃ দিনহাটা তাং ১মখণ্ড নাজনিরা মধ্যে ৮৫৬৯ নং তৌঃ লিঃ ৮৮।০৷০ ধুর জমির কাত বাঃ ৮৸০ আনা জমার পঃ স্বত্ব

৭৮১ নং সাটঃ ১৯৪৬।৪৭ ইং। বাঃ ডিঃ ১০।৬ মোঃ।

সরকার বাহাদুর বঃ আছিরণ নেছা গং

তপশীল সম্পত্তি।

পঃ দিনহাটা ৫৯৮ নং থাক তাং বড়নাচিনা মধ্যে ৫৬৩৮ নং তৌঃ লিঃ ৬৬১/০ ধুর জমির কাত বাঃ ৩৷৶০ আনা জমার পঃ স্বত্ব।

৮৩৩ নং ১৯৪৬।৪৭ ইং। বাঃ ডিঃ ১২২৸৶৯ মোঃ।

সরকার বাহাদুর বঃ উদ্যাবাস গং

তপশিল সম্পত্তি।

পঃ দিনহাটা ৫৭৭ নং থাক তাং বাজেরর্মা পক্ষিহাগা মধ্যে ৫২৮৪ নং তৌঃ লিঃ ৬৷১৷০ ধুর জমির কাত বাঃ ৯৲ টাকা জমার পঃ স্বত্ব।

৮৫৪ নং ১২৪৬।৪৭ ইং। বাঃ ডিঃ ১৪৲ মোঃ।

সরকার বাহাদুর বঃ জুরবুদ্দিন

তপশিল সম্পত্তি।

পঃ দিনহাটা তাং বামনগঞ্জ মধ্যে ১৫৮৩ নং তৌঃ লিঃ ১১ কাঠা জমির কাত বাঃ ২৲ টাকা জমার পং স্বত্ব।

৮৭৩ নং ১২৪৬।৪৭ ইং। বাঃ ডিঃ ১০০।৶৹ মোঃ।

সরকার বাহাদুর বঃ তারিণীপ্রসাদ রায় মণ্ডল গং

তপশিল সম্পত্তি।

পঃ দিনহাটা ৬০২ নং থাক তাং ছোটগারালদাগারী মধ্যে ৩২৪৫ নং তৌঃ লিঃ ২৪৷১৷৴৹ ধুর জমির কাত বাঃ ৩৸৶৭ আনা জমার পং স্বত্ব।

DWIJENDRA CHANDRA SEN, *Certificate Officer.*

দেওয়ানী কার্য্যবিধি আইনের ২১ হুকুম, ৬৬ নিয়মের ঘোষণাপত্র।

জারীর মহকুমা তুফানগঞ্জের দেঃ আদালত।

এতদ্দ্বারা সর্ব্বসাধারণকে জানান যাইতেছে যে, দায়ীকগণের নিম্নলিখিত সম্পত্তি আগামী ১৯৪৭ সনের ৩রা নভেম্বর মোঃ ১৩৫৪ সনের ১৬ই কার্ত্তিক তারিখে দিবা ১ ঘটিকার সময় প্রকাশ্য নিলাম আরম্ভ হইবে।

৪ নং ১৯৪৭।৪৮ ইং। বাঃ ডিঃ ৩২৲৹ মোঃ।

ডিঃ— রঘুনাথ সরকার সাং শীলবাপরী

দেঃ— টেপুচন্দ্র দাস সাং বালাকুটী

তপশিল সম্পত্তি।

পঃ তুফানগঞ্জ ১১৩৮ নং থাক তাং বালাকুটী মধ্যে ১৪৬ নং তৌঃ লিঃ ৮/৷৷৶৹ ধুর জমির কাত বাঃ ৮৶৹ আনা জমার দঃ চুঃ।

H. BARMA, *Naib Ahilkar.*

NOTICE.

THE CIVIL SUPPLIES DEPARTMENT.

(Cloth Section.)

Cooch Behar, the 12th September, 1947.

It is hereby notified for the information of those who are concerned that the validity of cloth licenses renewed after the 25th September 1946, will expire on the 25th September, 1947. Licenses are therefore required to be submitted to the Civil Supplies Offices with applications for renewal on eight-anna stamp paper with the renewal fee of Re. 1 (Rupee one) on or before the 25th September, 1947. Defaulters shall have to pay the full fee of Rs. 5 (Rupees five) only.

H. B. BISWAS,
Civil Supplies Commissioner, Cooch Behar.

The Cooch Behar Gazette.

১৪ই আশ্বিন, বুধবার] WEDNESDAY, OCTOBER 1,1947 [১৩৫৪ সাল ৪৩৮রাজশক

PART II.

NOTICES.

ছানী নিলামী ইস্তাহার কাছারী মাল মোতালেক নিজ বেহার এলাকে মেখলিগঞ্জ সব ৪৩ শকা
মোতাবেক সন ১৩৫৪ সাল তারিখ ১০।৯।১৯৪৭ ইং তারিখ।

এতদ্বারা সংবাদ দেওয়া যাইতেছে যে, নিম্নলিখিত সায়রাত মহাল আগামী ৭।১০।৪৭ মোতাবেক ২০ আশ্বিন দিবা দুই প্রহরের সময় বৎসর মেয়াদে নিলাম সর্ব্বোচ্চ ডাক কমার বন্দোবস্ত হইবেক। পত্তনেচ্ছুক ব্যক্তিরা নির্দ্ধারিত দিবসে নিয়মিত সময়ে সরকারী নিলাম ঘরে উপস্থিত হইয়া ডাক করে।

১।	১১২ নং থাক ২ নং তৌঃ ১ নং লাট পঃ মেখলীগঞ্জ মধ্যে তাং উঃ কুচলিবাড়ী মধ্যে জাবু বিড়ো হাট	নসীরউদ্দিন খাঁ	২০৲
২।	১৫৪ নং থাক ৪ নং তৌঃ ১ নং লাট পঃ মেখলীগঞ্জ মধ্যে তাং চাংড়াবান্ধা মধ্যে চাংড়াবান্ধা হাট	শিউপূজন তেওয়ারী	৪০০০৲
৩।	৬ নং তৌঃ ১ নং লাট তাং আলোকঝারী মধ্যে রাণীর হাট ...	শৈলেন্দ্রমোহন ঘোষ	৩০৫৩৲
৪।	৭০ নং থাক ১৩ নং তৌঃ ১ নং লাট মেখলীগঞ্জ তহবাজার ...	ক্ষীরোদচন্দ্র ঘোষ	৩০২৲
৫।	২৫, ৩০, ৩৪—৩৯, ৪৫, ৪৮ নং দেহা ১৩—১৬, ৪৩, ৪৬, ৫৪, ৮২ নং থাক ৬ নং তৌঃ ১ নং লাট তাং হুজুমডাঙ্গা মধ্যে বুড়া তিস্তা নদী	আহেচানউদ্দিন সরকার	৭০৲
৬।	২৬—২৯, ৩১—৩৩ নং দেহা ১৩,১৬ নং থাক ৭ নং তৌঃ ১ নং লাট তাং হুজুমডাঙ্গা মধ্যে গিরিয়া নদী ৪ তাং জয়লবণ মধ্যে গিরিয়া নদী ঐ ৩ মোট ৭	লখিরাম সাহা	৫১৲
৭।	৬০—৬২ নং দেহা ১৪৭ নং থাক ১০ নং তৌঃ ১ নং লাট তাং জোটবাড়ী মধ্যে যাথানী কুড়া ও শিলা নদী	ললিতমোহন সরকার	১১৯৲
৮।	৯০ নং দেহা ১৮ নং তৌঃ ১ নং লাট জারী তিস্তা নদী ১ম খণ্ড ও কুড়া...	লক্ষ্মীরাম সাহা	৩৪০৲

KUMAR P. NARAYAN, *Naib Ahilkar.*

রাজকীয় প্রাপ্য আদায় বিষয়ক ১৯৪৩ ইং সনের ১০ আইনের ২ সিডিউলের ৪৬ নিয়মের ঘোষণাপত্র।

রাজ্য কোচবিহারের সদর খাস মহাল আদালত।

এতদ্বারা সর্বসাধারণকে জানান যাইতেছে যে, দাবীকগণের নিম্নলিখিত সম্পত্তি আগামী ১৯৪৭ সনের ২রা অক্টোবর মোঃ ১৩৫৪ সনের ১৫ই আশ্বিন তারিখে দিবা ১ ঘটিকার সময় সদর খাসমহাল আদালতে প্রকাশ্য নিলাম আরম্ভ হইবে।

৭০ নং ১৯৪২।৪৩ ইং। বাঃ ডিঃ ৮৭৫৲ মোঃ।

সরকার বাহাদুর বঃ লক্ষ্মীন্দ্র নারায়ণ বসুনীয়া

তপশিল সম্পত্তি।

পং বেহার তাং হাতীরামশালবাড়ী মধ্যে ৮৭২৯ নং পঃ তৌঃ লিঃ ৩/৪৪/০ ধুর জমির কাত বাঃ ৪।৴০ আনা জমার পঃ স্বত্ব।

৪৩৪ নং ১৯৪৪।৪৫ ইং বাঃ ডিঃ ৩৪৶৩ মোঃ।

সরকার বাহাদুর বঃ হরিশ্চন্দ্র বর্ম্মণ

তপশিল সম্পত্তি।

পং বেহার ৮০৮ নং থাক তাং দেওয়ানবশ মধ্যে ৭৮৭৬ নং পং তৌঃ লিঃ ॥৪॥০ ধুর জমির কাত বাঃ ২৸৶০ আনা জমার পঃ স্বত্ব।

৩৬১ নং ১৯৪৫।৪৬ ইং। বাঃ ডিঃ ১৪৯॥৶২ মোঃ।

সরকার বাহাদুর বঃ ধুতু অধিকারী গং

তপশিল সম্পত্তি

পং বেহার ৮১২ নং থাক তাং অমর ভাণ্ডারথানা মধ্যে ৯৮৫৭ নং পঃ তৌঃ লিঃ ৩১৸২৶০ ধুর জমির কাত বাঃ ৩৮৶০ আনা জমার পঃ স্বত্ব।

৩৮২ নং ১৯৪৫।৪৬ ইং। বাঃ ডিঃ ৮১।৬ মোঃ।

সরকার বাহাদুর বঃ রূপনারায়ণ দাস

তপশিল সম্পত্তি।

পং বেহার ৮১৫ নং থাক তাং শালবাড়ী মধ্যে ৮৫৪৫ নং পঃ তৌঃ লিঃ ৮॥৪।০ ধুর জমির কাত বাঃ ১১॥০ আনা জমার পঃ স্বত্ব।

৪১৯ নং ১৯৪৫।৪৬ ইং। বাঃ ডিঃ ৭০।৩ মোঃ।

সরকার বাহাদুর বঃ বজরী দাস

তপশিল সম্পত্তি

পং বেহার ৮৩৫ নং থাক তাং শিতলাবশ মধ্যে ৮৩৫৫ নং পঃ তৌঃ লিঃ ৬।২৪/০ ধুর জমির কাত বাঃ ১০।/০ আনা জমার পং স্বত্ব।

৪২০ নং সাট্ট ১৯৪৫।৪৬ ইং। বাঃ ডিঃ ৩৮৲৩ মোঃ।

সরকার বাহাদুর বঃ দোবাজিরা দাস

তপশিল সম্পত্তি।

পং বেহার ৮৩৫ নং থাক তাং শিতলাবশ মধ্যে ৮৩৫৬ নং পঃ তৌঃ লিঃ ৫।০৸৶০ ধুর জমির কাত বাঃ ১১৶০ আনা জমার পঃ স্বত্ব।

৪৩৪ নং ১৯৪৫।৪৬ ইং। বাঃ ডিঃ ১৩৩৸৩ মোঃ।

সরকার বাহাদুর বঃ জোনাচু বর্ম্মণ গং

তপশিল সম্পত্তি।

পং বেহার ৮৩৯ নং থাক তাং চান্দামারী মধ্যে ৪২৪৮ নং পঃ তৌঃ লিঃ ১৮৸২৪০ ধুর জমির কাত বাঃ ২৩৶০ আনা জমার পং স্বত্ব।

৪৯৬ নং ১৯৪৫।৪৬ ইং। বাঃ ডিঃ ২২৮/৬ মোঃ।

সরকার বাহাদুর বঃ ময়না দাস গং

তপশিল সম্পত্তি।

পং বেহার ৮৫৩ নং থাক তাং রাণীডাঙ্গা মধ্যে ৮২৭৬ নং পঃ তৌঃ লিঃ ২/৩৸৶০ ধুর জমির কাত বাঃ ২৲ টাকা জমার পঃ স্বত্ব।

৫৬৩ নং সাট্ট ১৯৪৫।৪৬ ইং। বাঃ ডিঃ ৬৪।৶০ মোঃ।

সরকার বাহাদুর বঃ অভয়া দাস

তপশিল সম্পত্তি।

পং বেহার ৮৩০ নং থাক তাং কাশীয়াবাড়ী মধ্যে ৩৯৩২ নং পঃ তৌঃ লিঃ ।১/০ ধুর জমির কাত বাঃ ।০ আনা জমার পং স্বত্ব।

৫২৭ নং ১৯৪৫।৪৬ ইং। বাঃ ডিঃ ২০৭।৵৩ মোঃ।

সরকার বাহাদুর বঃ মাজাজ উদ্দিন মিঞা গং

তপশিল সম্পত্তি

পঃ বেহার নং থাক তাং শিমুলগুড়ী মধ্যে ৮৩২ নং পঃ তৌঃ লিঃ ২০।১৪৸৵০ ধুর জমির কাত বা ২০৴০ আনা জমার পঃ স্বত্ব।

৭২৫ নং ১৯৪৫।৪৬ ইং। বাঃ ডিঃ ১৪৷৵০ মোঃ।

সরকার বাহাদুর বঃ আইনুদ্দিন মিঞা গং

তপশীল সম্পত্তি।

পঃ বেহার ৯২৪ নং থাক তাং নবাবগঞ্জবাগানী মধ্যে ৩৭৮০ নং পঃ তৌঃ লিঃ ২।৪ কাঠা জমির কাত বাঃ ৮৵০ আনা জমার পঃ স্বত্ব।

৮৪০ নং সাটঃ ১৯৪৫।৪৬ ইং। বাঃ ডিঃ ৭৮৶১ মোঃ।

সরকার বাহাদুর বঃ জয়কান্ত দাস

তপশীল সম্পত্তি।

পঃ বেহার ৮৬৮ নং থাক তাং ছোটআঠারকোটা মধ্যে ৮০৮ নং পঃ তৌঃ লিঃ ২।২৷৶০ ধুর জমির কাত বাঃ ২৷৶০ আনা জমার পঃ স্বত্ব।

৮৮৩ নং ১৯৪৫।৪৬ ইং। বাঃ ডিঃ ৩৭৷৶০ মোঃ।

সরকার বাহাদুর বঃ রবীন্দ্র নারায়ণ নন্দি

তপশিল সম্পত্তি।

পঃ বেহার ১০৪১ নং থাক তাং চাপাগুড়ী মধ্যে ১৩১৯ নং পঃ তৌঃ লিঃ ৬.০।০ ধুর জমির কাত বাঃ ৬৷৵০ আনা জমার পঃ স্বত্ব।

৮৮৬ নং ১৯৪৫।৪৬ ইং। বাঃ ডিঃ ৪৩৷৶৯ মোঃ।

সরকার বাহাদুর বঃ অক্ষয় শিকারী গং

তপশিল সম্পত্তি।

পঃ বেহার ১০৪১ নং থাক তাং চাপাগুড়ী মধ্যে ১৩৩০ নং পঃ তৌঃ লিঃ ১৬/১৷৵০ ধুর জমির কাত বাঃ ১৭৸৴০ আনা জমার আং পঃ স্বত্ব।

১০২৮ নং সাট্ট ১৯৪৫।৪৬ ইং। বাঃ ডিঃ ৬৮৷০ মোঃ।

সরকার বাহাদুর বঃ বিশ্বনাথ দাস

তপশিল সম্পত্তি।

পঃ বেহার ৮৮০ নং থাক তাং গুধেরকুঠী মধ্যে ১০৬৮৭ নং পঃ তৌঃ লিঃ ৮/৩৸৶০ ধুর জমির কাত বাঃ ৯৷৶০ আনা জমার পঃ স্বত্ব।

২৮ নং সাট্ট ১৯৪৬।৪৭ ইং। বাঃ ডিঃ ২২।৶৯ মোঃ।

সরকার বাহাদুর বঃ বীরেন রায়

তপশিল সম্পত্তি

পঃ বেহার ১০৭৮ এ, নং থাক তাং ছাটগিরিয়ারী মধ্যে ৩১০৪ নং পঃ তৌঃ লিঃ ৮/২৶০ ধুর জমির কাত বাঃ ৭৶০ আনা জমার পঃ স্বত্ব।

২৬৭ নং সাট্ট ১৯৪৬।৪৭ ইং। বাঃ ডিঃ ৩৪৷০ মোঃ।

সরকার বাহাদুর বঃ কৃষ্ণমোহন দাস

তপশিল সম্পত্তি।

পঃ বেহার ৮৫৫ নং থাক তাং শিতলাবাস মধ্যে ৯০৬২ নং পঃ তৌঃ লিঃ ৯৸২৶০ ধুর জমির কাত বাঃ ১৩৷৵০ আনা জমার পঃ স্বত্ব।

৩১৫ নং সাট্ট ১৯৪৬।৪৭ ইং। বাঃ ডিঃ ৪৬৸১১ মোঃ।

সরকার বাহাদুর বঃ শুখে দাস

তপশিল সম্পত্তি।

পঃ বেহার ৮৫৫ নং থাক তাং প.টহড়া মধ্যে ৪০৮ নং পঃ তৌঃ লিঃ ৩/।৶০ ধুর জমির কাত বাঃ ৭।৵০ আনা জমার পঃ স্বত্ব।

৩.৮ নং ১৯৪৬।৪৭ ইং। বাঃ ডিঃ ৪৯৶২ মোঃ।

সরকার বাহাদুর বঃ কুশল দাস

তপশিল সম্পত্তি।

পঃ বেহার ৮৫৫ নং থাক তাং পাটহড়া মধ্যে ৪৭১ নং পঃ তৌঃ লিঃ ৫৸৪৶০ ধুর জমির কাত বাঃ ৭৷০ আনা জমার পঃ স্বত্ব।

৩২৮ নং ১৯৪৬।৪৭ ইং। বাঃ ডিঃ ২৩/৬ মোঃ।

সরকার বাহাদুর বঃ ছিকল দাস গং

তপশিল সম্পত্তি।

পং বেহার ৮৫৫ নং থাক তাং পাটছড়া মধ্যে ৫৯৯ নং পাঃ তৌঃ লিঃ ২৪/১৮/০ খুব জমির কাত বাঃ ৩৮।/০ আনা জমার পং স্বত্ব।

৩৩১ নং সা ১.৪২।৪৭ ইং। বাঃ ডিঃ ১২৩৮/৬ মোঃ।

সরকার বাহাদুর বঃ ধনমস্ত দাস

তপশিল সম্পত্তি।

পং বেহার ৮৫৫ নং থাক তাং পাটছড়া মধ্যে ৭৯৬০ নং পাঃ তৌঃ লিঃ ২৬।০৮০ খুব জমির কাত বাঃ ২৭৲ টাকা জমার পং স্বত্ব।

৩৪৩ নং সার্ট ১৯৪৬।৪৭ ইং। বাঃ ডিঃ ৩৯৶/৯ মোঃ।

সরকার বাহাদুর বঃ অবিউদ্দিন মিঞা

তপশিল সম্পত্তি।

পং বেহার ৮৬০ নং থাক তাং ১মখণ্ড শিয়ালদহ মধ্যে ৯৯১৪ নং পাঃ তৌঃ লিঃ ২০।৪।৶/০ খুব জমির কাত বাঃ ১০৸৶/০ জমার পং স্বত্ব।

৩৪৯ নং সার্ট ১৯৪৬।৪৭ ইং। বাঃ ডিঃ ৫৫।৶/৯ মোঃ।

সরকার বাহাদুর বঃ কেরকেটু বর্ম্মণ গং

তপশিল সম্পত্তি।

পং বেহার ৮৫৪ নং থাক তাং খারিজানলধোন্দয়া মধ্যে ৭৩৭৬ নং পাঃ তৌঃ লিঃ ১৫৸০৬/০ খুব জমির কাত বাঃ ১৩।৶/০ আনা জমার পং স্বত্ব।

৪০৪ নং সার্ট ১৯৪৬।৪৭ ইং। বাঃ ডিঃ ১২২।৵/৬ মোঃ।

সরকার বাহাদুর বঃ হরেন্দ্র দাস গং

তপশিল সম্পত্তি

পং বেহার ৯২৮ নং থাক তাং পানিশালা মধ্যে ২০৩৬ নং পাঃ তৌঃ লিঃ ৩০৸০।/০ খুব জমির কাত বাঃ ৪৩।০ আনা জমার পং স্বত্ব।

DWIJENDRA CHANDRA SEN, *Certificate Officer.*

রাজকীয় প্রাপ্য আদায় বিষয়ক ১৯৪৩ ইং সনের ১০ আইনের ২ সিডিউলের ৪৬ নিয়মের ঘোষণাপত্র।

রাজ্য কোচবিহারের সদর খাস মহাল আদালত।

এতদ্দ্বারা সর্ব্বসাধারণকে জানান যাইতেছে যে দাবীকগণের নিম্নলিখিত সম্পত্তি আগামী ১৯৪৭ ইং সনের ৪ঠা অক্টোবর মোঃ ১৩৫৪ সনের ১৭ই আশ্বিন তারিখে দিবা ১ ঘটিকার সময় দুকানগর খাস মহাল আফিসে খাস মহাল আফিসার কর্ত্তৃক প্রকাশ্য নিলাম আরম্ভ হইবে।

১০২ নং ১৯৪৬।৪৭ ইং। বাঃ ডিঃ ১১৮/৬মোঃ।

সরকার বাহাদুর বঃ সবদল সেখ গং।

তপশিল সম্পত্তি।

পং তুফানগঞ্জ ১১১১ নং থাক তাং বালসাই মধ্যে ১৪৩৮ নং পাঃ তৌঃ লিঃ ১৮/৩।/০ খুব জমির কাত বাঃ ২০৲ টাকা জমার পং স্বত্ব।

২ নং ১৯৪৬।৪৭ ইং। বাঃ ডিঃ ৫৩।৶/৯ মোঃ।

সরকার বাহাদুর বঃ সহরউদ্দিন সেখ গং।

তপশিল সম্পত্তি।

পং তুফানগঞ্জ ৯৪৩ নং থাক তাং রামরামপুর মধ্যে ১২৫ নং পাঃ তৌঃ লিঃ ২৬৮০।/০ খুব জমির কাত বাঃ ৩৫।০ আনা জমার পং স্বত্ব।

৯১ নং ১৯৪৬।৪৭ ইং। বাঃ ডিঃ ৩০।/০ মোঃ।

সরকার বাহাদুর বঃ জালীমাদুর সেখ গং।

তপশিল সম্পত্তি।

পং তুফানগঞ্জ ১০৯৭ নং থাক তাং লাঙ্গলগ্রাম মধ্যে ৪৪১ নং পং তৌঃ লিঃ ২৪৮৪৮৶০ ধুর জমির কাত বাঃ ৩১৮৶০ আনা জমার পং স্বত্ব।

১০৯ নং ১৯৪৬।৪৭ ইং। বাঃ ডিঃ ৩৩৷৶০ মোঃ।

সরকার বাহাদুর বঃ কান্তেশ্বর বর্ম্মণ।

তপশিল সম্পত্তি

পং তুফানগঞ্জ ১১১৩ নং থাক তাং বারকোদালী মধ্যে ১৯০৯ নং পঃ তৌঃ লিঃ ১৬৷২৶০ ধুর জমির কাত বাঃ ২৮৲ টাকা জমার পঃ স্বত্ব।

৯৭৪ নং ১৯৪১'৪২ ইং। বাঃ ডিঃ ১০৩.৶৯ মোঃ।

সরকার বাহাদুর বঃ মনবর অধিকারী।

তপশিল সম্পত্তি।

পং তুফানগঞ্জ ১১৭৬ নং থাক তাং কেরসাবাড়ী মধ্যে ২২৩৬ নং পঃ তৌ. লিঃ ৪;২৶০ ধুর জমির কাত বাঃ ৪৵০ আনা জমার পঃ স্বত্ব।

DWIJENDRA CHANDRA SEN, *Certificate Officer.*

রাজকীয় প্রাপ্য আদায় বিষয়ক ১৯৪৩ ইং সনের ১০ আইনের ২ সিডিউলের ৪৬ নিয়মের ঘোষণাপত্র।

রাজ্য কোচবিহারের সদর খাস মহাল আদালত।

এতদ্দ্বারা সর্ব্বসাধারণকে জানান যাইতেছে যে, দায়ীকগণের নিম্নলিখিত সম্পত্তি আগামী ১৯৪৭ সনের ৭ই অক্টোবর মোঃ ১৩৫৪ সনের ২০শে আশ্বিন তারিখে দিবা ১ ঘটিকার সময় মাথাভাঙ্গা খাসমহাল আদালতে প্রকাশ্য নিলাম আরম্ভ হইবে।

১০৩১ নং ১৯৩২।৪৩ ইং। বাঃ ডিঃ ৩৮৷৶০ মোঃ।

সরকার বাহাদুর বঃ কান্তেশ বন্দ্যোপাধ্যায় নাঃ গং।

তপশিল সম্পত্তি।

পং মাথাভাঙ্গা ২৬০ নং থাক তাং ভোজনের ছড়া মধ্যে ৯২৩ নং পঃ তৌঃ লিঃ ১৩৮১৷৵০ ধুর জমির কাত বাঃ ১৪৷০ আনা জমার পঃ স্বত্ব।

২২৫ নং ১৯৪৪।৪৫ ইং। বাঃ ডিঃ ১৯৬৸৶৬ মোঃ।

সরকার বাহাদুর বঃ একাব্বর সেখ গং

তপশিল সম্পত্তি।

পং মাথাভাঙ্গা ৪০০ নং থাক তাং গড়খোলা মধ্যে ২৫২১ নং পং তৌঃ লিঃ ৯২৷০৶০ ধুর জমির কাত বাঃ ৭৮৵০ আনা জমার পং স্বত্ব।

৮০ নং ১৯৪৫,৪৬ ইং। বাঃ ডিঃ ৭২৷০৶৬ মোঃ।

সরকার বাহাদুর বঃ হরেন্দ্র দাস গং

তপশিল সম্পত্তি।

পং মেহার ৮২৫ নং থাক তাং কলিমারী মধ্যে ৮৮৯৯ নং প তৌঃ লিঃ ১০৷৪৶০ ধুর জমির কাত বাঃ ১০৯০ আনা জমার পং স্বত্ব।

২৪৩ নং ১৯৪৫।৪৬ ইং বাঃ ডিঃ ১৩৷০ মোঃ।

সরকার বাহাদুর বঃ জুলুম মুচি গং।

তপশিল সম্পত্তি।

পং মাথাভাঙ্গা ৪৫৯ নং থাক তাং বড়গদাইখোড়া মধ্যে ৩৮১৩ নং পঃ তৌঃ লিঃ ৫৮১৶০ ধুর জমির কাত বাঃ ৪৷০ আনা জমার পং স্বত্ব।

৭৪০ নং ১৯৪৫।৪৬ ইং। বাঃ ডিঃ ৮২৶৩ মোঃ।

সরকার বাহাদুর বঃ ভুলা দাস গং।

তপশিল সম্পত্তি

পং মাথাভাঙ্গা ৩৪৩ নং থাক তাং মাটীয়ারকুটী মধ্যে ৩২৭৮ নং পঃ তৌঃ লিঃ ১৪।১ কাঠা জমির কাত বাঃ ১১৮৵০ আনা জমার পং স্বত্ব।

৭৭০ নং ১৯৪৫।৪৬ ইং। বাঃ ডিঃ ১৯৮৷৶০ মোঃ।

সরকার বাহাদুর বঃ লুন্ট রাম সরকার গং

তপশিল সম্পত্তি।

পং মাথাভাঙ্গা ৩৫৬ নং থাক তাং খড়িমারী মধ্যে ২১২৫ নং প. তৌ লিঃ ৪২/১৷/০ ধুর জমির কাত বাঃ ৩৫৶৬ আনা জমার পঃ স্বত্ব।

৮২২ নং ১৯৪৫।৪৬ ইং। বাঃ ডিঃ ১৭০৸/৯ মোঃ।

সরকার বাহাদুর বঃ মহানন্দ দাস

তপশিল সম্পত্তি

পং মাথাভাঙ্গা ৩৭৪ নং থাক তাং ২য়খণ্ড শালমারা মধ্যে ৫৫৫১ নং পাঃ তৌঃ লিঃ ৩৪।৪৶০ ধুম জমির কাত বাঃ ৩০৸০ আনা জমার পাঃ খব।

১৮৩ নং ১৯৪৬।৪৭ ইং। বাঃ ডিঃ ৮৮।৵৩ মোঃ।

সরকার বাহাদুর বঃ হরেন্দ্রদেব সিংহ নাং গং

তপশীল সম্পত্তি।

পং মাথাভাঙ্গা ৪০৩ নং থাক তাং রুইডাঙ্গা মধ্যে ৭১০ নং পাঃ তৌঃ লিঃ ১৬।৪/০ ধুম জমির কাত বাঃ ২২।০ আনা জমার পাং খব।

১৮৪ নং ১৯৪৬।৪৭ ইং। বাঃ ডিঃ ২৫৮/৫ মোঃ।

সরকার বাহাদুর বঃ সমসের আলী নাঃ

তপশীল সম্পত্তি।

পং মাথাভাঙ্গা ৪০৩ নং থাক তাং রুইডাঙ্গা মধ্যে ৭২৫ নং পাঃ তৌঃ লিঃ ১৮/২৸০ ধুম জমির কাত বাঃ ১৪৸৶০ আনা জমার পাঃ খব।

২০৩ নং ১৯৪৬।৪৭ ইং। বাঃ ডিঃ ১৬৷/০ মোঃ।

সরকার বাহাদুর বঃ মনেশ্বরী বর্মাণী গং

তপশিল সম্পত্তি।

পং মাথাভাঙ্গা ৩২৪ নং থাক তাং উপনীর বাড় মধ্যে ১৪৫১ নং পাঃ তৌঃ লিঃ ১৩।০ কাঠা জমির কাত বাঃ ১৮৸৶০ আনা জমার পাঃ খব।

২০৭ নং ১৯৪৬।৪৭ ইং। বাঃ ডিঃ ১৩৸/৬ মোঃ

সরকার বাহাদুর বঃ সুরেন্দ্র অধিকারী গং

তপশিল সম্পত্তি।

১। পং মাথাভাঙ্গা ৩৪২ নং থাক তাং তেররেকোরী মধ্যে ৪০৪৭ নং পাঃ তৌঃ লিঃ ১১০/০ ধুম জমির কাত বাঃ ২৪/০ আনা জমার অং পাং খব।

২। পং মাথাভাঙ্গা ৩৪২ নং থাক তাং তেররেকোরী মধ্যে ১৯২৪ নং পাঃ তৌঃ লিঃ ১/৪ কাঠা জমির কাত বাঃ ১৫ পাই জমার অং পাং খব।

৪৫৮ নং ১৯৪৬।৪৭ ইং। বাঃ ডিঃ ৫৪৸/৩ মোঃ।

সরকার বাহাদুর বঃ যোগেন বর্মণ নাঃ গং

তপশিল সম্পত্তি।

পং লালবাজার তাং পানাগুড়ী মধ্যে ১৯২ নং পাঃ তৌঃ লিঃ ৬।২৪/০ ধুম জমির কাত বাঃ ৭৶০ আনা জমার পাং খব।

৪৯৬ নং ১৯৪৬।৪৭ ইং। বাঃ ডিঃ ২৮।৶৬ মোঃ।

সরকার বাহাদুর বঃ রজনী প্রসাদ ঈশর গং

তপশিল সম্পত্তি।

পং মাথাভাঙ্গা ২৭১ নং থাক তাং বারঘরিয়া পাকচুটা মধ্যে ১৫০ নং পাঃ তৌঃ লিঃ ১২৸২৪৶০ ধুম জমির কাত বাঃ ২০৶০ আনা জমার পাং খব।

৪৯৯ নং ১৯৪৬।৪৭ ইং। বাঃ ডিঃ ১১৪৸/১১ মোঃ।

সরকার বাহাদুর বঃ উমানন্দ মুনসিয়া গং

তপশিল সম্পত্তি

পং মাথাভাঙ্গা ৩৪২ নং থাক তাং তোরসামা মধ্যে ৪৮০৫ নং পাঃ তৌঃ লিঃ ১২৪১৶০ ধুম জমির কাত বাঃ ১৬।৵০ আনা জমার পাং খব।

৫৯২ নং ১৯৪৬।৪৭ ইং। বাঃ ডিঃ ১০৮৸/৩ মোঃ।

সরকার বাহাদুর বঃ কৃষ্ণ বর্মণ

তপশিল সম্পত্তি।

পং মাথাভাঙ্গা ৪২০ নং থাক তাং মধ্যম মধুসূদন মধ্যে ৮০৩ নং পাঃ তৌঃ লিঃ ৭২৪১ কাঠা জমির কাত বাঃ ৮৩৸০ আনা জমার পাঃ খব।

৬৪৪ নং ১৯৪৬।৪৭ ইং। বাঃ ডিঃ ৩২।৶৭ মোঃ।

সরকার বাহাদুর বঃ টোনেয়া বর্মণ গং

তপশিল সম্পত্তি।

পং মাথাভাঙ্গা ৪৩২ নং থাক তাং শিবপুর মধ্যে ২।৪৷০ ধুম জমির কাত বাঃ ৫৪৵০ আনা জমার পাং খব।

৬৪৬ নং ১৯৪৬।৪৭ ইং। বাঃ ডিঃ ১২৪৶০ মোঃ।

সরকার বাহাদুর বঃ দেবীপ্রসাদ বর্মন

তপশিল সম্পত্তি।

পং মাথাভাঙ্গা ৪০৩ নং থাক তাং দুর্গানামী মধ্যে ৩৭৮৪ নং পাং তৌঃ লিঃ ১৪।১।৶০ ধুম জমির কাত বাঃ ২।৶০ আনা জমার পাং খব।

৬৬৫ নং ১৩৪৬।৪৭ ইং। বাঃ ডিঃ ৬৪৸৶৬ মোঃ।

সরকার বাহাদুর বঃ পেলা মিঞা গং

তপশিল সম্পত্তি।

পং মাথাভাঙ্গা ৪৬২ নং থাক তাং দেওয়ানেরকোট অবস্থার মধ্যে ১২১২ নং পঃ তৌঃ লিঃ ২।৮৹৸৶৹ ধুর জমির কাত, বাঃ ৩৮৴৹ আনা জমার পং খব।

৬৮৯ নং ১৩৪৬।৪৭ ইং বাঃ ডিঃ ৫৮৷৹ মোঃ।

সরকার বাহাদুর বঃ আনছার উদ্দিন আহাম্মদ গং

তপশিল সম্পত্তি।

পং মাথাভাঙ্গা ৪৬২ নং থাক তাং দেওয়ানেরকোট অবস্থার মধ্যে ১২০৯ নং পঃ তৌঃ লিঃ ১১/৪৶৹ ধুর জমির কাত বাঃ ১৩৷৹ আনা জমার পং খব।

৬৯০ নং ১৩৪৬।৪৭ ইং। বাঃ ডিঃ ১১৩৴৹ মোঃ।

সরকার বাহাদুর বঃ আনছার উদ্দিন আহাম্মদ গং

তপশিল সম্পত্তি।

পং মাথাভাঙ্গা ৪৬২ নং থাক তাং দেওয়ানেরকোট অবস্থার মধ্যে ১২১১ নং পঃ তৌঃ লিঃ ২৯/৮৹ ধুর জমির কাত বাঃ ৩৪৷৴৹ আনা জমার পং খব।

৮০৩ নং সা ১৩৪৬।৪৭ ইং। বাঃ ডিঃ ১২৪৶৹ মোঃ।

সরকার বাহাদুর বঃ শ্রীমন্ত বর্ম্মণ গং

তপশীল সম্পত্তি।

পং লালবাজার ৪৫৫ নং থাক তাং ভাঙ্গরথানা মধ্যে ১১৫১ নং পঃ তৌঃ লিঃ মোট ১০৫৷৹৴৹ ধুর জমির কাত বাঃ ১৭৴৹ আনা জমার আং খব।

৫ নং সাট ১৩৪৭।৪৮ ইং। বাঃ ডিঃ ৩৭৸৶৯ মোঃ।

সরকার বাহাদুর বঃ চন্দ্রনাথ বর্ম্মণ

তপশিল সম্পত্তি।

পং মাথাভাঙ্গা ৩৪০ নং থাক তাং মাটীয়ারকুটী মধ্যে ৩২৭৩ নং পঃ তৌঃ লিঃ ২১০৸৶৹ ধুর জমির কাত বাঃ ৩৶৹ আনা জমার পং খব।

DWIJENDRA CHANDRA SEN, *Certificate Officer.*

ইং ১৯১০ সালের ৫ আইনের ৫৩ ধারার ২ প্রকরণ মতে নিলামী ইস্তাহার।

জারীর মহকুমা মাথাভাঙ্গার মাল আদালত।

এতদ্বারা সর্ব্বসাধারণকে জানান যাইতেছে যে, প্রতিবাদীর দাবীর বাকী খাজানা আদায় না করায় তাহার নিম্নলিখিত ক্রোকী সম্পত্তি আগামী ১৩৫৪ সনের ১৯শে আশ্বিন মোতাবেক ১৯৪৭ সনের ৬ই অক্টোবর তারিখে বেলা ১ ঘটিকার সময় প্রকাশ্য নিলাম আরম্ভ হইবে।

১২৮ নং ১৩৪৭।৪৮ ইং। বাঃ খাঃ ৩১১৸৶৩ মোঃ।

ডিঃ—প্রিয়নাথ জমাদার মোঃ মাথাভাঙ্গা।

দেঃ—ধনচাঁদ শেঠিয়া মোঃ বৈরাগীর হাট ঠেঃ পাটগ্রাম জেঃ জলপাইগুড়ী।

তপশিল সম্পত্তি।

পং মাথাভাঙ্গা ৩১৩ নং থাক তাং পানীগ্রাম মধ্যে ৪৪ নং তৌঃ লিঃ ৪৭৸২৮৶৹ ধুর জমির কাত বাঃ ৬৲৶৹ আনা জমার চুঃ খব।

১২৭ নং ১৩৪৭।৪৮ ইং। বাঃ খাঃ ৩০৸৶৬ মোঃ।

ডিঃ—প্রিয়নাথ জমাদার মোঃ মাথাভাঙ্গা।

দেঃ—ধনচাঁদ শেঠিয়া মোঃ বৈরাগীর হাট ঠেঃ পাটগ্রাম জেঃ জলপাইগুড়ী।

তপশীল সম্পত্তি।

পং মাথাভাঙ্গা ৩১৩ নং থাক তাং পানীগ্রাম মধ্যে ৪৪ নং তৌঃ লিঃ ৪২/২৷৹ ধুর জমির কাত বাঃ ৬২৸৴৹ আনা জমার চুঃ খব।

১৭৩ নং ১৩৪৭।৪৮ ইং। বাঃ খাঃ ১৭৬৬ মোঃ।

ডিঃ—প্রিয়নাথ জমাদার মোঃ মাথাভাঙ্গা।

দেঃ—ভোলাগোবিন্দ বর্ম্মণ সাং বড়খাটিখোয়া ঠেঃ শীতলকুচী

তপশীল সম্পত্তি।

পং লালবাজার ৪৪৯ নং থাক তাং শীতলকুচী মধ্যে ৪০০ নং তৌঃ লিঃ ২০৮৩৷৶৹ ধুর জমির কাত বাঃ ৩০৷৶৹ আনা জমার চুঃ খব।

১৩৫ নং ১৯৪৭।৪৮ ইং। বাঃ খাঃ মোঃ ১০৩৸৵০

ডিঃ—প্রিয়নাথ তরফদার মোঃ মাথাভাঙ্গা।

দেঃ—রহমান মিঞা গং সাং গোলেনওহাটী টেঃ শীতলখুচী।

তপশিল সম্পত্তি।

পং লালবাজার ৪৬৬ নং থাক তাং গোলেনওহাটী মধ্যে ১১৫৯ নং খতের লিঃ ৭৮ ৵০ ধুর জমির কাত বাঃ ১৬৲ টাকা জমার দরচুঃ স্বত্ব।

১৩৪ নং ১৯৪৭।৪৮ ইং। বাঃ খাঃ ২৫৲

ডিঃ—প্রিয়নাথ তরফদার মোঃ মাথাভাঙ্গা।

দেঃ—শশীমোহন বর্ম্মণ সাং মধ্যমমধুসূদন

তপশিল সম্পত্তি

পং লালবাজার ৪২০ নং থাক তাং মধ্যমমধুসূদন মধ্যে ১৩৬ নং তৌঃ লিঃ ৪৭৵০ ধুর জমির কাত বাঃ ৪৵০ আনা জমার দরচুঃ স্বত্ব।

MANABENDRA NATH BHATTACHARJEE, *Naib Ahilkar*.

ইং ১৯১০ সালের ৫ আইনের ৫৩ ধারার ২ প্রকরণ মতে নিলামী ইস্তাহার।

জারীর মহকুমা মাথাভাঙ্গার এঃ ডিঃ নাঃ আ মাল আদালত।

এতদ্দ্বারা সর্ব্বসাধারণকে জানান যাইতেছে যে, প্রতিবাদীর দাবীর বাকী খাজনা আদায় না করায় তাহার নিম্নলিখিত ক্রোকী সম্পত্তি আগামী ১৩৫৪ সনের ১৯শে আশ্বিন মোতাবেক ১৯৪৭ সনের ৬ই অক্টোবর, তারিখে বেলা ১ ঘটিকার সময় প্রকাশ্য নীলাম আরম্ভ হইবে।

১২৯ নং ১৯৪৭।৪৮ ই বাঃ খাঃ ২৩১৵৯ মোঃ

ডিঃ—প্রিয়নাথ তরফদার মোঃ মাথাভাঙ্গা।

দেঃ—এক্রামউদ্দিন মিঞা গং।

তপশিল সম্পত্তি

পং লালবাজার ৬৬৩ নং থাক তাং গোলেনওহাটী মধ্যে ২২ নং তৌঃ লিঃ ৫০১৮৵০ ধুর জমির কাত বাঃ ৯৬.৬ পাই জমার দরচুঃ স্বত্ব।

১৩০ নং ১৯৪৭।৪৮ ইং। বাঃ খাঃ ৬৭৵০ মোঃ।

ডিঃ—প্রিয়নাথ তরফদার মোঃ মাথাভাঙ্গা।

দেঃ—আলীজান নেছাবিবি সাং শীতলখুচী।

তপশিল সম্পত্তি।

পং লালবাজার ৪৪৯ নং থাক তাং শীতলখুচী মধ্যে ৫০৪ নং তৌঃ লিঃ ১০৸৪ কাঠা জমির কাত বাঃ ১২ টাকা জমার দরচুঃ স্বত্ব।

১৩১ নং ১৯৪৭।৪৮ ইং। বাঃ খাঃ ১২৸৵০ মোঃ।

ডিঃ—প্রিয়নাথ তরফদার মোঃ মাথাভাঙ্গা।

দেঃ—ছপিরউদ্দিন মিঞা সাং গোলেনওহাটি টেঃ শীতলখুচী।

তপশিল সম্পত্তি।

পং লালবাজার ৪৬৬ নং থাক তাং গোলেনওহাটি মধ্যে ২৩ নং তৌঃ লিঃ ১৩৸১৵০ ধুর জমির কাত বাঃ ২৯৸৵০ আনা জমার দরচুঃ স্বত্ব।

TINKARI MOHAN MUKERJEE, *Addl. Naib Ahilkar*.

দেওয়ানী কার্য্যবিধি আইনের ২১ হুকুম, ৬৬ নিয়মের ঘোষণাপত্র।

জারীর মহকুমা মাথাভাঙ্গার নাঃ দেঃ আদালত।

এতদ্দ্বারা সর্ব্বসাধারণকে জানান যাইতেছে যে, দাবীকগণের নিম্নলিখিত সম্পত্তি আগামী ১৯৪৭ সনের ১১শে নবেম্বর মোঃ ১৩৫৪ সনের ৩রা অগ্রহায়ণ তারিখে দিবা ১২ ঘটিকার সময় প্রকাশ্য নিলাম আরম্ভ হইবে।

১৩ নং ১৯৪৭।৪৮ ইং। বাঃ ডিঃ ২৭৩৵০ মোঃ।

ডিঃ—ভবানীপ্রসন্ন তালুকদার মোঃ মাথাভাঙ্গা।

দেঃ—রেয়াজউদ্দিন মিঞা সাং বড়ুিমুচী।

তপশিল সম্পত্তি

পং লালবাজার ৪১৩ নং থাক তাং বড়ুিমুচী মধ্যে ১০০ নং তৌঃ লিঃ ৭৭৸৭৵০ ধুর জমির কাত বাঃ ২৩৸৵০ আনা জমার দরচুঃ স্বত্ব।

MANABENDRA NATH BHATTACHARJEE, *Naib Ahilkar*.

The Cooch Behar Gazette.

SUPPLEMENTARY.

১৪ই আশ্বিন, বুধবার] WEDNESDAY, OCTOBER 1, 1947 [১৩৫৪ সাল ৪৩৮রাজশক

PART II.

NOTICES.

ইং ১৯১০ সালের ৫ আইনের ৫৩ ধারার ২ প্রকরণ মতে নিলামী ইস্তাহার।

জারীর মহকুমা মেখলীগঞ্জের মাল আদালত।

এতদ্দ্বারা সর্ব্বসাধারণকে জানান যাইতেছে যে, প্রতিবাদীর দাবীর বাকী খাজনা আদায় না করায় তাহার নিম্নলিখিত ক্রোকী সম্পত্তি আগামী ১৩৫৪ সনের ১৯শে আশ্বিন মোতাবেক ১৯৪৭ সনের ৬ই অক্টোবর, তারিখে বেলা ১ ঘটিকার সময় প্রকাশ্য নীলাম আরম্ভ হইবে।

৫৯ নং ১৯৪৭।৪৮ ই বাঃ খাঃ ২৩৩।৫/০ মোঃ

ডিঃ—ফজলুলকরিম প্রধান সাং কিসামত ফতেমামুদ।

দেঃ—পবনেশ্বর রায় গং সাং নিজতরফ।

তপশিল সম্পত্তি।

পং মেখলিগঞ্জ ১৩৫ নং খাস তাং পানীশালা মধ্যে হাঃ ১৭৭৪ নং তৌঃ লিঃ ১০৮২।১/ ধুর জমির কাত বাঃ ২৭৮০ আনা জমার দরচুকানী স্বত্ব।

৬০ নং ১৯৪৭।৪৮ ইং। বাঃ খাঃ ১৯৬।৩

ডিঃ—ফজলুলকরিম প্রধান গং সাং কিসামত ফতেমামুদ।

দেঃ—যামিনী বর্ম্মণ গং সাং তথা।

তপশিল সম্পত্তি।

পং মেখলীগঞ্জ ৭৩ নং খাস তাং খাষবশ বাজে জমা মধ্যে ৭৮১ নং তৌঃ লিঃ ২৩২৮০ ধুর জমির কাত বাঃ ৪৪৲ টাকা জমার দরচুকানী স্বত্ব।

৬২ নং ১৯৪৭।৪৮ ইং। বাং খাঃ ১৬১৩মোং।

ডিঃ—নগেন্দ্রচন্দ্র লাহিড়ী গং মোঃ মেখলীগঞ্জ।

দেঃ—আত্তেশ্বরী বর্ম্মণী গং সাং ফুলকার ডাবরী।

তপশিল সম্পত্তি

পং মেখলীগঞ্জ ২৯ নং খাস তাং ফুলকার ডাবরী মধ্যে ১৫৬০ নং তৌঃ লিঃ ৪০।১৫৮৫/০ ধুর জমির কাত বাঃ ৪৪৮।১/০ আনা জমার কৃষিপ্রজা স্বত্ব।

৬৩ নং ১৩৪৭।৪৮ ইং। বাঃ খাঃ ৩১১৸৶/১ মোঃ।

ডি—রায় চৌধুরী ভরেশচন্দ্র মুস্তকী গঃ মোঃ বেহার।

দেঃ—যমুনা প্রসাদ সিংহ গঃ সাং উজলপুখরী।

তপশিল সম্পত্তি।

পাঃ মেখলীগঞ্জ ১৮৭ নং থাক তাং খারিজা গোপালপুর মধ্যে ১৯৭৫ নং তৌঃ লিঃ ৩২২৸৩৷৶০ যুব জমির কাত বাঃ ৪৬৵০ আনা জমায় চুকানী স্বত্ব।

৫৪ নং ১৩৪৭।৪৮ ইং। বাঃ খাঃ ৬৬৷৶০ মোঃ।

ডিঃ—রবিউল ইছলাম সাং গোথামারী।

দেঃ—সাবারউদ্দীন গঃ সাং গোথামারী চৌঃ মেখলীগঞ্জ।

তপশিল সম্পত্তি।

পাঃ মেখলীগঞ্জ ২৪ নং থাক তাং গোথামারী মধ্যে ৫৸৩৷০ যুব জমীর কাত বাঃ ১১৸০ আনা জমায় কৃষীপ্রজা।

৫৫ নং ১৩৪৭।৪৮ ইং। বাঃ খাঃ ১৪১৸৴/১ মোঃ।

ডিঃ—রবিউল ইছলাম সাং গোথামারী।

দেঃ—সাবারউদ্দীন গঃ সাং গোথামারী চৌঃ মেখলীগঞ্জ।

তপশিল সম্পত্তি

পাঃ মেখলীগঞ্জ ২৪ নং থাক তাং গোথামারী মধ্যে ১৪৪৩৷০ যুব জমীর কাত বাঃ ২৫৸/০ আনা জমায় কৃষীপ্রজা।

৫৬ নং ১৩৪৭।৪৮ ইং। বাঃ খাঃ ৯৷০ মোঃ।

ডিঃ—ধরনীকান্ত রায় সাং হেমকুমারী।

দেঃ—রামেশ্বরী বর্ম্মনী সাং হেমকুমারী চৌঃ হলদীবাড়ী।

তপশিল সম্পত্তি।

পাঃ মেখলীগঞ্জ ৫৫ নং থাক তাং হেমকুমারী মধ্যে ২৫০ নং তৌঃ বাঃ।২৸৶০ যুব জমীর কাত বাঃ ৸/০ আনা জমায় কৃষীপ্রজা।

৫৭ নং ১৩৪৭।৪৮ ইং। বাঃ খাঃ ৩৪৫৶৩ মোঃ।

ডিঃ—ভবানীপ্রসন্ন তালুকদার মোঃ ও চৌঃ মেখলীগঞ্জ।

দেঃ—কাউয়া মহাম্মদ গং সাং জামালদহ বালাপুখরী চৌঃ মেখলীগঞ্জ।

তপশিল সম্পত্তি।

পাঃ মেখলীগঞ্জের অন্তর্গত ১২১ নং তাং জামালদহ বালাপুখরী মধ্যে ১৭২৭ নং তৌঃ লিঃ ৩৪৸৩৸৶০ যুব জমির কাত বাঃ ৬৲৸/০ আনা জমায় চুঃ স্বত্ব।

৫৮ নং ১৩৪৭।৪৮ ইং বাঃ খাঃ ১৯/১ মোঃ।

ডিঃ—কাশীনাথ কৌঃব গং মোঃ হেমকুমারী চৌঃ মেখলীগঞ্জ।

দেঃ—ফজলুলকরিম প্রধান গঃ সাং কিং কুচমারুল।

তপশিল সম্পত্তি।

পাঃ মেখলীগঞ্জ ৩১নং থাক তাং নিজতরফ মধ্যে ৭৫৭ নং তৌঃ লিঃ ৮৩৷৶০ যুব জমির কাত বাং ১৩৲ টাকা জমায় বঃচু-স্বত্ব।

KUMAR P. NARAYAN, *Naib Ahilkar*.

The Cooch Behar Gazette.

২৯শে আশ্বিন, বৃহস্পতিবার; THURSDAY, OCTOBER 16, 1947 [১৩৫৪ সাল, ৪৩৮ রাজশক

PART II.

NOTICES.

ইং ১৯১০ সালের ৫ আইনের ৫৩ ধারার ২ প্রকরণ মতে নিলামী ইস্তাহার।

রাজ্য কোচবিহারের এঃ সিঃ জজ আদালত।

এতদ্বারা সর্ব্বসাধারণকে জানান যাইতেছে যে, প্রতিবাদীর দাবীর বাকী খাজানা আদায় না করায় তাহার নিম্নলিখিত ক্রোকী সম্পত্তি আগামী ১৩৫৪ সনের ৩রা অগ্রহায়ণ মোতাবেক ১৯৪৭ সনের ১৯শে নভেম্বর তারিখে বেলা ১ ঘটিকার সময় প্রকাশ্য নিলাম আরম্ভ হইবে।

১৩৫ নং ১৯৪৭।৪৮ ইং। বাঃ খাঃ ২৩৶৩ মোঃ।

ডিঃ—দি কুচবিহার ব্যাঙ্কিং করপোরেশন মোঃ বেহার ষ্টেঃ কোতয়ালী

দেঃ—মহিম চন্দ্র বর্ম্মণ নাঃ গং সাং ফলিমারী ষ্টেঃ কোতয়ালী

তপশিল সম্পত্তি।

পঃ বেহার ৮২৮ নং থাক তাং ব্রহ্মত্তর কশালডাঙ্গা মধ্যে ২২ নং খতের বাবদ ৩৮.০৷৶০ ধুর জমির কাত বাঃ ২৷০ আনা জমার কৃষিপ্রজা স্বত্ব।

১৩৪ নং ১৯৪৭।৪৮ ইং। বাঃ খাঃ ১৬।১৫৶০ মোঃ।

ডিঃ—দি কুচবিহার ব্যাঙ্কিং করপোরেশন লিমিটেড মোঃ বেহার ষ্টেশন কোতয়ালী

দেঃ—জ্ঞানদাসুন্দরী দেবী জঃ শশীধর বসুনীয়া সাং কশালডাঙ্গা ষ্টেঃ কোতয়ালী।

তপশীল সম্পত্তি।

পঃ বেহার ৮২৮ নং থাক তাং ব্রহ্মত্তর কশালডাঙ্গা মধ্যে ১০৮ নং খতের বাবদ ৩৭৸০৷৶০ ধুর জমির কাত বাঃ ৫৫৲ টাকা জমার চুঃ স্বত্ব।

৯২ নং ১৯৪৭।৪৮ ইং। বাঃ খাঃ ১০।৷০ মোঃ।

ডিঃ—দি কুচবিহার ব্যাঙ্কিং করপোরেশন লিমীটেড মোঃ বেহার ষ্টেশন কোতয়ালী

দেঃ—জগন্নাথ বর্ম্মণ গং পীং মৃত অ বাক বর্ম্মণ সাং কদমীমারী ষ্টেঃ কোতয়ালী।

তপশিল সম্পত্তি।

পঃ বেহার ৮২৮ নং থাক তাং ব্রহ্মত্তর কশালডাঙ্গা মধ্যে ৬১৩ নং খতের বাবদ ২৯/৪৫৶০ ধুর জমীর কাত বাঃ ৩০৸০ আনা জমার জোত স্বত্ব।

F. AHMED, *Offg. Asst. Civil Judge.*

MALCUCHERY NOTICE.

ইস্তাহারনামা কাছারী মাল মোকাম কোচবেহার, সন ১৯ তারীখ
মোতাবেক বাঙ্গালা ১৩৫৪ সন তারীখ।

পঃ মাথাভাঙ্গা এলাকাধীন ৩৯০ নং থাক তালুক শৌলমারী অন্তর্গত কোচবেহার চা বাগানের জন্ত অত্র অদালতের ১৯৪৭।৪৮ ইং সনের ১৮ নং ভূমিগ্রহণের মোকদ্দমার ১৮।৮।৪৭ ইং তারীখের আদেশ সূত্রে নিম্নলিখিত বাবাদযুক্ত ভূমী ১৩৫৪ সনের শুরু হইতে সরকারে গৃহীত হইয়া উক্ত কোচবেহার চা বাগানের সামীল হওয়ায় সর্ব্ব সাধারণের অবগতী জন্ত এই ইস্তাহার প্রচারিত হইল। ইতী

১। পঃ মাথাভাঙ্গা ৩৯০ নং থাক তাং শৌলমারী ১১ নং বাঃ ২৪৩৭ নং তৌঃ ১০৪ নং স্বত্ব জোত মালদার পিং দৌলতরাম ভাদানী হরেকচাদ পিং গোলাপচাদ ভাদানী মোঃ বেহার বাঃ জমি ১৮৭।৪৶০ ধুর জমা ১৪১॥০ আনা গৃহীত জমি ১৮৭৮৪৶০ ধুর জমা ১৪১॥০ আনা।

বিবরং

স্বত্ব নং ১০৫ সিট নং ২ দাগ নঃ ৮৫—১০৮, ১১৭—১২৩, ১২৫—১৩৩, ১৬১, ২১৬, ২১৭, ৮৪১ ৮৫২—৮৫৫, ১০০২—১০০৮ চুঃ চলকা পিং গুল দাস মহেন্দ্রনাথ বর্ম্মণ পিং নোকর দাস বাঃ জমি ১৮৭৮৪।৶০ ধুর জমা ১৯১/০ আনা গৃহীত জমি ১৮৭৮৪।৶০ ধুর জমা ১৯১/০ আনা।

২। পঃ মাথাভাঙ্গা ৩৯০ নং থাক তাং শৌলমারী বাঃ নং ১২ তৌঃ নং ২৪৩৮ স্বত্ব নং ১০৬ জোত মালদার পিং দৌলতরাম ভাদানী হরেকচাদ পিং গোলাপচাদ ভাদানী বাঃ জমি ১০৫/॥৶০ ধুর জমা ৪৫।০ আনা গৃহীত জমি ১০১/১৶০ ধুর জমা ৪৪৸৶৮ পাই।

বিবরং

স্বত্ব নং ১০৭ সিট নং ২ দাগ নং ১৩৪, ১৫৫, ১৩৭, ১৩৯, ১৪১, ১৪৭, ১৪৮, ১৫২, ৬৭৭, ৬৭৮, ৮৩৬—৮৪০, ৮৫১, ৯২১, ৯৫৬ চুঃ চলকা পিং গুল দাস বাঃ জমি ৪৫/৪॥/০ ধুর জমা ৩০।০ আনা গৃহীত জমি ৪২॥৪।০ ধুর জমা ৩০৶২ পাই।

বাঃ নং ১২ তৌঃ নং ২৪৩৮ স্বত্ব নং ১০৮ সিট নং ২ দাগ নং ১৩৬, ১৩৮, ১৫০—১৪৪, ১৪৯, ১৪৯—১৫১ ৬৭৫, ৬৭৬, ৬৭৯, ৮৭৯, ৮৫০, ৯১৯,—১০০১ চুঃ শুকুরচাদ নাঃ পক্ষে উহি মাতা কন্যামতি দাস্যা বাঃ নীলু বর্ম্মণ নাঃ রমেশচন্দ্র পিং রুদ্র বর্ম্মণ বাঃ জমি ৬১৸১ কাঠা জমা ৩১।০ আনা গৃঃ জমি ৫৮।৭৶০ ধুর জমা ৩০॥৶২

৩। পঃ মাথাভাঙ্গা ৩৯০ নং থাক তাং শৌলমারী বাঃ নং ১৩ তৌঃ নং ২৪৩৯ স্বত্ব নং ১০৯ জোত যোগেন্দ্রকুমার জ্ঞানেন্দ্রকুমার পিং হরেন্দ্রকুমার রায় চৌধুরী গিরীন্দ্রকুমার রায় চৌধুরী পিং গজেন্দ্রকুমার রায় চৌধুরী ধীরেন্দ্র কুমার জীতেন্দ্রকুমার পিং রাজেন্দ্রকুমার রায় চৌধুরী মোঃ মাথাভাঙ্গা তৌঃ সূত্রে রেখা বাগ কঃ ক্ষিতীশচন্দ্র বাগ ইন্দুবালা জঃ সত্যেন্দ্র কুমার সাহা মোঃ মাথাভাঙ্গা বাঃ জমি ৩৭৫/১ জমা ২২১।০ গৃহীত জমি ৩৪৫॥৪৮/০ ধুর জমা ২১৭।/৮ পাই।

বিবরং

সিট নং ২ দাগ নং ৫৩৫, ৯৬০ নিজ দখল ১৭॥৶০ ধুর।

১১০ নং স্বত্ব ২ নং সিট চুঃ রঘুনাথ পিঃ রামপ্রসাদ দাস বাঃ জমি ৩১১৸১৶০ ধুর জমা ২৫৩, টাকা গৃহীত জমি ২৮২.৪৸৫০ ধুর জমা ২৪৮৯ পাই।

বিবরং

দাগ নং ১৬৩—১৭৩, ১৭৯, ১৮১, ১৯০, ১৯১, ১৯২, ২০৪, ২০৭, ২১৫, ২৭০, ৩৬৬, ৩৮৮, ৩৭৭, ৩৭৮, ৩৮০, ৩৮১, ৩০৯, ৩৯০, ৩৯৭, ৪০৭, ৪০৮, ৪১০, ৪১৭, ৪১৯, ৪২০, ৪২১, ৪২৪, ৪২৫, ৪২৭, ৪৩১, ৪৪৬, ৪৯৯, ৫২০, ৫২১, ৫০২, ৫৩৩, ৫৩৬, ৫৪০, ৫৪৮, ৫৫৩, ৬৬০, ৬৮১, ৭২১, ৮৪০, ৮৮২, ৮৮৩, ৮৮৭, ৮৯৭, ৯১১, ৯১৩, ৯১৭, ৯৯০, ৯৯৮, ৯০০ নিজ দখল জমি ১০০৪২৫/০ ধুর।

পাঃ, থাক, তাং শৌলমারী ১৩ নং বাঃ ১৪৩৯ নং তৌঃ ১১২ নং স্বত্ব ২ নং সিট ১৮২, ১৯৮, ২০৩, ২৫৮, ২৮২, ২৮৩, ২৯৬, ৪৫৯, ৪০৩, ৪১৩, ৪০৭, ৪১৫, ৫১৭, ৫১৬, ৫২৬, ৫৭৮, ৫৭০, ৫৪৭, ৯৭১, ৯৭৪, ৯৮৪, ৯৮৯ নং দাগ দরচুঃ টোমা পিং গরীব বর্ম্মণ পদ্ম দাস পিং বৈদ্য বর্ম্মণ নাঃ পক্ষে উহি পিতামহী শাকালী দাস্যা বাঃ জমি ১৮॥০৸০ ধুর জমা ২০৶০ আনা গৃহীত জমি ১৮॥৸০ ধুর জমা ২০৶০ আনা।

১১৩ নং স্বত্ব ২ নং সিট ১৮০, ১৯৪, ২১০, ৩৭৫, ৩৮৭, ৩৯২, ৪০৪, ৪১৪, ৪৪০, ৪৪৪, ৫০৩, ৫০৬, ৫১৭, ৫২৪, ৫৪৫, ৮৮৬, ৯৭৫, ৯৮১ নং দাগ দঃ চুঃ অমরনাথ বর্ম্মণ পিং অভিন দাস বাঃ জমি ১৭১।৪॥/০ ধুর জমা ২১৶০ আনা গৃহীত জমি ১৭৪৪॥৶০ ধুর জমা ২১৶০ আনা।

পাঃ, থাক, তাং শৌলমারী ১৩ নং বাঃ ১৪৪৯ নং তৌঃ ১১৪ নং স্বত্ব ২ নং সিট ১৮৩, ১৯৪, ১৯৯, ২১৬, ২০৭, ২০২, ২০৭, ৩৭৭, ৩৮৪, ৩৯১, ৪০১, ৪২২, ৪২৩, ৫০৭, ৫০৮, ৫১৩, ৫১৫, ৫২৭, ৫২৯, ৫৩৯, ৫৪২, ৮৫৬, ৮৮০, ৮৯১, ৮৯১, ৮৯৬, ৯৭৮, ৯৮৮ নং দাগ দরচুঃ যুগল বর্ম্মণী জঃ টুনী বর্ম্মণ বাঃ জমি ১৭৸৩।/০ ধুর জমা ২২৸৶০ আনা গৃহীত জমি ১৭৸৩।/০ ধুর জমা ২২৸৶০ আনা।

১১৫ নং স্বত্ব ২ নং সিট ১৭৬, ২১৪, ৩৭৭, ৩৭৯, ৩৮২, ৩৯৪, ৪০০, ৪১১, ৫২২, ৫৩৭, ৫৪৭, ৮৮১, ৮৯০, ৮৯৮, ৯০১, ৯০২, ৯৭৭, ৯৮৯ নং দাগ দরচুঃ সোনাইন, হরিশঙ্কর পিং ভুবিয়া বর্ম্মণ বাঃ জমি ১৪॥৩৸০ ধুর জমা ১৫৸/০ আনা গৃহীত জমি ১৪৸৩৸০ ধুর জমা ১৫৸/০ আনা।

১১৭ নং স্বত্ব ২ নং সিট ১৭৭, ২১৩, ৩৬৯, ৩০৮, ৩৯১, ৪০৬, ৪১৬, ৫২৫, ৫৪৪, ৯৮২, ৯৮৩ নং দাগ দরচুঃ দিল হাজ্জা জঃ অধোয়া বর্ম্মণ বঃ জমি ১২॥০॥০ ধুর জমা ১১৮৶০ আনা গৃহীত জমি ১২॥০॥০ ধুর জমা ১১৸৶০ আনা।

১১৮ নং স্বত্ব ২ নং সিট ৮১, ১৯১, ১৯২, ২০১, ২০৯, ২৭১, ৩৭৬, ৩৮৬, ৩৯১, ৪০২, ৪১৫, ৪৪১, ৪৪২, ৫০০—৫০২, ৫০৫, ৫১৮, ৫১৩, ৫৪৬, ৯৭৬, ৯৮০, ৯৮৬ নং দাগ দরচুঃ নিপুছা পিং টেপু দাস বঃ জমি ২০৩৸৶০ ধুর জমা ২৩৷৴০ আনা গৃহীত জমি ২০৩৷৶০ ধুর জমা ২৩৷৴০ আনা।

প, থাক, তাং তথা ১৩ নং বঃ ২৪৫৯ নং তৌঃ ১১৯ নং স্বত্ব ২ নং সিট ১৭৮, ১৮৮, ১৮৯, ২০৫, ২১১, ৩৭৪, ৩৭৯, ৩৯৮, ৪০৯, ৪২২, ৪১৩, ৪৩৬, ৪৩—৪৪০, ৪৯৮, ৫০৪, ৫০৯—৫১১, ৫৫০, ৫৩৪, ৫৪১, ৮৮৮, ৮৮৯, ৯৮৫, ৯৯৭ নং দাগ দরচুঃ মেঘচাদ, খগেশ্বর পিং পতনেশ্বর বর্ম্মণ বঃ জমি ৩৯৮৪৸০ ধুর জমা ৪৭৷৴০ আনা গৃহীত জমি ৩৯৸৪৸০ ধুর জমা ৪৭৷৴০ আনা।

১২০ নং স্বত্ব ২ নং সিট ২১১, ৫৪৯, ৫৫৭, ৬৬১—৬৭৪, ৬৮২—৬৮৪, ৬৯০, ৮৮৪, ৮৮৫, ৮৯২—৮৯৪, ৮৯৯, ৯০৩, ৯০৬, ৯১২—৯১৬, ৯২২ নং দাগ চুঃ রথীনাথ পিং রামপ্রসাদ দাস বঃ জমি ৪৴১॥৴০ ধুর জমা ২৮৶০ আনা গৃহীত জমি ৪০৴১॥৴০ ধুর জমা ২৮৶০ আনা।

১২১ নং স্বত্ব চুঃ হরকচাদ পিং গোলাপচাদ ভাদানী মালচাদ পিং দৌলতরাম ভাদানী নাঃ পক্ষে সাঃ প্রাপ্ত উঁহি হরকচাদ ভাদানী বঃ জমি ২১৫০৷৶০ ধুর জমা ১৭৷৴ আনা গৃহীত জমি ২১॥০॥৶০ জমা ১৭৷৴০ আনা।

১৩ নং বঃ ১৪৯ নং তৌঃ ১২২ নং স্বত্ব ২ নং সিট ১৭৪, ১৭৫, ১৮৬, ১৮৭, ৩৯৯, ৪২৬, ৪২৮—৪৩০, ৫১৯, ৫৩২, ৫৫, ৫৫১ নং দাগ দরচুঃ হরিপ্রসাদ পিং নেন্দা বর্ম্মণ সাং রামঠেঙ্গা বঃ জমি ২১॥০॥৶০ ধুর জমা ২২৶০ আনা গৃহীত জমি ২১॥০॥৶০ ধুর জমা ২২৶০ আনা।

পঃ মাথাভাঙ্গা ৩৯০ নং থাক তাং শৌলমারী ১৪ নং বঃ ২৬৪০ নং তৌঃ জোত লালবিহারী মিছির পিং মহাবীর মিছির মোঃ মাথাভাঙ্গা তৌ. স্বত্রে গুরুপ্রসাদ প্রয়াগ দত্ত শুকুল মোঃ মাথাভাঙ্গা বঃ জমি ১৪৪৷৪৸৶০ ধুর জমা ১১৮৶০ গৃহীত জমি ১৪৪৷৫৸৶০ ধুর জমা ১১৮৶০ আনা।

বিক্রং

১২৩ নং স্বত্ব ২ নং সিট ৯২১ নং দাগ নিজ দখল ২৴৩॥৴০ ধুর।

১২৪ নং স্বত্ব চুঃ মালচাদ পিং দৌলতরাম ভাদানী হরেকচাদ পিং গোলাপচাদ ভাদানী মোঃ মাথাভাঙ্গা বঃ জমি ১৩৮৩৶০ ধুর জমা ১৫৮৷০ আনা গৃহীত জমি ১৫৮৷৪৷০ ধুর জমা ১৫৮॥০ আনা।

বিক্রং

১২৫ নং স্বত্ব ২ নং সিট ৪৭৬, ৪৮১, ৪৮, ৪৮৭—৪৯, ৪৯২, ৪৯৬, ৪৯৭, ৬৪৯, ৬৫২, ৬৫৪, ৬৫৮, ৮০৪, ৮৩৭, ৮৭৯, ৮৭৬ নং দাগ দরচুঃ অধোয়া পিং পাটিয়া বর্ম্মণ বঃ জমি ১৮২৸০ ধুর জমা ৩১৸০ আনা গৃহীত জমি ৮॥২৸০ ধুর জমা ৩১৸৶০ আনা।

১২৬ নং স্বত্ব ২ নং সিট ৪৭—৪৮০, ৪৮২, ৪৮৪—৪৮৬, ৬০৫, ৮৭০, ৮৭৩—৮৭৫, ৯৯৬ নং দাগ দরচুঃ নিপুছা পিং টেপু বর্ম্মণ বঃ জমি ১৩৷০॥৴০ ধুর জমা ২০৸৶০ আনা গৃহীত জমি ১৩০॥৴ ধুর জমা ২০৸৶০

১২৭ নং স্বত্ব ২ নং সিট ৪৭২—৪৭৫, ৪৯০, ৪২৫, ৫৫৩, ৮৭১, ৮৭১, ৮৭৭—৮৭৯ নং দাগ দরচুঃ দুধা, ভবেশ্বর পিং বুদু বর্ম্মণ বঃ জমি ১০৷৪৷৴০ ধুর জমা ১৬৶০ আনা গৃহীত জমি ১০৷৪৷৴ ধুর জমা ১৬॥৶০

১৪ নং বঃ ১৫১২ নং তৌঃ ১২৮ নং স্বত্ব ২ নং সিট ৪৯১, ৪২৩, ৪৯৪, ৬৩৯, ৬৪০, ৬৫২—৬৫৮, ৬৫০, ৬৫১, ৭৭৯—৭৮, ৮০৮, ৯২৪, ৯৯৫ নং দাগ দরচুঃ চলকা পিং গুরু দাস বঃ জমি ৬১৴২॥৴০ ধুর জমা ৯৫৲ গৃহীত জমি ৬১৴২॥৴০ ধুর জমা ৯৫ টাকা।

১২৯ নং স্বত্ব ২ নং সিট ৪৫৭—৪৫৯, ৯৯৩ নং দাগ দরচুঃ ব্রজনাথ পিং ছিয়াম বর্ম্মণ বঃ জমি ১৬৴১৴০ ধুর জমা ১৯৶ আনা গৃহীত জমি ১৬৴১৴০ ধুর জমা ১৯৷৶০ আনা।

১৩০ নং স্বত্ব ২ নং সিট ৭২৭, ৭২৮, ৭৪৮ নং দাগ দরচুঃ যোগনাথ পিং শিবনাথ শর্ম্মা বঃ জমি ১৮৸১৮৶০ ধুর জমা ১৪৷৶০ আনা গৃহীত জমি ১৮৸১৮৶০ ধুর জমা ১৪॥৶০ আনা।

১৩১ নং স্বত্ব ২ নং সিট চুঃ মালচাদ পিং দৌলতরাম ভাদানী হরেকচাদ পিং গোলাপচাদ ভাদানী মোঃ মাথাভাঙ্গা বঃ জমি ৩৸৩ কাঠা জমা ॥৶০ আনা গৃহীত জমি ৩৸৩ কাঠা জমা ॥৶০ আনা।

বিক্রং

১৩২ নং স্বত্ব ২ নং সিট ৯৬১ নং দাগ দরচুঃ দৈর্ঘ্য নাথ পিং জীবনাথ বর্ম্মণ বঃ জমি ৩৸৩ কাঠা জমা ৸৴০ আনা গৃহীত জমি ৩৸৩ কাঠা জমা ৸৴০ আনা।

পঃ মাথাভাঙ্গা ৩৯০ নং থাক তাং শৌলমারী ২৪৪১ নং তৌঃ জোত শিবদত্ত পিং রামচন্দ্র মিছির পার্ব্বতী দেব্যা জঃ চন্দ্রনাথ মিছির শিবলি, বৃন্দাবন পিং শিবদয়াল মিছির মোঃ পাথরবাড়ী, শিবকণ্ঠ পিং সূর্য্যপ্রসাদ মিছির মোঃ মাথাভাঙ্গা বঃ জমি ১৬০৴৩৸০ ধুর জমা ১৫২৶০ আনা গৃহীত জমি ১৬০৴৩৸৶০ জমা ১৫২৶০ আনা।

বিক্রং

১৩৩ নং স্বত্ব ২ নং সিট ৭৬২ নং দাগ নিজ দখল জমী ১১ কাঠা।

১৩৪ নং স্বত্ব ২ নং সিট ৬১১—৬১৩, ৬১৯, ৬২১—৬৩০, ৭৫৫, ৭২৬, ৮৬১ নং দাগ চুঃ গুরুচাদ নাঃ পক্ষে উঁহি মাতা বজামাত্ত দাস্তা জঃ শীতল চন্দ্র নারায়ণ পিং রুদ্রবর্ম্মণ বঃ জমী ৫৩৴২৶০ ধুর জমা ৮৩॥০ আনা গৃহীত জমী ৫৩৴২৶০ ধুর জমা ৮৩॥৶০ আনা।

বিবরং

নিজ দখল জমী ৩ ৪৩/০ ধুর।

১৩৫ নং খত ২ নং সিট ৮২০ নং দাগ রুবিপ্রজা গোবিন্দ পিং গু'র বর্ম্মণ বঃ জমী ।৩৶০ ধুর জমা ৷/০ আনা গৃহীত জমী ।৩৶০ ধুর জমা ৷/০ আনা।

১৩৬ নং খত ২ নং সীট ৬১৮, ৬১১, ৬৬৭, ৬৬৮, ৮৫০, ৭৩৪—৭৭৩, ৭৭৫—৭৯৭, ৭৫৪—৭৬১, ৭৬১—৭৮৫, ৮৬২, ৮৬৩, ৯৯৭ নং দাগ চুঃ যোগনাথ পিং শিবনাথ শর্ম্মা জগন্নাথ পীং কমলনাথ শর্ম্মা রাধানাথ পীং কাশীনাথ শর্ম্মা ভৈরবদত্ত পীং শিবনাথ শর্ম্মা বঃ জমী ৬৫/২৶০ ধুর জমা ৮০৲ টাকা গৃহীত জমি ৬৫/২৶০ ধুর জমা ৮০৲ টাকা।

১৩৭ নং খত ২ নং সীট ৬৩২, ৬৩৫, ৬৩৬ ৭৪৬, ৭৪৮, ৭৫১, ৭৫২, ৭৬০, ৭৬৫—৭৬৭ নং দাগ চুঃ যোগনাথ পীং শিবনাথ শর্ম্মা জগন্নাথ পীং কমলনাথ শর্ম্মা রাধানাথ পীং কাশীনাথ শর্ম্মা বঃ জমী ৩০৷৩৷/০ ধুর জমা ৪১৷৶০ আনা গৃহীত জমী ৩০৷৩৷/০ ধুর জমা ৪১৷৶০ আনা।

বিবরং

নিজ দখল জমী ১০৷২৶০ ধুর।

১৫ নং বঃ ১৪২০ নং তৌঃ ১০৮ নং খত ২ নং সীট ৬৭৭, ৬৩৭, ৭৫০, ৭৫৩, ৭৫৩, ৭৫০, ৭৫৮, ৭৬৩, ৭৬৪, ৭৬৮ নং দাগ দচুঃ গোবিন্দ পীং ছেপু বর্ম্মণ বঃ জমী ১৫/১৷৶০ ধুর জমা ২৪৸৶০ আনা গৃহীত জমী ১৫/১৷৶০ ধুর জমা ২৪৸৶০ আনা।

৬। পঃ মাথাভাঙ্গা ৩৯০ নং থাক তাং শৌলমারী ১৬ নং বঃ ২৪৪২ নং তৌঃ ১০০ নং খত ২ নং সীট জোত মালচাদ পীং দৌলতরাম ভাদানী হরেকচাদ পীং গোপালচাদ ভাদানী মোঃ মাথাভাঙ্গা তৌঃ সূত্রে হরেকচাদ ভাদানী বঃ জমী ১৫১/৩৸৶০ ধুর জমা ৪৪৷/০ আনা গৃহীত জমী ১৯/৩৶০ ধুর জমা ১৸৪ পাই।

বিবরং

১৪০ নং খত ২ নং সীট ২২৭/২ নং দাগ চুঃ বসী পীং রামপ্রসাদ দাস গেন্দগেলা পীং সাদা বুদ নস্ত মহেন্দ্রনাথ বর্ম্মণ পীং লোকর দাস বঃ জমী ১৫১/১৸৶০ ধুর জমা ৬০৶০ আনা গৃহীত জমী ১৪/৩৶০ জমা ২৸/৩ পাই।

৭। পঃ মাথাভাঙ্গা ৩৯০ নং থাক তাং শৌলমারী ২৯৭১ নং তৌঃ ২১ নং খত ২ নং সীট ৭২৬, ৯২৮ নং দাগ জোত ধৈর্য্যনারায়ণ বর্ম্মণ পীং জীবনাথ বর্ম্মণ সাং রামঠেঙ্গা তৌ সূত্রে জগৎচন্দ্র বর্ম্মণ বঃ জমী ৫,০৸৶০ ধুর জমা ৫৷৶০ আনা গৃহীত জমী ৫০৸৶০ ধুর জমা ৫৷৶০ আনা।

৮। পঃ মাথাভাঙ্গা ৩৯০ নং থাক তাং শৌলমারী ২৯৮১ নং তৌঃ ২ নং সীট ৬৫৭, ৭২২, ৭২৩, ৯১৪—৯২৭ নং দাগ জোত ধৈর্য্যনারায়ণ বর্ম্মণ পীং মৃত জীবনারায়ণ বর্ম্মণ সাং রামঠেঙ্গা তৌ সূত্রে জগৎচন্দ্র বর্ম্মণ বঃ জমী ২১৷২৶০ ধুর জমা ৭৷৶০ আনা গৃহীত জমী ২১৷২৶০ ধুর জমা ৭৷০ আনা।

চৌহদ্দী :—উঃ সীং ৩৯০ নং থাক তাং শৌলমারী অন্তর্গত চা বাগান বাবদ খাষ ভূমি ও জিলা জলপাইগুড়ী, দঃ সীং তাং নিজ অন্তর্গত চা বাগান বাবদ খাষ ভূমি ও ৩৯১ নং থাক তাং রামঠেঙ্গা, পঃ সীং তাং নিজ সিট নং ৩ ও ৪, পূঃ সীং তাং নিজ ২ নং সিট অন্তর্গত ২১৮, ৫২০, ৬৬৭, ৩২৫, ৩২৭, ৩৬৫, ৫৬৪, ৩৫২, ৫৫৭, ৯৫৮, ৫৫৬, ৫৯৯, ৬০৫, ৬১০, ৬১৪, ৬১৬, ৬১৭, ৭৮৯, ৭৮৮, ৭৮৭, ৭৮৬ নং দাগ বাবদ ভূমি।

K C GANGULI,
Revenue Minister of the
Cooch Behar State.

দেওয়ানী কার্য্যবিধি আইনের ২১ হুকুম, ৬৬ নিয়মের ঘোষণাপত্র।

জারীর মহকুমা মেখলীগঞ্জের দেঃ আদালত।

এতদ্দারা সর্ব্বসাধারণকে জানান যাইতেছে যে, দায়ীকগণের নিম্নলিখিত সম্পত্তি আগামী ১৯৪৭ সনের ১৯শে নভেম্বর মোঃ ১৩৫৪ সনের ৩রা অগ্রহায়ণ তারিখে দিবা ১২ ঘটিকার সময় প্রকাশ্য নিলাম আরম্ভ হইবে।

৭ নং ১৯৪৭।৪৮ ইং। বাঃ ডিঃ ২৪৫৶৩ মোঃ।

ডিঃ—মৃনালীনী বিশ্বাস পং মোঃ মেখলীগঞ্জ।

দেঃ—সতীশচন্দ্র বীশ্বাস মোঃ মেখলীগঞ্জ।

তপশিল সম্পত্তি।

পং মেখলীগঞ্জের অন্তর্গত ১৭৫ নং থাক তাং উচলপুখরী মধ্যে ২৫৭৷২৶০ ধুর জমীর কাত বাঃ ৩৮০৷৶০ আনা জমার আং দরচুঃ স্বত্ব।

KUMAR P. NARAYAN, *Naib Ahilkar.*

ইং ১৯১০ সালের ৫ আইনের ৫৩ ধারার ২ প্রকরণ মতে নিলামী ইস্তাহার।

আরীর মহকুমা মেখলীগঞ্জের মাল আদালত।

এতদ্বারা সর্বসাধারণকে জানান যাইতেছে যে, প্রতিবাদীর দাবীর বাকী খাজনা আদায় না করায় তাহার নিম্নলিখিত ক্রোকী সম্পত্তি আগামী ১৩৫৪ সনের ৩রা অগ্রহায়ণ মোতাবেক ১৯৪৭ সনের ১৯শে নবেম্বর, তারিখে বেলা ১২ঘটিকায় সদর প্রকাশ্য নীলাম আরম্ভ হইবে।

৬৩ নং ১৯৪৭/৪৮ ই বাঃ খাঃ ১,৮৵৩ মোঃ

ডিঃ—আব্দুল আজিজ পাটোয়ারী গং সাং বকসীগঞ্জ টেঃ হলদিবাড়ী

দেঃ—আশরাফ উদ্দিন আহম্মদ সাং বকসীগঞ্জ

তপশিল সম্পত্তি।

থাং মেখলীগঞ্জের অন্তর্গত ১১ নং থাক তাং বকসীগঞ্জ মধ্যে ১২৭ নং তৌঃ লিঃ ৮০৶০ খুব জমির কাত বাঃ ১৷৶০ আনা জমার ক্ষ দখল খব।

৬৭ নং ১৯৪৭/৪৮ ইং। বাঃ খাঃ ৮১৲৩

ডিঃ—সৌদামিনী দেব্যা জঃ মৃত শ্রীনারায়ণ চক্রবর্ত্তী মোঃ ও টেঃ মাথাভাঙ্গা

দেঃ—জ্যোতীশচন্দ্র রায় চৌধুরী পিং মৃত সাধুরাম রায় চৌধুরী সাং আলোকঝাড়ী।

তপশিল সম্পত্তি

থাং মেখলীগঞ্জের অন্তর্গত ১৫১ নং থাক তাং আলোকঝাড়ী মধ্যে ৯০নং খতের ৩৩৮২৷৶০ খুব জমির কাত বাঃ ৬১৮/০ আনা জমার দরচুঃ খব।

৬৯ নং ১৯৪৭/৪৮ ইং। বাঃ খাঃ ২৪৭৷৶৩ মোঃ।

ডিঃ—নগেন্দ্রচন্দ্র লাহিড়ী গং মোঃ মেখলীগঞ্জ।

দেঃ—হিসাবউদ্দিন মহাম্মদ সাং ধবলগুড়ী।

তপশিল সম্পত্তি

থাং মেখলীগঞ্জের অন্তর্গত ১০৫ নং থাক তাং বাঘডোকরা মধ্যে ৬৮নং খতের লিঃ ৫৩১৬৮৶০ খুব জমির কাত বাঃ ৩০৷৶০ আনা জমার চুঃ খব।

৭০ নং ১৯৪৭/৪৮ ইং। বাঃ খাঃ ১৪৪৷৩ মোঃ।

ডিঃ—নগেন্দ্রচন্দ্র লাহিড়ী মোঃ মেখলীগঞ্জ।

দেঃ—যোগেন্দ্র পাটোয়ারী গং সাং হেমকুমারী

তপশিল সম্পত্তি।

থাং মেখলীগঞ্জের অন্তর্গত ৫৫ নং থাক তাং হেমকুমারী মধ্যে ৩৯৪ নং খতের লিঃ ৫১৷৷০ খুব জমির কাত বাঃ ৭৮৲ টাকা জমার চুঃ খব।

৭১ নং ১৯৪৭/৪৮ ইং। বাঃ খাঃ ৫৩৮৷৶৩ মোঃ।

ডিঃ—নগেন্দ্রচন্দ্র লাহিড়ী গং মোঃ মেখলীগঞ্জ।

দেঃ—চিত্তরঞ্জনরায় পাটোয়ারী গং সাং হেমকুমারী।

তপশিল সম্পত্তি

থাং মেখলীগঞ্জের অন্তর্গত ৫৫ নং থাক তাং হেমকুমারী মধ্যে ২৮৩ নং তৌঃ লিঃ ১০২/১৮৶০ খুব জমির কাত বাঃ ১৫০৮৵০ আনা জমার চুঃ খব।

৭২ নং ১৯৪৭/৪৮ ইং। বাঃ খাঃ ১৬৬৷৶০ মোঃ।

ডিঃ—নজরউদ্দিন মহাম্মদ গং সাং খাবরশ টেঃ হলদিবাড়ী।

দেঃ—সুরাতআলী গং সাং খাবরশ টেঃ হলদিবাড়ী।

তপশিল সম্পত্তি।

থাং মেখলীগঞ্জের অন্তর্গত ৪৫ নং থাক তাং প্রাণমজুমদার মধ্যে ৩১ নং সিটের লিঃ ১/৪৮৶০ খুব জমির কাত বাঃ ১৪৵৮ পাই জমার দরচুঃ খব।

৭৩ নং ১৯৪৭/৪৮ ইং। বাঃ খাঃ ৫৭৷৶৩ মোঃ।

ডিঃ—মাসেতুল্যা সরকার পিং মৃত তাজমামুদ সরকার সাং হেমকুমারী টেঃ হলদিবাড়ী।

দেঃ—সুরেন্দ্রনাথ বর্ম্মণ পিং অন্নদাচরণ বর্ম্মণ সাং গোবনাডি টেঃ ডোমার জেলা রংপুর।

তপশিল সম্পত্তি।

থাং মেখলীগঞ্জের অন্তর্গত ৫৫ নং থাক তাং হেমকুমারী মধ্যে ৪৮৫ নং তৌঃ লিঃ ১২৷৩৲০ খুব জমির কাত বাঃ ৩০৮০ আনা জমার চুঃ খব।

৭৪ নং ১৯৪৭/৪৮ ইং বাঃ খাঃ ১১৯৷৶৫ মোঃ।

ডিঃ—সৌদামিনী দেব্যা জঃ মৃত শ্রীনারায়ণ চক্রবর্ত্তী মোঃ মাথাভাঙ্গা।

দেঃ—জ্যোতীশচন্দ্র রায় চৌধুরী সাং আলোকঝাড়ী

তপশিল সম্পত্তি।

থাং মেখলীগঞ্জের অন্তর্গত ১৫১ নং থাক তাং আলোকঝাড়ী মধ্যে ১নং তৌঃ লিঃ ২২৷৷৶০ খুব জমির কাত বাঃ ৩৭৷০ আনা জমার কবিপ্রজা খব।

৮১ নং ১৩৪৭।৪৮ ইং। বাঃ খাঃ ৫৪৸৵৯ মোঃ।

ডিঃ—মহাম্মদ খোখার উদ্দিন পিং মৃত বেহারু মহাম্মদ সাং বলরামবাদা চৌঃ হলদিবাড়ী।

দেঃ—নছিরণ নেছা বিবি অঃ শ্রীবেহারউ মহাম্মদ সাং বলরামবাদা চৌঃ হলদিবাড়ী।

তপশিল সম্পত্তি।

পঃ মেখলীগঞ্জের অন্তর্গত ৩২ নং থাক ১১৯০ নং তৌঃ লিঃ ২৫৸৩/০ ধুম জমির কাত বাঃ ১৩।/০ আনা জমার চুঃ খণ্ড।

৮২ নং ১৩৪৭।৪৮ ইং। বাঃ খাঃ ২৮৸৶০ মোঃ।

ডিঃ—মজিবর রহমান সরকার সাং হলুমডাঙ্গা।

দেঃ—মহিরউদ্দিন সরকার পঃ সাং হলুমডাঙ্গা।

তপশিল সম্পত্তি।

পঃ মেখলীগঞ্জ ১৩ নং থাক তাং হলুমডাঙ্গা মধ্যে ৫২ নং তৌঃ লিঃ ৯।৩।৶৩ কড়া জমির কাত বাঃ ৫।৵১০ পাই জমার দরচুঃ।

৮৩ নং ১৩৪৭।৪৮ ইং। বাঃ খাঃ ৫০৷৶৯ মোঃ।

ডিঃ—মজিবর রহমান সরকার সাং হলুমডাঙ্গা চৌঃ হলদীবাড়ী।

দেঃ—সফিরউদ্দিন মহম্মদ পঃ সাং হেমকুমারী।

তপশিল সম্পত্তি।

পঃ মেখলীগঞ্জ ১৩ নং থাক তাং হলুমডাঙ্গা মধ্যে ১৫৫ নং তৌঃ লিঃ ১৪৸৩৸/০ ধুম জমির কাত বাঃ ১৯৲ টাকা জমার দরচুঃ।

৮৬ নং ১৩৪৭।৪৮ ইং। বাঃ খাঃ ১৯৫৸৶৮ মোঃ।

ডিঃ—রমনীমোহন সিংহ চৌঃ মেখলীগঞ্জ।

দেঃ—তারাকান্ত পাখাধরা পঃ চৌঃ পাটগ্রাম জেলা জলপাইগুড়ী।

তপশিল সম্পত্তি।

পঃ মেখলীগঞ্জ ১১৩ নং থাক তাং বারিকামারী মধ্যে ১৯১২ নং তৌঃ লিঃ ১১৫।৪৪৷/০ ধুম জমির কাত বাঃ ৯৫।৶০ আনা জমার চুঃ।

৮৭ নং ১৩৪৭।৪৮ ইং বাঃ খাঃ ৫০৶০ মোঃ।

ডিঃ—সৌদামিনী দেব্যা মোঃ বাখাডাঙ্গা।

দেঃ—ক্ষোতীশচন্দ্র রায় চৌধুরী সাং আলোকঝাড়ী।

তপশিল সম্পত্তি।

পঃ মেখলীগঞ্জ ১২৯ নং থাক তাং আলোকঝাড়ী মধ্যে ১ নং তৌঃ লিঃ ২৮।১৸/০ ধুম জমির কাত বাঃ ৩৫৶০ পাই জমার অংশ কৃষিপ্রজা।

৮৮ নং ১৩৪৭।৪৮ ইং। বাঃ খাঃ ১৩৶৪ মোঃ।

ডিঃ—ফজলুলকরিম প্রধান পঃ সাং কিং কয়েমামুদ চৌঃ হলদিবাড়ী।

দেঃ—আব্বাজআলি মহম্মদ সাং নিজতরফ চৌঃ মেখলীগঞ্জ।

তপশিল সম্পত্তি

পঃ মেখলীগঞ্জ ৩৪ নং থাক তাং বাকেঙ্গা মধ্যে ৭৩৯ নং তৌঃ লিঃ ৪২ কাঠা জমির কাত বাঃ ১৶৯ পাই জমার দরচুঃ।

৮৯ নং ১৩৪৭।৪৮ ইং। বাঃ খাঃ ১৯৷/৯ মোঃ।

ডিঃ—ফজলুলকরিম প্রধান পঃ সাং কিসামত কয়েমামুদ চৌঃ হলদিবাড়ী।

দেঃ—নবিজান নেছা সাং বড়লা খাগড়াবাড়ী চৌঃ হলদিবাড়ী।

তপশিল সম্পত্তি।

পঃ মেখলীগঞ্জ তাং বড়লা খাগড়াবাড়ী মধ্যে ২১০৫ নং তৌঃ লিঃ ৩।৩ কাঠা জমির কাত বাঃ ।।০ আনা জমার চুঃ।

৯১ নং ১৩৪৭।৪৮ ইং। বাঃ খাঃ ৮৩৷৹ মোঃ।

ডিঃ—মুরলীধর ভট্টাচার্য্য মোঃ সহর কোচবিহার।

দেঃ—গেয়াসউদ্দিন ওঃ গয়েসউদ্দিন মহম্মদ পঃ সাং উপনচৌকী ভাজনী।

তপশিল সম্পত্তি।

পঃ মেখলীগঞ্জ তাং বালাপাড়া খাগড়াবাড়ী মধ্যে ২১৬৩ নং তৌঃ লিঃ ৯৮৸।৶০ ধুম জমির কাত বাঃ ২৯৸৶০ আনা জমার দরচু।

Kumar P. Narayan, *Naib Ahilkar.*

The Civil Supplies Department.

Dated, Cooch Behar the 15th October, 1947.

NOTICE.

It is hereby notified for the information of the general public that the distribution of Cloth for the October-December, 1947 quarter in the Sudder Sub-division will commence from the 16th October, 1947 and will continue upto the 15th November, 1947. The yardage of Dhuti Saree and other cloth as allotted will be 1½ yards each per head in the Urban Areas, while that in the Rural Areas will be 1 yard Dhuti Saree and 1 yard other cloth per head.

H. Biswas,
Civil Supplies Commissioner, Cooch Behar.

The Cooch Behar Gazette.

২৯শে আশ্বিন বৃহস্পতিবার] THURSDAY, OCTOBER 16, 1947 [১৩৫৪ সাল ৪৩৮ রাজশক

Part II B.

Police Supplement.

Annexed is the scheme for the Cooch Behar Auxiliary Police Force sanctioned by His Highness the Maharaja Bhup Bahadur in Council (*vide* State Council letter No. 2210-11 dated the 21st July, 1947).

It is proposed to organise groups at the following centres at the first instance :—

1. Haldibari.
2. Mekligunj.
3. Changrabandha.
4. Jamaldah.
5. Mathabhanga.
6. Sitalkhunchi Bandar.
7. Sitai Bandar.
8. Dinhata.
9. Choudhurihat.
10. Bamanhat.
11. Tufangunj.
12. Balarampur.
13. Bakshirhat.

The Circle Inspectors and Officers-in-charge concerned are directed to give publicity to the scheme and enlist public support in its favour.

The organisation will have as little official control or interference as possible. It is intended that the control of the Commissioner of Police with regard to the internal administration of the organisation will be of an advisory nature.

The leading members of the public at each centre should be requested to form at first a small Committee which will be entrusted with the work of enlisting members and organising the group. Such Committees will form the nucleous of the organisation.

It may be noted here that relaxation may here to be made about the rule enjoining that the members will provide themselves with certain articles of dress.

The Circle Inspectors and Officers-in-charge will report as soon as possible about the prospect of organising groups at their respective centres.

J. M. CHATTERJEE.
Commissioner of Police,
Cooch Behar.

COOCH BEHAR AUXILIARY POLICE FORCE.

1. The Cooch Behar Auxiliary Police Force is established under section 8 of Cooch Behar Police Act, 1947. The object of the organisation is to assist the regular police in the State in any emergency in the maintenance of law and order.

2. The organisation is purely voluntary and non-official and is open to gentlemen who are Cooch Beharis, Cooch Behar subjects or Cooch Behar residents with landed property in the State and who are not already members of any other auxiliary force unit. The members shall be over 18 years of age.

3. On appointment each member of the Auxiliary Force will receive a certificate of enrolment under section 8 of the Cooch Behar Police Act, 1947, and every member so appointed shall have the same privileges as the members of the regular Police Force.

4. Every member shall receive from the Commissioner of Police a badge of an approved pattern and a whistle. He will be required to provide himself with Khaki Shirts, Khaki Shorts and a Half lathi.

5. The members shall be grouped conveniently according to the places of their residence or occupation and shall not normally be required to serve at any considerable distance from their homes. Each group shall be under a group leader who shall be required to maintain a list of the members of the group with their addresses. A group shall be divided into two sections, each under a section leader. Each section of a group will take up duty alternately in order to allow reliefs and prevent the necessity of keeping the members out for long hours without rest or food or to interfere unduly with their normal occupation.

6. The authorities competent to call upon the members to report for duty are ;—

1. Commissioner of Police.
2. Fouzdari Ahilkar.
3. Naib Ahilkar in charge of Sub-division.

When called for duty the members shall work under the direction of the Commissioner of Police received either direct from him or through the Officer-in-charge of the Police Station concerned but they must not be treated as paid subordinates of the Police Department. The members should always be treated with respect and consideration due to gentlemen who have generously offered their services free in public interest at considerable personal inconvenience.

7. The members of the Auxiliary Police Force will be given training in drill and when possible in the use of fire-arms. Arrangements will be made for their training at the respective group headquarters or at other convenient centres.

8. **Powers and duties of the members of the Auxiliary Police Force.**

(1) Members of the Auxilary Police Force have the power to arrest without warrant any person found in possession of implements of house-breaking or of property suspected to be stolen and any person who is concerned or suspected to be concerned in any of the serious offences enumerated in Schedule A.

(2) Every member may interpose for the purpose of preventing, and shall, to the best of his ability, prevent, the commission of any of the offences mentioned in the sub-rule (1) above.

(3) Every member receiving information of a design to commit any offence shall forthwith communicate such information through his group leader to the Commissioner of Police or to the Officer-in-charge of the nearest Police Station.

(4) A member knowing of a design to commit any of the offences enumerated in schedule A may arrest, without order from a Magistrate and without warrant, the person so designing, if it appears to such members that the commission of the offence cannot be otherwise prevented.

(5) It is the duty of all members to arrest any person committing in their view any of the offences enumerated in schedule A.

(6) In making an arrest no more force is to be used than what is absolutely necessary.

(7) All persons arrested by the members of the Auxiliary Police Force shall forthwith be taken to the nearest police station and made over to the custody of the Officer-in-charge with a full report of the circumstances in which the arrests were made.

(8) When on duty in the areas handed over by the police to a group of the Auxiliary Police Force for watch and ward the members shall patrol such areas with a view to safeguarding life and property in those areas and to prevent offences against persons and property.

(9) All members shall assist the authorities in every way when engaged in maintaining peace and order.

9. The powers of the members of the Auxiliary Police Force as set forth in clause 8 above are exercisable only when they are called upon to report for duty by a competent authority.

10. The members shall not turn out with privately owned fire-arms unless specially instructed to do so. When privately owned fire-arms are taken out to suppress a riot the use of any ammunition other than an ordinary non-explosive spherical ball is strictly forbidden.

11 (*a*) Firing by an individual member or an order to fire given by a group leader or section leader on his own initiative as strictly forbidden except in circumstances where the firing is imperative in the exercise of the right of private defence. The responsibility of proving that the circumstances were such as to necessitate firing rests on the individual who fires or gives order to fire. In other circumstances, no member of the Auxiliary Police Force shall fire except under the order of a Magistrate or, when a Magistrate is not present, a Police Officer of or above the rank of an Officer-in-charge of a Police Station.

(*b*) Firing shall be so directed as to be at once effective and such as with the minimum injury, to convince the crowd of the necessity of dispersing

(*c*) Before firing, full and sufficient warning of the intention to fire must be given and firing must cease as soon as the crowd shows the slightest inclination to retire or disperse.

(*d*) Any member of the Auxiliary Police Force concerned in firing shall immediately submit a report through his group leader to the Commissioner of Police narrating the circumstances which necessitated firing, the number of rounds fired, the apparent results and the steps taken to succour casualties, if any.

(*e*) The law with regard to the right of private defence as contained in section 96 to 106 of the Cooch Behar Penal Code has been inserted in schedule B.

J. M. CHATTERJEE.

Commissioner of Police, Cooch Behar.

SCHEDULE A.

(Rule 8.)

Cooch Behar Penal Code.

Section 131.— Serious crime, *i. e.*, attempting to seduce an officer, soldier, etc.

Sections 143 to 147. — Being members of an unlawful assembly ; rioting.

Section 231.—Counterfeiting coins.

Section 302.—Murder.

Section 307.—Attempted murder.

Sections 324 to 326.—Causing hurt by a dangerous weapon or means ; causing grievous hurt.

Section 328.—Administration of stupefying drugs.

Sections 341 to 342.—Wrongfully restraining or confining any person.

Section 353.—Assault or use of criminal force on a public servant to deter him from discharging his duties

Section 354 —Assault on a woman..

Section 376.—Rape.

Sections 379 to 382, 392.—Theft, theft with voilence (robbery).

Section 428.—Mischief by killing or rendering useless any animal valued at Rs. 10 or more.

Sections 448, 454 to 457. - House trespass, lurking house trespass and house-breaking.

Cooch Behar Public Security Act, 1947.

Section 34.—Sabotage.

Section 36.—Carrying or possessing corrosive or explosive substance.

SCHEDULE 'B'.

(Rule 11)

Section 96 to 106 of the Cooch Behar Penal Code.

Section 96.—**Things done in private defence.**—Nothing is an offence which is done in the exercise of the right of private defence.

Section 97.— **Right of private defence of the body and of property.**—Every person has a right, subject to the restrictions contained in section 99, to defend—

First—his own body, and the body of any other person, against any offence affecting the human body ;

Secondly—the property, whether movable or immovable, of himself or of any other person, against any act which is an offence falling under the definition of theft, robbery, mischief or criminal tresspass, or which is an attempt to commit theft, robbery, mischief or criminal trespass.

Section 98.— **Right of private defence against the act of a person of unsound mind, etc.**—When an act, which would otherwise be a certain offence, is not that offence by reason of the youth, the want of maturity of understanding, the unsoundness of mind, or the intoxication of the person doing that act or by reason of any misconception on the part of that person, every person has the same right of private defence against that act which he would have if the act were that offence.

Illustration —(*a*) Z, under the influence of madness, attempts to kill A ; Z is guilty of no offence. But A has the same right of private defence which he whould have if Z were sane.

(*b*) A enters by night a house which A is legally entitled to enter. Z, in good faith, taking A for a house-breaker, attacks A. Here Z by attacking A under this misconception, commits no offence. But A has the same right of private defence against Z, which he would have if Z were not acting under that misconception.

Section 99.—**Acts against which there is no right of private defence.**—There is no right of private defence against an act which does not reasonably, cause the apprehension of death or of grievous hurt, if done, or attempted to be done, by a public servant acting in good faith under colour of his office, though that act may not be strictly justifiable by law.

There is no right of private defence against an act which does not reasonably cause the apprehension of death or of grievous hurt, if done, or attempted to be done, by the direction of a public servant acting in good faith under colour of his office, though that direction may not be strictly justifiable by law.

There is no right of private defence in cases in which there is time to have recourse to the protection of the public authorities.

Extent to which the right may be exercised :—The right of private defence in no case extends to the inflicting of more harm than it is necessary to inflict for the purpose of defence.

Explanation 1—A person is not deprived of the right of private defence against an act done, or attempted to be done, by a public servant, as such, unless he knows, or has reason to believe, that the person doing the act is such public servant.

Explanation 2—A person is not deprived of the right of private defence against an act done, or attempted to be done, by the direction of a public servant, unless he knows, or has reason to believe, that the person doing the act is acting by such direction, or unless such person states the authority under which he acts, or if he has authority in writing, unless he produces such authority, if demanded.

Section 100.—**When the right of private defence of the body extends to causing death.**—The right of private defence of the body extends, under the restrictions mentioned in the last preceding section, to the voluntary causing of death or of any other harm to the assailant, if the offence which occasions the exercise of the right be of any of the descriptions hereinafter enumerated, namely :—

First—such an assault as may reasonably cause the apprehension that death will otherwise be the consequence of such assault ;

Secondly - such an assault as may reasonably cause the apprehension that grievous hurt will otherwise be the consequence of such assault;

Thirdly—an assault with the intention of committing rape ;

Fourthly—an assault with the intention of gratifying unnatural lust ;

Fifthly—an assault with the intention of kidnapping or abducting ;

Sixthly—an assault with the intention of wrongfully confining a person, under circumstances which may reasonably cause him to apprehend that he will be unable to have recourse to the public authorities for his release.

Section 101.—**When such right extends to causing any harm other than death.**—If the offence be not of any of the descriptions enumerated in the last preceding section, the right of private defence of the body does not extend to the voluntary causing of death to the assailant, but does extend, under the restrictions mentioned in section 99, to the voluntary causing to the assailant of any harm other than death.

Section 102.—**Commencement and continuance of the right of private defence of the body.**—The right of private defence of the body commences as soon as a reasonable apprehension of danger to the body arises from an attempt or threat to commit the offence though the offence may not have been committed ; and it continues as long as such apprehension of danger to the body continues.

Section 103.—**When the right of private defence of property extends to causing death.**—The right of private defence of property extends, under the restrictions mentioned in section 99, to the voluntary causing of death or of any other harm to the wrong-doer, if the offence, the committing of which, or the attempting to commit which, occasions the exercise of the right, be an offence of any of the descriptions hereinafter, namely :—

First—robbery ;

Second—house-breaking by night ;

Thirdly—mischief by fire committed on any building, tent or vessel, which building, tent or vessel is used as a human dwelling, or as a place for the custody of property ;

Fourthly—theft, mischief or house-trespass, under such circumstances as may reasonably cause apprehension that death or grievous hurt will be the consequence, if such right of private defence is not exercised.

Section 104.—**When such right extends to causing any harm other than death.**—If the offence, the committing of which or the attempting to commit which, occasions the exercise of the right of private defence, be theft, mischief, or criminal trespass, not of any of the descriptions enumerated in the last preceding section, that right does not extend to the voluntary causing of death, but does extend subject to the restrictions mentioned in section 99, to the voluntary causing to the wrong-doer of any harm other than death.

Section 105.—**Commencement and continuance of the right of private defence of property.**—The right of private defence of property commences when a reasonable apprehension of danger to the property commences.

The right of private defence of property against theft continues till the offender has effected his retreat with the property or either the assistance of the public authorities is obtained, or the property has been recovered.

The right of private defence of property against robbery continues as long as the offender causes or attempts to cause to any person death or hurt or worngful restraint or as long as the fear of instant death or of instant hurt or of instant personal restraint continues.

The right of private defence of property against criminal trespass or mischief continue as long as the offender continues in the commission of criminal trespass or mischief.

The right of private defence of property against house-breaking by night continues as long as the house-trespass which has been begun by such house-breaking continues.

Section 106.—**Right of private defence against deadly assault when there is risk of harm to innocent person.**—If in the exercise of the right of private defence against an assault which reasonably cause of apprehension of death, the defender be so situated that he cannot effectually exercise that right without risk of harm to an innocent person, his right of private defence extends to the running of that risk.

Illustration.—A is attacked by a mob who attempts to number him. He cannot effectually exercise his right of private defence without firing on the mob, and he cannot fire without risk of harming young children who are mingled with the mob.

A commits no offence if by so firing he harms any of the children.

General Notice under section 26(2) of the Cooch Behar Police Act III of 1898.

Whereas I, the Commissioner of Police, Cooch Behar, am satisfied that it is intended by certain persons or class of persons to convene or collect assemblies or to form processions on the public roads or in the public streets or thoroughfares in the Towns of Cooch Behar, Dinhata, Tufangunj, Mathabhanga, Mekligunj and Haldibari.

And whereas such assembly or procession, if uncontrolled, would be likely to cause a breach of the peace.

Now, therefore, in exercise of the powers conferred by sub-section (2) of section 2 of the Cooch Behar Police Act 1898 (Act III of 1898) I do hereby require the persons convening or collecting such assembly or directing or promoting such procession to submit to me, at least 5 days before any date that may be fixed for such assembly and procession, the times of such assembly and procession, the place at which such assembly will meet or from which such procession will start, the route by which such procession will pass and the number of persons who are likely to attend such assembly or to take part in such procession, together with all other details required to be included in such license. This order will remain in force for three months from the date of issue.

J. M. CHATTERJEE,
Commissioner of Police, Cooch Behar.

The Cooch Behar Gazette.

১৪ই কার্ত্তিক, শনিবার ; SATURDAY, NOVEMBER 1, 1947 [১৩৫৪ সাল ৪৩৮ রাজশক

PART II.

NOTICES.

হাটী নিলামী ইস্তাহার কাচ রী খাস মোতালকে দিন হাটার এলাকে তুফানগঞ্জ সন ৪৩৮ শকা মোতাবেক সন ১৩১৪ সাল তারিখ ২২শে আশ্বিন ইং তারিখ ৯।১০।৪৭

এতদ্বারা সংবাদ দেওয়া যাইতেছে যে, নিম্নলিখিত হাট, ঘাট জমা আগামী ১০।১১।৪৭ মোতাবেক ২৩শে কার্ত্তিক দিবা ১২ই প্রহরের সময় বৎসর মেয়াদে নিলামে সর্ব্বোচ্চ ডাক কারীর বন্দোবস্ত হইবেক। পসন্দেচ্ছুক ব্যক্তিরা নির্দ্ধারিত দিবসে নিয়মিত সময়ে সরকারী নিলাম ঘরে উপস্থিত হইয়া ডাক করে

১।	৯৪৩ নং খাক ৭ নং তৌঃ পঃ ক্রেতার ডাং বলরামপুর মধ্যে কালজানী নদীতে (১) তুফানগঞ্জ ঘাট প্রঃ শ্রেণী (২) আরামপুর ঘাট প্রঃ শ্রেণী (৩) শিশাবাড়ী ঘাট ৩য় শ্রেণী	নগিনা ওঝা গং	১৫৫০৲
২।	৫০ নং দেহা ১৩ নং তৌঃ ১৪ নং লাট জারী কালজানী নদী	শ্রি রমাকান্ত চক্রবর্ত্তী	৯২৫৲
৩।	৫১ নং দেহা ১৪ নং তৌঃ ১৫ নং লাট জারী তোর্ষা নদী	ঐ	৫৬১৲
৪।	১১৭১ নং খাক ১ নং তৌঃ পঃ তুফানগঞ্জ ডাং ছোট লাউকুঠী মধ্যে শিবগঞ্জ ওঃ বক্সী হাট ...	গোবিন্দচন্দ্র সরকার	৫২২৫৲
৫।	১০৭৯ নং খাক ৫ নং তৌঃ ডাং চিলাখানা মধ্যে ঘোড়ামারা হাট ...	গিরিজাকান্ত চক্রবর্ত্তী	১০২৫৲
৬।	১১৫৭ নং খাক ৮ নং তৌঃ অন্দরান ফুলবাড়ী মধ্যে বলরামপুর হাট পোহাটা দোল মেলায় ৪ হাট বাদ ...	গোবিন্দ সিং	৬০৫১৲
৭।	১০৪৮ নং খাক ৯ নং তৌঃ পঃ তুফানগঞ্জ ডাং ধলপাল মধ্যে দেওয়ানগঞ্জ হাট	সুনীলকুমার বাগচী	৭০৲
৮।	১১৪৫ নং খাক ১০ নং তৌঃ শালবাড়ী মধ্যে নাককাটি হাট ...	গিরিজাকান্ত চক্রবর্ত্তী	১১০৫৲
৯।	১১৫৭ নং খাক ১৮ নং তৌঃ অন্দরান ফুলবাড়ী মধ্যে তুফানগঞ্জ টাউনস্থিত দৈনিক বাজার (হাট বার ও দোল মেলায় ২ দিন বাদ) ...	সুখদেব সিং	৭৫১৲
১০।	১০৭০ নং খাক ১ নং তৌঃ চিলাখানা মধ্যে কালজানী নদীতে ঘোড়ামারা ঘাট ২য় শ্রেণী পাড়া ইত্যাদ ১ম শ্রেণী ...	রামসেবক চৌধুরী	১২০৫৲
১১।	১০৮১ নং খাক ১১ নং তৌঃ ঘোগারকুঠী মধ্যে গদাধর নদীর ঘাট মাঝর ৩য় শ্রেণী ...	মটর মহরী	১১২২৲
১২।	১১৭৫ নং খাক ৩১ নং তৌঃ অন্দরকুমারী গদাধর নদীর ত্রিমোহিনীর ঘাট ২য় শ্রেণী	মেঘরাজ আগরওয়াল	১০০০৲
১৩।	১১০০ নং খাক ৩৮ নং তৌঃ আবশী চিলাখানা মধ্যে গদাধর নদীর ঘাট ৩য় শ্রেণী	ভগবান চৌধুরী	১০২৲
১৪।	৭০২ নং দেহা ১০৮৪ নং খাক ৫ নং তৌঃ ৫ নং লাট বালাভূত [illegible]	নগেন্দ্রনাথ ব্যাপারী	৮৫১৲

১৫। ৭০—৭৩ নং মেৌ ১১২৭ নং খাং ২৮ নং চৌঃ ২৮ নং দাগ জোয়ানেটা মধ্যে মানতামী মতীর হক্কা ... কমলনীর উকিল ৬৪০৲
১৬। ১১৭ নং মেৌ ৪৯ নং তৌঃ ৪৯ নং দাগ কারী গদাধর বর্মী ... গিরিজাকান্ত চক্রবর্ত্তী ৪০১.
১৭। ১২১ নং মেৌ ৫৩ নং তৌঃ ৫৩ নংদাগ কারী বুড়া মামেক বর্মী এবং টাকোবামাতী বর্মী এওয়ন কারী গদাধর বর্মী ... ... আশুতোষ চক্রবর্ত্তী ১৬০০৲

H. BARMA, *Naib Ahilkar.*

ইং ১৯১০ সালের ৫ আইনের ৫৩ ধারার ২ প্রকরণ মতে নিলামী ইস্তাহার।

আলীর মহকুমা মেখলীগঞ্জের মাল আদালত।

এতদ্দ্বারা সর্ব্বসাধারণকে জানান যাইতেছে যে, প্রতিবাদীর দাবীর বাকী খাজনা আদায় না করায় তাহার নিম্নলিখিত ক্রোকী সম্পত্তি আগামী ১৩৫৪ সনের ১২ই অগ্রহায়ণ মোতাবেক ১৯৪৭ সনের ১লা ডিসেম্বর, বেলা ১ ঘটিকার সময় প্রকাশ্য নীলাম আরম্ভ হইবে।

৮১ নং ১৯৪৬।৪৭ ইং বাঃ খাঃ ১০৪।৫ মোঃ।

ডিঃ—সুনকরণ কোঠারী মোঃ চাংড়াবান্ধা।
দেঃ—জ্যোতিষচন্দ্র রায় চৌঃ পঃ শূচ সাং আলোকবাড়ী।

[illegible] সম্পত্তি।

পঃ মেখলীগঞ্জ ১৫১ নং খাং তাং আলোকবাড়ী মধ্যে ২৫৪।০/০ খুঃ জমির কাত খাঃ ৩১৷৶০ আনা জমার আং চুঃ।

১০ নং ১৯৪৭।৪৮ ইং বাঃ খাঃ ২৫৬৷০ মোঃ

ডিঃ—মুরলীধর ভট্টাচার্য্য মোঃ মেখলা।
দেঃ—মহেশচন্দ্র পঃ সাং উপকড়ি ভাজনী চৌঃ মেখলীগঞ্জ।

তপশিল সম্পত্তি।

পঃ মেখলীগঞ্জ ২১৬৩ নং তৌঃ তাং বালাপাড়া খাগড়াবাড়ী মধ্যে ২১৬০।৶ খুঃ জমির কাত খাঃ ৩৪৶০ আনা জমার মধ্যের চুঃ।

১৭ নং ১৯৪৭।৪৮ ইং। বাঃ খাঃ ৫।৵০

ডি—বীরেন্দ্রচন্দ্র মিত্র মোঃ পৌলবাড়ী।
দেঃ—মনি মহম্মদ পঃ সাং ভোটাডাবরী চৌঃ মেখলীগঞ্জ।

তপশিল সম্পত্তি

পঃ মেখলীগঞ্জ ১৬১ নং খাং তাং ভোটাডাবরী মধ্যে ১৯৷৶০ জমির কাত খাঃ ২।৷৶ পাই জমার আং চুঃ।

১৫ নং ১৯৪৭।৪৮ ইং। বাঃ খাঃ ৮৵৶০ মোঃ।

ডিঃ—মুরলীধর ভট্টাচার্য্য মোঃ মেখলা।
দেঃ—মহিমচন্দ্র সরকার পঃ সাং বালাপাড়া খাগড়াবাড়ী চৌঃ কুচলিবাড়ী।

তপশিল সম্পত্তি

পঃ মেখলীগঞ্জ ২১৭৩ নং তৌঃ তাং বালাপাড়া খাগড়াবাড়ী মধ্যে ১৬৷০ কঠা জমির কাত খাঃ ১৯৵ পাই জমার দরচুঃ।

১৬ নং ১৯৪৭।৪৮ ইং। বাঃ খাঃ ২০৷৵০ মোঃ।

ডিঃ——নছিরননেছা বিবি পঃ সাং শ্রীরামপুর।
দেঃ—ফেলটু মহম্মদ পঃ সাং পানীশালা।

তপশিল সম্পত্তি।

পঃ মেখলীগঞ্জ ১৫২ নং খাং তাং পানীশালা মধ্যে ৪০৮১৵০ খুঃ জমির কাত খাঃ ৫০৲ টাকা জমার দরচুঃ।

১০১ নং ১৯৪৭।৪৮ ইং। বাঃ খাঃ ৯৭৷৶০ মোঃ।

ডিঃ—শরৎচন্দ্র মিত্র পঃ মোঃ মেখলীগঞ্জ।
দেঃ—কালাকৃষ্ণ বর্ম্মণ পঃ মোঃ পাড় মেখলীগঞ্জ।

তপশিল সম্পত্তি

পঃ মেখলীগঞ্জ ৫৪ নং খাং তাং নগর সাহেবগঞ্জ মধ্যে ৫০৮, ৫২৭ নং তৌঃ ফিঃ ৫৬১৷৶০ খুঃ জমির কাত খাঃ ৩২৶০ আনা জমার চুকানী স্বত্ব।

২৬ নং ১৯৪৭।৪৮ ইং। বাঃ খাঃ ৮৬৷৶০ মোঃ।

ডিঃ—শরৎচন্দ্র মিত্র পঃ মোঃ মেখলীগঞ্জ।
দেঃ—কালীকৃষ্ণ বর্ম্মণ সাং পাড় মেখলীগঞ্জ।

১০৩ নং ১৩৫৭।৪৮ ইং। বাঃ খাঃ [illegible] মোঃ।

ডিঃ—জামবল হুসেন মোঃ মেখলীগঞ্জ।

দেঃ—মহাবাহু[illegible] বৰ্ম্মণী সাঃ মোঃ মেখলীগঞ্জ।

তপশিল সম্পত্তি।

সাঃ মেখলীগঞ্জ ১০১ নং খাত্তা তাং চুলকাম ভাবরী মধ্যে ১৪৩৭ নং তৌঃ লিঃ ২৭।৴৹ [illegible] কাত বাঃ ২৫৷৴৹ আনা জমায় চুকানী স্বত্ব।

১০৪ নং ১৩৫৭।৪৮ ইং। বাঃ খাঃ ৫৮৸৫ মোঃ।

ডিঃ—৺মহিকুমার রায় গং সাং পাত্র মেখলীগঞ্জ।

দেঃ—মোবারক আলী মিঞা গং সাং পাত্র মেখলীগঞ্জ।

তপশীল সম্পত্তি।

সাঃ মেখলীগঞ্জ ৭৪ নং খাত তাং নিজ ভরক মধ্যে ৩/৬৩৭ নং তৌঃ লিঃ ৮।৩।৹ খুর জমির কাত বাঃ ৩।৴৬ পাই জমার চুকানী স্বত্ব।

১০৫ নং ১৩৫৭।৪৮ ইং। বাঃ খাঃ ৯১৵৹ মোঃ।

ডিঃ—কালীমোহন রায় সাং উচল পুখরী।

দেঃ—শিবো বৰ্ম্মণী গং সাং হেমকুমারী।

তপশিল সম্পত্তি

সাঃ মেখলীগঞ্জ ১৪৯ নং খাত তাং কালেক বাড়ী মধ্যে ৭ নং তৌঃ লিখিত ২৩৷৩৮৴৹ খুর জমির কাত বাঃ ৪৪৵৹ আনা জমার আং চুকানী স্বত্ব।

KUMAR P. NARAYAN, *Naib Ahilkar.*

দেওয়ানী কাৰ্য্যবিধি আইনের ২১ হুকুম, ৬৬ নিয়মের ঘোষণাপত্র।

তারীর মহকুমা মেখলীগঞ্জের দেঃ আদালত।

এতদ্বারা সর্ব্বসাধারণকে জানান যাইতেছে যে, দায়ীকগণের নিম্নলিখিত সম্পত্তি আগামী ১৩৫৭ সনের ১লা ডিসেম্বর মোঃ ১৩৫৪ সনের ১৫ই অগ্রহায়ণ তারিখে দিবা ১২ ঘটিকার সময় প্রকাশ্য নিলাম আরম্ভ হইবে।

৬ নং ১৩৫৭।৪৮ ইং। বাঃ ডিঃ ৬১৷৴৹ মোঃ।

ডিঃ—অজাবউদ্দিন আহাম্মদ সাং পানিশালা।

দেঃ—ক[illegible] উদ্দিন মামুদ সাং তথা।

তপশিল সম্পত্তি।

সাঃ মেখলীগঞ্জ ১৫০ নং খাত তাং পানিশালা মধ্যে ৩৬৭ নং হাঃ তৌঃ লিঃ ৮৸৶৹ খুর জমির কাত বাঃ ১০৶৹ আনা জমার আং বন্ধকী স্বত্ব।

KUMAR P. NARAYAN, *Naib Ahilkar.*

সিভিল সাপ্লাইজ কমিশনার ও কন্ট্রোলার অব প্রাইসেস্ আফিস, কুচবিহার।

বিজ্ঞাপন।

(মূল্য নিয়ন্ত্রণ)

সিভিল সাপ্লাইজ কমিশনারের উপর প্রদত্ত এবং ন্যস্ত ক্ষমতাবলে কোচবিহার Essential Supplies (Temporary Powers) Act 1946 এর ৩ ধারার অন্তর্গত ২ উপধারার সি ক্লজ অনুযায়ী নিম্নলিখিত দ্রব্যাদির সর্ব্বোচ্চ মূল্য নির্দ্ধারণপূর্ব্বক বাধ্য করা হইল এবং তাহা কুচবিহার গেজেটে প্রকাশিত হওয়ার তারিখ হইতে পুনরাদেশ না হওয়া পর্য্যন্ত বলবৎ থাকিবে। এতদ্বিষয়ক পূর্ব্ব বিজ্ঞপ্তি বাতিল করা হইল। কোন ব্যক্তি নির্দ্ধারিত মূল্যের অতিরিক্ত মূল্যে বিক্রয় করিলে বা দ্রব্যাদি বিক্রয়ার্থ আনিয়া নির্দ্ধারিত মূল্যে বিক্রয় করিতে অস্বীকার করিলে উপরোক্ত আইনের ৭ ধারা অনুযায়ী দণ্ডনীয় হইবে। ইতি ৩১শে অক্টোবর ১৯৪৭।

কেরোসিন—হলদিবাড়ী বন্দরের দর—

লাল কেরোসিন প্রতি টিন ৪৸৵ টিন সমেত প্রতি সের ৶৴

সাদা কেরোসিন প্রতি টিন ৫৶০ (ঐ) প্রতি সের ।৵

কয়লা—কয়লার দর মাত্র কুচবিহার সহরের জন্য নির্দ্ধারিত হইল।

মফঃস্বলের দর—কোচবিহার টাউন, দিনহাটা বন্দর, হলদিবাড়ী বন্দর, চাকলাবাজার বন্দর ব্যতীত অন্যান্য স্থানের দর নিম্নলিখিত দর অপেক্ষা (ধান্য, চাউল, সরিষা ও গম ব্যতীত) মণ প্রতি এক টাকা চারি আনা অর্থাৎ সের প্রতি দুই পয়সা বেশী হইবে। কিন্তু যে সকল ক্ষেত্রে রাজ্যের অন্যান্য স্থানের দর পৃথক ভাবে ধার্য্য আছে সেই সব ক্ষেত্রে ঐ নির্দ্ধারিত দরই প্রযোজ্য হইবে।

পাইকারী দর—দশ সেরের নীচে আড়াই সের পর্য্যন্ত খরিদ বিক্রী হইলে মণ প্রতি ।০ চারি আনা বেশী হইবে। কিন্তু এই নিয়ম, চাউল, সরিষা, গম, সম্বন্ধে প্রযোজ্য হইবে না এবং রেশন দোকানে ইহা প্রযোজ্য হইবে না; তথায় কেবলমাত্র নির্দ্ধারিত খুচরা দরে কেনা বেচা হইবে।

স্ট্যাণ্ডার্ড বস্তা—লবণ ১৬৯ সের বস্তা সহ।

চিনি ২৮১ সের বস্তা সহ।

	পণ্য দ্রব্যের নাম	প্রতি সের	প্রতি মণ	প্রতি ষ্ট্যাণ্ডার্ড বস্তা	মন্তব্য
১।	গুড়—দেশী আখের	৶০	৭৲		
	ঐ বড়দানা পাঞ্জাবী আখের		২০৸০		
২।	চিনি	৸৵০	২৪৷০	৬৭।৵০ (কোচবিহার সহর, দিনহাটা বন্দর, চাকলাবাজার বন্দর, হলদিবাড়ী বন্দরের জন্য) প্রতি ষ্ট্যাণ্ডার্ড বস্তা ৭০৸৵০ আনা	
	ঐ	৸৶০	২৭৲	(রাজ্যের অন্যান্য স্থানের দর)	
	বাতাসা, কদমা, তিলুয়া	৸৴	৩১৲		
	মিশ্রী	৸৴১০	৩২।০		
	রসগোল্লা	১।০	×		
	সন্দেশ (উৎকৃষ্ট)	২।০	×		
	ঐ (সাধারণ)	১৸০	×		
৩।	আটা	।৶০	১৫৸০		
৪।	ময়দা	৷৴০	২৮৲		
৫।	কয়লা		১৸৵০		
৬।	লবণ } ঐ (করকচ) }	৵০			
৭।	কেরোসিন তৈল (সাদা)	।৶ প্রতি বোতল		৫৸৵০ প্রতি টিন (টিন সমেত) ৫৴০ (৪ গ্যালন) টিন ছাড়া।	
	ঐ (লাল)	।০		৫।৵০ প্রতি টিন (টিন সমেত)। ৪৸০ (৪ গ্যালন) টিন ছাড়া।	
৮।	সাবান (পাঁচ খাসী)		৯৸০ প্রতি সের		
৯।	পাটকাটা পাটও	৸৶০			
	ঐ ৫ টাক	৸৶০			
১০।	চুন		তিন সের প্রতি টাকা (এই দর ছোট মোকাম কোচবিহার প্রযোজ্য নহে)		
১১।	জুতা চট মোটা গানি		২৭৶০		
	ঐ পোলা কচ	৸৶০			
১২।	অরহর ডাল (বড়দানা)	৸৵০ খুচরা প্রতি সের			৩৬।০ পাইকারী প্রতিমণ
	ঐ (ছোটদানা)	৸০ ,,			৩৪৸৵০ ,, ,,
১৩।	চালানি ছাতি মসুর	৸০ পাই ,,			৯২৶৵০ ,, ,,

The Cooch Behar Gazette.

১লা অগ্রহায়ণ, সোমবার; MONDAY, NOVEMBER 17, 1947 [১৩৫৪ সাল ৪৩৮ রাজশক

PART II.

NOTICES.

দেওয়ানী কার্য্যবিধি আইনের ২১ হুকুম, ৬৬ নিয়মের ঘোষণাপত্র।

রাজ্য কোচবিহারের ষ্টেঃ নং ৩য় আদালত।

এতদ্দ্বারা সর্ব্বসাধারণকে জানান যাইতেছে যে, দায়ীকগণের নিম্নলিখিত সম্পত্তি আগামী ১৯৪৭ সনের ১৯শে নবেম্বর মোঃ ১৩৫৪ সনের ৩রা অগ্রহায়ণ তারিখে দিবা ১ ঘটিকার সময় প্রকাশ্য নিলাম আরম্ভ হইবে।

৫৫ নং ১৯৪৭।৪৮ ইং। বাঃ ডিঃ ২৬৮৸০ মোঃ।

ডি—সুরেন্দ্রমোহন চক্রবর্ত্তী মোঃ বেহার ষ্টেঃ কোতয়ালী।

দেঃ—রাজেন্দ্রনাথ সাহা মোঃ বেহার ষ্টেঃ কোতয়ালী।

তপশিল সম্পত্তি।

পঃ বেহার ৯১০ নং থাক তাং খুণ্ডারী মধ্যে ২৫।৷৵০ ধুম জমির ৷০ আনা অংশ।

F. AHMED, *Asst. Civil Judge.*

ইং ১৯১০ সালের ৫ আইনের ৫৩ ধারার ২ প্রকরণ মতে নিলামী ইস্তাহার।

জাহির মহকুমা দিনহাটার নাঃ আঃ মাল আদালত।

এতদ্দারা সর্ব্বসাধারণকে জানান যাইতেছে যে, প্রতিবাদীর দাবীর বাকী খাজনা আদায় না করায় তাহার নিম্নলিখিত ক্রোকী সম্পত্তি আগামী ১৩২৪ সনের ১২ই অগ্রহায়ণ মোতাবেক ১৯১৭ সনের ১লা ডিসেম্বর তারিখে বেলা ১ ঘটিকার সময় প্রকাশ্য নীলাম আরম্ভ হইবে।

৮২ নং ১৯১৭।১৮ ইং। বাঃ খাঃ ৩১৮৶৩ মোঃ।

ডিঃ—মহব্বৎআলি মিঞা গং সাং কায়েতেরবাড়ী।

দেঃ—গোলাম ছোবাহানআলি মিঞা গং সাং ১ম খণ্ড সেউটী।

তপশিল সম্পত্তি।

পঃ দিনহাটা তাং ১ম খণ্ড সেউটী মধ্যে ৬।১৷৶০ ধুর জমির কাত বাঃ ৮।০ আনা জমার আং চুঃ।

AHAMED HOSAIN PRODHAN, *Naib Ahilkar.*

ইং ১৯১০ সালের ৫ আইনের ৫৩ ধারার ২ প্রকরণ মতে নিলামী ইস্তাহার।

জাহির মহকুমা দিনহাটার এঃ ডিঃ নাঃ আঃ মাল আদালত।

এতদ্দারা সর্ব্বসাধারণকে জানান যাইতেছে যে, প্রতিবাদীর দাবীর বাকী খাজানা আদায় না করায় তাহার নিম্নলিখিত ক্রোকী সম্পত্তি আগামী ১৩২৪ সনের ১৫ই অগ্রহায়ণ মোতাবেক ১৯১৭ সনের ১লা ডিসেম্বর তারিখে বেলা ১ ঘটিকার সময় প্রকাশ্য নিলাম আরম্ভ হইবে।

১১৪ নং ১৯১৭।১৮ ইং। বাঃ খাঃ ২৭৩৷৶০ মোঃ।

ডিঃ—তুলসীরাম ভাগা গং পিতাযুক্ত বিশ্বরচাঁদ ভাগা মোঃ গোসানীমারী ষ্টেশন দীনহাটা।

দে—সতীশ চন্দ্র ভট্টাচার্য্য পিতা মৃত উপেন্দ্রনাথ ভট্টাচার্য্য সাং ২য় খণ্ড ভাঙ্গনী ষ্টেশন দীনহাটা।

চনং দওরা পং দীনহাটার অন্তর্গত ৫৫২ নং থাক তাং খালিশা গোসানীমারী মধ্যে ৩ নং রেজেষ্টরীর লিখিত ৪১৯ নং স্বত্বে মঃ ৪৯১০৷৶০ ধুর জামর ব্রহ্মত্র হাল তেভিয়ে জেনদারের ।০ আনা ও বানীনাথ স্বায় শক.নন ।০ দীননাথ ০ আনা দেখা যায় উক্ত ব্রহ্মত্তরের জেনদারের ৷০ আনা অংশ মালিক জমিন সরকার বাহাদুর অনুমান মূল্য ৪০৲ টাকা।

GIRISH CHANDRA LAHIRI, *Addl. Naib Ahilkar.*

MALCUCHERY NOTICE.

ইস্তাহারনামা কাছারী মাল মোকামকে কোচবেহার, সন ১৯১৭ তারীখ ১৬ই অক্টোবর মোতাবেক বাঙ্গালা ১৩২৪ সন তারীখ ২৯শে আশ্বিন।

পঃ মাথাভাঙ্গা এলাকাধীন ৩১০ নং থাক তালুক শৌলমারী অন্তর্গত কোচবিহার চা বাগানের জন্য ডক্ত অদালতের ১৯১৭।১৮ ইং সনের ১৪ নং ভূমীগ্রহণের মোকদ্দমায় ১১। ১০ ৪৭ ইং তারীখের আদেশ হুজুর নিম্নলিখিত বীবরণযুক্ত ভূমী ১৩২৫ সনের শেষ ৭ মাস হইতে সরকারে গৃহীত হইয়া কোচবিহার চা বাগানের সামীল হওয়ায় সর্ব্ব সাধারণের অবগতী জন্য এই ইস্তাহার প্রচারিত হইল। ইতী

১। পং মাথাভাঙ্গা ৫১০ নং থাক তাং শৌলমারী বঃ নং ১৩ তৌঃ নং ১৪১১ ১০৯ নং জোত স্বত্ব যোগেন্দ্র কুমার ৶১৩।—জ্ঞানেন্দ্র কুমার ৶১৩,—পিং হরেন্দ্র কুমার রায় চৌধুরী। শিশির কুমার।৵৩,—পিং গজেন্দ্র কুমার রায় চৌধুরী ধরেন্দ্র কুমার ৶১৩।—জীতেন্দ্র কুমার ৶১৩।—পিং রাজেন্দ্র কুমার রায় চৌধুরী। মোঃ মাথাভাঙ্গা। বর্ত্তমান জমি ২৯।১৶০ ধুর জমা ৩।৫০ আনা গৃহীত জমী ২৯,৩৵০ ধুর জমা ৩৶০ পাই।

বিঃ

১১০ নং চুকানী স্বত্ব। বদিনাথ সিং রামপ্রসাদ দাস। বর্ত্তমান জমি ২৯।১৶০ ধুর জমা ৪৸৶০ আনা সিট নং ২ দাগ নং ২৭৬ গৃহীত জমি ২৯/৩৷০ ধুর জমা ৪৸৶৯ পাই।

২। পং মাথাভাঙ্গা ৩১০ নং থাক তাং শৌলমারী বঃ নং ১৩ তৌঃ নং ২০৩৩ ১৩৯ নং জোত স্বত্ব মাকচাঁদ জালানী ৷০ পিং দৌলতরাম জালানী হরকচাঁদ জালানি ৷০ পিং গোলকচাঁদ জালানী বর্ত্তমান জমি ১৩৭।৷৶০ ধুর জমা ৪২৸৶০ আনা গৃহীত জমি ১৩৭/৷৶০ ধুর জমা ৪২৸০ আনা।

পং মাথাভাঙ্গা ৩১০ নং থাক তাং শৌলমারী বঃ নং ১৩ তৌঃ নং ২০৩৪ নং ১৪০ চুকানী স্বত্ব বনী ৷০ পিং রামপ্রসাদ দাস গেলগেলা ।৶০ পিং রাজা মাধুর মহেন্দ্রনাথ বর্ম্মণ ৶০ পিং গোকুল দাস বর্ত্তমান জমি ১৩৭/৶০ ধুর জমা ৫৭৸৶০ আনা গৃহীত জমি ১৩৭/৷০ ধুর জমা ৫৭৸৶০ আনা।

বিতং

নিজদখল সিট নং ২ দাগ নং ২২৪, ২২৫, ২২৭, ২২৮, ২২৭/১০২১, ২২৭/১০২২, ২১১, গৃহীত জমি ৮৮॥২১ ০ ধুর।

১৪১ নং কৃষিপ্রজা স্বঃ চন্দকা ॥০ পিং গুরুদাস তারিনী ॥০ পিং পুটকন দাস বর্ত্তমান জমি ৫৮/।৶০ ধুর জমা ২৬৷০ আনা সিট নং ২ দাগ নং ২২০, ২২১, ২২২, ২২৩, ২২৬, গৃহীত জমি ৪৮৩/০ ধুর জমা ২৫৫৶/৭ পাই

৩। পঃ মাথাভাঙ্গা ৩৯০ নং থাক তাং শৌলমারী বঃ নং ১৭ তৌঃ নং ১৩১৮ ১৪২ নং জোতস্বত্ব লালবিহারী পিং মহাবীর বিভির সাং মাথাভাঙ্গা বর্ত্তমান জমি ১২৮৷১।৶০ ধুর জমা ৯২৫/০ আনা গৃহীত জমি ১২৪, ৪৶০ ধুর জমা ৮৮৶৫ পাই।

বিতং

নিজদখল সিট নং ২ দাগ নং ২৩১ গৃহীত জমি ২১৪ কাঠা।

১৪৩ নং চুকানী স্বত্ব টুমু বর্ম্মাণী জঃ সত্যনারায়ণ বর্ম্মণ বর্ত্তমান জমি ৩১॥৪।৶০ ধুর জমা ৪০।৶০ আনা। গৃহীত জমি ৩১॥৪।৶০ ধুর জমা ৪০।৶০ আনা।

বিতং

নিজদখল সিট নং ২ দাগ নং ২৮৬, ২৮৭, ২৮৮, ২৮৯, ২৯২, ২৯৩, গৃহীত জমি ১১/৪।৶০ ধুর।

পঃ মাথাভাঙ্গা ৩৯০ নং থাক তাং শৌলমারী ১৭ নং বঃ ১৪১৮ নং তৌঃ ১৪৪ নংস্বত্ব কৃষিপ্রজা আরা ॥০ পিং আরা দাস মব ॥০ পিং মঙ্গলু দাস বঃ জমি ২০॥০৶০ ধুর জমা ৩১।৶০ আনা ২নং সিট ২৬৯—২৫৫, ২৭০—২৭২, ২৭৪, ২৭৫, ২৬৪/১০৩০, ২৬৪/১০৩১, ২৬৪/১০৩২, ২৬৭/১০৩৩ নং দাগ গৃহীত জমি ২০॥০৶০ ধুর জমা ৩১।৶০ আনা।

১৪৫ নং স্বত্ব চুকানী স্বত্ব নবাস্থ পিং দেওয়ান মামুদ বঃ জমি ৫৪/।৶০ ধুর জমা ৫৩/০ আনা গৃহীত জমি ৪২৮৩॥৶০ ধুর জমা ৪৭৶৮ পাই।

পঃ মাথাভাঙ্গা ৩৯০ নং থাক তাং শৌলমারী ১৪ নং বঃ ১৪১৮ নং তৌ নিজ দখলী ২ নং সিট ২৩০, ২৪১—২৪৮, ২৫০, ২৫০, ২০৮, ২৫০/১০২৩, ২৩০/১০২৫, ২৩০/১০২৬, নং দাগ গৃহীত জমি ১৭৬১।/০ ধুর

১৪৬ নং স্বত্ব কৃষিপ্রজা আন পিং শ্যাম দাস বঃ জমি ৩১।৶০ ধুর জমা ৪০॥৵০ আনা ২নং সিট ২২৯, ২৩২—২৪৫, ২৪১ নং দাগ গৃহীত জমি ৩১/৩৶০ ধুর জমা ৩৩৷৶/২ পাই।

১৪৭ নং স্বত্ব চুঃ স্বত্ব নবাস্থ পিং দেওয়ান মহম্মদ বঃ জমি ৪০/১/০ ধুর জমা ৩১।৶০ আনা ২ নং সিট ২৫১—২৫৭, ২৫৯, ২৬০, ২৬৬—২৬৯, ২৯০, ২৯১, ২৫১/১০২৪, ২৬৮/১০২৭, ২৬৮/১০২৮, ২৬৮/১০২৯ নং দাগ গৃহীত জমি ৪০/১/০ ধুর জমা ৩১॥৶০ আনা।

৪। পঃ মাথাভাঙ্গা ৩৯০ নং থাক তাং শৌলমারী মধ্যে ১৮ নং বঃ ১৭১১ নং তৌঃ ১৪৮ নং স্বত্ব জোত মূল তৌজি বৃন্দাবন স্বয়ং /৬॥= চন্দ্রকান্ত /৬।= চন্দ্র শেখর /৬।= নাঃ পক্ষে উঁছি জ্যেষ্ঠ ভ্রাতা বৃন্দাবন শুকুল পিং প্রাণ দত্ত শুকুল সাং কুশারবাড়ী বঃ জমি ২৭২,৩৶০ ধুর জমা ১৮৯॥০ আনা গৃঃ জমি ২৬৮।০৮৶০ ধুর জমা ১৮৫৶/০ আনা।

(ক) তৌজি

রামমোহন ৮০ পিং পাতান মুনসির সাং কুশারবাড়ী।

বিতং

নিজ দখল ২ নং সিট ৯৫৮/৯৫১ নং দাগ গৃঃ জমি ।২।০ ধুর।

১৪৯ নং স্বত্ব কৃষি প্রজা গোবিন্দ পিং শ্যাম দাস বঃ জমি ৮।৪।৶০ জমা ৭।০ আনা ২ নং সিট ৩০৭/৩০৮ নং দাগ গৃঃ জমি ৩/৪৮০ ধুর জমা ১॥৵ ৩ পাই।

১৫০ নং স্বত্ব কৃষি প্রজা গলিমামুদ পিং গুমান মিঞা। বর্ত্তমান জমি ১২৪১।৶০ ধুর জমা ১৬৲ টাকা ২ নং সিট ২৮৩ ২৮৪, ২৮৫, ২৮৫/৯৫, ২৮২/৯২৬ নং দাগ গৃঃ জমি ১২॥১॥৶০ ধুর জমা ১৬৲ টাকা।

১৫১ নং স্বত্ব কৃষি প্রজা গোবিন্দ পিং শ্যাম দাস। বর্ত্তমান জমি ১৪।৪৶০ ধুর জমা ১০৵০ আনা ২ নং সিট ২৭৮—২৮১ নং দাগ গৃহীত জমি ১৪।২৶০ জমা ১০৵০ আনা।

১৫২ নং স্বত্ব কৃষি প্রজা চান্দবর নাঃ পক্ষে উঁছি মাতা দীনেশ্বরী দাস্যা জঃ বদি দাস বঃ জমি ৯১৪।৶০ ধুর জমা ৫॥/০ আনা ২ নং সিট ৩০৮/২৬৭, ৩০৮/৯৯৮, ৩০৮/২৬৯, ৩০৭/৯১০ নং দাগ গৃঃ জমি ৯৪।৫০ ধুর জমা ৫॥/০ আনা।

১৫৩ নং স্বত্ব কৃষি প্রজা বৈদ্যনাথ পিং জীবন দাস বঃ জমি ৫॥০/৮০ জমা ৩৮/০ আনা ২ নং সিট ৩২৪, ৩১৫ নং দাগ গৃঃ জমি ৫॥০৮ জমা ২৮/০ আনা।

১৫৪ নং স্বত্ব কৃষি প্রজা নারায়ণ ।০ মোহন ।০ পিং উজ্জ্বক বর্ম্মণ শীতল ॥০ পিং ভবানী বর্ম্মণ বঃ জমি ১১।৫৶০ ধুর জমা ৭।০ আনা ২ নং সিট ২৮২, ৩৩৬, ৩১৭, ৩১৮, ৩২০ নং দাগ গৃঃ জমি ১১।৫৶০ ধুর জমা ৭।০ আনা।

১৫৫ নং স্বত্ব চুকানী টুলী বর্ম্মণী বঃ সত্যনারায়ণ বর্ম্মণ বঃ জমি ৭৬৸৪৸৶০ ধুর জমা ৭৮৷৶০ আনা গৃঃ জমি ৭৬৸৪৸৶০ ধুর জমা ৭৮৷৶০ আনা।

বিভং

নিজ দখল ২ নং সিট ৩২০, ৩২১ নং দাগ গৃঃ জমি ১৪/০ ধুর।

১৫৬ নং স্বত্ব কঃ প্রজা গোবিন্দ পিং শ্যাম দাস বঃ জমি ২০।৩৮৶০ ধুর জমা ১২৸৶০ আনা ২ নং সিট ৩২১, ৩২৫, ৩৬৭, ৫২৩/২৬৪ নং দাগ গৃঃ জমি ২০।২৸৶০ ধুর জমা ১২৸৶০ আনা।

পঃ মাথাভাঙ্গা ৩১০ নং থাক তাং গৌলমারী ব নং ১৮ তৌঃ নং ১৪২১ নং ১৫৭ দরচুকানী স্বত্ব মেকডান্দ পিং পরমেশ্বর বর্ম্মণ বঃ জমি ২০।৩৶০ ধুর জমা ২৬৮৶০ আনা সিট নং ২ দাগ নং ৩২৩, ৩২৬ গৃহীত জমি ২০॥৫৶০ ধুর জমা ২৬৮৶০ আনা।

১৫৮ নং দরচুকানী স্বত্ব মথুরানাথ পিং হরচন্দ্র গুহ মোঃ কালাকাটা বঃ জমি ৩৪/৩৷৶০ ধুর জমা ৪৪৸৶০ আনা ২ নং সিট ৩১২, ৫১৮, ৩১৯ নং দাগ গৃঃ জমি ৩৪/৩॥৶০ ধুর জমা ৪৬॥৶০ আনা।

১৫৯ নং চুকানী স্বত্ব সুন্দরী মুরজিয়ানী জঃ রামসুন্দর মুরজিয়া বঃ জমি ১৮/২৶০ ধুর জমা ১২৸০ আনা ২ নং সিট ২৪২—২৪৫ নং দাগ গৃঃ জমি ১৮/২৷৶ ধুর জমা ১২৸০ আনা।

১৬০ নং চুকানী স্বত্ব মনেশ্বর।০ ফুলেশ্বর।০ পিং মাটিরা মুরজিয়া ছান্দু।০ মান্দু।০ পিং তেজু মুরজিয়া বঃ জমি ৩৪/৩॥৶০ ধুর জমা ২০॥৶০ আনা ২ নং সিট ৩২৯—৩৪১, ৩৪৬—৩৪৯ নং দাগ গৃঃ জমি ৩৪/৩॥৶০ ধুর জমা ২০।৶০ আনা।

১৬১ নং চুকানী স্বত্ব বৈদ্যনাথ পিং জীবনাথ বর্ম্মণ সাং রামঠেঙ্গা বঃ জমি ৬১।৪।৶০ ধুর জমা ৬৪ ০ আনা গৃঃ জমি ৬১।৪।৶০ ধুর জমা ৬৪/০ আনা।

বিভং

নিজ দখল ২ নং সিট ২৫১ নং দাগ গৃঃ জমি ২১০।৶০ ধুর।

১৬২ নং দরচুকানী স্বত্ব কেলাশী দাস্যা জঃ রামকমল দাস বঃ জমি ৫৯/২৮৸৶০ ধুর জমা ৭৩৸৶০ আনা ২ নং সিট ২২৭—৩৩৩, ৩৫৯—৩৭৫ নং দাগ গৃঃ জমি ৫৯/৩৸৶০ ধুর জমা ৭৩৸৶০ আনা।

১৬৩ নং চুকানী টুলী বর্ম্মণী জঃ সত্যনারায়ণ বর্ম্মণ বঃ জমি ২০।৪৩॥০ ধুর জমা ৩৫৲ টাকা গৃঃ জমি ২০।৪।০ ধুর জমা ৩৫৲ টাকা।

১৬৪ নং স্বত্ব দরচুঃ গোবিন্দ পিং শ্যাম দাস। বর্ত্তমান জমি ২৪॥৩॥০ ধুর জমা ৪১।৶০ আনা ২ নং সিট ২৯৪—৩০৬, ৩০৯—৩১৭ নং দাগ গৃহীত জমি ২০॥৪॥০ ধুর জমা ৪১।৶০ আনা।

৫। পঃ মাথাভাঙ্গা ৩২০ নং থাক তাং গৌলমারী মধ্যে ২৯ নং বঃ ১৪১৬ তৌঃ ১৬৫ নং স্বত্ব জোত শিবদত্ত।০ আনা পিং রামচন্দ্র মিশির পার্ব্বতী দেব্যা ৶১৩।— ক্রান্তি জঃ চন্দ্রনাথ মিশির শিবদলা ৶১৩।— ক্রান্তি বৃন্দাবন ৶১৩।— ক্রান্তি পিং শিবদান মিছির মোঃ গয়বাড়ী শিবকণ্ঠ।০ আনা পিং সূর্য্যপ্রসাদ মিছির মোঃ মাথাভাঙ্গা। বর্ত্তমান জমি ২৬৮।১৶০ ধুর জমা ২৫৫৶০ আনা গৃহীত জমি ২০৭৸১৸০ ধুর জমা ১৯২॥৶৫ পাই।

বিভং

নিজ দখল ২ সিট ৭৯১, ৮০৫, ৮৩৫, ৫৩৫ ৯৫৮ নং দাগ গৃহীত জমি ২॥১।৶০ ধুর।

১৬৬ নং স্বত্ব চুকানী বৈদ্যনাথ পিং জীবনাথ বর্ম্মণ সাং রামঠেঙ্গা। বর্ত্তমান জমি ৯৮৸০৸৶০ ধুর জমা ১০০৶০ আনা ২ নং সিট ৮১০ দাগ গৃহীত জমি ৭৭০।৶০ ধুর জমা ৮৪৶২ পাই।

নিজ দখল ২॥৩।০ ধুর।

১৬৭ নং স্বত্ব কৃষিপ্রজা তুল দাস্যা জঃ অনাদিল দাস। বর্ত্তমান জমি ৩১।৪৸৶০ ধুর জমা ৪৬।/০ আনা ২ নং সিট ৫৫৪—৫৬১, ৫৬৪, ৫৬৬, ৫৬৭ নং দাগ গৃহীত জমি ৩১।৪৸/০ ধুর জমা ৪৫॥/০ আনা।

১৬৮ নং স্বত্ব দরচুঃ মনেশ্বর দাস পিং মাটিয়া মুরজিয়া। বর্ত্তমান জমি ১৩।৩৸৶০ ধুর জমা ১১।৶০ আনা ২ নং সিট ৫৯১, ৮০৬, ৮০৯, ৮২০, ৮২১ নং দাগ গৃহীত জমি ৪।৪॥০ ধুর জমা ১৩ পাই।

পঃ মাথাভাঙ্গা ৩১০ নং থাক তাং গৌলমারী বঃ নং ১৯ তৌঃ নং ১৪১৬ নং ১৬৯ দরচুকানী স্বত্ব ফুলদাস্যা জঃ অনাদিল দাস বর্ত্তমান জমি ৩৮/৪০ ধুর জমা ৩৮৶০ আনা সিট নং ২ দাগ নং ৫৭৪, ৫৮৭, ৫৯০, ৫৯৫, ৫৯৬, ৫৯৯, ৬০৪, ৬০৫, ৬০৬, ৬০৮, ৬১০, ৬১৭, গৃহীত জমি ২৮৸০৸৶০ ধুর জমা ৩২॥৮ পাই।

১৭০ নং দরচুকানী স্বত্ব টেপু পিং বিরচরণ দাস বঃ জমি ১৩/৩॥৶০ ধুর জমা ২০৶০ আনা সিট নং ২ দাগ নং ৭৮৭, ৭৯৩, ৮১১, ৮১২, ৮১৫, ৮১৬ গৃঃ জমি ৯।৪৸০ ধুর জমা ১৪৶১০ পাই।

পং মাথাভাঙ্গা ৩৯০ নং থাক তাং শৌলমারী বঃ নং ১৯ তৌঃ নং ১৪১৬ নং ১১১ চুকানী স্বত্ব মনেশ্বর ৴৮ কুলেশ্বর ৵৮ পিং মাটিয়া মুরজিয়া মাম্পু ৵৬ ছাত্ত ৵৮ পিং ভেন্তু মুরজিয়া সুন্দরী মুরজীয়ানী ।৵৮ জঃ রামসুন্দর মুরজিয়া বর্ত্তমান জমি ৭৩৪৫।৵০ ধুর জমা ১০১৵০ আনা গৃহীত জমি ৫২৬০৩৮৴০ ধুর জমা ৭৭৶১০ পাই।

বিতং

মিজমাথলা সিট নং ২ দাগ নং ৫৬২, ৫৬৩, ৫৬৫, ৫৬৮—৫৭৩, ৫৭৫—৫৮৬, ৫৮৮, ৫৮৯, ৫৯২, ৫৯৪, ৫৯৮ ৬০০, ৬০১, ৬০২, ৬০৭, ৬০৯, ৬১৫, ৬১৭, ৭৯০, ৭৯৫, ৭৯৮, ৮১৪, ৮২৭, ৮২৮, ৮৩০, ৯৫২।

গৃহীত জমি ৪৩।১৮৶০ ধুর।

১৭২ নং স্বত্ব কৃষি প্রজা তোলা পিং মহাই মুরজিয়া বঃ জমি ৬।২৴০ ধুর জমা ৯৴০ আনা ২ নং সিট ৫৯২, ৫২৭, ৬০৩, ৮১৩ নং দাগ গৃঃ জমি ৬।২৴০ ধুর জমা ৯৴০ আনা।

১৭৩ নং স্বত্ব চকানী হরমোহন বর্ম্মণ পিং চোটাই দাস বঃ জমি ১১॥৪৶০ ধুর জমা ১৫।০ আনা ২ নং সিট ৭৮৯, ৭৯৯, ৮০০, ৮০৪, ৮২৪, ৮২৯, ৮৩০, ৮৩৩, ৮৩৪ নং দাগ গৃঃ জমি ৯৴১।৫০ ধুর জমা ১২৶২ পাই।

১৭৪ নং স্বত্ব চুকানী বুধী ॥০ পিং বানাকু বর্ম্মণ নাকশালা ৶১৩।৴০ কেটু ৶১৩।৴০ বিষাত্ত ৶১৩।৴০ পিং টোকরাই বর্ম্মণ বঃ জমি ৫৩॥২৴০ ধুর জমা ৬৮।৶০ আনা ২ নং সিট ৭৮৬, ৭৯২, ৭৯৩, ৮১৬—৮১৯, ৮২২, ৮২৩, ৮২৬, ৮৩৭—৮৪০, ৮১৩/৮৫৮, ৮৩০/৯৫৩ নং দাগ গৃঃ জমি ৪১।১।৶০ ধুর জমা ৫৯৶২ পাই।

১৭৫ নং স্বত্ব চুকানী গোবিন্দ ॥০ পিং টেপা বর্ম্মণ নারায়ণ ৶০ চন্দ্র ৶০ পিং রুদ্র বর্ম্মণ শুকচাঁদ।০ নাঃ পক্ষে উক্ত মাতা কন্যা মতী দাস্যা জঃ শীতল বর্ম্মণ বঃ জমী ২৭৮৩।৶০ ধুর জমা ৩১৮৶০ আনা ২ নং সিট ৬১৬ ৭৯৭ ৮০২, ৮০৭, ৮৩২, ৮০২/৮১৯, ৭৯৭/৮৬০, ৭৮৮, ৭৯৬, ৮০১, ৮০৩, ৮০৮, ৮২৫, ৮৩১, ৮২৫/৫৫৭ নং দাগ গৃঃ জমি ২১৮২৮৶০ ধুর জমা ২৬।৶২ পা।

। পঃ মাথাভাঙ্গা ৩৯০ নং থাক তাং শৌলমারী ২৭ নং বঃ ১৭২০ নং তৌঃ ২৬৩ নং জোত স্বত্ব অধকরণ॥০ পিং ভকুমচাঁদ বধেন মোহন লাল ॥০ পিং মালচাঁদ বধেন মোঃ মাথাভাঙ্গা বঃ জমি ২২৮৮০৶০ ধুর জমা ২০॥০ আনা গৃঃ জমি ৩৴৪৮০ ধুর জমা ২০৶১ পাই।

বিতং

২৭২ চুকানী স্বত্ব মনেশ্বর ৶০ কুলেশ্বর ৶০ পিং মাটিয়া মুরজিয়া মাম্পু ৶০ ছাম্পু ৶০ পিং ভেন্দু মুরজিয়া ধরাম দত্ত ৶০ পিং দুর্গাপ্রসাদ মুকুল ভূষণ ৶০ পিং কাশীচন্দ্র দাস তেওয়ারী বঃ জমা ৭॥৩৶০ ধুর জমা ১০॥০ আনা ২ নং সিট ৯২৩ নং দাগ বঃ জমি ৭॥৩৶০ ধুর জমা ১০॥০ আনা গৃঃ জমি ৩৴৪৮০ ধুর জমা ৫॥১ পাই

চৌঃ—উত্তর সিমানা—তাং রামঠেঙ্গা ষ্টেং ফালাকাটা জিলা জলপাইগুড়ী। দক্ষিণ সিমানাঃ—৩০৭ নং থাক তাং রামঠেঙ্গা ও ২০১ হইতে ২০৫ নং দাগ ২১০, ২১২, ২১৩, ২১৫, ২০৮, ২৭৭, ২৫২, ২৫৩, ৮৮৫, ৮৮৪ নং দাগ বাবদ ভূমি। পূর্ব্ব সিমানা ঃ—তাং নিজ সিট নং ১। পশ্চিম সিমানা ঃ—২২৭/১, ২২৭/২, ২২৬/৪, ২৭৭, ৫৬৮, ৫৬৬, ৩৭৩, ৩৭৪, ৮১ ৫৮২, ৯৭৮, হইতে ৯৮২, ৯৯৮, ৫৫৩, ৫৪৮, ৯০০, ৫৪০ হইতে ৫৪৭, ৬১১, হইতে ৬১৩, ৬১৮, ৭৮৫।

K C GANGULI,
Revenue Minister of the
Cooch Behar State.

ইং ১৯১০ সালের ৫ আইনের ৫৩ ধারার ২ প্রকরণ মতে নিলামী ইস্তাহার।

জারির মহকুমা মাথাভাঙ্গার নাঃ তঃ মাল আদালত।

এতদ্বারা সর্ব্বসাধারণকে জানান যাইতেছে যে, প্রাতবাদীর দাবীর বাকী খাজনা আদায় না করায় তাহার নিম্নলিখিত ক্রোকী সম্পত্তি আগামী ১৩৫৪ সনের ৩রা অগ্রহায়ণ মোতাবেক ১৯৪৭ সনের ১৯শে নবেম্বর তারিখে বেলা ১ ঘটিকায় সময় প্রকাশ্য নীলাম আরম্ভ হইবে।

১৮৩ নং ১৯৪৭।৪৮ ইং। বা: পাঃ ৪৫৭৲ মোঃ।

ডিঃ—রত্নেশ্বর সিংহ মোঃ মাথাভাঙ্গা।

দেঃ—সুধ্য বর্ম্মণ সাং খাট্টেরবাড়ী।

তপশীল সম্পত্তি।

পঃ মাথাভাঙ্গা ৩৮৫ নং থাক তাং খাটেরবাড়ী মধ্যে ৪৩৮ নং তৌ. লিঃ ৭২।৪৶০ ধুর জমির কাত বাঃ ১০৪৲ টাকা জমার বকেয়া।

১৫৮ নং ১৯১৭।১৪৮ ইং। বাঃ খাঃ ২৫৫।৶৵ মোঃ।

ডিঃ—মোহনলাল বয়েদ গঃ মোঃ মাথাভাঙ্গা।

দেঃ—মহেন্দ্র ওঃ খাপালু বর্ম্মণ সাং বড় শিমলগুড়ী।

তপশিল সম্পত্তি।

পঃ মাথাভাঙ্গা ৩৬১ নং থাক তাং খোপাচুলী মধ্যে ২৩।২৶০ পুর জমির কাত বাঃ ৪১৸৶০ জমার চুঃ।

১২০ নং ১৯১৭।১৪৮ ইং। বাঃ খাঃ ২০১৸৶০ মোঃ।

ডিঃ—মোহনলাল বয়েদ গঃ মোঃ মাথাভাঙ্গা।

দেঃ—কালীয়া বর্ম্মণ গঃ সাং আঙ্গারকাটা পাঞ্চুগী।

তপশিল সম্পত্তি।

পঃ মাথাভাঙ্গা ৪০৫ নং থাক তাং আঙ্গারকাটা পাঞ্চুগী মধ্যে ১৫।২৸৶০ পুর জমির কাত ৭৩।৶০ আনা জমার অংশ বাবদ ২৪৬ নং।

১৯৭ নং ১৯১৭।১৪৮ ইং। বাঃ খাঃ ৩৮৫।৶

ডিঃ—মোহনলাল বয়েদ গঃ মোঃ মাথাভাঙ্গা।

দেঃ—রাজকান্ত বর্ম্মণ গঃ সাং চেঙ্গারখাতা খাগড়াবাড়ী।

তপশিল সম্পত্তি।

পঃ মাথাভাঙ্গা ৩০৯ নং থাক তাং চেঙ্গারখাতা খাগড়াবাড়ী মধ্যে ৫৭।১৩।০ পুর জমির কাত বাঃ ২০৸৶০ অংশ জমার দঃচুঃ।

২০৪ নং ১৯১৭।১৪৮ ইং। বাঃ খাঃ ৬২৸৶০ মোঃ।

ডিঃ—মোহনলাল বয়েদ গঃ মোঃ মাথাভাঙ্গা।

দেঃ—বেশরবি বিবি গঃ সাং উনিশবিশা।

তপশিল সম্পত্তি

পঃ মাথাভাঙ্গা ৩১৮ নং থাক তাং উনিশবিশা মধ্যে ২৬।২।০ পুর জমির কাত বাঃ ২৮৶০ আনা জমার দরচুঃ।

১৭১ নং ১৯১৭।১৪৮ ইং। বাঃ খাঃ ৪৬।৶০ মোঃ।

ডিঃ—মোহনলাল বয়েদ গঃ মোঃ মাথাভাঙ্গা।

দেঃ—অক্ষেশ্বর বর্ম্মণ সাং বড় শিমলগুড়া চৈঃ মাথাভাঙ্গা।

তপশিল সম্পত্তি।

পঃ মাথাভাঙ্গা ৩৮০ নং থাক ২৬১০ নং তৌঃ তাং বড় শিমলগুড়া মধ্যে ৭৸০ কাঠা জমির কাত বাঃ ৬।৶০ আনা জমার দরাদর চুঃ।

১৬৯ নং ১৯১৭।১৪৮ ইং। বাঃ খাঃ ১১৫৶৵ মোঃ।

ডিঃ—মোহনলাল বয়েদ গঃ মোঃ মাথাভাঙ্গা।

দেঃ—রাজেশ্বর দাস গঃ সাং কোদালকেতা চৈঃ মাথাভাঙ্গা।

তপশিল সম্পত্তি

পঃ মাথাভাঙ্গা ৩৩২ নং থাক ২৫ নং তৌঃ তাং কোদালকেতা মধ্যে ২৩।১ কাঠা জমির কাত বাঃ ৪।১৶০ আনা জমার দরচুঃ।

১৬৪ নং ১৯১৭।১৪৮ ইং। বাঃ খাঃ ১৩১৶১০ মোঃ।

ডিঃ—মোহনলাল বয়েদ গঃ মোঃ মাথাভাঙ্গা।

দেঃ—রাজমোহন বর্ম্মণ গঃ সাং বড় শিমলগুড়ী।

তপশিল সম্পত্তি।

পঃ মাথাভাঙ্গা ৪০১ নং থাক ১৫৭৩ নং তৌঃ তাং ছোট শিমলগুড়ী মধ্যে ৫৩।০ কাঠা জমির কাত বাঃ ৪২ আনা জমার দরচুঃ।

১৯১ নং ১৯১৭।১৪৮ ইং। বাঃ খাঃ ১৩৯৭০ মোঃ

ডিঃ—প্রিয়নাথ সরকার মোঃ মাথাভাঙ্গা।

দেঃ—মোহনপ্রসাদ বর্ম্মণ সাং বারবরিয়া পাথচুটা চৈঃ মাথাভাঙ্গা।

তপশিল সম্পত্তি

পঃ মাথাভাঙ্গা ২৭১ নং থাক ২৭৭ নং তৌঃ তাং বারবরিয়া পাথচুটা মধ্যে ১০৭।৶০ পুর জমির কাত বাঃ ৭।৶০ আনা জমার চুঃ।

১৭৮ নং ১৯৪৭।৪৮ ইং। বাঃ খাঃ ১২০৮৵০ মোঃ।

ডিঃ—প্রিয়নাথ তরফদার পিং মৃত দ্বারকানাথ তরফদার মোঃ মাথাভাঙ্গা।

দেঃ—জহরউদ্দিন মিঞা গং বাদে ক্রমিক হর্তাগ্র ঘরে মর্হাযর আলা মিঞা পিং মৃত সদাগর মিঞা সাং শিংপুর

তপশিল সম্পত্তি।

পং লালবাজার ৪৩২ নং খাক তাং শিংপুর মধ্যে ২৫২ নং তৌ লিখিত ১৩৷৷০।৵০ থুং জমির কাত বাঃ ২৪৸৵০ আনা জমার চুঃ স্বত্ব।

৪৬ নং ১৯৪৭।৪৮ ইং। বাঃ খাঃ ৪২৫৷১৩ মোঃ।

ডিঃ—মোহনলাল বয়েদ গং পিং মৃত মাগচাঁদ বয়েদ মোঃ মাথাভাঙ্গা।

দেঃ—দয়ালদেব সিংহ গং সাং ভাউরাগুড়ী।

তপশিল সম্পত্তি।

পং মাথাভাঙ্গা ৪০০ নং খাক তাং ভাউরাগুড়ী মধ্যে ১৫৫৭ নং সাঃ তৌঃ লিখিত ১।৩৷৵০ থুং জমির কাত বাঃ ১।০ আনা জমার কবিপ্রজা স্বত্ব।

১৯০ নং ১৯৪৭।৪৮ ইং। বাঃ খাঃ ৩৯৯৲৬ মোঃ।

ডিঃ—প্রিয়নাথ তরফদার পিং মৃত দ্বারকানাথ তরফদার মোঃ মাথাভাঙ্গা।

দেঃ—মগরআলী সেখ গং সাং বড়মধুসূদন চৌং শীতলখুচী।

তপশিল সম্পত্তি।

পং লালবাজার ৪২১ নং খাক তাং বড়মধুসূদন মধ্যে ৬৩ নং স্বত্বের লিখিত ৫৮৸২৸৵০ থুং জমির কাত বাঃ ৭১৸০ আনা জমার চুঃ স্বত্ব।

১৮৯ নং ১৯৪৭।৪৮ ইং। বাঃ খাঃ ৪১৫৷৵৯ মোঃ।

ডিঃ—প্রিয়নাথ তরফদার পিং মৃত দ্বারকানাথ তরফদার মোঃ মাথাভাঙ্গা।

দেঃ—মগরআলী সেখ গং সাং বড় মধুসূদন চৌং শীতলখুচী।

তপশিল সম্পত্তি।

পং লালবাজার ৪২১ নং খাক তাং বড়মধুসূদন মধ্যে ১৩৯ নং তৌঃ লিখিত ৬।৸১৸৩ থুং জমির কাত বাঃ ৮৮৸৵০ আনা জমার চুঃ স্বত্ব।

৮ নং ১৯৪৭।৪৮ ইং। বাঃ খাঃ ৫৭।৵০ মোঃ।

ডিঃ—গুডকরণ বয়েদ গং মোঃ মাথাভাঙ্গা।

দেঃ—ভান্দারী বর্মণী গং সাং খেংচী।

তপশিল সম্পত্তি।

পং লালবাজার ৪৫২ নং খাক ৫৯২ নং তৌঃ তাং খেংচী মধ্যে ৭১৴২।৵০ থুং জমার কাত বার্ষিক ১১১৸৵০ আনা জমার আং দরাব চুকানী।

১৯৭ নং ১৯৪৭।৪৮ ইং। বাঃ খাঃ ২৫৸৵৩ মোঃ।

ডিঃ—অটামলাল বয়েদ মোঃ মাথাভাঙ্গা।

দেঃ—শাহউদ্দিন মিঞা গং সাং সাতপাও মোঃ মাথাভাঙ্গা।

তপশিল সম্পত্তি।

পং মাথাভাঙ্গা ২৩৭ নং খাক ৫৩০ক নং তৌঃ তাং সাতপাও মধ্যে ১৩৴২।০ থুং জমির কাত বার্ষিক ২১৲ টাকা জমার চুকানী স্বত্ব।

১৯৬ নং ১৯৪৭।৪৮ ইং বাঃ খাঃ ২৭৸৩ মোঃ

ডিঃ—অটামলাল বয়েদ মোঃ মাথাভাঙ্গা।

দেঃ—শাহউদ্দিন মিঞা সাং সাতপাও চৌং মাথাভাঙ্গা।

তপশিল সম্পত্তি।

পং মাথাভাঙ্গা ২৩০ নং খাক ৫৮০ক নং তৌঃ তাং সাতপাও মধ্যে ৯৷২৸৵০ থুং জমির কাত বার্ষিক ৬৸৵০ আনা জমার চুকানী স্বত্ব।

১৭৫ নং ১৯৪৭।৪৮ ইং বাঃ সুঃ ২২৸৹ মোঃ।

ডিঃ—শিবনাথ তরফদার দেঃ মাথাভাঙ্গা।

দেঃ—সুরবালা দাঃ গঃ সাং শীতলখুচী।

তপশিল সম্পত্তি

পঃ লালবাজার ৪৪৯ নং খাং ৪২০ নং তৌঃ তাং শীতলখুচী মধ্যে ২/২৸৶০ ধুর জমির কাত বার্ষিক ৩৸৴০ আনা জমার কৃষিপ্রজা স্বত্ব।

MANABENDRA NATH BHATTACHARJEE, *Naib Ahilkar.*

ইং ১৯১০ সালের ৫ আইনের ৫৩ ধারার ২ প্রকরণ মতে নিলামী ইস্তাহার।

তারীর মহকুমা মাথাভাঙ্গার ৫ঃ ডিঃ নাঃ আঃ স্রাল আদালত।

এতদ্বারা সর্ব্বসাধারণকে জানান যাইতেছে যে, প্রতিবাদীর দাবীর বাকী থাকায় আদায় না হওয়ায় তাহার নিম্নলিখিত ক্রোকী সম্পত্তি আগামী ১৩৫৪ সনের ৩রা অগ্রহায়ণ মোতাবেক ১৯৪৭ সনের ১৯শে নবেম্বর তারিখে বেলা ১ ঘটিকার সময় প্রকাশ্য নিলাম আরম্ভ হইবে।

১১৫ নং ১৯৪৭।৪৮ ইং। বাঃ খাঃ ১৭৩৷৶৩ মোঃ।

ডিঃ—শিবনাথ তরফদার মোঃ মাথাভাঙ্গা।

দেঃ—আনন্দ বর্ম্মণ গঃ সাং চোরাডাবরা খাগড়ীবাড়ী দেঃ মাথাভাঙ্গা।

তপশিল সম্পত্তি

পঃ [illegible] ৩০৯ নং খাং তাং চোরাডাবরা খাগড়ীবাড়ী মধ্যে সাঃ ৭৩৯ নং তৌঃ দিঃ ৪।৩৸৴০ ধুর জমির কাত বাঃ ৬৸৷৶০ আনা জমার চুঃ।

১২৬ নং ১৯৪৭।৪৮ ইং। বাঃ খাঃ ১২৯৸০ মোঃ।

ডিঃ—বেশরীচাঁদ ভাণ্ডারী গঃ মোঃ মাথাভাঙ্গা।

দেঃ—ছাদুরী ওঃ গিরিবালা বর্ম্মণী গঃ সাং কেকেরকুটী জলিসাবারী।

তপশিল সম্পত্তি।

পঃ মাথাভাঙ্গা ৯২৩ নং খাং তাং শালমারা মধ্যে ১৭২ নং তৌঃ দিঃ ৩৸।৷৴০ ধুর জমির কাত বাঃ ৮।৶০ আনা জমার আং বরচুঃ।

১৭৬ নং ১৯৪৭।৪৮ ইং। বাঃ খাঃ ৩৮৸৶৩ মোঃ।

ডিঃ—ভবানীপ্রসন্ন তালুকদার মোঃ মাথাভাঙ্গা।

দেঃ—গেন্দর বর্ম্মণ গঃ সাং বাটিয়ারকুঠি।

তপশিল সম্পত্তি।

পঃ মাথাভাঙ্গা ৩৩৪ নং খাং তাং নলাইগ্রাম মধ্যে ৮।২ কাঠা জমির কাত বাঃ ১৲ টাকা জমার দরচুঃ।

১৮৩ নং ১৯৪৭।৪৮ ইং। বাঃ খাঃ ৪ ..৩ মোঃ।

ডিঃ—মোহনলাল নন্দী গঃ মোঃ মাথাভাঙ্গা।

দেঃ—পঞ্চেশ্বর বর্ম্মণ গঃ সাং নিত্যানন্দী।

তপশিল সম্পত্তি।

পঃ মাথাভাঙ্গা ৩১৫ নং খাং তাং ছাট পশিয়ারা মধ্যে সাঃ ৮০৪ নং তৌঃ দিঃ ৪।২।০ ধুর জমির কাত বাঃ ৸৶০ আনা জমার দরচুঃ।

১৮১ নং ১৯৪৭।৪৮ ইং। বাঃ খাঃ ১০৪৷৶৩ মোঃ।

ডিঃ—মোহনলাল নন্দী গঃ মোঃ মাথাভাঙ্গা।

দেঃ—টেকা বর্ম্মণ গঃ সাং মোহনপুর দেঃ মাথাভাঙ্গা।

তপশিল সম্পত্তি।

পঃ মাথাভাঙ্গা ২৮৩ নং খাং তাং নদীর ভোগা মধ্যে সাঃ ৪৩৮ নং তৌঃ দিঃ ২।৪৸০ ধুর জমির কাত বাঃ ২৲ টাকা জমার দরচুঃ।

The Cooch Behar Gazette.

১লা অগ্রহায়ণ সোমবার] MONDAY, NOVEMBER 17, 1947. [১৩৫৪ সাল, ৪৩৮ রাজশক

Part II B.

Police Supplement.

NOTICE.

In supersession of the previous notices issued under section 30 (2) of the Cooch Behar Police Act, 1947, the following fresh notice is issued. :—

"General Notice under section 30 (2) of the Cooch Behar Police Act, 1947".

Whereas I, the Commissioner of Police, Cooch Behar, am satisfied that it is intended by certain persons or class of persons to convene or collect assemblies or to form processions on the public roads or in the public streets or thoroughfares in the Towns of Cooch Behar, Dinhata, Tufangunj, Mathabhanga, Mekligunj and Haldibari.

And whereas such assembly or procession, if uncontrolled, would be likely to cause a breach of peace.

Now, therefore, in exercise of the powers conferred by sub-section (2) of section 30 of the Cooch Behar Police Act, I do hereby require the persons convening or collecting such assembly or directing or promoting such procession to submit to me, at least 5 days before any date that may be fixed for such assembly and procession, an application for a license and to state therein the reason for such assembly and procession, the times fixed for such assembly and procession, the place at which such assembly will meet or from which such procession will start, the route by which such procession will pass and the number of persons who are likely to attend such assembly or to take part in such procession, together with all other details required to be included in such license. This order will remain in force for three months from the date of issue.

COOCH BEHAR,
The 3rd November, 1917.

J. M. CHATTERJEE,
Commissioner of Police,
Cooch Behar.

The Cooch Behar Gazette.

১৩ই অগ্রহায়ণ, সোমবার, MONDAY, DECEMBER 1, 1947 [১৩৫৪ সাল ৪৩৮ রাজশক

PART II.

NOTICES.

ইস্তাহারনামা সব-রেজেষ্টারী আফিস, সবডিবিসন মোতালকে

রাজ্য কোচবিহার। ইতি সন ১৯৪৭। তারিখ

এতদ্দ্বারা সর্ব্বসাধারণ জনগণকে জানান যাইতেছে যে, ইং ১৮৭৭ সালের ৩ আইনের ৮২ ধারা ও অত্র রাজ্যের প্রচলিত বিধানানুসারে মহকুমা সদর সব-রেজেষ্টারী আফিসের দাতা ও গৃহিতাগণ কর্ত্তৃক ওয়াপোষ না লওয়ায় নিম্নলিখিত দলীল সমস্ত আগামী ১৯৪৮ সনের ৫ই জানুয়ারী মোঃ বাং ১৩৫৪ সনের ২০শে পৌষ দিবা ১২ ঘটিকার সময় অত্রাফিসের সম্মুখে প্রকাশ্য জ্বালাইয়া দেওয়া যাইবেক। অতএব দলীল গৃহিতাগণ নির্দ্ধারিত তারিখের পূর্ব্বে আপন আপন উচিত জরিমানা সহ উপস্থিত হইয়া দলীল ওয়াপোষ লইতে পারে। নচেৎ ঐ সমস্ত দলীল সম্বন্ধে ভবিষ্যতে কাহারও কোন দাবী দাওয়া শুনা যাইবে না।

দাখিলের তাং	দলীলের প্রকার	দাতার নাম	গৃহিতার নাম	দলীলের নং
৩০।৩।৪৪	কবিলনামা	এছাকউদ্দিন মিঞা	বিবিছন নেছা	১
১০।৩।৪৪	রেহান	আবদুল কাদের মিঞা	সেখ এমাদউদ্দিন আহম্মদ	১৩
৮।৪।৪৪	কবলা	মোছাম্মৎ ছাবরণ খাতুন	বাগেশ্বরী দাস	৮৪
১৭।৪।৪৪	ঐ	রসমালী সেখ	আহাম্মদ সেখ	১৫১
১৮।৪।৪৪	দান পত্র	টৈরা বর্ম্মণী	নৃপেন্দ্রনাথ রায়	১৭০
২৪।৪।৪৪	কবলা	আমেনা নেছা বিবি	জমেরজেহা বিবি	২০৩
”	ঐ	কছিমুদ্দিন সেখ উকিল	সমসের সেখ গং	২০৬
”	কবুলিয়ৎ	মহম্মদ মামুদ মিঞা	মহম্মদ জাহেরউদ্দিন আহম্মদ	২০৮
”	ঐ	ঐ	ঐ	২১৬
[illegible]	[illegible]	চারুচন্দ্র ভট্ট	চেয়ারম্যান টাউন কমিটি	৮
”	ঐ	প্রফুল্লচন্দ্র রায়	ঐ	৯
১৩।৫।৪৪	কাবিলনামা	আবদুল জব্বার মিঞা	মোছাম্মৎ সকিরণ নেছা	২৫৩
[illegible]	[illegible]	মুক্তি দাস	চন্দ্রনাথ দাস	২৯১
[illegible]	[illegible]	[illegible]	[illegible]	[illegible]

The Cooch Behar Gazette.

[illegible]] TUESDAY, JULY 1, 1947. [[illegible]]

PART IV.

Important Papers and References.

Return showing the rain-fall, character of weather and prospects of crops in Cooch Behar for the fortnight ending the 19th April 1947.

SUB-DIVISION.	Rain-fall in inches.	Character of the weather in the District as far as known.	State and prospects of the crops and state of health at date.
Sudder 8th April ...	Nil	Seasonable ...	Preparation of lands for *bitri* paddy and jute and sowing of the same going on. Price of common rice is Rs. 16 per maund. No case of small pox or cholera reported. Public health generally good. No cattle disease reported. Fodder and water sufficient.
Ditto. 15th April ...	Nil	Do ...	Preparation of lands for *bitri* paddy and jute and sowing of the same going on. Price of common rice is Rs. 16 per maund. No case of small-pox or cholera reported. Public health generally good. No cattle disease reported. Fodder and water sufficient.
Dinhata 8th April ...	Nil	Do ...	Preparation of lands for *bitri* paddy and jute finished. Sowing of jute still going on in some places. Sowing of *bitri* paddy finished. No report of damage of any crop reported. Prices of common rice, *haimanti* paddy, jute, and mustard seeds are Rs. 15, Rs. 10, Rs. 27 and Rs. [illegible] respectively.
Ditto. 15th April ...	Nil	Do ...	Return not received.

PRICE-CURRENT of food-grains, Jute, Tobacco and Salt in the

RETAIL SALE:—Quantities per Rupee

	Wheat. Present return.	Wheat. Next preceding return.	Wheat. Corresponding return of last year.	Rice best sort. Present return.	Rice best sort. Next preceding return.	Rice best sort. Corresponding return of last year.	Rice common sort. Present return.	Rice common sort. Next preceding return.	Rice common sort. Corresponding return of last year.
Sub-divisions.	s. ch.	s. ch.	s. ch.	ch.	s. ch.	s. ch.	s. ch.	s. ch.	s. ch
Cooch Behar	......	......	......	......	......	......	2 8	2 5	4 0
Dinhata	......	......	......	......	......	......	2 4	2 8	3 4
Mathabhanga	......	......	......	......	......	......	......	......	......
Mekligunj	......	......	......	......	......	......	......	......	......
Tufangunj	......	......	......	2 0	2 0	2 14	2 4½	2 14	3 8

WHOLE-SALE PRICES CURRENT of food-grains, Jute, Tobacco and Salt in

WHOLE-SALE—Price

Markets.	Rs. A. P.	Rs. A. P.	Rs. A. P.	Rs. A. P.	Rs. A. P.	Rs. A. P.	Rs. A. P.	Rs. A. P.	Rs. A. P.
Cooch Behar	......	......	......	......	......	......	16 0 0	19 0 0	10 0 0
Dewanhat	......	......	......	......	......	......	16 0 0	19 0 0	10 0 0
Chowrahat	......	......	......	18 0 0	16 0 0	12 0 0	......	......	......
Choudl irhat	......	......	......	14 8 0	16 0 0	10 0 0	......	......	......
Ranirhat	......	......	......	......	......	......	......	......	......
Buxirhat	......	......	......	......	......	......	......	......	......
Sitaihat	......	......	......	16 0 0	16 0 0	10 0 0	......	......	......
Kaligunjhat	......	......	......	......	......	......	......	......	......
Gosanimarihat	......	......	......	19 0 0	16 0 0	12 0 0	......	......	......
Nazirerhat	......	......	......	......	......	......	......	......	......
Mathabhangahat ...	......	......	......	......	......	......	......	......	......
Shibporehat	......	......	......	......	......	......	......	......	......
Moraagahat	......	......	......	......	......	......	......	......	......
Sitalkhuchihat	......	......	......	......	......	......	......	......	......
Mekligunj	......	......	......	......	......	......	......	......	......
Changrabanda	......	......	......	......	......	......	......	......	......
Haldibari	......	......	......	......	......	......	......	......	......
Jamaldahe ...	......	......	......	......	......	......	......	......	......
Ranirhat	......	......	......	20 0 0	20 0 0	15 0 0	17 8 0	15 0 0	11 8 0
Balarampur	......	......	......	21 0 0	20 0 0	15 0 0	17 8 0	15 0 0	11 8 0
Buxirhat	......	......	......	20 0 0	20 0 0	15 0 0	16 0 0	16 0 0	11 8 4
Gheramarahat	......	......	......	20 0 0	20 0 0	15 0 0	17 8 0	15 8 0	11 8 0

Haimanti paddy.			Bitri paddy.			Tobacco.			Salt		
Present return	Next preceding return.	Corresponding return of last year.*	Present return.	Next preceding return.	Corresponding return of last year.	Present return.	Next preceding return.	Corresponding return of last year	Present return	Next preceding return.	Corresponding return last year
s. ch.	s. ch	s. ch	s. ch.	s. ch	s. ch	s. ch	s. ch	s. ch	s. ch	s. ch	s. ch
4 0	5 0	5 13	......	......	......	0 8	0 8	1 0	5 8	5 8	5 8
4 0	4 0	6 6	......	......	......	......	......	0 11	3 4	4 0	4½ 0
......	......	......	......	......	......	......	......	......	......	......	......
......	......	......	......	......	......	......	......	......	......	......	......
......	......	......	......	......	......	......	......	......	......	......	......

Rs A P.	Rs. A P.	Rs. A P.	Rs. A P.	Rs. A P.	Rs. A P	Rs A P	Rs A. P.	Rs A. P	Rs. A. P.	Rs A. P.	Rs A P
10 0 0	8 0 0	7 0 0	......	......	......	80 0 0	80 0 0	40 0 0	7 8 0	7 8 0	7 8 0
10 0 0	8 0 0	7 0 0	......	......	......	80 0 0	80 0 0	40 0 0	7 8 0	7 8 0	7 8 0
10 0 0	10 0 0	6 0 0	......	......	......	......	......	50 0 0	7 8 0	10 0 0	8 12 0
10 0 0	10 0 0	5 8 0	......	......	......	......	100 0 0	......	......	......	......
......	......	......	......	......	......	......	......	......	......	......	......
......	......	......	......	......	......	......	......	......	......	......	......
10 0 0	10 0 0	5 8 0	......	......	......	......	......	......	......	......	......
......	......	......	......	......	......	......	......	......	......	......	......
10 0 0	10 0 0	6 0 0	......	......	......	80 0 0	......	......	7 8 0	10 0 0	......
......	......	......	......	......	......	......	......	......	......	......	......
......	......	......	......	......	......	......	......	......	......	......	......
......	......	......	......	......	......	......	......	......	......	......	......
......	......	......	......	......	......	......	......	......	......	......	......
......	......	......	......	......	......	......	......	......	......	......	......
......	......	......	......	......	......	......	......	......	......	......	......
......	......	......	......	......	......	......	......	......	......	......	......
......	......	......	......	......	......	......	......	......	......	......	......
......	......	......	......	......	......	......	......	......	......	......	......
9 8 0	9 0 0	5 8 0	......	......	......	120 0 0	120 0 0	60 0 0	6 4 0	6 4 0	9 6 0
9 8 0	9 0 0	5 8 0	......	......	......	120 0 0	120 0 0	60 0 0	6 4 0	6 4 0	9 6 0
9 8 0	9 0 0	5 8 0	......	......	......	120 0 0	120 0 0	60 0 0	6 4 0	6 4 0	9 6 0
9 8 0	9 0 0	5 8 0	......	......	......	120 0 0	120 0 0	60 0 0	6 4 0	6 4 0	9 6 0

Chena.			Kaon			Mustard seed			Mustard seed oil		
Present return	Next preceding return.	Corresponding return of last year	Present return.	Next preceding return.	Corresponding return of last year	Present return.	Next preceding return.	Corresponding return of last year.	Present return.	Next preceding return	Corresponding return of last year
ch	s. ch.	s. ch.	s. ch.	s. ch	s. ch.	s. ch.	s. ch.	s. ch.	s. ch.	s. ch.	s. ch.
......	......	......	......	......	......	2 0	2 8	2 8	0 10	0 10	0 13
......	......	......	......	......	......	1 8½	1 8½	2 8	0 5½	0 5½	0 10
......	......	......	......	......	......	......	......	......	......	......	......
......	......	......	......	......	......	......	......	......	......	......	......
......	......	......	......	......	......	......	......	......	......	......	......

R. A. P.	Rs. A. P.	Rs. A. P.	Rs. A. P.	Rs. A. P.	Rs. A. P.	Rs. A. P.	Rs. A. P.	Rs. A. P.	Rs. A. P.	Rs. A. P.	Rs. A. P.
......	......	......	......	......	......	20 0 0	16 0 0	16 0 0	62 8 0	62 8 0	50 0 0
......	......	......	......	......	......	20 0 0	16 0 0	16 0 0	62 8 0	62 8 0	50 0 0
......	......	......	......	......	......	26 0 0	26 0 0	16 0 0	120 0 0	120 0 0	60 0 0
......	......	......	......	......	......	......	28 0 0	16 0 0	1[illegible]0 0 0	100 0 0	60 0 0
......	......	......	......	......	......	......	......	......	......	......	......
......	......	......	......	......	......	......	......	......	......	......	......
......	......	......	......	......	......	2[illegible] 0 0	25 0 0	16 0 0	100 0 0	100 0 0	60 0 0
......	......	......	......	......	......	......	......	......	......	......	......
......	......	......	......	......	......	26 0 0	26 0 0	15 0 0	120 0 0	120 0 0	60 0 0
......	......	......	......	......	......	......	......	......	......	......	......
......	......	......	......	......	......	......	......	......	......	......	......
......	......	......	......	......	......	......	......	......	......	......	......
......	......	......	......	......	......	......	......	......	......	......	......
......	......	......	......	......	......	......	......	......	......	......	......
......	......	......	......	......	......	......	......	......	......	......	......
......	......	......	......	......	......	......	......	......	......	......	......
......	......	......	......	......	......	......	......	......	......	......	......
......	......	......	......	......	......	......	......	......	......	......	......
......	......	......	......	......	......	20 0 0	18 0 0	16 0 0	80 0 0	80 0 0	60 0 0
......	......	......	......	......	......	20 0 0	18 0 0	16 0 0	80 0 0	8[illegible] 0 0	6[illegible] 0 0
......	......	......	......	......	......	20 0 0	18 0 0	16 0 0	80 0 0	80 0 0	60 0 0
......	......	......	......	......	......	20 0 0	18 [illegible] 0	16 0 0	8[illegible] 0 0	8[illegible] [illegible] [illegible]	6[illegible] 0 [illegible]

...ase of Cooch Behar for the fortnight ending the 19th April 1947.

...y the Seer of 80 Tolas.

JUTE.			KHESARI KALAI.			OIL CAKE.			REMARKS.
Present return	Next preceding return.	Corresponding return of last year.	Present return.	Next preceding return.	Corresponding return of last year.	Present return.	Next preceding return.	Corresponding return of last year.	
s. ch	s. ch	s. ch.	s. ch.	s. ch.	s. ch.	s. ch.	s. ch.	s ch.	
1 7	1 6	4 8	3 4	3 4	5 11	8 0	8 0	9 0	
2 10	1 9	3 11	3 7	......	5 0	6 14	6 6	8 0	
......	......	......	......	......	......	......	......	......	
......	......	......	......	......	......	......	......	......	
......	......	......	......	......	......	......	......	......	

...the Principal marts of Cooch Behar for the fortnight ending the 19th April 1947

per maund of 40 seers.

Rs. A. P	Rs. A. P.	Rs. A. P	Rs. A. P.	Rs. A. P.	Rs. A. P.	Rs. A. P.	Rs. A. P.	Rs. A. P
27 0 0	26 0 0	9 0 0	12 0 0	12 0 0	7 0 0	5 0 0	5 0 0	4 8 0
27 0 0	26 0 0	9 0 0	12 0 0	12 0 0	7 0 0	5 0 0	5 0 0	4 8 0
27 0 0	25 0 0	11 0 0	12 0 0	......	8 0 0	6 0 0	6 0 0	5 0 0
25 0 0	25 0 0	11 0 0	12 0 0	......	10 0 0	8 0 0	6 0 0	5 0 0
......	......	......	......	......	......	......	......	......
......	......	......	......	......	......	......	......	......
......	......	......	......	......	......	4 0 0	4 0 0	4 0 0
......	......	......	......	......	......	......	......	......
......	25 0 0	......	......	......	......	6 0 0	6 0 0	4 0 0
......	......	......	......	......	......	......	......	......
......	......	......	......	......	......	......	......	......
......	......	......	......	......	......	......	......	......
......	......	......	......	......	......	......	......	......
......	......	......	......	......	......	......	......	......
......	......	......	......	......	......	......	......	......
......	......	......	......	......	......	......	......	......
......	......	......	......	......	......	......	......	......
......	......	......	......	......	......	......	......	......
26 0 0	28 0 0	12 0 0	15 0 0	15 0 0	7 8 0	5 0 0	6 0 0	4 0 0
26 0 0	28 0 0	12 0 0	15 0 0	15 0 0	7 8 0	5 0 0	6 0 0	4 0 0
26 0 0	28 0 0	12 0 0	15 0 0	15 0 0	7 8 0	5 0 0	6 0 0	4 0 0
26 0 0	28 0 0	12 0 0	15 0 0	15 0 0	7 8 0	5 0 0	6 0 0	4 0 0

Return showing the rain-fall, character of weather and prospects of crops in Cooch Behar for the fortnight ending the 19th April 1947.

SUB-DIVISION.	Rain-fall in inches.	Character of the weather in the district as far as known.	State and prospects of the crops and State of health at date.
Mathabhanga 8th April	Nil	Seasonable ...	Sowing of *bitri* paddy and curing of tobacco are going on. The remaining 3 cases of "Galafoila" cattle disease have been cured and no any other epidemic was reported during the week. Price of paddy, rice mustard seeds are Rs. 8 to Rs. 8-8, Rs. 16 and Rs. 26 per maund respectively.
Mathabhanga 15th April ...	Nil	Do	Sowing of *bitri* paddy and curing of tobacco are going on. Price of paddy, rice and mustard seeds are Rs. 9, Rs. 16 and Rs. 26 per maund respectively. One case of small-pox was reported during the week.
Mekliganj 8th April ...	Nil	Fair ...	Preparation of lands for *bitri* paddy and jute going on. Prices of common rice, *haimanti* paddy and tobacco are Rs. 16, Rs. 8-2 to Rs. 10 and Rs. 50 to Rs. 75 per maund respectively. Out of 11 fresh cases of cattle desease (pox) reported from Mekliganj police Station 5 ended fatally and 6 are still lingering. Fodder and water sufficient. Public health generally good.
Mekliganj 15th April ...	Nil	Do ...	Return not received.
Tufanganj 8th April	Nil	Do ...	Weeding of *bitri* paddy and sowing of jute going on. Prices of common rice, mustard seeds and jute are Rs. 17-8, Rs. 24 and Rs. 28 per maund respectively. Condition of standing crops fair. 5 cases of cholera reported during the week of which 4 ended fatally and the remaining one case is still pending. The one case of small-pox reported during the last week was diognised as a case of chicken pox. Fodder and water sufficient.
Tufanganj 15th April ...	Nil.	Do ...	Weeding of *bitri* paddy and sowing of jute going on. Condition of standing crops fair. The one case of cholera is cured and no fresh attack is reported during the week. Prices of common rice, mustard seeds and jute are Rs. 15, Rs. 20 and Rs. 28 respectively. Fodder and water sufficient.

L. M. Bakshi,
Development Commissioner, Cooch Behar.

The Cooch Behar Gazette.

৩১শে আষাঢ় বুধবার] WEDNESDAY, JULY 16, 1947. [১৩৫৪ সাল, ৪৩৮ রাজশকা

PART IV.

Important Papers and References.

Return showing the rain-fall, character of weather and prospects of crops in Cooch Behar for the fortnight ending the 3rd May 1947.

SUB-DIVISION.	Rain-fall in inches.	Character of the weather in the District as far as known.	State and prospects of the crops and state of health at date.
Sadder 22nd April ...	Nil	Seasonable ...	Preparation of lands for *bitri* paddy and jute and sowing of the same going on. Weeding of the same commenced. Price of common rice is Rs. 16 per maund. No case of small pox or cholera reported. Public health generally good. No cattle disease reported. Fodder and water sufficient.
Ditto. 29th April ...	Nil	Do ...	Preparation of lands for *bitri* paddy and jute and sowing of the same going on. Weeding is commencing. Price of common rice is Rs. 16 per maund. No case of small-pox or cholera reported. Public health generally good. No cattle disease reported. Fodder and water sufficient.
Dinhata 22nd April ...	Nil	Do ...	Preparation of lands for jute and *bitri* paddy and sowing of their seeds finished. Weeding of jute and *bitri* paddy going on. Prospects and condition of the standing crops tolerable. No report of damage of any crops reported. Prices of common rice, *haimanti* paddy, jute and mustard seeds are Rs. 18, Rs. 10, Rs. 27, and Rs. 26 respectively.
Ditto. 29th April ..	Nil	Do ...	Preparation of lands for *haimanti* paddy and sowing of *haimanti* seeds going on. Weeding of jute and *bitri* paddy going on. Prospects and condition of standing crops tolerable. No report of damage of any crops reported. Prices of common rice, *haimanti* paddy, jute, mustard seeds and tobacco are Rs. 18, Rs. 11-8 Rs. 27, Rs 24 and Rs. 60 respectively.

PRICE-CURRENT of food-grains, Jute, Tobacco and Salt in the

RETAIL SALE:—Quantities per Rupee

Sub-divisions.	Wheat. Present return	Next preceding return.	Corresponding return of last year.	Rice best sort. Present return.	Next preceding return	Corresponding return of last year.	Rice common sort. Present return.	Next preceding return.	Corresponding return of last year.
	s. ch.	s. ch.	s. ch.	ch.	s. ch.	s. ch.	s. ch.	s. ch.	s. ch.
Cooch Behar	......	......	......	......	......	......	2 1	2 8	3 10
Dinhata	......	......	......	......	......	......	2 4	2 4	5 4
Mathabhanga	......	......	......	......	......	......	......	......	......
Mekligunj	......	......	......	2 0	2 0	3 0	2 8	2 8	3 0
Tufangunj	......	......	......	2 0	2 0	2 14	2 4½	2 14	3 8

WHOLE-SALE PRICES CURRENT of food-grains, Jute, Tobacco and Salt in

WHOLE-SALE—Price

Markets.	Rs. A. P.	Rs. A. P.	Rs. A. P.	Rs. A. P.	Rs. A. P.	Rs. A. P.	Rs. A. P.	Rs. A. P.	Rs. A. P.
Cooch Behar	......	......	......	......	......	......	19 0 0	16 0	12 0
Dewanhat	......	......	......	......	......	......	19 0 0	16 0	10 12
Chowrahat	......	......	......	......	......	......	18 0 0	18 0	2 0
Chaudhurihat	......	......	......	......	......	......	14 0 0	14 8	1 0 0
Ranirhat	......	......	......	......	......	......	......	......	......
Baxirhat	......	......	......	......	......	......	......	......	......
Sitaihat	......	......	......	......	......	......	20 0 0	16 0	10 0 0
Kaliganjhat	......	......	......	......	......	......	......	......	......
Gosanimarihat	......	......	......	......	......	......	19 0	18 0	......
Nazirerhat	......	......	......	......	......	......	......	......	......
Mathabhangahat ...	......	......	......	......	......	......	......	......	......
Shibporehat	......	......	......	......	......	......	......	......	......
Moranggahat	......	......	......	......	......	......	......	......	......
Sitalkhuchihat	......	......	......	......	......	......	......	......	......
Mekligunj	......	......	......	20 0 0	20 0 0	13 0 0	16 0 0	16 0	13 0 0
Changrabandha	......	......	......	20 0 0	20 0 0	18 0 0	16 0 0	16 0 0	18 0
Haldibari	......	......	......	20 0 0	20 0 0	20 0 0	16 0 0	16 0 0	18 0
Jamaldaha	......	......	......	20 0 0	20 0 0	20 0 0	16 0 0	16 0 0	13 0 0
Ranirhat	......	......	......	20 0 0	20 0 0	15 0 0	17 8 0	17 8 0	11 8 0
Balarampur	......	......	......	20 0 0	20 0 0	15 0 0	17 8	17 8	11 8
Baxirhat	......	...	......	20 0 0	20 0 0	15 0 0	16 0	15 0 0	11 8
Ghoramarahat	...	......	......	20 0 0	20 0	15 0 0	17 8 0	17 0 0	11 8 0

CHEENA.			KAON			MUSTARD SEED			MUSTARD SEED OIL		
Present return	Next preceding return.	Corresponding return of last year	Present return.	Next preceding return.	Corresponding return of last year	Present return.	Next preceding return.	Corresponding return of last year.	Present return.	Next preceding return	Corresponding return of last year
ch.	s. ch.	s. ch.	s. ch.	s. ch.	s. ch.	s. ch.	s. ch.	s. ch.	s. ch.	s. ch.	s. ch.
......	......	......	......	......	......	2 0	2 0	2 8	0 10	0 10	0 13
......	......	......	......	......	......	1 9½	1 8½	2 8	7 4	0 5½	0 10
......	......	......	......	......	......	......	......	......	......	......	......
......	......	......	......	......	......	1 8	1 0	1 8	0 6	1 4	0 10½
......	......	......	......	......	......	2 0	2 0	2 8	0 8	0 8	0 10

R. A. P.	Rs. A. P.	Rs. A. P.	Rs. A. P.	Rs. A. P.	Rs. A. P.	Rs. A. P.	Rs. A. P.	Rs. A. P.	Rs. A. P.	Rs. A. P.	Rs. A. P.
......	......	......	......	......	......	20 0 0	20 0 0	16 0 0	62 8 0	62 8 0	50 0 0
......	......	......	......	......	......	20 0 0	20 0 0	16 0 0	62 8 0	62 8 0	50 0 0
......	......	......	......	......	......	24 0 0	26 0 0	16 0 0	100 0 0	120 0 0	60 0 0
......	......	......	......	......	......	......	......	16 0 0	100 0 0	100 0 0	65 0 0
......	......	......	......	......	......	......	......	......	......	......	......
......	......	......	......	......	......	......	......	......	......	......	......
......	......	......	......	......	......	22 0 0	25 0 0	16 0 0	100 0 0	100 0 0	60 0 0
......	......	......	......	......	......	......	......	......	......	......	......
......	......	......	......	......	......	26 0 0	26 0 0	......	100 0 0	120 0 0	60 0 0
......	......	......	......	......	......	......	......	......	......	......	......
......	......	......	......	......	......	......	......	......	......	......	......
......	......	......	......	......	......	......	......	......	......	......	......
......	......	......	......	......	......	......	......	......	......	......	......
......	......	......	......	......	......	......	......	......	......	......	......
......	......	......	......	......	......	27 0 0	40 0 0	27 0 0	100 0 0	100 0 0	60 0 0
......	......	......	......	......	......	27 0 0	40 0 0	27 0 0	100 0 0	100 0 0	60 0 0
......	......	......	......	......	......	27 0 0	40 0 0	27 0 0	100 0 0	100 0 0	60 0 0
......	......	......	......	......	......	27 0 0	40 0 0	27 0 0	100 0 0	100 0 0	60 0 0
......	......	......	......	......	......	20 0 0	20 0 0	18 0 0	80 0 0	80 0 0	60 0 0
......	......	......	......	......	......	20 0 0	28 0 0	18 0 0	80 0 0	80 0 0	60 0 0
......	......	......	......	......	......	20 0 0	20 0 0	18 0 0	80 0 0	80 0 0	60 0 0
......	......	......	......	......	......	20 0 0	20 0 0	18 0 0	80 0 0	80 0 0	[illegible]

State of Cooch Behar for the fortnight ending the 3rd May 1947.

by the Seer of 80 Tollas.

Jute			Kheshari Kalai			Oil Cake			Remarks
Present return	Next preceding return.	Corresponding return of last year.	Present return.	Next preceding return.	Corresponding return of last year.	Present return.	Next preceding return.	Corresponding return of last year.	
s. ch.	s. ch.	s. ch.	s. ch.	s. ch.	s. ch.	s. ch.	s. ch.	s. ch.	
1 7	1 7	4 0	3 4	3 4	5 11	9 0	8 0	8 0	
1 8½	1, 10	4 0	3 4	3 7	5 0	5 11	6 14	8 0	
......	......	......	......	......	......	......	......	......	
2 9	1 8	3 5	......	......	......	4 0	4 0	8 0	
1 5	1 7	2 6	2 14	2 14	5 4	8 0	8 0	10 0	

the Principal marts of Cooch Behar for the fortnight ending the 3rd May 1947

per maund of 40 seers.

Rs. A. P.	Rs. A. P.	Rs. A. P.	Rs. A. P.	Rs. A. P.	Rs. A. P.	Rs. A. P.	Rs. A. P.	Rs. A. P.
27 0 0	27 0 0	10 0 0	12 0 0	12 0 0	7 0 0	4 8 0	5 0 0	5 0 0
27 0 0	27 0 0	10 0 0	12 0 0	12 0 0	7 0 0	4 8 0	5 0 0	5 0 0
27 0 0	27 0 0	10 0 0	12 0 0	12 0 0	8 0 0	7 0 0	6 0 0	5 0 0
25 0 0	25 0 0	10 0 0	13 0 0	12 0 0	8 0 0	6 0 0	6 0 0	4 0 0
......	......	......	......	......	......	......	......	......
......	......	......	......	......	......	......	......	......
......	......	......	......	......	......	4 0 0	4 0 0	3 12 0
......	......	......	......	......	......	......	......	......
25 0 0	......	......	......	......	......	6 0 0	6 0 0	4 0 0
......	......	......	......	......	......	......	......	......
......	......	......	......	......	......	......	......	......
......	......	......	......	......	......	......	......	......
......	......	......	......	......	......	......	......	......
......	......	......	......	......	......	......	......	......
17 8 0	24 0 0	12 0 0	......	......	......	10 0 0	10 0 0	5 0 0
17 8 0	24 0 0	12 0 0	......	......	......	10 0 0	10 0 0	5 0 0
17 8 0	24 0 0	12 0 0	......	......	......	10 0 0	10 0 0	5 0 0
17 8 0	24 0 0	12 0 0	......	......	......	10 0 0	10 0 0	5 0 0
26 0 0	26 0 0	12 0 0	15 0 0	15 0 0	7 8 0	5 0 0	5 0 0	4 0 0
26 0 0	26 0 0	12 0 0	15 0 0	15 0 0	7 8 0	5 0 0	5 0 0	4 0 0
26 0 0	26 0 0	[illegible]	15 0 0	15 0 0	7 8 0	5 0 0	5 0 0	4 0 0
26 0 0	26 0 0	12 0 0	15 0 0	15 0 0	7 8 0	5 0 0	5 0 0	4 0 0

Return showing the rain-fall, character of weather and prospects of crops in Cooch Behar for the fortnight ending the 3rd May 1947.

SUB-DIVISION.	Rain-fall in inches.	Character of the weather in the district as far as known.	State and prospects of the crops and State of health at date.
Mathabhanga 22nd April ...	Nil	Seasonable ...	Sowing of *bitri* paddy and jute going on. One case of cholera was reported during the week and the case proved fatal. Price of paddy, rice are Rs. 9, Rs. 16 per maund respectively.
Ditto. 29th April ...	Nil	Do ..	Sowing of *bitri* paddy and jute going on. Price of paddy and rice is Rs. 9, Rs. 16 per maund respectively. No case of any epidemic was reported during the week.
Mekligunj 22nd April ...	Nil	Do ...	Preparation of lands for *bitri* paddy and jute going on. Prices of common rice, *haimanti* paddy and tobacco are Rs. 16, Rs. 8-2 to Rs. 10 and Rs. 50 to Rs. 2 per maund respectively. Lingering 6 cases of cattle disease (pox) are still lingering. Fodder and water sufficient. Public health generally good.
Ditto 29th April	Nil	Do ...	Preparation of lands for *bitri* paddy and jute going on. Weeding operation has also commenced. Prices of common rice, *haimanti* paddy and tobacco are Rs. 16-2 to Rs. 10 and Rs. 75 to Rs. 100 respectively. There are 2 fresh cases of cattle disease (Pox). These together with 6 lingering cases of the previous week made up a total of 8 cases out of which 7 ended fatally and 1 is still lingering. Out of 9 cases of cholera reported from Mekliganj P. S. 7 ended fatally and 2 got cured. Otherwise public health generally good. Fodder and water sufficient.
Tufangunj 22nd April ...	Nil	Do ..	Weeding of *bitri* paddy and sowing of jute going on. Condition of standing crops fair. Prices of common rice, mustard seeds and jute are Rs. 16-4, Rs. 20 and Rs. 26 respectively. Fodder and water sufficient. 3 cases of small-pox reported during the week out of which one cured and the remaining 2 cases are lingering.
Ditto 29th April ..	Nil	Do ..	Weeding of *bitri* paddy and sowing of jute going on. Condition of standing crops fair. Prices of common rice, mustard seeds and jute are Rs. 17-8, Rs 18 and Rs. 26 respectively. Fodder and water sufficient. One case of Cholera reported during the week and got cured. Out of the 2 lingering cases of small pox one got cured and the other ended fatally.

L. M. BAKSHI,

Development Commissioner, Cooch Behar.

The Cooch Behar Gazette.

১৫ই শ্রাবণ শুক্রবার] FRIDAY, AUGUST 1, 1947. [১৩৫৪ সাল, ৪৩৮ রাজশকা

PART IV.

Important Papers and References.

Return showing the rain-fall, character of weather and prospects of crops in Cooch Behar for the fortnight ending the 17th May 1947.

SUB-DIVISION.	Rain-fall in inches.	Character of the weather in the District as far as known.	State and prospects of the crops and state of health at date.
Sadder 6th May ...	Nil	Seasonable ...	Preparation of lands for *bitri* paddy and jute and sowing and weeding of the same going on. Price of common rice is Rs. 18 per maund. No case of small pox or cholera reported. Public health generally good. No cattle disease reported. Fodder and water sufficient.
Ditto. 13th May ...	Nil	Do ...	Preparation of lands for *bitri* paddy and jute finished. Sowing and weeding of the same going on. Price of common rice is Rs. 19 per maund. No case of small-pox or cholera reported. Public health generally good. No cattle disease reported. Fodder and water sufficient.
Dinhata 6th May ...	Nil	Do ...	Preparation of lands for *haimanti* paddy and sowing of *haimanti* seeds going on. Weding of jute and *bitri* paddy still going on. Prospect and condition of standing crops tolerable. No report of damage of any crops reported. Prices of common rice, *haimanti* paddy, tobacco, jute and mustard seeds are Rs. 18, Rs. 11-8, Rs. 60, Rs. 27 and Rs. 24 per maund respectively.
Ditto. 13th May ...	Nil	Do ...	Preparation of lands for *haimanti* paddy and sowing of *haimanti* seeds still going on. Weeding of jute and *bitri* paddy going on. Prospect and condition of standing crops tolerable. No report of any damage of any crops reported. Prices of common rice, *haimanti* paddy, tobacco, jute, and mustard seeds are Rs. 19, Rs. 11-8, Rs. 60, Rs. 27 and Rs. 24 per maund respectively.

PRICE-CURRENT of food-grains, Jute, Tobacco and Salt in th

Retail Sale:—Quantities per Rupee

Sub divisions.	Wheat. Present return	Wheat. Next preceding return	Wheat. Corresponding return of last year	Rice best sort. Present return	Rice best sort. Next preceding return	Rice best sort. Corresponding return of last year	Rice common sort. Present return	Rice common sort. Next preceding return	Rice common sort. Corresponding return of last year
	s. ch.	s. ch.	s. ch.	s. ch.	s. ch.	s. ch.	s. ch.	s. ch.	s. ch.
Cooch Behar	......	......	......	......	......	......	2 0	2 8	3 10
Dinhata	......	......	......	......	......	......	......	......	......
Mathabhanga	......	......	......	......	......	......	......	......	......
Mekligunj	......	......	......	2 0	2 0	2 0	2 6	2 6	3 0
Tufangunj	......	......	......	2 0	2 0	2 14	2 4½	2 4½	2 8

WHOLE-SALE PRICES CURRENT of food-grains, Jute, Tobacco and Salt in

Whole-sale—Price

Markets.	Rs. A. P.	Rs. A. P.	Rs. A. P.	Rs. A. P.	Rs. A. P.	Rs. A. P.	Rs. A. P.	Rs. A. P.	Rs. A. P.
Cooch Behar	......	......	......	......	......	......	19 0 0	16 0 0	10 12 0
Dewanhat	......	......	......	......	......	......	19 0 0	16 0 0	10 12 0
Chowrahat	......	......	......	......	......	......	19 0 0	18 0 0	12 8 0
Choudhurihat	......	......	......	......	......	......	16 0 0	14 0 0	10 0 0
Ranirhat	......	......	......	......	......	......	......	......	......
Buxirhat	......	......	......	......	......	......	......	......	......
Sitaihat	......	......	......	......	......	......	16 0 0	20 0 0	11 0 0
Kaligunjhat	......	......	......	......	......	......	......	......	......
Gosanimarihat	......	......	......	......	......	......	19 0 0	19 0 0	......
Nazirerhat	......	......	......	......	......	......	15 0 0	......	......
Mathabhangahat ...	......	......	......	......	......	......	......	......	......
Shibporehat	......	......	......	......	......	......	......	......	......
Morangahat	......	......	......	......	......	......	......	......	......
Sitalkhuchihat	......	......	......	......	......	......	......	......	......
Mekligunj	......	......	......	20 0 0	20 0 0	20 0 0	16 8 0	16 8 0	13 0 0
Changrabanda	......	......	......	20 0 0	20 0 0	20 0 0	16 8 0	16 8 0	13 0 0
Haldibari	......	......	......	20 0 0	20 0 0	20 0 0	16 8 0	16 8 0	13 0 0
Jamaldaha	......	......	......	20 0 0	20 0 0	20 0 0	16 8 0	16 8 0	13 0 0
Ranirhat	......	......	......	20 0 0	20 0 0	15 0 0	17 8 0	17 8 0	11 4 0
Balarampur	......	......	......	20 0 0	[illegible]	15 9 0	17 8 0	17 8 0	11 4 0
Buxirhat	......	......	......	20 0 0	[illegible]	15 0 0	16 0 0	15 0 0	11 4 0
Ghoramarahat	......	......	......	20 0 0	[illegible]	15 0 0	17 8 0	17 8 0	11 4 0

Cheena. Present return	Cheena. Next preceding return.	Cheena. Corresponding return of last year	Kaon. Present return.	Kaon. Next preceding return.	Kaon. Corresponding return of last year	Mustard seed. Present return.	Mustard seed. Next preceding return.	Mustard seed. Corresponding return of last year.	Mustard seed oil. Present return.	Mustard seed oil. Next preceding return	Mustard seed oil. Corresponding return of last year
s. ch.	s. ch.	s. ch.	s. ch.	s. ch.	s. ch.	s. ch.	s. ch.	s. ch.	s. ch.	s. ch.	s. ch.
......	......	......	......	......	......	2 0	2 0	2 8	0 10	0 10	0 1[illegible]
......	......	......	......	......	......	......	......	......	......	......	......
......	......	......	......	......	......	......	......	......	......	......	......
......	......	......	......	......	......	1 6	1 0	1 8	0 7	0 [illegible]	0 10
......	......	......	......	......	......	2 0	2 0	2 14	0 8	0 8	0 10

R. A. P.	Rs. A. P.	Rs. A. P.	Rs. A. P.	Rs. A. P.	Rs. A. P.	Rs. A. P.	Rs. A. P.	Rs. A. P.	Rs. A. P.	Rs. A. P.	Rs. A. P.
......	......	......	......	......	......	20 0 0	20 0 0	16 0 0	62 8 0	62 8 0	50 0
......	......	......	......	......	......	20 0 0	20 0 0	16 0 0	62 8 0	62 8 0	50 0
......	......	......	......	......	......	26 0 0	24 0 0	16 0 0	100 0 0	100 0 0	62 0
......	......	......	......	......	......	......	......	16 0 0	100 0 0	100 0 0	60 0
......	......	......	......	......	......	......	......	......	......	......	......
......	......	......	......	......	......	......	......	......	......	......	......
......	......	......	......	......	......	22 0 0	22 0 0	16 0 0	100 0 0	100 0 0	60 0
......	......	......	......	......	......	......	......	......	......	......	......
......	......	......	......	......	......	36 0 0	26 0 0	16 0 0	100 0 0	100 0 0	60 0
......	......	......	......	......	......	22 0 0	......	......	100 0 0	......	......
......	......	......	......	......	......	......	......	......	......	......	......
......	......	......	......	......	......	......	......	......	......	......	......
......	......	......	......	......	......	......	......	......	......	......	......
......	......	......	......	......	......	......	......	......	......	......	......
......	......	......	......	......	......	30 0 0	40 0 0	27 0 0	90 0 0	100 0 0	60 0
......	......	......	......	......	......	30 0 0	40 0 0	27 0 0	90 0 0	100 0 0	60 0
......	......	......	......	......	......	30 0 0	40 0 0	37 0 0	90 0 0	100 0 0	60 0
......	......	......	......	......	......	30 0 0	40 0 0	27 0 0	90 0 0	100 0 0	60 0
......	......	......	......	......	......	30 0 0	30 0 0	15 0 0	80 0 0	80 0 0	60 0
......	......	......	......	......	......	30 0 0	30 0 0	15 0 0	80 0 0	80 0 0	60 0
......	......	......	......	......	......	20 0 0	20 0 0	15 0 0	80 0 0	80 0 0	80 0
......	......	......	......	......	......	30 0 0	20 0 0	15 0 0	80 0 0	80 0 0	60 0

State of Cooch Behar for the fortnight ending the 17th May 1947.

by the Seer of 80 Tollas.

JUTE			KHESARI KALAI.			OIL CAKE.			REMARKS
Present return	Next preceding return.	Corresponding return of last year.	Present return.	Next preceding return.	Corresponding return of last year.	Present return.	Next preceding return.	Corresponding return of last year.	
s. ch	s. ch	s. ch	s. ch.	s. ch.	s. ch.	s. ch.	s. ch.	s. ch.	
1 7	1 7	4 0	3 4	3 4	5 11	9 0	8 0	8 0	
......	......	......	......	......	......	......	......	......	
......	......	......	......	......	......	......	......	......	
2 9	1 7	3 5	......	......	......	4 0	4 0	8 0	
1 5	1 5	3 8	2 14	2 14	5 4	8 0	8 0	10 0	

the Principal marts of Cooch Behar for the fortnight ending the 17th May 1947
per maund of 40 seers.

Rs. A. P.	Rs. A. P.	Rs. A. P.	Rs. A. P.	Rs. A. P.	Rs. A. P.	Rs. A. P.	Rs. A. P.	Rs. A. P.
27 0 0	27 0 0	10 0 0	12 0 0	12 0 0	7 0 0	4 8 0	5 0 0	5 0 0
27 0 0	27 0 0	10 0 0	12 0 0	12 0 0	7 0 0	4 8 0	5 0 0	5 0 0
26 0 0	27 0 0	......	12 0 0	12 0 0	8 0 0	7 0 0	7 0 0	5 0 0
25 0 0	25 0 0	1[illegible] 0 0	12 0 0	13 0 0	8 0 0	6 0 0	6 0 0	5 0 0
......	......	......	......	......	......	......	......	......
......	......	......	......	......	......	......	......	......
......	......	......	......	......	......	4 0 0	4 0 0	4 0 0
......	......	......	......	......	......	......	......	......
25 0 0	25 0 0	......	......	......	......	6 0 0	6 0 0	4 0 0
25 0 0	......	......	11 0 0	......	......	5 0 0	......	......
......	......	......	......	......	......	......	......	......
......	......	......	......	......	......	......	......	......
......	......	......	......	......	......	......	......	......
......	......	......	......	......	......	......	......	......
17 8 0	28 0 0	12 0 0	......	......	......	10 0 0	10 0 0	5 0 0
17 8 0	28 0 0	12 0 0	......	......	......	10 0 0	10 0 0	5 0 0
17 8 0	17 8 0	12 0 0	......	......	......	10 0 0	10 0 0	5 0 0
17 8 0	17 8 0	12 0 0	......	......	......	10 0 0	10 0 0	5 0 0
26 0 0	26 0 0	12 0 0	15 0 0	15 0 0	7 8 0	5 0 0	5 0 0	4 0 0
26 9 0	26 0 0	12 0 0	15 0 0	15 0 0	7 8 0	5 0 0	5 0 0	4 0 0
26 0 0	26 0 0	12 0 0	15 0 0	15 0 0	7 8 0	5 0 0	5 0 0	4 0 0
26 0 0	26 0 0	12 0 0	15 0 0	15 0 0	7 8 0	5 0 0	5 0 0	4 0 0

Return showing the rain-fall, character of weather and prospects of crops in Cooch Behar for the fortnight ending the 17th May 1947.

Sub-Division.	Rain-fall in inches	Character of the weather in the district as far as known.	State and prospects of the crops and State of health at date.
Mathabhanga 6th May ...	Nil	Seasonable ...	Sowing of *bitri* paddy and jute finished. Prices of paddy and mustard seed are Rs. 10 and Rs. 24 per maund respectively. No case of any epidemic was reported during the week.
Ditto. 13th May ...	Nil	Do. ..	Price of *haimanti* paddy sells at Rs. 10 per maund and rice sells at 2½ seer per rupee. Mustard seeds sell at Rs. 24 per maund. No case of any epidemic was reported during the week.
Mekliganj 6th May ...	Nil	Fair ...	Weeding operation of *bitri* paddy and jute going on. Prices of common rice, *haimanti* paddy and tobacco are Rs.17-4, Rs. 8-2 to Rs. 10 and Rs. 75 to Rs. 100 per maund respectively. There were 12 fresh cases of cattle disease (pox) during the week of report. These together with 1 pending case of the last week made up a total of 13 cases out of which 12 ended fatally and one lingering. One case of cholera was reported from Mekliganj Police Station. This case is lingering. Otherwise Public health generally good. Fodder and water sufficient.
Ditto 13th May ..	Nil	Do ...	Weeding operation of *bitri* paddy and jute going on. Prices of common rice, *haimanti* paddy and tobacco are Rs. 17-4, Rs. 8-2 to Rs. 10 end Rs. 75 to Rs. 110 per maund respectively. There were 42 fresh cases of cattle disease (cholera) during the week of report these together 1 lingering case of the last week made up a total 43 cases of which 2 ended fatally and 41 are still lingering. 8 cases of cholera reported from Mekliganj Police Station. These together with 1 case of the last week made up a total of 9 cases of which 8 ended in death and 1 is still lingering. Public health generally good. Fodder and water sufficient.
Tufanganj 6th May ...	Nil	Seasonable ...	Weeding of *bitri* paddy and sowing of jute going on. Condition of standing crops fair. Fodder and water sufficient. Prices of common rice, mustard seeds and jute are Rs. 17-5, Rs. 20 and Rs. 26 respectively. No cases of small-pox and cholera reported reported during the week under report.
Ditto 13th May ...	Nil	Do ...	Weeding of *bitri* paddy and jute going on. Condition of standing crops fair. Fodder and water sufficient. Prices of common rice, mustard seeds and jute are Rs. 17-8, Rs. 20 and Rs. 26 respectively. No case of small-pox and Cholera reported during the week under report.

L. M. Bakshi.
Development Commissioner, Cooch Behar.

The Cooch Behar Gazette.

২রা ভাদ্র মঙ্গলবার] TUESDAY, AUGUST 19, 1947. [১৩৫৪ সাল, ৪৩৮ রাজশকা

PART IV.

Important Papers and References.

Return showing the rain-fall, character of weather and prospects of crops in Cooch Behar for the fortnight ending the 31st May 1947.

SUB-DIVISION.	Rain-fall in inches.	Character of the weather in the District as far as known.	State and prospects of the crops and state of health at date.
Sudder 20th May ...	Nil	Seasonable	Sowing of *bitri* paddy and jute almost finished. Weeding of the same continuing. Price of common rice is Rs. 19 per maund. No case of small pox or cholera reported. Public health generally good. No cattle disease reported. Fodder and water sufficient.
Ditto. 27th May ...	Nil	Do ...	Sowing of *bitri* paddy and jute finished. weeding of the same going on. Price of common rice is Rs. 19 per maund. No case of small-pox or cholera reported. Public health generally good. No cattle disease reported. Fodder and water sufficient.
Dinhata 20th May ...	Nil	Do ...	Preparation of lands for *haimanti* paddy and sowing of *haimanti* seeds still going on. Weeding of jute and *bitri* paddy still going on. Weeding of jute and *bitri* paddy still going on. Prospect and condition of standing crops tolerable. No report of any damage of standing crops reported. Prices of common rice, *haimanti* paddy tobacco, jute and mustard seeds are Rs. 19, Rs. 11, Rs. 60, Rs. 26 and Rs. 24 per maund respectively.
Ditto. 27th May ...	Nil	Do ...	Preparation of lands for *haimanti* paddy and sowing of *haimanti* seeds going on. Weeding of *bitri* paddy and jute finished. Prospect and condition of standing crops tolerable. No report of any damage of any crops reported. Prices of common rice, paddy, tobacco, jute, and mustard seeds are Rs. 20, Rs. 12, Rs. 60, Rs. 26 and Rs. 26 per maund respectively.
Mathabhanga 20th May	Nil	Do ...	Price of *haimanti* paddy is Rs. 1 -8 per maund and price of rice 2 seers per rupee and mustard seeds Rs. 25 per maund. No case of any epidemic was reported during the week.
Ditto. 27th May	Nil	Do ...	Price of *haimanti* paddy Rs. 10-8 and rice at Rs. 20 per maund. No case of any epidemic was reported during the week.

PRICE-CURRENT of food-grains, Jute, Tobacco and Salt in the

Retail Sale:—Quantities per Rupee

	Wheat.			Rice best sort.			Rice common sort.		
	Present return	Next preceding return.	Corresponding return last year.	Present return.	Next preceding return	Corresponding return of last year.	Present return.	Next preceding return.	Corresponding return of last year.
Sub-divisions.	s. ch.	s. ch.	s. ch.	s. ch.	s. ch.	s. ch.	s. ch.	s. ch.	s. ch.
Cooch Behar	......	......	......	......	......	......	2 2	2 8	3 10
Dinhata	......	......	......	......	......	......	2 0	2 2	3 0
Mathabhanga	......	......	......	......	......	......	......	......	......
Mekligunj	......	......	......	2 0	2 0	2 0	2 6	2 6	3 0
Tufangunj	......	......	......	2 0	2 0	2 14	2 4½	2 4½	3 8

WHOLE-SALE PRICES CURRENT of food-grains, Jute, Tobacco and Salt in

Whole-sale—Price

Markets.	Rs. A. P.	Rs. A. P.	Rs. A. P.	Rs. A. P.	Rs. A. P.	Rs. A. P.	Rs. A. P.	Rs. A. P.	Rs. A. P.
Cooch Behar	......	......	......	......	......	......	19 0 0	16 0 [illegible]	10 12 0
Dewanhat	......	......	......	......	......	......	19 0 0	16 0 0	10 12 0
Chowrahat	......	......	......	......	......	......	20 0 0	13 0 0	......
Choudhurirhat	......	......	......	......	......	......	16 0 0	16 0 0	......
Ranirhat	......	......	......	......	......	......	......	......	......
Buxirhat	......	......	......	......	......	......	......	......	......
Sitaihat	......	......	......	......	......	......	20 0 0	16 0 0	1[illegible] 0 0
Kaligunjhat	......	......	......	......	......	......	......	......	......
Nazirerhat	......	......	......	......	......	......	20 0 0	15 0 0	......
Gosanimarihat	......	......	......	......	......	......	20 0 0	19 0 0	......
Mathabhangahat ..	......	......	......	......	......	......	......	......	......
Shibporehat	......	......	......	......	......	......	......	......	......
Morangahat	......	......	......	......	......	......	......	......	......
Sitalkhuchihat	......	......	......	......	......	......	......	......	......
Mekligunj	......	......	......	20 0 0	20 0 0	20 0 [illegible]	16 8 0	16 8	13 0 0
Changrabanda	......	......	......	20 0 0	20 0 0	20 0 0	16 [illegible] 0	16 8 0	13 0 0
Haldibari	......	......	......	20 0 0	20 0 0	20 0 0	16 8 0	16 8 0	13 0 [illegible]
Jamaldaha	......	......	......	20 0 0	20 0 0	20 0 0	16 8 0	16 8 0	13 0 0
Ranirhat	......	......	......	20 0 0	20 0 0	15 0 0	13 12 0	17 8 0	11 4 0
Balarampur	......	......	......	20 0 0	20 0 0	15 8 0	20 0 0	17 5 0	11 4 0
Buxirhat	......	...	......	20 0 0	20 0 0	15 0 0	17 8 0	15 0 0	11 4 0
Gh[illegible]ramarahat	...	......	......	20 0 0	20 0 0	15 0 0	17 8 0	17 8 0	11 4 0

State of Cooch Behar for the fortnight ending the 31st May 1947.

by the Seer of 80 Tollas.

Jute			Khesari Kalai.			Oil Cake.			Remarks.
Present return.	Next preceding return.	Corresponding return of last year.	Present return.	Next preceding return.	Corresponding return of last year.	Present return.	Next preceding return.	Corresponding return of last year.	
s. ch.	s. ch.	s. ch.	s. ch.	s. ch.	s. ch.	s. ch.	s. ch.	s. ch.	
1 7	1 7	4 8	3 4	3 4	5 11	8 0	8 0	8 0	
1 6½	1 4	4 0	3 6	4 0	4 0	5 0	4 12	8 0	
	......	......	......	......	......	......	......	......	
2 9	1 8	8 8	......	...	......	4 0	4 0	8 0	
1 5	1 5	8 8	2 14	2 14	5 4	8 0	8 0	8 0	

the Principal marts of Cooch Behar for the fortnight ending the 31st May 1947
per maund of 40 seers.

Rs. A. P.	Rs. A. P.	Rs. A. P.	Rs. A. P.	Rs. A. P.	Rs. A. P.	Rs. A. P.	Rs. A. P.	Rs. A. P.
27 0 0	27 0 0	10 0 0	12 0 0	12 0 0	7 0 0	5 0 0	5 0 0	5 0 0
27 0 0	27 0 0	10 0 0	12 0 0	12 0 0	7 0 0	5 0 0	5 0 0	5 0 0
28 0 0	26 0 0	11 0 0	12 0 0	12 0 0	10 0 0	8 0 0	7 0 0	5 0 0
25 0 0	25 0 0	12 0 0	14 0 0	12 0 0	8 0 0	5 0 0	6 0 0	5 0 0
......	......	......	......	......	......	......	......	......
......	......	......	......	......	......	......	......	...
......	......	......	......	......	......	4 0 0	4 0 0	4 0 0
......	......	......	......	......	......	......	......	......
25 0 0	25 0 0	......	12 0 0	11 0 0	......	4 0 0	5 0 0	......
......	25 0 0	......	17 0 0	......	......	5 0 0	6 0 0	6 0 0
......	......	......	......	......	......	......	......	......
......	......	......	......	......	......	...	......	......
..	......	......	......	......	......	......	......	......
......	......	......	......	......	......	......	......	......
17 8 0	18 0 0	12 0 0	......	......	......	10 8 0	10 0 0	5 0 0
17 8 0	18 0 0	12 0 0	......	......	......	10 0 0	10 0 0	5 0 0
17 8 0	18 8 0	12 0 0	......	......	......	10 0 0	10 0 0	5 0 0
17 8 0	18 8 0	12 0 0	......	......	......	10 0 0	10 0 0	5 0 0
26 0 0	26 0 0	12 0 0	15 0 0	15 0 0	7 8 0	5 0 0	5 0 0	4 0 0
26 0 0	26 0 0	12 0 0	15 [illegible] 0	15 0 0	7 8 0	5 0 0	5 0 0	4 0 0
26 0 0	26 0 0	12 0 0	15 0 0	15 0 0	7 8 0	5 0 0	5 0 0	4 0 0
26 0 0	[illegible]	12 0 0	15 0 0	15 0 0	7 8 0	5 0 0	5 0 0	4 0 0

Return showing the rain-fall, character of weather and prospects of crops in Cooch Behar for the fortnight ending the 31st May 1947.

Sub-division.	Rainfall in inches	Character of the weather in the district as far as known.	State of prospects of the crops and State of health at date.
Mekliganj 20th May ...	Nil	Seasonable ..	Weeding operation of *bitri* paddy and jute going on. Prices of common rice, *haimanti* paddy, jute and tobacco are Rs. 16, Rs. 8, Rs. 17-8 Rs. 80 per maund respectively. One fresh case of cholera reported during the week from the Mekliganj Police Station. This together with one old case of the last week made up a total of 2 cases. These two cases got cured. No cattle disease reported. Public health generally good. Fodder and water sufficient.
Ditto 27th May ..	Nil	Do	Weeding operation of *bitri* paddy and jute going on. Prices of common rice, tobacco and jute are Rs. 16, Rs. 80 and Rs. 17 8 per maund respectively. 7 cases of cholera reported during the week of which 1 died and 6 cases are lingering. No cattle disease reported. Public health generally good. Fodder and water sufficient.
[illegible] 20th May ...	Nil	Do ...	Weeding of *bitri* paddy and sowing of jute going on. Condition of standing crops fair. Fodder and water sufficient. 1 fresh case of small pox reported during this week was cured. 4 fresh cases of cholera reported during the week of which 1 got cured and 3 proved fatal.
Ditto 27th May	Nil	Do ...	Weeding of *bitri* paddy and sowing of jute going on. Condition of standing crops fair. Price of mustard seeds, common rice and jute are Rs. 21, Rs. 17-8 and Rs. 26 respectively No case of cattle disease reported during the week. Public health generally good.

L. M. BAKSHI,
Development Commissioner, Cooch Behar.

The Cooch Behar Gazette.

১৫ই ভাদ্র [illegible]] MONDAY, SEPTEMBER 1, 1947. [১৩৫৪ সাল, [illegible]

PART IV.

Important Papers and References.

Return showing the rain-fall, character of weather and prospects of crops in Cooch Behar for the fortnight ending the 14 June 1947.

SUB-DIVISION.	Rain-fall in inches.	Character of the weather in the District as far as known.	State and prospects of the crops and state of health at date.
Sadder 3rd June ...	Nil	Seasonable	Weeding of *bitri* paddy and jute almost finished. Preparation of land for *haimanti* seedbed and sowing of the same in the nursery going on. Price of common rice is Rs. 19 per maund. No case of small pox or Cholera reported. Public health generally good. No cattle disease reported. Fodder and water sufficient.
Ditto, 1[illegible]th June ...	Nil	Do ...	Weeding of *bitri* paddy and jute almost finished. Preparation of land for *haimanti* seedbed and sowing of the same in the nursery going on. Price of common rice is Rs. 19 per maund. No case of small-pox or Cholera reported. Public health generally good. No cattle disease reported. Fodder and water sufficient.
Dinhata 3rd June ...	Nil	Do ...	Preparation of lands for *haimanti* paddy and sowing of *haimanti* seeds going on. Weeding of jute and *bitri* paddy finished. Prospect and condition of standing crops tolerable. No report of any damage of any crops reported. Public health is generally good. Prices of common rice, *haimanti* paddy, tobacco, jute and mustard seeds are Rs. 20, Rs. 11-8, Rs. [illegible], Rs. [illegible] and Rs. 22-8 per maund respectively.
Ditto, 10th June ...	Nil	Do	Preparation of lands for *haimanti* paddy and sowing of *haimanti* seeds going on. Prospect and condition of standing crops good. No report of any damage of any crops reported. Transplantation will commence in same places within a short time. Price of common rice, *haimanti* paddy, tobacco, jute and mustard seeds are Rs. 21, Rs. 12, Rs. 60, Rs. [illegible], Rs. 22 8 per maund respectively.
Mathabhanga	Nil	Do	Return not received.
Ditto, 10th June	Nil	Do	Preparation of land for *haimanti* paddy is going on. Price of *haimanti* paddy, rice, is Rs. 1[illegible], Rs. 26 per maund respectively. No case of any [illegible] during the week.

PRICE-CURRENT of food-grains, Jute, Tobacco and Salt i n th e

RETAIL SALE :—Quantities per Rupee

	Wheat.			Rice best sort.			Rice common sort.		
	Present return.	Next preceding return.	Corresponding return of last year.	Present return.	Next preceding return.	Corresponding return of last year.	Present return.	Next preceding return.	Corresponding return of last year.
Sub-divisions.	s. ch.	s. ch.	s. ch.	ch.	s. ch.	s. ch.	s. ch.	s. ch.	s. ch
Cooch Behar	......	......	......	......	......	......	2 2	2 8	3 10
Dinhata	......	......	......	......	......	......	2 2	2 0	......
Mathabhanga	......	......	......	......	......	......	......	......	......
Mekligunj	......	......	......	2 0	2 0	2 0	2 4	2 8	3 1
Tufanganj	......	......	......	2 0	2 0	2 14	2 1¼	2 1¼	3 0

WHOLE-SALE PRICES CURRENT of food-grains, Jute, Tobacco and Salt in

WHOLE-SALE— Price

Markets.	Rs. A. P.	Rs. A. P.	Rs. A. P.	Rs. A. P.	Rs. A. P.	Rs. A. P.	Rs. A. P.	Rs. A. P.	Rs. A. P.
Cooch Behar	......	......	......	......	......	......	19 0 0	16 0 0	10 12 0
Dewanhat	......	......	......	......	......	......	19 0 0	16 0 0	10 12 0
Chowrahat	......	......	......	......	......	......	19 0 0	20 0 0	12 8 0
Choudhurirhat	......	......	......	......	......	......	16 0 0	16 0 0	12 12 0
Ranirhat	......	......	......	......	......	......	......	......	......
Baxirhat	......	......	......	......	......	......	......	......	......
Sitaihat	......	......	......	......	......	......	18 0 0	20 0 0	12 0 0
Kaligunjhat	......	......	......	......	......	......	......	......	......
Nasirerhat	......	......	......	......	......	......	16 0 0	20 0 0	......
Gosanimarihat	......	......	......	......	......	......	20 0 0	19 0 0	12 8 0
Mathabhangahat ...	......	......	......	......	......	......	......	......	......
Shibporehat	......	......	......	......	......	......	......	......	......
Morangahat	......	......	......	......	......	......	......	......	......
Sitalkhuchihat	......	......	......	......	......	......	......	......	......
Mekligunj	......	......	......	20 0 0	20 0 0	20 0 0	18 0 0	16 8 0	13 0 0
Changrabanda	......	......	......	20 0 0	20 0 0	20 0 0	16 8 0	16 8 0	13 0 0
Haldibari	......	......	......	20 0 0	20 0 0	20 0 0	16 8 0	16 8 0	13 0 0
Jamaldaha	......	......	......	20 0 0	20 0 0	20 0 0	16 8 0	16 8 0	13 0 0
Ranirhat	......	......	......	20 0 0	20 0 0	15 0 0	18 12 0	18 12 0	12 8 0
Balasampur	......	......	......	20 0 0	20 0 0	15 0 0	20 0 0	20 0 0	12 8 0
Baxirhat	......	......	......	20 0 0	20 0 0	15 0 0	17 8 0	17 8 0	12 8 0
Ghoramarahat	......	......	......	20 0 0	20 0 0	15 0 0	17 8 0	17 8 0	12 8 0

State of Cooch Behar for the fortnight ending the 14th June 1947.

by the Seer of 80 Tollas.

Jute			Khesari Kalai.			Oil Cake.			Remarks
Present return	Next preceding return.	Corresponding return of last year.	Present return.	Next preceding return.	Corresponding return of last year.	Present return.	Next preceding return.	Corresponding return of last year.	
s. ch	s. ch	s. ch	s. ch.	s. ch.	s. ch.	s. ch.	s. ch.	s. ch.	
1 7	1 7	4 0	3 4	3 4	5 11	8 0	8 0	8 0	
1 6	1 6½	......	3 5	3 6	......	5 0	5 0	......	
	......	......	......	......	......	......	......	......	
1 7	2 9	3 5	......	......	......	4 0	4 0	8 0	
1 5	1 5	3 8	2 14	2 14	5 4	8 0	8 0	10 0	

the Principal marts of Cooch Behar for the fortnight ending the 14th June 1947
per maund of 40 seers.

Rs. A. P	Rs. A. P.	Rs. A. P.	Rs. A. P.	Rs. A. P.	Rs. A. P.	Rs. A. P.	Rs. A. P.	Rs. A. P.
27 0 0	27 0 0	10 0 0	12 0 0	12 0 0	7 8 0	5 0 0	5 0 0	5 0 0
27 0 0	27 0 0	10 0 0	12 0 0	12 0 0	7 0 0	5 0 0	5 0 0	5 0 0
28 0 0	28 0 0	13 0 0	12 0 0	12 0 0	......	8 0 0	8 0 0	5 0 0
28 0 0	25 0 0	12 0 0	14 0 0	14 0 0	......	5 0 0	5 0 0	4 0 0
......	......	......	......	......	......	......	......	......
......	......	......	......	......	......	......	......	......
......	......	......	......	......	......	5 0 0	4 0 0	4 8 0
......	......	......	......	......	......	......	......	......
25 0 0	25 0 0	......	12 0 0	12 0 0	......	4 0 0	4 0 0	......
......	......	......	20 0 0	17 0 0	......	6 0 0	6 0 0	5 0 0
......	......	......	......	......	......	......	......	......
......	......	......	......	......	......	......	......	......
......	......	......	......	......	......	......	......	......
......	......	......	......	......	......	......	......	......
28 0 0	17 8 0	12 0 0	......	......	......	10 0 0	10 0 0	5 0 0
26 0 0	17 8 0	18 0 0	......	......	......	10 0 0	10 0 0	5 0 0
25 0 0	17 8 0	12 0 0	......	......	......	10 0 0	10 0 0	5 0 0
25 0 0	17 8 0	12 0 0	......	......	......	10 0 0	10 0 0	5 0 0
26 0 0	26 0 0	12 0 0	15 0 0	15 0 0	7 8 0	5 0 0	5 0 0	4 0 0
26 0 0	26 0 0	12 0 0	15 0 0	15 0 0	7 8 0	5 0 0	5 0 0	4 0 0
26 0 0	26 0 0	12 0 0	16 0 0	15 0 0	7 8 0	5 0 0	5 0 0	4 0 0
26 0 0	25 0 0	12 0 0	15 0 0	15 0 0	7 8 0	5 0 0	5 0 0	4 0 0

Return showing the rain-fall, character of weather, and prospects of crops in Cooch Behar for the fortnight ending the 14th June 1947.

SUBDIVISION.	Rain-fall in inches.	Character of the weather in the district as far as known.	State and prospects of the crops and State of health at date.
[illegible]gunj 3rd June ...	Nil	Seasonable ...	Weeding operation of *bitri* and june finished. Sowing of seeds for *haimanti* paddy going on. Prices of common rice, tobacco and jute Rs. 16-8 Rs. 66, Rs. 17-4 per maund respectively. 2 fresh cases of cholera reported during the week with the previous 6 cases there were altogether 8 cases of which 2 cases died and 6 cases got cured. No cattle disease reported. Fodder and water sufficient. Public health generally good.
Ditto 10th June ...	Nil	Do	Sowing of seeds for *haimanti* paddy going on. Prices of common rice, tobacco and jute are Rs. 16-8, Rs. 6 and Rs. 17-4 per maund respectively. No cholera and cattle disease reported during the week. Fodder and water sufficient. Public health generally good.
[illegible]gunj 3rd June ...	[illegible]	Do	[illegible] of *bitri* paddy and jute finished. [illegible]eparation of lands for *haimanti* seedlings going on. Prices of common rice, *haimanti* paddy, mustard seeds and jute are Rs. 17-8, Rs. 10, Rs. [illegible]1 and Rs 26 per maund respectively. No cattle disease reported. Condition of standing crops fair. Public health generally good.
Ditto 10th June	Nil	Do	Preparation of lands for *haimanti* paddy and sowing of said seedlings going on. Prices of common rice, *haimanti* paddy, mustard seeds and jutes are Rs. 18-12, Rs. 9-8, Rs. 22 and Rs. 27 per maund respectively. No cattle disease reported. Condition of standing crops fair Public health generally good.

L. M. BAKSHI,
Development Commissioner, Cooch Behar.

The Cooch Behar Gazett

৩০শে ভাদ্র মঙ্গলবার] TUESDAY, SEPTEMBER 16, 1947. [১৩৫৪ সাল; ৪৩৮ রাজশকাব্দ

PART IV.

Important Papers and References.

Return showing the rain-fall, character of weather and prospects of crops in Cooch Behar for the fortnight ending the 28th June 1947.

SUB-DIVISION.	Rain-fall in inches.	Character of the weather in the District as far as known.	State and prospects of the crops and state of health at date.
Sudder 17th June ...	Nil	Seasonable ..	Weeding of *bitri* paddy and jute finished. Preparation of lands for *haimanti* paddy and sowing of the same seeds in the nursery going on. Price of common rice is Rs. 19 per maund. No case of small-pox or cholera reported. Public health generally good. No cattle disease reported. Fodder and water sufficient.
Ditto. 24th June ...	Nil	Do ...	Preparation of lands for cultivation of *haimanti* paddy and sowing of the seeds in the nursery going on. Price of common rice is Rs. 19 per maund. No case of small-pox or cholera reported. Public health generally good. No cattle disease reported. Fodder and water sufficient.
Dinhata 17th June ...	Nil	Do ...	Preparation of lands for *haimanti* paddy and sowing of *haimanti* seeds going on. Transplantation of the *haimanti* seedlings going on in some places. Cutting of *bitri* paddy, jute and kaon going on. Prospect and condition of standing crops good. No report of any damage of any crop reported. Prices of common rice, *haimanti* paddy, tobacco, jute and mustard seeds are Rs. 19, Rs. 11, Rs. 70, Rs. 28, Rs. 26 per maund respectively.
Ditto. 24th June ...	Nil	Do ...	Return not received.
Mathabhanga 17th June ...	Nil	Do ...	Sowing of *haimanti* seeds is going on. No case of any epidemic was reported during the week. Price of paddy and rice is Rs. 10-8 and Rs. 20 per maund respectively.
Ditto. 24th June ...	Nil	Do ...	Sowing of *haimanti* seeds is going on. No case of any epidemic was reported during the week. Price of paddy, rice is selling at Rs. 10-8, Rs. 20 per maund respectively.

PRICE-CURRENT of food-grains, Jute, Tobacco and Salt in the

RETAIL SALE:—Quantities per Rupee

Sub-divisions.	Wheat. Present return	Wheat. Next preceding return.	Wheat. Corresponding return of last year.	Rice best sort. Present return.	Rice best sort. Next preceding return	Rice best sort. Corresponding return of last year.	Rice common sort. Present return.	Rice common sort. Next preceding return.	Rice common sort. Corresponding return of last year.
	s. ch.	s. ch.	s. ch.	ch.	s. ch.	s. ch.	s. ch.	s. ch.	s. ch
Cooch Behar	......	......	......	......	......	......	1 13	2 2	2 8
Dinhata	......	......	......	......	......	......	......	......	......
Mathabhanga	......	......	......	......	......	......	......	......	......
Mekligunj	......	......	......	1 10	1 10	2 0	1 12	1 12	3 1
Tufangunj	......	......	......	1 8	2 0	2 8	1 12	2 1¼	3 8

WHOLE-SALE PRICES CURRENT of food-grains, Jute, Tobacco and Salt in

WHOLE-SALE—Price

Markets.	Rs. A. P.	Rs. A P.	Rs. A. P.	Rs. A. P.	Rs. A. P.	Rs A. P.	Rs. A. P	Rs. A. P.	Rs. A P
Cooch Behar	......	......	......	......	......	......	22 0 0	19 0 0	16 0 0
Dewanhat	......	......	......	......	......	......	22 0 0	9 0 0	16 0 0
Chowrahat	......	......	......	......	......	......	20 0 0	19 0 0	13 0 0
Choudhurihat	......	......	......	......	......	......	20 0 0	16 0 0	13 0 0
Ranirhat	......	......	......	......	......	......	......	......	......
Baxirhat	......	......	......	......	......	......	......	......	......
Sitaihat	......	......	......	......	......	......	18 0 0	18 0 0	12 0 0
Kaligunjhat	......	......	......	......	......	......	......	......	......
Nazirerhat	......	......	......	......	......	......	18 0 0	16 0 [illegible]	......
Gosanimarihat	......	......	......	......	......	......	22 0 0	20 0 0	16 0 0
Mathabhangahat ..	......	......	......	......	......	......	......	......	......
Shitporehat	......	......	......	......	......	......	......	......	......
Morangahat	......	......	......	......	......	......	......	......	......
Sitalkuchihat	......	......	......	......	......	......	......	......	......
Mekligunj	......	......	......	26 0 0	26 0 0	20 0 [illegible]	23 0 0	23 0 [illegible]	18 0 0
Changrabandha	......	......	......	26 0 0	26 0 0	20 0 0	23 0 0	23 0 0	18 0 0
Haldibari	......	......	......	26 0 0	26 0 0	20 0 0	23 0 0	23 0 0	18 0 [illegible]
Jamaldaha	......	......	......	24 0 0	24 0 0	20 0 0	2[illegible] 0 0	20 0 0	13 0 0
Ranirhat	......	......	......	25 0 0	20 0 0	15 0 0	22 8 0	16 12 0	11 4 0
Balarampur	......	......	......	25 0 0	20 0 0	15 6 0	22 8 0	18 12 0	11 4 0
Baxirhat	......	...	......	2[illegible] 0 0	20 0 0	15 0 0	22 8 0	18 12 0	11 4 0
Ghoramarahat	...	......	......	25 0 0	20 0 0	15 0 0	22 8 0	18 12 0	11 4 0

State of Cooch Behar for the fortnight ending the 28th June 1947,

by the Seer of 80 Tolias,

	JUTE.			KHESARI KALAI.			OIL CAKE.			REMARKS.
	Present return	Next preceding return.	Corresponding return of last year.	Present return.	Next preceding return.	Corresponding return of last year.	Present return.	Next preceding return.	Corresponding return of last year.	
	s. ch	s. ch	s. ch	s. ch.	s. ch.	s. ch.	s. ch.	s. ch.	s. ch.	
	1 7	1 7	4 0	3 4	3 4	5 11	8 0	8 0	8 0	
	......	......	......	......	......	......	......	......	......	
	. .	......	......	......	......	......	......	......	......	
	1 9½	1 6½	3 5	......	......	......	8 0	8 0	8 0	
	1 5	1 5	3 8	2 17¼	2 3⅗	5 4	6 3⅗	8 3⅗	4 0	

the Principal marts of Cooch Behar for the fortnight ending the 28th June 1947
per maund of 40 seers.

	Rs. A. P.	Rs. A. P.	Rs. A. P.	Rs. A. P.	Rs. A. P.	Rs. A. P.	Rs. A. P.	Rs. A. P.	Rs. A. P.
	27 0 0	27 0 0	10 0 0	12 0 0	12 0 0	7 0 0	5 0 0	5 0 0	5 0 0
	27 0 0	27 0 0	10 0 0	12 0 0	12 0 0	7 0 0	5 0 0	5 0 0	5 0 0
	28 0 0	28 0 0	......	......	12 0 0	......	8 0 0	8 0 0	5 0 0
	26 0 0	28 0 0	13 0 0	......	14 0 0	......	5 0 0	5 0 0	......
	......	......	......	......	......	......	......	......	......
	......	......	......	......	......	......	......	......	......
	......	......	......	18 0 0	......	......	3 12 0	5 0 0	4 0 0
	......	......	......	......	......	......	......	......	......
	27 0 0	25 0 0	......	12 0 0	12 0 0	......	5 0 0	4 0 0	......
	......	......	......	......	20 0 0	......	6 0 0	6 0 0	4 0 0
	......	......	......	......	......	......	......	......	......
	......	......	......	......	......	......	......	......	......
	......	......	......	......	......	......	......	......	......
	......	......	......	......	......	......	......	......	......
	25 0 0	28 0 0	12 0 0	......	......	......	5 0 0	5 0 0	5 0 0
	25 0 0	28 0 0	18 0 0	......	......	......	5 0 0	5 0 0	5 0 0
	25 0 0	28 0 0	13 0 0	......	......	......	5 0 0	5 0 0	5 0 0
	25 0 0	26 0 0	12 0 0	......	......	......	5 0 0	5 0 0	5 0 0
	26 0 0	26 0 0	12 0 0	15 0 0	15 0 0	7 8 0	6 0 0	5 0 0	4 0 0
	26 0 0	26 0 0	12 0 0	15 0 0	15 0 0	7 8 0	6 0 0	5 0 0	4 0 0
	[illegible]	26 0 0	[illegible]	15 0 0	15 0 0	7 8 0	6 0 0	5 0 0	4 0 0
	26 0 0	26 0 0	12 0 0	15 0 0	15 0 0	7 8 0	6 0 0	5 0 0	4 0 0

Return showing the rain-fall, character of weather and prospects of crops in Cooch Behar for the fortnight ending the 28th June 1947.

SUB-DIVISION.	Rain-fall in inches.	Character of the weather in the district as far as known.	State and prospects of the crops and State of health at same.
Mekligunj 17th June ...	5·95	Seasonable ...	Sowing of seeds in the nursery and preparation of lands for *haimanti* paddy going on. Prices of common rice, tobacco and jute are Rs. 2 , Rs. 6) and Rs. 17-4 per maund respectively. No cattle disease and cholera reported during the week. Public health generally good. Fodder and water sufficient.
Ditto 24th June ..	Nil	Hot ..	Sowing of seeds in the nursery for *haimanti* paddy and preparation of lands for the same are in progress. Prices of common rice, tobacco and jute are Rs. 20, Rs. 6) and Rs. 17-4 per maund respectively. One case of cholera reported from Mekligunj town during the week ended fatally. No fresh case reported. Public health generally good. Fodder and water sufficient.
Tufangunj 17th June ...	UN	Seasonable ...	Preparation of lands for *haimanti* paddy and sowing of said seedlings going on. Prices of common rice, *haimanti* paddy, mustard seeds and jute are Rs. 18-12, Rs. 9-8, Rs. 23 and Rs. 27 per maund respectively. No cattle disease reported. Condition of standing crops fair. Public health generally good.
Ditto 24th June ...	Nil	Do ..	Return not received.

L. M. Bakshi,
Development Commissioner, Cooch Behar.

The Cooch Behar Gazette.

১৪ই আশ্বিন বুধবার] WEDNESDAY, OCTOBER 1, 1947. [১৩৫৪ সাল, ৪৩৮ রাজশক

PART IV.

Important Papers and References.

Return showing the rain-fall, character of weather and prospects of crops in Cooch Behar for the fortnight ending the 12th July 1947.

SUB-DIVISION.	Rain-fall in inches.	Character of the weather in the District as far as known.	State and prospects of the crops and state of health at date.
Sudder 1st July ...	Nil	Seasonable ...	Preparation of lands for *haimanti* paddy and sowing of the same seeds in the nursery going on. Price of common rice is Rs. 20 per maund. No case of small-pox or cholera reported. Public health generally good. No cattle disease reported. Fodder and water sufficient.
Ditto. 8th July ...	Nil	Do	Preparation of lands for of *haimanti* paddy and sowing of the seeds in the nursery going on. Transplantation of the seedlings, harvesting of *bitri* paddy and cutting of jute commenced. Price of common rice is Rs. 24 per maund. No case of small-pox or cholera reported. Public health generally good. No cattle disease reported. Fodder aud water sufficient.
Dinhata 1st July ...	Nil	Do	Preparation of lands for *haimanti* paddy and sowing of *haimanti* seeds and transplantation of seedlings going on. Cutting of jute going on in same places. Harvesting of *bitri* paddy going on. No report of any damage of any crop reported. Prices of common rice, *haimanti* paddy, *bitri* paddy, jute, tobacco, and mustard seeds are Rs. 20, Rs. 12-8, Rs. 8, Rs. 28, Rs. 70 and Rs. 26 per maund respectively.
Ditto. 8th July ...	Nil	Do ...	Preparation of lands for *haimanti* paddy and sowing of *haimanti* seeds and transplantation of *haimanti* seedlings going on. Cutting and steeping of jute going on. Harvesting of *bitri* paddy on. No report of any damage of any crop reported. Prices of common rice, *haimanti* paddy, jute, tobacco and mustard seed are Rs. 26, Rs. 13, Rs. 38, Rs. 70, Rs. 26 per maund respectively.

PRICE-CURRENT of food-grains, Jute, Tobacco and Salt in the

RETAIL SALE:—Quantities per Rupee

Sub-divisions.	Wheat.			Rice best sort.			Rice common sort.		
	Present return.	Next preceding return.	Corresponding return of last year.	Present return.	Next preceding return.	Corresponding return of last year.	Present return.	Next preceding return.	Corresponding return of last year.
	s. ch.	s. ch.	s. ch.	s. ch.	s. ch.	s. ch.	s. ch.	s. ch.	s. ch.
Cooch Behar	......	......	......	......	......	......	1 13	2 2	2 8
Dinhata	......	......	......	......	......	......	1 12	......	......
Mathabhanga	......	......	......	......	......	......	......	......	......
Mekligunj	......	......	......	1 10	1 10	2 0	1 12	1 12	3 1
Tufangunj	......	......	......	1 7½	1 7½	2 14	1 8	1 8	3 0

WHOLE-SALE PRICES CURRENT of food-grains, Jute, Tobacco and Salt in

WHOLE-SALE—Price

Markets.	Rs. A. P.	Rs. A. P.	Rs. A. P.	Rs. A. P.	Rs. A. P.	Rs. A. P.	Rs. A. P.	Rs. A. P.	Rs. A. P.
Cooch Behar	......	......	......	......	......	......	22 0 0	19 0 0	16 0 0
Dewanhat	......	......	......	......	......	......	22 0 0	19 0 0	16 0 0
Chowrahat	......	......	......	......	......	......	23 0 0	20 0 0	......
Chowdhurirhat	......	......	......	......	......	......	25 0 0	20 0 0	13 6 0
Ranirhat	......	......	......	......	......	......	......	......	......
Baxirhat	......	......	......	......	......	......	......	......	......
Sitaihat	......	......	......	......	......	......	20 0 0	18 0 0	......
Kaligunjhat	......	......	......	......	......	......	......	......	......
Nazirerhat	......	......	......	......	......	......	20 0 0	18 0 0	......
Gosanimarihat	......	......	......	......	......	......	26 0 0	22 0 0	16 0 0
Mathabhangahat	......	......	......	......	......	......	......	......	......
Shibpurehat	......	......	......	......	......	......	......	......	......
Morangahat	......	......	......	......	......	......	......	......	......
Sitalkhuchihat	......	......	......	......	......	......	......	......	......
Mekligunj	......	......	......	30 0 0	26 0 0	30 0 0	23 0 0	23 0 0	13 0 0
Changrabanda	......	......	......	30 0 0	26 0 0	30 0 0	23 0 0	23 0 0	13 0 0
Haldibari	......	......	......	30 0 0	26 0 0	30 0 0	23 0 0	23 0 0	13 0 0
Jamaldaha	......	......	......	26 0 0	24 0 0	20 0 0	23 0 0	20 0 0	13 0 0
Ranirhat	......	......	......	27 8 0	27 8 0	15 0 0	25 0 0	25 0 0	12 8 0
Balarampur	......	......	......	27 8 0	27 8 0	15 0 0	25 0 0	25 0 0	12 8 0
Baxirhat	......	......	......	27 8 0	27 8 0	15 0 0	25 0 0	25 0 0	12 8 0
Ghoramarahat	......	......	......	27 8 0	27 8 0	15 0 0	25 0 0	25 0 0	12 8 0

State of Cooch Behar for the fortnight ending the 12th July 1947.

by the S[illegible] of 80 Tollas.

Jute			Khesari Kalai			Oil Cake			Remarks
Present return.	Next preceding return.	Corresponding return of last year.	Present return.	Next preceding return.	Corresponding return of last year.	Present return.	Next preceding return.	Corresponding return of last year.	
s. ch.	s. ch.	s. ch.	s. ch.	s. ch.	s. ch.	s. ch.	s. ch.	s. ch.	
1 6	1 7	1 7	3 4	3 4	5 11	5 11	8 0	8 0	
1 9	......	......	......	......	......	5 0	......	......	
	......	......	......	......	......	......	......	......	
......	......	......	......	......	......	8 0	8 0	8 0	
1 15	1 8	2 10¼	2 4	2 4	4 0	6 3	6 3	8 0	

the Principal marts of Cooch Behar for the fortnight ending the 12th July 1947

per maund of 40 seers.

Rs. A. P.	Rs. A. P.	Rs. A. P.	Rs. A. P.	Rs. A. P.	Rs. A. P.	Rs. A. P.	Rs. A. P.	Rs. A. P.
28 0 0	27 0 0	27 0 0	12 0 0	12 0 0	7 0 0	7 0 0	5 0 0	5 0 0
28 0 0	27 0 0	27 0 0	12 0 0	12 0 0	7 0 0	7 0 0	5 0 0	5 0 0
25 0 0	28 0 0	15 0 0	......	......	......	8 0 0	8 0 0	5 0 0
26 0 0	26 0 0	14 0 0	......	......	......	6 0 0	5 0 0	4 0 0
......	......	......	......	......	......	......	......	......
......	......	......	......	......	......	......	......	......
......	......	......	18 0 0	18 0 0	......	4 0 0	3 12 0	......
......	......	......	......	......	......	......	......	......
27 0 0	27 0 0	......	12 0 0	12 0 0	......	5 0 0	5 0 0	......
......	......	......	......	......	......	6 0 0	6 0 0	4 0 0
......	......	......	......	......	......	......	......	......
......	......	......	......	......	......	......	......	......
......	......	......	......	......	......	......	......	......
......	......	......	......	......	......	......	......	......
25 0 0	28 0 0	12 0 0	......	......	......	5 0 0	5 0 0	5 0 0
25 0 0	28 0 0	18 0 0	......	......	......	5 0 0	5 0 0	5 0 0
25 0 0	28 0 0	12 0 0	......	......	......	5 0 0	5 0 0	5 0 0
25 0 0	28 0 0	12 0 0	......	......	......	5 0 0	5 0 0	5 0 0
24 0 0	26 0 0	15 0 0	17 8 0	17 8 0	10 0 0	6 0 0	6 0 0	5 0 0
24 0 0	26 0 0	15 0 0	17 8 0	17 8 0	10 0 0	6 0 0	6 0 0	5 0 0
22 0 0	26 0 0	16 0 0	17 8 0	17 8 0	10 0 0	6 0 0	6 0 0	5 0 0
22 0 0	26 0 0	15 0 0	17 8 0	17 8 0	10 0 0	6 0 0	6 0 0	5 0 0

Return showing the rain-fall, character of weather and prospects of crops in Cooch Behar for the fortnight ending the 12th July 1947.

SUB-DIVISION.	Rain-fall in inches.	Character of the weather in the district as far as known.	State and prospects of the crops and State of health at else.
Mathabhanga 1st July ...	5·95	Seasonable ...	Transplantation of *haimanti* seedlings in some places in Dola land commenced. Price of paddy and rice is selling at Rs. 10-8 to Rs. 11 and Rs. 20 per maund respectively. No case of any epidemic was reported during the week.
Ditto 8th July		Do	Transplantation of *haimanti* seedlings in Dola going on. Prices of rice, paddy are Rs. 2) Rs. 11 to Rs. 12 per md. respectively. No case of any epidemic was reported during the week.
Mekligunj 1st July ...	Nil	Hot	Sowing of seeds in the nursery for *haimanti* paddy and preparation of lands for *haimanti* paddy are being retarded for want of rains. Prices of common rice, tobacco and jute are Rs. 20, Rs. 60 to Rs. 100 and Rs. 25 per maund respectively. One fresh case of cholera reported from Mekliganj Police Station is cured. No cattle disease reported. Public health generally good. Fodder and water sufficient.
Ditto 8th July ..	8 56	Rainy	Prospect etc. of crops—transplantation of *haimanti* paddy has commenced. Cutting and steeping of jute have commenced in places. Prices of common rice, tobacco and jute are Rs. 22-8, Rs. 80, to Rs. 120 and Rs. 22 per maund respectively. Public health generally good. Fodder and water sufficient.
Tufangunj 1st July ...			Return not received.
Ditto 8th July	Nil	Seasonable	Harvesting of *bitri* paddy & transplantation of *haimanti* paddy commenced in places. Prices of common rice, *haimanti* paddy, mustard seeds and jute are Rs. 18-12, Rs. 9-8, Rs. 24 and Rs. 27 per maund respectively. 4 fresh cases of small-pox reported during this week. Out of these 4 cases 3 cured and one case is still lingering. Condition of standing crops fair. Public health generally good.

L. M. BAKSHI,
Development Commissioner, Cooch Behar.

The Cooch Behar Gazette.

২৯শে আশ্বিন বৃহস্পতিবার] THURSDAY, OCTOBER 16, 1947. [১৩৫৪ সাল, ৪৩৮ রাজশক]

PART IV.

Important Papers and References.

Return showing the rain-fall, character of weather and prospects of crops in Cooch Behar for the fortnight ending the 26th July 1947.

SUB-DIVISION.	Rain-fall in inches.	Character of the weather in the District as far as known.	State and prospects of the crops and state of health at date.
Sudder 15th July ...	Nil	Seasonable ...	Preparation of lands for *haimanti* paddy, sowing of the seeds in the nursery and transplantation of the seedlings going on. Harvesting of *bitri* paddy and cutting of jute continuing. Price of common rice is Rs. 22 per maund. No case of small-pox or cholera reported. Public health generally good. No cattle disease reported. Fodder and water sufficient.
Ditto. 22nd July ...	Nil	Do ...	Preparation of lands for *haimanti* paddy and sowing of the seeds in the nursery and transplantation of the seedlings going on. Harvesting of *bitri* paddy, cutting, steeping and washing of jute continuing. Price of common rice is Rs. 20 per maund. No case of small-pox or cholera reported. Public health generally good. No cattle disease reported. Fodder and water sufficient.
Dinhata 15th July ...	Nil	Do ...	Preparation of lands for *haimanti* paddy, sowing and transplantation of *haimanti* seedlings going on. Cutting of *bitri* paddy and jute going on. Harvesting of *bitri* paddy also going on. No report of damage of any crops reported. Prices of common rice, paddy, jute, tobacco and mustard seeds are Rs. 25, Rs. 13, Rs. 27, Rs. 70 and Rs. 26 per maund respectively.
Ditto. 22nd July ...	Nil	Do ...	Preparation of lands for *haimanti* paddy and transplantation of *haimanti* seedlings going on. Harvesting of *bitri* paddy going on. Cutting and steeping of jute going on. No report of damage of any crops reported. Prices of common rice, *haimanti* paddy, jute, tobacco and mustard seeds are Rs. 23, Rs. 13-3, Rs. 25 and Rs. 25 per maund respectively.

PRICE-CURRENT of food-grains, Jute, Tobacco and Salt in the

Retail Sale :—Quantities per Rupee

Sub-divisions.	Wheat. Present return	Wheat. Next preceding return.	Wheat. Corresponding return of last year.	Rice best sort. Present return.	Rice best sort. Next preceding return	Rice best sort. Corresponding return of last year.	Rice common sort. Present return.	Rice common sort. Next preceding return.	Rice common sort. Corresponding return of last year.
	s. ch.	s. ch.	s. ch.	ch.	s. ch.	s. ch.	s. ch.	s. ch.	s. ch
Cooch Behar	......	......	......	......	......	......	1 10	1 13	2 8
Dinhata	......	......	......	......	......	......	1 8	1 12	......
Mathabhanga	......	......	......	......	......	......	......	......	......
Mekligunj	......	......	......	1 8	1 8	2 0	1 10	1 10	2 0
Tufangunj	......	......	......	1 7½	1 7½	2 14	1 8	1 8	3 0

WHOLE-SALE PRICES CURRENT of food-grains, Jute, Tobacco and Salt in

Whole-sale—Price

Markets.	Rs. A. P.	Rs. A. P.	Rs. A. P.	Rs. A. P.	Rs. A. P.	Rs. A. P.	Rs. A. P.	Rs. A. P.	Rs. A. P.
Cooch Behar	......	......	......	......	......	......	25 0 0	22 0 0	16 0 0
Dewanhat	......	......	......	......	......	......	25 0 0	22 0 0	16 0 0
Chowrahat	......	......	......	......	......	......	27 0 0	23 0 0	12 8
Choudhurirhat	......	......	......	......	......	......	25 0 0	23 0 0	13 4 0
Ranirhat	......	......	......	......	......	......	......	......	......
Buxirhat	......	......	......	......	......	......	......	......	......
Sitaihat	......	......	......	......	......	......	27 0 0	20 0 0	10 0
Kaligunjhat	......	......	......	......	......	......	......	......	......
Nazirerhat	......	......	......	......	......	......	20 0 0	20 0 0	......
Gosanimarihat	......	......	......	......	......	......	27 0 0	28 0 0	20 0 0
Mathabhangahat ...	......	......	......	......	......	......	......	......	......
Shibporehat	......	......	......	......	......	......	......	......	......
Norangahat	......	......	......	......	......	......	......	......	......
Sitalkhuchihat	......	......	......	......	......	......	......	......	......
Mekligunj	......	......	......	26 0 0	26 0 0	20 0 0	22 0 0	22 0 0	20 0 0
Changrabanda	......	......	......	26 0 0	26 0 0	20 0 0	22 0 0	22 0 0	20 0 0
Haldibari	......	......	......	26 0 0	26 0 0	20 0 0	22 0 0	22 0 0	20 0 0
Jamaldaha	......	......	......	26 0 0	26 0 0	20 0 0	22 0 0	22 0 0	20 0 0
Ranirhat	......	......	......	27 8 0	27 8 0	15 0 0	25 0 0	25 0 0	12 8 0
Balarampur	......	......	......	27 8 0	27 8 0	15 0 0	25 0 0	25 0 0	12 8 0
Buxirhat	......	......	......	27 8 0	27 8 0	15 0 0	25 0 0	25 0 0	12 8 0
Ghoramarahat	......	......	......	27 8 0	27 8 0	15 0 0	25 0 0	25 0 0	12 8 0

Return showing the rain-fall, character of weather and prospects of crops in Cooch Behar for the fortnight ending the 26th July 1947.

SUB-DIVISION.	Rain-fall in inches.	Character of the weather in the district as far as known.	State and prospects of the crops and State of health at date.
Mathabhanga 15th July ...	Nil	Seasonable ..	Transplantation of *haimanti* seedlings in Dola going on. No case of any epidemic was reported during the week. Price of paddy and rice sells at Rs. 11 8, Rs. 20 per maund respectively.
Ditto, 22nd July ...	Nil	Do ...	Transplantation of *haimanti* seedlings in Dola is going on. No case of any epidemic was reported during the week. Price of paddy. rice sells at Rs. 12-8, Rs. 20 per maund respectively.
Mekligunj 15th July ...	6.97"	Do ..	Transplantation of *haimanti* paddy going on vigorously. Cutting and steeping of jute going on. Prices of common rice, tobacco and jute are Rs. 26, Rs. 80 to Rs. 120 and Rs. 22 per maund respectively. Public health generally good. Fodder and water sufficient.
Ditto, 22nd July ..	4·12"	Do ...	Transplantation of *haimanti* paddy going on. Cutting, steeping and washing of jute going on. Prices of common rice, tobacco and jute are Rs. 26, Rs. 80 to Rs. 12 , Rs. 25 per maund respectively. 13 cattle disease (Diarrhoea) reported from Mekligunj Police Station and all are lingering. Public health generally good. Fodder and water sufficient.
Tufangunj 15th July ...	N	Do ...	Harvesting of *bitri* paddy and transplantation of *haimanti* paddy going on. Prices of common rice, *haimanti* paddy, jute and mustard seeds are Rs. 22-8, Rs. 11, Rs. 8, Rs. 28 and Rs. 25 per maund respectively. No cattle disease reported. 1 previous case of small-pox cured. Condition of standing crops fair. Fodder and water sufficient.
Ditto, 22nd July ...	Nil	Do ...	Harvesting of *bitri* paddy and tranplantation of *haimanti* paddy going on. Price of common rice, *haimanti* paddy, *bitri* paddy, *bitri* rice. mustard seeds and jute are Rs. 22-8, Rs. 12-8, Rs. 8-8, Rs. 16-4, Rs. 28 and Rs. 28 per maund respectively. 4 fresh cases of cattle disease reported during the week which are lingering. Condition of standing crops fair. Fodder and water sufficient.

L. M. BAKSHI,
Development Commissioner, Cooch Behar.

The Cooch Behar Gazette.

১৫ই কার্ত্তিক শনিবার] SATURDAY, NOVEMBER 1, 1947. [১৩৫৪ সাল, ৩৮ রাজশকা

PART IV.

Important Papers and References.

Return showing the rain-fall, character of weather and prospects of crops in Cooch Behar for the fortnight ending the 9th August 1947.

SUB-DIVISION.	Rain-fall in inches.	Character of the weather in the District as far as known.	State and prospects of the crops and state of health at date.
Sadder 29th July ...	Nil	Seasonable ..	Preparation of lands for *haimanti* paddy, and sowing of the seeds in the nursery and transplantation of the seedlings going on. Harvesting of *bitri* paddy and cutting, steeping and washing of jute continuing. Price of common rice is Rs. 22 per maund. No case of small-pox or cholera reported. Public health generally good. No cattle disease reported. Fodder and water sufficient.
Ditto. 5th August ...	Nil	Do ...	Preparation of lands for *haimanti* paddy and transplantation of the seedlings going on. Harvesting of *bitri* paddy, cutting, steeping and washing of jute continuing. Price of common rice is Rs. 24 per maund. No case of small-pox or cholera reported. Public health generally good. No cattle disease reported. Fodder and water sufficient.
Dinhata 29th July ...	Nil	Do ...	Transplantation of *haimanti* seedlings and Harvesting and thrashing of *bitri* paddy still going on. Cutting and steeping of jute going on. No report of any damage of any crop reported. Prices of common rice, *haimanti* paddy, jute, mustard seeds and tobacco are Rs. 25, Rs. 14, Rs. 27, Rs. 36 and Rs. 60 per maund respectively.
Ditto. 5th August ...	Nil	Do ...	Transplantation of *haimanti* seedlings going on. Harvesting and thrashing of *bitri* paddy going to be finished. Cutting and steeping of jute going on. No report of damage of any crops reported. Prices of common rice, *haimanti* paddy, *bitri* paddy mustard seeds and jute are Rs. 27, Rs. 15, Rs. 12-8 Rs. 27 and Rs. 26 per maund respectively.

The Cooch Behar Gazette.

১লা অগ্রহায়ণ সোমবার] MONDAY, NOVEMBER 17, 1947. [১৩৫৪ সাল, ৪:৮ রাজশকা

PART IV.

Important Papers and References.

Return showing the rain-fall, character of weather and prospects of crops in Cooch Behar for the fortnight ending the 23rd August 1947.

SUB-DIVISION.	Rain-fall in inches.	Character of the weather in the District as far as known.	State and prospects of the crops and state of health at date.
Sudder 12th August ...	Nil	Seasonable ...	Preparation of lands of *haimanti* paddy and transplantation of the seedlings going on. Harvesting of *bitri* paddy and cutting, steeping and washing of jute continuing. Price of common rice is Rs. 25 per maund. No case of small-pox or cholera reported. Public health generally good. No cattle disease reported. Fodder and water sufficient.
Ditto. 19th August ...	Nil	Do ...	Preparation of lands for *haimanti* paddy and transplantation of the seedlings going on. Harvesting of *bitri* paddy, cutting, steeping and washing of jute continuing. Price of common rice is Rs. 25 per maund. No case of small-pox or cholera reported. Public health generally good. No cattle disease reported. Fodder and water sufficient.
Dinhata 12th August ...	Nil	Do ...	Transplantation of *haimanti* seedling going on. Harvesting and thrashing of *bitri* paddy going to be finished. Harvesting and thrashing of *bitri* paddy going to be finished. Cutting and steeping of jute going on. No report of damage of any crop reported. Prospect and condition of standing crop tolerable. Prices of common rice, *haimanti* paddy, *bitri* paddy, jute and mustared seed are Rs 25, Rs. 16, Rs. 13, Rs. 24 and Rs. 25 per maund respectively.
Ditto. 19th August ...	Nil	Do ...	Transplantation of *haimanti* seedlings going on. Harvesting and thrashing of *bitri* paddy finished. Steeping and cutting of jute still going on. No report of any damage of any crop reported. Prospect and condition of standing crops tolerable. Prices of common rice, *haimanti* paddy, *bitri* paddy, jute and mustared seed are Rs. 25-10, Rs. 16, Rs. 13, Rs. 24 and Rs. 25 per maund respectively.

The Cooch Behar Gazette.

৩০শে অগ্রহায়ণ মঙ্গলবার] TUESDAY, DECEMBER 16, 1947. [১৩৫৪ সাল, ৪·৮ রাজশক

PART IV.

Important Papers and References.

Return showing the rain-fall, character of weather and prospects of crops in Cooch Behar for the fortnight ending the 20th September 1947.

SUB-DIVISION.	Rain-fall in inches.	Character of the weather in the District as far as known.	State and prospects of the crops and state of health at date.
Sudder 9th September ...	Nil	Seasonable ...	Preparation of lands for *haimanti* paddy and transplantation of the seedlings going on. Cutting, steeping and washing of jute continuing. Price of common rice is Rs. 26 per maund. No case of small pox or cholera reported. Public health generally good. No cattle disease reported. Fodder and water sufficient.
Ditto. 16th September ...	Nil	Do ...	Preparation of lands for *haimanti* paddy and transplantation of the seedlings going on. Cutting, steeping and washing of jute continuing. Price of common rice is Rs. 26 per maund. No case of small pox or cholera reported. Public health generally good. No cattle disease reported. Fodder and water sufficient.
Dinhata 9th September ...	Nil	Do ...	Transplantation of *haimanti* seedling still going on. Steeping and washing of jute going on. Prospect and condition of standing crops tolerable. No report of any damage of any crop reported. Prices of common rice, *haimanti* paddy, *bitri* paddy, jute and mustared seeds are Rs. [illegible]2, Rs. 16, Rs. 13, Rs. 22 and Rs. [illegible]7 per maund respectively.
Ditto. 16th September ...	Nil	Do ...	Transplantation of *haimanti* seedlings going on. Steeping, thrashing and washing of jute going on. Prospect and condition of standing crops tolerable. No report of damage of any crops reported. Prices of common rice, *haimanti* paddy, *bitri* paddy and jute are Rs. 30, Rs. 15, Rs. 21 per maund respectively.

PRICE-CURRENT of food-grains, Jute, Tobacco and Salt in the

RETAIL SALE:—Quantities per Rupee

	WHEAT.			RICE BEST SORT.			RICE COMMON SORT.		
	Present return	Next preceding return.	Corresponding return of last year.	Present return.	Next preceding return	Corresponding return of last year.	Present return.	Next preceding return.	Corresponding return of last year.
Sub divisions.	s. ch.	s. ch.	s. ch.	ch.	s. ch.	s. ch.	s. ch.	s. ch.	s. ch
Cooch Behar	......	......	......	......	......	......	1 7	1 7	2 8
Dinhata	......	......	......	......	......	......	1 5	1 4	......
Mathabhanga	......	......	......	......	......	......	......	......	......
Mekligunj	......	......	......	1 4	1 2	2 0	1 11	1 9	2 0
Tufangunj	......	......	......	1 7½	1 5	2 0	1 8	1 8	2 8

WHOLE-SALE PRICES CURRENT of food-grains, Jute, Tobacco and Salt in

WHOLE-SALE—Price

Markets.	Rs. A. P.	Rs. A. P.	Rs. A. P.	Rs. A. P.	Rs. A. P.	Rs. A. P.	Rs. A. P.	Rs. A. P.	Rs. A. P.
Cooch Behar	......	......	......	......	......	......	27 0 0	27 0 0	16 0 0
Dewanhat	......	......	......	......	......	......	27 0 0	27 0 0	16 0 0
Chowrahat	......	......	......	......	......	......	20 0 0	30 0 0	......
Choudhurirhat	......	......	......	......	......	......	30 0 0	26 0 0	20 0 0
Ranirhat	......	......	......	......	......	......	......	......	......
Buxirhat	......	......	......	......	......	......	......	......	......
Sitaihat	......	......	......	......	......	......	27 0 0	26 0 0	12 0 0
Kaligunjhat	......	......	......	......	......	......	......	......	......
Nazirerhat	......	......	......	......	......	......	26 0 0	22 0 0	......
Gosanimarihat	......	......	......	......	......	......	32 0 0	27 0 0	30 0 0
Mathabhangahat ..	......	......	......	......	......	......	......	......	......
Shibporehat	......	......	......	......	......	......	......	......	......
Morangahat	......	......	......	......	......	......	......	......	......
Sitalkhuchihat	......	......	......	......	......	......	......	......	......
Mekligunj	......	......	......	30 0 0	35 0 0	10 0 [illegible]	23 0 0	35 0 [illegible]	20 0 [illegible]
Changrabanda	......	......	......	30 0 0	35 0 0	30 0 0	23 0 0	25 0 0	20 0 0
Haldibari	......	......	......	30 0 0	35 0 0	30 0 0	24 0 0	35 0 0	30 0 [illegible]
Jamaldaha	......	......	......	30 0 0	35 0 0	20 0 0	23 0 0	[illegible] 0 0	30 0 0
Ranirhat	......	......	......	27 8 0	30 0 0	20 0 0	[illegible] 0 0	25 0 0	17 8 0
Bularampur	......	......	......	27 8 0	30 0 0	30 0 0	25 0 0	25 0 0	17 8 0
Buxirhat	......	...	......	27 8 0	30 0 0	30 0 0	25 0 0	25 0 0	17 8 0
Ghoramarahat	......	......	......	27 8 0	30 0 0	30 0 0	25 0 0	25 0 0	17 8 0

The Cooch Behar Gazette.

৩১শে আষাঢ় বুধবার] WEDNESDAY, JULY 16, 1947. [১৩৫৪ সাল, ৪৩৮ রাজশক

PART V.

Advertisements

Sale Notice

The following Sal, Sissu and Teak Lots will be sold by public auction at the Forest Office, Cooch Behar on the 30th July, 1947.

Lot Nos. 1 to 4 of 1947-48 ... Mahismuri Sal Forest—Sal trees.

„ No. 5 of 1947-48 ... Nababgunj Balashi Forest—Sissu and Simul trees.

„ Nos. 6 to 11 of 1947-48 ... Nilkuthi Forest—Teak and a few Sal trees.

Intending purchasers are requested to inspect the Lots before sale and write to the undersigned for particulars. Some more trees, which are being marked, will also be put up in the auction on the 30th July, 1947.

B. N. Roy, B. F. S. (Retd.)
Conservator of Forests, Cooch Behar State.

নোটিশ।

এতদ্বারা সর্ব্বসাধারণকে জানান যাইতেছে যে শামুক সহর কোচবিহার মধ্যে কৌজচালা ষ্টেটের উত্তর পার্শ্বে শ্রীযুক্ত বাবু চাম্পালাল সেঠিয়া ও মোহনলাল সেঠিয়া মহাশয়ের মালিক ৮ নং তৌজির লিখিত ৩৪।৶০ খুদ জমির কাত বার্ষিক ৪৫৮৶০ জমার চুকানী স্বত্ব বিশিষ্ট জোত কবলা বিক্রয় হইবেক ক্রয়েচ্ছুক ব্যক্তিগণ নিম্নলিখিত ঠিকানায় অনুসন্ধান করুন। ইতি—

ঠিকানা—
শ্রীহুকুমচন্দ সেঠিয়া,
ভূতপূর্ব্ব কানুরাম নথমল সেঠিয়ার কারবার
কোচবিহার

List of State Acts, Laws and Codes for sale in the State Press, Cooch Behar.

	Rs.	A.	P.
Act of 1874 Limitation (English)* ...	0	12	0
,, Ditto (Bengali) ...	0	12	0
,, of 1882 Cattle Trespass* ,, ...	0	2	0
মুদ্রিত কাগজ সম্বন্ধীয় নিয়মাবলী ...	0	2	0
Act of 1888 Sub-infeudation* ...	0	1	0
,, I of 1890 লোক সংখ্যা গ্রহণ বিষয়ক আইন	0	0	6
,, I of 1892 Private Fisheries Protection (English and Bengali combined.)	0	1	0
,, II of 1892 Amendment of Limitation (Engish and Bengali combined.)	0	1	0
,, III of 1892 Jurisdiction (English)*	0	1	3
,, Ditto (Bengali)*	0	1	0
,, IV 1892 Merchandise Marks (Eng.)*	0	2	0
,, I of 1893 Legal Practitioners ,, *	0	1	3
,, Ditto ditto (Bengali)	0	1	0
,, II of 1893 Amendment of Town Committee (English).	0	0	3
,, III of 1893 Village Chowkidari (English)	0	1	6
,, IV of 1893 Amendment of Revenue Sale (English).	0	0	3
,, IV of 1893 Amendment Revenue Sale (Bengali)	0	0	3
,, V of 1893 Cess (English)	0	1	0
,, Ditto (Bengali)	0	1	0
,, VI of 1893 Amendment of Legal Practitioners (English and Bengali combined.)*	0	0	3
,, I of 1894 Amendment of Town Committee.*	0	0	3
,, II of 1894 Amendment of Voluntary Sale of under-tenures.	0	0	3
,, III of 1894 Amendment of Village Chowkidari.*	0	0	6
,, I of 1895 Small Cause Courts Act (English).	0	0	9
,, I of 1896 Amendment of Cooch Behar Stamp Act (English).*	0	0	3
,, I of 1896 Amendment of Cooch Behar Stamp Act (Bengali).*	0	0	3
,, II of 1896 Preservation of Boundary Act (English).	0	0	6
,, III of 1896 Amendment of Village Chowkidari Act (English).	0	0	3
,, I of 1897 Amendment of Cooch Behar Town Committee Act (Eng.)	0	0	3
,, II of 1897 Mahomedan Inheritance Act (English).	0	0	3
,, III of 1897 Oaths Act (English)*	0	0	6
,, IV of 1897 Amendment of Stamp rules (English.)	0	0	3
,, V of 1897 Revenue Sale Act (English).	0	3	0
,, V of 1897 Revenue Sale Act (Bengali).	0	3	0
,, VI of 1897 Wards Act (English)	0	1	0
,, I of 1898 Kist Act ,,	0	0	
,, Ditto (Bengali)	0	0	
,, II of 1898 Amendment of Revenue Sale Act (English).	0	0	
,, Ditto (Bengali)	0	0	3
,, III of 1898 Police Act (English)	0	2	0
,, Ditto (Bengali.)	0	2	0

	Rs.	A.	P.
Act IV of 1898 Bridge Toll Act (Eng.)*	0	0	6
,, of Ditto ditto (Bengali)	0	0	6
,, V of 1898 Succession Certificate Act (English)	0	2	0
,, Ditto ditto (Bengali)	0	2	0
,, VI of 1898 Amendment of Voluntary Sales of under-tenures (Eng.)	0	0	9
,, Ditto ditto (Bengali)	0	0	9
,, VII of 1898 Amendment of Village Chowkidari Act (English)	0	0	3
,, Ditto ditto (Bengali)	0	0	3
,, VIII of 1898 Revenue Sales Act ,,	0	0	3
,, Ditto (English)	0	0	3
,, I of 1899 Cow Killing Act ,,	0	0	3
,, Ditto (Bengali)	0	0	3
,, II of 1899 Public Demands Recovery Act (Eng.)	0	3	0
,, Ditto ditto (Bengali)	0	3	0
,, III of 1899 Amendment of Limitation Act (English)	0	0	3
,, Ditto ditto (Bengali)	0	0	3
,, IV of 1899 State Demands Act (English and Bengali combined)	0	0	6
,, V of 1899 Civil Marriage Act (Eng.)	0	1	6
,, Ditto ditto (Bengali)	0	1	6
,, I of 1900 Amendment of Civil Procedure Code (English)	0	2	0
,, II of 1900 Census Act (English)	0	1	3
,, Ditto ditto (Bengali)	0	1	0
,, I of 1901 C. B. Telegraph Act ,,	0	1	0
,, I of 1903 C. B. Stamp Act (Eng.)	0	6	0
,, Ditto Ditto (Beng.)	0	6	0
,, II of 1903 Drainage Act (Eng.)	0	0	6
,, Ditto (Bengali)	0	0	6
,, III of 1903 Amendment of Cooch Behar Limitation Act (English).	0	1	6
,, Ditto (Bengali)	0	1	6
Act IV of 1903 C. B. Town Committee Act (English).	0	6	0
V of 1903 Amendment of Civil Procedure Code.	0	1	6
,, VI of 1903 Vaccination Act (Eng)*	0	2	0
,, Ditto Ditto (Beng.)	0	2	0
Act I of 1904 Registration Act (Eng.)	0	0	6
,, II of 1904 Amendment of Village Chowkidari (Eng.)	0	1	0
,, Ditto Ditto (Beng.)	0	1	0
,, I of 1905 Amendment of Stamp Act (English).	0	0	6
,, II of 1905 Unclaimed Intestate Property.	0	0	6
,, I of 1906 Encumbered Estate Act (English)	0	0	6
,, II of 1906 Companies Act (English).	0	1	0
,, III of 1906 Evidence Act Amendment.	0	0	6
,, IV of 1906 Amendment of Village Chaukidari Act.	0	0	6
,, V of 1906 Small Cause Court Act (English)	0	3	0
,, VI of 1906 Wills Act (English)	0	0	3
,, VII of 1906 Probate and Administration Act.	0	0	6

* Out of stock.

	Rs.	A.	P.
Act I of 1907 Amendment Town Committee Act.	0	0	6
,, II of 1907 Succession Act (English),	0	0	6
,, III of 1907 Amendment Vaccination Act (Bengali).	0	1	0
,, IV of 1907 Penal Code Act ...	0	0	6
,, I of 1908 Amendment of Stamp Act.	0	1	0
,, II of 1908 Forest Act ...	0	2	0
,, I of 1909 The Code of Criminal Procedure.	0	2	0
,, II of 1909 Act for the Legislative Council.	0	0	6
,, I of 1910 Registration of Births and Deaths (English).	0	1	0
Ditto (Bengali)	0	1	0
,, II of 1910 Amendment of Succession Certificate Act.	0	1	0
,, III of 1910 Provisions for the care of lunatics.	0	0	6
Act IV of 1910 Census Act (Eng. & Beng)	0	1	0
Act V of 1910 Tenancy Act (English)	0	8	0
,, V ,, ,, (Bengali)	0	11	0
,, I of 1913 Survey ,, Eng.)	0	2	0
,, ,, ,, (Beng.)	0	[illegible]	0
Letters and Proceedings having the force of Law.	0	10	0
Law Reports Vol. I*	0	8	0
,, Vol. II*	2	4	0
,, Vol. III	1	0	0
Law Report Vol IV (1911—Jan. 1314)	0	12	0
Vol. V (Mar. 1914-Dec. 1920)	0	8	0
Law Report Vol. VI.	0	12	0
,, Vol. VII	0	12	0
Act I of 1920 Census Act (Eng.)	0	2	0
,, ,, ,, (Beng.)	0	2	0
,, I of 1921 General Clauses Act	0	4	0
,, II ,, Code of Civil Procedure Act.	0	5	0
,, III ,, Transfer of Property ,,	0	2	0
,, IV ,, Limitation Act ...	0	3	0
,, V ,, Majority ,, ...	0	2	0
,, VI ,, Registration ,, ...	0	2	0
,, VII ,, Guardians and Wards Act.	0	2	0
,, VIII ,, Negotiable instruments Act.	0	2	0
,, IX ,, Criminal Tribes Act	0	3	0
,, X ,, Interest ,,	0	2	0
,, XI ,, Suits Valuations ,,	0	2	0
,, XII ,, Bankers' Books evidence (amendment.)	0	1	0
,, I of 1923 Regulation E.B.R. Arbitration.	0	1	0
,, I of 1923 Excise, Opium & Drugs	0	5	0
,, I of 1929 (amending the Cooch Behar Town Committee Act IV of 1903)	0	1	0
,, I of 1930 Criminal Law (amendt.)	0	1	0
,, II ,, Census Act ...	0	2	0
,, III ,, Co-operative Societies Act	0	4	0
,, III , 1930 ,, (Sec. 43) ...	0	3	0
,, I of 1931 Christian Marriage Act	0	1	0
,, I of 1932 Motor Vehicles Act	0	2	0
Act I of 1933 Cooch Behar Penal Code Amendment Act.	0	0	3

	Rs.	A.	P.
Act II of 1933 Cooch Behar Companies Act.	0	2	0
,, III of 1933 Code of Criminal Procedure.	0	4	0
,, I of 1934 The Lepers Act ...	0	2	0
,, III of 1934 Cooch Behar Revenue Sale Amendment Act.	0	1	0
Act No. IV of 1934 Hindu widow Marriage Act (Eng. & Beng).	0	1	0
,, I of 1935 Cooch Behar Matches (Excise Duty) Act.	0	2	0
,, I of 1937 Cooch Behar Hat toll protection Act.	0	0	6
Act II of 1937 Act for Prevention of Cruelty to Animals.	0	6	0
,, I of 1938 C.B. Public gambling Act	0	2	0
,, II of 1938 C.B. Amusement Tax Act	0	2	0
,, I of 1939 Amendment of C.B.T.C.	0	0	6
Act I of 1940 Census Act... ...	0	2	0
,, II of 1940 C. B. Penal Code Amendment Act.	0	0	6
,, I of 1941 Amendment of C. B. Tenancy Act.	0	0	6
,, II of 1941 C. B. Food Adulteration	0	3	0
,, III of 1941 Legislative Council Act	0	2	0
,, IV of 1941 C. B. Electricity Act	0	4	0
Act V of 1941 C. B. Income Tax Act	0	8	0
,, VI of 1941 C. B. Export Duty Act	0	1	0
Act VII of 1941 Motor Vehicles	1	0	0
,, VIII of 1941 Village choukidary Amendment	0	2	0
,, IX of 1941 Town Committee Amendment	0	1	0
,, X of 1941 General Amending	0	6	0
,, XI of 1941 Cow killing Amendment	0	0	3
,, XII of 1941 Tenancy (second Amend.) Act No. XII of 1941	0	0	3
,, I of 1942 Standard of weight	0	1	0
,, II of 1942 foreigner's Act	0	1	0
,, III of 1942 Penal Code Act	2	12	0
,, IV of 1942 Companies (Amend)	0	1	0
,, V of 1942 Public Demands recovery (Amend)	0	1	0
,, VI of 1942 Incometax (Amend)	0	1	0
Act VII of 1942 (An Act to Amend the C. B. General Clauses Act I of 1921	0	0	6
,, VIII of 1942 (Transfer of Property Amendment) Act 1942	0	1	0
,, IX of 1942 (C. B. Registration Amendment) Act 1942	0	0	6
,, X of 1942 (C. B. Limitation Amendment) Act 1942	0	1	0
,, No. XI of 1942 (C. B. Town Committee) Amendment Act	0	0	6
Live Stock Census Report	0	4	0
Schedule of rates*	2	8	0
Cottage Industry	2	0	0
History of Cooch Behar (Paper bound) Bengali	2	0	0
Do Do (cloth bound)	3	0	0
Hand Book of Circular orders	2	0	0
History of Cooch Behar (Englsh version)	5	0	0

* Out of stock.

	Rs.	A.	P.
Act I of 1943 Legal Practitioners Act	0	4	0
,, II of 1943 Stamp Act ...	0	14	0
,, III of 1943 Excess Profits Tax Act	0	6	0
,, IV of 1943 Patents Act ...	0	4	0
,, V of 1943 Public Health Act ...	0	8	0
,, VI of 1943 (An Act to provide for the Prevention and Control of Contagions deseases affecting Animals.)	0	2	0
,, VII of 1943 Army Act ...	0	8	0
,, VIII of 1943 Workmen's Compensation Act.	0	1	0
,, IX of 1943 Factories Act	0	1	0
,, X of 1943 Public Demand Recovery Act.	1	12	0
,, XI of 1943 Civil Procedure Code (amendment) Act.	0	2	0
,, XII of 1943 Pension (Exemption) Act.	0	0	6
,, XIII of 1943 Insolvency Act ...	0	8	0
,, XIV of 1943 Succession Act ...	0	1	0
,, XV of 1943 Extradition Act ...	0	8	0
,, XVI of 1943 Muli (Regulating) Act	0	0	6
,, XVII of 1943 Interest (amendment) Act.	0	0	6
,, XVIII of 1943 Revenue sale (amendment) Act.	0	0	6
,, XIX of 1943 Land Acquisition Act	0	4	0
,, XX of 1943 Forest (amendment) Act.	0	0	6
Act XXI of 1943 Tenancy (amendment) Act 1943.	0	6	0
Act XXII of 1943 Cooch Behar Co-operation Societies Act 1943.	0	2	0
Act XXIII of 1943 Village Chaukidary (amendment).	0	1	0
Act XXIV of 1943 Cooch Behar Incometax (amendment) Act 1943.	0	1	0
Act XXV of 1943 Tobacco (Excise Duty) Act.	0	3	0
Act XXVI of 1943 Bengal and Assam Railway Arbitration Act.	0	2	0
Table of rates of Advalorem Fees laviable on the institution of Suits under the Cooch Behar Stamp Act II of 1943.	0	2	0
Rules made under section 52 of the Income-tax Act 1941.	0	2	0
Lives-stock Census Report	0	4	0
Act II of 1921 (as amended up to Cooch Behar Civil procedure 1921 (Cooch Behar State).	0	5	0
Cooch Behar Tenancy Act, Act V of 1910 (as amended upto 1943) Cooch Behar State.	0	11	0
Act I of 1944 Cooch Beher Agriculturists' Loans Act.	0	0	6
,, II of 1944 Cooch Behar Land Improvement Loans Act.	0	2	0
,, III of 1944 Cooch Behar Municipal Act	1	8	0
,, IV of 1944 C. B. Prevention of Cruelty to Animals Act. (Amendement.)	0	2	6
V of 1944 Cooch Behar Vaccination Act. (Amendement.)	0	2	0
,, VI of 1944 The Cooch Behar Medical Act.	0	6	0
VII of 1944 Cooch Behar Opium Smoking Act.	0	2	0
VIII of 1944 Cooch Behar Arms Act.	0	6	0
Act IX of 1944 Cooch Behar Police (incitement to Disaffection) Act.	0	1	6
Act X of 1944 The Cow killing Temporary Amendment Act.	0	0	6
The Government of Cooch Behar Act (not for sale).			
Act No. I of 1945 Cooch Behar Income Tax (Amendment) Act.	0	1	0
,, II of 1945 Cooch Behar Excess Profit Tax (Amendment) Act.	0	1	0
,, III of 1945 Cooch Behar Special Excise Act.	0	6	0
,, IV of 1945 The Cooch Behar Land Encroachment Act.	0	4	0
,, V of 1945 The Cooch Behar Orphanage Act.	0	2	0
,, VI of 1945 The Cooch Behar Tea Cultivation Control Act.	0	2	0
,, VII of 1945 The Cooch Behar Penal Code (Amendment) Act.	0	1	0
,, VIII of 1945 The Cooch Behar Ferries Act.	0	4	0
,, IX of 1945 The Cooch Behar Stamp (Amendment) Act.	0	1	0
,, X of 1945 The Cooch Behar Food Adultaration (Amendment) Act.	0	1	0
,, XI of 1945 The Cooch Behar Chowkidari (Amendment) Act.	0	1	0
,, XII of 1945 The Cooch Behar Export Duty (Amendment) Act.	0	1	0
,, XIII of 1945 The Cooch Behar Criminal Procecure Code.	6	6	0
Live-stock Census Report 1945	0		0
Rules made under section 2 of the Agriculturists Loans Act (I of 1944)	0	4	0
,, made under section 9 of the Land Improvement Loans Act II of 1944	0	4	0
,, made under sections 5 and 26 of the Special Excise Act 1945	2	0	0
,, I of 1946 (Forest Act) ...	0	4	0
,, II of 1946 (C. B. Foreign Companies Act 1946)	0	2	0
,, III of 1946 (The C. B. Reciprocity Act 1946.	0	1	0
Act No. IV of 1946 (C. B. Criminal Procedure Code (Amend) Act 1946)	0	1	0
,, V of 1946 C. B. Factories (Amend) Act 1946,	0	1	0
,, VI of 1946 (C. B Patents (Amend) Act 1946.	0	1	0
Act No. VII of 1946 (C. B. Excise Act).	0	12	0
,, VIII of 1946 (C. B. Opium Act).	0	2	0
,, IX of 1946 (C. B. Dangerous Drugs Act).	0	7	0
,, X of 1946 (C. B. Excess Profits (Repealing) Act 1946).	0	1	0
,, XI of 1946 C. B, Ferries (Amend) Act 1946	0	1	0
,, XII of 1946 (The Industrial Statistics Act.).	0	1	0
,, XIII of 1946 (C B. Requisitioned Land Act.)	0	1	0
, XIV of 1946 (C. B. Essential Supplies Act).	0	2	0
,, XV of 1946 Requisitioned Land (Amendment) Act 1946.	0	1	6
,, XVI of 1946 (C. B. Aircraft Act). 1946.	0	2	0
,, I of 1947 (C. B. Essential Supplies (Tem. powers) Amendment 1947.	0	2	0

A. BAGCHI,
Superintendent, State Press, Cooch Behar.

NOTICES.

Applications are invited for the following posts. Applicants must be at least Matriculates.

Apply stating age, qualifications, past experience & with copies of testimonials & with Father's name, Home address (P.O., Village, P.S. & District), Present address and place of last residence.

Applications must reach the Chairman, Public Service Commission, Cooch Behar within the 30th July, 1947.

Vacancies.

Name of post.	Scale.
5th Master Baneswar M. E. School.	25-2½/2-35
4th Master Dewanhat „ „	Do
3rd Pundit, Natabari Model „	Do
3rd Mistress or Master Mekligunj Girls' M. E. School.	Do
2nd & 4th Master Nishimayee M. E. School	Do
3rd Master Gosanimari „ „	Do
2nd do Shoulmari „ „	Do
4th do Mamat Changrabandha „ „	Do
2nd & 4th Master Khetti „ „	Do
3rd Master Junglebosh „ „	Do
2nd do Dharmeswari „ „	Do
2nd Mistress or Master Tufangunj Girls' M. E.	Do
2nd Master Per-mekligunj M. E.	Do
2nd 3rd Master Shitalkhuchi „	Do
4th Master Balarampur „	Do
Head Master Shikarpur „	35-3/2-50-2-60
Do Krishnapur „	Do
Head Mistress or Master Tufangunj M. E.	Do

Applications are invited from suitable candidates for the post of Supervisor, Dinhata - Tufanganj Circle for Development Department, Cooch Behar on a scale pay of Rs. 60-5/2-80 plus the usual D. A. and interim special pay.

Preference will be given to one who has fair knowledge in Agriculture as well as some practical experience in this line.

Applications are invited for the post of a Mechanic in the transport Department on Rs. 80 in the scale of Rs. 80-4-100.

The post is temporary but likely to be permanent at the close of the year. Preference will be given to one who has thorough conversance in Motor Mechanism.

Apply stating age, qualification, past experience and with copies of testimonials if any and with Father's name, Home address (P. O., Vill., P. S. & District), present address and place of last residence.

Applications will be received by the Chairman, Public Service Commission, Cooch Behar up to the 30th July, 1947.

B. RAHAMAN,
Chairman,
Public Service Commission, Cooch Behar.

বিজ্ঞাপন

এতদ্বারা সর্বসাধারণকে জানান যাইতেছে যে কুচবিহার পুলিশ ফোর্সের জন্য বর্তমানে অস্থায়ী ভাবে একজন কুচবিহারি এসিষ্ট্যান্ট সাবইন্সপেক্টর ও দুই জন কনেষ্টবল লওয়া হইবে। আগামি ১৫ই আগষ্ট (১৯৪৭ ইং) মধ্যে যে কোন দিবসে বেলা ৮টা হইতে ১২টার মধ্যে প্রার্থীগণকে নির্বাচনের জন্য উপস্থিত হইতে হইবে।

এসিষ্ট্যান্ট সাবইন্সপেক্টরের বেতন ২৫-২/১-৫৫, ইহা ব্যতীত মাসিক প্রচলিত ডিয়ারনেস্ এলাউন্স পাইবেন এবং উপর পঞ্চ সাইকেলভাতা ৫, ও অতিরিক্ত বেতন ৬, ।

কনেষ্টবলগণের বেতন ১৮-১/২-২৫, ইহা ব্যতীত মাসিক প্রচলিত ডিয়ারনেস্ এলাউন্স ও অতিরিক্ত বেতন ৩, ।

এসিষ্ট্যান্ট সাব ইন্সপেক্টর অন্তত পক্ষে ম্যাট্রিকুলেশন পাশ হওয়া আবশ্যক এবং কনেষ্টবলের জন্য সাধারণ বাংলা লেখাপড়া জানা আবশ্যক। প্রার্থীদের লম্বা ন্যূন পক্ষে ৫ ফুট ৪ ইঞ্চি, ছাতি ৩১ ইঞ্চি ও বয়স ১৮ হইতে ২৫ বৎসর হওয়া আবশ্যক।

U. BISWAS,
for Commissioner of Police, Cooch Behar.

Registered No. C 1023

The Cooch Behar Gazette.

১৬ই শ্রাবণ শুক্রবার FRIDAY, AUGUST 1, 1947 [১৩৫৪ সাল ৪৩৮ রাজশক

PART V.

Advertisements

NOTICE.

It is hereby notified for general information that some packing boxes and batten papers will be sold by auction sale on Saturday the 9th August, 1947 at 2 P. M. in the State Press premises. The value of the articles will have to be desposited just after the the auction is over.

A. BAGCHI,
Controller of Stationery, Cooch Behar.

নোটিশ

এতদ্দ্বারা সর্ব্ব-সাধারণকে জানান যাইতেছে যে আগামী ৯ই আগষ্ট শনিবার বেলা ২ ঘটিকার সময় ষ্টেট প্রেসের বারান্দায় কতকগুলি প্যাকিং বাক্স এবং তিন বাঁধার বেটেন কাগজ নিলাম হইবে। ডাক শেষের অব্যবহিত পরেই জিনিষের দাম জমা দিতে হইবে। ইতি।

এ. বাগচি।
কণ্ট্রোলার অব ষ্টেশনারী,
কোচবিহার।

NOTICE.

Applications are invited from female candidates for posts of Probationer Trainee Nurses at the Maharaja Jitendra Narayan Hospital. The course is for 3 years and will commence on the 1st October 1947. The Candidates will receive a stipend of Rs. 30 per mensem. They should be between the ages of 18 and 25 years and must have read up to Class VIII of the Matriculation standard. This may be relaxed in the case of suitable candidates. Cooch Behari candidates are preferred. Applications in candidates' own handwriting should reach the undersigned on or before the 25th August 1947.

বিজ্ঞাপন

এজন্য শ্রী মহারাজা জিতেন্দ্র-নারায়ণ হাসপাতালে নার্স এর কার্য্যে শিক্ষালাভ করিবার জন্য মহিলাদিগের নিকট হইতে দরখাস্ত আহ্বান করা যাইতেছে। আগামী ১লা অক্টোবর হইতে ঐ বিষয়ে ক্লাস আরম্ভ হইবে এবং দরখাস্তকারিণীদিগকে তিন বৎসর শিক্ষা গ্রহণ করিতে হইবে। শিক্ষাধীন কালে তাঁহারা মাসিক ৩০৲ টাকা হিসাবে ভাতা পাইবেন। শিক্ষার্থিনীগণের ম্যাট্রিকুলেশন ষ্ট্যাণ্ডার্ডের অষ্টম মান (Class VIII) পর্য্যন্ত শিক্ষালাভ যোগ্যতা আবশ্যক এবং ট্রেনিং ক্লাস আরম্ভের সময় তাঁহাদের বয়স ১৮-২৫ বৎসর প্রয়োজন। বিশেষ ক্ষেত্রে বয়সের বাধা বর্জ্জিত হইবে না এবং কোচবিহারী প্রার্থিনীদিগকে অগ্রগণ্য বলিয়া বিবেচিত হইবে। শিক্ষার্থিনীগণ স্বহস্তে দরখাস্ত লিখিয়া নিম্নস্বাক্ষরকারীর নিকট ২৫।৮।৪৭ তারিখের পূর্ব্বে দরখাস্ত করুন।

S. C. CHATTERJEE,
Chief Medical Officer & Secretary,
Medical & Public Health Departments,
Cooch Behar.

List of State Acts, Laws and Codes for sale in the State Press, Cooch Behar.

	Rs.	A.	P.
Act of 1874 Limitation (English)* ...	0	12	0
" Ditto (Bengali) ...	0	12	0
" of 1882 Cattle Trespass* " ...	0	2	0
মুদ্রিত কাগজ সম্বন্ধীয় নিয়মাবলী ...	0	2	0
Act of 1888 Sub-infeudation* ...	0	1	0
" I of 1890 লোক সংখ্যা গ্রহণ বিষয়ক আইন	0	0	6
" I of 1892 Private Fisheries Protection (English and Bengali combined.)	0	1	0
" II of 1892 Amendment of Limitation (Engish and Bengali combined.)	0	1	0
" III of 1892 Jurisdiction (English)*	0	1	0
" Ditto (Bengali)*	0	1	0
" IV 1892 Merchandise Marks (Eng.)*	0	2	0
" I of 1893 Legal Practitioners " *	0	1	3
" Ditto ditto (Bengali)	0	1	0
" II of 1893 Amendment of Town Committee (English).	0	0	3
" III of 1893 Village Chowkidari (English)	0	1	6
" IV of 1893 Amendment of Revenue Sale (English).	0	0	3
" IV of 1893 Amendment Revenue Sale (Bengali)	0	0	3
" V of 1893 Cess (English)	0	1	0
" Ditto (Bengali)	0	1	0
" VI of 1893 Amendment of Legal Practitioners (English and Bengali combined.)*	0	0	3
" I of 1894 Amendment of Town Committee.*	0	0	3
" II of 1894 Amendment of Voluntary Sale of under-tenures.	0	0	3
" III of 1894 Amendment of Village Chowkidari.*	0	0	6
" I of 1895 Small Cause Courts Act (English).	0	0	9
" I of 1896 Amendment of Cooch Behar Stamp Act (English).*	0	0	3
" I of 1896 Amendment of Cooch Behar Stamp Act (Bengali).*	0	0	3
" II of 1896 Preservation of Boundary Act (English).	0	0	6
" III of 1896 Amendment of Village Chowkidari Act (English).	0	0	3
" I of 1897 Amendment of Cooch Behar Town Committee Act (Eng.)	0	0	3
" II of 1897 Mahomedan Inheritance Act (English).	0	0	3
" III of 1897 Oaths Act (English)*	0	0	6
" IV of 1897 Amendment of Stamp rules (English.)	0	0	3
" V of 1897 Revenue Sale Act (English).	0	3	0
" V of 1897 Revenue Sale Act (Bengali).	0	3	0
" VI of 1897 Wards Act (English)	0	1	0
" I of 1898 Kist Act "	0	0	
" Ditto (Bengali)	0	0	
" II of 1898 Amendment of Revenue Sale Act (English).	0	0	
" Ditto (Bengali)	0	0	3
" III of 1898 Police Act (English)	0	2	0
" Ditto (Bengali.)	0	2	0

	Rs.	A.	
Act IV of 1898 Bridge Toll Act (Eng.)	0	0	6
" of Ditto ditto (Bengali)	0	0	6
" V of 1898 Succession Certificate Act (English)	0	2	0
" Ditto ditto (Bengali)	0	2	0
" VI of 1898 Amendment of Voluntary Sales of under-tenures (Eng.)	0	0	9
" Ditto ditto (Bengali)	0	0	9
" VII of 1898 Amendment of Village Chowkidari Act (English)	0	0	3
" Ditto ditto (Bengali)	0	0	3
" VIII of 1898 Revenue Sales Act "	0	0	3
" Ditto (English)	0	0	3
" I of 1899 Cow Killing Act "	0	0	3
" Ditto (Bengali)	0	0	3
" II of 1899 Public Demands Recovery Act (Eng.)	0	3	0
" Ditto ditto (Bengali)	0	3	0
" III of 1899 Amendment of Limitation Act (English)	0	0	3
" Ditto ditto (Bengali)	0	0	3
" IV of 1899 State Demands Act (English and Bengali combined).	0	0	6
" V of 1899 Civil Marriage Act Eng.)	0	1	6
" Ditto ditto (Bengali)	0	1	6
" I of 1900 Amendment of Civil Procedure Code (English)	0	2	0
" II of 1900 Census Act (English)	0	1	3
" Ditto ditto (Bengali)	0	1	0
" I of 1901 C. B. Telegraph Act "	0	1	0
" I of 1903 C. B. Stamp Act (Eng.)	0	6	0
" Ditto Ditto (Beng.)	0	6	
" II of 1903 Drainage Act (Eng.)	0	0	6
" Ditto (Bengali)	0	0	6
" III of 1903 Amendment of Cooch Behar Limitation Act (English).	0	1	6
" Ditto (Bengali)	0	1	6
Act IV of 1903 C. B. Town Committee Act (English).	0	6	0
V of 1903 Amendment of Civil Procedure Code.	0	1	6
" VI of 1903 Vaccination Act (Eng)*	0	2	0
" Ditto Ditto (Beng.)	0	2	0
Act I of 1904 Registration Act (Eng.)	0	0	6
" II of 1904 Amendment of Village Chowkidari (Eng.)	0	1	0
" Ditto Ditto (Beng.)	0	1	0
" I of 1905 Amendment of Stamp Act (English).	0	0	6
" II of 1905 Unclaimed Intestate Property.	0	0	6
" I of 1906 Encumbered Estate Act (English)	0	0	6
" II of 1906 Companies Act (English).	0	1	0
" III of 1906 Evidence Act Amendment	0	0	6
" IV of 1906 Amendment of Village Chaukidari Act.	0	0	6
" V of 1906 Small Cause Court Act (English)	0	3	0
" VI of 1906 Wills Act (English)	0	0	3
" VII of 1906 Probate and Administration Act	0	0	6

* Out of stock.

	Rs.	A.	P.
Act I of 1907 Amendment Town Committee Act.	0	0	6
„ II of 1907 Succession Act (English).	0	0	6
„ III of 1907 Amendment Vaccination Act (Bengali).	0	1	0
„ IV of 1907 Penal Code Act ...	0	0	6
„ I of 1908 Amendment of Stamp Act.	0	1	0
„ II of 1908 Forest Act ...	0	2	0
„ I of 1909 The Code of Criminal Procedure.	0	2	0
„ II of 1909 Act for the Legislative Council.	0	0	6
„ I of 1910 Registration of Births and Deaths (English).	0	1	0
Ditto (Bengali)	0	1	0
„ II of 1910 Amendment of Succession Certificate Act.	0	1	0
„ III of 1910 Provisions for the care of lunatics.	0	0	6
Act IV of 1910 Census Act (Eng. & Beng)	0	1	0
Act V of 1910 Tenancy Act (English)	0	8	0
„ V „ „ (Bengali)	0	11	0
„ I of 1913 Survey „ Eng.)	0	2	0
„ „ „ „ (Beng.)	0	3	0
Letters and Proceedings having the force of Law.	0	10	0
Law Reports Vol. I*	0	8	0
„ Vol. II*	2	4	0
„ Vol. III	1	0	0
Law Report Vol IV (1911—Jan. 1314)	0	12	0
Vol. V (Mar. 1914-Dec. 1920)	0	8	0
Law Report Vol. VI.	0	12	0
„ Vol. VII	0	12	0
Act I of 1920 Census Act (Eng.)	0	2	0
„ „ „ (Beng)	0	2	0
„ I of 1921 General Clauses Act	0	4	0
„ II „ Code of Civil Procedure Act.	0	5	0
„ III „ Transfer of Property „	0	2	0
„ IV „ Limitation Act ...	0	8	0
„ V „ Majority „ ...	0	2	0
„ VI „ Registration „ ...	0	2	0
„ VII „ Guardians and Wards Act.	0	2	0
„ VIII „ Negotiable instruments Act.	0	2	0
„ IX „ Criminal Tribes Act	0	3	0
„ X „ Interest „	0	2	0
„ XI „ Suits Valuations „	0	2	0
„ XII „ Bankers' Books evidence (amendment.)	0	1	0
„ I of 1923 Regulation E.B.R. Arbitration.	0	1	0
„ I of 1923 Excise, Opium & Drugs	0	5	0
„ I of 1929 (amending the Cooch Behar Town Committee Act IV of 1902)	0	1	0
„ I of 1930 Criminal Law (amendt.)	0	1	0
„ II „ Census Act ...	0	2	0
„ III „ Co-operative Societies Act	0	4	0
„ III „ 1930 „ (Sec. 43) ...	0	3	0
„ I of 1931 Christian Marriage Act	0	1	0
„ I of 1932 Motor Vehicles Act	0	2	0
Act I of 1933 Cooch Behar Penal Code Amendment Act.	0	0	3

	Rs.	A.	P.
Act II of 1933 Cooch Behar Companies Act.	0	2	0
„ III of 1933 Code of Criminal Procedure.	0	4	0
„ I of 1934 The Lepers Act ...	0	2	0
„ III of 1934 Cooch Behar Revenue Sale Amendment Act.	0	1	0
Act No. IV of 1934 Hindu widow Marriage Act (Eng. & Beng).	0	1	0
„ I of 1935 Cooch Behar Matches (Excise Duty) Act.	0	2	0
„ I of 1937 Cooch Behar Hat toll protection Act.	0	0	6
Act II of 1937 Act for Prevention of Cruelty to Animals.	0	6	0
„ I of 1938 C.B. Public gambling Act	0	2	0
„ II of 1938 C.B. Amusement Tax Act	0	2	0
„ I of 1939 Amendment of C.B.T.C.	0	0	6
Act I of 1940 Census Act... ...	0	2	0
„ II of 1940 C. B. Penal Code Amendment Act.	0	0	6
„ I of 1941 Amendment of C. B. Tenancy Act.	0	0	6
„ II of 1941 C. B. Food Adulteration	0	3	0
„ III of 1941 Legislative Council Act	0	2	0
„ IV of 1941 C. B. Electricity Act	0	4	0
Act V of 1941 C. B. Income Tax Act	0	8	0
„ VI of 1941 C. B. Export Duty Act	0	1	0
Act VII of 1941 Motor Vehicles	1	0	0
„ VIII of 1941 Village choukidary Amendment	0	2	0
„ IX of 1941 Town Committee Amendment	0	1	0
„ X of 1941 General Amending	0	6	0
„ XI of 1941 Cow killing Amendment	0	0	3
„ XII of 1941 Tenancy (second Amend.) Act No. XII of 1941	0	0	3
„ I of 1942 Standard of weight	0	1	0
„ II of 1942 foreigner's Act	0	1	0
„ III of 1942 Penal Code Act	2	12	0
„ IV of 1942 Companies (Amend)	0	1	0
„ V of 1942 Public Demands recovery (Amend)	0	1	0
„ VI of 1942 Incometax (Amend)	0	1	0
Act VII of 1942 (An Act to Amend the C. B. General Clauses Act I of 1921	0	0	6
„ VIII of 1942 (Transfer of Property Amendment) Act 1942	0	1	0
„ IX of 1942 (C. B. Registration Amendment) Act 1942	0	0	6
„ X of 1942 (C. B. Limitation Amendment) Act 1942	0	1	0
„ No. XI of 1942 (C. B. Town Committee) Amendment Act	0	0	6
Live Stock Census Report	0	4	0
Schedule of rates*	2	8	0
Cottage Industry	2	0	0
History of Cooch Behar (Paper bound) Bengali	2	0	0
Do Do (cloth bound)	3	0	0
Hand Book of Circular orders	2	0	0
History of Cooch Behar (English version)	5	0	0

* Out of stock.

	Rs.	A.	P.
Act I of 1943 Legal Practitioners Act	0	4	0
„ II of 1943 Stamp Act ...	0	14	0
„ III of 1943 Excess Profits Tax Act	0	6	0
„ IV of 1943 Patents Act	0	4	0
„ V of 1943 Public Health Act ...	0	3	0
„ VI of 1943 (An Act to provide for the Prevention and Control of Contagious deseases affecting Animals.)	0	2	0
„ VII of 1943 Army Act ...	0	8	0
„ VIII of 1943 Workmen's Compensation Act.	0	1	0
„ IX of 1943 Factories Act ...	0	1	0
„ X of 1943 Public Demand Recovery Act.	1	12	0
„ XI of 1943 Civil Procedure Code (amendment) Act.	0	2	0
„ XII of 1943 Pension (Exemption) Act.	0	0	6
„ XIII of 1943 Insolvency Act ...	0	8	0
„ XIV of 1943 Succession Act ...	0	1	0
„ XV of 1943 Extradition Act ...	0	3	0
„ XVI of 1943 Muli (Regulating) Act	0	0	6
„ XVII of 1943 Interest (amendment) Act.	0	0	6
„ XVIII of 1943 Revenue sale (amendment) Act.	0	0	6
„ XIX of 1943 Land Acquisition Act	0	4	0
„ XX of 1943 Forest (amendment) Act.	0	0	6
Act XXI of 1943 Tenancy (amendment) Act 1943.	0	6	0
Act XXII of 1943 Coch Behar Co-operation Societies Act 1943.	0	2	0
Act XXIII of 1943 Village Chaukidary (amendment).	0	1	0
Act XXIV of 1943 Cooch Behar Incometax (amendment) Act 1943.	0	1	0
Act XXV of 1943 Tobacco (Excise Duty) Act.	0	3	0
Act XXVI of 1943 Bengal and Assam Railway Arbitration Act.	0	2	0
Table of rates of Advalorem Fees laviable on the institution of Suits under the Cooch Behar Stamp Act II of 1943.	0	2	0
Rules made under section 52 of the Income-tax Act 1941.	0	2	0
Lives-stock Census Report	0	4	0
Act II of 1921 (as amended up to Cooch Behar Civil procedure 1921 (Cooch Behar State).	0	5	0
Cooch Behar Tenancy Act, Act V of 1910 (as amended upto 1943) Cooch Behar State.	0	11	0
Act I of 1944 Cooch Beher Agriculturists' Loans Act.	0	0	6
„ II of 1944 Cooch Behar Land Improvement Loans Act.	0	2	0
„ III of 1944 Cooch Behar Municipal Act	1	8	0
„ IV of 1944 C. B. Prevention of Cruelty to Animals Act. (Amendament.)	0	2	6
„ V of 1944 Cooch Behar Vaccination Act. (Amendement.)	0	2	0
„ VI of 1944 The Cooch Behar Medical Act.	0	6	0
VII of 1944 Cooch Behar Opium Smoking Act.	0	2	0
VIII of 1944 Cooch Behar Arms Act.	0	6	0

	Rs.	A.	P.
Act IX of 1944 Cooch Behar Police (incitement to Disaffection) Act.	0	1	6
Act X of 1944 The Cow killing Temporary Amendment Act.	0	0	6
The Government of Cooch Behar Act (not for sale).			
Act No. I of 1945 Cooch Behar Income Tax (Amendment) Act.	0	1	0
„ II of 1945 Cooch Behar Excess Profit Tax (Amendment) Act	0	1	0
„ III of 1945 Cooch Behar Specia Excise Act.	0	6	0
„ IV of 1945 The Cooch Behar Land Encroachment Act	0	4	0
„ V of 1945 The Cooch Behar Orphanage Act.	0	2	0
„ VI of 1945 The Cooch Behar Tea Cultivation Control Act.	0	2	0
„ VII of 1945 The Cooch Behar Penal Code (Amendment) Act.	0	1	0
„ VIII of 1945 The Cooch Behar Ferries Act.	0	4	0
„ IX of 1945 The Cooch Behar Stamp (Amendment) Act.	0	1	0
„ X of 1945 The Cooch Behar Food Adultaration (Amendment) Act.	0	1	0
„ XI of 1945 The Cooch Behar Chowkidari (Amendment) Act.	0	1	0
„ XII of 1945 The Cooch Behar Export Duty (Amendment) Act.	0	1	0
„ XIII of 1945 The Cooch Behar Criminal Procecure Code.	1	6	0
Live-stock Census Report 1945	0	4	0
Rules made under section 2 of the Agriculturists Loans Act (I of 1944)	0	4	0
„ made under section 9 of the Land Improvement Loans Act II of 1944	0	4	0
„ made under sections 5 and 26 of the Special Excise Act 1945	2	0	0
„ I of 1946 (Forest Act) ...	0	4	0
„ II of 1946 (C. B. Foreign Companies Act 1946)	0	2	0
„ III of 1946 (The C. B. Reciprocity Act 1946.	0	1	0
Act No. IV of 1946 (C. B. Criminal Procedure Code (Amend) Act 1946)	0	1	0
„ V of 1946 C. B. Factories (Amend) Act 1946,	0	1	0
„ VI of 1946 (C. B Patents (Amend) Act 1946.	0	1	0
Act No. VII of 1946 (C. B. Excise Act).	0	12	0
„ VIII of 1946 (C. B. Opium Act).	0	2	0
„ IX of 1946 (C. B. Dangerous Drugs Act).	0	7	0
„ X of 1946 (C. B. Excess Profits (Repealing) Act 1946).	0	1	0
„ XI of 1946 C. B. Ferries (Amend) Act 1946	0	1	0
„ XII of 1946 (The Industrial statistics Act.)	0	1	0
„ XIII of 1946 (C B. Requisitioned Land Act.)	0	1	
„ XIV of 1946 (C. B. Essential Supplies Act).	0	2	0
„ XV of 1946 (Requisitioned Land (Amendment) Act 1946.	0	1	0
„ XVI of 1946 (C. B. Aircraft Act). 1946.	0	2	0
„ I of 1947 (C. B. Essential Supplies (Tem. powers) Amendment 1947.	0	2	0

A. BAGCHI,
Superintendent, State Press, Cooch Behar.

The Cooch Behar Gazette.

২রা ভাদ্র মঙ্গলবার] TUESDAY, AUGUST 19, 1947. [১৩৫৪ সাল, ৪৩৮...

PART V.

Advertisements

NOTICE.

Tenders are invited for supply of Bazar materials for the use of the Public Works Department for the period from 1st October, 1947 to 31st March, 1948. The name of articles, units of measurements & rates are to be clearly and legibly written serially according to the present schedule. The tenders are to be submitted to this office in sealed covers at or before 15th September, 1947.

The selected tenderer will have to stock all materials of approved quality to be delivered at the shortest notice.

The undersigned does not bind himself to accept the lowest or any other tender.

Any quotation as Market Rate will not be accepted.

S. Stern,
Chief Engineer, P. W. D.,
Cooch Behar

বিজ্ঞাপন :

কোচবিহার মোকাম চাঙ্গারাবান্ধা ৺যদুনাথ সিদ্ধান্তের পুত্র শ্রীযুক্ত উপেন্দ্রনাথ সিদ্ধান্ত মহাশয়কে আমরা আমমোক্তার নিযুক্ত করিয়াছিলাম, গত আষাঢ় মাস হইতে তাঁহাকে কার্য্য হইতে অপসারিত করা হইয়াছে এতদ্দ্বারা তাহার আমমোক্তারনামা খারিজ করা হইল, অত পর তাহার কার্য্যের আমরা কোন রূপে দায়ী হইব না। ইতি—১৩৫৪ সাল তারিখ ২ শে শ্রাবণ

বালচাঁদ ওসোয়াল
দেওচাঁদ ওসোয়াল
কারম পক্ষে আমমোক্তার
শ্রীহুকুমচাঁদ ওসোয়াল
সাং চাঙ্গারাবান্ধা।

জমি বিক্রয় !

নিউটাউনের পাকা রাস্তার ধারে ১১½ কাঠা জমি বিক্রয় হইবে। ক্রয়েচ্ছু ব্যক্তি নিম্নঠিকানায় অনুসন্ধান করুন।

শ্রীতারাপদ বন্দ্যোপাধ্যায়।
হেড ক্লার্ক, ষ্টেটপ্রেস, কুচবিহার।

List of State Acts, Laws and Codes for sale in the State Press, Cooch Behar.

	Rs.	A.	P.
Act of 1874 Limitation (English)* ...	0	12	0
" Ditto (Bengali) ...	0	12	0
" of 1882 Cattle Trespass* ,, ...	0	2	0
মুদ্রিত কাগজ সম্বন্ধীয় নিয়মাবলী ...	0	2	0
Act of 1888 Sub-infeudation* ...	0	1	0
" I of 1890 লোক সংখ্যা গ্রহণ বিষয়ক আইন	0	0	6
" I of 1892 Private Fisheries Protection (English and Bengali combined.)	0	1	0
" II of 1892 Amendment of Limitation (Engish and Bengali combined.)	0	1	0
" III of 1892 Jurisdiction (English)*	0	1	0
" Ditto (Bengali)*	0	1	0
" IV 1892 Merchandise Marks (Eng.)*	0	2	0
" I of 1893 Legal Practitioners ,, *	0	1	3
" Ditto ditto (Bengali)	0	1	0
" II of 1893 Amendment of Town Committee (English).	0	0	[illegible]
" III of 1893 Village Chowkidari (English)	0	1	6
" IV of 1893 Amendment of Revenue Sale (English).	0	0	3
" IV of 1893 Amendment Revenue Sale (Bengali)	0	0	3
" V of 1893 Cess (English)	0	1	0
" Ditto (Bengali)	0	1	0
" VI of 1893 Amendment of Legal Practitioners (English and Bengali combined.)*	0	0	3
" I of 1894 Amendment of Town Committee.*	0	0	3
" II of 1894 Amendment of Voluntary Sale of under-tenures.	0	0	3
" III of 1894 Amendment of Village Chowkidari.*	0	0	6
" I of 1895 Small Cause Courts Act (English).	0	0	9
" I of 1896 Amendment of Cooch Behar Stamp Act (English).*	0	0	3
" I of 1896 Amendment of Cooch Behar Stamp Act (Bengali).*	0	0	3
" II of 1896 Preservation of Boundary Act (English).	0	0	6
" III of 1896 Amendment of Village Chowkidari Act (English).	0	0	3
" I of 1897 Amendment of Cooch Behar Town Committee Act (Eng.)	0	0	3
" II of 1897 Mahomedan Inheritance Act (English).	0	0	3
" III of 1897 Oaths Act (English)*	0	0	6
IV of 1897 Amendment of Stamp rules (English.)	0	0	3
" V of 1897 Revenue Sale Act (English).	0	3	0
" V of 1897 Revenue Sale Act (Bengali).	0	3	0
" VI of 1897 Wards Act (English)	0	1	0
" I of 1898 Kist Act ,,	0	0	
" Ditto (Bengali)	0	0	
" II of 1898 Amendment of Revenue Sale Act (English).	0	0	
" Ditto (Bengali)	0	0	3
" III of 1898 Police Act (English)	0	2	0
" Ditto (Bengali.)	0	2	0

	Rs.	A.	
Act IV of 1898 Bridge Toll Act (Eng.)	0	0	6
" of Ditto ditto (Bengali)	0	0	6
" V of 1898 Succession Certificate Act (English)	0	2	0
" Ditto ditto (Bengali)	0	2	0
" VI of 1898 Amendment of Voluntary Sales of under-tenures (Eng.)	0	0	9
" Ditto ditto (Bengali)	0	0	9
" VII of 1898 Amendment of Village Chowkidari Act (English)	0	0	3
" Ditto ditto (Bengali)	0	0	3
" VIII of 1898 Revenue Sales Act ,,	0	0	3
" Ditto (English)	0	0	3
" I of 1899 Cow Killing Act ,,	0	0	3
" Ditto (Bengali)	0	0	3
" II of 1899 Public Demands Recovery Act (Eng.)	0	3	0
" Ditto ditto (Bengali)	0	3	
" III of 1899 Amendment of Limitation Act (English)	0	0	3
" Ditto ditto (Bengali)	0	0	3
" IV of 1899 State Demands Act (English and Bengali combined)	0	0	6
" V of 1899 Civil Marriage Act (Eng.)	0	1	6
" Ditto ditto (Bengali)	0	1	6
" I of 1900 Amendment of Civil Procedure Code (English)	0	2	0
" II of 1900 Census Act (English)	0	1	3
" Ditto ditto (Bengali)	0	1	0
" I of 1901 C. B. Telegraph Act ,,	0	1	0
" I of 1903 C. B. Stamp Act (Eng.)	0	6	0
" Ditto Ditto (Beng.)	0	6	0
" II of 1903 Drainage Act (Eng.)	0	0	6
" Ditto (Bengali)	0	0	6
" III of 1903 Amendment of Cooch Behar Limitation Act (English).	0	1	6
" Ditto (Bengali)	0	1	6
Act IV of 1903 C. B. Town Committee Act (English).	0	6	0
V of 1903 Amendment of Civil Procedure Code.	0	1	6
" VI of 1903 Vaccination Act (Eng)*	0	2	0
" Ditto Ditto (Beng.)	0	2	0
Act I of 1904 Registration Act (Eng.)	0	0	6
" II of 1904 Amendment of Village Chowkidari (Eng.)	0	1	0
" Ditto Ditto (Beng.)	0	1	0
" I of 1905 Amendment of Stamp Act (English).	0	0	6
" II of 1905 Unclaimed Intestate Property.	0	0	6
" I of 1906 Encumbered Estate Act (English)	0	0	6
" II of 1906 Companies Act (English).	0	1	0
" III of 1906 Evidence Act Amendment	0	0	6
" IV of 1906 Amendment of Village Chaukidari Act.	0	0	6
" V of 1906 Small Cause Court Act (English)	0	3	0
" VI of 1906 Wills Act (English)	0	0	3
" VII of 1906 Probate and Administration Act	0	0	6

* Out of stock.

	Rs.	A.	P.
Act I of 1907 Amendment Town Committee Act.	0	0	6
,, II of 1907 Succession Act (English).	0	0	6
,, III of 1907 Amendment Vaccination Act (Bengali).	0	1	0
,, IV of 1907 Penal Code Act ...	0	0	6
,, I of 1908 Amendment of Stamp Act.	0	1	0
,, II of 1908 Forest Act ...	0	2	0
,, I of 1909 The Code of Criminal Procedure.	0	2	0
,, II of 1909 Act for the Legislative Council.	0	0	6
,, I of 1910 Registration of Births and Deaths (English).	0	1	0
Ditto (Bengali)	0	1	0
,, II of 1910 Amendment of Succession Certificate Act.	0	1	0
,, III of 1910 Provisions for the care of lunatics.	0	0	6
Act IV of 1910 Census Act (Eng. & Beng)	0	1	0
Act V of 1910 Tenancy Act (English)	0	8	0
,, V ,, ,, (Bengali)	0	11	0
,, I of 1913 Survey ,, Eng.)	0	2	0
,, ,, ,, (Beng.)	0	-	0
Letters and Proceedings having the force of Law.	0	10	0
Law Reports Vol. I*	0	8	0
,, Vol. II*	2	4	0
,, Vol. III	1	0	0
Law Report Vol IV (1911—Jan. 1314)	0	12	0
Vol. V (Mar. 1914-Dec. 1920)	0	8	0
Law Report Vol. VI.	0	12	0
,, Vol. VII	0	12	0
Act I of 1920 Census Act (Eng.)	0	2	0
,, ,, ,, (Beng.)	0	[illegible]	[illegible]
,, I of 1921 General Clauses Act	0	4	0
,, II ,, Code of Civil Procedure Act.	0	5	0
,, III ,, Transfer of Property ,,	0	2	0
,, IV ,, Limitation Act ...	0	3	0
,, V ,, Majority ,, ...	0	2	0
,, VI ,, Registration ,, ...	0	2	0
,, VII ,, Guardians and Wards Act.	0	2	0
,, VIII ,, Negotiable instruments Act.	0	2	0
,, IX ,, Criminal Tribes Act	0	3	0
,, X ,, Interest ,,	0	2	0
,, XI ,, Suits Valuations ,,	0	2	0
,, XII ,, Bankers' Books evidence (amendment.)	0	1	0
,, I of 1923 Regulation E.B.R. Arbitration.	0	1	0
,, I of 1923 Excise, Opium & Drugs	0	5	0
,, I of 1929 (amending the Cooch Behar Town Committee Act IV of 1907)	0	1	0
,, I of 1930 Criminal Law (amendt.)	0	1	0
,, II ,, Census Act ...	0	2	0
,, III ,, Co-operative Societies Act	0	4	0
,, III ,, 1930 ,, (Sec. 43) ...	0	3	0
,, I of 1931 Christian Marriage Act	0	1	0
,, I of 1932 Motor Vehicles Act	0	2	0
Act I of 1933 Cooch Behar Penal Code Amendment Act.	0	0	3

	Rs.	A.	P.
Act II of 1933 Cooch Behar Companies Act.	0	2	0
,, III of 1933 Code of Criminal Procedure.	0	4	0
,, I of 1934 The Lepers Act ...	0	2	0
,, III of 1934 Cooch Behar Revenue Sale Amendment Act.	0	1	0
Act No. IV of 1934 Hindu widow Marriage Act (Eng. & Beng).	0	1	0
,, I of 1935 Cooch Behar Matches (Excise Duty) Act.	0	2	0
,, I of 1937 Cooch Behar Hat toll protection Act.	0	0	6
Act II of 1937 Act for Prevention of Cruelty to Animals.	0	6	0
,, I of 1938 C.B. Public gambling Act	0	2	0
,, II of 1938 C.B. Amusement Tax Act	0	2	0
,, I of 1939 Amendment of C.B.T.C.	0	0	6
Act I of 1940 Census Act... ...	0	2	0
,, II of 1940 C. B. Penal Code Amendment Act.	0	0	6
,, I of 1941 Amendment of C. B. Tenancy Act.	0	0	6
,, II of 1941 C. B. Food Adulteration	0	3	0
,, III of 1941 Legislative Council Act	0	2	0
,, IV of 1941 C. B. Electricity Act	0	4	0
Act V of 1941 C. B. Income Tax Act	0	8	0
,, VI of 1941 C. B. Export Duty Act	0	1	0
Act VII of 1941 Motor Vehicles	1	0	0
,, VIII of 1941 Village choukidary Amendment	0	2	0
,, IX of 1941 Town Committee Amendment	0	1	0
,, X of 1941 General Amending	0	6	0
,, XI of 1941 Cow killing Amendment	0	0	3
,, XII of 1941 Tenancy (second Amend.) Act No XII of 1941	0	0	3
,, I of 1942 Standard of weight	0	1	0
,, II of 1942 foreigner's Act	0	1	0
,, III of 1942 Penal Code Act	2	12	0
,, IV of 1942 Companies (Amend)	0	1	0
,, V of 1942 Public Demands recovery (Amend)	0	1	0
,, VI of 1942 Incometax (Amend)	0	1	0
Act VII of 1942 (An Act to Amend the C. B. General Clauses Act I of 1921	0	0	6
,, VIII of 1942 (Transfer of Property Amendment) Act 1942	0	1	0
,, IX of 1942 (C. B. Registration Amendment) Act 1942	0	0	6
,, X of 1942 (C. B. Limitation Amendment) Act 1942	0	1	0
,, No. XI of 1942 (C. B. Town Committee) Amendment Act	0	0	6
Live Stock Census Report	0	4	0
Schedule of rates*	2	8	0
Cottage Industry	2	0	0
History of Cooch Behar (Paper bound) Bengali	2	0	0
Do Do (cloth bound)	3	0	0
Hand Book of Circular orders	2	0	0
History of Cooch Behar (Englsh version)	5	0	0

* Out of stock.

	Rs.	A.	P.
Act I of 1943 Legal Practitioners Act	0	4	0
,, II of 1943 Stamp Act ...	0	14	0
,, III of 1943 Excess Profits Tax Act	0	6	0
,, IV of 1943 Patents Act ...	0	4	0
,, V of 1943 Public Health Act ...	0	3	0
,, VI of 1943 (An Act to provide for the Prevention and Control of Contagious deseases affecting Animals.)	0	2	0
,, VII of 1943 Army Act ...	0	8	0
,, VIII of 1943 Workmen's Compensation Act.	0	1	0
,, IX of 1943 Factories Act ...	0	1	0
,, X of 1943 Public Demand Recovery Act	1	12	0
,, XI of 1943 Civil Procedure Code (amendment) Act.	0	2	0
,, XII of 1943 Pension (Exemption) Act.	0	0	6
,, XIII of 1943 Insolvency Act ...	0	8	0
,, XIV of 1943 Succession Act ...	0	1	0
,, XV of 1943 Extradition Act ...	0	3	0
,, XVI of 1943 Muli (Regulating) Act	0	0	6
,, XVII of 1943 Interest (amendment) Act.	0	0	6
,, XVIII of 1943 Revenue sale (amendment) Act.	0	0	6
,, XIX of 1943 Land Acquisition Act	0	4	0
,, XX of 1943 Forest (amendment) Act.	0	0	6
Act XXI of 1943 Tenancy (amendment) Act 1943.	0	6	0
Act XXII of 1943 Coch Behar Co-operation Societies Act 1943.	0	2	0
Act XXIII of 1943 Village Chaukidary (amendment).	0	1	0
Act XXIV of 1943 Cooch Behar Incometax (amendment) Act 1943.	0	1	0
Act XXV of 1943 Tobacco (Excise Duty) Act.	0	3	0
Act XXVI of 1943 Bengal and Assam Railway Arbitration Act.	0	2	0
Table of rates of Advalorem Fees laviable on the institution of Suits under the Cooch Behar Stamp Act II of 1943.	0	2	0
Rules made under section 52 of the Income-tax Act 1941.	0	2	0
Lives-stock Census Report	0	4	0
Act II of 1921 (as amended up to Cooch Behar Civil procedure 1921 (Cooch Behar State).	0	5	0
Cooch Behar Tenancy Act, Act V of 1910 (as amended upto 1943) Cooch Behar State.	0	11	0
Act I of 1944 Cooch Beher Agriculturists' Loans Act.	0	0	6
,, II of 1944 Cooch Behar Land Improvement Loans Act.	0	2	0
,, III of 1944 Cooch Behar Municipal Act	1	8	0
,, IV of 1944 C. B. Prevention of Cruelty to Animals Act. (Amendement.)	0	2	6
V of 1944 Cooch Behar Vaccination Act. (Amendement.)	0	2	0
,, VI of 1944 The Cooch Behar Medical Act.	0	6	0
VII of 1944 Cooch Behar Opium Smoking Act.	0	2	0
VIII of 1944 Cooch Behar Arms Act.	0	6	0
Act IX of 1944 Cooch Behar Police (incitement to Disaffection) Act.	0	1	6

	Rs.	A.	P.
Act X of 1944 The Cow killing Temporary Amendment Act.	0	0	6
The Government of Cooch Behar Act (not for sale).			
Act No. I of 1945 Cooch Behar Income Tax (Amendment) Act.	0	1	0
,, II of 1945 Cooch Behar Excess Profit Tax (Amendment) Act.	0	1	0
,, III of 1945 Cooch Behar Specia Excise Act.	0	6	0
,, IV of 1945 The Cooch Behar Land Encroachment Act.	0	4	0
,, V of 1945 The Cooch Behar Orphanage Act.	0	2	0
,, VI of 1945 The Cooch Behar Tea Cultivation Control Act.	0	2	0
,, VII of 1945 The Cooch Behar Penal Code (Amendment) Act.	0	1	0
,, VIII of 1945 The Cooch Behar Ferries Act.	0	4	0
,, IX of 1945 The Cooch Behar Stamp (Amendment) Act.	0	1	0
,, X of 1945 The Cooch Behar Food Adulteration (Amendment) Act.	0	1	0
,, XI of 1945 The Cooch Behar Chowkidari (Amendment) Act.	0	1	0
,, XII of 1945 The Cooch Behar Export Duty (Amendment) Act.	0	1	0
,, XIII of 1945 The Cooch Behar Criminal Procecure Code.	1	6	0
Live-stock Census Report 1945	0	4	0
Rules made under section 2 of the Agriculturists Loans Act (1 of 1944)	0	4	0
,, made under section 9 of the Land Improvement Loans Act II of 1944	0	4	0
,, made under sections 5 and 26 of the Special Excise Act 1945	2	0	0
,, XIV of 1945 the Cooch Behar Army (Amendment) Act 1945.	0	2	[illegible]
,, I of 1946 (Forest Act) ...	0	4	[illegible]
,, II of 1946 (C. B. Foreign Companies Act 1946)	0	2	[illegible]
,, III of 1946 (The C. B. Reciprocity Act 1946.	0	1	[illegible]
Act No. IV of 1946 (C. B. Criminal Procedure Code (Amend) Act 1946)	0	1	[illegible]
,, V of 1946 C. B. Factories (Amend) Act 1946,	0	1	[illegible]
,, VI of 1946 (C. B Patents (Amend) Act 1946.	0	1	[illegible]
Act No. VII of 1946 C. B. Excise Act).	0	12	[illegible]
,, VIII of 1946 (C. B. Opium Act).	0	2	[illegible]
,, IX of 1946 (C. B. Dangerous Drugs Act).	0	7	
,, X of 1946 (C. B. Excess Profits (Repealing) Act 1946).	0	1	[illegible]
,, XI of 1946 C. B. Ferries (Amend) Act 1946	0	1	[illegible]
,, XII of 1946 (The Industrial Statistics Act.)	0	1	[illegible]
,, XIII of 1946 (C. B. Requisitioned Land Act.)	0	1	
,, XIV of 1946 (C. B. Essential Supplies Act).	0	2	
,, XV of 1946 (Requisitioned Land (Amendment) Act 1946.	0	1	
,, XVI of 1946 (C. B. Aircraft Act). 1946.	0	2	
,, I of 1947 (C. B. Essential Supplies (Tem. powers) Amendment 1947.	0	2	
,, II of 1947 the Cooch Behar Public Security Act, 1947.	0	6	[illegible]

A. BAGCHI,
Superintendent, State Press, Cooch Behar

The Cooch Behar Gazette.

১৫ই ভাদ্র সোমবার] MONDAY, SEPTEMBER 1, 1947. [১৩৫৪ সাল, ৫৮শ ভাগ

PART V

Advertisements

WANTED.

Applications are invited from Cooch Behari candidates for undergoing Forest Ranger Course Training in the Indian Forest Ranger College at Dehra Dun as a State stipendiary,

Minimum qualification should be Intermediate passed of any recognised Indian University with one or more of the following subjects :—

Mathematics, Physics, Chemistry, Botany and Zoology.

Age of the candidates must not be less than 18 years nor more than 25 years on the 1st April, 1948.

The selected candidate will have to furnish a bond to the effect that on completion of his training, he will serve the State at least for 5 years.

The selected candidate will have to work in the Cooch Behar Forest Department on a suitable stipend for a couple of months before appearing for a qualifying Examination at Dehra Dun. Further particulars may be had from the office of the undersigned.

Applications stating age, qualification and with copies of testimonials including a certificate from the Sub-divisional Officer concerned will be received by the undersigned on or before 15th September, 1947.

J. C. Goon

For Public Health & Education Minister,
Cooch Behar.

নোটিশ।

এতদ্দ্বারা সর্ব্বসাধারণকে অবগত করান যাইতেছে যে মোকাম বেহারের শ্রীযুক্ত মানদানন্দ ভট্টাচার্য্য মহাশয় আমাদের ইষ্টেটের আমমোক্তার ছিলেন। তাঁহার কার্য্যতায় সন্দেহ হওয়ায় তাঁহাকে আমমোক্তারনামা হইতে খারিজ করা গেল। অদ্য হইতে তিনি আমাদের ইষ্টেট সংক্রান্ত কোন কার্য্য করিলে আমরা বাধ্য হইব না ও আইনতঃ তাহা অগ্রাহ্য হইবেক। ইতি—২৭।৩।৪৭ ইং

ইষ্টেট—শ্রীলাবণ্যময়ী দেবী,
বওজে শ্রীযুক্ত মাধবানন্দ ভট্টাচার্য্য,
মোকাম বেহার।

List of State Acts, Laws and Codes for sale in the State Press, Cooch Behar.

	Rs.	A.	P.
Act of 1874 Limitation (English)* ...	0	12	0
,, Ditto (Bengali) ...	0	12	0
,, of 1882 Cattle Trespass* ,, ...	0	2	0
মুদ্রিত কাগজ সম্বন্ধীয় নিয়মাবলী ...	0	2	0
Act of 1888 Sub-infeudation* ...	0	1	0
,, I of 1890 লোক ও পশু গ্রহণ বিষয়ক আইন	0	0	6
,, I of 1892 Private Fisheries Protection (English and Bengali combined.)	0	1	0
,, II of 1892* Amendment of Limitation (English and Bengali combined.)	0	1	0
,, III of 1892 Jurisdiction (English)*	0	1	0
,, Ditto (Bengali)*	0	1	0
,, IV 1892 Merchandise Marks (Eng.)*	0	2	0
,, I of 1893 Legal Practitioners ,, *	0	1	3
,, Ditto ditto (Bengali)	0	1	0
,, II of 1893 Amendment of Town Committee (English).	0	0	9
,, III of 1893 Village Chowkidari (English)	0	1	6
,, IV of 1893 Amendment of Revenue Sale (English).	0	0	3
,, IV of 1893 Amendment Revenue Sale (Bengali)	0	0	3
,, V of 1893 Cess (English)	0	1	0
,, Ditto (Bengali)	0	1	0
,, VI of 1893 Amendment of Legal Practitioners (English and Bengali combined.)*	0	0	9
,, I of 1894 Amendment of Town Committee.*	0	0	3
,, II of 1894 Amendment of Voluntary Sale of under-tenures.	0	0	3
,, III of 1894 Amendment of Village Chowkidari.*	0	0	6
,, I of 1895 Small Cause Courts Act (English).	0	0	9
,, I of 1896 Amendment of Cooch Behar Stamp Act (English).*	0	0	3
,, I of 1896 Amendment of Cooch Behar Stamp Act (Bengali).*	0	0	3
,, II of 1896 Preservation of Boundary Act (English).	0	0	6
,, III of 1896 Amendment of Village Chowkidari Act (English).	0	0	3
,, I of 1897 Amendment of Cooch Behar Town Committee Act (Eng.)	0	0	3
,, II of 1897 Mahomedan Inheritance Act (English).	0	0	3
,, III of 1897 Oaths Act (English)*	0	0	6
,, IV of 1897 Amendment of Stamp rules (English.)	0	0	3
,, V of 1897 Revenue Sale Act (English).	0	3	0
,, V of 1897 Revenue Sale Act (Bengali).	0	3	0
,, VI of 1897 Wards Act (English)	0	1	0
,, I of 1898 Kist Act ,,	0	0	
,, Ditto (Bengali)	0	0	
,, II of 1898 Amendment of Revenue Sale Act (English).	0	0	
,, Ditto (Bengali)	0	0	3
,, III of 1898 Police Act (English)	0	2	0
,, Ditto (Bengali.)	0	2	0

	Rs.	A.
Act IV of 1898 Bridge Toll Act (Eng.)	0	0
,, of Ditto ditto (Bengali)	0	0
,, V of 1898 Succession Certificate Act (English)	0	2
,, Ditto ditto (Bengali)	0	2
,, VI of 1898 Amendment of Voluntary Sales of under-tenures (Eng.)	0	0
,, Ditto ditto (Bengali)	0	0
,, VII of 1898 Amendment of Village Chowkidari Act (English)	0	0
,, Ditto ditto (Bengali)	0	0
,, VIII of 1898 Revenue Sales Act ,,	0	0
,, Ditto (English)	0	0
,, I of 1899 Cow Killing Act ,,	0	0
,, Ditto (Bengali)	0	0
,, II of 1899 Public Demands Recovery Act (Eng.)	0	3
,, Ditto ditto (Bengali)	0	3
,, III of 1899 Amendment of Limitation Act (English)	0	0
,, Ditto ditto (Bengali)	0	0
,, IV of 1899 State Demands Act (English and Bengali combined)	0	0
,, V of 1899 Civil Marriage Act Eng.)	0	1
,, Ditto ditto (Bengali	0	1
,, I of 1900 Amendment of Civil Procedure Code (English)	0	2
,, II of 1900 Census Act (English)	0	1
,, Ditto ditto (Bengali)	0	1
,, I of 1901 C. B. Telegraph Act ,,	0	1
,, I of 1903 C. B. Stamp Act (Eng.)	0	6
,, Ditto Ditto (Beng.)	0	6
,, II of 1903 Drainage Act (Eng.)	0	0
,, Ditto (Bengali)	0	0
,, III of 1903 Amendment of Cooch Behar Limitation Act (English).	0	1
,, Ditto (Bengali)	0	1
Act IV of 1903 C. B. Town Committee Act (English).	0	6
V of 1903 Amendment of Civil Procedure Code.	0	1
,, VI of 1903 Vaccination Act (Eng)*	0	2
,, Ditto Ditto (Beng.)	0	2
Act I of 1904 Registration Act (Eng.)	0	0
,, II of 1904 Amendment of Village Chowkidari (Eng.)	0	1
,, Ditto Ditto (Beng.)	0	1
,, I of 1905 Amendment of Stamp Act (English).	0	0
,, II of 1905 Unclaimed Intestate Property.	0	0
,, I of 1906 Encumbered Estate Act (English)	0	0
,, II of 1906 Companies Act (English).	0	1
,, III of 1906 Evidence Act Amendment	0	0
,, IV of 1906 Amendment of Village Chaukidari Act.	0	0
,, V of 1906 Small Cause Court Act (English)	0	3
,, VI of 1906 Wills Act (English)	0	0
,, VII of 1906 Probate and Administration Act	0	0

* Out of stock.

	Rs.	A.	P.
Act I of 1907 Amendment Town Committee Act.	0	0	6
„ II of 1907 Succession Act (English)	0	0	6
„ III of 1907 Amendment Vaccination Act (Bengali).	0	1	0
„ IV of 1907 Penal Code Act ...	0	0	6
„ I of 1906 Amendment of Stamp Act	0	1	0
„ II of 1908 Forest Act ...	0	2	0
„ I of 1909 The Code of Criminal Procedure.	0	2	0
„ II of 1909 Act for the Legislative Council.	0	0	6
„ I of 1910 Registration of Births and Deaths (English).	0	1	0
Ditto (Bengali)	0	1	0
„ II of 1910 Amendment of Succession Certificate Act.	0	1	0
„ III of 1910 Provisions for the care of lunatics.	0	0	6
Act IV of 1910 Census Act (Eng. & Beng)	0	1	0
Act V of 1910 Tenancy Act (English)	0	8	0
„ V „ „ (Bengali)	0	11	0
„ I of 1913 Survey „ (Eng.)	0	2	0
„ „ „ (Beng.)	0		0
Letters and Proceedings having the force of Law.	0	10	0
Law Reports Vol. I*	0	8	0
„ Vol. II*	2	4	0
„ Vol. III	1	0	0
Law Report Vol. IV (1911—Jan. 1914)	0	12	0
Vol. V (Mar. 1914-Dec. 1920)	0	8	0
Law Report Vol. VI.	0	12	0
„ Vol. VII	0	12	0
Act I of 1920 Census Act (Eng.)	0	2	0
„ „ „ (Beng)	0	2	0
„ I of 1921 General Clauses Act	0	4	0
„ II „ Code of Civil Procedure Act.	0	5	0
„ III „ Transfer of Property „	0	2	0
„ IV „ Limitation Act ...	0	8	0
„ V „ Majority „ ...	0	2	0
„ VI „ Registration „ ...	0	2	0
„ VII „ Guardians and Wards Act.	0	2	0
„ VIII „ Negotiable instruments Act.	0	2	0
„ IX „ Criminal Tribes Act	0	8	0
„ X „ Interest „	0	2	0
„ XI „ Suits Valuations „	0	2	0
„ XII „ Bankers' Books evidence (amendment.)	0	1	0
„ I of 1923 Regulation E.B.R. Arbitration.	0	1	0
„ I of 1923 Excise, Opium & Drugs	0	5	0
„ I of 1929 (amending the Cooch Behar Town Committee Act IV of 1903)	0	1	0
„ I of 1930 Criminal Law (amendt.)	0	1	0
„ II „ Census Act ...	0	2	0
„ III „ Co-operative Societies Act	0	4	0
„ III „ 1930 „ (Sec. 43) ...	0	3	0
„ I of 1931 Christian Marriage Act	0	1	0
„ I of 1932 Motor Vehicles Act	0	2	0
Act I of 1933 Cooch Behar Penal Code Amendment Act.	0	0	5

	Rs.	A.	P.
Act II of 1933 Cooch Behar Companies Act.	0	2	0
„ III of 1933 Code of Criminal Procedure.	0	4	0
„ I of 1934 The Lepers Act ...	0	2	0
„ III of 1934 Cooch Behar Revenue Sale Amendment Act.	0	1	0
Act No. IV of 1934 Hindu widow Marriage Act (Eng. & Beng).	0	1	0
„ I of 1935 Cooch Behar Matches (Excise Duty) Act.	0	2	0
„ I of 1937 Cooch Behar Hat toll protection Act.	0	0	6
Act II of 1937 Act for Prevention of Cruelty to Animals.	0	6	0
„ I of 1938 C B. Public gambling Act	0	2	0
„ II of 1938 C.B. Amusement Tax Act	0	2	0
„ I of 1939 Amendment of C.B.T.C.	0	0	6
Act I of 1940 Census Act... ...	0	2	0
„ II of 1940 C. B. Penal Code Amendment Act.	0	0	6
„ I of 1941 Amendment of C. B. Tenancy Act.	0	0	6
„ II of 1941 C. B. Food Adulteration	0	3	0
„ III of 1941 Legislative Council Act	0	2	0
„ IV of 1941 C. B. Electricity Act	0	4	0
Act V of 1941 C. B. Income Tax Act	0	8	0
„ VI of 1941 C. B. Export Duty Act	0	1	0
Act VII of 1941 Motor Vehicles	1	0	0
„ VIII of 1941 Village choukidary Amendment	0	2	0
„ IX of 1941 Town Committee Amendment	0	1	0
„ X of 1941 General Amending	0	6	0
„ XI of 1941 Cow killing Amendment	0	0	3
„ XII of 1941 Tenancy (second Amend) Act No XII of 1941	0	0	3
„ I of 1942 Standard of weight	0	1	0
„ II of 1942 foreigner's Act	0	1	0
„ III of 1942 Penal Code Act	2	12	0
„ IV of 1942 Companies (Amend)	0	1	0
„ V of 1942 Public Demands recovery (Amend)	0	1	0
„ VI of 1942 Incometax (Amend)	0	1	0
Act VII of 1942 (An Act to Amend the C. B. General Clauses Act I of 1921	0	0	6
„ VIII of 1942 (Transfer of Property Amendment) Act 1942	0	1	0
„ IX of 1942 (C. B. Registration Amendment) Act 1942	0	0	6
„ X of 1942 (C. B. Limitation Amendment) Act 1942	0	1	0
„ No. XI of 1942 (C. B. Town Committee) Amendment Act	0	0	6
Live Stock Census Report	0	4	0
Schedule of rates*	2	8	0
Cottage Industry	2	0	0
History of Cooch Behar (Paper bound) Bengali	2	0	0
Do Do (cloth bound)	3	0	0
Hand Book of Circular orders	2	0	0
History of Cooch Behar (English version)	5	0	0

* Out of stock.

	Rs.	A.	P.
Act I of 1943 Legal Practitioners Act	0	4	0
,, II of 1943 Stamp Act ...	0	14	0
,, III of 1943 Excess Profits Tax Act	0	6	0
,, IV of 1943 Patents Act ...	0	4	0
,, V of 1943 Public Health Act ...	0	8	0
,, VI of 1943 (An Act to provide for the Prevention and Control of Contagious deseases affecting Animals.)	0	2	0
,, VII of 1943 Army Act ...	0	8	0
,, VIII of 1943 Workmen's Compensation Act.	0	1	0
,, IX of 1943 Factories Act ...	0	1	0
,, X of 1943 Public Demand Recovery Act	1	12	0
,, XI of 1943 Civil Procedure Code (amendment) Act.	0	2	0
,, XII of 1943 Pension (Exemption) Act.	0	0	6
,, XIII of 1943 Insolvency Act ...	0	8	0
,, XIV of 1943 Succession Act ...	0	1	0
,, XV of 1943 Extradition Act ...	0	8	0
,, XVI of 1943 Muli (Regulating) Act	0	0	6
,, XVII of 1943 Interest (amendment) Act.	0	0	6
,, XVIII of 1943 Revenue sale (amendment) Act.	0	0	6
,, XIX of 1943 Land Acquisition Act	0	4	0
,, XX of 1943 Forest (amendment) Act.	0	0	6
Act XXI of 1943 Tenancy (amendment) Act 1943.	0	6	0
Act XXII of 1943 Cooch Behar Co-operation Societies Act 1943.	0	2	0
Act XXIII of 1943 Village Chaukidary (amendment).	0	1	0
Act XXIV of 1943 Cooch Behar Incometax (amendment) Act 1943.	0	1	0
Act XXV of 1943 Tobacco (Excise Duty) Act.	0	3	0
Act XXVI of 1943 Bengal and Assam Railway Arbitration Act.	0	2	0
Table of rates of Advalorem Fees laviable on the institution of Suits under the Cooch Behar Stamp Act II of 1943.	0	2	0
Rules made under section 52 of the Income-tax Act 1941.	0	2	0
Lives-stock Census Report	0	4	0
Act II of 1921 (as amended up to Cooch Behar Civil procedure 1921 (Cooch Behar State).	0	5	0
Cooch Behar Tenancy Act, Act V of 1910 (as amended upto 1943) Cooch Behar State.	0	11	0
Act I of 1944 Cooch Beher Agriculturists' Loans Act.	0	0	6
,, II of 1944 Cooch Behar Land Improvement Loans Act.	0	2	0
,, III of 1944 Cooch Behar Municipal Act	1	8	0
,, IV of 1944 C. B. Prevention of Cruelty to Animals Act. (Amendement.)	0	2	6
V of 1944 Cooch Behar Vaccination Act. (Amendement)	0	2	0
,, VI of 1944 The Cooch Behar Medical Act.	0	6	0
VII of 1944 Cooch Behar Opium Smoking Act.	0	2	0
VIII of 1944 Cooch Behar Arms Act.	0	6	0
Act IX of 1944 Cooch Behar Police (incitement to Disaffection) Act.	0	1	6

	Rs.	A.	P.
Act X of 1944 The Cow killing Temporary Amendment Act.	0	0	6
The Government of Cooch Behar Act (not for sale).			
Act No. I of 1945 Cooch Behar Income Tax (Amendment) Act.	0	1	0
,, II of 1945 Cooch Behar Excess Profit Tax (Amendment) Act	0	1	0
,, III of 1945 Cooch Behar Specia Excise Act.	0	6	0
,, IV of 1945 The Cooch Behar Land Encroachment Act	0	4	0
,, V of 1945 The Cooch Behar Orphanage Act.	0	2	0
,, VI of 1945 The Cooch Behar Tea Cultivation Control Act.	0	2	0
,, VII of 1945 The Cooch Behar Penal Code (Amendment) Act.	0	1	0
,, VIII of 1945 The Cooch Behar Ferries Act.	0	4	0
,, IX of 1945 The Cooch Behar Stamp (Amendment) Act.	0	1	0
,, X of 1945 The Cooch Behar Food Adulteration (Amendment) Act.	0	1	0
,, XI of 1945 The Cooch Behar Chowkidari (Amendment) Act.	0	1	0
,, XII of 1945 The Cooch Behar Export Duty (Amendment) Act.	0	1	0
,, XIII of 1945 The Cooch Behar Criminal Proceepre Code.	1	6	0
Live-stock Census Report 1945	0	4	0
Rules made under section 2 of the Agriculturists Loans Act (I of 1944)	0	4	0
,, made under section 9 of the Land Improvement Loans Act II of 1944	0	4	0
,, made under sections 5 and 26 of the Special Excise Act 1945	2	0	0
,, XIV of 1945 the Cooch Behar Army (Amendment) Act 1945.	0	2	0
,, I of 1946 (Forest Act) ...	0	4	0
,, II of 1946 (C. B. Foreign Companies Act 1946)	0	2	0
,, III of 1946 (The C. B. Reciprocity Act 1946.	0	1	0
Act No. IV of 1946 (C. B. Criminal Procedure Code (Amend) Act 1946)	0	1	0
,, V of 1946 C. B. Factories (Amend) Act 1946.	0	1	0
,, VI of 1946 (C. B Patents (Amend) Act 1946.	0	1	0
Act No. VII of 1946 (C. B. Excise Act)	0	12	0
,, VIII of 1946 (C. B. Opium Act).	0	2	0
,, IX of 1946 (C. B. Dangerous Drugs Act).	0	7	0
,, X of 1946 (C. B. Excess Profits (Repealing) Act 1946).	0	1	0
,, XI of 1946 C. B. Ferries (Amend) Act 1946	0	1	0
,, XII of 1946 (The Industrial Statistics Act.)	0	1	0
,, XIII of 1946 (C. B. Requisitioned Land Act.)	0	1	0
,, XIV of 1946 (C. B. Essential Supplies Act).	0	2	0
,, XV of 1946 (Requisitioned Land (Amendment) Act 1946.	0	1	0
,, XVI of 1946 (C. B. Aircraft Act). 1946.	0	2	0
,, I of 1947 (C. B. Essential Supplies (Tem. powers) Amendment 1947.	0	2	0
,, II of 1947 the Cooch Behar Public Security Act, 1947.	0	6	0

A. BAGCHI,
Superintendent, State Press, Cooch Behar.

The Cooch Behar Gazette.

৩১শে ভাদ্র মঙ্গলবার] TUESDAY, SEPTEMBER 16, 1947. [১৩৫৪ সাল, ৪৩৮ রাজশক

PART V.

Advertisements

NOTICE.

Applications are invited for the post of 2nd pandit Panigram State Model school on Rs. 25 per mensem plus usual dearness allowance and special allowance.

. Apply stating age, qualifications, past experience if any and with Father's name, Home address, Present address and place of last residence.

Applications will be received by the Chairman, Public Service Commission, Cooch Behar up to the 30th September, 1947.

B. RAHAMAN,
Chairman,
Public Service Commission, Cooch Behar.

বিজ্ঞাপন।

ডিপার্টমেন্ট অব ইনডাষ্ট্রীজ, কোচবিহার।

সাবান প্রস্তুত শিক্ষা ও মফঃস্বল কেন্দ্রে সাবান ফ্যাক্টরী স্থাপন।

সাবান প্রত্যেক গৃহস্থের নিত্য প্রয়োজনীয় জিনিষ। কোচবিহার রাজ্যে বহু সাবান কাটতি হয় উহার পরিমাণ নিতান্ত কম নহে। লক্ষ টাকারও অধিক মূল্যের সাবান প্রতি বৎসর বাহির হইতে কোচবিহারে আমদানী ও বিক্রয় হয়। এই সমস্ত পয়সাই বিদেশীয় মহাজন ও কারিকরেরা কোচবিহার হইতে পাইতেছে।

যুদ্ধাবসানে সাবান প্রস্তুত করিবার তৈল ও কষ্টিকসোডা প্রভৃতি আবার সুলভ হইতেছে। কোচবিহার শিল্পবিভাগে সাবান-প্রস্তুত শিক্ষা করার যথেষ্ট সুযোগ আছে। যাহারা সাবান প্রস্তুত শিক্ষা করিতে ইচ্ছুক তাহারা নিম্নস্বাক্ষরকারীর নিকট দরখাস্ত করিলে সাবান শিক্ষা দেওয়ার ব্যবস্থা করা হইবে।

শ্রীশ্রীমহারাজা ভূপ বাহাদুর ইচ্ছা করেন, তাঁহার রাজ্যের বিভিন্ন মফঃস্বল কেন্দ্রে যাহাতে সাবানের ছোট ছোট কারখানা গড়িয়া উঠে সেই উদ্দেশ্যে সাবান প্রস্তুত শিক্ষার্থিগণকে শিক্ষা সমাপ্ত হইলে ফ্যাক্টরী স্থাপন করিবার জন্য প্রয়োজনীয় অর্থ বা সরঞ্জামাদির সাহায্যে ও ঋণদান কারণার্থ ব্যবস্থা সরকার হইতে করা হইবে। যে সমস্ত শিক্ষার্থিগণ মফঃস্বল হইতে কোচবিহার সহরে আসিয়া সাবান প্রস্তুত শিক্ষা করিতে পারিবে না, তাহাদের শিক্ষার জন্য শিল্পবিভাগ হইতে ভ্রাম্যমান সাবান শিক্ষার কেন্দ্র শিক্ষার্থিগণের বাসস্থানের নিকট স্থাপন করিয়া শিক্ষা দেওয়ার বন্দোবস্ত করা যাইতে পারে। এক এক স্থান হইতে ৫।৬ জন উপযুক্ত শিক্ষার্থী একত্রে দরখাস্ত করিলে মফঃস্বল শিক্ষাকেন্দ্র স্থাপন করিবার বিষয় বিবেচনা করা হইবে। শিক্ষিত ব্যক্তিগণকে সাবান শিক্ষা সমাপ্ত হইলে সাবানের কারখানা স্থাপন করিতে হইবে এইরূপ সর্ত্তে সাবান শিক্ষা দেওয়া হইবে।

শিক্ষার্থিগণ নিম্নস্বাক্ষরকারীর নিকট শিল্পবিভাগে আবেদন করিবেন।

ইনডাষ্ট্রিজ ডিপার্টমেন্ট,
কোচবিহার,
৫।৯।৪৭

শ্রীললিতমোহন বক্সী,
ডেভেলোপমেন্ট কমিশনার,
কোচবিহার।

List of State Acts, Laws and Codes for sale in the State Press, Cooch Behar.

	Rs.	A.	P.
Act of 1874 Limitation (English)* ...	0	12	0
„ Ditto (Bengali) ...	0	12	0
„ of 1882 Cattle Trespass* „ ...	0	2	0
মুদ্রিত কাগজ সম্বন্ধীয় নিয়মাবলী ...	0	2	0
Act of 1888 Sub-infeudation* ...	0	1	0
„ I of 1890 লোকসংখ্যা গ্রহণ বিষয়ক আইন	0	0	6
„ I of 1892 Private Fisheries Protection (English and Bengali combined.)	0	1	0
„ II of 1892 Amendment of Limitation (Engish and Bengali combined.)	0	1	0
„ III of 1892 Jurisdiction (English)*	0	1	0
„ Ditto (Bengali)*	0	1	0
„ IV 1892 Merchandise Marks (Eng.)*	0	2	0
„ I of 1893 Legal Practitioners „ *	0	1	3
„ Ditto ditto (Bengali)	0	1	0
„ II of 1893 Amendment of Town Committee (English).	0	0	3
„ III of 1893 Village Chowkidari (English)	0	1	6
„ IV of 1893 Amendment of Revenue Sale (English).	0	0	3
„ IV of 1893 Amendment Revenue Sale (Bengali)	0	0	3
„ V of 1893 Cess (English)	0	1	0
„ Ditto (Bengali)	0	1	0
„ VI of 1893 Amendment of Legal Practitioners (English and Bengali combined.)*	0	0	3
„ I of 1894 Amendment of Town Committee.*	0	0	3
„ II of 1894 Amendment of Voluntary Sale of under-tenures.	0	0	3
„ III of 1894 Amendment of Village Chowkidari.*	0	0	6
„ I of 1895 Small Cause Courts Act (English).	0	0	9
„ I of 1896 Amendment of Cooch Behar Stamp Act (English).*	0	0	3
„ I of 1896 Amendment of Cooch Behar Stamp Act (Bengali).*	0	0	3
„ II of 1896 Preservation of Boundary Act (English).	0	0	6
„ III of 1896 Amendment of Village Chowkidari Act (English).	0	0	3
„ I of 1897 Amendment of Cooch Behar Town Committee Act (Eng.)	0	0	3
„ II of 1897 Mahomedan Inheritance Act (English).	0	0	3
„ III of 1897 Oaths Act (English)*	0	0	6
„ IV of 1897 Amendment of Stamp rules (English.)	0	0	3
„ V of 1897 Revenue Sale Act (English).	0	3	0
„ V of 1897 Revenue Sale Act (Bengali).	0	3	0
„ VI of 1897 Wards Act (English)	0	1	0
„ I of 1898 Kist Act „	0		
„ Ditto (Bengali)	0		
„ II of 1898 Amendment of Revenue Sale Act (English).	0		
Ditto (Bengali)	0	0	3
„ III of 1898 Police Act (English)	0	2	0
„ Ditto (Bengali.)	0	2	0

	Rs.	A.	
Act IV of 1898 Bridge Toll Act (Eng.)	0	0	6
„ of Ditto ditto (Bengali)	0	0	6
„ V of 1898 Succession Certificate Act (English)	0	2	0
„ Ditto ditto (Bengali)	0	2	0
„ VI of 1898 Amendment of Voluntary Sales of under-tenures (Eng.)	0	0	9
„ Ditto ditto (Bengali)	0	0	9
„ VII of 1898 Amendment of Village Chowkidari Act (English)	0	0	3
„ Ditto ditto (Bengali)	0	0	3
„ VIII of 1898 Revenue Sales Act „	0	0	3
„ Ditto (English)	0	0	3
„ I of 1899 Cow Killing Act „	0	0	3
„ Ditto (Bengali)	0	0	3
„ II of 1899 Public Demands Recovery Act (Eng.)	0	3	0
„ Ditto ditto (Bengali)	0	3	0
„ III of 1899 Amendment of Limitation Act (English)	0	0	3
„ Ditto ditto (Bengali)	0	0	3
„ IV of 1899 State Demands Act (English and Bengali combined)	0	0	6
„ V of 1899 Civil Marriage Act (Eng.)	0	1	6
„ Ditto ditto (Bengali)	0	1	6
„ I of 1900 Amendment of Civil Procedure Code (English)	0	2	0
„ II of 1900 Census Act (English)	0	1	3
„ Ditto ditto (Bengali)	0	1	0
„ I of 1901 C. B. Telegraph Act „	0	1	0
„ I of 1903 C. B. Stamp Act (Eng.)	0	6	0
„ Ditto Ditto (Beng.)	0	6	0
„ II of 1903 Drainage Act (Eng.)	0	0	6
„ Ditto (Bengali)	0	0	6
„ III of 1903 Amendment of Cooch Behar Limitation Act (English).	0	1	6
„ Ditto (Bengali)	0	1	6
Act IV of 1903 C. B. Town Committee Act (English).	0	6	0
V of 1903 Amendment of Civil Procedure Code.	0	1	6
„ VI of 1903 Vaccination Act (Eng)*	0	3	0
„ Ditto Ditto (Beng.)	0	3	0
Act I of 1904 Registration Act (Eng.)	0	0	6
„ II of 1904 Amendment of Village Chowkidari (Eng.)	0	1	0
„ Ditto Ditto (Beng.)	0	1	0
„ I of 1905 Amendment of Stamp Act (English).	0	0	6
„ II of 1905 Unclaimed Intestate Property.	0	0	6
„ I of 1906 Encumbered Estate Act (English)	0	0	6
„ II of 1906 Companies Act (English).	0	1	0
„ III of 1906 Evidence Act Amendment	0	0	6
„ IV of 1906 Amendment of Village Chaukidari Act.	0	0	6
„ V of 1906 Small Cause Court Act (English)	0	3	0
„ VI of 1906 Wills Act (English)	0	0	3
„ VII of 1906 Probate and Administration Act	0	0	6

* Out of stock.

	Rs.	A.	P.
Act I of 1907 Amendment Town Committee Act.	0	0	6
,, II of 1907 Succession Act (English).	0	0	6
,, III of 1907 Amendment Vaccination Act (Bengali).	0	1	0
,, IV of 1907 Penal Code Act ...	0	0	6
,, I of 1908 Amendment of Stamp Act.	0	1	0
,, II of 1908 Forest Act ...	0	2	0
,, I of 1909 The Code of Criminal Procedure.	0	2	0
,, II of 1909 Act for the Legislative Council.	0	0	6
,, I of 1910 Registration of Births and Deaths (English).	0	1	0
Ditto (Bengali)	0	1	0
,, II of 1910 Amendment of Succession Certificate Act.	0	1	0
,, III of 1910 Provisions for the care of lunatics.	0	0	6
Act IV of 1910 Census Act (Eng. & Beng)	0	1	0
Act V of 1910 Tenancy Act (English)	0	8	0
,, V ,, ,, (Bengali)	0	11	0
,, I of 1913 Survey ,, Eng.)	0	2	0
,, ,, ,, (Beng.)	0		0
Letters and Proceedings having the force of Law.	0	10	0
Law Reports Vol. I*	0	8	0
,, Vol. II*	2	4	0
,, Vol. III	1	0	0
Law Report Vol IV (1911—Jan. 1314)	0	12	0
Vol. V (Mar. 1914-Dec. 1920)	0	8	0
Law Report Vol. VI.	0	12	0
,, Vol. VII	0	12	0
Act I of 1920 Census Act (Eng.)	0	2	0
,, ,, ,, (Beng)	0	2	0
,, I of 1921 General Clauses Act	0	4	0
,, II ,, Code of Civil Procedure Act.	0	5	0
,, III ,, Transfer of Property ,,	0	2	0
,, IV ,, Limitation Act ...	0	8	0
,, V ,, Majority ,, ...	0	2	0
,, VI ,, Registration ,, ...	0	2	0
,, VII ,, Guardians and Wards Act.	0	2	0
,, VIII ,, Negotiable instruments Act.	0	2	0
,, IX ,, Criminal Tribes Act	0	3	0
,, X ,, Interest ,,	0	2	0
,, XI ,, Suits Valuntions ,,	0	2	0
,, XII ,, Bankers' Books evidence (amendment.)	0	1	0
,, I of 1923 Regulation E.B.R. Arbitration.	0	1	0
,, I of 1923 Excise, Opium & Drugs	0	5	0
,, I of 1929 (amending the Cooch Behar Town Committee Act IV of 1902)	0	1	0
,, I of 1930 Criminal Law (amendt.)	0	1	0
,, II ,, Census Act ...	0	2	0
,, III ,, Co-operative Societies Act	0	4	0
,, III , 1930 ,, (Sec. 43) ...	0	3	0
,, I of 1931 Christian Marriage Act	0	1	0
,, I of 1932 Motor Vehicles Act	0	2	0
Act I of 1933 Cooch Behar Penal Code Amendment Act.	0	0	3

	Rs.	A.	P.
Act II of 1933 Cooch Behar Companies Act.	0	2	0
,, III of 1933 Code of Criminal Procedure.	0	4	0
,, I of 1934 The Lepers Act ...	0	2	0
,, III of 1934 Cooch Behar Revenue Sale Amendment Act.	0	1	0
Act No. IV of 1934 Hindu widow Marriage Act (Eng. & Beng).	0	1	0
,, I of 1935 Cooch Behar Matches (Excise Duty) Act.	0	2	0
,, I of 1937 Cooch Behar Hat toll protection Act.	0	0	6
Act II of 1937 Act for Prevention of Cruelty to Animals.	0	6	0
,, I of 1938 C.B. Public gambling Act	0	2	0
,, II of 1938 C.B. Amusement Tax Act	0	2	0
,, I of 1939 Amendment of C.B.T.C.	0	0	6
Act I of 1940 Census Act... ...	0	2	0
,, II of 1940 C. B. Penal Code Amendment Act.	0	0	6
,, I of 1941 Amendment of C. B. Tenancy Act.	0	0	6
,, II of 1941 C. B. Food Adulteration	0	3	0
,, III of 1941 Legislative Council Act	0	2	0
,, IV of 1941 C. B. Electricity Act	0	4	0
Act V of 1941 C. B. Income Tax Act	0	8	0
,, VI of 1941 C. B. Export Duty Act	0	1	0
Act VII of 1941 Motor Vehicles	1	0	0
,, VIII of 1941 Village choukidary Amendment	0	2	0
,, IX of 1941 Town Committee Amendment	0	1	0
,, X of 1941 General Amending	0	6	0
,, XI of 1941 Cow killing Amendment	0	0	3
,, XII of 1941 Tenancy (second Amend) Act No XII of 1941	0	0	3
,, I of 1942 Standard of weight	0	1	0
,, II of 1942 foreigner's Act	0	1	0
,, III of 1912 Penal Code Act	2	12	0
,, IV of 1942 Companies (Amend)	0	1	0
,, V of 1942 Public Demands recovery (Amend)	0	1	0
,, VI of 1942 Incometax (Amend)	0	1	0
Act VII of 1942 (An Act to Amend the C. B. General Clauses Act I of 1921	0	0	6
,, VIII of 1942 (Transfer of Property Amendment) Act 1942	0	1	0
,, IX of 1942 (C. B. Registration Amendment) Act 1942	0	0	6
,, X of 1942 (C. B. Limitation Amendment) Act 1942	0	1	0
,, No. XI of 1942 (C. B. Town Committee) Amendment Act	0	0	6
Live Stock Census Report	0	4	0
Schedule of rates*	2	8	0
Cottage Industry	2	0	0
History of Cooch Behar (Paper bound) Bengali	2	0	0
Do Do (cloth bound)	3	0	0
Hand Book of Circular orders	2	0	0
History of Cooch Behar (English version)	5	0	0

* Out of stock.

	Rs.	A.	P.
Act I of 1948 Legal Practitioners Act	0	4	0
„ II of 1943 Stamp Act ...	0	14	0
„ III of 1943 Excess Profits Tax Act	0	6	0
„ IV of 1943 Patents Act ...	0	4	0
„ V of 1943 Public Health Act ...	0	3	0
„ VI of 1943 (An Act to provide for the Prevention and Control of Contagious deseases affecting Animals.)	0	2	0
„ VII of 1943 Army Act ...	0	8	0
„ VIII of 1943 Workmen's Compensation Act.	0	1	0
„ IX of 1943 Factories Act ...	0	1	0
„ X of 1943 Public Demand Recovery Act	1	12	0
„ XI of 1943 Civil Procedure Code (amendment) Act.	0	2	0
„ XII of 1943 Pension (Exemption) Act.	0	0	6
„ XIII of 1943 Insolvency Act ...	0	8	0
„ XIV of 1943 Succession Act ...	0	1	0
„ XV of 1943 Extradition Act ...	0	3	0
„ XVI of 1943 Muli (Regulating) Act	0	0	6
„ XVII of 1943 Interest (amendment) Act.	0	0	6
„ XVIII of 1943 Revenue sale (amendment) Act.	0	0	6
„ XIX of 1943 Land Acquisition Act	0	4	0
„ XX of 1943 Forest (amendment) Act.	0	0	6
Act XXI of 1943 Tenancy (amendment) Act 1943.	0	6	0
Act XXII of 1943 Coch Behar Co-operation Societies Act 1943.	0	2	0
Act XXIII of 1943 Village Chaukidary (amendment).	0	1	0
Act XXIV of 1943 Cooch Behar Incometax (amendment) Act 1943.	0	1	0
Act XXV of 1943 Tobacco (Excise Duty) Act.	0	3	0
Act XXVI of 1943 Bengal and Assam Railway Arbitration Act.	0	2	0
Table of rates of Advalorem Fees leviable on the institution of Suits under the Cooch Behar Stamp Act II of 1943.	0	2	0
Rules made under section 52 of the Income-tax Act 1941.	0	2	0
Lives-stock Census Report	0	4	0
Act II of 1921 (as amended up to Cooch Behar Civil procedure 1921 (Cooch Behar State).	0	5	0
Cooch Behar Tenancy Act, Act V of 1910 (as amended upto 1943) Cooch Behar State.	0	11	0
Act I of 1944 Cooch Behar Agriculturists' Loans Act.	0	0	6
„ II of 1944 Cooch Behar Land Improvement Loans Act.	0	2	0
„ III of 1944 Cooch Behar Municipal Act	1	8	0
„ IV of 1944 C. B. Prevention of Cruelty to Animals Act. (Amendement.)	0	2	6
V of 1944 Cooch Behar Vaccination Act. (Amendement.)	0	2	0
„ VI of 1944 The Cooch Behar Medical Act.	0	6	0
VII of 1944 Cooch Behar Opium Smoking Act.	0	2	0
VIII of 1944 Cooch Behar Arms Act.	0	6	0
Act IX of 1944 Cooch Behar Police (Incitement to Disaffection) Act,	0	1	6

	Rs.	A.	P.
Act X of 1944 The Cooch Behar Temporary Amendment Act.	[illegible]	[illegible]	[illegible]
The Government of Cooch Behar Act	(not for sale).		
Act No. I of 1945 Cooch Behar Income Tax (Amendment) Act.	0	1	0
„ II of 1945 Cooch Behar Excess Profit Tax (Amendment) Act	0	1	0
„ III of 1945 Cooch Behar Special Excise Act.	0	6	0
„ IV of 1945 The Cooch Behar Land Encroachment Act	0	4	0
„ V of 1945 The Cooch Behar Orphanage Act.	0	2	0
„ VI of 1945 The Cooch Behar Tea Cultivation Control Act.	0	2	0
„ VII of 1945 The Cooch Behar Penal Code (Amendment) Act.	0	1	0
„ VIII of 1945 The Cooch Behar Ferries Act.	0	4	0
„ IX of 1945 The Cooch Behar Stamp (Amendment) Act.	0	1	0
„ X of 1945 The Cooch Behar Food Adultaration (Amendment) Act.	0	1	0
„ XI of 1945 The Cooch Behar Chowkidari (Amendment) Act.	0	1	0
„ XII of 1945 The Cooch Behar Export Duty (Amendment) Act.	0	1	0
„ XIII of 1945 The Cooch Behar Criminal Proceedure Code.	1	6	0
Live-stock Census Report 1945	0	4	0
Rules made under section 2 of the Agriculturists Loans Act (1 of 1944)	0	4	0
„ made under section 9 of the Land Improvement Loans Act II of 1944	0	4	0
„ made under sections 5 and 26 of the Special Excise Act 1945	2	0	0
„ XIV of 1945 the Cooch Behar Army (Amendment) Act 1945.	0	2	0
„ I of 1946 (Forest Act) ...	0	4	0
„ II of 1946 (C. B. Foreign Companies Act 1946)	0	2	0
„ III of 1946 (The C. B. Reciprocity Act 1946.	0	1	0
Act No. IV of 1946 (C. B. Criminal Procedure Code (Amend) Act 1946)	0	1	0
„ V of 1946 C. B. Factories (Amend) Act 1946,	0	1	0
„ VI of 1946 (C. B Patents (Amend) Act 1946.	0	1	0
Act No. VII of 1946 (C. B. Excise Act).	0	12	0
„ VIII of 1946 (C. B. Opium Act).	0	2	0
„ IX of 1946 (C. B. Dangerous Drugs Act).	0	7	0
„ X of 1946 (C. B. Excess Profits (Repealing) Act 1946).	0	1	0
„ XI of 1946 C. B. Ferries (Amend) Act 1946	0	1	0
„ XII of 1946 (The Industrial Statistics Act.)	0	1	0
„ XIII of 1946 (C B. Requisitioned Land Act.)	0	1	0
„ XIV of 1946 (C. B. Essential Supplies Act).	0	2	0
„ XV of 1946 (Requisitioned Land (Amendment) Act 1946.	0	1	0
„ XVI of 1946 (C. B. Aircraft Act). 1946.	0	2	0
„ I of 1947 (C. B. Essential Supplies (Tem. powers) Amendment 1947.	0	2	0
„ II of 1947 the Cooch Behar Public Security Act, 1947.	0	6	0

A. BAGCHI,
Superintendet, State Press, Cooch Behar.

The Cooch Behar Gazette.

১৪ই আশ্বিন বুধবার] WEDNESDAY, OCTOBER 1, 1947. [১৩৫৪ সাল, ৪৩৮ রাজশক

PART V.

Advertisements

ADVERTISEMENT.

Applications are invited and will be received by the undersigned till 10th October, 1947 from intending Cooch Behari candidates for obtaining specialised training in Dairying for I. D. Diploma at State cost.

Candidates applying must be at least matriculates.

L. M. BAKSI,
Development Commissioner, Cooch Behar.

NOTICES.

WANTED immediately a Store Keeper for the Electricity Department, Cooch Behar temporarily for 3 months for the present with prospect of being made permanent on a pay of Rs. 40 p. m. with usual dearness allowance and special pay in the grade of Rs. 40-5/2-80. Preference will be given to the candidate who has got some experience of maintaining store. Applications will be received by the undersigned on or before the 6th October, 1947.

G. NARAYAN,
Major,
Actg. Chief Engineer,
Electricity Department,
Cooch Behar.

Applications are invited for the post of a Paid Probationer of the Fouzdari Office.

None need apply who is not a registered candidate.

Apply stating age, qualifications and past experience if any and with Father's name, Home address (P. O., Vill., P. S. and Dist.) and with present address and place of last residence.

Applications will be received by the Chairman, Public Service Commission, Cooch Behar up to the 11th October, 1947.

B. RAHAMAN,
Chairman,
Public Sevice Commission, Cooch Behar.

নোটিশ

এতদ্বারা সর্বসাধারণকে জ্ঞাত করা যাইতেছে যে পাঞ্জাব হইতে আনীত একটী হরিয়ানা ষাঁড় তুফানগঞ্জ মহকুমার বলরামপুর বন্দরে আগামী ইংরাজী অক্টোবর মাসের ৫ই তারিখে বেলা ৪ ঘটিকার প্রকাশ্য নিলামে বিক্রয় হইবে। সুতরাং ক্রয়েচ্ছু ব্যক্তিগণ উক্ত দিবস উক্ত স্থানে উপস্থিত হইয়া উহা ক্রয় করিতে পারেন।

[illegible] ম, বক্সী
[illegible]ন্ট কমিশনার।

List of State Acts, Laws and Codes for sale in the State Press, Cooch Behar.

	Rs.	A.	P.
Act of 1874 Limitation (English)* ...	0	12	0
" Ditto (Bengali) ...	0	12	0
" of 1882 Cattle Trespass* ,, ...	0	2	0
মুদ্রিত কাগজ সম্বন্ধীয় নিয়মাবলী ...	0	2	0
Act of 1888 Sub-infeudation* ...	0	1	0
" I of 1890 লোক ও খত গ্রহণ বিষয়ক আইন	0	0	6
I of 1892 Private Fisheries Protection (English and Bengali combined.)	0	1	0
" II of 1892 Amendment of Limitation (English and Bengali combined.)	0	1	0
III of 1892 Jurisdiction (English)*	0	1	3
" Ditto (Bengali)*	0	1	0
" IV 1892 Merchandise Marks (Eng.)*	0	2	0
" I of 1893 Legal Practitioners ,, *	0	1	3
" Ditto ditto (Bengali)	0	1	0
" II of 1893 Amendment of Town Committee (English).	0	0	9
" III of 1893 Village Chowkidari (English)	0	1	6
" IV of 1893 Amendment of Revenue Sale (English).	0	0	3
" IV of 1893 Amendment Revenue Sale (Bengali)	0	0	3
" V of 1893 Cess (English)	0	1	0
" Ditto (Bengali)	0	1	0
" VI of 1893 Amendment of Legal Practitioners (English and Bengali combined.)*	0	0	8
" I of 1894 Amendment of Town Committee.*	0	0	3
" II of 1894 Amendment of Voluntary Sale of under-tenures.	0	0	3
" III of 1894 Amendment of Village Chowkidari.*	0	0	6
" I of 1895 Small Cause Courts Act (English).	0	0	9
" I of 1896 Amendment of Cooch Behar Stamp Act (English).*	0	0	3
" I of 1896 Amendment of Cooch Behar Stamp Act (Bengali).*	0	0	3
" II of 1896 Preservation of Boundary Act (English).	0	0	6
" III of 1896 Amendment of Village Chowkidari Act (English).	0	0	3
" I of 1897 Amendment of Cooch Behar Town Committee Act (Eng.)	0	0	3
" II of 1897 Mahomedan Inheritance Act (English).	0	0	3
" III of 1897 Oaths Act (English)*	0	0	6
" IV of 1897 Amendment of Stamp rules (English.)	0	0	3
" V of 1897 Revenue Sale Act (English).	0	3	6
" V of 1897 Revenue Sale Act (Bengali).	0	3	0
" VI of 1897 Wards Act (English)	0	1	0
" I of 1898 Kist Act ,,	0	0	6
" Ditto (Bengali)	0	0	6
" II of 1898 Amendment of Revenue Sale Act (English).	0	0	3
" Ditto (Bengali)	0	0	3
" III of 1898 Police Act (English)	0	2	0
" Ditto (Bengali.)	0	2	0
Act IV of 1898 Bridge Toll Act (Eng.)	0	0	6
" of Ditto ditto (Bengali)	0	0	6
" V of 1898 Succession Certificate Act (English)	0	2	0
" Ditto ditto (Bengali)	0	2	0
" VI of 1898 Amendment of Voluntary Sales of under-tenures (Eng.)	0	0	9
" Ditto ditto (Bengali)	0	0	9
" VII of 1898 Amendment of Village Chowkidari Act (English)	0	0	3
" Ditto ditto (Bengali)	0	0	3
" VIII of 1898 Revenue Sales Act ,,	0	0	8
" Ditto (English)	0	0	3
" I of 1899 Cow Killing Act ,,	0	0	3
" Ditto (Bengali)	0	0	3
" II of 1899 Public Demands Recovery Act (Eng.)	0	3	0
" Ditto ditto (Bengali)	0	3	0
" III of 1899 Amendment of Limitation Act (English)	0	0	3
" Ditto ditto (Bengali)	0	0	3
" IV of 1899 State Demands Act (English and Bengali combined)	0	0	6
" V of 1899 Civil Marriage Act (Eng.)	0	1	6
" Ditto ditto (Bengali)	0	1	6
" I of 1900 Amendment of Civil Procedure Code (English)	0	2	0
" II of 1900 Census Act (English)	0	1	3
" Ditto ditto (Bengali)	0	1	0
" I of 1901 C. B. Telegraph Act ,,	0	1	0
" I of 1903 C. B. Stamp Act (Eng.)	0	6	0
" Ditto Ditto (Beng.)	0	6	0
" II of 1903 Drainage Act (Eng.)	0	0	6
" Ditto (Bengali)	0	0	6
" III of 1903 Amendment of Cooch Behar Limitation Act (English).	0	1	6
" Ditto (Bengali)	0	1	6
Act IV of 1903 C. B. Town Committee Act (English).	0	6	0
V of 1903 Amendment of Civil Procedure Code.	0	1	6
" VI of 1903 Vaccination Act (Eng)*	0	2	0
" Ditto Ditto (Beng.)	0	2	0
Act I of 1904 Registration Act (Eng.)	0	0	6
" II of 1904 Amendment of Village Chowkidari (Eng.)	0	1	0
" Ditto Ditto (Beng.)	0	1	0
" I of 1905 Amendment of Stamp Act (English).	0	0	6
" II of 1905 Unclaimed Intestate Property.	0	0	6
" I of 1906 Encumbered Estate Act (English)	0	0	6
" II of 1906 Companies Act (English).	0	1	0
" III of 1906 Evidence Act Amendment.	0	0	6
" IV of 1906 Amendment of Village Chaukidari Act.	0	0	6
" V of 1906 Small Cause Court Act (English)	0	3	0
" VI of 1906 Wills Act (English)	0	0	3
" VII of 1906 Probate and Administration Act.	0	0	6

* Out of stock.

	Rs.	A.	P.
Act I of 1907 Amendment Town Committee Act.	0	0	6
,, II of 1907 Succession Act (English).	0	0	6
,, III of 1907 Amendment Vaccination Act (Bengali).	0	1	0
,, IV of 1907 Penal Code Act ...	0	0	6
,, I of 1908 Amendment of Stamp Act.	0	1	0
,, II of 1908 Forest Act ...	0	2	0
,, I of 1909 The Code of Criminal Procedure.	0	2	0
,, II of 1909 Act for the Legislative Council.	0	0	6
,, I of 1910 Registration of Births and Deaths (English).	0	1	0
Ditto (Bengali)	0	1	0
,, II of 1910 Amendment of Succession Certificate Act.	0	1	0
,, III of 1910 Provisions for the care of lunatics.	0	0	6
Act IV of 1910 Census Act (Eng. & Beng)	0	1	0
Act V of 1910 Tenancy Act (English)	0	8	0
,, V ,, ,, (Bengali)	0	11	0
,, I of 1913 Survey ,, (Eng.)	0	2	0
,, ,, ,, ,, (Beng.)	0	[illegible]	0
Letters and Proceedings having the force of Law.	0	10	0
Law Reports Vol. I*	0	8	0
,, Vol. II*	2	4	0
,, Vol. III	1	0	0
Law Report Vol IV (1911—Jan. 1314)	0	12	0
Vol. V (Mar. 1914-Dec. 1920)	0	8	0
Law Report Vol. VI.	0	12	0
,, Vol. VII	0	12	0
Act I of 1920 Census Act (Eng.)	0	2	0
,, ,, ,, (Beng.)	0	2	0
,, I of 1921 General Clauses Act	0	4	0
,, II ,, Code of Civil Procedure Act.	0	5	0
,, III ,, Transfer of Property ,,	0	2	0
,, IV ,, Limitation Act ...	0	3	0
,, V ,, Majority ,, ...	0	2	0
,, VI ,, Registration ,, ...	0	2	0
,, VII ,, Guardians and Wards Act.	0	2	0
,, VIII ,, Negotiable instruments Act.	0	2	0
,, IX ,, Criminal Tribes Act	0	3	0
,, X ,, Interest ,,	0	2	0
,, XI ,, Suits Valuations ,,	0	2	0
,, XII ,, Bankers' Books evidence (amendment.)	0	1	0
,, I of 1923 Regulation E.B.R. Arbitration.	0	1	0
,, I of 1923 Excise, Opium & Drugs	0	5	0
,, I of 1929 (amending the Cooch Behar Town Committee Act IV of 1902)	0	1	0
,, I of 1930 Criminal Law (amendt.)	0	1	0
,, II ,, Census Act ...	0	2	0
,, III ,, Co-operative Societies Act	0	4	0
,, III ,, 1930 ,, (Sec. 43) ...	0	3	0
,, I of 1931 Christian Marriage Act	0	1	0
,, I of 1932 Motor Vehicles Act	0	2	0
Act I of 1933 Cooch Behar Penal Code Amendment Act.	0	0	3

	Rs.	A.	P.
Act II of 1933 Cooch Behar Companies Act.	0	2	0
,, III of 1933 Code of Criminal Procedure.	0	4	0
,, I of 1934 The Lepers Act ...	0	2	0
,, III of 1934 Cooch Behar Revenue Sale Amendment Act.	0	1	0
Act No. IV of 1934 Hindu widow Marriage Act (Eng. & Beng).	0	1	0
,, I of 1935 Cooch Behar Matches (Excise Duty) Act.	0	2	0
,, I of 1937 Cooch Behar Hat toll protection Act.	0	0	6
Act II of 1937 Act for Prevention of Cruelty to Animals.	0	6	0
,, I of 1938 C.B. Public gambling Act	0	2	0
,, II of 1938 C.B. Amusement Tax Act	0	2	0
,, I of 1939 Amendment of C.B.T.C.	0	0	6
Act I of 1940 Census Act... ...	0	2	0
,, II of 1940 C. B. Penal Code Amendment Act.	0	0	6
,, I of 1941 Amendment of C. B. Tenancy Act.	0	0	6
,, II of 1941 C. B. Food Adulteration	0	3	0
,, III of 1941 Legislative Council Act	0	2	0
,, IV of 1941 C. B. Electricity Act	0	4	0
Act V of 1941 C. B. Income Tax Act	0	8	0
,, VI of 1941 C. B. Export Duty Act	0	1	0
Act VII of 1941 Motor Vehicles	1	0	0
,, VIII of 1941 Village choukidary Amendment	0	2	0
,, IX of 1941 Town Committee Amendment	0	1	0
,, X of 1941 General Amending	0	6	0
,, XI of 1941 Cow killing Amendment	0	0	3
,, XII of 1941 Tenancy (second Amend.) Act No XII of 1941	0	0	3
,, I of 1942 Standard of weight	0	1	0
,, II of 1942 foreigner's Act	0	1	0
,, III of 1942 Penal Code Act	2	12	0
,, IV of 1942 Companies (Amend)	0	1	0
,, V of 1942 Public Demands recovery (Amend)	0	1	0
,, VI of 1942 Incometax (Amend)	0	1	0
Act VII of 1942 (An Act to Amend the C. B. General Clauses Act I of 1921	0	0	6
,, VIII of 1942 (Transfer of Property Amendment) Act 1942	0	1	0
,, IX of 1942 (C. B. Registration Amendment) Act 1942	0	0	6
,, X of 1942 (C. B. Limitation Amendment) Act 1942	0	1	0
,, No. XI of 1942 (C. B. Town Committee) Amendment Act	0	0	6
Live Stock Census Report	0	4	0
Schedule of rates*	2	8	0
Cottage Industry	2	0	0
History of Cooch Behar (Paper bound) Bengali	2	0	0
Do Do (cloth bound)	3	0	0
Hand Book of Circular orders	2	0	0
History of Cooch Behar (Englsh version)	5	0	0

* Out of stock.

	Rs.	A.	P.
Act I of 1943 Legal Practitioners Act	0	4	0
„ II of 1943 Stamp Act ...	0	14	0
„ III of 1943 Excess Profits Tax Act	0	6	0
„ IV of 1943 Patents Act ...	0	4	0
„ V of 1943 Public Health Act ...	0	8	0
„ VI of 1943 (An Act to provide for the Prevention and Control of Contagious deseases affecting Animals.)	0	2	0
„ VII of 1943 Army Act ...	0	8	0
„ VIII of 1943 Workmen's Compensation Act.	0	1	0
„ IX of 1943 Factories Act ...	0	1	0
„ X of 1943 Public Demand Recovery Act	1	12	0
„ XI of 1943 Civil Procedure Code (amendment) Act.	0	2	0
„ XII of 1943 Pension (Exemption) Act.	0	0	6
„ XIII of 1943 Insolvency Act ...	0	8	0
„ XIV of 1943 Succession Act ...	0	1	0
„ XV of 1943 Extradition Act ...	0	3	0
„ XVI of 1943 Muli (Regulating) Act	0	0	6
„ XVII of 1943 Interest (amendment) Act.	0	0	6
„ XVIII of 1943 Revenue sale (amendment) Act.	0	0	6
„ XIX of 1943 Land Acquisition Act	0	4	0
„ XX of 1943 Forest (amendment) Act.	0	0	6
Act XXI of 1943 Tenancy (amendment) Act 1943.	0	6	0
Act XXII of 1943 Coch Behar Co-operation Societies Act 1943.	0	2	0
Act XXIII of 1943 Village Chaukidary (amendment).	0	1	0
Act XXIV of 1943 Cooch Behar Incometax (amendment) Act 1943.	0	1	0
Act XXV of 1943 Tobacco (Excise Duty) Act.	0	3	0
Act XXVI of 1943 Bengal and Assam Railway Arbitration Act.	0	2	0
Table of rates of Advalorem Fees laviable on the institution of Suits under the Cooch Behar Stamp Act II of 1943.	0	2	0
Rules made under section 52 of the Income-tax Act 1941.	0	2	0
Lives-stock Census Report	0	4	0
Act II of 1921 (as amended up to Cooch Behar Civil procedure 1921 (Cooch Behar State).	0	5	0
Cooch Behar Tenancy Act, Act V of 1910 (as amended upto 1943) Cooch Behar State.	0	11	0
Act I of 1944 Cooch Beher Agriculturists' Loans Act.	0	0	6
„ II of 1944 Cooch Behar Land Improvement Loans Act.	0	2	0
„ III of 1944 Cooch Behar Municipal Act	1	8	0
„ IV of 1944 C. B. Prevention of Cruelty to Animals Act. (Amendement.)	0	2	6
V of 1944 Cooch Behar Vaccination Act. (Amendement.)	0	2	0
„ VI of 1944 The Cooch Behar Medical Act.	0	6	0
VII of 1944 Cooch Behar Opium Smoking Act.	0	2	0
VIII of 1944 Cooch Behar Arms Act.	0	6	0
Act IX of 1944 Cooch Behar Police (incitement to Disaffection) Act.	0	1	6

	Rs.	A.	P.
Act X of 1944 The Cow killing Temporary Amendment Act.	0	0	6
The Government of Cooch Behar Act	(not for sale).		
Act No. I of 1945 Cooch Behar Income Tax (Amendment) Act.	0	1	0
„ II of 1945 Cooch Behar Excess Profit Tax (Amendment) Act.	0	1	0
„ III of 1945 Cooch Behar Special Excise Act.	0	6	0
„ IV of 1945 The Cooch Behar Land Encroachment Act	0	4	0
„ V of 1945 The Cooch Behar Orphanage Act.	0	2	0
„ VI of 1945 The Cooch Behar Tea Cultivation Control Act.	0	2	0
„ VII of 1945 The Cooch Behar Penal Code (Amendment) Act.	0	1	0
„ VIII of 1945 The Cooch Behar Ferries Act.	0	4	0
„ IX of 1945 The Cooch Behar Stamp (Amendment) Act.	0	1	0
„ X of 1945 The Cooch Behar Food Adultaration (Amendment) Act.	0	1	0
„ XI of 1945 The Cooch Behar Chowkidari (Amendment) Act.	0	1	0
„ XII of 1945 The Cooch Behar Export Duty (Amendment) Act.	0	1	0
„ XIII of 1945 The Cooch Behar Criminal Proceeure Code.	1	6	0
Live-stock Census Report 1945	0	4	0
Rules made under section 2 of the Agriculturists Loans Act (I of 1944)	0	4	0
„ made under section 9 of the Land Improvement Loans Act II of 1944	0	4	0
„ made under sections 5 and 26 of the Special Excise Act 1945	2	0	0
„ XIV of 1945 the Cooch Behar Army (Amendment) Act 1945.	0	2	0
„ I of 1946 (Forest Act) ...	0	4	0
„ II of 1946 (C. B. Foreign Companies Act 1946)	0	2	0
„ III of 1946 (The C. B. Reciprocity Act 1946.	0	1	0
Act No. IV of 1946 (C. B. Criminal Procedure Code (Amend) Act 1946)	0	1	0
„ V of 1946 C. B. Factories (Amend) Act 1946.	0	1	0
„ VI of 1946 (C. B Patents (Amend) Act 1946.	0	1	0
Act No. VII of 1946 (C. B. Excise Act).	0	12	0
„ VIII of 1946 (C. B. Opium Act).	0	2	0
„ IX of 1946 (C. B. Dangerous Drugs Act).	0	7	0
„ X of 1946 (C. B. Excess Profits (Repealing) Act 1946).	0	1	0
„ XI of 1946 C. B. Ferries (Amend) Act 1946	0	1	0
„ XII of 1946 (The Industrial Statistics Act.)	0	1	0
„ XIII of 1946 (C B. Requisitioned Land Act.)	0	1	0
„ XIV of 1946 (C. B. Essential Supplies Act).	0	2	0
„ XV of 1946 (Requisitioned Land (Amendment) Act 1946.	0	1	0
„ XVI of 1946 (C. B. Aircraft Act) 1946.	0	2	0
„ I of 1947 (C. B. Essential Supplies (Tem. powers) Amendment 1947.	0	2	0
„ II of 1947 the Cooch Behar Public Security Act, 1947.	0	6	0

A. BAGCHI,
Superintendent State Press, Cooch Behar.

The Cooch Behar Gazette.

২৯শে আশ্বিন বৃহস্পতিবার] THURSDAY, OCTOBER 16, 1947 [১৩৫৪ সাল ৪৩৮ রাজশক

PART V.

Advertisements

SALE NOTICE.

The following unsold lots will be sold by public auction at the Forest Office, Cooch Behar on the 5th November 1947, beginning at 1 P. M. :—

Lot Nos. 1 to 3 of 1947-48	Sal trees in Mahismuri Sal Forest.
Lot No, 5 of 1947-48	Sissu and a few Simul trees in Nababgunj Balashi Forest.
Lot Nos. 6 to 12 of 1947-48	Teak trees in Nilkuthi Teak Forest.
Lot Nos. 14 and 15 of 1947-48	Sissu and a few Simul trees in Nababgunj Balashi Forest.
Lot No. 16 of 1947-48	Sissu logs in the depot at Cooch Behar Town.

B. N. Roy,
Conservator of Forests,
Cooch Behar.

ADVERTISEMENT.

Tenders are invited for earthwork (for construction and repairs to Rural Paths) and timber bridges and cement concrete ring culverts under the Development Department of this State for the current year. The tenders must reach this office in sealed covers by the 7th November 1947 at the latest. Further particulars may be had from this office.

L. M. Baksi,
Development Commissioner, Cooch Behar.

বিজ্ঞাপন।

শহরের মধ্যস্থলে অবস্থিত মোকদ্দমী স্বত্বের উৎকৃষ্ট জমী বিক্রয় হইবে। নিম্নলিখিত ঠিকানায় অনুসন্ধান করুন।

শ্রীমোহিনীমোহন বক্সী,
জমিদার।

List of State Acts, Laws and Codes for sale in the State Press, Cooch Behar.

	Rs.	A.	P.
Act of 1874 Limitation (English)* ...	0	12	0
,, Ditto (Bengali) ...	0	12	0
,, of 1882 Cattle Trespass* ,, ...	0	2	0
মুদ্রিত কাগজ সম্বন্ধীয় নিয়মাবলী ...	0	2	0
Act of 1888 Sub-infeudation* ...	0	1	0
,, I of 1890 লোক সংখ্যা গ্রহণ বিষয়ক আইন	0	0	6
I of 1892 Private Fisheries Protection (English and Bengali combined.)	0	1	0
,, II of 1892 Amendment of Limitation (Engish and Bengali combined.)	0	1	0
III of 1892 Jurisdiction (English)*	0	1	0
,, Ditto (Bengali)*	0	1	0
,, IV 1892 Merchandise Marks (Eng.)*	0	2	0
,, I of 1893 Legal Practitioners ,, *	0	1	3
,, Ditto ditto (Bengali)	0	1	0
,, II of 1893 Amendment of Town Committee (English).	0	0	3
,, III of 1893 Village Chowkidari (English)	0	1	6
,, IV of 1893 Amendment of Revenue Sale (English).	0	0	3
,, IV of 1893 Amendment Revenue Sale (Bengali)	0	0	3
,, V of 1893 Cess (English)	0	1	0
,, Ditto (Bengali)	0	1	0
,, VI of 1893 Amendment of Legal Practitioners (English and Bengali combined.)*	0	0	8
,, I of 1894 Amendment of Town Committee.*	0	0	3
,, II of 1894 Amendment of Voluntary Sale of under-tenures.	0	0	8
,, III of 1894 Amendment of Village Chowkidari.*	0	0	6
,, I of 1895 Small Cause Courts Act (English).	0	0	9
,, I of 1896 Amendment of Cooch Behar Stamp Act (English).*	0	0	3
,, I of 1896 Amendment of Cooch Behar Stamp Act (Bengali).*	0	0	8
,, II of 1896 Preservation of Boundary Act (English).	0	0	6
,, III of 1896 Amendment of Village Chowkidari Act (English).	0	0	3
,, I of 1897 Amendment of Cooch Behar Town Committee Act (Eng.)	0	0	3
,, II of 1897 Mahomedan Inheritance Act (English).	0	0	3
,, III of 1897 Oaths Act (English)*	0	0	6
,, IV of 1897 Amendment of Stamp rules (English.)	0	0	8
,, V of 1897 Revenue Sale Act (English).	0	3	6
,, V of 1897 Revenue Sale Act (Bengali).	0	3	0
,, VI of 1897 Wards Act (English)	0	1	0
,, I of 1898 Kist Act ,,	0	0	6
,, Ditto (Bengali)	0	0	6
,, II of 1898 Amendment of Revenue Sale Act (English).	0	0	3
,, Ditto (Bengali)	0	0	3
,, III of 1898 Police Act (English)	0	2	0
,, Diuu (Bengali.)	0	2	C

	Rs.	A.
Act IV of 1898 Bridge Toll Act (Eng.)	0	0
,, of Ditto ditto (Bengali)	0	0
,, V of 1898 Succession Certificate Act (English)	0	2
,, Ditto ditto (Bengali)	0	2
,, VI of 1898 Amendment of Voluntary Sales of under-tenures (Eng.)	0	0
,, Ditto ditto (Bengali)	0	0
,, VII of 1898 Amendment of Village Chowkidari Act (English)	0	0
,, Ditto ditto (Bengali)	0	0
,, VIII of 1898 Revenue Sales Act ,,	0	0
,, Ditto (English)	0	0
,, I of 1899 Cow Killing Act ,,	0	0
,, Ditto (Bengali)	0	0
,, II of 1899 Public Demands Recovery Act (Eng.)	0	3
,, Ditto ditto (Bengali)	0	3
,, III of 1899 Amendment of Limitation Act (English)	0	0
,, Ditto ditto (Bengali)	0	0
,, IV of 1899 State Demands Act (English and Bengali combined)	0	0
,, V of 1899 Civil Marriage Act (Eng.)	0	1
,, Ditto ditto (Bengali)	0	1
,, I of 1900 Amendment of Civil Procedure Code (English)	0	2
,, II of 1900 Census Act (English)	0	1
,, Ditto ditto (Bengali)	0	1
,, I of 1901 C. B. Telegraph Act ,,	0	1
,, I of 1903 C. B. Stamp Act (Eng.)	0	6
,, Ditto Ditto (Beng.)	0	6
,, II of 1903 Drainage Act (Eng.)	0	0
,, Ditto (Bengali)	0	0
,, III of 1903 Amendment of Cooch Behar Limitation Act (English).	0	1
,, Ditto (Bengali)	C	1
Act IV of 1909 C. B. Town Committee Act (English).	0	6
V of 1903 Amendment of Civil Procedure Code.	0	1
,, VI of 1903 Vaccination Act (Eng)*	0	2
,, Ditto Ditto (Beng.)	0	2
Act I of 1904 Registration Act (Eng.)	0	0
,, II of 1904 Amendment of Village Chowkidari (Eng.)	0	1
,, Ditto Ditto (Beng.)	0	1
,, I of 1905 Amendment of Stamp Act (English).	0	0
,, II of 1905 Unclaimed Intestate Property.	0	0
,, I of 1906 Encumbered Estate Act (English)	0	0
,, II of 1906 Companies Act (English).	0	1
,, III of 1906 Evidence Act Amendment	0	0
,, IV of 1906 Amendment of Village Chaukidari Act.	0	0
,, V of 1906 Small Cause Court Act (English)	0	3
,, VI of 1906 Wills Act (English)	0	0
,, VII of 1906 Probate and Administration Act.	0	0

* Out of stock.

	Rs.	A.	P.
Act I of 1907 Amendment Town Committee Act.	0	0	6
,, II of 1907 Succession Act (English).	0	0	6
,, III of 1907 Amendment Vaccination Act (Bengali).	0	1	0
,, IV of 1907 Penal Code Act ...	0	0	6
,, I of 1908 Amendment of Stamp Act.	0	1	0
,, II of 1908 Forest Act ...	0	2	0
,, I of 1909 The Code of Criminal Procedure.	0	2	0
,, II of 1909 Act for the Legislative Council.	0	0	6
,, I of 1910 Registration of Births and Deaths (English).	0	1	0
Ditto (Bengali)	0	1	0
,, II of 1910 Amendment of Succession Certificate Act.	0	1	0
,, III of 1910 Provisions for the care of lunatics.	0	0	6
Act IV of 1910 Census Act (Eng. & Beng)	0	1	0
Act V of 1910 Tenancy Act (English)	0	8	0
,, V ,, ,, (Bengali)	0	11	0
,, I of 1913 Survey ,, Eng.)	0	2	0
,, ,, ,, ,, (Beng.)	0	2	0
Letters and Proceedings having the force of Law.	0	10	0
Law Reports Vol. I*	0	8	0
,, Vol. II*	2	4	0
,, Vol. III	1	0	0
Law Report Vol IV (1911—Jan. 1314)	0	12	0
Vol. V (Mar. 1914-Dec. 1920)	0	8	0
Law Report Vol. VI.	0	12	0
,, Vol. VII	0	12	0
Act I of 1920 Census Act (Eng.)	0	2	0
,, ,, ,, (Beng.)	0	2	0
,, I of 1921 General Clauses Act	0	4	0
,, II ,, Code of Civil Procedure Act.	0	5	0
,, III ,, Transfer of Property ,,	0	2	0
,, IV ,, Limitation Act ...	0	3	0
,, V ,, Majority ...	0	2	0
,, VI ,, Registration ,, ...	0	2	0
,, VII ,, Guardians and Wards Act.	0	2	0
,, VIII ,, Negotiable instruments Act.	0	2	0
,, IX ,, Criminal Tribes Act	0	3	0
,, X ,, Interest ,,	0	2	0
,, XI ,, Suits Valuations ,,	0	2	0
,, XII ,, Bankers' Books evidence (amendment.)	0	1	0
,, I of 1923 Regulation E.B.R. Arbitration.	0	1	0
,, I of 1923 Excise, Opium & Drugs	0	5	0
,, I of 1929 (amending the Cooch Behar Town Committee Act IV of 1902)	0	1	0
,, I of 1930 Criminal Law (amendt.)	0	1	0
,, II ,, Census Act ...	0	2	0
,, III ,, Co-operative Societies Act	0	4	0
,, III ,, 1930 ,, (Sec. 43) ...	0	3	0
,, I of 1931 Christian Marriage Act	0	1	0
,, I of 1932 Motor Vehicles Act	0	2	0
Act I of 1933 Cooch Behar Penal Code Amendment Act.	0	0	3

	Rs.	A.	P.
Act II of 1933 Cooch Behar Companies Act.	0	2	0
,, III of 1933 Code of Criminal Procedure.	0	4	0
,, I of 1934 The Lepers Act ...	0	2	0
,, III of 1934 Cooch Behar Revenue Sale Amendment Act.	0	1	0
Act No. IV of 1934 Hindu widow Marriage Act (Eng. & Beng).	0	1	0
,, I of 1935 Cooch Behar Matches (Excise Duty) Act.	0	2	0
,, I of 1937 Cooch Behar Hat toll protection Act.	0	0	6
Act II of 1937 Act for Prevention of Cruelty to Animals.	0	6	0
,, I of 1938 C.B. Public gambling Act	0	2	0
,, II of 1938 C.B. Amusement Tax Act	0	2	0
,, I of 1939 Amendment of C.B.T.C.	0	0	6
Act I of 1940 Census Act... ...	0	2	0
,, II of 1940 C. B. Penal Code Amendment Act.	0	0	6
,, I of 1941 Amendment of C. B. Tenancy Act.	0	0	6
,, II of 1941 C. B. Food Adulteration	0	3	0
,, III of 1941 Legislative Council Act	0	2	0
,, IV of 1941 C. B. Electricity Act	0	4	0
Act V of 1941 C. B. Income Tax Act	0	8	0
,, VI of 1941 C. B. Export Duty Act	0	1	0
Act VII of 1941 Motor Vehicles	1	0	0
,, VIII of 1941 Village choukidary Amendment	0	2	0
,, IX of 1941 Town Committee Amendment	0	1	0
,, X of 1941 General Amending	0	6	0
,, XI of 1941 Cow killing Amendment	0	0	3
,, XII of 1941 Tenancy (second Amend.) Act No. XII of 1941	0	0	3
,, I of 1942 Standard of weight	0	1	0
,, II of 1942 foreigner's Act	0	1	0
,, III of 1942 Penal Code Act	2	12	0
,, IV of 1942 Companies (Amend)	0	1	0
,, V of 1942 Public Demands recovery (Amend)	0	1	0
,, VI of 1942 Incometax (Amend)	0	1	0
Act VII of 1942 (An Act to Amend the C. B. General Clauses Act I of 1921	0	0	6
,, VIII of 1942 (Transfer of Property Amendment) Act 1942	0	1	0
,, IX of 1942 (C. B. Registration Amendment) Act 1942	0	0	6
,, X of 1942 (C. B. Limitation Amendment) Act 1942	0	1	0
,, No. XI of 1942 (C. B. Town Committee) Amendment Act	0	0	6
Live Stock Census Report	0	4	0
Schedule of rates*	2	8	0
Cottage Industry	2	0	0
History of Cooch Behar (Paper bound) Bengali	2	0	0
Do Do (cloth bound)	3	0	0
Hand Book of Circular orders	2	0	0
History of Cooch Behar (Englsh version)	5	0	0

* Out of stock.

	Rs.	A.	P.
Act I of 1943 Legal Practitioners Act	0	4	0
„ II of 1943 Stamp Act ...	0	14	0
„ III of 1943 Excess Profits Tax Act	0	6	0
„ IV of 1943 Patents Act ...	0	4	0
„ V of 1943 Public Health Act ...	0	3	0
„ VI of 1943 (An Act to provide for the Prevention and Control of Contagious deseases affecting Animals.)	0	2	0
„ VII of 1943 Army Act ...	0	8	0
„ VIII of 1943 Workmen's Compensation Act,	0	1	0
„ IX of 1943 Factories Act ...	0	1	0
„ X of 1943 Public Demand Recovery Act.	1	12	0
„ XI of 1943 Civil Procedure Code (amendment) Act.	0	2	6
„ XII of 1943 Pension (Exemption) Act.	0	0	6
„ XIII of 1943 Insolvency Act ...	0	8	0
„ XIV of 1943 Succession Act ...	0	1	0
„ XV of 1943 Extradition Act ...	0	3	0
„ XVI of 1943 Muli (Regulating) Act	0	0	6
„ XVII of 1943 Interest (amendment) Act.	0	0	6
„ XVIII of 1943 Revenue sale (amendment) Act.	0	0	6
„ XIX of 1943 Land Acquisition Act	0	4	0
„ XX of 1943 Forest (amendment) Act.	0	0	6
Act XXI of 1943 Tenancy (amendment) Act 1943.	0	6	0
Act XXII of 1943 Coch Behar Co-operation Societies Act 1943.	0	2	0
Act XXIII of 1943 Village Chaukidary (amendment).	0	1	0
Act XXIV of 1943 Cooch Behar Incometax (amendment) Act 1943.	0	1	0
Act XXV of 1943 Tobacco (Excise Duty) Act.	0	3	0
Act XXVI of 1943 Bengal and Assam Railway Arbitration Act.	0	2	0
Table of rates of Advalorem Fees laviable on the institution of Suits under the Cooch Behar Stamp Act II of 1943.	0	2	0
Rules made under section 52 of the Income-tax Act 1941.	0	2	0
Lives-stock Census Report	0	4	0
Act II of 1921 (as amended up to Cooch Behar Civil procedure 1921 (Cooch Behar State).	0	5	0
Cooch Behar Tenancy Act, Act V of 1910 (as amended upto 1943) Cooch Behar State.	0	11	0
Act I of 1944 Cooch Beher Agriculturists' Loans Act,	0	0	6
„ II of 1944 Cooch Behar Land Improvement Loans Act.	0	2	0
„ III of 1944 Cooch Behar Municipal Act	1	8	0
„ IV of 1944 C. B. Prevention of Cruelty to Animals Act. (Amendement.)	0	2	6
V of 1944 Cooch Behar Vaccination Act. (Amendement.)	0	2	0
„ VI of 1944 The Cooch Behar Medical Act.	0	6	0
VII of 1944 Cooch Behar Opium Smoking Act.	0	2	0
VIII of 1944 Cooch Behar Arms Act.	0	6	0
Act IX of 1944 Cooch Behar Police (incitement to Disaffection) Act,	0	1	6

	Rs.	A.	P.
Act X of 1944 The Cow killing Temporary Amerdment Act.	0	0	6
The Government of Cooch Behar Act	(not for sale).		
Act No. I of 1945 Cooch Behar Income Tax (Amendment) Act.	0	1	0
„ II of 1945 Cooch Behar Excess Profit Tax (Amendment) Act.	0	1	0
„ III of 1945 Cooch Behar Special Excise Act.	0	6	0
„ IV of 1945 The Cooch Behar Land Encroachment Act	0	4	0
„ V of 1945 The Cooch Behar Orphanage Act,	0	2	0
„ VI of 1945 The Cooch Behar Tea Cultivation Control Act.	0	2	0
„ VII of 1945 The Cooch Behar Penal Code (Amendment) Act.	0	1	0
„ VIII of 1945 The Cooch Behar Ferries Act.	0	4	0
„ IX of 1945 The Cooch Behar Stamp (Amendment) Act.	0	1	0
„ X of 1945 The Cooch Behar Food Adultaration (Amendment) Act.	0	1	0
„ XI of 1945 The Cooch Behar Chowkidari (Amendment) Act.	0	1	0
„ XII of 1945 The Cooch Behar Export Duty (Amendment) Act.	0	1	0
„ XIII of 1945 The Cooch Behar Criminal Procecure Code.	1	6	0
Live-stock Census Report 1945	0	4	0
Rules made under section 2 of the Agriculturists Loans Act (I of 1944)	0	4	0
„ made under section 9 of the Land Improvement Loans Act II of 1944	0	4	0
„ made under sections 5 and 26 of the Special Excise Act 1945	2	0	0
„ XIV of 1945 the Cooch Behar Army (Amendment) Act 1945.	0	2	0
„ I of 1946 (Forest Act) ...	0	4	0
„ II of 1946 (C. B. Foreign Companies Act 1946)	0	2	0
„ III of 1946 (The C. B. Reciprocity Act 1946.	0	1	0
Act No. IV of 1946 (C. B. Criminal Procedure Code (Amend) Act 1946)	0	1	0
„ V of 1946 C. B. Factories (Amend) Act 1946,	0	1	0
„ VI of 1946 (C. B Patents (Amend) Act 1946.	0	1	0
Act No. VII of 1946 (C. B. Excise Act).	0	12	0
„ VIII of 1946 (C. B. Opium Act).	0	2	0
„ IX of 1946 (C. B. Dangerous Drugs Act).	0	7	0
„ X of 1946 (C. B. Excess Profits (Repealing) Act 1946).	0	1	0
„ XI of 1946 C. B. Ferries (Amend) Act 1946	0	1	0
„ XII of 1946 (The Industrial Statistics Act.)	0	1	0
„ XIII of 1946 (C B. Requisitioned Land Act.)	0	1	0
„ XIV of 1946 (C. B. Essential Supplies Act).	0	2	0
„ XV of 1946 (Requisitioned Land (Amendment) Act 1946,	0	1	0
„ XVI of 1946 (C. B. Aircraft Act). 1946,	0	2	0
„ I of 1947 (C. B. Essential Supplies (Tem. powers) Amendment 1947.	0	2	0
„ II of 1947 the Cooch Behar Public Security Act, 1947.	0	6	0

A. BAGCHI,
Superintendet State Press, Cooch Behar.

Serial No.	Name of articles.	Previous rate. Rs.	A.	P.	Proposed rate. Rs.	A.	P.	Unit of rates.
128	Glass panes upto 2 Sft. (Belgium) ..	1	8	0	1	8	0	per sft.
129	Do. above 2 sft. up to 4 sft. ...	1	8	0	1	8	0	"
130	Do. Do. 4 sft. ...	1	8	0	1	8	0	"
131	Do. frosted upto 2 sft. ...	1	12	0	1	12	0	"
132	Do. above 2 sft. upto 4 sft. ...	2	0	0	2	0	0	"
133	Do. above 4sft. ...	2	4	0	2	0	0	"
134	1/8" Glass panes up to 2 sft. ...	3	0	0	3	4	0	"
135	Gunny (36" wide)	0	6	0	0	6	0	per yard
136	Do. (40" wide)	0	8	0	0	8	0	"
137	Do. (48" wide)	0	10	0	0	10	0	"
138	Green ink powder	0	3	0	0	4	0	per packet
139	Green ink powder (English) ...	2	12	0	....			"
140	Gold powder (best)	1	4	0	1	4	0	"
141	Green powder (English)	4	0	0	2	0	0	"
142	Grease	0	12	0	0	12	0	per lb
143	Glue	3	0	0	3	0	0	per seer
144	Gum	2	8	0	2	8	0	"
145	Galvanised Staples	2	0	0	2	8	0	"
146	Hemp rope	1	8	0	1	8	0	"
147	Hemp sutli	2	0	0	2	0	0	"
148	Hack Saw blade	0	6	0	0	4	0	each
149	Iron Hinges 2"	0	7	0	0	7	0	per pair
150	Do. 2½"	0	8	0	0	7	0	"
151	Do. 3"	0	10	0	0	8	0	"
152	Do 3½"	0	12	0	0	9	0	"
153	Do. 4"	0	11	0	0	10	0	"
154	Iron Door Bolts 4"	0	6	0	0	6	0	each
155	Do. 5"	0	8	0	0	8	0	"
156	Do. 6"	0	9	0	0	9	0	"
157	Do. 7"	0	10	0	0	10	0	"
158	Do. 8"	0	11	0	0	11	0	"
159	Iron Patent hasps and staples 3" (English)	0	6	0	0	5	0	"
160	Do. 4" "	0	8	0	0	6	0	"
161	Do. 5" "	0	10	0	0	8	0	"
162	Ink powder (lamp black)	0	3	0	0	4	0	per packet
163	!vory black	2	0	0	2	0	0	"
164	Iron Nuts 1/8"	0	0	3	0	0	6	each
165	Iron Nuts ¼"	0	0	3	0	0	6	"
166	Iron Nuts 5 16"	0	0	3	0	0	6	"
167	Iron Nuts 3/8"	0	1	0	0	1	9	"
168	Iron Nuts ½"	0	2	0	0	2	0	"
169	Iron Nuts 5/8"	0	2	6	0	3	0	"
170	Iron Nuts ¾"	0	3	0	0	3	6	"
771	Iron Nuts 7/8"	0	4	0	0	4	0	"
172	Iron Nuts 1"	0	6	0	0	7	0	"
173	Iron Nuts 1¼"	0	6	0	0	8	0	"
174	Do. washers 1/8"	0	2	0	0	3	0	per dozen
175	Do. washers ¼"	0	2	0	0	3	0	"
176	Do. washers 5/16"	0	3	0	0	3	0	"
177	Do. washers 8/8"	0	0	6	0	0	6	each
178	Do. washers ½"	0	0	6	0	0	-6	"
179	Do. washers 5/8"	0	0	6	0	1	0	"
180	Do. washers 3/4"	0	0	9	0	1	0	"
181	Do. washers 7/8"	0	0	9	0	1	0	"
182	Do. washers 1"	0	0	9	0	1	0	"
183	Do. washers 1¼"	0	0	9	0	1	0	"
184	Iron Nuts & Bolts 6" × 5/8" ...	0	8	0	0	8	0	each
185	Do. 4" × 5/8" ...	0	6	0	0	6	0	"
186	Do. 6" × 1/2" ...	0	6	0	0	6	0	"
187	Do. 4" × 1/2" ...	0	4	0	0	5	0	"
188	Do. 3" × 1/2" ...	0	4	0	0	4	0	"
189	Do. 2" × 1/2" ...	0	4	0	0	4	0	"
190	Do. 1½" × 1/2" ...	0	3	0	0	3	0	"
191	Do. 1" × 3/8" ...	0	2	0	0	2	0	"
192	Do. 1½" × 3/8" ...	0	2	0	0	2	0	"
193	Do. 2" × 3/8" ...	0	2	0	0	2	0	"
194	Do. 2½" × 3/8" ...	0	2	0	0	4	0	"
195	Do. 3" × 3/8" ...	0	2	6	0	4	6	"
196	Iron door chain	0	4	0	0	4	0	"
197	Iron door rings	0	4	0	0	4	0	per pair
198	Iron (M. S. Round)	15	8	0	....			per maund

Serial No.	Name of articles.		Previous rate: Rs.	A.	P.	Proposed rate: Rs.	A.	P.	Unit of [illegible]
199	Iron (M. S. Flat)	... ...	15	8	0	....			per maund
200	Do. (Sheet)	... ...	15	8	0	....			,,
201	Jute	... ...	0	12	0	0	12	0	per seer
202	Jute rope (fine)	... ...	1	0	0	1	4	0	,,
203	Do. (ordinary)	... ...	0	14	0	1	0	0	,,
204	Jonsons' sofeda	... ...	8	12	0	4	0	0	,,
205	Khun kharap	... ...	0	2	0	0	2	0	per tola
206	Khoyeri brown	... ...	1	12	0	2	8	0	per packet
207	Linseed oil pale boiled (Gouripur)	...	10	0	0	10	0	0	per gallon
208	Linseed oil boiled (Double)	...	10	0	0	10	0	0	,,
209	Do raw (Gouripur)	...	9	12	0	9	8	0	,,
210	Do Do	...	2	12	0	2	8	0	per seer
211	Loban	... ...	1	4	0	1	0	0	,,
212	Limpet washers	... ...	0	7	0	0	7	0	per gross
213	Lamp black (English)	... ...	1	4	0	1	4	0	per lb.
214	Mina paint	... ...	0	7	0	0	4	0	per tola.
215	Matting tape	... ...	0	1	0	0	1	0	per yard
216	Machine thread	... ...	0	8	0	0	8	0	,,
217	Malacca cane	... ...	0	4	0	0	4	0	each
218	Mata cloth	... ...	0	5	0	0	5	0	per yard
219	Mustard oil	...	1	12	0	2	4	0	per seer
220	Muratic acid	... ...	4	0	0	4	0	0	,,
221	Mehagoni powder	... ...	0	6	0	0	6	0	per tola
222	Newar	... ...	4	0	0	2	0	0	per seer
223	Paint (Hubbucks) white zinc	..	150	0	0	150	0	0	per Cwt
224	Do Do	... ...	4	0	0	4	0	0	per seer
225	Paint (Hubbucks) green	...	100	0	0	100	0	0	per Cwt
226	Do Do	...	2	0	0	2	0	0	per seer
227	Paint (Hubbucks) red oxide	...	90	0	0	90	0	0	per Cwt
228	Do Do	... ...	1	12	0	1	12	0	per seer
229	Paint (Hubbucks) buff paint	...	100	0	0	100	0	0	per Cwt
230	Do Do	...	2	0	0	2	0	0	per seer
231	Linseed oil (boiled)	... ...	2	12	0	2	8	0	per seer
232	Paint white zinc (English)	...	2	0	0	2	0	0	,,
233	Do (Umbrella brand) (Jenson & Nicholson)	...	2	0	0	2	0	0	,,
234	Paint green (English)	... ...	1	8	0	1	8	0	,,
235	Paint red (English)	... ...	1	8	0	1	8	0	,,
236	Paint Shalimar red corrugal	...	16	8	0	15	8	0	per gallon
237	Paint Shalimar green corrugal	..	17	8	0	16	8	0	,,
238	Patent nails 2" to 8" (Eng.)	...	1	4	0	1	8	0	per seer
239	Puri (English)	... ...	3	8	0	3	0	0	per lb
240	Prussian blue	... ...	1	0	0	4	0	0	per seer
241	Painting Round Brush No. 2 (Eng. Wolf Brand).	...	1	0	0	1	4	0	each
242	Do Do No 3	...	1	4	0	1	4	0	,,
243	Do Do No 4	...	1	4	0	1	4	0	,,
244	Do Do No 6 & 7	...	1	6	0	1	6	0	,,
245	Do Do No 11		1	8	0	1	8	0	,,
246	Do Do No 11 (Country)		1	0	0	1	0	0	,,
247	Prepared wax polished (U S A.)	...	3	8	0	3	8	0	per lb.
248	Quill brush (small)	... ...	0	8	0	0	8	0	each
249	Do (medium)	..	0	12	0	0	12	0	,,
250	Rivet iron fine ¼", ½", ¾" & 1"	...	3	0	0	6	0	0	per seer
251	Rivet iron	... ...	2	0	0	4	12	0	,,
252	Rope for tents	... ...	1	8	0	2	8	0	,,
253	Resin	... ...	1	8	0	3	0	0	,,
254	Rung	... ...	15	0	0	18	0	0	,,
255	Raw sienna	... ...	2	0	0	2	8	0	per packet
256	Red earth	... ...	0	8	0	0	8	0	per seer
257	Do (Eng.)	... ...	1	0	0	1	4	0	,,

Serial No.	Name of articles.	Previous rate. Rs.	A.	P.	Proposed rate. Rs.	A.	P.	Unit of rate.
258	Rothas cement	4	0	0	....			per bag
259	Do (Retail sale) ...	0	1	0	....			per seer
260	Steel (Broken)	2	8	0	2	8	0	,,
261	Sand paper Nos. 1, 2 and 3 (Eng.)...	3	0	0	3	0	0	per dozen
262	Sajimati	0	8	0	0	8	0	per seer
263	Soda	0	6	0	0	6	0	,,
264	Silver powder	1	0	0	1	0	0	per packet
265	Stone Lime (Sylhet) ...	4	4	0	4	0	0	per md.
266	,, (Jainty)	3	0	0	2	0	0	,,
267	,, (Paste) for white washing (½ Md. tin)	4	0	0	3	8	0	per tin
268	,, Do (16 sr. ,,)	3	4	0	3	4	0	,,
269	Do. Do. (12 seer tin)	2	12	0	2	12	0	,,
270	Sapoline (40 oz.) ...	3	0	0	2	0	0	,,
271	Tacks (small)	2	0	0	2	0	0	per packet.
272	Twine thread (small)	0	4	0	0	4	0	each
273	Do. (large)	0	6	0	0	6	0	,,
274	Thread red and blue	0	3	0	0	3	0	,,
275	Thread red and blue (Country) ...	0	3	0	0	3	0	,,
276	Thread cotton	5	0	0	....			per seer
277	Turkey Umber	1	12	0	2	8	0	per packet
278	Turpentine (Hubbucks)	12	0	0	12	0	0	per gallon
279	Do. Do	4	0	0	4	0	0	per seer
280	Turpentine (Country)	10	0	0	10	0	0	per gallon
281	Do Do	4	0	0	4	0	0	per seer
282	Venetian Hook	4	0	0	8	0	0	per cent
283	Verminia red	4	0	0	....			per packet
284	Whiting (Eng.)	15	0	0	15	0	0	per md.
285	Wood oil	8	0	0	4	0	0	per gallon
286	Wax	4	0	0	4	0	0	per seer
287	Water filter net	5	0	0	....			per sft
288	Wood Screw ½"	3	0	0	3	0	0	per gross
289	Do. 3"	6	0	0	6	0	0	,,
290	Do. 3½"	6	0	0	8	8	0	,,
291	Do. 4"	6	8	0	6	8	0	,,
292	Do. 5"	7	0	0	7	0	0	,,
293	Yellow Ochre	0	8	0	0	8	0	per seer
294	Do. (English) ...	1	0	0	1	0	0	,,
295	Copal varnish (Umbrella Brand) (J. & N.)	12	0	0	12	0	0	per gallon
296	French polish (Do. Do.)	17	0	0	17	0	0	,,
297	White zinc paint stiff (J. & N.) ...	100	0	0	100	0	0	per Cwt.
298	Turpentine, (Umbrella Brand).	12	0	0	12	0	0	per gallon
299	Dry distemper	54	0	0	....			per Cwt.
300	Wood Screw ¾"	....			4	8	0	per gross
301	Do. 1"	....			2	12	0	,,
302	Do. 1¼"	....			3	0	0	,,
303	Do 1½"	....			3	8	0	,,
304	Do 1¾"	....			4	0	0	,,
305	Do. 2"	....			4	8	0	Do.
306	Do. 2¼"	....			4	4	0	Do.

G. NARAYAN,
MAJOR,
Actg. Chief Engineer, P. W. D.,
Cooch Behar State.

The Cooch Behar Gazette.

১লা অগ্রহায়ণ সোমবার] MONDAY, NOVEMBER 17, 1947 [১৩৫৪ সাল ৪৩৮ রাজশক

PART V.

Advertisements

NOTICES.

It is hereby notified that the sale of bricks by any authorised P. W. D. Contractor, or the receipt of bricks by any member of the public in the State, is illegal except when a Permit for the sale of bricks has been issued by the Chief Engineer, P. W. D. Permits are strickly non-transferable and any surplus bricks not required by the Consumer should be surrendered to the Chief Engineer at the controlled rate of sale.

G. NARAYAN,
Major,
Actg. Chief Engineer, Cooch Behar.

Notice is hereby given for general information that time for subscription of shares of the Cooch Behar Tea Estate, Ltd. by the State residents, is extended up to the 30th November, 1947.

M. GUPTA,
Officer-in-charge,
The Cooch Behar Tea Estate Ltd.

WANTED.

Applications are invited from Cooch Behari candidates for undergoing Forest Ranger Course Training in the Indian Forest Ranger College at Dehra Dun as a State stipendiary.

Minimum qualification should be intermediate passed of any recognised Indian University with one or more of the following subjects :—Mathematics, Physics, Chemistry, Botany and Zoology.

Age of the candidates must not be less than 18 years nor more than 25 years on the 1st April, 1948.

The selected candidate will have to furnish a bond to the effect that on completion of his training, he will serve the State at least for 5 years, if required.

The selected candidate will have to work in the Cooch Behar Forest Department on a suitable stipend for a couple of months before appearing for a qualifying Examination at Dehra Dun. Further particulars may be had from the office of the undersigned.

Applications stating age, qualification and with copies of testimonials including a certificate from the Sub-divisional Officer concerned, will be received by the undersigned on or before the 5th December, 1947.

S. C. ROY SINGH SARKAR,
Public Health & Education Minister.

Sale ! **Sale !!** **Sale !!!**

It is notified for general information that 14 Harianа cows of the State Model Dairy Farm will be sold out in public auction to the highest bidder on the 28th November, 1947 at 2 P. M. in the Dairy premises.

The bid money will have to be deposited within an hour after the auction.

I. NARAYAN,
Lt. Col.,
Dy: Development Commissioner
for Development Commissioner, Cooch Behar

বিক্রয় ! **বিক্রয় !!** **বিক্রয় !!**

এতদ্বারা সর্ব্বসাধারণকে জানান যাইতেছে যে আগামী ২৮শে নভেম্বর বেলা ২ ঘটিকায় ষ্টেট মডেল ডায়েরী ফার্মে পাঞ্জাব হইতে আনীত ১৪টি হারিয়ানা গাভী প্রকাশ্য নিলামে বিক্রয় করা হইবে।

নিলামডাকের টাকা ১ ঘণ্টার মধ্যেই দাখিল করিতে হইবে।

আই, নারায়ণ,
ডেপুটি ডেভলপমেন্ট কমিশনার,
কোচবিহার।

নীলামের বিজ্ঞাপন।

এতদ্বারা সর্ব্বসাধারণকে জানান যাইতেছে যে, আগামী ২১শে নভেম্বর ১৯৪৭ তারিখে বেলা ২ ঘটিকার সময় অত্র কুচবিহার কলেক্টর আফিসে নীলকুঠি, চরকেরকুঠী ও ইছামারী চাপাগুড়ীর ছনখড় বাগান প্রকাশ্য নীলামে বিক্রয় করা হইবে। ক্রয়েচ্ছুক ব্যক্তিগণ উক্ত তারিখে আসিয়া নির্দ্ধারিত সময়ে ডাক করিবেন।

প্রকাশ থাকে যে ডাক খতমে অর্দ্ধেক টাকা জমা দিতে হইবেক।

স্বাঃ—বি, এম, রায়।
কলেক্টর অফ কলেক্টর, কুচবিহার।

নোটীশ।

(আমমোক্তারনামা খারিজ)

এতদ্বারা সর্ব্বসাধারণকে জ্ঞাত করান যাইতেছে যে আমার ইষ্টেটের কার্য্য নির্ব্বাহের জন্য পুনীবালা সাকিনের মৃত হুরমামুদ মিঞার পুত্র আব্দুল জব্বর মহাশয় ও ঐ সাকিনের মৃত গফুরমামুদ মহাশয়ের পুত্র সহরউল্যা মহাশয়কে গত ৩।১১।৪৭ ইং তারিখে ৫৬ নং আমমোক্তারনামা দলীলের দ্বারা আমার ইষ্টেটের কার্য্য পরিচালনা করার নিমিত্ত আমমোক্তার নিযুক্ত করিয়াছিলাম। আমি অদ্য হইতে তাহাদিগকে আমমোক্তারনামার কার্য্য হইতে বরখাস্ত করিলাম। অদ্য হইতে তাহারা আমার ইষ্টেটের যে কোন কার্য্য করিবেন তাহা সম্পূর্ণ বাতিল হইবেক। ইতি—তাং ১১।১১।৪৭ ইং

শ্রীহেমলতা দাস্যা বস্ত ও
শ্রীদিব্যনাথ দাস নাবালক
পক্ষে উহি অং পিতামহী
শ্রীহেমলী দাস্যা।

The Cooch Behar Gazette.

১৫ই অগ্রহায়ণ সোমবার] MONDAY, DECEMBER 1, 1947 [১৩৫৪ সাল ৪৩৮ রাজশক

PART V.

Advertisements

Tenders are invited separately for clearing the water weeds from the water surfaces of "Dangurai Dighi" and "Chandan Dighi" under the Fishery Department of this State. Tenders must reach this office in sealed covers by the 7th December, 1947 at the latest. Further particulars may be had from this office.

I. NARAYAN,
Dy. Development Commissioner,
in charge, Fishery Department,
Cooch Behar.

NOTICES.

Applications are invited for the post of a Graduate Mistress for the Sunity Academy in the grade of Rs. 60-5/2-100 plus the usual dearness allowance and the special pay.

Apply stating qualifications and past experience and with copies of testimonials if any and with Father's name, Home address and place of last residence.

Applications will be received by the Chairman, Public Service Commission, Cooch Behar up to the 15th December, 1947.

B. RAHAMAN,
Chairman,
Public Service Commission, Cooch Behar.

WANTED.

Applications are invited from the Cooch Beharis or Cooch Behar Subjects for the posts of Foresters on a pay of Rs. 40-2-50-2-60 for a period of 3 months for the present.

The candidates may be permanently appointed, if they are found suitable. The Foresters will have to stay in out-lying places, *viz.*, Nagrurhat, Garodhat or Patlakhawa etc.

Minimum qualification—Matriculates.

Applications will be received up to the 10th December, 1947.

B. N. ROY,
Conservator of Forests,
Cooch Behar.

J. C. GOON,
Assistant Secretary, General Secretariat,
Cooch Behar.

ADVERTISEMENT.

WANTED six temporary Time keepers on a monthly pay of Rs. 40 plus usual allowances for the supervision of works in rural areas under this Department. Preference to be given to those who can calculate earth works and Bridge works correctly.

Application must reach this office on or before 7th December, 1947.

L. M. BAKSI,
Development Commissioner, Cooch Behar.

নোটিশ।

এতদ্দ্বারা সর্ব্বসাধারণকে জ্ঞাত করান যাইতেছে যে আগামী ১৯৪৭ সনের ১১ই ডিসেম্বর তারিখে মোতাবেক ১৩৫৪ সনের ২৫শে অগ্রহায়ণ তারিখ দিবা ১০ ঘটিকার সময় অত্র সহর কুচবিহারের সরকারী কবিরাজি-বাগানের পশ্চিম পার্শ্বস্থ আমাদের দোকানে জমাজাতি তামাক ৫৭/৭ সের ও মজিহার বিবপাতা তামাক ৩০/ মণ প্রকাশ্য নিলামে বিক্রয় হইবে। এবং নিলামে পণবাহার মুদ্রা ডাক খতমের পর দাখিল করিতে হইবে। ক্রয়েচ্ছু ব্যক্তিগণ উপস্থিত হইয়া নিলাম ডাকিতে পারেন। ইতি—

এম, কে, সেন
ও
এস, সি, দত্ত
কুচবিহার।

নোটিশ।

এতদ্দ্বারা জানান যাইতেছে যে নোয়াখালি নিবাসী মঃ সোলায়মান মিঞা যিনি মোহরমি বিবি ও মোঃ হানিফ মিঞার ইষ্টেটের আমমোক্তার ছিলেন তাঁহাকে ১৩৫৪ সনের ১২ই অগ্রহায়ণ হইতে কার্য্য হইতে অপসারিত করা হইল। উক্ত তারিখের পর হইতে তাঁহার কোন কার্য্যকারিতার আমরা বাধ্য থাকিব না। ইতি ১৩।৮।৫৪ বাং

মোঃ হানিফ মিঞা
কোচবিহার।

Registered No. C 1085

The Cooch Behar Gazette.
EXTRAORDINARY

২২শে আষাঢ় সোমবার] MONDAY, JULY 7, 1947 [১৩৫৪ সাল ৪৩৮ রাজশক

THE STATE COUNCIL, COOCH BEHAR.

GENERAL AND EXECUTIVE DEPARTMENT.

NOTIFICATION.

(Jute)

No. G/17.—*Dated the 2nd July, 1947.*

Under Section 4 (1) of the Cooch Behar Export Duty Act (VI of 1941), the Durbar are pleased to notify in modification of any previous notification in this respect that the rate of export duty on jute shall until further orders be raised from annas 4 to annas 6 (annas six) per maund of 40 seers of 80 tolas of each seer subject to a decrease from annas 4 to annas 2 per maund in respect of all British Indian Jute re-exported from the bundar of Haldibari.

The above order takes effect from the date of its publication in the *Cooch Behar Gazette.*

By order,
J. C. GOON,
Asstt. Secretary, General Secretariat, Cooch Behar.

THE STATE COUNCIL, COOCH BEHAR.

GENERAL & EXECUTIVE DEPARTMENT.

NOTIFICATION.

(Tobacco)

No. G/18.—*Dated the 2nd July, 1947.*

Under Section 4 (1) of the Cooch Behar Export Duty Act (VI of 1941), the Durbar are pleased to notify in modification of any previous notification in this respect that the rate of export duty on tobacco shall until further orders be raised from Re. 1 to Rs. 1-4 per maund of 40 seers of 80 tolas of each seer.

The above order takes effect from the date of its publication in the *Cooch Behar State Gazette.*

By order,
J. C. GOON,
*Assistant Secretary, General Secretariat,
Cooch Behar.*

Registered No. C 1085.

The Cooch Behar Gazette.

EXTRAORDINARY

৪ঠা শ্রাবণ সোমবার] MONDAY, JULY 21, 1947 [১৩৫৪ সাল ৪৩৮ রাজশক

SPECIAL COOCH BEHAR STATE FORCES ORDER
BY
HIS HIGHNESS THE CHIEF COMMANDANT.

Cooch Behar, the 15th July, 1947.

His Highness the Maharaja Bhup Bahadur has kindly consented to become the 'COLONEL-IN-CHIEF' of the NARAYAN GUARDS Regiment of the Cooch Behar State Forces.

By order,
B. P. WALAWALKER,
LT. COLONEL,
Deputy Chief Commandant.

THE STATE COUNCIL, COOCH BEHAR.
GENERAL & EXECUTIVE DEPARTMENT.
NOTIFICATION.
(Revenue.)

No. G/21.—*Dated the 4th July, 1947.*

It is notified for general information that the Durbar have been pleased to order that owing to improvement in economic conditions, the Naib Ahilkars will, in future, declare jotes khas under section 19 of the Revenue Sale Act at the time of sale instead of passing of such orders on some subsequent date.

By order,
J. C. GOON,
Assistant Secretary, General Secretariat,
Cooch Behar.

THE STATE COUNCIL, COOCH BEHAR.
General and Executive Department.
NOTIFICATION.
(Excise)

No. G/24.—*Dated the 9th July, 1947.*

In exercise of powers conferred by section 5(d) of the Cooch Behar Opium Act 1946 and in supersession of all previous orders and notifications regulating the rates of retail prices for sale of smaller weights of opium the Durbar is pleased to fix the following rates for retail sale of opium :—

OPIUM.

Wights.	Prices. Rs.	As.	P.
1¾ grains	0	0	6
2⅞ ,,	0	1	0
5¼ ,,	0	2	0
9 ,,	0	3	6

OPIUM.

Weights.	Prices. Rs.	As.	P.
⅛ tola	0	8	9
¼ ,,	1	1	6
½ ,,	2	3	0
1 ,,	4	6	0

By order,
J. C. Goon,
Assistant Secretary, General Secretariat,
Cooch Behar.

THE STATE COUNCIL, COOCH BEHAR.
General and Executive Department.
NOTIFICATION.
(Excise)

No. G/25.—*Dated the 9th July, 1947.*

In exercise of powers conferred by sub-section 2 of section 88 of Cooch Behar Excise Act VII of 1945 and in supersession of all previous orders and notifications regulating the rates of retail prices for sale of smaller weights of Ganja, the Durbar is pleased to fix the following rates for retail sale of Ganja :–

Weights.		Prices. Rs.	A.	P.
1½ grains	...	0	0	6
3 ,,	...	0	1	0
6 ,,	...	0	2	0
$\frac{1}{16}$ Tola	...	0	3	9

Weights.		Prices. Rs.	A.	P.
⅛ Tola	...	0	7	6
¼ ,,	...	0	15	0
½ ,,	...	1	14	0
1 ,,	...	3	12	0

By order,
J. C. Goon,
Assistant Secretary, General Secretariat,
Cooch Behar.

Registered No. C 1085

The Cooch Behar Gazette.

EXTRAORDINARY

৭ই শ্রাবণ বৃহস্পতিবার] THURSDAY, JULY 24, 1947 [১০৫৪ সাল ৪৩৮ রাজশক

GENERAL SECRETARIAT, COOCH BEHAR.

GENERAL & EXECUTIVE DEPARTMENT.

NOTIFICATION No. 5.

The 23rd July, 1947.

It is notified for general information that His Highness the Maharaja Bhup Bahadur in Council has been pleased to make the following orders in supersession of all orders on the subject :—

The following monthly tuition fees for the Victoria College and seat rents of the Hostel attached to it, are introduced with effect from the beginning of the new session.

(*a*) **Tution fee :—**

I. A.	I. Sc.	B. A.	B. A. (honours)
Rs. 7	Rs. 8	Rs. 9	Rs. 9

(*b*) **Admission fee.**—An amount equivalent to one month's tuition fee as before.

(*c*) **Seat rent of the Hostel :—**

Rs. 3—Ground floor. Rs. 4—First floor.

The seat rent is leviable for 12 months in a session.

2. His Highness the Maharaja Bhup Bahadur in Council has further been pleased to order that all Cooch Behari boys and girls should receive education in the Victoria College, free of tuition fees, and any one residing in the Hostel, would not have to pay any seat rent. They are further exempted from payment of any admission fees. This concession in part or in whole, may, at the discretion of the Minister-in-charge, be extended to the deserving sons and daughters of Cooch Behar subjects and of State servants as well. To compensate the cost, the Minister-in-charge will provide for as many stipends as are required according to the number of such boys and girls admitted in the College year by year and will make budget provisions accordingly.

All previous orders regarding grant of free-studentships in the College are hereby withdrawn, but the procedure for grant of free-studentship as was in force before will apply for grant of stipends to the sons and daughters of Cooch Behar subjects and State servants.

3. It is further decided that in supersession of all previous order, all scholarships from the Victoria College will be confined to the Cooch Beharis only and that unless specially ordered, no such scholarship will be available outside this College. But any sanctioned scholarship or free-studentship should continue till the period of sanction is over.

S. C. ROY SINGHA SARKAR,
Public Health & Education Minister,
Cooch Behar.

Registered No. C1033

The Cooch Behar Gazette.

EXTRAORDINARY

২২শে আশ্বিন বুধবার] WEDNESDAY, OCTOBER 8, 1947. [১৩৫৪ সাল, ৪৩৮ রাজশক

THE STATE COUNCIL, COOCH BEHAR.

GENERAL AND EXECUTIVE DEPARTMENT.

NOTIFICATION.

No. G/38.—*Dated the 4th October, 1947.*

With the object of developing and extending the town of Cooch Behar, His Highness the Maharaja Bhup Bahadur in Council is pleased to accord sanction to the establishment of a Development Board consisting of the Chief Minister as Chairman, the Revenue Minister and the Finance Minister as Members and the Chief Engineer as Member and Secretary.

It will be the duty of the Development Board to examine all schemes for extension and development of the town of Cooch Behar, to submit revised rules for leases of land and to allot lands from time to time to applicants. To meet the cost of acquisition of land and developing it, suitable advances will be made to the Board from time to time. The Board will be expected to make each scheme a financial success.

This supersedes all previous orders on the subject,

By Order,
J. C. GOON,
Assistant Secretary,
General Secretariat, Cooch Behar.

HIGH COURT NOTIFICATION.

CRIMINAL PROCEDURE.

Dated, the 27th September, 1947.

In exercise of the powers conferred by Section 554 of the Indian Code of Criminal Procedure, 1898, as adopted in the State, the High Court is pleased to prescribe, with the previous sanction of the Durbar, the following Bond and Bail Bond Forms (both in English and in Bengali) for use in the State in appropriate cases with such variation in individual cases, if any as may be necessary, in supersession of the Forms III, XXV and XLII in Schedule V of the aforesaid Code.

By order,
R. R. BANERJEE,
for Registrar, High Court Cooch Behar.

BOND AND BAIL BOND—FORM A.

After arrest under a Warrant.

(See Sections 76, 168, 496, 497 and 499 (2)).

I, son of
of village Sub-division being brought
before the $\frac{\text{Ahilkar of}}{\text{officer-in-charge of} \quad \text{Police Station}}$ under a warrant
to compel my appearance to answer the charge of
do hereby bind myself to attend in the Court of or
in any other Court to which the case may be transferred on the
day of next to answer to the said charge and to continue so to attend until otherwise directed by the Court (and should the case be sent for trial by the Court of Session to appear before the said Court when called upon to answer the charge against me) and in the case of my making default herein, I bind myself to forfeit to His Highness the Maharaja Bhup Bahadur, the sum of rupees

Dated this day of 19

(Signature)

$\frac{\text{I}}{\text{We}}$ son(s) of
of village Sub-division do hereby
$\frac{\text{declare myself surety}}{\text{jointly and severally declare ourselves and each of us sureties}}$ for the above mentioned of that he shall attend in the Court of or in any other Court to which the case may be transferred on the day of next to answer to the charge on which he has been arrested and shall continue so to attend until otherwise directed by the Court (and should the case be sent for trial by the Court of Session to appear before the said Court when called upon to answer the charge against him) and in the case of his making default therein, $\frac{\text{I}}{\text{We}}$ bind $\frac{\text{myself}}{\text{ourselves}}$ to forfeit to His Highness the Maharaja Bhup Bahadur the sum of rupees

Dated this day of 19

(Signature)

BOND AND BAIL BOND—FORM B.

During the Pendency of Appeal or Motion.

(*Sections 426, 435 & 498.*)

son of

of Sub-division having preferred $\frac{\text{an appeal}}{\text{a motion}}$ in the Court of against the order of conviction passed on me by the Court of under Sec. C. B. P. C., I bind myself to attend the Court of on the day of and all subsequent dates of hearing of the $\frac{\text{appeal}}{\text{motion}}$ and surrender myself if and when ordered to do so, and in the case of my making default herein, I bind myself to forfeit to His Highness the Maharaja Bhup Bahadur,-the sum of rupees

Dated this day of 19

(*Signature.*)

We Son(s) of

of village Sub-division do hereby $\frac{\text{declare myself surety}}{\text{jointly and severally declare ourselves and each of us sureties}}$ for the above named of that he shall attend the Court of on the day of and all subsequent dates of hearing of the $\frac{\text{appeal}}{\text{motion}}$ and surrender himself, if and when ordered to do so and in the case of his making default herein $\frac{\text{I}}{\text{We}}$ bind $\frac{\text{myself}}{\text{ourselves}}$ to forfeit to His Highness the Maharara Bhup Bahadur, the sum of rupees

Dated this day of 19

(*Signature.*)

BOND AND BAIL BOND—FORM C.

Interim Bond or Bail Bond till Appeal is filed.

(*Section 426 (2A)*).

I, son of of having been convicted under Section C. B. P. C. by the Court of on the day of and intending to file an appeal against the said order of conviction in the Court of I do hereby bind myself to appear before this Court on or any other date hereafter fixed for the purpose, if no appeal is presented or no bail is obtained from the appellate Court before the said date and in case of my making default herein, I bind myself to forfeit to His Highness the Maharaja Bhup Bahadur, the sum of rupees

Dated this day of 19

(*Signature.*)

I/We ... son(s) of ... of village ... Sub-division ... do hereby ~~jointly and severally declare ourselves, and each of us sureties~~ declore myself surety for the above named ... of ... that he shall attend this Court on ... or any other date hereafter fixed for the purpose, if no appeal is preferred or no bail is obtained from the appellate Court before that date and in case of his making default herein, I/We bind myself/ourselves to forfeit to His Highness the Maharaja Bhup Bahadur, the sum of of rupees

Dated this ... day of ... 19

(*Signature.*)

মুচলিকা ও জামিননামা ফরম—ক।

ওয়ারেন্ট বাগে ধৃত ব্যক্তির মুচলিকা ও জামিননামা।

(৭৬, ১৬৯, ৪২৬, ৪৯৭ ও ৪৯৯-(২) ধারা)

আমি শ্রী ... পিতা ... সাকিন ... সাবডিভিসান ... আমাকে হাজির করিবার উদ্দেশ্যে জারীকৃত ওয়ারেন্টমূলে ধৃত হইয়া, আমার বিরুদ্ধে আনীত ... ধারা মতে অভিযোগের উত্তরদায়ক হইবার জন্য আদালতের মহোদয়ের / থানার ভারপ্রাপ্ত কর্মচারীর সম্মুখে উপস্থিত হইয়া এতদ্দ্বারা অঙ্গীকার করিতেছি যে আমার বিরুদ্ধে আনীত অভিযোগের উত্তর দিবার জন্য আমি ... তারিখে এবং তৎপরবর্তী মোকদ্দমার শুনানি তারিখে ... আদালতে কিংবা মোকদ্দমা বিচারার্থ অন্য আদালতে প্রেরিত কিংবা সেসন্স আদালতে সোপর্দ হইলে সেই আদালতে, আদালত কর্তৃক অন্য আদেশ না হওয়া পর্যন্ত, উপস্থিত হইব ও হাজির থাকিব। ইহাতে কোনরূপ অন্যথা বা ত্রুটী হইলে আমি শ্রীশ্রী৺মহারাজা ভূপবাহাদুরের সরকারে ... টাকা দণ্ড দিতে বাধ্য থাকিব। এতদর্থে এই মুচলিকা পত্র লিখিয়া দিলাম। ইতি

অদ্য সন ... তারিখ

(দস্তখত)

আমি ... পিতা ... সাকিন ... সাবডিভিসান ... ও আমি ... পিতা ... সাকিন ... সাবডিভিসান ... আমি/আমরা উপরোক্ত ... সাকিনের ... আসামীর একযোগে ও পৃথকভাবে জামিন হইয়া এতদ্দ্বারা অঙ্গীকার করিতেছি যে তাহার বিরুদ্ধে আনীত অভিযোগের উত্তর দিবার জন্য উক্ত আসামী ... তারিখে ... আদালতে অথবা বিচারার্থ মোকদ্দমা অন্য আদালতে প্রেরিত কিংবা সেসন্স আদালতে সোপর্দ হইলে সেই আদালতে, আদালত কর্তৃক অন্য আদেশ না হওয়া পর্যন্ত, প্রতি তারিখে উপস্থিত হইবে এবং হাজির থাকিবে। ইহাতে আসামী কোনরূপ অন্যথা বা ত্রুটী করিলে আমি/আমরা শ্রীশ্রী৺মহারাজা ভূপ বাহাদুরের সরকারে ... টাকা দণ্ড দিতে বাধ্য থাকিব। ইতি

অদ্য সন ... তারিখ

(দস্তখত)

Registered
No. C 1085

The Cooch Behar Gazette.

EXTRAORDINARY,

২১শে আশ্বিন বুধবার — WEDNESDAY, OCTOBER 8, 1947. [১৩৫৪ সাল, ৪৩৮ রাজশক

THE STATE COUNCIL, COOCH BEHAR.

(Obituary).

Dated the 8th October, 1947.

Council have heard with deep regret of the death of Mr. Benoy Ghose, formerly Financial Secretary to His Highness the Maharaja Bhup Bahadur in the Audit Department and Debutter Department of the Cooch Behar State, and desire to send their profound sympathy to the members of the bereaved family.

By order,
J. C. Goon,
Assistant Secretary,
General Secretariat, Cooch Behar.

Registered No. C 1085.

The Cooch Behar Gazette.

EXTRAORDINARY,

২৩শে আশ্বিন শুক্রবার FRIDAY, OCTOBER 10, 1947. [১৩৫৪ সাল, ৪৩৮ রাজশক

THE STATE COUNCIL, COOCH BEHAR.

GENERAL & EXECUTIVE DEPARTMENT.

NOTIFICATION.

G/40.—*Dated the 4th October, 1947.*

It is notified for general information that the Durbar in continuation of the State Council Notification No. G. 36 dated the 2nd October 1947 published in the *Cooch Behar Gazette* (Extra-ordinary) dated the 3rd October 1947, are pleased to order that the aforesaid Notification be amended by the addition of the following proviso :—

"Provided that when the Durbar are satisfied that in any special case the use of a microphone is in the public interest, they may authorise its use. Such authority shall be given in writing.

By order,

J. C. GOON,

Assistant Secretary,

General Secretariat, Cooch Behar.

ORDER.

The 9th October, 1947.

In modification of the recent order regarding Puja holidays, 27th and 28th October, 1947 are also allowed as holidays, the result being that there will be a continuous holiday from the 19th October to the 30th October, 1947.

H. SINGH,

Chief Minister, Cooch Behar State.

The Cooch Behar Gazette.

EXTRAORDINARY

২২শে কার্ত্তিক শনিবার | SATURDAY, NOVEMBER 8, 1947. [১৩৫৪ সাল, [illegible]

THE STATE COUNCIL, COOCH BEHAR.

GENERAL & EXECUTIVE DEPARTMENT.

NOTIFICATION.

(Day of Remembrance).

No. R/80.—*Dated the 6th November, 1947.*

The day of remembrance will be observed in the State on Sunday, the 9th November 1947 to commemorate the wars of 1914-18 and 1939-45.

At 11 A. M. (Railway time) on that day a State Military force gun will be fired and again at 11-2 A. M. Two minutes' complete silence should be observed individually in commemoration during the space between the gun fires.

By order,

J. C G ON,

Assistant Secretary, General Secretariat, Cooch Behar.

Registered No. C 1085.

The Cooch Behar Gazette.

EXTRAORDINARY

২৩শে কার্ত্তিক সোমবার]   MONDAY, NOVEMBER 10, 1947.   [১৩৫৪ সাল, ৪৩৮ রাজশক

ORDERS BY THE STATE COUNCIL, COOCH BEHAR.

APPOINTMENT.—*The 3rd November, 1947.*—Srijut Jyotish Chandra Goon, M. A. (Com.), Assistant Secretary, General Secretariat, Cooch Behar is appointed Registrar of Marriages under Act V of 1899 for the State of Cooch Behar with effect from the 31st October, 1947.

H. Singh,
Chief Minister, & Vice-President,
State Council, Cooch Behar.

The Cooch Behar Gazette.

EXTRAORDINARY

২৬শে অগ্রহায়ণ শুক্রবার] FRIDAY, DECEMBER 12, 1947. [১৩৫৪ সাল, ৪৩৮ রাজশক

THE STATE COUNCIL, COOCH BEHAR.

GENERAL AND EXECUTIVE DEPARTMENT.

NOTIFICATION.

No. L/18—*Dated the 8th December, 1947.*

His Highness the Maharaja Bhup Bahadur has, in exercise of the powers specified in section 4 of the Government of Cooch Behar Act, 1941, been pleased to enact the Act given hereafter to have immediate force in the State :—

Act No. IX of 1947.

(An Act to amend the Cooch Behar Essential Supplies (Temporary powers) Act, 1946.)

Preamble.

Whereas it is expedient to amend the Cooch Behar Essential Supplies (Temporary Powers) Act, 1946, XIV of 1946, for the purposes hereinafter appearing ;

It is hereby enacted as follows :—

Short title and commencement.

1 (1) This Act may be called the Cooch Behar Essential Supplies (Temporary Powers) (Amendment) Act, 1947.

(2) It shall come into force at once.

Amendment of the Preamble to Act XIV of 1946.

2. In the Preamble to the Cooch Behar Essential Supplies (Temporary Powers) Act, 1946, (hereinafter referred to as the said Act), the following words be added at the end, namely :—

"and also any other commodity as the Durbar in their discretion declare to be an essential commodity "

Amendment of Section 2 (a) of Act XIV of 1946.

3. In section 2 (a) of the said Act, add the following item at the end, namely :—

"(ix) any other commodity which the Durbar from time to time by notified order declare to be an essential commodity".

By Command,

K. C. GANGULI,

Revenue Minister,

for Chief Minister, Cooch Behar

Registered No. C1035

The Cooch Behar Gazette.

EXTRAORDINARY

২৯শে অগ্রহায়ণ সোমবার] MONDAY, DECEMBER 15, 1947. [১৩৫৪ সাল, ৪৩৮ রাজশক

THE STATE COUNCIL, COOCH BEHAR.

General and Executive Department.

NOTIFICATION.

(Decontrol of Sugar).

No. R/32—*Dated the 12th December, 1947.*

The Government of India having decided to decontrol Sugar and Gur with immediate effect, it is ordered that Sugar and Gur will be decontrolled within the State with effect from the 20th of December 1947. There will be no internal control exercised over the movements, distribution and price of any grade of Sugar and Gur but movements to foreign countries including Pakisthan will be subject to the control of the State. With effect from that date the existing stock of Sugar will, until it is exhausted, continue to be distributed under the control of the Civil Supplies Department, Cooch Behar. During this period the price, the scale and distribution of Sugar per Ration Card in the urban and rural ration areas, will be the same as now. On and from the 20th December, 1947 individual Rationees and Establishments will be free to buy any amount of Sugar and Gur from the open market but will be allowed to purchase only their allotted quota from Ration Shops.

By order,

J. C. Goon,

Asstt. Secretary, General Secretariat, Cooch Behar.

GYAN

DISTRICT GAZETTEERS OF INDIA {IN 245 BINDINGS}

ASSAM DISTRICT GAZETTEERS

11 VOLUMES

ISBN: 9788121285933 (PB Set)
Price: 6500/

BENGAL DISTRICT GAZETTEERS

52 VOLUMES

ISBN: 9789362089151 (PB Set)
Price: 35000/

GAZETTEER OF THE BOMBAY PRESIDENCY

27 VOLUMES
(IN 35 BINDINGS)

ISBN: 9788121285605 (PB Set)
Price: 90000/

CENTRAL PROVINCES DISTRICT GAZETTEERS

30 VOLUMES
(IN 33 BINDINGS)

ISBN: 9789362085399 (PB Set)
Price: 23000/

MADRAS DISTRICT GAZETTEERS

23 VOLUMES
(IN 25 BINDINGS)

ISBN: 9789362085627 (PB Set)
Price: 32000/

PUNJAB DISTRICT GAZETTEERS

36 VOLUMES
(IN 37 BINDINGS)

ISBN: 9789362084033 (PB Set)
Price: 46000/

RAJPUTANA DISTRICT GAZETTEERS

3 VOLUMES

ISBN: 9789362084781 (PB Set)
Price: 6000/

District Gazetteers of India {In 245 Bindings}
(Rs. 530000/- Hardcover)
(Rs. 370000/- Softcover)
Crown Size

UNITED PROVINCES OF AGRA AND OUDH DISTRICT GAZETTEERS

49 VOLUMES

ISBN: 9789362082183 (PB Set)
Price: 86404/